A BIBLIOGRAPHY OF SOURCES IN CHRISTIANITY AND THE ARTS

Daven Michael Kari

Studies in Art and Religious Interpretation
Volume 16

The Edwin Mellen Press
Lewiston/Queenston/Lampeter

Library of Congress Cataloging-in-Publication Data

Kari, Daven Michael.
    A bibliography of sources in Christianity and the arts / Daven
Michael Kari.
        p.   cm. -- (Studies in art and religious interpretation ; v.
16)
    Includes and index.
    ISBN 0-7734-9094-9
    1. Christianity and the arts--Bibliography.   I. Title.
II. Series.
Z7776.68.K37   1994
[BR115.A8   1994
016.246--dc20   94-9769
                                                                          CIP

This is volume 16 in the continuing series
Studies in Art and Religious Interpretation
Volume 16 ISBN 0-7734-9094-9
SARI Series ISBN 0-88946-956-3

A CIP catalog record for this book is available from the British Library.

The Edwin Mellen Press   The Edwin Mellen Press
        Box 450   Box 67
Lewiston, New York   Queenston, Ontario
USA 14092-0450   CANADA L0S 1L0

The Edwin Mellen Press, Ltd.
Lampeter, Dyfed, Wales
UNITED KINGDOM SA48 7DY

Printed in the United States of America

To my beloved Priya

whose devotion to God

and delight in life

ever inspire my own

TABLE OF CONTENTS

INTRODUCTION

As the title of this book implies, *A Bibliography of Sources in Christianity and the Arts* has been developed around several axiomatic concepts. First, this bibliography is offered as a statement of faith in the capacity of the Christian church to become involved in meaningful ways with virtually all forms of art. For those dedicated to serving God in the name of Jesus Christ and through the Holy Spirit, expressions of faith through the arts are both possible and necessary. The process for achieving this good objective is long and arduous. Great art is rarely born overnight, and great Christian art can never be merely an echo of popular culture. The spiritual and intellectual training essential to significant Christian art requires years of diligence, perhaps a generation or two of nurture to come to fruition. This bibliography on Christianity and the arts is offered as a contribution toward the development of art appropriate to Christian worship and living.

Second, this bibliography is designed to help people doing research in the ways Christianity has been and can be blended with the fine arts. Such a blend implies a certain theological perspective about the nature of life and creativity. For human beings to be created in the image of God suggests more than a similarity of shape, although that too may be involved. The *imago Dei* reflects the spiritual qualities of God, including the capacity to create. While God alone can create from nothing, people can re-create and thereby replicate in some small way the original creation of the world. This capacity to create is central to spirituality, and an active use of creativity is axiomatic to a healthy spiritual life.

One of the most fascinating developments in western Christianity during the past two decades has been the resurgence of the arts as an integral part of Christian worship and lifestyles. A growing recognition of the value of the five senses in worshiping God has led many denominations to re-evaluate their use of the visual arts and dance, as well as the dramatic arts, which have roots in medieval worship services. The Christian church may well be on the verge of a renaissance, a re-birth which will once again allow room in worship for both the planned and the spontaneous forms of art.

Third, the title of this bibliography suggests that it is selective, reflecting specific criteria. In addition to the other criteria listed below, entries in this bibliography have been selected for the specific purpose of helping readers explore the fine arts as they are blended with the Christian faith. Because Christianity must always be defined in a cultural context, many works not directly related to Christianity have been included to provide a larger perspective. Furthermore, some categories of the arts--such as graffiti, photography, and posters--have rarely been connected with the Christian faith and are of necessity included here as media studied primarily from secular perspectives.

The current challenge for Christians seeking to develop skills in the arts is that most schools and many resources treating the arts are in no way linked with Christianity. Because art involves craft, Christians can learn much from secular artists as well as religious ones. Yet Christians also have a great need for discovering ways of blending their faith with the crafts of art. Achieving a fruitful synthesis between art and faith is rarely easy. Many books and articles have been written on religion and the arts, but finding a resource which leads one to the most useful ones is difficult. The last major source containing a variety of units for such research was John G. Barrow's *A Bibliography on Bibliographies in Religion* [BBI-030] completed in 1955. Since that time many bibliographies of bibliographies have appeared, but few of them have dealt specifically with Christianity and the arts. *The Christian Resource Directory* [LIR-010] of 1988 by Jonathan and Jeanette Gainsbrugh contains many references to works related to the arts, but does not focus specifically on the arts. While Diane Peters' recent bibliography, *Christianity and the Visual Arts: A Bibliography* [VAR-020], offers an interesting treatment of the resources in one major library, it is somewhat limited as a resource for other libraries.

To help amend the lack of a current research guide, this bibliography is primarily designed to assist English speaking westerners in conducting research in the arts, especially as they are related to western Christianity. While many works treating other cultures and religions are included, these non-Christian or non-western sources are presented primarily to provide a frame of reference. Those interested in conducting additional research in non-Christian religions can find ready help in various bibliographies of bibliographies and in specialized bibliographies such as that by John W. Cook included in *Art as Religious Studies* [VAR-050], edited by Doug Adams and Diane Apostolos-Cappadona, and that by John F. Butler in *Christianity in Asia and America: After A.D. 1500* [VAR-190], both listed in Chapter 12.

Finally, as the title further indicates, in addition to the connecting point between the Christian faith and the fine arts, the first criterion for including works in this bibliography has been utility in conducting research. Bibliographies and works with bibliographies have therefore been given first priority as sources. Where possible, the size of each bibliographical source has been indicated by page numbers, and (when information is available) by the number of entries in that source, the latter figure being indicated by a number in brackets. When the bibliography does not appear within twenty pages of the end of the work listed, and when no specific bibliography appears in that work, then the total number of pages is also given to indicate the size of the source. When prefatory pages number more than twenty, these too are listed to alert readers to lengthy introductions, some of which contain all of the commentary in illustrated texts. Preference has been given to current sources, since these usually provide references to the most readily available works. Many older books, however, have been included simply because they list classic works of particular interest to the specialists. Preference has also been given to works of substantial size, usually of forty pages or more for books, and twenty pages or more for bibliographies. Many brief bibliographies of four to twenty pages were produced for the U. S. Library of Congress during the first few decades of the twentieth century, but these have been omitted because of their scant size and unavailability to most readers. Those interested in such small works will find them all given in Theodore Besterman's fine bibliographies on bibliographies listed near the beginning of this bibliography. Also note that this bibliography primarily lists books, and only a few major journals and individual articles have been given. For those looking for additional journal titles, consult the latest edition of *Ulrich's International Periodical Directory* (New Providence, N.J.: R. R. Bowker), or, for more discriminating and annotated lists, see Bill Katz's and Linda Sternberg Katz's *Magazines for Libraries* (New Providence, N.J.: R. R. Bowker, 1992), now in its seventh edition.

To aid in making this bibliography concise, reference sources have typically been listed only once in the category which best suits the work. In the few instances when reference sources are split evenly between several different disciplines, cross references have been used to indicate alternate classifications for certain works. By this means repetition has been minimized and virtually eliminated for the more than 5,200 works listed. Those conducting a thorough search for sources will want to investigate all relevant and related categories.

Like all selective bibliographies, this one works within fairly narrow boundaries. This bibliography excludes most works of a "how to" nature since these applicatory works rarely move beyond mechanical issues and seldom provide bibliographies. A few of the "how to" books have been included in categories in which little else was available. Sometimes, as in the overly technical yet nonetheless masterful works of Ansel Adams on photography, important aesthetic principles are disclosed in the midst of discussions about the craft, so some of these technical works have been included even when they have lacked bibliographies. Furthermore, this bibliography provides only a general treatment of music, although sources listed treat most of the major aspects of that discipline, including folk music, hymns, musical drama, and opera. Specialized bibliographies on music have been listed, along with the major encyclopedias and handbooks on this topic. Many works on arts and crafts have also been omitted simply because they constitute another large category usually treated separately from the fine arts, although crafts and fine arts do sometimes overlap, as in fabric arts. Some categories, such as the decorative arts and jewelry, are included in the general discussions of architecture and the visual arts, respectively, although some might well argue that these art forms deserve separate treatment. While the decorative arts and jewelry have often been used to illustrate aspects of the Christian faith, careful studies of these art forms as expressions of Christian theology are rare, suggesting yet another topic worthy of fresh research and analysis.

This bibliography also focuses chiefly on works treating art movements and groups of individuals. Numerous bibliographies are available on almost every major artist, musician, and writer in the western culture, and these can be found readily in the bibliographies on bibliographies listed in Chapter 1. In covering the painters of Europe, however, several individuals have been selected for special treatment since they help define major religious movements in the West. Also note that works on lithographs typically treat individual artists, thus necessitating a deviation from this pattern of including only works covering more than one artist.

Works on religion and the arts abound, and are proliferating at an astonishing rate. With the help of this bibliography one can at least begin to explore this fecund and inspiring world of study. To make the best use of this bibliography, one will do well to begin by reading the introductions to relevant sections where introductory texts and other important studies are identified. Those conducting a more exhaustive study will want to work through relevant sections of bibliographies on bibliographies and entire bibliographies devoted to the selected area of research. Most of the major reference works listed in this book can be found in major libraries in America, Australia, Canada, and Great Britain. Rare works and those available only in foreign languages have been included only when they are of primary importance to the study of a given topic. Some specialized bibliographies and studies may be found only in specialty libraries, but even these can be obtained through the help of major library systems which allow inter-library loans.

The organization of this bibliography is primarily alphabetical, although the function of categories sometimes necessitates a deviation from this pattern. For example, for the sake of facilitating the locating of reference works, this book begins with a chapter on bibliographies of bibliographies, and introduces a section on bibliographies at the beginning of each chapter and most sections within the chapters. Since theoretical works are important for foundational studies in any discipline, these are listed second when such a category is large enough to be represented separately, as in Chapter 9 on literature and Chapter 10 on music. In Chapter 9, works on criticism of literature have been separated from those concentrating on theory, and because these works tend to be more specific and application oriented, they are given after works on literary theory. To facilitate references to works in this bibliography, a code system has been employed which is identified in the table of contents. Like the book as a whole, this code is basically alphabetical, with the exception of bibliographies being given first and works associated with religion being given last in each chapter. For example, Chapter 9 on literature begins with items numbered [BLI-010], the "B" standing for bibliography, and the "LI" standing for literature. Works on literary theory are identified by [LIT-010] and following numbers, the "T" standing for theory.

Research for this bibliography has taken many forms. At the outset, the author made use of several major libraries and concentrated on works available in those places. As the volume grew, the author added to the works discovered those listed in OCLC's international library system. A variety of alternate computer search services have been used for those categories particularly difficult to research, such as graffiti and, in the last chapter, wit and humor and religion. Reviews of major bibliographies and key works have also alerted the author to which works belong in this present volume. For most categories covered in this bibliography, searches have gone from the present back to 1960, although major works written before this time have also been included. In a few general categories, such as architecture and sculpture, an extended search was not manageable, so most of the works date back no further than the 1970s. Older key works not listed in these sections may readily be found in the numerous bibliographies on architecture and sculpture listed immediately before these two general categories. For other categories, such as Albrecht Dürer and Matthias Grünewald, the search had to be extended into the 1950s or earlier just to find the standard reference works and studies recognized as being the best of their kind, such as the work by Erwin Panofsky on Dürer.

With a few exceptions, this bibliography follows *The Chicago Manual of Style*, primarily because it offers a more readable bibliographical form than does the style used by the Modern Language Association. In particular, the states of countries are abbreviated according to the Chicago style, instead of MLA's zip code style. However, at several points the abbreviations used by MLA have been adopted to save space. For example, "ed." after a writer's name indicates "editor," "eds." after two or more writers' names means "editors," and "Ed." before writers listed after the title should be interpreted as "Edited by." A similar pattern is used for compilers and translators. Alphabetizing is self-explanatory, except that "Mc" has been treated as if it were spelled out as "Mac." Similarly, in the Index of Titles, works beginning with arabic numerals have been listed as if they were spelled out. Also note that titles beginning with "Ä" have been listed separately after the titles beginning with "A."

This selective bibliography on Christianity and the arts is offered with the full understanding that it can be just a beginning. Works listed herein are presented as doors leading to rooms with resources and more doors leading to still more rooms with additional resources. The careful researcher will find a mansion of opportunities for learning in each of the categories listed. No doubt, the furnishings of these rooms will be adjusted and updated many times over the years. In this process of collecting and arranging such resources, suggestions are welcome from all readers since research is at best a community effort. Additionally, this bibliography can alert readers to the need for more books treating the arts from a Christian perspective. For example, categories such as collage, embroidery, graffiti, photography, posters, and wood carving are rarely treated in connection with their use in the church. Much work remains to be done.

As with all works of more than passing significance, this bibliography has been the product of many people's efforts. I owe many thanks to William L. Hendricks for alerting me to the need for such a resource tool and for offering preliminary suggestions for its organization. I am also deeply indebted to the staff members of the many libraries which have assisted me in collecting information, including the James P. Boyce Centennial Library at Southern Baptist Theological Seminary, the William F. Ekstrom Library and the Margaret M. Bridwell Art Library at the University of Louisville, the St. Louis Public Library, Main Branch, the Jung-Kellogg Library at Missouri

Baptist College, the Annie Gabriel Library at California Baptist College, the Thomas Rivera Library at the University of California at Riverside, and the Central Library of Riverside, California. The librarians in each have demonstrated time and again that library research is more than a science; such research is itself an art. Many people have offered helpful comments about key works which belong in this bibliography, and to these persons I must offer a word of thanks summarily since they are too numerous to list. Those whose wisdom about specific art forms has proven invaluable are Robert Jackson for insights into the literature on cinema and religion, Mike Jones for assistance in exploring the literature of numismatics, and Melissa Conway Luther for advice about illuminated manuscripts. Most of all, I owe a special debt of gratitude to my wife, Priya, for her infinite patience in allowing me to frequent libraries while she has tended to our infant sons. Her own love for the arts and insights into them, as well as her fine editing skills, have influenced this bibliography at many points. Research is in one sense a solitary undertaking, but in another sense a community endeavor, beginning at home.

CHAPTER 1

BIBLIOGRAPHIES OF BIBLIOGRAPHIES

The following bibliographies of bibliographies represent the beginning point for most research projects. For those wishing to study the arts in connection with Christianity, many bibliographies will offer pertinent categories, but only a few will afford a major concentration in this interdisciplinary focus. John G. Barrow's work [BBI-030] represents the most complete treatment of Christianity and the arts until the appearance of this present bibliography. *The Christian Resource Directory* of 1988 by Jonathan and Jeanette Gainsbrugh (listed as LIR-010 in Chapter 9 on literature) contains many references to works related to the arts, but does not focus specifically on the arts. The third volume of Walford and Taylor's work [BBI-570] offers the most current bibliography of bibliographies treating the arts, however, it does not treat in particular Christian themes and concerns. Although not a bibliography of bibliographies, Diane Peters' recent bibliography, *Christianity and the Visual Arts: A Bibliography* [VAR-020], offers a useful selection of works treating Christianity and the arts, but her volume is focused on a single library's collection and is, therefore, somewhat limited as a research tool for other libraries.

Of the works listed below, those by Theodore Besterman and cohorts [BBI-060 to BBI-110], including a supplemental work by Alice F. Toomey [BBI-560], represent the best products up to their time. For more current bibliographies, see the *Bibliographic Index* [BBI-130], or periodicals--such as the *Bibliographical Bulletin* [BBI-160], *Bibliographical Society of America. Papers* [BBI-140], *Bulletin of Bibliography* [BBI-180], and *The Library: The Transactions of the Bibliographical Society* [BBI-410]--and recent works developed from them, such as the summary work by Naomi Caldwell-Wood and Patrick W. Wood [BBI-190], which also offer more readily accessible information than that in the works by Besterman. For reasonably current works treating dance and drama and other performing arts, see *Bibliographies and Indexes in the Performing Arts* [BBI-150].

The following section also includes specialized bibliographies of bibliographies which should be consulted in connection with categories such as aesthetics, film, feminism, literature, and music. These bibliographies are also mentioned in the head notes to pertinent sections given below. The older bibliographies listed, such as William P. Courtney's work [BBI-260] and Joseph Sabin's work [BBI-500], are offered as a means for discovering works which have been significant in past eras but may have been set aside or overlooked by later generations. Another work of special interest to researchers is Michael M. Reynold's bibliography [BBI-480] treating theses and dissertations, which often provide extensive bibliographies. Several other guides to dissertations are also given below, including [BBI-200], [BBI-240], [BBI-270], and [BBI-390]. Specialized versions of these guides appear in many categories of this bibliography. Finally, one should take special note of the bibliographies treating international bibliographies since these are not often emphasized elsewhere in this book. Those conversant in other languages or interested in topics treated extensively in non-western cultures (as is calligraphy in middle-eastern and far eastern cultures) will want to consider these international bibliographies carefully.

[BBI-010] Arnim, Max. *Internationale Personalbibliographie, 1800-1943.* 2nd ed. 2 vols. Stuttgart: Hiersemann, 1944-1952. Gerhard Bock and Franz Hodes. Vol. 3: 1944-1959. 1963. 659 pp. Franz Hodes. 2nd ed of vol. 3. 3 vols. 1978-.

[BBI-020] Ballou, Patricia K. *Women: A Bibliography of Bibliographies.* 2nd ed. Women's Studies Publications. Boston: G. K. Hall, 1986. 268 pp.

[BBI-030] Barrow, John G[raves]. *A Bibliography of Bibliographies in Reli-gion*. Ann Arbor: Edwards Brothers, Inc., 1955.

[BBI-040] Beaudiquez, Marcelle, ed. *Inventaire général des bibliographies nationales rétrospectives/Retrospective National Bibliogra-phies: An International Bibliography*. IFLA Publications 35. Munich: Saut, 1986. 189 pp.

[BBI-050] Bell, Barbara L. *An Annotated Guide to Current National Bibliog-raphies*. Government Documents Bibliographies. Alexan-dria: Chadwyck-Healey, 1986. 407 pp.

[BBI-060] Besterman, Theodore. *Art and Architecture: A Bibliography of Bibliographies*. Totowa, N.J.: Rowman and Littlefied, 1971. 216 pp.

[BBI-070] ------. *Literature, English and American: A Bibliography of Bibliog-raphies*. Totowa, N.J.: Rowman and Littlefield, 1971. 457 pp.

[BBI-080] ------. *Music and Drama: A Bibliography of Bibliographies*. Totowa, N.J.: Rowman and Littlefield, 1971.

[BBI-090] ------. *A World Bibliography of African Bibliographies*. Rev. J. D. Pearson. Totowa, N.J.: Rowman, 1975. 105 pp.

[BBI-100] ------. *A World Bibliography of Bibliographies*. 4th ed. 5 vols. Lausanne: Societas Bibliographica, 1965. 339 pp.

[BBI-110] ------. *A World Bibliography of Oriental Bibliographies*. Rev. J. D. Pearson. Totowa, N.J.: Rowman and Littlefield, 1975.

[BBI-120] Bewsey, Julia J. "Festschriften Bibliographies and Indexes." *Bulle-tin of Bibliography* 42 (1985): 193-202.

[BBI-130] *Bibliographic Index: A Cumulative Bibliography of Bibliographies*. New York: H. W. Wilson Co., 1937-. Annual.

[BBI-140] *Bibliographical Society of America. Papers*. New York: Biblio-graphical Society of America, 1904-. Quarterly.

[BBI-150] *Bibliographies and Indexes in the Performing Arts*. Westport, Conn.: Greenwood Press, 1984-. Irregular.

[BBI-160] *Bibliographische Berichte/Bibliographical Bulletin*. Frankfurt am Main: Klostermann, 1959-. Supersedes *Zeitschrift für Bibli-othekswesen un Bibliographie* 1-5 (1954-1958).

[BBI-170] Briney, Robert E., and Edward Wood. *SF Bibliographies: An Annotated Bibliography of Bibliographical Works on Science*

4

Fiction and Fantasy Fiction. Chicago: Advent Publishers, 1972.

[BBI-180] *Bulletin of Bibliography.* Westport, Conn.: GP Subscription Publications, 1897-. Quarterly.

[BBI-190] Caldwell-Wood, Naomi, and Patrick W. Wood. *Checklist of Bibliographies Appearing in the Bulletin of Bibliography, 1897-1987.* Wesport, Conn.: Meckler Corporation, 1989. 144 pp.

[BBI-200] *Canadian Theses/Theses canadiennes [1961-].* Ottawa: National Library of Canada, 1963-. 2 per year with cumulative index. *1947-1960.* 2 vols. 1973. Continues *Canadian Graduate Theses in the Humanities and Social Sciences, 1921-1946/ Theses des gradues canadiens dans les humanites et les sciences sociales.* Ottawa: Cloutier, 1951. 194 pp.

[BBI-210] Coatsworth, Patricia A., Mary Ravenhall, and James Hecimovich. *An Annotated Bibliography and Index Covering CPL Bibliographies 1-253, January 1978-December 1989.* Chicago: Council of Planning Librarians, [1989].

[BBI-220] Collison, Robert. *Published Library Catalogues: An Introduction to Their Contents and Use.* London: Mansell Information/ Publishing, Ltd., 1973. 184 pp.

[BBI-230] *Commonwealth National Bibliographies: An Annotated Directory.* 2nd ed. Comp. IFLA International Office for UBC. N.p.: Commonwealth Secretariat, 1982. 69 pp.

[BBI-240] *Comprehensive Dissertation Index, 1861-1972.* 37 vols. Ann Arbor: Xerox, 1973. Annual supplements, with cumulation for 1973-1982.

[BBI-250] Cordasco, Francesco. *A Register of 18th Century Bibliographies and References: A Chronological Quarter-Century Survey Relating to English Literature, Booksellers, Newspapers, Periodicals, Printing and Publishing, Aesthetics, Art and Music, Economics, History and Science: A Preliminary Contribution.* Chicago: V. Giorgio, 1950. Reprint. Detroit: Gale Research, 1968. 74 pp.

[BBI-260] Courtney, William P. *A Register of National Bibliography.* 3 vols. London: Constable, 1905-1912.

[BBI-270] *Dissertation Abstracts International.* Ann Arbor: University Microfilms International, 1938-. Monthly. Formerly *Index to American Doctoral Dissertations [1955-1963],* and *Doctoral Dissertations Accepted by American Universities [1933-1955].*

[BBI-280] Domay, Friedrich. *Bibliographie der nationalen Bibliographien/ Bibliographie mondiale des bibliographies nationales/A World Bibliography of National Bibliographies.* Hiersemanns Bibliographische Handbucher 6. Stuttgart: Hiersemann, 1987. 557 pp.

[BBI-290] Downs, Robert B. *American Library Resources: A Bibliographical Guide.* Chicago: American Library Association, 1951. 428 pp. *Supplement, 1950-1961.* 1962. 226 pp. *Supplement, 1961-1970.* 1972. 244 pp. *Supplement, 1971-1980.* 1981. 209 pp. American Library Resources: *Cumulative Index, 1870-1970.* Comp. Clara D. Keller. 1981. 89 pp.

[BBI-300] ------. *British and Irish Library Resources: A Bibliographical Guide.* London: Mansell, 1981. 427 pp.

[BBI-310] Eager, Alan R. *A Guide to Irish Bibliographical Material: A Bibliography of Irish Bibliographies and Sources of Information.* 2nd ed. Westport, Conn.: Greenwood Press, 1980. 502 pp.

[BBI-320] Gorman, G. E., and Lyn Gorman. *Theological and Religious Reference Materials.* 4 vols. Bibliographies and Indexes in Religious Studies 1-2, 7. Westport, Conn.: Greenwood Press, 1984-. Vol. 1: *General Resources and Biblical Studies.* 1984. 526 pp. Vol. 2: *Systematic Theology and Church History.* 1985. 401 pp. Vol. 3: *Practical Theology.* 1986. 388 pp. Vol. 4: *Judaism and Islam.* c. 1991.

[BBI-330] Guerry, Herbert. *A Bibliography of Philosophical Bibliographies.* Westport, Conn.: Greenwood Press, 1977. 332 pp. [2,353]

[BBI-340] Gray, Richard A., comp. *Serial Bibliographies in the Humanities and Social Sciences.* Ann Arbor: Pierian, 1969. 345 pp.

[BBI-350] Hartman, Donald K., and Jerome Drost. *Themes and Settings in Fiction: A Bibliography of Bibliographies.* San Jose, Calif.: Dibco Press, 1972.

[BBI-360] Henige, David, comp. *Serial Bibliographies and Abstracts in History: An Annotated Guide.* Bibliographies and Indexes in World History 2. Westport, Conn.: Greenwood Press, 1986. 220 pp.

[BBI-370] Howard-Hill, T[revor] H[oward]. *Index to British Literary Bibliography.* Oxford: Clarendon, 1969-.

[BBI-380] Hurd, John Coolidge. *A Bibliography of New Testament Bibliographies.* New York: Seabury Press, 1966.

[BBI-390] *Index to Theses with Abstracts Accepted for Higher Degrees by the*

6

Universities of Great Britain and Ireland and the Council for National Academic Awards. London: Aslib, 1953-. Quarterly.

[BBI-400] Jordan, Alma, and Barbara Comissiong. *The English-Speaking Caribbean: A Bibliography of Bibliographies.* Reference Publication in Latin American Studies. Boston: G. K. Hall, 1984. 411 pp.

[BBI-410] *Library, The: The Transactions of the Bibliographical Society.* Oxford: Oxford University Press, 1889-. Quarterly.

[BBI-420] Lochhead, Douglas, comp. *Bibliography of Canadian Bibliographies/Bibliographie des bibliographies canadiennes.* 2nd ed. Toronto: University of Toronto Press, in association with Bibliographical Society of Canada, 1972. 312 pp.

[BBI-430] Meggett, Joan M. *Music Periodicals: An Annotated Bibliography of Indexes and Bibliographies.* Metuchen, N.J.: Scarecrow Press, 1978.

[BBI-440] Nelson, Bonnie R. *A Guide to Published Library Catalogs.* Metuchen, N.J.: Scarecrow Press, 1982. 342 pp.

[BBI-450] Newman, Richard, comp. *Black Access: A Bibliography of Afro-American Bibliographies.* Westport, Conn.: Greenwood Press, 1984. 249 pp.

[BBI-460] Nilon, Charles H., ed. *Bibliography of Bibliographies in American Literature.* New York: R. R. Bowker Co., 1970.

[BBI-470] Northup, Clark Sutherland. *A Register of Bibliographies of the English Language and Literature.* 1925. Reprint. New York: Hafner Pub. Co., 1962. 507 pp.

[BBI-480] Reynolds, Michael M. *A Guide to Theses and Dissertations: An International Bibliography of Bibliographies.* Rev. ed. Phoenix: Oryx, 1985. 263 pp.

[BBI-490] Rouse, Richard H. *Serial Bibliographies for Medieval Studies.* Publications of the Center for Medieval and Renaissance Studies 3. Berkeley: University of California Press, 1969. 150 pp.

[BBI-500] Sabin, Joseph. *A Bibliography of Bibliography.* New York: J. Sabin and Sons, 1877. 150 pp. Annotated.

[BBI-510] Sheehy, Eugene P., ed. *Guide to Reference Books.* 10th ed. Chicago: American Library Association, 1986. 1,560 pp.

[BBI-520] Shields, Allan. *A Bibliography of Bibliographies in Aesthetics*. San Diego: San Diego State University Press, 1974. 79 pp.

[BBI-530] Shunami, Shlomo. *Bibliography of Jewish Bibliographies*. 2nd ed. Jerusalem: The Magnes Press, 1969. 997 pp. [4727] Supplement, 1975.

[BBI-540] Smith, Wilbur M. *A List of Bibliographies of Theological and Biblical Literature Published in Great Britain and America, 1595-1931*. Coatesville, Pa.: N.p., 1931. 62 pp. [300 entries]

[BBI-550] Szabe, Charles, et al. *Bibliography of Articles on the Humanities: British and American Festschriften Through 1980*. 2 vols. New York: Kraus International Publications, 1989.

[BBI-560] Toomey, Alice F. *A World Bibliography of Bibliographies: 1964-1974*. 2 vols. Totowa, N.J.: Rowman and Littlefield, 1977.

[BBI-570] Walford, A. J., and L. J Taylor, eds. *Walford's Guide to Reference Material*. 4th ed. 3 vols. London: Library Association, 1980-1987. Vol. 1: *Science and Technology*. 1980. 697 pp. Vol. 2: *Social and Historical Sciences, Philosophy and Religion*. 1982. 812 pp. Vol. 3: *Generalia, Language and Literature, the Arts*. 1987. 872 pp.

[BBI-580] Weeks, Elizabeth Harriet. *A Bibliography of Seventeenth Century Bibliographies: A List of the Bibliographies Cited on the Catalog Cards for the Titles in Wing's Short Title Catalog, 1641-1700*. Ann Arbor: University Microfilms International, 1978.

[BBI-590] Williamson, Jane. *New Feminist Scholarship: A Guide to Bibliographies*. Old Westbury: Feminist Press, 1979. 139 pp.

[BBI-600] Wortman, William A. *A Guide to Serial Bibliographies for Modern Literatures*. Selected Bibliographies in Language and Literature 3. New York: MLA, 1982. 124 pp.

[BBI-610] Wulff, Hans Jurgen, ed. *Bibliography of Film Bibliographies/Bibliographie der Filmbibliographien*. Munich: K. G. Saur, 1987. 326 pp. New York: K. G. Saur, 1987. 480 pp.

CHAPTER 2

AESTHETICS

BIBLIOGRAPHIES ON AESTHETICS

Although the body of literature treating aesthetics is vast, the number of bibliographies treating this particular topic is relatively small, and those available are often not as current as one would hope. The most timely general bibliographies in English given below include the Aesthetic Education Program's work [BAE-010], Mary Vance's two volume work [BAE-200], and Irena Wojnar's *Aesthetic Education* [BAE-210]. To find more current bibliographies in aesthetics one should consult Hans Bolliger's German and English bibliography [BAE-060], or Franco Fanizza's and J. Koller's *Antico e Moderno: L'estetica e la sua Storia* [BAE-090], which offers summaries in English. For those most concerned about the history of aesthetics, several additional works will be particularly helpful, including [BAE-020], [BAE-030], [BAE-050], [BAE-070], [BAE-080], [BAE-110], [BAE-120], [BAE-180], and [BAE-190]. For more tightly focused studies treating ethnic or specialized approaches to aesthetics, consult [BAE-040], [BAE-100], [BAE-130], [BAE-140], [BAE-150], and [BAE-160]. To locate additional bibliographies not given here, consult *A Bibliography of Bibliographies in Aesthetics* [BBI-520] and other bibliographies of bibliographies given in Chapter 1. Many of the most recent works in aesthetics may be located below in sections entitled Key works

10

in Aesthetics and Key Works in Aesthetics and Religion. The bibliographies in these works will also prove useful to the researcher as one traces sources to related works.

[BAE-010] Aesthetic Education Program. *The Aesthetic Education Program: A Bibliography, Current as of February 1976.* [St. Louis]: CEMREL, 1976. 23 pp.

[BAE-020] Albert, Ethel M., et al. *A Selected Bibliography on Values, Ethics, and Esthetics in the Behavioral Sciences and Philosophy, 1920-1958.* Glencoe, Ill.: N.p., 1959. 342 pp. [2006]

[BAE-030] Baldwin, James Mark. *Dictionary of Philosophy and Psychology.* 4 vols. in 3. New ed. 1925. Reprint. Gloucester, Mass.: Peter Smith, 1949. See vol. 3, Benjamin Rand, *Bibliography of Philosophy, Psychology, and Cognate Subjects.*

[BAE-040] Baxandall, Lee. *Marxism and Aesthetics: A Selective Annotated Bibliography: Books and Articles in the English Language.* New York: Humanities Press, 1973. xxii, 261 pp.

[BAE-050] Belknap, George N. *A Guide to Reading in Aesthetics and Theory of Poetry.* University of Oregon: Studies in College Teaching, Bulletin 5. Eugene, Oreg.: University of Oregon, 1934. 91 pp. [100 on aesthetics] (See [LIT-120])

[BAE-060] Bolliger, Hans, ed. *Dokumentations-Bibliothek zur Kunst des 20. Jahrhunderts/Bibliography of 20th Century Art Publications.* San Francisco: Alan Wofsy Fine Arts, 1991.

[BAE-070] Chandler, Albert Richard, and Edward Norton Barnhart. *A Bibliography of Psychological and Experimental Aesthetics, 1864-1937.* Berkeley: University of California Press, 1938. Reprint. New York: AMS Press, 1979. 190 pp.

[BAE-080] Draper, John William. *Eighteenth Century English Aesthetics: A Bibliography.* 1931. Reprint. New York: Octagon Books, 1968. 140 pp. [1300]

[BAE-090] Fanizza, Franco, and J. Koller. *Antico e Moderno: L'estetica e la sua Storia.* Palermo: Centro Internationale Studi di Estetica, 1989. 91 pp. Summary in English.

[BAE-100] Fowler, Carolyn. *Black Arts and Black Aesthetics: A Bibliography.* 2nd ed. [Georgia?]: First World, 1981. xliii, 211 pp.

[BAE-110] Gayley, Charles Mills, and Fred Newton Scott. *A Guide to the*

11

Literature of Aesthetics. Library Bulletin, no. 11. Berkeley: University of California, 1890. Reprint. Burt Franklin Bibliography and Reference Series, no. 498. New York: Burt Franklin Reprints, 1974. 116 pp. [1750]

[BAE-120] Hammond, William Alexander. *A Bibliography of Aesthetics and of the Philosophy of the Fine Arts from 1900-1932*. Rev. ed. 1934. Reprint. New York: Russell and Russell, 1967. 205 pp. [2191]

[BAE-130] Kiell, Norman. *Psychiatry and Psychology in the Visual Arts and Aesthetics: A Bibliography*. Madison: University of Wisconsin Press, 1965. 250 pp.

[BAE-140] Lawford, Paul. *Marxist Aesthetics: A Short Bibliography of Works in English, with a Supplement on Russian Formalism, Structuralism, Semiotics*. Keele, Staffordshire, England: Department of Sociology and Social Anthropology, University of Keele, 1977. 51 pp.

[BAE-150] Manova, N. V. *Problems of Marxist-Leninist Esthetics and Esthetic Education*. Wright-Patterson Air Force Base, Ohio: Translation Division, Foreign Technology Division, 1965. 152 pp.

[BAE-160] Mitra, Haridas. *Contribution to a Bibliography of Indian Art and Aesthetics*. 2nd ed. Santiniketan: Visva-Bharati Research Publications Committee, 1980. 237 pp. Bib. refs. (See [BVA-510])

[BAE-170] Nugent, Elinor Roth. *Design for Living: An Annotated Bibliography of the Aesthetics*. [East Lansing]: Michigan State University, 1966. 78 pp.

[BAE-180] Schimmelman, Janice Gayle. *American Imprints on Art Through 1865: Books and Pamphlets on Drawing, Painting, Sculpture, Aesthetics, Art Criticism, and Instruction: An Annotated Bibliography*. Boston: G. K. Hall, 1990. 419 pp.

[BAE-190] ------. *A Checklist of European Treatises on Art and Essays on Aesthetics Available in America Through 1815*. Worcester, Mass.: American Antiquarian Society, 1983. 79 pp.

[BAE-200] Vance, Mary. *Aesthetics: Monographs*. 2 vols. Monticello, Ill.: Vance Bibliographies, 1984. 258 pp.

[BAE-210] Wojnar, Irena. *Aesthetic Education*. Paris: Unesco; Geneva: IBE, 1978. 84 pp.

KEY WORKS ON AESTHETICS

The writings listed below represent only a small number of the numerous works available on aesthetics. While this brief list includes standard works dating back to 1909, most have been selected because of their currency, dating primarily from 1980 to the present. Furthermore, this section includes only works which treat aesthetics in its broader, philosophical context. Works treating aesthetics as linked to specific disciplines, such as architecture or music, have been included in chapters focusing on those subjects. Even with this abbreviated list of works included in Chapter 2, the number of titles available on aesthetics can be bewildering unless one knows where to begin reading. As an introduction to the study of aesthetics, Stephen David Ross's *Art and Its Significance: An Anthology of Aesthetic Theory* [AES-1440] offers an excellent selection of the major statements by the most prominent aestheticians from Plato and Aristotle to Gadamer and Derrida, most of whom are treated in greater detail by other titles in this section. Other anthologies which provide useful selections of key statements by aestheticians include Moshe Barasch's *Theories of Art: From Plato to Winckelmann* [AES-110], George Dickie's, R. J. Sclufani's, and Ronald Roblin's *Aesthetics: A Critical Anthology* [AES-510], and Trevor Pateman's *Key Concepts: A Guide to Aesthetics, Criticism, and the Arts in Education* [AES-1300]. For a lucid and reliable survey of the history of aesthetics, read Monroe C. Beardsley's *Aesthetics from Classical Greece to the Present: A Short History* [AES-140]. Also consider Harold Osborne's *Aesthetics and Art Theory: An Historical Introduction* [AES-1280] as a useful overview. Beyond reading these foundational works, one will do well to consult several reference works, including David Cooper's *A Companion to Aesthetics* [AES-380], Richard L. Gregory's and O. L. Zongwill's *Oxford Companion to the Mind* [AES-720], or, for more extensive studies, Paul Edwards' eight volume work, *The Encyclopedia of Philosophy* [AES-570].

While many of the works listed below make notable contributions to the study of aesthetics, a few have been written with such eloquence that they promise to be memorable for many years to come. Some of the most noteworthy authors and titles are Jacques Barzun's *The Use and Abuse of Art*

[AES-130], Susanne Katherina Langer's *Feeling and Form: A Theory of Art* [AES-990], and her *Philosophy in a New Key: A Study of the Symbolism of Reason, Rite and Art* [AES-1000], Rollo May's *The Courage to Create* [AES-1150], and Jose Ortega y Gasset's *The Dehumanization of Art: And other Essays on Art, Culture, and Literature* [AES-1260]. A number of the works in this section treat specialized topics, or focus on specific eras. Some of the more prominent categories are as follows: anthropology and aesthetics [AES-390], [AES-1110]; comparative aesthetics [AES-330], [AES-340], [AES-1020], [AES-1090], [AES-1250], [AES-1290], [AES-1450], [AES-1540], [AES-1830]; feminism and aesthetics [AES-790], [AES-1850]; Marxist aesthetics [AES-540], [AES-1390], [AES-1760]; modernism and aesthetics [AES-180] [AES-280], [AES-300], [AES-700], [AES-1340], [AES-1720]; postmodernism and aesthetics [AES-320], [AES-420], [AES-650], [AES-960]. For the most current and scholarly discussions on aesthetics, see the following journals: *The British Journal of Aesthetics* [AES-250], *The Journal of Aesthetic Education* [AES-870], and the *Journal of Aesthetics and Art Criticism* [AES-880]. For works treating aesthetics and specific disciplines, consult the sections of the pertinent disciplines given in subsequent chapters.

[AES-010]   Aagaard-Mogensen, Lars, and Luk de Vos, eds. *Text, Literature, and Aesthetics: In Honor of Monroe C. Beardsley*. Elementa, Bd. 45. Wurzburg: Konigshausen and Neumann; Amsterdam: Rodopi, 1986. 224 pp.

[AES-020]   Adler, Mortimer Jerome. *Six Great Ideas: Truth, Goodness, Beauty, Liberty, Equality, Justice: Ideas we Judge by, Ideas we Act on*. New York: Collier Books; London: Collier Macmillan, 1981. 243 pp.

[AES-030]   Adorno, Theodor W., Gretel Adorno, and Rolf Tiedemann. *Aesthetic Theory*. Trans. *Ästhetische Theorie*. London; Boston: Routledge and Kegan Paul, 1983. Bib. refs. pp. 499-511.

[AES-040]   Alexenberg, Melvin L. *Aesthetic Experience in Creative Process*. Romat Gan, Israel: Bar-Ilan University Press, 1981. Bib. pp. 203-205.

[AES-050]   Anderberg, Thomas, Tore Nilstun, and Ingmar Persson. *Aesthetic Distinction: Essays Presented to Goran Hermeren on his 50th Birthday*. Lund: Lund University Press; Bromley: Chart-

14

well-Bratt, 1988. Bib. pp. 115-117.

[AES-060] Anderson, Howard Peter, and John S. Shea, eds. *Studies in Criticism and Aesthetics, 1660-1800: Essays in Honor of Samuel Hold Monk*. Minneapolis, University of Minnesota Press, [1967]. 419 pp. Bib.

[AES-070] Appelbaum, David. *Making the Body Heard: The Body's Way Toward Existence*. New York: Peter Lang, 1988. Bib. pp. 195-204.

[AES-080] Aristotle. *The Poetics of Aristotle: Translation and Commentary*. Trans. and ed. Stephen Halliwell. Chapel Hill: University of North Carolina Press, 1987. Bib. p. 185.

[AES-090] Aschenbrenner, Karl. *The Concept of Coherence in Art*. Dordrecht; Boston: D. Reidel Publishing Co., 1985. Dist. Kluwer Academic Publishers, Hingham, Mass. Bib. p. 239.

[AES-100] Baldwin, James Mark, ed. *Dictionary of Philosophy and Psychology*. New ed. New York: Peter Smith, 1940.

[AES-110] Barasch, Moshe. *Theories of Art: From Plato to Winckelmann*. New York: New York University Press, 1985. 394 pp. Bib. refs. in notes.

[AES-120] Barilli, Renato. *A Course on Aesthetics*. Minneapolis: University of Minnesota Press, 1993. Bib. refs.

[AES-130] Barzun, Jacques. *The Use and Abuse of Art*. A. W. Mellon Lectures, 1973. Bollingen Series, no. 35. Princeton: Princeton University Press, 1974. 150 pp.

[AES-140] Beardsley, Monroe C. *Aesthetics from Classical Greece to the Present: A Short History*. 1966. Reprint. Tuscaloosa: University of Alabama Press, 1975. Bib. pp. 389-398

[AES-150] Beardsley, Monroe C., Michael J. Wreen, and Donald M. Callen. *The Aesthetic Point of View: Selected Essays*. Ithaca: Cornell University Press, 1982. Bib. pp. 371-378.

[AES-160] Berenson, Bernard. *Aesthetics and History*. 1948. Reprint. Ann Arbor, Mich.: University Microfilms International, 1990. 242 pp.

[AES-170] Berleant, Arnold. *Art and Engagement*. Philadelphia: Temple University Press, 1991. Bib. refs. pp. 215-245.

[AES-180] Bernstein, J[ay] M. *The Fate of Art: Aesthetic Alienation from Kant to Derrida and Adorno*. Cambridge: Polity, 1992.

292 pp.

[AES-190] Bersani, Leo. *Arts of Impoverishment: Beckett, Rothko, Resnais*. Cambridge, Mass.; London: Harvard University Press, 1993. Bib. refs.

[AES-200] Best, David. *Feeling and Reason in the Arts*. Boston: Allen and Unwin, 1985. Bib. pp. 195-197.

[AES-210] Bloch, Ernst, ed. *Aesthetics and Politics*. London: Verso, 1977. 220 pp. Bib. refs.

[AES-220] Bonville, W. J. *Footnotes to a Fairytale: A Study of the Nature of Expression in the Arts*. St. Louis, Mo.: Warren H. Green, Inc., 1979. Bib. pp. 168-170.

[AES-230] Boullart, K. E. *Aesthetic Values: Special Aspects*. Gent, Belgium: Philosophica, 1986. 153 pp. Bib. refs.

[AES-240] Bowie, Andrew. *Aesthetics and Subjectivity from Kant to Nietzsche*. Manchester; New York: Manchester University Press, 1990. 284 pp. Bib. refs.

[AES-250] *British Journal of Aesthetics, The*. London: Oxford University Press, 1960-.

[AES-260] Buber, Martin. *On Intersubjectivity and Cultural Creativity*. Ed. S. N. Eisenstadt. Chicago: University of Chicago Press, 1992. 264 pp.

[AES-270] Bungay, Stephen. *Beauty and Truth: A Study of Hegel's Aesthetics*. Oxford Modern Languages and Literature Monographs. Oxford: Oxford University Press, 1984. 256 pp. Bib.

[AES-280] Burger, Peter. *The Decline of Modernism*. Cambridge: Polity Press, 1992. Bib. refs. pp. 162-182.

[AES-290] Burke, Edmund. *On the Sublime and the Beautiful*. 1980. Reprint. Charlottesville, Va.: Ibis Pub., 1989. 342 pp.

[AES-300] Calinescu, Matei. *Five Faces of Modernity: Modernism, Avant-Garde, Decadence, Kitsch, Postmodernism*. Rev. ed. of *Faces of Modernity*, 1977. Durham: Duke University Press, 1987. Bib. pp. 365-385.

[AES-310] Campbell, Walter. *The Five Pillars of Wisdom: A Dialogue*. Manchester, England: W. Campbell, 1984. 79 pp.

[AES-320] Carroll, David. *Paraesthetics: Foucault, Lyotard, Derrida*. New York: Methuen, 1987. Reprint. New York: Routledge,

16

1989. 219 pp. Bib. refs.

[AES-330] Chaudhary, Angraj. *Comparative Aesthetics, East and West.*
Delhi: Eastern Book Linkers, 1991. Bib. refs. pp. 266-284.

[AES-340] Chaudhury, Prabas Jivan. *Studies in Comparative Aesthetics.* 2nd
ed. Santiniketan: Visva-Bharati Research Publications,
1990. 127 pp. Bib. refs.

[AES-350] Child, Irvin Long. *Development of Sensitivity to Esthetic Values.*
New Haven: Yale University, 1964. Bib. p. 51

[AES-360] Chipp, Herschel B. *Theories of Modern Art: A Source Book by Artists and Critics.* Berkeley: University of California Press,
1968. Bib. pp. 631-651.

[AES-370] Cloutier, Cecile, and Calvin Seerveld, eds. *Opuscula Aesthetica
Nostra: A Volume of Essays on Aesthetics and the Arts in
Canada.* Edmonton, Alberta: Academic Print. and Pub.,
1984. Bib. pp. 189-191.

[AES-380] Cooper, David E[dward], ed. *A Companion to Aesthetics.* Blackwell Companions to Philosophy. Oxford: Blackwell Refer-
ence, 1992. 466 pp. Bibs.

[AES-390] Coote, Jeremy, and Anthony Shelton. *Anthropology, Art and Aesthetics.* Oxford Studies in the Anthropology of Cultural
Forms. Oxford: Clarendon, 1992. 281 pp. Bibs.

[AES-400] Cothey, A[ntony] L. *The Nature of Art.* The Problems of Philosophy. London; New York: Routledge, 1990. Bib. refs. pp.
190-193.

[AES-410] Croce, Benedetto. *Aesthetic as Science of Expression and General
Linguistic.* Rev. ed. Trans. Douglas Ainslie. New York:
Noonday Press, [1953]. Bib. pp. 475-489.

[AES-420] Crowther, Paul. *Critical Aesthetics and Postmodernism.* Oxford:
Clarendon Press, 1993. 214 pp. Bib. refs.

[AES-430] ------. *The Kantian Sublime: From Morality to Art.* Oxford Philosophical Monographs. Oxford: Clarendon, 1989. 200 pp.

[AES-440] Currie, Gregory. *An Ontology of Art.* Basingstoke: Macmillan
Publishing Co., with Scots Philosophical Club, 1989. Bib.
pp. 135-138.

[AES-450] Della Volpe, Galvano. *Critique of Taste.* Trans. *Critica del Gusto.*
London; New York: Verso, 1991. 272 pp. Bib. refs.

[AES-460] Denvir, Bernard. *The Late Victorians: Art, Design, and Society, 1852-1910*. New York: Longman, 1986. Bib. pp. 249-263.

[AES-470] Deutsch, Eliot. *Studies in Comparative Aesthetics*. [Honolulu]: University Press of Hawaii, 1975. Bib. pp. 90-95.

[AES-480] Dewey, John. *Art as Experience*. New York: Minton, Balch and Co., [1934]. Reprint. New York: Perigee Books, 1980. 355 pp.

[AES-490] Dickie, George. *The Art Circle: A Theory of Art*. New York: Haven, 1984. 116 pp. Bib. refs.

[AES-500] ------. *Evaluating Art*. Philadelphia: Temple University Press, 1988. 193 pp.

[AES-510] Dickie, George, R. J. Sclufani, and Ronald Roblin, eds. *Aesthetics: A Critical Anthology*. 2nd ed. New York: St. Martin's Press, 1989. Bib. pp. 651-666.

[AES-520] Dipert, Randall R. *Artifacts, Art Works, and Agency*. Philadelphia: Temple University Press, 1993. Bib. refs. pp. 249-261.

[AES-530] Dufrenne, Mikel, Mark S. Roberts, and Dennis Gallagher. *In the Presence of the Sensuous: Essays in Aesthetics*. Atlantic Highlands, N.J.: Humanities Press International, 1990. xxv, 213 pp. Bib. pp. 199-207.

[AES-540] Eagleton, Terry. *The Ideology of the Aesthetic*. Oxford: Basil Blackwell Publishing, 1990. 400 pp.

[AES-550] Eaton, Marcia Muelder. *Aesthetics and the Good Life*. Rutherford, N.J.: Fairleigh Dickinson University Press; London; Toronto: Associated University Presses, 1989. Bib. pp. 194-203.

[AES-560] ------. *Basic Issues in Aesthetics*. Belmont, Calif.: Wadsworth Publishing Co., 1987. 154 pp. Bibs.

[AES-570] Edwards, Paul, ed. *The Encyclopedia of Philosophy*. 8 vols. New York: Macmillan Publishing Co., 1967. Bibs.

[AES-580] Eldridge, Richard Thomas. *On Moral Personhood: Philosophy, Literature, Criticism, and Self-Understanding*. Chicago: University of Chicago Press, 1989. 210 pp.

[AES-590] *Empirical Studies of the Arts*. Farmingdale, N.Y.: Baywood Publishing Co., 1983-.

[AES-600] Erwin, John W. *Annunciations to Anyone: The Disclosure of Au-*

18

thority in Writing and Painting. New York: Peter Lang, 1990. Bib. refs. pp. 269-273.

[AES-610] Farley, Frank H., and Ronald W. Neperud. *The Foundations of Aesthetics, Art and Art Education.* New York: Frederick A. Praeger Publishers, 1988. Bib. pp. 365-402.

[AES-620] Fekete, John, ed. *Life after Postmodernism: Essays on Value and Culture.* CultureTexts. Houndmills, Basingstoke, Hampshire: Macmillan Education, 1988. 197 pp. Bibs.

[AES-630] Feldman, Edmund Burke. *Becoming Human Through Art: Aesthetic Experience in the School.* Englewood Cliffs, N.J.: Prentice-Hall Press, [1970]. Bib. pp. 384-385.

[AES-640] ------. *Varieties of Visual Experience.* 2nd ed. Englewood Cliffs, N.J.: Prentice-Hall Press, 1981. Bib. pp. 504-506.

[AES-650] Foster, Hal. *The Anti-Aesthetic: Essays on Postmodern Culture.* Port Townsend, Wash.: Bay Press, 1983. 159 pp. Bib. refs.

[AES-660] Fowler, Barbara Hughes. *The Hellenistic Aesthetic.* Madison, Wis.: University of Wisconsin Press, 1989. Bib. pp. 201-213.

[AES-670] French, Peter A., Theodore E. Uehling, and Howard K. Wettstein. *Philosophy and the Arts.* Midwest Studies in Philosophy, vol. 16. Notre Dame: University of Notre Dame Press, 1991. 496 pp.

[AES-680] Fuller, Peter. *Theoria: Art and the Absence of Grace.* London: Chatto and Windus, 1988. 224 pp.

[AES-690] Furniss, Tom. *Edmund Burke's Aesthetic Ideology: Language, Gender, and Political Economy in Revolution.* Cambridge; New York: Cambridge University Press, 1993. Bib. refs.

[AES-700] Gauss, Charles Edward. *The Aesthetic Theories of French Artists from Realism to Surrealism.* Baltimore: Johns Hopkins Press, 1949. Bib. pp. 100-107.

[AES-710] Geiger, Moritz, and Klaus Berger. *The Significance of Art: A Phenomenological Approach to Aesthetics.* Trans. *Die Bedeutung der Kunst.* Current Continental Research, no. 402. Washington, D.C.: Center for Advanced Research in Phenomenology with University Press of America, 1986. 217 pp. Bib. refs.

[AES-720] Gregory, Richard L., and O. L. Zongwill. *Oxford Companion to the Mind.* New York: Oxford University Press, 1987. 920 pp.

[AES-730] Hanfling, Oswald, ed. *Philosophical Aesthetics: An Introduction.* Oxford: Basil Blackwell Publishing; Cambridge, Mass.: Open University, 1991. 496 pp.

[AES-740] Hanke, John W. *Maritain's Ontology of the Work of Art.* Hague, Netherlands: Martinus Nijhoff Publications, 1973. Bib. pp. 125-129.

[AES-750] Harrell, Jean G[abbert]. *Profundity: A Universal Value.* University Park, Pa.: Pennsylvania State University Press, 1992. Bib. refs. pp. 183-188.

[AES-760] Haskell, Francis. *Past and Present in Art and Taste: Selected Essays.* New Haven: Yale University Press, 1987. Bib. pp. 227-249.

[AES-770] ------. *Rediscoveries in Art: Some Aspects of Taste, Fashion and Collecting in England and France.* Ithaca: Cornell University Press, 1976. Bib. pp. 231-242.

[AES-780] Hayward, Frank Herbert. *The Lesson in Appreciation: An Essay on the Pedagogics of Beauty.* New York: Macmillan Publishing Co., 1925. Bib. pp. 225-230.

[AES-790] Hein, Hilde S., and Carolyn Korsmeyer. *Aesthetics in Feminist Perspective.* Bloomington: Indiana University Press, 1993. Bib. refs.

[AES-800] Hermeren, Goran. *Aspects of Aesthetics.* Lund: CWK Gleerup, 1983. Bib. pp. 261-271.

[AES-810] Hospers, John. *Understanding the Arts.* Englewood Cliffs, N.J.: Prentice-Hall Press, 1982. 431 pp. Bibs.

[AES-820] Ingarden, Roman. *Selected Papers in Aesthetics.* Ed. Peter J. McCormick. Philosophia Resources Library. Washington, D.C.: Catholic University of America Press; Munich: Philosophia Verlag, 1985. Bib. pp. 183-261.

[AES-830] Iser, Wolfgang. *Walter Pater: The Aesthetic Moment.* Trans. *Die Autonomie des Ästhetischen.* European Studies in English Literature. Cambridge, England; New York: Cambridge University Press, 1987. Bib. pp. 194-204.

[AES-840] Israel, Calvin, ed. *Discoveries and Considerations: Essays on Early American Literature and Aesthetics: Presented to Harold Jantz.* Albany: State University of New York Press, 1976. 216 pp. Bibs.

[AES-850] Jhanji, Rekha. *Aesthetic Meaning: Some Recent Theories.* Delhi:

20

Ajanta Publications, 1980. Bib. pp. 187-196.

[AES-860]   Johnson, Robert Vincent. *Aestheticism*. London: Methuen, [1969]. Bib. pp. 87-92.

[AES-870]   *Journal of Aesthetic Education, The*. Urbana: University of Illinois Press, 1966-. Quarterly.

[AES-880]   *Journal of Aesthetics and Art Criticism, The*. [Philadelphia]: American Society for Aesthetics, 1941-. Quarterly.

[AES-890]   Keefe, Robert, and Janice A. Keefe. *Walter Pater and the Gods of Disorder*. Athens: Ohio University Press, 1988. Bib. pp. 171-178.

[AES-900]   Kemal, Salim. *Kant's Aesthetic Theory: An Introduction*. Houndmills, Basingstoke, Hampshire: Macmillan Publishing Co., 1992. Bib. refs. pp. 170-193.

[AES-910]   Knobler, Nathan. *Visual Dialogue: An Introduction to the Appreciation of Art*. 3rd ed. New York: Holt, Rinehart and Winston, 1980. Bib. pp. 301-305.

[AES-920]   Knoepflmacher, U. C., and G. B. Tennyson. *Nature and the Victorian Imagination*. Berkeley: University of California Press, 1977. 519 pp. Bib.

[AES-930]   Knudsen, Donald L[ee]. *A Crushing Truth for Art: Martin Heidegger's Meditation on Truth and the Work of Art in Der ursprung des Kunstwerkes*. Toronto: Institute for Christian Studies, 1988. Bib. pp. 131-142.

[AES-940]   Kostelanetz, Richard. *Esthetics Contemporary*. Rev. ed. Buffalo, N.Y.: Prometheus Books, 1989. Bib. pp. 451-464.

[AES-950]   Kovach, Francis Joseph. *Philosophy of Beauty*. Norman, Okla.: University of Oklahoma Press, 1974. Bib. pp. 318-337.

[AES-960]   Kroker, Arthur, and David Cook. *The Postmodern Scene: Excremental Culture and Hyper-Aesthetics*. 2nd ed. New York: St. Martin's Press, 1988. Bib. pp. 291-320.

[AES-970]   Krukowski, Lucian. *Art and Concept: A Philosophical Study*. Amherst: University of Massachusetts Press, 1987. Bib. pp. 115-123.

[AES-980]   Kubler, George. *The Shape of Time: Remarks on the History of Things*. New Haven: Yale University Press, 1962. 136 pp.

[AES-990]   Langer, Susanne Katherina (Knauth). *Feeling and Form: A*

Theory of Art. New York: Charles Scribner's Sons, 1953. Bib. 417-423.

[AES-1000] ------. *Philosophy in a New Key: A Study of the Symbolism of Reason, Rite and Art.* New York: The New American Library, [1942]. 248 pp.

[AES-1010] Lankford, E. Louis. *Aesthetics, Issues and Inquiry.* Reston, Va.: National Art Education Association, 1992. 106 pp. Bib. refs.

[AES-1020] Li, Tse-hou. *The Path of Beauty: A Study of Chinese Aesthetics.* Beijing: Morning Glory Publishers, 1988. 270 pp.

[AES-1030] Lovell, Terry. *Pictures of Reality: Aesthetics, Politics, Pleasure.* N.p.: British Film Institute, 1980. Bib. pp. 102-111.

[AES-1040] McCloskey, Mary A. *Kant's Aesthetic.* Albany: State University of New York Press, 1987. Bib. pp. 178-181.

[AES-1050] McCormick, Peter [J.]. *Modernity, Aesthetics, and the Bounds of Art.* Ithaca: Cornell University Press, 1990. 349 pp. Bib. refs.

[AES-1060] MacDiarmid, Hugh. *Aesthetics in Scotland.* Edinburgh: Mainstream, 1984. 99 pp. Bib. refs.

[AES-1070] McEvilley, Thomas. *Art and Discontent: Theory at the Millennium.* Kingston, N.Y.: McPherson and Co., 1991. 186 pp. Bib. refs.

[AES-1080] McFarland, Thomas. *Originality and Imagination.* Baltimore: Johns Hopkins University Press, 1985. Bib. pp. xvii-xxxvi.

[AES-1090] McLaren, Ronald, and Donald Keene. *Aesthetic and Ethical Values in Japanese Culture.* Richmond, Ind.: Institute for Education on Japan, Earlham College, 1990. 48 pp. Bibs.

[AES-1100] Malek, James S. *The Arts Compared: An Aspect of Eighteenth-Century British Aesthetics.* Detroit: Wayne State University Press, 1974. 175 pp. Bibs.

[AES-1110] Maquet, Jacques. *The Aesthetic Experience: An Anthropologist Looks at the Visual Arts.* New Haven: Yale University Press, 1986. Bib. pp. 256-260. New Haven; London: Yale University Press, 1988. 283 pp.

[AES-1120] Margolis, Joseph Zalman, ed. *Philosophy Looks at the Arts: Contemporary Readings in Aesthetics.* Rev. ed. Philadelphia: Temple University Press, 1978. Bibs., annotated.

22

[AES-1130] Marvin, Walter Taylor. *An Introduction to Systematic Philosophy.* New York: Columbia University Press, 1909. Bib. p. 568. Pt. V, Aesthetics.

[AES-1140] Mattick, Paul. *Eighteenth-Century Aesthetics and the Reconstitution of Art.* New York: Cambridge University Press, 1993.

[AES-1150] May, Rollo. *The Courage to Create.* New York: W. W. Norton and Co., 1975. 143 pp. Bib. refs.

[AES-1160] Mayo, Donald H. "Carl G. Jung: A Solution to the Problem of the Aesthetic Experience." Ph.D. Thesis, American University, 1988. Bib. pp. 201-207.

[AES-1170] Meerbote, Ralf, and Hud Hudson. *Kant's Aesthetics.* Atascadero, Calif.: Ridgeview, 1991. Bib. pp. 129-143.

[AES-1180] Meynell, Hugo Anthony. *The Nature of Aesthetic Value.* London: Macmillan Publishing Co., 1986. Bib. pp. 134-153.

[AES-1190] Michelson, Peter. *Speaking the Unspeakable: A Poetics of Obscenity.* Rev. of *Aesthetics of Pornography.* Albany: State University of New York Press, 1993. Bib. pp. 301-312.

[AES-1200] Milazzo, Richard. *Beauty and Critique.* New York: TSL, 1982. 175 pp. Bib. refs.

[AES-1210] Mitias, Michael H. *Aesthetic Quality and Aesthetic Experience.* Elementa, Bd. 50. Amsterdam: Rodopi; Wurzburg: Konigshausen and Neumann, 1988. 176 pp. Bib. refs.

[AES-1220] ------. *What Makes an Experience Aesthetic?* Elementa, Bd. 51. Amsterdam: Rodopi; Wurzburg: Konigshausen and Neumann, 1988.

[AES-1230] Moravcsik, J. M. E., and Philip Temko. *Plato on Beauty, Wisdom, and the Arts.* Totowa, N.J.: Rowman and Allanheld, 1982. 150 pp. Bib. refs.

[AES-1240] Mothersill, Mary. *Beauty Restored.* New York: Oxford University Press, 1984. Bib. pp. 429-434.

[AES-1250] Mukherji, Ramaranjan. *Comparative Aesthetics: Indian and Western.* Calcutta: Sanskrit Pustak Bhandar, 1991. Bib. refs. pp. 156-161.

[AES-1260] Ortega y Gasset, Jose. *The Dehumanization of Art: And other Essays on Art, Culture, and Literature.* Trans. *La deshumanizacion del arte.* 1948. Reprint. Princeton: Princeton University Press, 1968. 204 pp. Bib. refs. in footnotes.

23

[AES-1270] Osborne, Harold, comp. *Aesthetics*. Oxford Readings in Philosophy. London: Oxford University Press, 1972. Bib. pp. 178-184.

[AES-1280] ------. *Aesthetics and Art Theory: An Historical Introduction*. New York: E. P. Dutton and Co., Inc., 1970. Bib. pp. 308-313.

[AES-1290] Pandey, Kanti Chandra. *Comparative Aesthetics*. 2nd ed. 2 vols. Chowkhamba Sanskrit Studies, vol. 2, no. 4. Varanasi: Chowkhamba Sanskrit Series Office, 1990.

[AES-1300] Pateman, Trevor. *Key Concepts: A Guide to Aesthetics, Criticism, and the Arts in Education*. The Falmer Press Library on Aesthetic Education. London; New York: Falmer Press, 1991. Bib. refs. pp. 193-202.

[AES-1310] Pawlowski, Tadeusz. *Aesthetic Values*. Nijhoff International Philosophy Series, vol. 31. Dordrecht; Boston: Kluwer Academic, 1989. 138 pp. Bib. refs.

[AES-1320] Philipson, Morris H., and Paul J. Gudel. *Aesthetics Today*. Rev. ed. New York: New American Library, 1980. Bib. pp. 569-592.

[AES-1330] Pole, David, and George Roberts. *Aesthetics, Form and Emotion*. London: Duckworth, 1983. 248 pp. Bib. refs.

[AES-1340] Rader, Melvin Miller, ed. *Modern Book of Esthetics: An Anthology*. 5th ed. New York: Holt, Rinehart and Winston, 1979. Bib. pp. 523-552.

[AES-1350] Ramesh, G. *Aesthetics and Education*. New Delhi: South Asian Publishers, 1988. Bib. pp. 174-188. (Herbert Edward Read.)

[AES-1360] Read, Herbert Edward, and A[rthur] H[ilary] Armstrong. *On Beauty*. Eranos Lectures, no. 6. Dallas, Tex.: Spring Publications, 1987. 73 pp.

[AES-1370] Redfern, H[ildred] B[etty]. *Questions in Aesthetic Education*. Introductory Studies in Philosophy of Education. London; Boston: Allen and Unwin, 1986. Bib. pp. 114-118.

[AES-1380] Richardson, John Adkins. *Art: The Way It Is*. 2nd ed. New York: Harry N. Abrams, 1980. Bib. pp. 358-363, annotated.

[AES-1390] Rose, Margaret A. *Marx's Lost Aesthetic: Karl Marx and the Visual Arts*. Cambridge, England; New York: Cambridge University Press, 1988. Bib. pp. 199-207.

24

[AES-1400] Roskill, Mark W., and David Carrier. *Truth and Falsehood in Visual Images*. Amherst: University of Massachusetts Press, 1983. 145 pp. Bib. refs.

[AES-1410] Ross, Malcolm. *The Aesthetic Impulse*. Oxford; Elmsford, N.Y.: Pergamon Press, 1984. Bib. p. 148.

[AES-1420] ------. *The Arts: A Way of Knowing*. Oxford; New York: Pergamon Press, 1983. 244 pp. Bibs.

[AES-1430] ------. *The Development of Aesthetic Experience*. Curriculum Issues in Arts Education, vol. 3. Oxford; New York: Pergamon Press, 1982. 210 pp. Bibs.

[AES-1440] Ross, Stephen David, ed. *Art and Its Significance: An Anthology of Aesthetic Theory*. 2nd ed. Albany: State University of New York Press, 1987. 638 pp.

[AES-1450] Roy, Pabitrakumar. *Beauty, Art, and Man: Studies in Recent Indian Theories of Art*. Monograph n. 67. Simla: Indian Institute of Advanced Study with Munshiram Manoharlal Publishers, New Delhi, 1990. Bib. refs. pp. 121-123.

[AES-1460] Rufenacht, Claude R. *Fundamentals of Esthetics*. Chicago: Quintessence Publishing Co., 1990. 373 pp. Bib. refs.

[AES-1470] Santayana, George. *The Sense of Beauty: Being the Outlines of Aesthetic Theory*. Ed. William G. Holzberger, and Herman J. Saatkamp. Critical ed. Cambridge: MIT Press, 1988. xxviii, 248 pp. Bib. pp. 173-188.

[AES-1480] Schelling, F. W. J. *The Philosophy of Art*. Trans. and ed. Douglas W. Stott. Theory and History of Literature, vol. 58. Minneapolis: University of Minnesota Press, 1989. 396 pp.

[AES-1490] Schiller, Friedrich. *On the Aesthetic Education of Man: In A Series of Letters*. Trans. *Briefe uber die Ästhetische Erziehung des Menschen*. 1954. Reprint. New York: Continuum, 1984. 146 pp.

[AES-1500] Schimmelman, Janice Gayle. *A Checklist of European Treatises on Art and Essays on Aesthetics Available in America Through 1815*. Worcester, Mass.: American Antiquarian Society, 1983. pp. 95-195. Reprinted from *Proceedings of the American Antiquarian Society*, vol. 93, part 1, April 1983.

[AES-1510] Schor, Naomi. *Reading in Detail: Aesthetics and the Feminine*. London: Methuen, 1987. 210 pp. Bib.

[AES-1520] Schwartz, Ellen. *Beauties and Beasts, or, What Makes Great Art*

Great? N.p.: Pratt Manhattan Center Gallery, 1984. 71 pp. Bib. refs.

[AES-1530] Scruton, Roger. *The Aesthetic Understanding: Essays in the Philosophy of Art and Culture.* London; New York: Methuen, 1983. 259 pp. Bib. refs.

[AES-1540] Sharma, Kaushal Kishore. *Rabindranath Tagore's Aesthetics.* New Delhi: Abhinav Publications, 1988. Bib. pp. 105-111.

[AES-1550] Sharpe, R. A. *Contemporary Aesthetics: A Philosophical Analysis.* Modern Revivals in Philosophy. Brighton, Sussex: Harvester, 1983. Reprint. Aldershot: Gregg Revivals, 1991. Bib. pp. 187-194.

[AES-1560] Sheppard, Anne. *Aesthetics: An Introduction to the Philosophy of Art.* Oxford; New York: Oxford University Press, 1987. Bib. pp. 165-166.

[AES-1570] Shusterman, Richard. *Analytic Aesthetics.* Oxford: Basil Blackwell Publishing, 1989. 240 pp. Bib. refs.

[AES-1580] ------. *Pragmatist Aesthetics: Living Beauty, Rethinking Art.* Oxford; Cambridge, Mass.: Basil Blackwell Publishing, 1992. Bib. refs. pp. 262-310.

[AES-1590] Sircello, Guy. *Love and Beauty.* Princeton: Princeton University Press, 1989. Bib. pp. 211-249.

[AES-1600] Smith, Richard Candida. "Margins of the Modern: Aesthetics and Subjectivity in California Art and Poetry Movements, 1925-1975." 2 vols. Ph.D. Thesis, UCLA, 1992. 863 pp. Bib. refs.

[AES-1610] Spariosu, Mihai. *Dionysus Reborn: Play and the Aesthetic Dimension in Modern Philosophical and Scientific Discourse.* Ithaca: Cornell University Press, 1989. 317 pp. Bib. refs.

[AES-1620] Sparshott, Francis Edward. *The Theory of the Arts.* Princeton: Princeton University Press, 1982. Bib. pp. 685-711.

[AES-1630] Stein, Charles. *Being Equals Space Times Action: Searches for Freedom of Mind Through Mathematics, Art, and Mysticism.* Berkeley, Calif.: North Atlantic Books, 1988. 433 pp. Bibs.

[AES-1640] Stein, Roger B. *John Ruskin and Aesthetic Thought in America, 1840-1900.* Cambridge, Mass.: Harvard University Press, 1967. Bib. in notes pp. 267-307.

[AES-1650] Steinkraus, Warren E., and Kenneth L. Schmitz. *Art and Logic in*

Hegel's Philosophy. Atlantic Highlands, N.J.: Humanities Press; [Brighton], Sussex: Harvester Press, 1980. Bib. pp. 238-270.

[AES-1660] Stephan, Michael. *A Transformational Theory of Aesthetics.* London: New York: Routledge, 1990. Bib. refs. pp. 223-233.

[AES-1670] Summers, David. *The Judgment of Sense: Renaissance Naturalism and the Rise of Aesthetics.* New York: Cambridge University Press, 1987. Bib. pp. 337-349.

[AES-1680] Swanger, David. *Essays in Aesthetic Education.* Lewiston, N.Y.: Edwin Mellen Press, 1991. 168 pp.

[AES-1690] Sychrava, Juliet. *Schiller to Derrida: Idealism in Aesthetics.* Cambridge: Cambridge University Press, 1989. Bib.

[AES-1700] Talbot, Emile. *Stendhal and Romantic Esthetics.* French Forum Monographs, no. 61. Lexington, Ky.: French Forum, 1985. Bib. pp. 175-181.

[AES-1710] Taminiaux, Jacques. *Poetics, Speculation, and Judgment: The Shadow of the Work of Art from Kant to Phenomenology.* SUNY Series in Contemporary Continental Philosophy. Albany: State University of New York Press, 1993. Bib. refs.

[AES-1720] Thompson, James M[atheson]. *Twentieth Century Theories of Art.* Ottawa: Carleton University Press, 1990. 547 pp. Bib. refs.

[AES-1730] Tilghman, Benjamin R. *Wittgenstein, Ethics, and Aesthetics: The View from Eternity.* Albany: State University of New York Press, 1991. Bib. refs. pp. 179-189.

[AES-1740] Tollefsen, Olaf. *Foundationalism Defended: Essays on Epistemology, Ethics, and Aesthetics.* Manchester, N.H.: Sophia Institute Press, 1993. Bib. refs.

[AES-1750] *Toward an Aesthetic Education.* Washington, D.C.: Music Educators National Conference, [1971]. Bib. pp. 170-190.

[AES-1760] Truitt, Willis H. *Mainstreams in American Aesthetics: A Marxist Analysis.* New York: Haven Publishing Co., 1991. 154 pp. Bib. refs.

[AES-1770] Tuan, Yi-fu. *Passing Strange and Wonderful: Aesthetics, Nature, and Culture.* Washington, D.C.: Shearwater Books, 1993. 288 pp. Bib. refs.

[AES-1780] Turner, Frederick. *Beauty: The Value of Values*. Charlottesville: University Press of Virginia, 1991. 140 pp.

[AES-1790] Virilio, Paul. *The Aesthetics of Disappearance*. New York: Semiotext(e), 1991. 127 pp. Bib. refs.

[AES-1800] von Morstein, Petra. *On Understanding Works of Art: An Essay in Philosophical Aesthetics*. Lewiston, N.Y.: Edwin Mellen Press, 1986. 275 pp.

[AES-1810] Wall, Kevin Albert. *A Classical Philosophy of Art: The Nature of Art in the Light of Classical Principles*. Washington, D.C.: University Press of America, 1982. Bib. p. 100.

[AES-1820] Weiss, Allen S. *The Aesthetics of Excess*. SUNY Series in Aesthetics. Albany: State University of New York Press, 1989. Bib. refs. pp. 181-208.

[AES-1830] Welsh-Asante, Kariamu. *The African Aesthetic: Keeper of the Traditions*. New York: Greenwood Press, 1993. 263 pp. Bib. refs.

[AES-1840] Williams, Carolyn. *Transfigured World: Walter Pater's Aesthetic Historicism*. Ithaca: Cornell University Press, 1989. Bib. refs.

[AES-1850] Wolf, Naomi. *The Beauty Myth*. London: Chatto and Windus, 1990. Bib. pp. 243-276.

[AES-1860] Wolff, Janet. *Aesthetics and the Sociology of Art*. 2nd ed. Ann Arbor: University of Michigan Press, 1993. Bib. refs.

[AES-1870] Wollheim, Richard. *Art and Its Objects*. 2nd ed. New York: Cambridge University Press, 1980. Bib. pp. 241-270, annotated.

[AES-1880] Wolterstorff, Nicholas. *Works and World of Art*. Clarendon Library of Logic and Philosophy. Oxford: Clarendon Press; New York: Oxford University Press, 1980.

[AES-1890] Young, Julian. *Nietzsche's Philosophy of Art*. Cambridge; New York: Cambridge University Press, 1992. Bib. pp. 153-166.

KEY WORKS ON AESTHETICS AND RELIGION

Good books treating aesthetics and religion, especially from a Christian perspective, are relatively rare. Too many books attempting to treat this topic resort to dogmatics and prescriptions before offering clear, balanced thinking. Other works are written by prominent theologians who simply do not have adequate expertise in the arts. Although often well meaning, such theologians remain outsiders in the world of art, foreigners to the field who attempt to make art speak in a theological idiom rather than on its own terms. For example, Hans Küng's *Art and the Question of Meaning* [AER-460] and Paul Tillich's *Theology of Culture* [AER-750] both offer intriguing theological insights, but are not especially useful in helping one understand the arts. Still other writings, such as Hans Urs von Balthasar's fascinating seven volume work, *The Glory of the Lord: A Theological Aesthetics* [AER-030], are erudite, but overwritten and not entirely clear. (For assistance in sifting the wheat from the chaff in von Balthasar's recondite work, see Louis Roberts' *The Theological Aesthetics of Hans Urs von Balthasar* [ARE-650].) Those who can write widely and well about theological and aesthetic concerns are few.

The following list primarily represents writing completed since 1960, but includes a good number of works from the rest of the twentieth century as well. While most of the works listed here make significant contributions to the discussion of aesthetics, a few are particularly noteworthy as explorations of religious sensibilities in relation to the arts. John Dillenberger's *A Theology of Artistic Sensibilities: The Visual Arts and the Church* [AER-160] offers a fine overview of the subject and therefore provides a solid beginning point for understanding this topic. His preface also gives a useful critique of recent writings in religion and aesthetics through 1985. Several authors have proven themselves masters of this subject, including John W. Dixon, in *Art and the Theological Imagination* [AER-170] and *Nature and Grace in Art* [AER-180], Umberto Eco, in *Art and Beauty in the Middle Ages* [AER-210], Mircea Eliade, in *Symbolism, the Sacred, and the Arts* [AER-230], Jacques Maritain, in *Creative Intuition in Art and Poetry* [AER-510], and Nicholas Wolterstorff, in *Art in Action: Toward a Christian Aesthetic* [AER-840]. Although more demanding than most of the works just mentioned, the writings of Hans Georg Gadamer, including *The Relevance of the Beautiful and Other Essays* [AER-280] and *Truth and Method* [AER-290], provide very useful distinctions which allow aesthetics to be understood on its own terms. For assistance in interpreting Gadamer's work, consult Joel Weinsheimer's *Gadamer's Herme-*

neutics: A Reading of Truth and Method [ARE-810].
For an evangelical interpretation of the arts and aesthetics, read Frank E. Gaebelein's *The Christian, The Arts, and Truth: Regaining The Vision of Greatness* [AER-300], Clyde S. Kilby's *Christianity and Aesthetics* [AER-450], and Franky Schaeffer's *Addicted to Mediocrity: 20th Century Christians and the Arts* [AER-690]. For discussions of aesthetics linked with particular disciplines, such as music or the visual arts, see the pertinent sections in subsequent chapters.

[AER-010] Aberbach, Alan David. *Ideas of Richard Wagner: An Examination and Analysis of His Major Aesthetic, Political, Economic, Social and Religious Thoughts*. Rev. ed. N.p.: University Press of America; Eurospan, 1988. 450 pp.

[AER-020] Auvenshine, Donnie Glenn. "The Theological Significance of Beauty in the Old Testament." Ph.D. Thesis, Southwestern Baptist Theological Seminary, 1987. Bib. pp. 210-231.

[AER-030] Balthasar, Hans Urs von. *The Glory of the Lord: A Theological Aesthetics*. 7 Vols. Trans. Andrew Louth, Oliver Davies, Brian McNeil, et al. Ed. Joseph Fessio, John Riches, and Brian McNeil. T. & T. Clarke: Edinburgh; New York: Crossroad, 1983-1991. Bib. refs.

[AER-040] Bolam, David W., and James L. Henderson. *Art and Belief*. New York: Schocken Books, 1970. 220 pp.

[AER-050] Bozarth-Campbell, Alla. *The Word's Body: An Incarnational Aesthetic of Interpretation*. University: University of Alabama Press, 1979. Bib. pp. 162-175.

[AER-060] Brandon, S. G. F. *Man and God in Art and Ritual: A Study of Iconography, Architecture and Ritual Action as Primary Evidence of Religious Belief and Practice*. New York: Charles Scribner's Sons, 1975.

[AER-070] Brown, Frank Burch. *Religious Aesthetics: A Theological Study of Making and Meaning*. N.p., England: Macmillan Publishing Co., 1989. 248 pp. Princeton: Princeton University Press, 1990. 248 pp. Bib. pp. 195-217.

[AER-080] Brueggemann, Walter. *The Prophetic Imagination*. Philadelphia: Fortress Press, 1978. Bib. refs.

[AER-090] Canfield, John V., ed. *Aesthetics, Ethics and Religion*. The

Philosophy of Wittgenstein Series, no. 14. New York; London: Garland Publishing, 1986. 376 pp. New York: Garland Publishing, 1987. 342 pp.

[AER-100] Cramer, Raymond L. *Psychology of Jesus and Mental Health.* Grand Rapids: Zondervan Press, 1981.

[AER-110] Danto, Arthur Coleman. *Beyond the Brillo Box: The Visual Arts in Post-Historical Perspective.* New York: Farrar Straus Giroux, 1992. 263 pp.

[AER-120] Dean, William D. *Coming to: A Theology of Beauty.* Philadelphia: Westminster Press, [1972]. 207 pp. Bib. refs.

[AER-130] Delattre, Roland A. *Beauty and Sensibility in the Thought of Jonathan Edwards: An Essay in Aesthetics.* New Haven: Yale University Press, 1968.

[AER-140] Delloff, Linda-Marie. "God as Artist: Aesthetic Theory in *The Christian Century* 1908-1955." Ph.D. Thesis, University of Chicago, Divinity School, 1985. Bib. pp. 234-238.

[AER-150] Desmond, William. *Philosophy and Its Others: Ways of Being and Mind.* SUNY Series in Systematic Philosophy. Albany, N.Y.: State University of New York Press, 1990. 396 pp.

[AER-160] Dillenberger, John. *A Theology of Artistic Sensibilities: The Visual Arts and the Church.* New York: Crossroad, 1986. London: SCM Press, 1987. 280 pp. Notes.

[AER-170] Dixon, John W. *Art and the Theological Imagination.* New York: Seabury Press, 1978. 165 pp. Bib. refs.

[AER-180] ------. *Nature and Grace in Art.* Chapel Hill: University of North Carolina Press, 1964. Bib. pp. 213-214.

[AER-190] Durka, Gloria, and Joanmarie Smith. *Aesthetic Dimensions of Religious Education.* New York: Paulist Press, 1979. 252 pp. Bibs.

[AER-200] Eco, Umberto. *The Aesthetics of Thomas Aquinas.* Trans. Hugh Bredin. Trans. *Il Problema estetico in Tommaso d'Aquino.* Cambridge, Mass.: Harvard University Press, 1988. Bib. pp. 268-278.

[AER-210] ------. *Art and Beauty in the Middle Ages.* Trans. Hugh Bredin. New Haven: Yale University Press, 1986. 131 pp. Bib. pp. 120-129.

[AER-220] Eliade, Mircea, ed. *The Encyclopedia of Religion.* 16 vols. New

York: Macmillan Publishing Co., 1987.

[AER-230] ------. *Symbolism, the Sacred, and the Arts*. Ed. Diane Apostolos-Cappadona. New York: Crossroad, 1985. Bib. pp. 178-179.

[AER-240] England, Daniel Briggs. "The Aesthetic Nature of God." Th.M. Thesis, Dallas Theological Seminary, 1951. Bib. refs. pp. 68-70.

[AER-250] Eversole, Finley, ed. *Christian Faith and the Contemporary Arts*. Nashville: Abingdon Press, 1962.

[AER-260] Forsyth, Peter Taylor. *Christ on Parnassus: Lectures on Art, Ethics, and Theology*. New York: Hodder and Stoughton, [c. 1911]. 297 pp. (architecture, art, music)

[AER-270] Fraser, Hilary. *Beauty and Belief: Aesthetics and Religion in Victorian Literature*. New York: Cambridge University Press, 1986. Bib. pp. 275-282.

[AER-280] Gadamer, Hans Georg. *The Relevance of the Beautiful and Other Essays*. Trans. Nicholas Walker. New York: Cambridge University Press, 1986. Bib. pp. 171-181.

[AER-290] ------. *Truth and Method*. 2nd rev. ed. Trans. Garrett Barden and John Cumming. Trans. rev. Joel Weinsheimer and Donald G. Marshall. Trans. *Wahrheit und Methode*. New York: Continuum, 1993. xxxviii, 594 pp. Bib. refs.

[AER-300] Gaebelein, Frank E. *The Christian, The Arts, and Truth: Regaining The Vision of Greatness*. Ed. D. Bruce Lockerbie. Portland, Oreg.: Multnomah Press, 1985. 261 pp.

[AER-310] Giles, Paul. *American Catholic Arts and Fictions: Culture, Ideology, Aesthetics*. Cambridge: Cambridge University Press, 1992. 547 pp.

[AER-320] Gill, Eric. *Art-Nonsense and Other Essays*. London: Cassell and Co., Ltd., 1929. 324 pp.

[AER-330] Gottner-Abendroth, Heidi. *The Dancing Goddess: Principles of a Matriarchal Aesthetic*. Trans. Maureen T. Krause. 1984. Reprint. N.p.: Beacon Press, 1991. 296 pp.

[AER-340] Harned, David B. *Theology and the Arts*. Philadelphia: Westminster Press, 1966.

[AER-350] Harries, Richard. *Art and the Beauty of God*. London; New York: Mowbray, 1994.

32

[AER-360] Hazelton, Roger. *A Theological Approach to Art.* Nashville: Abingdon Press, 1967.

[AER-370] ------. *Ascending Flame, Descending Dove.* Philadelphia: Westminster Press, 1976.

[AER-380] Holbrook, Clyde A. *The Ethics of Jonathan Edwards: Morality and Aesthetics.* N.p.: University of Michigan Press, 1973. 208 pp.

[AER-390] Hunter, Howard, ed. *Humanities, Religion and the Arts Tomorrow.* New York: Holt, Rhinehart and Winston, 1972.

[AER-400] Institute of Formative Spirituality. *Spiritual Formation and the Aesthetic Experience.* Studies in Formative Spirituality, vol. 4, no. 1 0193-2748. Pittsburgh, Pa.: Institute of Formative Spirituality, Duquesne University, 1983. Bib. pp. 161-169.

[AER-410] Johnston, William S. *The Mirror Mind: Zen-Christian Dialogue.* N.p.: Fordham University Press, 1990. 181 pp.

[AER-420] Jorgenson, Dale A. *Theological and Aesthetic Roots in the Stone-Campbell Movement.* N.p.: T. Jefferson University Press; N.p.: Eurospan, 1989. 360 pp.

[AER-430] Kant, Immanuel. *Observations on the Feeling of the Beautiful and Sublime.* 1961. Reprint. Berkeley: University of California Press, 1991. 124 pp. Bib. refs.

[AER-440] Kay, Jeffrey A. *Theological Aesthetics: Theology.* European University Studies, Series 23, vol. 60. New York: Peter Lang, 1976. 115 pp.

[AER-450] Kilby, Clyde S. *Christianity and Aesthetics.* IVP Series in Contemporary Christian Thought, 3. Chicago: Inter-Varsity Press, 1961. 43 pp. Bib.

[AER-460] Küng, Hans. *Art and the Question of Meaning.* Trans. Edward Quinn. New York: Crossroad, 1981. 71 pp.

[AER-470] Laeuchli, Samuel. *Religion and Art in Conflict.* Philadelphia: Fortress Press, 1980. Bib. pp. 189-193. (See [VAR-720])

[AER-480] MacGregor, Geddes. *Aesthetic Experience in Religion.* London: Macmillan Publishing Co., 1947. 264 pp.

[AER-490] McNally, Dennis. *Sacred Space: An Aesthetic for the Liturgical Environment.* N.p.: Cloverdale Library, 1990. 215 pp.

[AER-500] McSwain, Harold W. "A Relational Aesthetic: Toward a Theory of the Arts in Christian Ministry." Th.D. Thesis, Boston University, 1990. Bib. refs. pp. 216-222.

[AER-510] Maritain, Jacques. *Creative Intuition in Art and Poetry*. A. W. Mellon Lectures in the Fine Arts, 1952. Bollingen Series 35, no. 1. New York: Pantheon Books, 1953. Reprint. Princeton: Princeton University Press, 1978. 423 pp. Bib. refs. in footnotes.

[AER-520] Martin, David F. *Art and the Religious Experience: The "Language" of the Sacred*. Lewisburg: Bucknell University Press, 1972. 288 pp.

[AER-530] Martin, James Alfred, Jr. *Beauty and Holiness: The Dialogue Between Aesthetics and Religion*. Princeton: Princeton University Press, 1990. 269 pp. Bib. refs in notes, pp. 197-217.

[AER-540] Martland, Thomas R. *Religion as Art: An Interpretation*. New York: State University of New York Press, 1981. 221 pp. Bib. refs.

[AER-550] Maurer, Armand A[ugustine]. *About Beauty: A Thomistic Interpretation*. Houston: Center for Thomistics Studies, University of St. Thomas, 1983. 135 pp. Bib. refs.

[AER-560] Merton, Thomas. "Beauty is from God." Kansas City, Mo.: Credence Cassettes: National Catholic Reporter Publishing Co., 1988. 58 min. cassette.

[AER-570] Mitias, Michael H. *Creativity in Art, Religion, and Culture*. Elementa, Bd. 42. Wurzburd: Konigshausen and Neumann; Amsterdam: Rodopi, 1985. Dist. Humanities Press, Atlantic Highlands, N.J. 134 pp.

[AER-580] Mooney, Hilary A[nne-Marie]. *The Liberation of Consciousness: Bernard Lonergan's Theological Foundations in Dialogue with the Theological Aesthetics of Hans Urs von Balthasar*. Frankfurt am Main: J. Knecht, 1992. Bib. refs. pp. 265-281.

[AER-590] *New Catholic Encyclopedia*. 17 vols. New York: McGraw, 1967-1979.

[AER-600] Pattison, George. *Kierkegaard on Art and Communication*. New York: St. Martin's Press, 1992. 189 pp. Bib. refs.

[AER-610] ------. *Kierkegaard: The Aesthetic and the Religious--From the Magic Theatre to the Crucifixion of the Image*. Studies in Literature and Religion Series. N.p.: Macmillan Academic and Professional, 1992. 224 pp.

34

[AER-620] Pelikan, Jaroslav. *Human Culture and the Holy: Essays on the True, the Good, and the Beautiful.* London: SCM Press, Ltd., 1959. 172 pp.

[AER-630] Porter, Samuel Judson. *The Gospel of Beauty.* New York: George H. Doran Co., 1922. 118 pp.

[AER-640] Reese, William L. *Dictionary of Philosophy and Religion, Eastern and Western Thought.* Hassocks: Harvester; Atlantic Highlands: Humanities, 1980. 644 pp.

[AER-650] Roberts, Louis. *The Theological Aesthetics of Hans Urs von Balthasar.* Washington, D.C.: Catholic University of America Press, 1987. 266 pp. Bib. pp. 249-254. Reprint. N.p.: E.D.S., 1992.

[AER-660] Ross-Bryant, Lynn. *Imagination and the Life of the Spirit.* Chico: Polebridge Books, 1981.

[AER-670] Santayana, George. *Interpretations of Poetry and Religion: Critical Edition.* Ed. Herman J. Saatkamp and William G. Holzberger. Complete Works of George Santayana, vol. 3. Cambridge: MIT Press, 1990. 224 pp.

[AER-680] Sayers, Dorothy. *The Mind of the Maker.* Westport, Conn.: Greenwood Press, 1941. 229 pp. Bib. refs. in footnotes.

[AER-690] Schaeffer, Franky. *Addicted to Mediocrity: 20th Century Christians and the Arts.* Rev. ed. Illus. Kurt Mitchell. Westchester, Ill.: Crossway Books, 1985. 127 pp.

[AER-700] Seerveld, Colin. *Rainbows for the Fallen World: Aesthetic Life and Artistic Task.* N.p., England: Stride Publications, 1988. 224 pp.

[AER-710] Sherry, Patrick. *Spirit and Beauty: An Introduction to Theological Aesthetics.* Oxford; New York: Oxford University Press, 1992. Bib. refs. pp. 183-187.

[AER-720] Spero, Moshe Halevi. *Religious Objects as Psychological Structures: A Critical Integration of Object Relations Theory, Psychotherapy, and Judaism.* Chicago: University of Chicago Press, 1992. 242 pp.

[AER-730] Steiner, Rudolf. *Truth, Beauty & Goodness.* N.p.: Rudolf Steiner College Publications, Saint George Publications, 1986.

[AER-740] Taylor, Mark C. *Nots.* Religion and Postmoderism Series. Chicago: University of Chicago Press, 1993. 280 pp.

35

[AER-750] Tillich, Paul. *Theology of Culture*. Ed. Robert C. Kimball. 1959.
Reprint. New York: Oxford University Press, 1972.
213 pp.

[AER-760] Ts'ai, Yuan-P'ei. *On "Aesthetics Taking the Place of Religion"*.
National Peking University and Chinese Association for
Folklore, Folklore and Folkliterature Series, no. 101. N.p.:
Oriental Book Store, 1979. Chinese.

[AER-770] van der Leeuw, Gerardus. *Sacred and Profane Beauty: The Holy
in Art*. Trans. David E. Green. 1932. Reprint. New York:
Holt, Rhinehart and Winston; Nashville: Abingdon Press,
1963. Bib. refs. in notes, pp. 342-352.

[AER-780] Veith, Gene E., Jr. *The Gift of Art*. Downers Grove, Ill.: Inter-
Varsity Press, 1984. 120 pp.

[AER-790] Walton, Janet Roland. "The Contributions of Aesthetics to
Liturgical Renewal." Ed.D. Thesis, Columbia University,
1979. Bib. pp. 127-137.

[AER-800] Ward, Wendy. *Gift of God, Gift to God: Living the Word Through
Artistry*. [Philadelphia]: Geneva Press, 1984. 32 pp. Bib.
refs.

[AER-810] Weinsheimer, Joel. *Gadamer's Hermeneutics: A Reading of Truth
and Method*. New Haven: Yale University Press, 1985. Bib.
pp. 261-271.

[AER-820] Weiss, Paul. *Religion and Art*. Milwaukee: Marquette University
Press, 1963.

[AER-830] Wittgenstein, Ludwig. *Lectures and Conversations on Aesthetics,
Psychology, Religious Belief*. [Oxford]: Basil Blackwell Publishing, 1966. [Berkeley]: University of California Press,
1967. 72 pp.

[AER-840] Wolterstorff, Nicholas. *Art in Action: Toward a Christian Aesthetic*. N.p.: Paternoster Press; Grand Rapids: William B.
Eerdmanns, 1980. Bib. refs. in notes, pp. 223-237.

[AER-850] ------. *Art, Responsibility and Shalom*. Arlington, Va.: C. S. Lewis
Institute, 1981. 84 min. cassette.

CHAPTER 3

ARCHITECTURE

BIBLIOGRAPHIES ON ARCHITECTURE

The body of literature treating architecture is so vast that the following section can be just a sampling of available works. Because many works on architecture treat technical matters not directly related to the fine arts, the focus of this book, these more technical works have typically been omitted. The primary strength of this chapter is its lists of bibliographies, both the general list and the one treating architecture and religion. These lists include bibliographies dating back to 1914, but most strongly representing publications since 1960. For those looking for a one or two volume bibliography in architecture, three works by Georgia Bizios [BAR-060 to 080] provide current and reasonably concise references. Also see Donald L. Ehresmann's *Architecture: A Bibliographic Guide to Basic Reference Works, Histories, and Handbooks* [BAR-230]. Four other short, general bibliographies which are somewhat dated but still worth consulting are Don Gifford's *The Literature of Architecture* [BAR-260], the Library Association's *Readers' Guide to Books on Architecture* [BAR-370], Margaret Phillips' *Guide to Architectural Information* [BAR-500], and Denison Langley Smith's *How to find out in Architecture and Building: A Guide to Sources of Information* [BAR-590]. For those conducting exhaustive research, the largest and most comprehensive bibliographies are those produced by the Avery Memorial Architectural Library at Columbia University [BAR-030], [BAR-040], [BAR-140], and [BAR-510], the Library of the Graduate School of Design at Harvard University [BAR-310], and the Art and Architecture Division of the New York Public Library [BAR-050], [BAR-460], and [BAR-470].

In addition to consulting these larger bibliographies, one will do well to see the numerous and more specialized works produced by Vance Bibliographies [BAR-010], [BAR-020], [BAR-120], [BAR-130], [BAR-190], [BAR-200], [BAR-210], [BAR-240], [BAR-290], [BAR-610], and [BAR-700 to BAR-810]. Mary Vance and her colleagues have produced some of the most current bibliographies in architecture, and have written carefully focused works treating sundry categories of this profession, including topics such as aesthetics [BAR-200], garden landscaping [BAR-180, BAR-240, and BAR-780], and the mission style in architecture [BAR-290]. Beyond these and various other specialized bibliographies whose titles are self-explanatory, one should also note James M. Goode's *Bibliography of Doctoral Dissertations Relating to American Architectural History, 1897-1991* [BAR-270] for the extensive bibliographies often given with these studies. While works treating individual artists are rarely included in this book, several bibliographies concentrating on representative major architects have been listed below, including ones on Le Corbusier [BAR-100], Andrea Palladio [BAR-190], Giorgio Vasari [BAR-120], and Frank Lloyd Wright [BAR-670]. Bibliographies treating particular eras, geographical regions, and ethnic or special interest groups abound in the following section and may be identified readily by titles. Finally, to help one locate illustrations of various works of architecture, one should consult Edward H. Teague's *World Architecture Index: A Guide to Illustrations* [BAR-680]. For additional bibliographies, consult works given in Chapter 1, Bibliographies of Bibliographies, and see the bibliographies listed in the opening section of Chapter 12, Visual Arts I.

[BAR-010]   *Architecture Series: Bibliography*. No. A-1. Monticello, Ill.: Vance Bibliographies, June 1978-.

[BAR-020]   *Architecture Series: Bibliography: List of Architecture Series Bibliographies in Print 1987 to Present*. Monticello, Ill.: Vance

Bibliographies, Inc., 1991. 43 pp.

[BAR-030] *Avery Index to Architectural Periodicals.* Boston: Columbia University, 1963. [265,500] 12 supplements, Boston: G. K. Hall, to 1992, up to 4 vols. each.

[BAR-040] Avery Library. *Catalog of the Avery Memorial Architectural Library of Columbia University.* 2nd ed. Boston: G. K. Hall, 1972-.

[BAR-050] *Bibliographic Guide to Art and Architecture, 1989.* (c. Annually, 1977-). 2 vols. Boston: G. K. Hall, 1990.

[BAR-060] Bizios, Georgia. *Architectural Design, Human Behavior, Special Topics.* Durham, N.C.: Eno River Press, 1991. 449 pp.

[BAR-070] ------. *Architectural Theory and Criticism, Urban Design Theory, Architectural History.* Durham, N.C.: Eno River Press, 1991. 369 pp.

[BAR-080] ------. *Architecture Reading Lists and Course Outlines.* 2 vols. Durham, N.C.: Eno River Press, 1991.

[BAR-090] Boys, Jos, et al. *Making a Place for Women: A Resource Handbook on Women and the Built Environment.* London: Women's Design Service: South Bank Polytechnic, 1989. 74 pp.

[BAR-100] Brady, Darlene A. *Le Corbusier: An Annotated Bibliography.* Garland Reference Library of the Humanities, vol. 407. New York: Garland Publishing, 1985. 302 pp.

[BAR-110] Burke, Martin P. "Bridge Aesthetics Bibliography." Paper presented at annual meeting of the Transportation Research Board, Washington, D.C., January 1987.

[BAR-120] Cable, Carole. *Giorgio Vasari, Architect: A Selected Bibliography of Books and Articles.* Monticello, Ill.: Vance Bibliographies, 1985. 7 pp.

[BAR-130] ------. *Medieval Architectural Design and Structure: A Bibliography with Selected Annotations.* Monticello, Ill.: Vance Bibliographies, 1981.

[BAR-140] *Catalog of the Avery Memorial Architectural Library of Columbia University.* Boston: [Columbia University], 1958. [242,201]

[BAR-150] Coulson, William D. E., and Patricia N. Freiert. *Greek and Roman Art, Architecture, and Archaeology: An Annotated Bibliography.* 2nd ed. New York: Garland Publishing, 1987.

204 pp.

[BAR-160] Craven, Roy C. *Indian Art: A Bibliography of Holdings in the Architecture and Fine Arts Library, University of Florida*. Gainesville, Fla.: Department of Art, University of Florida, 1985. 45 pp.

[BAR-170] Davies, Martin. *Romanesque Architecture: A Bibliography*. A Reference Publication in Art History. Boston: G. K. Hall, 1993.

[BAR-180] Dearden, Philip. *Landscape Aesthetics: An Annotated Bibliography*. Exchange Bibliography--Council of Planning Librarians, no. 1220. Monticello, Ill.: Council of Planning Librarians, 1977. 19 pp.

[BAR-190] Doumato, Lamia. *Andrea Palladio*. Monticello, Ill.: Vance Bibliographies, 1982. 31 pp.

[BAR-200] ------. *Architectural Aesthetics*. Monticello, Ill.: Vance Bibliographies, 1985. 12 pp.

[BAR-210] Dunning, Glenna. *Architecture of the Pueblo Indians: An Annotated Bibliography*. Monticello, Ill.: Vance Bibliographies, 1988. 22 pp.

[BAR-220] Edinburgh City Libraries, Fine Art Department. *Architecture: A Teaching Resource*. Edinburgh: Edinburgh City Libraries, Fine Art Department, 1992. 24 pp.

[BAR-230] Ehresmann, Donald L. *Architecture: A Bibliographic Guide to Basic Reference Works, Histories, and Handbooks*. Littleton, Colo.: Libraries Unlimited, 1984. 338 pp.

[BAR-240] Ferguson, Bruce K. *Art and Aesthetics in Landscape Architecture Articles in "Landscape Architecture" Magazine, 1910-1979*. Architecture Series: Bibliography, A-534 0194-1356. Monticello, Ill.: Vance Bibliographies, 1981. 11 pp.

[BAR-250] Frank, Folker. *Asthetik und Architektur*. Stuttgart: IRB Verlag, 1986. 102 pp.

[BAR-260] Gifford, Don, ed. *The Literature of Architecture*. New York: E. P. Dutton and Co., 1966.

[BAR-270] Goode, James M. *Bibliography of Doctoral Dissertations Relating to American Architectural History, 1897-1991*. Philadelphia: Society of Architectural Historians, 1992. 138 pp.

[BAR-280] Hall, Robert de Zouche. *A Bibliography on Vernacular Architec-*

ture. Newton Abbot: David and Charles, 1972. 191 pp.

[BAR-290] Harmon, Robert Bartlett. *The Mission Style in American Architecture: A Brief Style Guide.* Monticello, Ill.: Vance Bibliographies, 1983. 15 pp.

[BAR-300] Harris, Eileen, and Nicholas Savage. *British Architectural Books and Writers 1556-1785.* Cambridge: Cambridge University Press, 1990.

[BAR-310] Harvard University. *Catalogue of the Library of the Graduate School of Design.* 44 vols. Boston: G. K. Hall, 1968. Supplement, 2 vols., 1970.

[BAR-320] Hitchcock, Henry Russell. *American Architectural Books: A List of Books, Portfolios, and Pamphlets on Architecture and Related Subjects Published in America Before 1895.* Rev. ed. 1962. Reprint. New York: Da Capo Press, 1976. 150 pp.

[BAR-330] Kaufman, Edward. *Medievalism: An Annotated Bibliography of Recent Research in the Architecture and Art of Britain and North America.* Garland Reference Library of the Humanities, vol. 791. New York: Garland Publishing, 1988. xlvii, 279 pp.

[BAR-340] Kaufmann, Thomas Da Costa. *Art and Architecture in Central Europe, 1550-1620: An Annotated Bibliography.* Boston: G. K. Hall, 1988. xxxvii, 316 pp.

[BAR-350] Kempton, Richard. *Art Nouveau: An Annotated Bibliography.* Art and Architecture Bibliographies, no. 4. Los Angeles: Hennessey and Ingalls, 1977. xxvi, 303 pp.

[BAR-360] Kleeman, Walter. *Interior Ergonomics: Significant Dimensions in Interior Design and Planning: A Selected Bibliography.* Monticello, Ill.: Council of Planning Librarians, 1972. 43 pp.

[BAR-370] Library Association. *Readers' Guide to Books on Architecture.* 2nd ed. [Durham]: Library Association, 1969.

[BAR-380] McCommons, Richard E., et al. *Guide to Architecture Schools in North America: Members and Affiliates of the ACSA.* Washington, D.C.; Silver Springs, Md.: Association of Collegiate Schools of Architecture Press, 1989. xxvii, 274 pp.

[BAR-390] McCoy, Esther, and Barbara Goldstein. *Guide to U.S. Architecture, 1940--1980.* Santa Monica, Calif.: Arts and Architecture Press, 1982. Bib. pp. 160-161.

42

[BAR-400] McGough, Melinda. *A Selected Bibliography: National Trust Historic Museums and Collections.* Washington, D.C.: National Trust for Historic Preservation, 1980. 21 pp.

[BAR-410] McParland, Edward. *A Bibliography of Irish Architectural History.* [Dublin]: Irish Historical Studies, 1988. Reprinted from *Irish Historical Studies*, vol. 26, no. 102 (Nov. 1988), pp. 161-212.

[BAR-420] Massey, James C., Nancy B. Schwartz, and Shirley Maxwell. *Historic American Buildings Survey/Historic American Engineering Record: An Annotated Bibliography.* [Washington, D.C.?]: Historic American Buildings Survey/Historic American Engineering Board, National Park Service, U.S. Department of the Interior, 1992. 170 pp.

[BAR-430] Maurstad, Betty L., ed. *Contemporary Architecture: A Bibliographical Survey of Selections from the Recent Literature and Basic Information Sources.* Detroit: Wayne State University, 1977. Bib. pp. 50-59.

[BAR-440] Mekkawi, Mod. *Bibliography on Traditional Architecture in Africa.* Washington, D.C.: Mekkawi, 1978. 105 pp.

[BAR-450] Neil, J. Meredith. *Paradise Improved: Environmental Design in Hawaii.* Charlottesville: University Press of Virginia, [1972]. 208 pp.

[BAR-460] New York Public Library. Art and Architecture Division. *Bibliographic Guide to Art and Architecture.* Boston: G. K. Hall, 1975-. Annual. Supplement to the *Dictionary Catalog of the Art and Architecture Division.*

[BAR-470] ------. *Dictionary Catalog of the Art and Architecture Division.* 30 vols. Boston: G. K. Hall, 1975.

[BAR-480] *Pan American Magazines Relating to Architecture, Art and Music.* Pan American Union. Washington, D.C.: Columbus Memorial Library, 1942. 13 pp. [100]

[BAR-490] Park, Helen. *A List of Architectural Books Available in America Before the Revolution.* Rev. ed. Los Angeles: Hennessey and Ingalls, 1973. 79 pp.

[BAR-500] Phillips, Margaret. *Guide to Architectural Information.* Lansdale, Pa.: Design Data Center, 1971. 89 pp.

[BAR-510] Placzek, Adolf K., and Angela Giral. *Avery's Choice: 5 Centuries of Great Architectural Books: A Book Prepared in Celebration of the Avery Architectural and Fine Arts Library of*

Columbia University. N.p., 1990. In progress. 32 pp.

[BAR-520] Powell, Antoinette Paris. *Bibliography of Landscape Architecture, Environmental Design, and Planning.* London: Mansell, 1987. 312 pp.

[BAR-530] [Rollins, Mary Harris]. *Catalogue of the Books Relating to Architecture Construction and Decoration.* 2nd ed. Public Library: Subject Catalogue, no. 10. Boston: [Boston Public Library], 1914. 535 pp. [16,500]

[BAR-540] Roos, Frank John, Jr. *Bibliography of Early American Architecture: Writings on Architecture Constructed Before 1860 in Eastern and Central United States.* Urbana: University of Illinois Press, 1968.

[BAR-550] Royal Institute of British Architects. *Catalogue of the Royal Institute of British Architects Library.* 2 vols. 1937-38. Reprint. Folkestone: Dawsons, 1972.

[BAR-560] Saunders, David. *A Manual of Architectural History Research.* 3 vols. Sydney: Power Institute of Fine Arts, University of Sydney, 1977. Bib. pp. 348-350.

[BAR-570] Sharp, Dennis. *Sources of Modern Architecture: A Critical Bibliography.* 2nd ed. London; New York: Eastview Ed., Inc., 1981. 192 pp.

[BAR-580] Simmins, Geoffrey. *Bibliography of Canadian Architecture.* Ottawa: Society for the Study of Architecture in Canada, 1992. 28 pp. English and French.

[BAR-590] Smith, Denison Langley. *How to find out in Architecture and Building: A Guide to Sources of Information.* New York: Pergamon Press, [1967]. 232 pp.

[BAR-600] Smith, G[eorge] E[verard] Kidder. *The Architecture of the United States.* Garden City, N.Y.: Anchor Press, 1981.

[BAR-610] Starbuck, James Carlton. *Geographic Index to Architecture Series, Bibliographies.* 2 vols. Monticello, Ill.: Vance Bibliographies, 1980.

[BAR-620] Stark, Ulrike. *Competitions: Operas, Theatres and Concert Buildings.* Stuttgart: IRB Verlag, 1990. 48 pp.

[BAR-630] ------. *Congress Buildings.* Stuttgart: IRB Verlag, 1990. 81 pp.

[BAR-640] Stiverson, Cynthia Zignego. *Architecture and the Decorative Arts: The A. Lawrence Kocher Collection of Books at the Colonial*

44

Williamsburg Foundation. West Cornwall, Conn.: Locust Hill Press, 1989. xli, 245 pp. Bib. pp. xxxi-xxxiii.

[BAR-650] Stoddard, Richard. *Theatre and Cinema Architecture: A Guide to Information Sources.* Detroit: Gale Research, 1978. 368 pp.

[BAR-660] Story, R. A., ed. *Architectural History and the Fine and Applied Arts: Sources in the National Register of Archives.* Comp. T. W. M. Jaine and Brenda Weeden. London: National Register of Archives, 1972.

[BAR-670] Sweeney, Robert L[awrence]. *Frank Lloyd Wright: An Annotated Bibliography.* Art and Architecture Bibliographies, no. 5. Los Angeles: Hennessey and Ingalls, 1978. xliv, 303 pp.

[BAR-680] Teague, Edward H. *World Architecture Index: A Guide to Illustrations.* Art Reference Collection, no. 12 0193-6867. New York: Greenwood Press, 1991. 447 pp.

[BAR-690] Tomlan, Michael A. "Popular and Professional American Architectural Literature in the Late Nineteenth Century." Ph.D. Thesis, Cornell University, 1983. Bib. pp. 455-486.

[BAR-700] Vance, Mary. *Architectural Acoustics: A Bibliography.* Monticello, Ill.: Vance Bibliographies, 1982. 21 pp.

[BAR-710] ------. *Architectural Criticism: A Bibliography.* Monticello, Ill.: Vance Bibliographies, 1983. 31 pp.

[BAR-720] ------. *Architecture and Society: A Bibliography.* Monticello, Ill.: Vance Bibliographies, 1982.

[BAR-730] ------. *Architecture Books Arranged by Style and Periods: A Selective Bibliography.* Monticello, Ill.: Vance Bibliographies, 1979. 61 pp.

[BAR-740] ------. *Baroque Architecture: Monographs Published 1970-1987.* Monticello, Ill.: Vance Bibliographies, 1988. 24 pp.

[BAR-750] ------. *Castles: Monographs.* Monticello, Ill.: Vance Bibliographies, 1984. 153 pp.

[BAR-760] ------. *Gothic Architecture: Monographs Published 1976-1986.* Monticello, Ill.: Vance Bibliographies, 1987. 12 pp.

[BAR-770] ------. *Islamic Architecture: Monographs Published 1970-1987.* Monticello, Ill.: Vance Bibliographies, 1988. 26 pp.

[BAR-780] ------. *Landscape and Nature Aesthetics: Monographs (A Revision of A 56).* Monticello, Ill.: Vance Bibliographies, 1986. 28 pp.

[BAR-790] ------. *New Publications for Architecture Libraries, Nov. 1979 [-Sept. 1980].* 11 vols. Monticello, Ill.: Vance Bibliographies, 1979-1980.

[BAR-800] ------. *New Publications for Architecture Libraries [1980-].* Monticello, Ill.: Vance Bibliographies, 1981-. c. Annual.

[BAR-810] ------. *Romanesque Architecture: Monographs Published 1970-1987.* Monticello, Ill.: Vance Bibliographies, 1988. 20 pp.

[BAR-820] Van Neste, W. Lane, and Virgil E. Baugh. *Preliminary Inventory of the Records of the Public Buildings Service.* Washington, D.C.: National Archives: Preliminary Inventories, no. 110, 1958. 108 pp.

[BAR-830] Vatsyayan, Kapila. *Indian Art: Recent Indian Publications on Jaina and Hindu Art and Architecture.* New Delhi: Educational Resources Center, 1978. 47 pp.

[BAR-840] Vulker, Judy, Douglas Smith, and Janet Smith. *The Sourcebook.* 2nd ed. Manuka, A.C.T.: The Royal Australian Institute of Architects, National Education Division, 1990. Bib. pp. 133-151.

[BAR-850] Wodehouse, Lawrence. *American Architects from the Civil War to the First World War: A Guide to Information Sources.* Detroit: Gale Research, 1976.

[BAR-860] ------. *American Architects from the First World War to the Present: A Guide to Information Sources.* Detroit: Gale Research, 1977. 305 pp.

KEY WORKS ON ARCHITECTURE

This section treating the general topic of architecture is primarily offered as a supplement to available bibliographies, only a few of which move beyond 1985. Accordingly, works given here primarily represent publications from 1985 to the present, although some date back as far as 1850. To facilitate locating works in this long list, the following classifications are offered, with the understanding that some overlap will occur between them. Careful researchers will therefore need to consult several categories for almost any given search. For assistance with the concepts and terminology of architecture, see [ARC-270], [ARC-460], [ARC-700], [ARC-1150], and [ARC-1540]. To locate works treating aesthetics and philosophy in architectural studies, see [ARC-090], [ARC-240], [ARC-630], [ARC-1080], [ARC-1130], [ARC-1360], and [ARC-1760]. For works with a wide scope, see [ARC-400], [ARC-410], [ARC-590], [ARC-760], [ARC-840], [ARC-870], [ARC-1040], [ARC-1050], [ARC-1080], [ARC-1160], [ARC-1190], [ARC-1250], [ARC-1310], [ARC-1370], [ARC-1390], [ARC-1440], [ARC-1480], [ARC-1510], [ARC-1560], [ARC-1650], [ARC-1750], [ARC-1810], and [ARC-1880].

Since many of the works treat specific eras of architectural history, the following works have been organized according to eras: Primitive [ARC-570]; Classical (Greek and Roman) [ARC-020], [ARC-100], [ARC-180], [ARC-260], [ARC-610], [ARC-890], [ARC-1040], [ARC-1180], [ARC-1380], [ARC-1630], [ARC-1730], [ARC-1740], [ARC-1800], [ARC-1900]; Medieval (Romanesque and Gothic) [ARC-310], [ARC-380], [ARC-900], [ARC-930], [ARC-940], [ARC-1230], [ARC-1670], [ARC-1710]; Renaissance [ARC-1430], [ARC-1690]; Baroque and Rococo [ARC-650], [ARC-880], [ARC-1660]; Neo-Classical [ARC-1490]; Romantic [ARC-390], [ARC-480], [ARC-640]; Victorian [ARC-320], [ARC-1260]; Modern [ARC-130], [ARC-420], [ARC-620], [ARC-670], [ARC-680], [ARC-920], [ARC-1080], [ARC-1090], [ARC-1110], [ARC-1340], [ARC-1410], [ARC-1680], [ARC-1930]. For additional works treating these eras, see those listed in the preceding paragraph.

Because the study of architecture is often linked with specific locations, many architectural works treat this topic according to national or regional expressions of architecture. Those treating regions include the following: Africa [ARC-210], [ARC-490], [ARC-1100], [ARC-1120], [ARC-1220]; America (North, Central, and South) [ARC-030], [ARC-080], [ARC-440], [ARC-600], [ARC-660], [ARC-810], [ARC-820], [ARC-950], [ARC-990], [ARC-1290], [ARC-1330], [ARC-1500], [ARC-1640], [ARC-1780], [ARC-1790], [ARC-1830]; Asia (Orient) [ARC-290], [ARC-370], [ARC-430], [ARC-550], [ARC-710], [ARC-750], [ARC-800], [ARC-860], [ARC-1000], [ARC-1020], [ARC-1070], [ARC-1240], [ARC-1890]; Australia and New Zealand [ARC-1420], [ARC-1600]; Europe [ARC-070], [ARC-170], [ARC-330], [ARC-360], [ARC-470], [ARC-740], [ARC-780], [ARC-1400], [ARC-1470],

[ARC-1520], [ARC-1860], [ARC-1870]; Middle East and Mediterranean [ARC-050], [ARC-530], [ARC-730], [ARC-830], [ARC-960], [ARC-1040], [ARC-1460], [ARC-1840]. For a journal treating architecture from a global perspective, see *World Architecture* [ARC-1820].

In addition to books treating regional architecture, many works also divide this subject matter according to national lines. Some of these works have been included in the regional studies identified above, such as the U.S. architecture being grouped with that in the Americas and Japanese architecture being listed with works on Asia. For European architectural studies, however, further subdivisions according to nationalities are essential. In the key works on architecture given below the following groups may be found: France [ARC-110], [ARC-120], [ARC-220], [ARC-970], [ARC-1140], [ARC-1570], [ARC-1770]; Germany [ARC-280], [ARC-850]; Great Britain [ARC-140], [ARC-160], [ARC-200], [ARC-300], [ARC-340], [ARC-350], [ARC-510], [ARC-520], [ARC-540], [ARC-690], [ARC-770], [ARC-910], [ARC-1170], [ARC-1200], [ARC-1210], [ARC-1270], [ARC-1280], [ARC-1490], [ARC-1550], [ARC-1580], [ARC-1610], [ARC-1620], [ARC-1720]; Holland [ARC-580]; Italy [ARC-190], [ARC-250], [ARC-900], [ARC-980], [ARC-1300], [ARC-1320], [ARC-1350], [ARC-1590]; Russia [ARC-060]; Spain [ARC-560], [ARC-1920]. For a useful beginning point for looking at European architecture, volumes by Doreen Yarwood are particularly helpful. Her works, *The Architecture of Europe* [ARC-1860] and its four volume revision [ARC-1870], as well as her *A Chronology of Western Architecture* [ARC-1880], are models of clarity and precision.

For additional studies treating architecture, see the section entitled Key Works on General Theory of Visual Arts in Chapter 12, Visual Arts I. Note especially the work of William Fleming, *Arts & Ideas* [VAT-340], for its relating of architecture to the other fine arts and the aesthetic movements behind them.

[ARC-010] Abercrombie, Stanley. *Architecture as Art.* New York: Van Nostrond Reinhold, 1984. Reprint. New York; London: Harper and Row, 1986. 176 pp.

[ARC-020] Adam, Robert. *Classical Architecture: A Comprehensive Hand-*

48

book to the Tradition of Classical Style. New York: Harry N. Abrams, 1991. 319 pp. Bib. refs.

[ARC-030] Adams, William Howard, ed. *The Eye of Jefferson*. Washington, D.C.: National Gallery of Art, 1976.

[ARC-040] Allen, Edward. *Architectural Detailing: Function Constructibility Aesthetics*. New York: Wiley, 1993. 281 pp. Bib. refs.

[ARC-050] Altun, Ara. *An Outline of Turkish Architecture in the Middle Ages*. Essay, Critique, and History Series, no. 6. Trans. *Ortacag Turk Mimarisinin Anahatlari icin bir Ozet*. Sirkeci, Istanbul: Arkeoloji ve Sanat Yayinlari, 1990. Bib. pp. 230-234.

[ARC-060] Anisimov, A[leksandr] V[iktorovich]. *Architectural Guide to Moscow*. Rotterdam: Uitgeverij, 1993. 159 pp.

[ARC-070] Asensio Cerver, Francisco. *European Masters*. 10 vols. Barcelona: Atrium, 1991.

[ARC-080] Bayer, Patricia. *Art Deco Architecture: Design, Decoration and Detail from the Twenties and Thirties*. London: Thames and Hudson, 1992. Bib. pp. 220-221.

[ARC-090] Benjamin, Andrew E. *Philosophy and Architecture*. London: Academy Editions; New York: St. Martin's Press, 1990. 96 pp.

[ARC-100] Boardman, John, Jasper Griffin, and Oswyn Murray, eds. *The Roman World*. Oxford; New York: Oxford University Press, 1988. 486 pp. Bibs.

[ARC-110] Braham, Allan. *The Architecture of the French Enlightenment*. 1980. Reprint. Berkeley: University of California Press, 1989. Bib. refs. pp. 279-282.

[ARC-120] Branner, Robert. *Burgundian Gothic Architecture*. 1960. Reprint. London: A. Zwemmer, 1985. 206 pp. Bib. refs.

[ARC-130] Broner, Kaisa, ed. *Modernity and Popular Culture*. [Jyvaskyla, Finland]: Alvar Aalto Museum; Helsinki: Museum of Finnish Architecture: Building Book, 1988. 144 pp. Bib. refs.

[ARC-140] Brown, Jane. *The Art and Architecture of English Gardens: Designs for the Garden from the Collection of the Royal Institute of British Architects, 1609 to the Present Day*. London: Weidenfeld and Nicolson, 1989. Bib. p. 314.

[ARC-150] Brown, Rosanna Sofia. "Humor in the Landscape." M.Arch.

Thesis, University of Texas at Arlington, 1990. Bib. refs. pp. 74-79.

[ARC-160] Brunskill, R[onald] W[illiam]. *Traditional Buildings of Britain: An Introduction to Vernacular Architecture.* New ed. London: Gollancz with Peter Crawley, 1992. Bib. pp. 181-182.

[ARC-170] Brusatin, Manlio, et al. *The Baroque in Central Europe: Places, Architecture and Art.* Venice: Marsilio Publishers, 1992. 319 pp. Bibs.

[ARC-180] Buitron-Oliver, Diana, ed. *New Perspectives in Early Greek Art.* Studies in the History of Art (Washington, D.C.), Symposium Papers, no. 16. Washington, D.C.: National Gallery of Art, 1991. Dist. University Press of New England, Hanover. 308 pp. Bib. refs.

[ARC-190] Burckhardt, Jacob, and Peter Murray. *The Architecture of the Italian Renaissance.* Trans. *Geschichte der Renaissance in Italien.* London: Secker and Warburg, 1985. Reprint. Harmondsworth: Penguin, 1987. xxxv, 283 pp. Bib. pp. xix-xxix.

[ARC-200] Byrne, Andrew. *London's Georgian Houses.* London: Georgian Press, 1986. Bib. p. 205.

[ARC-210] Carroll, Kevin. *Architectures of Nigeria: Architectures of the Hausa and Yoruba Peoples and of the Many Peoples Between--Tradition and Modernization.* [London]: Ethnographica, Ltd., with Lester Crook Academic Publishing for Society of African Missions, 1992. Bib. refs. pp. 121-122.

[ARC-220] Carlson-Reddig, Thomas. *An Architect's Paris.* Boston: Bulfinch Press, 1993. Bib. refs.

[ARC-230] Cole, Doris, Kren Cord Taylor, and Sylvia Moore. *The Lady Architects: Lois Lilley Howe, Eleanor Manning and Mary Almy: 1893-1937.* New York: Midmarch Arts Press, 1990. Bib. refs. pp. 143-144.

[ARC-240] Colomina, Beatriz, and Jennifer Bloomer, eds. *Sexuality and Space.* Princeton Papers on Architecture, no. 1. New York: Princeton Architectural Press, 1992. 389 pp. Bib. refs.

[ARC-250] Constant, Caroline. *The Palladio Guide.* Princeton: Princeton Architectural Press, 1985. Bib. p. 141.

[ARC-260] Curl, James Stevens. *Classical Architecture: An Introduction to its Vocabulary and Essentials, with a Select Glossary of Terms.* London: B. T. Batsford, 1992. Bib. pp. 223-225.

50

[ARC-270] ------. *Encyclopaedia of Architectural Terms*. London: Donhead, 1992. Bib. pp. 349-352.

[ARC-280] Dal Co, Francesco. *Figures of Architecture and Thought: German Architecture Culture, 1880-1920*. Rizzoli Essays on Architecture. New York: Rizolli International Publications, 1990. 344 pp.

[ARC-290] Danby, Miles. *Grammar of Architectural Design, with Special Reference to the Tropics*. New York: Oxford University Press, 1963. 243 pp. Bib.

[ARC-300] De la Bedoyere, Guy. *The Buildings of Roman Britain*. London: B. T. Batsford, 1991. 224 pp. Bib.

[ARC-310] Deuchler, Florens. *Gothic*. Trans. *Gotik*. Universe History of Art and Architecture. 1973. Reprint. New York: Universe Books, 1989. 200 pp.

[ARC-320] Dixon, Roger. *Victorian Architecture: With a Short Dictionary of Architects and 250 Illustrations*. 2nd ed. London: Thames and Hudson, 1991. 288 pp. Bib. pp. 250-251.

[ARC-330] Donnelly, Marian C[ard]. *Architecture in the Scandinavian Countries*. Cambridge, Mass.; London: MIT Press, 1992. Bib. pp. 373-391.

[ARC-340] Downes, Kerry. *The Architecture of Wren*. Rev. ed. Reading: Redhedge, 1988. Bib. pp. 132-133.

[ARC-350] Downing, Andrew Jackson. *The Architecture of Country Houses*. 1850. Reprint. New York: Dover Publications, n.d.

[ARC-360] Enge, Torsten Olaf, and Carl Friedrich Schroer. *Garden Architecture in Europe, 1450-1800: From the Villa Garden of the Italian Renaissance to the English Landscape Garden*. Trans. Aisa Mattaj. Trans. *Gartenkunst in Europa, 1450-1800*. Cologn: Benedikt Taschen, 1990. 236 pp.

[ARC-370] Engel, Heino. *The Japanese House: A Tradition for Contemporary Architecture*. 1964. Reprint. Rutland, Vt.: C. E. Tuttle Co., 1988. Bib. refs. pp. 489-490.

[ARC-380] Enlart, Camille, and David Hunt. *Gothic Art and the Renaissance in Cyprus*. Trans. *L'art gothique et la Renaissance en Chypre*. London: Trigraph with A. G. Leventis Foundation, 1987. xxi, 544 pp. Bib. refs. pp. 524-532.

[ARC-390] Etlin, Richard A. *Frank Lloyd Wright and Le Corbusier: The Romantic Legacy*. Manchester; New York: Manchester

51

University Press, 1993.

[ARC-400] Fleming, John, Hugh Honour, and Nikolaus Pevsner. *The Pen-guin Dictionary of Architecture*. Reissue: Penguin Books, 1991. 497 pp.

[ARC-410] Fletcher, Banister. *A History of Architecture*. 18th ed. Ed. J. C. Palmes. New York: Charles Scribner's Sons, 1975. 1,390 pp. Bibs.

[ARC-420] Frampton, Kenneth. *Modern Architecture: A Critical History*. 3rd ed. London: Thames and Hudson, 1992. Bib. refs. pp. 345-366.

[ARC-430] Frankfort, Henri. *The Art and Architecture of the Ancient Orient*. 1970. Reprint. London; New York: Penguin, 1989. Bib. pp. 415-436.

[ARC-440] Friedman, Joe, and Richard Berenholtz. *Inside New York: Dis-covering New York's Classic Interiors*. New York: Harper Collins Publishers, 1992. Bib. p. 122.

[ARC-450] Gaines, Thomas A. *The Campus as a Work of Art*. New York; London: Frederick A. Praeger Publishers, 1991. 168 pp. Bib. refs.

[ARC-460] Gelbrich, Uli. *Dictionary of Architecture and Building, English-German*. Amsterdam; New York: Elsevier, 1989. 418 pp.

[ARC-470] German Commission for UNESCO. *Art Noveau/Jugendstil Archi-tecture in Europe*. Architecture and Protection of Monu-ments and Sites of Historical Interest, vol. 26. [Bonn]: German Commission for UNESCO, 1988. 244 pp. Bib. refs.

[ARC-480] Gilchrist, Agnes Eleanor [Addison]. *Romanticism and the Gothic Revival*. 1938. Reprint. New York: Gordian Press, 1967. Bib. pp. 157-183.

[ARC-490] Gillispie, Charles Coulston, and Michel Dewachter, eds. *Monu-ments of Egypt: The Napoleonic Edition: The Complete Archaeological Plates from La Description de l'Egypte*. Princeton: Princeton Architectural Press with Architectural League of New York, J. Paul Getty Trust, 1987. 45 pp., 525 pp. of plates. Bib.

[ARC-500] Gippenreiter, Vadim Evgenevich. *Fabled Cities of Central Asia: Samarkand, Bukhara, Khiva*. New York: Abbeville Press, 1989. Bib. p. 187.

52

[ARC-510] Glancey, Jonathan. *New British Architecture*. New York: Thames and Hudson, 1990. Bib. p. 190.

[ARC-520] Goode, Patrick, and Michael Lancaster. *The Oxford Companion to Gardens*. Oxford; New York: Oxford University Press, 1991. Bib. pp. 629-635.

[ARC-530] Graham, James Walter. *The Palaces of Crete*. Rev. ed. Princeton: Princeton University Press, 1987. Bib. pp. 270-274.

[ARC-540] Grant, Lindy. *Medieval Art, Architecture and Archaeology in London*. [London]: British Archaeological Association, 1990. 172 pp. Bib. refs.

[ARC-550] Grewal, Bikram, and R. K. Bose. *Taj Mahal: A Visitor's Guide*. London: Heinemann, 1986. 51 pp. Bib.

[ARC-560] Guell, Xavier. *Spanish Contemporary Architecture: The Eighties*. Barcelona: G. Gili, 1990. Bib. pp. 190-191.

[ARC-570] Guidoni, Enrico. *Primitive Architecture*. Trans. Robert Erich Wolf. New York: Harry N. Abrams, Inc., 1978. Bib. pp. 359-368.

[ARC-580] Guillermo, Jorge. *Dutch Houses and Castles*. New York: M.T. Train/Scala Books, 1990. Bib. refs. pp. 206-207.

[ARC-590] Gutheim, Frederick, ed. *In the Cause of Architecture*. New York: Architectural Record, 1925.

[ARC-600] Hamlin, Talbot. *Greek Revival Architecture in America: Being an Account of Important Trends in American Architecture and American Life Prior to the War Between the States*. New York: Oxford University Press, 1944. Bib. pp. 383-409.

[ARC-610] Henig, Martin, ed. *Architecture and Architectural Sculpture in the Roman Empire*. Monograph/Oxford University Committee for Archaeology, no. 29. Oxford: Oxford University Committee for Archaeology, 1990. Dist. Oxbow Books. Bib. refs. pp. 161-162.

[ARC-620] Hitchcock, Henry Russell, and Philip Johnson. *The International Style*. New York: W. W. Norton and Co., 1966.

[ARC-630] Holgate, Alan. *Aesthetics of Built Form*. Oxford; New York: Oxford University Press, 1992. 289 pp.

[ARC-640] Holt, Elizabeth Basye Gilmore, ed. *From the Classicists to the Impressionists: A Documentary History of Art and Architecture in the 19th Century*. New York: New York University

Press, 1966. 552 pp.

[ARC-650] Hubala, Erich. *Baroque and Rococo*. Trans. *Barock und Rokoko*. 1976. Reprint. New York: Universe Books, 1989. Bib.

[ARC-660] Hunt, William Dudley, Jr. *American Architecture: A Field Guide to the Most Important Examples*. New York: Harper and Row, 1984. 320 pp.

[ARC-670] Jencks, Charles. *Architecture Today*. London: Academy Editions, 1988. Bib. pp. 344-345.

[ARC-680] ------. *Late-Modern Architecture and Other Essays*. New York: Rizolli International Publications, Inc., 1980. Bib. pp. 191-193.

[ARC-690] Jenner, Michael. *The Architectural Heritage of Britain and Ireland: An Illustrated A-Z of Terms and Styles*. London: Michael Joseph, 1993. 320 pp.

[ARC-700] Jones, Frederic H[icks]. *A Concise Dictionary of Interior Design*. Los Altos, Calif.: Crisp Publications, 1990. 215 pp.

[ARC-710] Keswick, Maggie, Judy Oberlander, and Joe Wai. *In a Chinese Garden: The Art and Architecture of the Dr. Sun Yat-Sen Classical Chinese Garden*. Vancouver: Dr. Sun Yat-Sen Garden Society of Vancouver, 1990. 63 pp. Bib. refs. p. 3.

[ARC-720] Khalili, Nader. *Ceramic Houses and Earth Architecture: How to Build your Own*. 1986. Reprint. Los Angeles: Burning Gate Press, 1990. 225 pp. Bibs.

[ARC-730] Khonsari, Mehdi. *Bazaars: Public Space in Traditional Persian Architecture*. Washington, D.C.: Mage, 1993.

[ARC-740] Kiel, Machiel. *Ottoman Architecture in Albania, 1385-1912*. Besiktas, Istanbul: Research Centre for Islamic History, Art and Culture, 1990. 342 pp. Bib. refs. pp. 301-319.

[ARC-750] Knapp, Ronald G. *The Chinese House: Craft, Symbol, and the Folk Tradition*. Hong Kong; New York: Oxford University Press, 1990. Bib. refs. pp. 84-85.

[ARC-760] Kostof, Spiro. *A History of Architecture: Settings and Rituals*. New York: Oxford University Press, 1985. 788 pp. Bib. refs.

[ARC-770] Krasner, Deborah. *Celtic: Living in Scotland, Ireland, and Wales*. London: Thames and Hudson, 1990. Bib. p. 254.

54

[ARC-780] Kraus, Wolfgang. *The Palaces of Vienna*. New York: Vendome Press, 1993. Dist. Rizolli International Publications, Inc. in USA and Canada.

[ARC-790] Kultermann, Udo. *Architecture in the 20th Century*. Trans. *Architektur im 20. Jahrhundert*. New York: Van Nostrand Reinhold, 1993. 306 pp. Bib. refs.

[ARC-800] Kurokawa, Kisho. *Rediscovering Japanese Space*. New York: Weatherhill, 1988. 128 pp.

[ARC-810] Lane, Mills. *Architecture of the Old South*. New York: Abbeville Press, 1993. Bib. refs.

[ARC-820] Larson, George A. *Chicago Architecture and Design*. New York: Harry N. Abrams, 1993. Bib. refs.

[ARC-830] Lawrence, A. W. *Greek Architecture*. 4th ed. Rev. R. A. Tombinson. Pelican History of Art. New York: Penguin Books, 1983. Bib. pp. 397-413.

[ARC-840] Leatherbarrow, David. *The Roots of Architectural Invention: Site, Enclosure, Materials*. Cambridge; New York: Cambridge University Press, 1993. Bib. refs.

[ARC-850] Lewis, Michael J. *The Politics of the German Gothic Revival: August Reichensperger (1808-1895)*. New York: Architectural History Foundation; Cambridge: MIT Press, 1993. Bib. refs.

[ARC-860] Liu, Laurence G. *Chinese Architecture*. London: Academy Editions, 1989. Bib. p. 281.

[ARC-870] Lucas, Oliver W. R. *The Design of Forest Landscapes*. Oxford: Oxford University Press, 1991. 381 pp. Bib.

[ARC-880] Lyttelton, Margaret. *Baroque Architecture in Classical Antiquity*. Ithaca: Cornell University Press, 1974. Bib. pp. 327-331.

[ARC-890] MacDonald, William L. *The Architecture of the Roman Period*. Rev. ed. 2 vols. New Haven: Yale University Press, 1982, 1986. Bib. Vol. 1, pp. 205-211; Vol. 2, pp. 290-301.

[ARC-900] McIntyre, Anthony. *Medieval Tuscany and Umbria*. London: Viking, 1992. Bib. p. 146.

[ARC-910] McKean, Charles. *Edinburgh: An Illustrated Architectural Guide*. [New ed.] Edinburgh: RIAS, 1992. 236 pp. Bib.

[ARC-920] Magnago Lampugnani, Vittorio, ed. *The Thames and Hudson*

Encyclopaedia of 20th Century Architecture. Rev. ed. Trans. Barry Bergdoll. Trans. *Hatje Lexikon der Architekur des 20. Jahrhunderts (1983).* London: Thames and Hudson, 1986. 384 pp. Bibs. Also called *Encyclopedia of 20th-Century Architecture* in U.S.

[ARC-930] Mahoney, Kathleen. *Gothic: An Exuberant Heritage.* New York: Viking Studio Books, 1993.

[ARC-940] Mark, Robert. *Experiments in Gothic Structure.* Cambridge: MIT Press, 1982. 135 pp. Bib. refs.

[ARC-950] Markovich, Nicholas C., Wolfgang F. E. Preiser, and Fred Gillette Sturm. *Pueblo Style and Regional Architecture.* New York; London: Van Nostrand Reinhold, 1990. 348 pp. Bibs.

[ARC-960] Martin, Roland. *Greek Architecture: Architecture of Crete, Greece, and the Greek World.* History of World Architecture. New York: Electa/Rizzoli, 1988. Bib. p. 197.

[ARC-970] Mehling, Franz N., Maria Paukert, and Bernhard Pollmann. *Paris and the Ile de France: A Phaidon Art and Architecture Guide.* Trans. *Knaurs Kulturfuhrer in Farbe, Paris und Ile de France.* New York: Prentice-Hall Press, 1987.

[ARC-980] Mehling, Marianne, Joachim Hertlein, and Albin Rohrmoser. *Florence and Tuscany.* Trans. *Knaurs Kulturfuhrer in Farbe, Florenz und Toskana.* A Phaidon Cultural Guide. New York: Prentice-Hall Press, 1986. 259 pp.

[ARC-990] Meyer, Richard E., ed. *Cemeteries and Gravemarkers: Voices of American Culture.* Logan, Utah: Utah State University Press, 1992. Bib. refs. pp. 329-339.

[ARC-1000] Michell, George, and Philip Davies. *The Penguin Guide to the Monuments of India.* 2 vols. London: Penguin, 1989. Bib.

[ARC-1010] Morriss, Richard K., and Ken Hoverd. *The Buildings of Bath.* Dover, N.H.: Alan Sutton, 1993. Bib. refs.

[ARC-1020] Nath, R. *The Taj Mahal and Its Incarnation: Original Persian Data on Its Builders, Material, Costs, Measurements, etc.* Jaipur: Historical Research Documentation Programme, 1985. 152 pp. Bibs.

[ARC-1030] Necipoglu, Gulru. *Architecture, Ceremonial, and Power: The Topkapi Palace in the Fifteenth and Sixteenth Centuries.* New York: Architectural History Foundation; Cambridge, Mass.; London: MIT, 1991. Bib. pp. 305-328. (Topkapi Sarayi Muzesi, Turkey.)

[ARC-1040] Negev, Avraham. *The Late Roman and Byzantine Periods*. [Jerusalem]: Institute of Archaeology, Hebrew University of Jerusalem, 1988. 116 pp. Bib. refs.

[ARC-1050] Norberg-Schulz, Christian. *Intentions in Architecture*. 1965. Reprint. Cambridge: MIT Press, 1988. Bib. refs. pp. 225-232.

[ARC-1060] Paine, Robert Treat, and Alexander Coburn Soper. *The Art and Architecture of Japan*. 3rd ed. Updated by D. B. Waterhouse and Bunji Kobayashi. 1981. Reprint. Harmondsworth, England; Baltimore: Penguin Books, 1985. Bib. pp. 455-489.

[ARC-1070] Pal, Pratapaditya. *Art and Architecture of Ancient Kashmir*. Bombay: Marg Publications, 1989. 136 pp. Bibs.

[ARC-1080] Papadakes, A. *The New Modern Aesthetic*. Architectural Design Profile, no. 86. *Architectural Design*, vol. 60, nos. 7-8, 1990. London: Academy Editions; New York: St. Martin's Press, 1990. 96 pp.

[ARC-1090] ------. *Pop Architecture*. Architecture Design Profile, no. 98. London: Academy Group Ltd.; New York: St. Martin's Press, 1992. xxiv, 96 pp.

[ARC-1100] Parker, Richard Bordeaux. *Islamic Monuments in Cairo: A Practical Guide*. 3rd ed. Rev. Caroline Williams. Cairo, Egypt: American University in Cairo Press, 1985. 334 pp. Bib. pp. 287-288.

[ARC-1110] Peel, Lucy. *An Introduction to 20th-Century Architecture*. London: Apple Press, 1989. Bib. p. 128.

[ARC-1120] Pemberton, Delia. *Ancient Egypt*. Architectural Guides for Travellers. London: Penguin, 1992. Bib. pp. 146-147.

[ARC-1130] Penning-Rowsell, Edmund C[harles]. *Landscape Meanings and Values*. London: Allen and Unwin, 1986. 160 pp. Bib.

[ARC-1140] Perouse de Montclos, Jean-Marie, and Robert Polidori. *Versailles*. New York: Abbeville Press, 1991. Bib. refs. p. 419.

[ARC-1150] Petersen, Toni, ed. *Art and Architecture Thesaurus*. 3 vols. New York: Oxford University Press for Getty Art History Information Program, 1990.

[ARC-1160] Placzek, Adolph K., ed. *Macmillan Encyclopedia of Architects*. 4 vols. New York: Free Press, 1982.

[ARC-1170] Platt, Colin. *The Architecture of Medieval Britain: A Social History.* New Haven: Yale University Press, 1990. Bib. refs. pp. 301-318.

[ARC-1180] Porphyrios, Demetri. *Classical Architecture.* London: Academy Editions, 1991. 155 pp. (Based on six lectures given at University of Virginia and Yale University in 1987 and 1989.)

[ARC-1190] Pothorn, Herbert. *Styles of Architecture.* Trans. Baustile. London: B. T. Batsford, 1971. 187 pp.

[ARC-1200] Prescott, Elizabeth. *The English Medieval Hospital: 1050-1640.* London: Seaby, 1992. Bib. refs. pp. 173-178.

[ARC-1210] Quiney, Anthony. *Kent Houses: English Domestic Architecture.* Woodbridge, Suffolk: Antique Collectors' Club, 1993. Bib. refs. pp. 275-279.

[ARC-1220] Quirke, Stephen, and A. Jeffrey Spencer. *The British Museum Book of Ancient Egypt.* New York: Thames and Hudson, 1992. Bib. refs. pp. 221-222.

[ARC-1230] Radding, Charles M. *Medieval Architecture, Medieval Learning: Builders and Masters in the Age of Romanesque and Gothic.* New Haven; London: Yale University Press, 1992. Bib. pp. 151-164.

[ARC-1240] Rai, Raghu, and Usha Rai. *Taj Mahal.* 2nd ed. New York: Vendome Press, 1987. Dist. Rizzoli International Publications. 160 pp.

[ARC-1250] Rees, Ronald. *Interior Landscapes: Gardens and the Domestic Environment.* Baltimore: Johns Hopkins University Press, 1993. Bib. refs. pp. 179-182.

[ARC-1260] Reynolds, Donald Martin. *Nineteenth-Century Architecture.* Cambridge Introduction to Art. Cambridge: Cambridge University Press, 1992. Bib. pp. 103-104.

[ARC-1270] Robinson, John Martin. *The Architecture of Northern England.* London: Macmillan London, 1986. Bib. pp. 348-349.

[ARC-1280] Rosenberg, Eugene, and Richard Cork. *Architect's Choice: Art in Architecture in Great Britain Since 1945.* London: Thames and Hudson, 1992. Bib. refs. pp. 170-171.

[ARC-1290] Roth, Leland M. *A Concise History of American Architecture.* New York: Harper and Row, 1979.

58

[ARC-1300] Ruskin, John. *The Stones of Venice.* 2 vols. 1892. Reprint. New York: Garland Publishing, 1977.

[ARC-1310] ------. *The Seven Lamps of Architecture: Architecture and Painting.* New York: E. P. Dutton and Co., [1906]. 228 pp.

[ARC-1320] Russell, Terence M. *Architecture in the Encyclopedie of Diderot and d'Alembert: The Letterpress Articles and Selected Engravings.* Aldershot: Scolar Press, 1993. 224 pp.

[ARC-1330] Rydell, Robert W. *Architecture and the American West.* Berkeley: Pacific Historical Review, 1985. Bib. refs. From *Pacific Historical Review*, vol. 54, no. 4 (1985), pp. 397-566.

[ARC-1340] Sailer, John. *The Great Stone Architects: Interviews with Philip Johnson, John Burgee, Michael Graves, Cesar Pelli, Helmut Jahn, John Portman and Der Scutt.* Oradell, N.J.: Trademark Publishing Co., 1991. 107 pp.

[ARC-1350] Satkowski, Leon George. *Giorgio Vasari: Architect and Courtier.* Princeton: Princeton University Press, 1993. Bib. refs.

[ARC-1360] Scruton, Roger. *The Aesthetics of Architecture.* Princeton Essays on the Arts, no. 8. Princeton: Princeton University Press, 1979. Bib. pp. 291-292.

[ARC-1370] Scully, Vincent Joseph. *Architecture: The Natural and the Manmade.* New York: St. Martin's Press, 1991. 388 pp. Bib. refs.

[ARC-1380] Sear, Frank. *Roman Architecture.* Rev. ed. Ithaca: Cornell University Press, 1989. Bib. refs. pp. 280-285.

[ARC-1390] Semper, Gottfried. *The Four Elements of Architecture and Other Writings.* RES Monographs in Anthropology and Aesthetics. Cambridge: Cambridge University Press, 1988. 314 pp.

[ARC-1400] Sestoft, Jorgen, and Jorgen Hegner Christiansen. *Guide to Danish Architecture.* Copenhagen: Arkitektens Forlag, 1991. Bib. refs. p. 271. Vol. 1, 1000-1960.

[ARC-1410] Sharp, Dennis. *Modern Architecture and Expressionism.* New York: George Braziller, [1967]. Bib. pp. 195-202.

[ARC-1420] Shaw, Peter, and Robin Morrison. *New Zealand Architecture: From Polynesian Beginnings to 1990.* Auckland: Hodder and Stoughton, 1991. Bib. p. 212.

[ARC-1430] Smith, Christine [Hunnikin]. *Architecture in the Culture of Early Humanism Ethics, Aesthetics, and Eloquence, 1400-1470.*

New York; Oxford: Oxford University Press, 1992. Bib. refs. in notes, pp. 217-267. Bib. pp. 269-290.

[ARC-1440] Smith, G[eorge] E[verard] Kidder. *Looking at Architecture.* New York: Harry N. Abrams, 1990. Bib. refs. p. 168.

[ARC-1450] Smitthi Siribhadra, Elizabeth H. Moore, and Michael Freeman. *Palaces of the Gods: Khmer Art and Architecture in Thailand.* Bangkok: River Books, 1992. Bib. p. 344.

[ARC-1460] Sozen, Metin, and Ilhan Aksit. *The Evolution of Turkish Art and Architecture.* Istanbul: Haset Kitabevi, 1987. Bib. pp. 323-327.

[ARC-1470] Steiner, Dietmar, and Johann Georg Gsteu. *Architecture in Vienna.* 2nd English ed. Trans. *Architektur in Wien.* Vienna: G. Prachner, 1992. Bib. refs. pp. 204-206.

[ARC-1480] Stierlin, Henri. *Encyclopaedia of World Architecture.* 2 vols. New York: Facts on File, 1977. 499 pp.

[ARC-1490] Stillman, Damie. *English Neo-Classical Architecture.* 2 vols. London: Zwemmer, 1988. Bib. pp. 601-626.

[ARC-1500] Stimpson, Miriam F. *A Field Guide to Landmarks of Modern Architecture in the United States: Touring Directory Including Maps, Illustrations, and Brief Histories.* Englewood Cliffs, N.J.: Prentice-Hall Press, 1985. Bib. pp. 427-429.

[ARC-1510] Stoddard, Richard. *Theatre and Cinema Architecture: A Guide to Information Sources.* Performing Arts Information Guide Series, vol. 5. Detroit: Gale Research, 1978. 368 pp.

[ARC-1520] Stoica, Georgeta. *Romanian Folk Architecture.* Bucharest: Meridiane Publishing House, 1989. Bib. refs. pp. 162-163.

[ARC-1530] Strachan, Paul. *Imperial Pagan: Art and Architecture of Burma.* Honolulu: University of Hawaii Press, 1990. 159 pp. Bib. refs.

[ARC-1540] Sturgis, Russell, et al. *A Dictionary of Architecture and Building: Biographical, Historical, and Descriptive.* 3 vols. New York: Macmillan Publishing Co., 1902-1904. Bib. Vol. 3, cols. 1141-1212.

[ARC-1550] Summerson, John Newenham. *Architecture in Britain, 1530-1830.* 7th ed. Harmondsworth; New York: Penguin Books, 1986. 624 pp. Bib. pp. 580-588.

[ARC-1560] ------. *The Classical Language of Architecture.* Cambridge: MIT

60

Press, 1966. Bib. pp. 53-56.

[ARC-1570] Sutcliffe, Anthony. *Paris: An Architectural History*. New Haven: Yale University Press, 1993. Bib. refs.

[ARC-1580] Symes, Michael. *The English Rococo Garden*. Shire Garden History, no. 5. Buckinghamshire, United Kingdom: Shire Publications, 1991. 72 pp. Bib. refs.

[ARC-1590] Tavernor, Robert. *Palladio and Palladianism*. World of Art. London: Thames and Hudson, 1991. Bib. refs. pp. 210-212.

[ARC-1600] Taylor, Jennifer. *Australian Architecture Since 1960*. 2nd ed. Red Hill, A.C.T.: National Education Division, Royal Australian Institute of Architects, 1990. Bib. pp. 255-256.

[ARC-1610] Thornton, Victoria, and Ken Allinson. *Guide to London's Contemporary Architecture*. Oxford; Boston: Butterworth Architecture, 1993.

[ARC-1620] Thurley, Simon. *The Royal Palaces of Tudor England: Architecture and Court Life, 1460-1547*. New Haven: Yale University Press, 1993. Bib. refs.

[ARC-1630] Tomlinson, R[ichard] A[llan]. *Greek Architecture*. Classical World Series. Bristol: Bristol Classical Press, 1989. Bib. pp. 100-101.

[ARC-1640] Townsend, Richard F., ed. *The Ancient Americas: Art from Sacred Landscapes*. Chicago: Art Institute of Chicago; Munich: Prestel Verlag, 1992. 397 pp. Bib. refs.

[ARC-1650] Trachtenbery, Marvin, and Isabelle Hyman. *Architecture: From Prehistory to Post-Modernism: The Western Tradition*. New York: Harry N. Abrams, Inc., 1986. Bib. pp. 589-593.

[ARC-1660] University Prints. *Baroque-XVIII Century Art and Architecture: A Special Study Set of Fine Art Reproductions*. 4 vols. Winchester, Mass.: University Prints, 1991.

[ARC-1670] ------. *Medieval Art and Architecture: A Special Study Set of Fine Art Reproductions*. 4 vols. Winchester, Mass.: University Prints, 1991.

[ARC-1680] ------. *Modern XIX-XX Century Art and Architecture: A Special Study Set of Fine Art Reproductions*. 5 vols. Winchester, Mass.: University Prints, 1991.

[ARC-1690] ------. *Renaissance Art and Architecture: A Special Study Set of Fine Art Reproductions*. 5 vols. Winchester, Mass.: University Prints, 1991.

[ARC-1700] Vlatseas, S. *A History of Malaysian Architecture*. Singapore: Longman, 1990. Bib. refs. p. 133.

[ARC-1710] Waldeier Bizzarro, Tina. *Romanesque Architectural Criticism: A Pre-History*. Cambridge: Cambridge University Press, 1992. Bib. pp. 213-246.

[ARC-1720] Wallace, Joyce M. *The Historic Houses of Edinburgh*. Edinburgh: John Donald, 1987. Dist. Humanities Press, Atlantic Highlands, N.J. Bib. p. 232.

[ARC-1730] Ward-Perkins, J[ohn] B[ryan]. *Roman Architecture*. History of World Architecture. New York: Electa/Rizzoli, 1988. Bib. pp. 205-207.

[ARC-1740] ------. *Roman Imperial Architecture*. The Pelican History of Art. New York: Viking Penguin, 1981. Bib. pp. 498-501.

[ARC-1750] Watkin, David. *A History of Western Architecture*. New York: Thames and Hudson, 1986. Bib. pp. 579-584.

[ARC-1760] Weber, Ralf P. "On the Aesthetics of Architectural Forms: A Psychological Approach to the Structure and the Order of Perceived Architectural Space." Ph.D. Thesis, University of California, Berkeley, 1986. Bib. refs. pp. 282-289.

[ARC-1770] White, Norval. *The Guide to the Architecture of Paris*. New York: Charles Scribner's Sons, 1993. xlvii, 446 pp.

[ARC-1780] Wilbur, C. Keith. *Home Building and Woodworking in Colonial America*. Old Saybrook, Conn.: Globe Pequot Press, 1992. 121 pp. Bib. refs.

[ARC-1790] Wilson, Richard Guy, and Sidney K. Robinson. *Modern Architecture in America: Visions and Revisions*. Ames: Iowa State University Press, 1991. 217 pp. Bib. refs.

[ARC-1800] Winter, Nancy A. *Greek Architectural Terracottas: From the Prehistoric Through to the Archaic Period*. Oxford Monographs on Classical Archaeology. Oxford: Clarendon Press; New York: Oxford University Press, 1993. Bib. refs.

[ARC-1810] Woods, Lebbeus. *Anarchitecture: Architecture is a Political Act*. Architectural Monographs, no. 22 0141-2191. London: Academy Editions/St. Martin's Press, 1992. Bib. p. 144.

[ARC-1820] *World Architecture*. London: Grosvenor Press International, 1990-. Bi-monthly.

62

[ARC-1830] Wright, Frank Lloyd. *An Autobiography*. New York: Horizon Press, 1937.

[ARC-1840] Wright, G[eorge] R. H. *Ancient Buildings in Cyprus*. 2 vols. Leiden; New York: E. J. Brill, 1992. Bib. refs.

[ARC-1850] Yamashita, Michael S., and Elizabeth Bibb. *In the Japanese Garden*. Washington, D.C.: Starwood, 1991. Bib. p. 107.

[ARC-1860] Yarwood, Doreen. *The Architecture of Europe*. [London]: Chancellor Press, 1974. Bib. pp. 565-572.

[ARC-1870] ------. *The Architecture of Europe*. 4 vols. London: B. T. Batsford, 1992. Bib. refs. Vol. 1: *The Ancient Classical and Byzantine World, 3000 B.C.-A.D. 1453*. 166 pp. Vol. 2: *Middle Ages, 650-1550*. 202 pp. Vol. 3: *Classical Architecture 1420-1800*. 202 pp. Vol. 4: *The Modern World*.

[ARC-1880] ------. *A Chronology of Western Architecture*. London: B. T. Batsford, 1987. Bib. pp. 216-217.

[ARC-1890] Yeang, Ken. *The Architecture of Malaysia*. Amsterdam: Pepin Press, 1992. Bib. refs. pp. 350-351.

[ARC-1900] Yegul, Fikret K[utlu]. *Baths and Bathing in Classical Antiquity*. New York: Architectural History Foundation; Cambridge, Mass.; London: MIT Press, 1992. Bib. pp. 474-486.

[ARC-1910] Yenisoganci, H. Veli. *Hagia Sophia and Hagia Eirene, Mosaic Museum, Imrahor Monument, Kariye Museum, Fethiye Museum, Tekfur Palace: Museums' Guide*. 1990? Reprint. Ankara: Donmez Offset Muze Eserleri Turistik Yayinlari, 1993. Bib. p. 109.

[ARC-1920] Zerbst, Rainer. *Gudi, 1852-1926: Antoni Gaudi i Cornet: A Life Devoted to Architecture*. Cologne: Benedikt Taschen Verlag, 1988. Bib. pp. 238-239.

[ARC-1930] Zevi, Bruno. *The Modern Language of Architecture*. Seattle: University of Washington Press, 1978. 241 pp.

KEY WORKS ON ARCHITECTURE AND RELIGION

The following bibliographies were primarily selected from publications completed since 1960. Nearly all of the recent bibliographies treating architecture and religion have been produced by Vance Bibliographies. Due to the relatively small size of most of the bibliographies on this topic, many shorter bibliographies have been included here. Although the main focus of this book is on Christianity and the fine arts, several bibliographies treating architecture and non-Christian religions have been included here to allow students of the arts to identify the extent to which Christian architecture reflects or differs from the arts of other cultures. The bibliographies treating non-Christian architecture include the following: [ARR-020], [ARR-060], [ARR-110], [ARR-120], [ARR-150], [ARR-160], [ARR-170], [ARR-190], [ARR-350], [ARR-430], [ARR-470], [ARR-480], [ARR-490], [ARR-500]. The other thirty-six bibliographies listing works treating Christian architecture range from the broadly theological, such as [ARR-010], [ARR-310], to the specifically focused, such as [ARR-070], [ARR-080], [ARR-130], and [ARR-140]. The titles of each are self-explanatory.

As for the texts treating architecture and religion, a strong sampling is given below. For the study of architecture and theological aesthetics see [ARR-510], [ARR-650], [ARR-830], [ARR-910], [ARR-990], [ARR-1400], [ARR-1580], [ARR-1900], [ARR-1940], [ARR-2100], and [ARR-2180]. To review this topic from a broad perspective, see the following survey works: [ARR-720], [ARR-1070], [ARR-1480], [ARR-1870]. For studies of architecture in pre-Christian or non-Christian cultures, see [ARR-550], [ARR-720], [ARR-740], [ARR-900], [ARR-950], [ARR-1140], [ARR-1150], [ARR-1160], [ARR-1170], [ARR-1380], [ARR-1440], [ARR-1460], [ARR-1480], [ARR-1600], [ARR-1770], [ARR-1840], [ARR-1850], and [ARR-1950].

To examine early Christian architecture, particularly in the Middle East and northern Africa, note Paul Corby Finney's recent work, *Art, Archaeology, and Architecture of Early Christianity* [ARR-1000], and also see [ARR-530], [ARR-720], [ARR-1090], [ARR-1250], [ARR-1590], [ARR-1730], [ARR-1780]. For studies of Byzantine, Romanesque, and other styles emerging during the Middle Ages, note especially Richard Krautheimer's and Slobodan Curcic's *Early Christian and Byzantine Architecture* [ARR-1390]. Also see [ARR-770], [ARR-850], [ARR-930], [ARR-1020], [ARR-1030], [ARR-1180], [ARR-1190], [ARR-1320], [ARR-1360], [ARR-1450], [ARR-1500], [ARR-1510], [ARR-1530], [ARR-1540], [ARR-1550], [ARR-1560], [ARR-1590], [ARR-1640], [ARR-1690], [ARR-1710], [ARR-1810], [ARR-

1860], [ARR-1900], [ARR-1990], [ARR-2070], and [ARR-2190].

If, as David W. Cook has suggested, the Gothic church is the most thoroughly Christian expression of theology in architecture, one will do well to begin with books emphasizing this style. The primary difficulty in studying this style is that it was often blended with earlier Norman and Romanesque styles. For a detailed and insightful review of the nature of Gothic architecture in churches, consult the profound and extensive works of Emile Mâle on Gothic churches in Medieval France, including [ARR-1520] and [VAR-740 to VAR-760] listed in Chapter 12, Visual Arts I. One will also benefit from reviewing Louis Grodecki's classic works [ARR-1110], [ARR-1120], Stephen Murray's more recent studies [ARR-1650 to 1670], which place the Gothic cathedral in its larger social context, and Erwin Panofsky's excellent work, *Gothic Architecture and Scholasticism* [ARR-1750]. Additional studies of Gothic churches can be found in the following volumes: [ARR-520], [ARR-540], [ARR-570], [ARR-600], [ARR-620], [ARR-640], [ARR-660], [ARR-680], [ARR-690], [ARR-700], [ARR-710], [ARR-780], [ARR-870], [ARR-880], [ARR-920], [ARR-960], [ARR-970], [ARR-1010], [ARR-1040], [ARR-1080], [ARR-1210], [ARR-1280], [ARR-1290], [ARR-1340], [ARR-1430], [ARR-1490], [ARR-1570], [ARR-1620], [ARR-1740], [ARR-1760], [ARR-1970], [ARR-1980], [ARR-2140], [ARR-2200], [ARR-2220].

For later centuries, see survey volumes, such as Doreen Yarwood's or other survey works identified in this section. Also note for seventeenth century architecture [ARR-750], [ARR-940], [ARR-1130]; for eighteenth and nineteenth century architecture [ARR-1330], [ARR-1350], [ARR-2130]; and for modern architecture [ARR-730], [ARR-2000]. Many volumes given in Chapter 12, Visual Arts I, treat architecture in connection with major art movements, and should therefore be considered as an augmentation to this short list.

Special Bibliographies

[ARR-010] Association of Christians in Planning and Architecture. *Christian Belief and the Built Environment: An Annotated Bibliography*. Rev. ed. Leicester: Universities and Colleges Christian Fellowship Associates for the Association of Christians in Planning and Architecture, 1987. 97 pp.

[ARR-020] Black, Linda Perlis. *Synagogue Architecture and Planning: An Annotated Bibliography.* Monticello, Ill.: Council of Planning Librarians, 1978. 24 pp.

[ARR-030] Breman, Paul, ed. *Churches of Italy.* London: Weinreb and Breman, 1967. 16 pp.

[ARR-040] Cable, Carole. *The Gothic Cathedral in France and England: Style, Form, and Sources.* Monticello, Ill.: Vance Bibliographies, 1985. 7 pp.

[ARR-050] Coppa and Avery Consultants. *Church Architecture: A Bibliographic Guide to Church Architecture in Selected Municipalities and Regions in the United States.* Monticello, Ill.: Vance Bibliographies, 1980. 10 pp.

[ARR-060] Creswell, K[eppel] A[rchibald] C[ameron]. *A Bibliography of the Architecture, Arts, and Crafts of Islam to 1st Jan. 1960.* 2nd ed. [Cairo]: American University in Cairo; Vaduz: Quarto Press, 1978. 1330 cols. *First Supplement, Jan. 1960 to Jan. 1972,* 1973. 336 cols. *Second Supplement, Jan. 1972 to Dec. 1980,* J[ames] D[ouglas] Pearson, Michael Meinecke, and George T. Scanlon, 1984. 578 cols.

[ARR-070] Doumato, Lamia. *The Byzantine Church of Hagia Sophia: Selected References.* Monticello, Ill.: Vance Bibliographies, 1980. 11 pp.

[ARR-080] ------. *Church of the Holy Sepulchre, Jerusalem.* Monticello, Ill.: Vance Bibliographies, 1981. 13 pp.

[ARR-090] ------. *Early Christian Architecture of Syria.* Monticello, Ill.: Vance Bibliographies, 1980. 17 pp.

[ARR-100] ------. *Mexican Churches: A Bibliography.* Monticello, Ill.: Vance Bibliographies, 1990. 9 pp.

[ARR-110] ------. *Mosques of the Near East.* Monticello, Ill.: Vance Bibliographies, 1979. 13 pp.

[ARR-120] ------. *Ptolemaic Temples of Egypt.* Monticello, Ill.: Vance Bibliographies, 1980. 10 pp.

[ARR-130] ------. *Sir Christopher Wren and St. Paul's Cathedral.* Monticello, Ill.: Vance Bibliographies, 1979. 16 pp.

[ARR-140] ------. *Strasbourg Cathedral: A Bibliography.* Monticello, Ill.:

66

Vance Bibliographies, 1990. 8 pp.

[ARR-150] ------. *The Temple of Athena Nike*. Monticello, Ill.: Vance Bibliographies, 1980. 5 pp.

[ARR-160] ------. *The Temple Ruins of Baalbek*. Monticello, Ill.: Vance Bibliographies, 1979. 9 pp.

[ARR-170] ------. *The Temples of Karnak and Luxor*. Monticello, Ill.: Vance Bibliographies, 1981. 8 pp.

[ARR-180] Dunning, Glenna. *Architecture of the California Missions*. Monticello, Ill.: Vance Bibliographies, 1982. 24 pp.

[ARR-190] Fairbanks, Dolores. *Islamic Architecture: A General Bibliography*. Cambridge: Aga Khan Program for Islamic Architecture at Harvard University and MIT, Documentation Center, 1981. 24 pp.

[ARR-200] Kleinbauer, W. Eugene. *Early Christian and Byzantine Architecture: An Annotated Bibliography and Historiography*. Boston: G. K. Hall, 1992. cxxiii, 779 pp.

[ARR-210] Meulen, Jan van der, Rudiger Hoyer, and Deborah Cole. *Chartres: Sources and Literary Interpretation: A Critical Bibliography*. Reference Publications in Art History. Boston: G. K. Hall, 1989. 1046 pp.

[ARR-220] Pagan, Hugh, ed. *Church Architecture and Architects in Britain*. London: B. Weinreb Architectural Books, 1976.

[ARR-230] Pevoto, Charlotte Wren. *Spanish Missions in Texas*. Monticello, Ill.: Vance Bibliographies, 1985. 9 pp.

[ARR-240] Phillips, James. *Christian Architecture: Its Origins, Early Forms, and Techniques*. Monticello, Ill.: Vance Bibliographies, 1982. 22 pp.

[ARR-250] ------. *Constantinian Architecture: The Lesser Sites*. Monticello, Ill.: Vance Bibliographies, 1982. 25 pp.

[ARR-260] ------. *Early Christian and Byzantine Constantinople*. 2 vols. Monticello, Ill.: Vance Bibliographies, 1982.

[ARR-270] ------. *Early Christian and Byzantine Constantinople, II: The Early Christian Period*. Monticello, Ill.: Vance Bibliographies, 1982. 14 pp.

[ARR-280] ------. *Early Christian Architecture in the City of Rome*. 3 vols. Monticello, Ill.: Vance Bibliographies, 1982.

[ARR-290] Starbuck, James C. *Modern American Religious Buildings*. 2 vols. Monticello, Ill.: Council of Planning Librarians, 1977.

[ARR-300] Swanick, Eric L. *Religious Architecture of Canada*. Monticello, Ill.: Vance Bibliographies, 1980. 8 pp.

[ARR-310] Universities and Colleges Christian Fellowship Associates. *Christian Belief and the Built Environment: An Annotated Bibliography*. Rev. ed. Leicester: Universities and Colleges Christian Fellowship Associates for the Association of Christians in Planning and Architecture, 1987. 97 pp.

[ARR-320] Vance, Mary A. *Abbeys: Journal Articles*. Monticello, Ill.: Vance Bibliographies, 1989. 18 pp.

[ARR-330] ------. *Abbeys: Monographs*. Monticello, Ill.: Vance Bibliographies, 1983. 26 pp.

[ARR-340] ------. *Altars and Altarpieces: Monographs*. Monticello, Ill.: Vance Bibliographies, 1983. 13 pp.

[ARR-350] ------. *Buddhist Temples: A Bibliography*. Monticello, Ill.: Vance Bibliographies, 1987. 17 pp.

[ARR-360] ------. *Byzantine Architecture: A Bibliography of English Language References*. Monticello, Ill.: Vance Bibliographies, 1982. 10 pp.

[ARR-370] ------. *Catacombs: Monographs*. Monticello, Ill.: Vance Bibliographies, 1984. 16 pp.

[ARR-380] ------. *Cathedrals: Monographs*. Monticello, Ill.: Vance Bibliographies, 1984. 175 pp.

[ARR-390] ------. *Cave Temples: A Bibliography*. Monticello, Ill.: Vance Bibliographies, 1987. 11 pp.

[ARR-400] ------. *Church Decorations and Ornament Monographs*. Monticello, Ill.: Vance Bibliographies, 1984. 43 pp.

[ARR-410] ------. *Church Furniture Monographs*. Monticello, Ill.: Vance Bibliographies, 1984. 9 pp.

[ARR-420] ------. *Church Portals: A Bibliography*. Monticello, Ill.: Vance Bibliographies, 1985. 7 pp.

[ARR-430] ------. *Hindu Temples: A Bibliography*. Monticello, Ill.: Vance Bibliographies, 1987. 17 pp.

[ARR-440] ------. *Monasteries: A Bibliography of Recent Journal Articles*.

68

Monticello, Ill.: Vance Bibliographies, 1989. 22 pp.

[ARR-450] ------. *Monographs on Church Architecture*. 2 vols. Monticello, Ill.: Vance Bibliographies, 1984. 249 pp.

[ARR-460] ------. *Sepulchral Monuments: Monographs*. Monticello, Ill.: Vance Bibliographies, 1983. 31 pp.

[ARR-470] White, Anthony G. *Religious Architecture, Hindu: A Selected Bibliography*. Monticello, Ill.: Vance Bibliographies, 1984. 5 pp.

[ARR-480] ------. *Religious Architecture, Islamic: A Selected Bibliography*. Monticello, Ill.: Vance Bibliographies, 1984. 17 pp.

[ARR-490] ------. *Religious Architecture: Judaism Before 1945: A Selected Bibliography*. Monticello, Ill.: Vance Bibliographies, 1984. 6 pp.

[ARR-500] ------. *Shaker Architecture: A Brief Bibliography*. Monticello, Ill.: Vance Bibliographies, 1986. 4 pp.

Key Works

[ARR-510] Abou-El-Haj, Barbara Fay. *The Medieval Cult of Saints: Formations and Transformations*. Binghamton: State University of New York, 1993. Bib. refs.

[ARR-520] Adams, Henry. *Mont-Saint-Michel and Chartre*. 1905. Reprint. Princeton: Princeton University Press, 1981.

[ARR-530] Al Syriany, Samuel, and Badii Habib. *Guide to Ancient Coptic Churches and Monasteries in Upper Egypt*. [Cairo, Egypt?]: Institute of Coptic Studies, Department of Coptic Architecture, 1990. 160 pp.

[ARR-540] Anderson, William. *The Rise of the Gothic*. Photo. Clive Hicks. Salem, N.H.: Salem House, 1985. Reprint. New York: Dorset Press, 1988. Bib. pp. 204-205.

[ARR-550] Andrews, Edward Deming. *The People Called Shakers*. New York: Dover Publications, 1963.

[ARR-560] Andrijisyn, Joseph, ed. *Millenium of Christianity in Ukraine: A Symposium*. Trans. *Mille ans de Chretiente en Ukraine*. Ottawa, Ontario: Saint Paul University, 1987. 303 pp. Bibs.

[ARR-570] Aubert, Marcel, J. A. Schmoll, and Hans H. Hofstatter. *High*

Gothic Art. London: Methuen, [1964]. Bib. pp. 205-217.

[ARR-580] Azevedo, Carlos de, and Chester E. V. Brummel. *Churches of Portugal*. New York: Scala Books, 1985. Dist. Harper and Row. Bib. p. 199.

[ARR-590] Baldwin, J. W. *Masters, Princes and Merchants*. 2 vols. Princeton: Princeton University Press, 1970.

[ARR-600] Barry, Siuban, John Bradley, and Adrian Empey. *A Worthy Foundation: The Cathedral Church of St. Canice, Kilkenny, 1285-1985: Essays*. Mountrath, Portlaoise, Ireland: Dolmen Press, 1985. Bib. pp. 102-103.

[ARR-610] Batcock, Neil, and Philip W[yn] Williams. *The Ruined and Disused Churches of Norfolk*. East Anglian Archaeology Report, no. 51 0307-2460. Dereham: Norfolk Archaeological Unit, Norfolk Museums Service, 1991. Bib. pp. 188-191.

[ARR-620] Beeson, Trevor. *Westminster Abbey*. 9th ed. Barcelona: Editorial Escudo de Oro, 1990. 62 pp.

[ARR-630] Beevers, David, Richard Marks, and John Roles. *Sussex Churches and Chapels*. Brighton: Royal Pavilion, Art Gallery and Museums, 1989. Bib. pp. 161-165.

[ARR-640] Begule, Lucien. *The Abbey of Fontenay*. 6th ed. Rev. Hubert Aynard. Trans. Kay Werner Simonson. Small Monographs of the Great Edifices of France. Malakoff, France: L. T. Henri Laurens, 1986. Bib. pp. 76-77.

[ARR-650] Bieler, Andre. *Architecture in Worship: The Christian Place of Worship*. Trans. Odette and Donald Elliott. Philadelphia: Westminster Press, [1965]. 96 pp.

[ARR-660] Blum, Pamela Z. *Early Gothic Saint-Denis: Restorations and Survivals*. Berkeley; Oxford: University of California Press, 1992. 187 pp. Bib. refs.

[ARR-670] Brabbs, Derry, and Nigel Nicolson. *English Country Churches*. London: Weidenfeld and Nicolson, 1985. Bib. p. 157.

[ARR-680] Branner, Robert. *The Cathedral of Bourges and Its Place in Gothic Architecture*. New York: Architectural History Foundation; Cambridge: MIT Press, 1989. xxvi, 278 pp. Bib. refs. pp. 247-256.

[ARR-690] Braunfels, Wolfgang. *Monasteries of Western Europe: The Architecture of the Orders*. Princeton: Princeton University Press, 1972.

70

[ARR-700] British Archaeological Association. *Medieval Art and Architecture at Gloucester and Tewkesbury.* Conference Transactions/ British Archaeological Association, no. 7 (1981). [London; Leeds: British Archaeological Association], 1985. 132 pp. Bibs.

[ARR-710] ------. *Medieval Art and Architecture at Lincoln Cathedral.* Conference Transactions/British Archaeological Association, no. 8 (1982). [London]: British Archaeological Association, 1987. 157 pp. Bibs.

[ARR-720] Brown, Richard. *Sacred Architecture, its Rise, Progress, and Present State. Embracing the Babylonian, Indian, Egyptian, Greek, and Roman Temples; the Byzantine, Saxon, Lombard, Norman, and Italian Churches, with an Analytical Inquiry into the Origin, Progress, and Perfection of the Gothic Churches in England.* London: Fisher, Son, and Co., [1845]. 304 pp.

[ARR-730] Bruggink, Donald J., and Carl H. Drappers. *When Faith Takes Form: Contemporary Churches of Architectural Integrity in America.* Grand Rapids: William B. Eerdmans, [1971]. 126 pp.

[ARR-740] Burdajewicz, Mariusz. *The Aegean Sea Peoples and Religious Architecture in the Eastern Mediterranean at the Close of the Late Bronze Age.* BAR International Series, no. 558. Oxford: BAR, 1990. 196 pp. Bib. refs. pp. 133-146.

[ARR-750] Burman, Peter. *St. Paul's Cathedral.* New Bell's Cathedral Guides. London: Bell and Hyman, 1987. Bib. pp. 181-182.

[ARR-760] Butikov, G[eorgii] P[etrovich]. *St. Isaac's Cathedral: Museum.* Leningrad: SMART, 1990. 80 pp. (St. Petersburg, Russia.)

[ARR-770] Butler, L[awrence] A. S., and Richard Morris, eds. *The Anglo-Saxon Church: Papers on History, Architecture, and Archaeology in Honour of Dr. H[arold] M[cCarter] Taylor.* London: Council for British Archaeology, 1986. 226 pp. Bibs.

[ARR-780] Carny, Lucien, and Eugene Canseliet. *Notre-Dame de Paris: Symbolisme hermetique et alchimique.* [Paris?]: Le Groupe des 3, 1969. Bib. refs. p. 128.

[ARR-790] Celedin, Gertrude. *Kirche, Kunstler und Konflikte: 100 Jahre Herz-Jesu-Kirche, Graz: ein Kulturhistorisches Dokument.* Graz: Styria, 1991. 179 pp. Bib. refs.

[ARR-800] Clifton-Taylor, Alec. *English Parish Churches as Works of Art.* 2nd ed. London: B. T. Batsford, 1986. Reprint. Oxford:

Oxford University Press, 1989. 256 pp.

[ARR-810] Cobb, Gerald. *London City Churches*. 3rd ed. Rev. Nicholas Redman. London: B. T. Batsford, 1989. Bib. pp. 178-188.

[ARR-820] Colchester, L[inzee] S[parrow]. *Wells Cathedral*. The New Bell's Cathedral Guides. London: Unwin Hyman, 1987. Bib. p. 184.

[ARR-830] Cope, Gilbert Frederick, ed. *Christianity and the Visual Arts: Studies in the Art and Architecture of the Church*. London: Faith Press, 1964. 107 pp.

[ARR-840] Costello, Peter. *Dublin Churches*. Dublin: Gill and Macmillan, 1989. Bib. p. 235.

[ARR-850] Couasnon, Charles. *The Church of the Holy Sepulchre in Jerusalem*. New York: Oxford University Press, 1974.

[ARR-860] Coulton, G[eorge] G[ordon]. *Art and the Reformation*. New York: Harper, [1958]. Bib. pp. xix-xxii.

[ARR-870] Crawford, B. E. *St. Magnus Cathedral and Orkney's Twelfth-Century Renaissance*. Aberdeen: Aberdeen University Press, 1988. 283 pp. Bib. refs.

[ARR-880] Crossley, Paul. *Gothic Architecture in the Reign of Kasimir the Great: Church Architecture in Lesser Poland, 1320-1380*. Biblioteka Wawelska, no. 7. Cracow: Ministerstwo Kultury i Sztuki, Zarzad Muzeow i Ochrony Zabytkow, 1985. 492 pp. Bib. pp. 459-465.

[ARR-890] Cruden, Stewart. *Scottish Medieval Churches*. Edinburgh: John Donald Publishers, 1986. Dist. Humanities Press, Atlantic Highlands, N.J., in U.S. and Canada. Bib. pp. 197-204.

[ARR-900] Dahmen-Dallapiccola, Anna Libera. *The Ramachandra Temple at Vijayanagara*. New Delhi: Manohar, American Institute of Indian Studies, 1992. Bib. refs. pp. 303-306.

[ARR-910] Davis, Ian, ed. *Christian Dimensions in Architecture and Planning*. [Leicester]: Universities and Colleges Christian Fellowship Associates for the Association of Christians in Planning and Architecture, 1985. 106 pp.

[ARR-920] Decker, Paul. *Gothic Architecture*. 1759. Reprint. Boston: Gregg Press (G. K. Hall), 1968.

[ARR-930] Detorakes, Theochares Eustratiou, and Nikos Psilakes, ed. *The Monasteries of Crete*. Athens: Bank of Crete, 1988. 247 pp.

72

Bib. refs.

[ARR-940] Donnelly, Marian C. *The New England Meeting Houses of the Seventeenth Century*. N.p.: Wesleyan University Press, 1968.

[ARR-950] Downey, Susan B. *Mesopotamian Religious Architecture: Alexander Through the Parthians*. Princeton: Princeton University Press, 1988. 197 pp. Bib. pp. xiii-xv.

[ARR-960] Duby, Georges. *The Europe of the Cathedrals: 1140-1280*. Trans. Stuart Gilbert. Geneva: Skira, [1966]. 220 pp.

[ARR-970] Evans, Sydney. *Salisbury Cathedral: A Reflective Guide*. Great Britain: Michael Russell, 1985. 63 pp.

[ARR-980] Fernie, E. C. *Architectural History of Norwich Cathedral*. Clarendon Studies in the History of Art Series. Oxford: Clarendon Press; Oxford; New York: Oxford University Press, 1993. Bib. p. 213.

[ARR-990] Fiddes, Victor. *The Architectural Requirements of Protestant Worship*. Toronto: Ryerson Press, 1961. 119 pp.

[ARR-1000] Finney, Paul Corby. *Art, Archaeology, and Architecture of Early Christianity*. Studies in Early Christianity, vol. 18. New York: Garland Publishing, 1993. Covers 30-600 A.D.

[ARR-1010] Fitchen, John. *The Construction of Gothic Cathedrals: A Study of Medieval Vault Erection*. Oxford: Clarendon Press, 1961. "Annotated bibliography of false-work literature," pp. 241-247; Bib. pp. 317-336.

[ARR-1020] Folda, Jaroslav. *The Nazareth Capitals and the Crusader Shrine of the Annunciation*. University Park, [Pa.]: Pennsylvania State University Press for College Art Association of America, 1986. Bib. pp. 87-94.

[ARR-1030] Forsyth, G., and Kurt Weitzmann. *The Monastery of Saint Catherine at Mount Sinai*. Ann Arbor: University of Michigan Press, 1973.

[ARR-1040] Frankel, Paul. *The Gothic*. Princeton: Princeton University Press, 1960.

[ARR-1050] Frere-Cook, Gervis. *Art and Architecture of Christianity*. Cleveland: Press of Case Western Reserve University, 1972. 296 pp. Also published as *The Decorative Arts of the Christian Church*. London: Cassell, 1972. 296 pp.

[ARR-1060] Galende, Pedro G. *Angels in Stone: Architecture of Augustinian Churches in the Philippines*. Metro Manila, Philippines: G. A. Formoso Pub., 1987. Bib. pp. 475-519. ·

[ARR-1070] Garrett, James Leo. *Free Church Architecture: Its History and Thought*. Nashville: Church Architecture Dept., Baptist Sunday School Board, [n.d.]. 135 pp.

[ARR-1080] Gerson, Paula Lieber, ed. *Abbot Suger and Saint-Denis: A Symposium*. New York: Metropolitan Museum of Art, 1986. 303 pp. Bibs.

[ARR-1090] Gerster, Georg. *Churches in Rock: Early Christian Art in Ethiopia*. Trans. Richard Hosking. London: Phaidon Press, Ltd.; New York: Phaidon Publishers, Inc., 1970. Dist. Frederick A. Praeger Publishers. Bib. pp. 144-146.

[ARR-1100] Gough, Michael. *The Early Christians*. Ancient Peoples and Places, vol. 19. London: Thames and Hudson; New York: Frederick A. Praeger Publishers, 1961. 268 pp. Bib. pp. 207-210.

[ARR-1110] Grodecki, Louis. *Gothic Architecture*. Trans. I. Mark Paris. History of World Architecture Series. New York: Rizzoli International Publications, 1985. Bib. pp. 207-212.

[ARR-1120] Grodecki, Louis, Anne Prache, and Roland Rect. *Gothic Architecture*. Trans. I. Mark Paris. New York: Harry N. Abrams, 1977. Bib. pp. 423-427.

[ARR-1130] Guildhall Library. *Sir Christopher Wren: The Design of St. Paul's Cathedral*. Ed. Kerry Downes. London: Trefoil with Guildhall Library, 1988. 191 pp.

[ARR-1140] Gutmann, Joseph. *The Dura-Europos Synagogue: A Re-evaluation (1932-1972)*. Atlanta: American Academy of Religion, 1973.

[ARR-1150] ------. *The Synagogue: Studies in Origins, Archeology and Architecture*. New York: KTAV Publishing House, 1975.

[ARR-1160] Hachlili, Rachel. *Ancient Jewish Art and Archaeology in the Land of Israel*. Leiden; New York: E. J. Brill, 1988. xxii, 427 pp. Bib. pp. 405-416.

[ARR-1170] ------, ed. *Ancient Synagogues in Israel: Third-Seventh Century C.E.: Proceedings of Symposium, University of Hafia [i.e. Haifa], May 1987*. BAR International Series, no. 499. Oxford: BAR, 1989. 105 pp. Bib. refs.

74

[ARR-1180] Harrison, R. M[artin]. *A Temple for Byzantium: The Discovery and Excavation of Anicia Juliana's Palace-Church in Istanbul*. Austin: University of Texas Press, 1989. Bib. pp. 145-147.

[ARR-1190] Hetherington, Paul. *Byzantine and Medieval Greece: Churches, Castles, and Art of the Mainland and Peloponnese*. London: J. Murray, 1991. 238 pp. Bib. refs.

[ARR-1200] Hewett, Cecil Alec. *English Cathedral and Monastic Carpentry*. Chichester, Sussex: Phillimore, 1985. 257 pp. Bib. pp. xii-xiv.

[ARR-1210] Hill, Derek Ingram, Peter Burton, and Harland Walshaw. *Canterbury Cathedral*. The New Bell's Cathedral Guides. London: Bell and Hyman, 1986. Bib. pp. 183-184.

[ARR-1220] Holroyd, Violet M. *Foundations of Faith: Historic Religious Buildings of Ontario*. Toronto, Ontario: Natural Heritage/Natural History, Inc., 1991. Bib. refs. pp. 171-174.

[ARR-1230] Horn, Walter. *The Plan of St. Gall*. [Berkeley]: University of California Press, 1980.

[ARR-1240] Huffman, Walter Costner. *Where We Worship*. Minneapolis: Augsburg Publishing House, 1987. 48 pp. Bib. refs.

[ARR-1250] Huskinson, J. M. *Concordia Apostolorum: Christian Propaganda at Rome in the Fourth and Fifth Centuries: A Study in Early Christian Iconography and Iconology*. Oxford: BAR, 1982. Bib. pp. 151-160.

[ARR-1260] *Introvert vs. Extrovert: The Orders of Byzantine and Roman Christianity*. [Clemson, S.C.]: Clemson University College of Architecture: Clemson University Communications Center, 1989. Videocassette, 40 min., 50 sec.

[ARR-1270] Jacoby, Mary Moore. *The Churches of Charleston and the Lowcountry*. Columbia, S.C.: University of South Carolina Press, 1993. Bib. refs.

[ARR-1280] James, John, and François Bucher. *The Traveler's Key to Medieval France: A Guide to the Sacred Architecture of Medieval France*. New York: Alfred A. Knopf, 1986. Bib. pp. 302-303.

[ARR-1290] Jantzen, Hans. *High Gothic*. [London]: Constable, 1962. 181 pp. (The Cathedrals of Chartres, Reims, and Amiens)

[ARR-1300] Jones, Lawrence E[lmore]. *County Guide to English Churches*.

Newbury: Countryside Books, 1992. 352 pp.

[ARR-1310] Kadiroglu, Mine. *The Architecture of the Georgian Church at Ishan*. European University Studies. Series XXVII, History of Art, Publications universitaires europeennes. Frankfurt am Main; New York: Peter Lang, 1991. Bib. refs. pp. 115-138.

[ARR-1320] Kahler, Heinz. *Hagia Sophia*. New York: Frederick A. Praeger Publishers, 1967.

[ARR-1330] Kalman, Harold. *Pioneer Churches*. Photo. John de Visser. New York: W. W. Norton and Co., 1976. Bib. pp. 185-189, annotated.

[ARR-1340] Kelly, Francis. *Medieval Art and Architecture at Exeter Cathedral*. British Archaeological Association Conference Transactions, no. 11. [London]: British Archaeological Association, 1991. Bib. pp. 219-229.

[ARR-1350] Kennedy, Roger G., and David Larkin. *Mission: The Story of Building on a Frontier*. Boston: Houghton Mifflin, 1993. Bib. refs.

[ARR-1360] Kostof, Spiro. *The Orthodox Baptistery of Ravenna*. New Haven: Yale University Press, 1965.

[ARR-1370] Kraeling, Carl. *The Christian Building*. N.p.: J. J. Augustin, 1967.

[ARR-1380] ------. *The Synagogue*. [New York]: KTAV Publishing House, 1979.

[ARR-1390] Krautheimer, Richard, and Slobodan Curcic. *Early Christian and Byzantine Architecture*. 4th ed. New Haven: Yale University Press; New York: Penguin Books, 1986. 553 pp. Bib. pp. 523-525.

[ARR-1400] Landreth, Charles Noel. "Process Theology as a Basis for Defining Stewardship in Landscape Architecture." M.L.A. Thesis, Louisiana State University, Baton Rouge, 1990. Bib. refs. pp. 53-55.

[ARR-1410] Lealman, Brenda. *Church Buildings*. N.p.: Christian Education Movement, 1990. 59 pp.

[ARR-1420] Leask, Harold G[raham]. *Irish Churches and Monastic Buildings*. 3rd ed. 3 vols. Dundalk, Ireland: Dundalgan Press, 1987. Bib. refs.

76

[ARR-1430] Lesser, George. *Gothic Cathedrals and Sacred Geometry.* 3 vols. London: A. Tiranti, 1957-1964. Bib. Vol. 1, pp. 161-163.

[ARR-1440] Levine, Lee I., ed. *The Synagogue in Late Antiquity.* Philadelphia: American Schools of Oriental Research, 1987. 218 pp. Bibs.

[ARR-1450] Lindholm, Dan, with Walther Roggenkamp. *Stave Churches in Norway: Dragon Myth and Christianity in Old Norwegian Architecture.* London: Rudolf Steiner Press, 1969. 208 pp.

[ARR-1460] Lindsay, Paul. *The Synagogues of London.* London; Portland, Oreg.: Vallentine Mitchell, 1992. Bib. refs.

[ARR-1470] Luciani, Roberto. *St. Mary in Trastevere.* Rome: Fratelli Palombi Editori, 1987. Bib. refs. p. 62.

[ARR-1480] Lyle, Emily B[uchanan]. *Sacred Architecture in the Traditions of India, China, Judaism and Islam.* Edinburgh: Edinburgh University Press, 1992. 220 pp.

[ARR-1490] Macaulay, David. *Cathedral: The Story of its Construction.* Boston: Houghton Mifflin, 1973. 77 pp. (Well written children's book.)

[ARR-1500] MacGibbon, David, and Thomas Ross. *The Ecclesiastical Architecture of Scotland: From the Earliest Christian Times to the Seventeenth Century.* 3 vols. Edinburgh: James Thin, 1991.

[ARR-1510] Mainstone, R[owland] J. *Hagia Sophia: Architecture, Structure, and Liturgy of Justinian's Great Church.* New York: Thames and Hudson, 1988. Bib. pp. 282-284.

[ARR-1520] Mâle, Emile. *The Gothic Image.* N.p.: Harper Torchbooks, 1958.

[ARR-1530] Mango, Cyril. *Byzantine Architecture.* New York: Harry N. Abrams, 1976.

[ARR-1540] Mathews, Thomas. *The Byzantine Churches of Istanbul.* University Park: Pennsylvania State University Press, 1976.

[ARR-1550] ------. *The Early Churches of Constantinople, Architecture and Liturgy.* University Park: Pennsylvania State University Press, 1971.

[ARR-1560] Mauropoulou-Tsioume, Chrysanthe. *The Church of St. Nicholas Orphanos.* Guides of the Institute for Balkan Studies (I.M.X.A.), no. 3. Thessalonica: Institute for Balkan Studies, 1986. Bib. p. 47.

Development Guide. Oxford; Boston: Butterworth Architecture, 1991. Bib. refs. pp. 87-92.

[ARR-1840] Ramanaiah, J[aesetty]. *Temples of South India: A Study of Hindu, Jain, and Buddhist Monuments of the Deccan.* New Delhi: Concept Publishing Co., 1989. xxi, 358 pp. Bib. pp. 256-264.

[ARR-1850] Reinhard, Johan. *Machu Picchu: The Sacred Center.* Lima, Peru: Nuevas Imagenes, 1991. Bib. refs. pp. 95-108.

[ARR-1860] Rodley, Lyn. *Byzantine Art and Architecture.* Cambridge, [England]; New York: Cambridge University Press, 1993.

[ARR-1870] Rodwell, Warwick. *Our Christian Heritage.* London: G. Philip, 1984. Bib. pp. 245-248.

[ARR-1880] Rosenau, Helen. *Vision of the Temple: The Image of the Temple of Jerusalem in Judaism and Christianity.* London: Oresko Books, Ltd., 1979. Bib. pp. 187-188.

[ARR-1890] Rotoff, Basil, Roman Yereniuk, and Stella M. Hryniuk. *Monuments of Faith: Ukrainian Churches in Manitoba.* [Winnipeg]: University of Manitoba Press, 1990. Bib. refs. pp. 188-191.

[ARR-1900] Ruggieri, Vincenzo. *Byzantine Religious Architecture (582-867): Its History and Structural Elements.* Orientalia Christiana Analecta, vol. 237. Rome: Pont. Institutum Studiorum Orientalium; Chicago: Loyola University Press, 1991. xli, 287 pp. Bib. refs. pp. xxiii-xxxix.

[ARR-1910] Saalman, Howard. *Brunelleschi: The Buildings.* University Park, Pa.: Pennsylvania State University Press, 1993. Bib. refs.

[ARR-1920] Saliba, Gary Elliot. "Construction and Christianity: Dealing with One While Keeping the Other." Writing for Certification by the National Association of Church Business Administrators, 1989.

[ARR-1930] Schwarz, Rudolf. *The Church Incarnate: The Sacred Function of Church Architecture.* Chicago: Henry Regnery, 1958.

[ARR-1940] Seta, Alessandro della. *Religion and Art: A Study in the Evolution of Sculpture, Painting and Architecture.* Trans. Marion Chilton Harrison. Ed. Eugenie [Sellers] Strong. New York: Charles Scribner's Sons, 1914. 415 pp.

[ARR-1950] Settar, S. *The Hoysala Temples.* 2 vols. Bangalore: Kala Yatra

80

Publications, 1991. Bib. refs., vol. 1, pp. 379-386.

[ARR-1960] Shipley, Debra. *Durham Cathedral*. London: Tauris Parke Books with KEA Pub. Services, 1990. Bib. p. 126.

[ARR-1970] Simson, Otto Georg von. *The Gothic Cathedral*. 1956. Reprint. Princeton: Princeton University Press, 1974.

[ARR-1980] ------. *The Gothic Cathedral: Origins of Gothic Architecture and the Medieval Concept of Order*. 3rd ed. Princeton: Princeton University Press, 1988. Bib. pp. 249-268.

[ARR-1990] ------. *The Sacred Fortress*. Chicago: University of Chicago Press, 1948. (Ravenna, Italy)

[ARR-2000] Smith, George Everard Kidder. *The New Churches of Europe*. New York: Holt, Rinehart and Winston, 1964. Bib. pp. 289-290.

[ARR-2010] Street, George Edmund. *Some Account of Gothic Architecture in Spain*. 2 vols. Ed. Georgiana Goddard King. New York: E. P. Dutton and Co., 1914.

[ARR-2020] Swinfen, Averil. *Forgotten Stones: Ancient Church Sites of the Burren and Environs*. Dublin: Lilliput Press, 1992. 151 pp. Bib. (Ireland.)

[ARR-2030] Texier, Charles Felix Marie. *Byzantine Architecture: Illustrated by Examples of Edifices Erected in the East During the Earliest Ages of Christianity: With Historical and Archaeological Descriptions*. 1894. Reprint. London: Day and Son, Lithographers to the Queen and to H.R.H. the Prince of Wales, 1990. 218 pp.

[ARR-2040] Tigerman, Stanley. *The Architecture of Exile*. New York: Rizolli International Publications, Inc., 1988. Bib. pp. 182-188.

[ARR-2050] Toker, Franklin. *The Church of Notre-Dame in Montreal: An Architectural History*. 2nd ed. Montreal: McGill-Queen's University Press, 1991. xxv, 124 pp. Bibs.

[ARR-2060] Treib, Marc, Dorothee Imbert. *Sanctuaries of Spanish New Mexico*. Berkeley: University of California Press, 1993. Bib. refs.

[ARR-2070] Turkoglu, Sabahattin. *Hagia Sophia*. 3rd ed. Istanbul: Net Turistik Yayinlar A.S., 1987. 60 pp.

[ARR-2080] Twitouridou, Anna. *The Church of the Panagia Chalkeon*. Trans. *Panagia ton Chalkeon*. Guides of the Institute for

Balkan Studies (I.M.X.A.), no. 7. Thessalonica: Institute for Balkan Studies, 1985. Bib. pp. 57-58.

[ARR-2090] Turkoglu, Sabahattin. *Hagia Sophia.* 6th ed. Istanbul: NET Turistik Yayinlar A.S., 1990. 60 pp.

[ARR-2100] Turner, Harold W. *From Temple to Meeting House: The Phenomenology and Theology of Places of Worship.* New York: Mouton, 1979. 404 pp. Bib.

[ARR-2110] Upton, Dell. *Holy Things and Profane: Anglican Parish Churches in Colonial Virginia.* New York: Architectural History Foundation; Cambridge: MIT Press, 1986. xxii, 278 pp. Bib. pp. 235-259.

[ARR-2120] Vigar, John E. *Exploring Sussex Churches.* Gillingham, Kent: Meresborough Books, 1986. Bib. refs. po. 118.

[ARR-2130] Wakely, David, and Thomas A. Drain. *A Sense of Mission: Churches of the Southwest.* San Francisco: Chronicle Books, 1994. Bib. refs.

[ARR-2140] *Westminster Abbey.* The New Bell's Cathedral Guides. London: Bell and Hyman, 1986. Bib. p. 184.

[ARR-2150] White, James F., and Susan J. White. *Church Architecture: Building and Renovating for Christian Worship.* Nashville: Abingdon Press, 1988. Bib. pp. 165-170.

[ARR-2160] White, Susan J. "The Liturgical Arts Society (1927-1972): Art and Architecture in the Agenda of the American Roman Catholic Liturgical Renewal." Ph.D. Thesis, University of Notre Dame, 1987. Bib. pp. 427-435.

[ARR-2170] Wigoder, Geoffrey. *The Story of the Synagogue.* Jerusalem: Domino Press, 1986. 208 pp. Bib. refs.

[ARR-2180] Wittich, John. *Churches, Cathedrals and Chapels.* Leominster: Gracewing, 1988. 137 pp. (London guide book.)

[ARR-2190] Whitting, Philip D., ed. *Byzantium: An Introduction.* New York: New York University Press, 1971. 178 pp. Bibs.

[ARR-2200] Wilson, Christopher. *The Gothic Cathedral: The Architecture of the Great Church 1130-1530.* Rev. ed. New York; London: Thames and Hudson, 1992. Bib. pp. 295-298.

[ARR-2210] Wischnitzer, Rachel. *The Architecture of the European Synagogue.* Philadelphia: Jewish Publication Society of America, 1964.

82

[ARR-2220]   Wolff, Arnold, Rainer Gaertner. *The Cologne Cathedral.* Cologne: Vista Point, 1990. 32 pp, and 80 pp. of plates. Bib. refs. p. 28.

[ARR-2230]   Wright, Frank Lloyd, and William Gannett. *The House Beautiful.* Chicago: N.p., 1896.

[ARR-2240]   Yates, W. Nigel. *Rug Chapel, Llangar Church, Gwydir Uchaf Chapel.* Cardiff: Cadw: Welsh Historic Monuments, 1993. 48 pp.

[ARR-2250]   Young, Elizabeth, Wayland Kennet, and Louisa Young. *London's Churches.* London: Grafton; Topsfield, Mass.: Salem House, 1986. 214 pp.

CHAPTER 4

CINEMA

BIBLIOGRAPHIES ON CINEMA

As the lengthy list of bibliographies given below indicates, cinema is rapidly becoming one of the most widely reviewed art forms of the twentieth century. Because cinemas are produced by a complex array of script writers, directors, actors, set designers, musicians, and technicians, bibliographies and indexes take a wide variety of forms, often specializing in one or more of these categories of participants or their respective products. For bibliographies treating cinema script writers, see [BCI-010] and [BCI-390]. To locate authors whose literary works have been translated into screen plays, see the following bibliographies and indexes: [BCI-300], [BCI-340], [BCI-370], [BCI-380], [BCI-460], [BCI-550], [BCI-560], [BCI-660], [BCI-800], [BCI-870], [BCI-890], [BCI-900], [BCI-1030], [BCI-1110]. For bibliographies and indexes of directors, see [BCI-320], [BCI-480], [BCI-540], [BCI-780], [BCI-930], and [BCI-940]. Studies of actors are listed in [BCI-050], [BCI-480], [BCI-770], and [BCI-950]. Costume designers are identified in [BCI-830]. For specialized studies of women in cinema, see [BCI-240] and [BCI-520]. Music in cinema is treated in [BCI-110], [BCI-120], [BCI-590], [BCI-600], [BCI-610], [BCI-670], [BCI-720], and [BCI-1040].

84

For assistance in locating films by title or subject matter, see the following bibliographies and indexes: [BCI-030], [BCI-060], [BCI-070], [BCI-090], [BCI-200], [BCI-210], [BCI-220], [BCI-230], [BCI-250], [BCI-260], [BCI-270], [BCI-280], [BCI-290], [BCI-310], [BCI-330], [BCI-350], [BCI-360], [BCI-410], [BCI-440], [BCI-470], [BCI-530], [BCI-570], [BCI-580], [BCI-730], [BCI-750], [BCI-810], [BCI-880], [BCI-920], [BCI-970], [BCI-1080], [BCI-1100]. For bibliographies listing resources for research of cinema, consult the following: [BCI-100], [BCI-130], [BCI-140], [BCI-150], [BCI-160], [BCI-170], [BCI-180], [BCI-190], [BCI-400], [BCI-420], [BCI-430], [BCI-450], [BCI-490], [BCI-500], [BCI-510], [BCI-620], [BCI-630], [BCI-640], [BCI-650], [BCI-680], [BCI-690], [BCI-700], [BCI-710], [BCI-740], [BCI-760], [BCI-790], [BCI-820], [BCI-840], [BCI-850], [BCI-910], [BCI-960], [BCI-980], [BCI-990], [BCI-1000], [BCI-1010], [BCI-1020], [BCI-1050], [BCI-1060], [BCI-1070], [BCI-1090]. Finally, for specialized studies on the audience of cinema, see [BCI-080].

Since this list of bibliographies may be intimidating for neophytes, the following works may prove useful as manageable beginning points for the study of cinema: Robert A. Armour's *Film: A Reference Guide* [BCI-040], Kim N. Fisher's *On the Screen: A Film, Television, and Video Research Guide* [BCI-430], and Frank Manchel's *Film Study: A Resource Guide* [BCI-680]. The standard reference works which one will want to consult when conducting extended research in cinema are the *British National Film Catalogue* [BCI-150], the *Educational Film and Video Locator* [BCI-350], the *Film Literature Index [1973-]: A Quarterly Author-Subject Index to the International Periodical Literature of Film and Television/Video* [BCI-420], the *International Directory of Film and TV Documentation Centers* [BCI-500], and Jay Robert Nash's and Stanley Ralph Ross's 12 volume *The Motion Picture Guide* along with its annual supplements [BCI-750]. While none of these bibliographies concentrates on Christianity in cinema, most usually have at least a small section or two devoted to Christian, religious, or moral themes.

[BCI-010]   Academy of Motion Picture Arts and Sciences and the Writers Guild of America, West. *Who Wrote the Movie and What Else did he Write? An Index of Screen Writers and Their Film Works, 1936-1969*. Los Angeles: n.p., 1970. 491 pp.

[BCI-020] American Council on Education. *Motion Pictures in Education: A Summary of the Literature.* Comp. Edgar Dale, et al. New York: Arno Press, 1970. 472 pp.

[BCI-030] *American Film Institute Catalog of Motion Pictures Produced in the United States.* 19 vols. Berkeley: University of California, 1971-. Covers 1893-1970.

[BCI-040] Armour, Robert A. *Film: A Reference Guide.* American Popular Culture. Westport, Conn.: Greenwood Press, 1980. 251 pp. Bibs.

[BCI-050] Aros, Andrew A. *An Actor Guide to the Talkies, 1965 Through 1974.* Metuchen, N.J.: Scarecrow Press, 1977. 781 pp.

[BCI-060] ------. *A Title Guide to the Talkies, 1964 Through 1974.* Metuchen, N.J.: Scarecrow Press, 1977. 344 pp.

[BCI-070] ------. *A Title Guide to the Talkies, 1975 Through 1984.* Metuchen, N.J.: Scarecrow Press, 1986. 355 pp.

[BCI-080] Austin, Bruce A. *The Film Audience: An International Bibliography of Research with Annotations and an Essay.* Metuchen, N.J.: Scarecrow Press, 1983. 224 pp.

[BCI-090] Banerjee, Shampa. *One Hundred Indian Feature Films: An Annotated Filmography.* Garland Reference Library of the Humanities, vol. 915. New York: Garland Publishing, 1988. 205 pp.

[BCI-100] Batty, Linda. *Retrospective Index to Film Periodicals, 1930-1971.* New York: R. R. Bowker Co., 1975. 425 pp.

[BCI-110] Benjamin, Ruth. *Movie Song Catalog: The Songs, Performers, and Songwriters Film-by-Film, 1928-1988.* Jefferson, N.C.: McFarland, 1993.

[BCI-120] Bloom, Ken. *Hollywood Song: The Complete Film Musical Companion.* 2 vols. New York: Facts on File, 1991.

[BCI-130] Bowles, Stephen E. *An Approach to Film Study: A Selected Booklist.* New York: Revisionist Press, 1974. 108 pp.

[BCI-140] ------, ed. *Index to Critical Film Reviews in British and American Periodicals, Together with Index to Critical Reviews of Books about Film.* 3 vols. New York: Franklin, 1974-1975. Covers through 1971.

[BCI-150] British Film Institute. *British National Film Catalogue.* London: British Film Institute, 1963-. Quarterly. *First Supplement of*

86

the Catalogue of the Book Library of the British Film Institute. Boston: G. K. Hall, 1983.

[BCI-160] *British Humanities Index.* London: The Library Association, 1962-. (Formerly called *The Subject Index to Periodicals,* 1915-1961.) See "Cinema."

[BCI-170] Bukalski, Peter J. *Film Research: A Critical Bibliography with Annotations and Essay.* Boston: G. K. Hall, 1972. 215 pp.

[BCI-180] ------. *1000 Books About Film.* Dayton, Ohio: n.p., [1972]. 54 pp.

[BCI-190] Burton, Julianne, comp. *The New Latin American Cinema: An Annotated Bibliography of Sources in English, Spanish, and Portuguese 1960-1980.* New York: Smyrna, 1983. 80 pp.

[BCI-200] Buteau, June D. *Nonprint Materials on Communication: An Annotated Directory of Select Films, Videotapes, Videocassettes, Simulations and Games.* Metuchen, N.J.: Scarecrow Press, 1976. 454 pp.

[BCI-210] Center for Southern Folklore, comp. *American Folklore Films and Videotapes: A Catalog.* 2nd ed. New York: R. R. Bowker, 1976.

[BCI-220] Cohen, Louis Harris. *The Soviet Cinema, Film, and Photography: A Selected Annotated Bibliography.* Rev. ed. Edwards Air Force Base, Calif.: Photographic Branch, DOETC, Air Force Flight Test Center, 1976. 492 pp.

[BCI-230] Combs, James. *American Political Movies: An Annotated Filmography of Feature Films.* Garland Reference Library of the Humanities. Series no. 970, no. 1. New York: Garland Publishing, 1990. 173 pp.

[BCI-240] Cook, Samantha. *Women and Film Bibliography.* 2nd ed. London: BFI Education, 1989. 130 pp.

[BCI-250] Cowie, Peter, ed. *International Film Guide.* (Annually, 1983-1989). New York: New York Zoetrope, 1983-1989. c. 500 pp. each.

[BCI-260] ------. *International Film Guide: 1990.* Cambridge, Mass.: Basil Blackwell Publishing, 1990.

[BCI-270] Cyr, Helen W. *A Filmography of the Third World, 1976-1983: An Annotated List of 16mm Films.* Metuchen, N.J.: Scarecrow Press, 1985. 285 pp.

[BCI-280] ------. *Filmography of the Third World.* Metuchen, N.J.: Scarecrow

Press, 1976, 1983.

[BCI-290] ------. *The Third World in Film and Video, 1984-1990*. Metuchen, N.J.: Scarecrow Press, 1991. 256 pp.

[BCI-300] Daisne, Johan. *Dictionnaire filmographique de la littérature mondiale/Filmographic Dictionary of World Literature/Filmographisches Lexikon der Weltliteratur/Filmografisch Lexicon der Wereldliteratuur*. 2 vols. Gand: Story-Scientia, 1971-1975. Supplement, 1978. 638 pp.

[BCI-310] Dimmit, Richard Bertrand. *A Title Guide to the Talkies: A Comprehensive Listing of 16,000 Feature-Length Films from October, 1927, Until December, 1963*. 2 vols. New York: Scarecrow Press, 1965. [See BCI-060 to BCI-070.]

[BCI-320] Dixon, Wheeler W. *The "B" Directors: A Biographical Directory*. Metuchen, N.J.: Scarecrow Press, 1985. 613 pp.

[BCI-330] Drew, Bernard A. *Motion Picture Series and Sequels: A Reference Guide*. Garland Reference Library of the Humanities, no. 1186. New York: Garland Publishing, 1990. 412 pp.

[BCI-340] Dyment, Alan R. *The Literature of the Film: A Bibliographical Guide to the Film as Art and Entertainment, 1936-1970*. London: White Lion, 1975. 398 pp. Annotated.

[BCI-350] *Educational Film and Video Locator of the University Film Centers and R. R. Bowker*. 4th ed. New Providence, N.J.: R. R. Bowker, 1990-1991.

[BCI-360] Ellis, Jack C., Charles Derry, and Sharon Kern. *The Film Book Bibliography: 1940-1975*. Metuchen, N.J.: Scarecrow Press, 1975. 764 pp. Annotated.

[BCI-370] Emmens, Carol A. *Short Stories on Film and Video*. 2nd ed. Littleton, Colo.: Libraries Unlimited, 1985. 337 pp.

[BCI-380] Enser, A. G. S. *Filmed Books and Plays: A List of Books and Plays from Which Films have been Made, 1928-1986*. Rev. ed. Alderhot, Hampshire: Gower Publishing Co., 1986. 770 pp.

[BCI-390] Fenton, Jill. *Women Writers, from Page to Screen*. Garland Reference Library of the Humanities, vol. 687. New York: Garland Publishing, 1990. 483 pp.

[BCI-400] Fielding, Raymond, comp. *A Bibliography of Theses and Dissertations on the Subject of Film, 1916-1979*. University Film Association Monograph 3. Houston: University Film

Association, 1979. 70 pp.

[BCI-410] *Film Index, The: A Bibliography.* 3 vols. White Plains: Kraus, 1941 (Vol. 1), 1985 (Vols. 2-3). Covers through 1935.

[BCI-420] *Film Literature Index [1973-]: A Quarterly Author-Subject Index to the International Periodical Literature of Film and Television/Video.* Albany, N.Y.: Film and Television Documentation Center, State University of New York at Albany, 1973-. Quarterly with annual cumulation.

[BCI-430] Fisher, Kim N. *On the Screen: A Film, Television, and Video Research Guide.* Reference Sources in the Humanities Series. Littleton, Colo.: Libraries Unlimited, 1986. 209 pp.

[BCI-440] Gartenberg, Jon, et al., eds. *The Film Catalog: A List of Holdings in the Museum of Modern Art.* Boston: G. K. Hall, 1985.

[BCI-450] Gerlach, John C., and Lana Gerlach. *The Critical Index: A Bibliography of Articles on Film in English, 1946-1973, Arranged by Names and Topics.* New York: Teachers College Press, 1974. 726 pp. Annotated.

[BCI-460] Gifford, Denis. *Books and Plays in Films, 1896-1915: Literary, Theatrical and Artistic Sources of the First Twenty Years of Motion Pictures.* London: Mansell, 1991. 206 pp.

[BCI-470] ------. *The British Film Catalogue, 1895-1985: A Reference Guide.* New York: Facts on File, 1986. N.p.

[BCI-480] Gray, John. *Blacks in Film and Television: A Pan-African Bibliography of Films, Filmmakers, and Performers.* New York: Greenwood Press, 1990. 496 pp.

[BCI-490] International Federation of Film Archives. *Union Catalogue of Books and Periodicals Published Before 1914 Held by the Film Archives Members of the International Federation of Film Archives.* [Brussels: Cinematheque Royale de Belgique, Palais des Beaux-arts], 1967. 89 pp.

[BCI-500] International Federation of Film Archives Documentation Center. *International Directory of Film and TV Documentation Centers.* 3rd ed. Chicago: St. James Press, 1988.

[BCI-510] *International Index to Film Periodicals.* New York: R. R. Bowker Co., 1972-.

[BCI-520] Kowalski, Rosemary R. *Women and Film: A Bibliography.* Metuchen, N.J.: Scarecrow Press, 1976. 287 pp.

[BCI-530] Krafsur, Richard, ed. *The American Film Institute Catalog of Motion Pictures: Feature Films, 1961-1970.* 2 vols. New York: R. R. Bowker, 1976.

[BCI-540] Langman, Larry. *A Guide to American Film Directors: The Sound Era: 1929-1979.* 2 vols. Metuchen, N.J.: Scarecrow Press, 1981. 718 pp.

[BCI-550] ------. *Writers on the American Screen: A Guide to Film Adaptations of American and Foreign Literary Works.* Garland Reference Library of the Humanities, no. 658. New York: Garland Publishing, 1986. 329 pp.

[BCI-560] Leonard, William T. *Theatre: Stage to Screen to Television.* 2 vols. Metuchen, N.J.: Scarecrow Press, 1981.

[BCI-570] Levitan, Eli L. *An Alphabetical Guide to Motion Pictures, Television and Videotape Production.* New York: McGraw-Hill, [1970]. 797 pp.

[BCI-580] Limbacher, James L. *Feature Films on 8 mm, 16 mm, and Videotape: A Directory of Feature Films Available for Rental, Sale, and Lease in the United States and Canada.* 8th ed. New York: R. R. Bowker, 1985.

[BCI-590] ------. *Film Music: From Violins to Video.* Metuchen, N.J.: Scarecrow Press, 1974. 835 pp.

[BCI-600] ------. *Keeping Score: Film Music, 1972-1979.* Metuchen, N.J.: Scarecrow Press, 1981. 519 pp.

[BCI-610] ------. *Keeping Score: Film and Television Music, 1980-1988: With Additional Coverage of 1921-1979.* Metuchen, N.J.: Scarecrow Press, 1991. 916 pp. Bib. refs. p. 7. Discography, pp. 664-762.

[BCI-620] ------. *Original Film Sources and Titles with Subsequent Remakes.* Dearborn, Mich.: Dearborn Public Library, [1964]. 42 pp.

[BCI-630] ------. *Sexuality in World Cinema.* 2 vols. Metuchen, N.J.: Scarecrow Press, 1983. 1,535 pp.

[BCI-640] Loughney, Katharine. *Film, Television, and Video Periodicals: A Comprehensive Annotated List.* Garland Reference Library of the Humanities, vol. 1032. New York: Garland Publishing, 1991. 431 pp.

[BCI-650] MacCann, Richard Dyer, and Edward S. Perry. *The New Film Index: A Bibliography of Magazine Articles in English, 1930-1970.* New York: E. P. Dutton and Co., 1975. 522 pp.

Annotated.

[BCI-660]   McCarty, Clifford. *Published Screenplays: A Checklist*. Kent, Ohio: Kent State University Press, [1971]. 127 pp.

[BCI-670]   ------. *Film Composers in America: A Checklist of their Work*. New York: Da Capo Press, 1972.

[BCI-680]   Manchel, Frank. *Film Study: A Resource Guide*. Rutherford, N.J.: Fairleigh Dickinson University Press, [1973]. 422 pp.

[BCI-690]   Manz, H. P. *International Film Bibliography: 1979-1980*. New York: New York Zoetrope, [1981]. 165 pp.

[BCI-700]   ------. *International Film Bibliography: 1981*. Vol. 2. New York: New York Zoetrope, 1982. 165 pp.

[BCI-710]   Media Referral Service. *The Film File, 1984-85*. 4th ed. Minneapolis: Media Referral Service, 1984.

[BCI-720]   Meeker, David. *Jazz in the Movies*. London: Talisman Books, 1981. 350 pp.

[BCI-730]   Munden, Kenneth W., ed. *The American Film Institute Catalog of Motion Pictures: Feature Films, 1921-1930*. 2 vols. New York: R. R. Bowker, 1971.

[BCI-740]   Nachbar, Jack. *Western Films 2: An Annotated Critical Bibliography from 1974 to 1987*. New York: London Garland, 1988. 308 pp.

[BCI-750]   Nash, Jay Robert, and Stanley Ralph Ross. *The Motion Picture Guide*. 12 vols. Chicago: Cinebooks, 1985-1987. Covers 1910-1983. Annual supplement: *The Motion Picture Guide Annual*, 1987-.

[BCI-760]   National Film Board of Canada, Reference Library. *Books on Film and Television in the Reference Library of the National Film Board of Canada*. Montreal: The Library, 1992. English and French.

[BCI-770]   Parish, James Robert. *Film Actors Guide: Western Europe*. Metuchen, N.J.: Scarecrow Press, 1977. 621 pp.

[BCI-780]   ------. *Film Directors Guide: Western Europe*. Metuchen, N.J.: Scarecrow Press, 1976. 300 pp.

[BCI-790]   Parker, David L., and Esther Siegel. *Guide to Dance in Films: A Guide to Information Sources*. Performing Arts Information Guide Series, vol. 3. Detroit: Gale Research, 1978. 240 pp.

[BCI-800] Parlato, Salvatore J., [Jr.] *Films Ex Libre: Literature in 16mm and Video*. Jefferson, N.C.: McFarland and Co., Inc., 1980. 283 pp.

[BCI-810] ------. *Superfilms: An International Guide to Award-Winning Educational Films*. Metuchen, N.J.: Scarecrow Press, 1976. 365 pp.

[BCI-820] Phillips, Leona Rasmussen. *Silent Cinema: Annotated Critical Bibliography*. New York: Gordon Press, 1978. 149 pp.

[BCI-830] Prichard, Susan P. *Film Costume: An Annotated Bibliography*. Metuchen, N.J.: Scarecrow Press, 1981. 577 pp.

[BCI-840] Rehrauer, George. *Cinema Booklist*. Metuchen, N.J.: Scarecrow Press, 1972. 473 pp. *Supplement One*, 1974, 405 pp. *Supplement Two*, 1977, 470 pp.

[BCI-850] ------. *The Macmillan Film Bibliography*. 2 vols. New York: Macmillan Publishing Co., 1982. Annotated.

[BCI-860] Reilly, Adam. *Current Film Periodicals in English*. Rev. ed. New York: Educational Film Library Association, [1972]. 25 pp.

[BCI-870] Ross, Harris. *Film as Literature, Literature as Film: An Introduction to and Bibliography of Film's Relationship to Literature*. Bibliographies and Indexes in World Literature 10. New York: Greenwood Press, 1987. 346 pp.

[BCI-880] Salz, Kay, ed. *Craft Films: An Index of International Films on Crafts*. New York: Neal-Schuman Publishers, Inc., 1979. 156 pp.

[BCI-890] Samples, Gordon. *The Drama Scholars' Index to Plays and Filmscripts: Vol. 2: A Guide to Plays and Filmscripts in Selected Anthologies, Series and Periodicals*. Metuchen, N.J.: Scarecrow Press, 1980. 750 pp.

[BCI-900] ------. *The Drama Scholars' Index to Plays and Filmscripts: Vol. 3: A Guide to Plays and Filmscripts in Selected Anthologies, Series and Periodicals*. Metuchen, N.J.: Scarecrow Press, 1986. 426 pp.

[BCI-910] ------. *How to Locate Reviews of Plays and Films: A Bibliography of Criticism from the Beginnings to the Present*. Metuchen, N.J.: Scarecrow Press, Inc., 1976. 114 pp.

[BCI-920] Scheuer, Steven H., ed. *The Complete Guide to Videocassette Movies*. New York: Holt, 1987.

92

[BCI-930] Schmidt, Nancy J. *Sub-Saharan African Films and Filmmakers: An Annotated Bibliography.* New York: Hans Zell Publishers, 1988. 401 pp. English and French.

[BCI-940] Schuster, Mel. *Motion Picture Directors: A Bibliography of Magazine and Periodical Articles, 1900-1969.* Metuchen, N.J.: Scarecrow Press, 1973. 418 pp.

[BCI-950] ------. *Motion Picture Performers: A Bibliography of Magazine and Periodical Articles, 1900-1969.* Metuchen, N.J.: The Scarecrow Press, 1971. 702 pp.

[BCI-960] Sheahan, Eileen. *Moving Pictures: A Bibliography of Selected Reference Works for the Study of Film, with Emphasis on Holdings in the Libraries of Yale University.* New Haven: Yale University Library, 1973. 78 pp.

[BCI-970] Slide, Anthony. *Films on Film History.* Metuchen, N.J.: Scarecrow Press, 1979. 242 pp.

[BCI-980] ------, ed. *International Film, Radio and Television Journals.* Westport, Conn.: Greenwood Publishing Group, Inc., 1985. 428 pp.

[BCI-990] ------. *Selected Film Criticism: 1896-1911.* Metuchen, N.J.: Scarecrow Press, 1982. 134 pp.

[BCI-1000] ------. *Selected Film Criticism: 1912-1920.* Metuchen, N.J.: Scarecrow Press, 1982. 325 pp.

[BCI-1010] ------. *Selected Film Criticism: 1921-1930.* Metuchen, N.J.: Scarecrow Press, 1982. 335 pp.

[BCI-1020] ------. *Selected Film Criticism: 1931-1940.* Metuchen, N.J.: Scarecrow Press, 1982. 292 Study of Film, with Emphasis on Holdings in the Libraries of Yale University. New Haven: Yale University Library, 1973. 78 pp.

[BCI-1030] *Screenplays and Production Stills.* 2 vols. Boston: G. K. Hall, 1972.

[BCI-1040] Stubblebine, Donald J. *Cinema Sheet Music: A Comprehensive Listing of Published Film Music from "Squaw Man" (1914) to "Batman" (1989).* Jefferson, N.C.: McFarland, 1991. 628 pp. Bib. refs. pp. 457-459.

[BCI-1050] United Nations Educational, Scientific and Cultural Organization. Department of Mass Communications. *The Influence of the Cinema on Children and Adolescents, An Annotated International Bibliography.* [Paris]: Unesco, 1961. 106 pp.

[BCI-1060] University Microfilms International. *Cinema: A Dissertation Catalog*. Ann Arbor: University Microfilms International, 1980. 11 pp.

[BCI-1070] Vincent, Carl, Riccardo Redi, and Franco Venturini. *General Bibliography of Motion Pictures*. 1953. Reprint. [New York]: Arno Press, 1972. 251 pp.

[BCI-1080] *Video Source Book, The*. Syosset: National Video Clearinghouse, 1979-. Annual.

[BCI-1090] Vieler-Porter, Chris. *Black and Third Cinema: Film and Television Bibliography*. London: BFI, 1991. 247 pp.

[BCI-1100] Weaver, Kathleen, ed. *Film Programmer's Guide to 16 mm. Rentals*. 3rd ed. Albany: Reel Research, 1980.

[BCI-1110] Welch, Jeffrey. *Literature and Film: An Annotated Bibliography, 1900-1977*. New York: Garland Publishing, 1981.   350 pp.

KEY WORKS ON CINEMA

The following section listing studies of cinema is designed to provide a context in which to interpret religious studies of this art form. Since works specifically focusing on religion and cinema are relatively few, these sources with a wider scope provide a crucial supplement to the study of Christianity and cinema. For studies introducing readers to the basics of film, see Jan Bone's and Ron Johnson's *Understanding the Film: An Introduction to Film Appreciation* [CIN-090], Bruce Kawin's *How Movies Work* [CIN-550], and John Mercer's *An Introduction to Cinematography* [CIN-700]. To help one interpret key terms and locate basic details, see Frank Beaver's *Dictionary of Film Terms* [CIN-080], Ephraim Katz's *The Film Encyclopedia* [CIN-540], Roger Manvell's *The International Encyclopedia of Film* [CIN-670], Virginia Oakey's *Dictionary of Film and Television Terms* [CIN-730], and Paul Petzold's older but still useful *All-in-One Movie Book* [CIN-760].

While all of the books listed in this section are useful for research, several offer specialized studies in cinema, including the following: aesthetics [CIN-020], [CIN-040], [CIN-050], [CIN-100], [CIN-260], [CIN-440], [CIN-490], [CIN-500], [CIN-590], [CIN-720], [CIN-890], [CIN-900], [CIN-920], [CIN-950], [CIN-970]; criticism and theory [CIN-110], [CIN-140], [CIN-180],

[CIN-200], [CIN-210], [CIN-340], [CIN-520], [CIN-660], [CIN-680], [CIN-750], [CIN-800], [CIN-810], [CIN-820], [CIN-860], [CIN-910], [CIN-950], noting especially [CIN-130] and [CIN-250] as beginning points; directors [CIN-430], [CIN-830]; history of cinema [CIN-010], [CIN-070], [CIN-170], [CIN-300], [CIN-570], [CIN-620], [CIN-780], [CIN-880], noting especially [CIN-290], [CIN-850] for their reference to D. W. Griffith as a watershed figure in cinema history; literature in cinema [CIN-640]; music [CIN-600]; sexuality [CIN-230], [CIN-580], [CIN-750]; technical aspects [CIN-060], [CIN-420], [CIN-550], [CIN-560], [CIN-690], [CIN-770], [CIN-790], [CIN-960]; third world cinema [CIN-280], [CIN-400], [CIN-940]; and writers [CIN-710]. For the most substantial and scholarly reviews of cinema, see especially the following journals listed below: [CIN-300 to CIN-380], [CIN-610]. As with the bibliographies on cinema, few of these key works concentrate on Christian themes, but many do make some references to religious and moral concerns or themes.

[CIN-010] Allen, Robert Clyde. *Film History: Theory and Practice*. Reading, Mass.: Addison-Wesley Publishing Co., 1985. Bib.

[CIN-020] Andrew, D. *Film in the Aura of Art*. Princeton: Princeton University Press, 1984. 217 pp.

[CIN-030] Annual Conference on Film. *Proceedings: Purdue University Fifth Annual Conference on Film, Oct. 30--Nov. 1, 1980*. [West Lafayette, Ind.]: Purdue University, 1980. 260 pp.

[CIN-040] Arnheim, Rudolf. *Film as Art*. Trans. 1958. Reprint. London: Faber and Faber, 1983. 194 pp.

[CIN-050] Aumont, J[acques]. *Aesthetics of Film*. Trans. *Esthétique du Film*. Austin: University of Texas Press, 1992. Bib. refs. pp. 253-269.

[CIN-060] Baddeley, Walter Hugh. *The Technique of Documentary Film Production*. 2nd ed. New York: Hastings House, [1969]. 268 pp.

[CIN-070] Balio, Tino, ed. *The American Film Industry*. Rev. ed. Madison: University of Wisconsin Press, 1985. Bib. pp. 633-643.

[CIN-080] Beaver, Frank. *Dictionary of Film Terms*. New York: McGraw-Hill, 1983. 392 pp.

95

[CIN-090] Bone, Jan, and Ron Johnson. *Understanding the Film: An Intro-duction to Film Appreciation.* 4th ed. Lincolnwood, Ill.: National Textbook Co., 1991. Bibs. 304 pp.

[CIN-100] Bordwell, David, and Kristin Thompson. *Film Art: An Introduction.* 4th ed. New York: McGraw-Hill, 1993. 508 pp. Bib. refs.

[CIN-110] Brunette, Peter, David Wills. *Screen/Play: Derrida and Film Theory.* Princeton: Princeton University Press, 1989. 210 pp.

[CIN-120] Bruno, Giuliana. *Streetwalking on a Ruined Map: Cultural Theory and the City Films of Elvira Notari.* Princeton: Princeton University Press, 1993. 424 pp.

[CIN-130] Bywater, Tim, and Thomas Sobchack. *An Introduction to Film Criticism: Major Critical Approaches to Narrative Film.* New York: Longman, 1989. 238 pp.

[CIN-140] Cadbury, William. *Film Criticism: A Counter Theory.* Ames: Iowa State University Press, 1982. Bib. pp. 285-292.

[CIN-150] Clover, Carol J. *Men, Women, and Chain Saws: Gender in the Modern Horror Film.* Princeton: Princeton University Press, 1993. 260 pp.

[CIN-160] Conley, Tom. *Film Hieroglyphs.* Minneapolis: University of Minnesota Press, 1991. 304 pp.

[CIN-170] Cook, David A. *A History of Narrative Film.* New York: W. W. Norton and Co., 1981. Bib. pp. 671-692.

[CIN-180] Curran, Trisha. *New Note on the Film: A Theory of Film Criticism Derived from Susan K. Langer's Philosophy of Art.* 3rd ed. New York: Holt, Rinehart and Winston, 1980. Bib. pp. 301-305.

[CIN-190] Dawidoff, Heidi G. *Between the Frames: Thinking about Movies.* Hamden, Conn.: Archon Books, 1989. Bib. pp. 203-204.

[CIN-200] Deleuze, Gilles. *Cinema 1: The Movement-Image.* Trans. Hugh Tomlinson and Barbara Habberjam. Minneapolis: University of Minnesota Press, 1986. 264 pp. (Philosophy)

[CIN-210] ------. *Cinema 2: The Time-Image.* Trans. Hugh Tomlinson and Robert Galeta. Minneapolis: University of Minnesota Press, 1989. 362 pp. (Philosophy)

[CIN-220] Dick, Bernard F. *Anatomy of Film.* 2nd ed. New York: St.

Martin's Press, 1990. 273 pp. Bib.

[CIN-230] Doane, Mary Ann. *Femmes Fatales: Feminism, Film Theory, Psychoanalysis*. London: Routledge, 1991. 312 pp.

[CIN-240] Earle, William. *A Surrealism of the Movies*. Chicago, Ill.: Precedent Pub., 1987. Bib. pp. 157-158.

[CIN-250] Eberwein, Robert T. *A Viewer's Guide to Film Theory and Criticism*. Metuchen, N.J.: Scarecrow Press, 1973. 243 pp.

[CIN-260] Edmonds, Robert. *The Sights and Sounds of Cinema and Television: How the Aesthetic Experience Influences Our Feelings*. New York: Teachers College, Columbia University, 1982. Bib. pp. 223-224.

[CIN-270] Eisenstein, Sergei. *The Film Sense*. London: Faber and Faber, 1986. Bib. pp. 211-216.

[CIN-280] Fabien, Rosemarie. *Third World Cinema*. Washington, D.C.: National Education Services, American Film Institute, 1977. Bib. pp. 20-27.

[CIN-290] Fell, John L., ed. *Film Before Griffith*. Berkeley: University of California Press, 1983. Bib. pp. 376-381.

[CIN-300] *Film and History*. Newark, N.J.: New Jersey Institute of Technology, 1972-. Quarterly.

[CIN-310] *Film Comment*. New York: Film Society of Lincoln Center, 1962-. Bi-monthly.

[CIN-320] *Film Criticism*. Meadville, Penn.: Allegheny College, 1976-. 3/year.

[CIN-330] *Film Culture: America's Independent Motion Picture Magazine*. New York: Film Culture, 1955-. Quarterly.

[CIN-340] *Film Evaluation Guide*. New York: Educational Film Library Association, 1946-1964, 1968, 1972-.

[CIN-350] *Film Facts*. Los Angeles: Division of Cinema of the University of Southern California, 1958-1977.

[CIN-360] *Film Quarterly*. Berkeley: University of California Press, 1945-. Quarterly. Formerly *Quarterly of Film, Radio, and Television*.

[CIN-370] *Film Review*. London: Orpheus Publications, 1954-. Monthly.

[CIN-380] *Films in Review.* New York: National Board of Review of Motion Pictures, Inc., 1950-. Monthly.

[CIN-390] *Focal Encyclopedia of Film and Television, The.* New York: Hastings House, [1969]. 1100 pp.

[CIN-400] Gabriel, Teshome H[abte]. *Third Cinema in the Third World: The Aesthetics of Liberation.* Ann Arbor, Mich.: UMI Research Press, 1982. Bib. pp. 135-141.

[CIN-410] Goldstein, Ruth M., and Edith Zornow. *The Screen Image of Youth: Movies about Children and Adolescents.* Metuchen, N.J.: Scarecrow Press, 1980. 384 pp.

[CIN-420] Halas, John, and Roger Manvell. *The Technique of Film Animation.* 3rd ed. New York: Hastings House, [1971]. Bib. p. 357.

[CIN-430] Heck-Rabi, Louise. *Women Filmmakers: A Critical Reception.* Metuchen, N.J.: Scarecrow Press, 1984. 408 pp.

[CIN-440] Hickey, James William. "Cinemaesthetics: A College-Level Curriculum in Film and Communication Theory, Aesthetics and Ethics, Critical Thinking, Reading, and Articulation Skills." Ph.D. Thesis, Teachers College, Columbia University, 1990. Bib. pp. 176-178. Filmography, pp. 182-191.

[CIN-450] Hollander, Anne. *Moving Pictures.* New York: Alfred A. Knopf, 1989. Reprint. London; Cambridge, Mass.: Harvard University Press, 1991. 512 pp. Bib. refs. pp. 475-480.

[CIN-460] Horton, Andrew, and Michael Brashinsky. *The Zero Hour: Glasnost and Soviet Cinema in Transition.* Princeton: Princeton University Press, 1992. 344 pp.

[CIN-470] Issari, Mohammad Ali. *Cinema Verite.* [East Lansing]: Michigan State University Press, [1971]. Bib. pp. 191-202.

[CIN-480] Issari, Mohammad Ali, and Doris A. Paul. *What is Cinema Verite?* Metuchen, N.J.: Scarecrow Press, 1979. 216 pp.

[CIN-490] Jacobs, Lewis. *The Emergence of Film Art: The Evolution and Development of the Motion Picture as an Art, from 1900 to the Present.* 2nd ed. New York: W. W. Norton and Co., 1979. Bib.

[CIN-500] Jameson, Fredric. *The Geopolitical Aesthetic: Cinema and Space in the World System.* Bloomington: Indiana University Press; London: BFI Pub., 1992. 220 pp. Bib. refs.

98

[CIN-510] Jarvie, I[an] C[harles]. *Movies as Social Criticism: Aspects of Their Social Psychology.* Metuchen, N.J.: Scarecrow Press, 1978. 225 pp.

[CIN-520] ------. *Philosophy of the Film: Epistemology, Ontology, Aesthetics.* New York: Routledge and Kegan Paul, 1987. Bib. pp. 364-375.

[CIN-530] Johnson, Lincoln F. *Film: Space, Time, Light, and Sound.* New York: Holt, Rinehart and Winston, [1974]. Filmography pp. 303-318; Bib. pp. 319-325.

[CIN-540] Katz, Ephraim. *The Film Encyclopedia.* New York: Crowell, 1979. 1,266 pp.

[CIN-550] Kawin, Bruce. *How Movies Work.* New York: Macmillan Publishing Co., 1986. 648 pp.

[CIN-560] Kindem, Gorham. *The Moving Image: Production Principles and Practices.* Glenview, Ill.: Scott, Foresman and Co., 1987. Bibs. 458 pp.

[CIN-570] Kirby, Lynne Elizabeth. "The Railroad and the Cinema, 1895-1929: Institutions, Aesthetics and Gender." Ph.D. Thesis, UCLA, 1989. Bib. pp. 427-458.

[CIN-580] Kuhn, Annette. *Cinema, Censorship and Sexuality: 1909-1925.* New York: Routledge Chapman and Hall, 1988. Bib. pp. 135-155.

[CIN-590] Landon, Brooks. *The Aesthetics of Ambivalence: Rethinking Science Fiction Film in the Age of Electronic (Re)production.* Westport, Conn.: Greenwood Press, 1992. Bib. refs. pp. 161-169.

[CIN-600] Larson, Randall D. *Musique Fantastique: A Survey of Film Music in the Fantastic Cinema.* Metuchen, N.J.: Scarecrow Press, 1985. 602 pp.

[CIN-610] *Literature Film Quarterly (LFQ).* Salisbury, Md.: Salisbury State College, 1973-. Quarterly.

[CIN-620] Lowry, Edward. *The Filmology Movement and Film Study in France.* Studies in Cinema, no. 33. Ann Arbor, Mich.: UMI Research Press, 1985. Bib. pp. 203-210.

[CIN-630] Madsen, Roy Paul. *The Impact of Film: How Ideas are Communicated Through Cinema and Television.* New York: Macmillan Publishing Co., [1973]. Bib. pp. 535-549.

[CIN-640] Magill, Frank N. *Cinema: The Novel in Film*. Pasadena, Calif.: Salem Press, 1980. 504 pp.

[CIN-650] Malkiewicz, J. Kris, and Robert E. Rogers. *Cinematography*. 2nd ed. New York: Prentice-Hall Press, 1988. Bib. pp. 205-206.

[CIN-660] Maltby, Richard. *Harmless Entertainment: Hollywood and the Ideology of Consensus*. Metuchen, N.J.: Scarecrow Press, 1983. 425 pp.

[CIN-670] Manvell, Roger, ed. *The International Encyclopedia of Film*. New York: Crown Publishers, 1972. 574 pp.

[CIN-680] Mast, Gerald, Marshall Cohen, and Leo Braudy, eds. *Film Theory and Criticism: Introductory Readings*. 4th ed. New York: Oxford University Press, 1992. Bib. pp. 791-797.

[CIN-690] Mathias, Harry, and Richard Patterson. *Electronic Cinematography: Achieving Photographic Control Over the Video Image*. Belmont, Calif.: Wadsworth Publishing Co., 1985. 251 pp.

[CIN-700] Mercer, John. *An Introduction to Cinematography*. Champaign, Ill.: Stipes Publishing Co., 1968. Bib. pp. 197-199.

[CIN-710] Morsberger, Robert E., Stephen O. Lesser, and Clark Randall, eds. *American Screenwriters*. Dictionary of Literary Biography, no. 26. Detroit: Gale Research, 1984. 382 pp.

[CIN-720] Nilsen, Vladimir. *The Cinema as Graphic Art*. Trans. Stephen Garry. Ed. Ivor Montagu. [London]: Newness, [1937].

[CIN-730] Oakey, Virginia. *Dictionary of Film and Television Terms*. New York: Harper and Row, 1982. 206 pp.

[CIN-740] O'Kane, John Russell. "Film and Cultural Politics after the Avant-garde." Ph.D. Thesis, University of Minnesota, 1988. 228 pp. Bib. refs.

[CIN-750] Penley, Constance, ed. *Feminism and Film Theory*. New York: Routledge; London: BFI Pub., 1988. 271 pp.

[CIN-760] Petzold, Paul. *All-in-One Movie Book*. New York: Amphoto, 1969. 222 pp.

[CIN-770] Pincus, Edward, and Jairus Lincoln. *Guide to Filmmaking*. Photos David N. Hancock. Drawings John E. Reid. Chicago: Regnery, [1972]. Bib. pp. 249-252.

[CIN-780] Quart, Leonard, and Albert Auster. *American Film and Society Since 1945*. New York: Frederick A. Praeger Publishers,

100

1984. Bib. pp. 147-148.

[CIN-790] Rabiger, Michael. *Directing: Film Techniques and Aesthetics.* Boston; London: Focal Press, 1989. Bib. pp. 400-404.

[CIN-800] Roberge, Gaston. *The Subject of Cinema.* The Rita Ray Memorial Lectures, 1987. Calcutta: Seagull Books, 1990. Bib. refs. pp. 221-240.

[CIN-810] ------. *The Ways of Film Studies: Film Theory and the Interpretation of Films.* Delhi: Ajanta Publications, 1992. Bib. refs. pp. 227-233.

[CIN-820] Rothman, William. *The "I" of the Camera: Essays in Film Criticism, History, and Aesthetics.* Cambridge Studies in Film. Cambridge: Cambridge University Press, 1988. 210 pp.

[CIN-830] Sadoul, Georges. *Dictionary of Film Makers.* Trans. Peter Morris. Berkeley, Calif.: University of California Press, 1972. 288 pp.

[CIN-840] ------. *Dictionary of Films.* Trans. Peter Morris. Berkeley, Calif.: University of California Press, 1972. 432 pp.

[CIN-850] Schickel, Richard. *D. W. Griffith: An American Life.* New York: Simon and Schuster, 1984. Bib. pp. 629-636. 672 pp.

[CIN-860] Sharff, Stefan. *The Elements of Cinema: Toward a Theory of Cinesthetic Impact.* New York: Columbia University Press, 1982. 187 pp.

[CIN-870] Shaviro, Steven. *The Cinematic Body.* Theory Out of Bounds, vol. 2. Minneapolis: University of Minnesota Press, 1993. Bib. refs.

[CIN-880] Staiger, Janet. *Interpreting Films: Studies in the Historical Reception of American Cinema.* Princeton: Princeton University Press, 1992. Bib. refs. pp. 259-269.

[CIN-890] Stephenson, Ralph, and Guy Phelps. *Cinema as Art.* Rev. ed. New York: Penguin, 1990. 320 pp.

[CIN-900] Sterling, Anna K., comp. *Cinematographers on the Art and Craft of Cinematography.* (Essays from 1929-1937.) Metuchen, N.J.: Scarecrow Press, 1987. 145 pp.

[CIN-910] Szekeres, Peter, and Gedeon P. Dienes. *All Time Great Films.* Trans. *Minden Idok Nagy Filmjei.* Budapest: Institute for Culture, 1984. Bib. pp. 41-43.

[CIN-920] Taylor, Richard, and Boris Mikhailovich Eikhenbaum, eds. *The Poetics of Cinema*. Trans. *Poetika Kino*. RPT Publications with Department of Literature, University of Essex, 1982. 126 pp.

[CIN-930] Thomas, Sari. *Film/Culture: Explorations of Cinema in its Social Context*. Metuchen, N.J.: Scarecrow Press, 1982. 281 pp.

[CIN-940] Thompson, Tracy. *Third World Cinema*. Rev. ed. Los Angeles American Film Institute, Educations Services, 1987. Bib. pp. 17-24.

[CIN-950] Watson, Robert. *Film and Television in Education: An Aesthetic Approach to the Moving Image*. The Falmer Press Library on Aesthetic Education. London; New York: Falmer Press, 1990. Bib. refs. pp. 151-168.

[CIN-960] Wheeler, Leslie J. *Principles of Cinematography: A Handbook of Motion Picture Technology*. 4th ed. London: Fountain, [1969]. Bib. pp. 383-429.

[CIN-950] Whitaker, Rod. *The Language of Film*. Englewood Cliffs, N.J.: Prentice-Hall Press, 1970. 178 pp. Bib.

[CIN-960] White, David Manning, and Richard Averson. *Sight, Sound, and Society: Motion Pictures and Television in America*. Boston: Beacon Press, 1968. 466 pp. Bibs.

[CIN-970] Zettl, Herbert. *Sight, Sound, Motion: Applied Media Aesthetics*. Belmont, Calif.: Wadsworth Publishing Co., [1973]. Bib. pp. 388-391.

KEY WORKS ON CINEMA AND RELIGION

The following list of works is the fruit of extensive research for resources treating Christianity and cinema. Many of these works tend to be censorious or primarily descriptive, but some provide significant insights into the aesthetic and spiritual dimensions of cinema. For basic information about films and their correlation or contrast with Christian values, see the following items: [CIR-010], [CIR-020], [CIR-080], [CIR-110], [CIR-260], [CIR-350], and [CIR-400], and take special note of Richard H. Campbell's and Michael R. Pitts's very useful work, *The Bible on Film: A Checklist, 1897-1980* [CIR-090]. To locate more developed and probing analyses of cinema and religion, consult the following works: [CIR-030 to CIR-070], [CIR-100], [CIR-130 to 170], [CIR-220 to 250], [CIR-270], [CIR-280], [CIR-300 to CIR-340], [CIR-360], [CIR-370 to CIR-420]. Note in particular Lloyd Billingsley's recent work, *The Seductive Image: A Christian Critique of the World of Film* [CIR-040]. Of special interest to students of cinema will be four critiques on the work of Ingmar Bergman [CIR-190], [CIR-200], [CIR-250], and [CIR-290], and three studies of the Star Wars Trilogy [CIR-180], [CIR-380], and [CIR-430]. These last three titles illustrate well the tension between various interpretations of creative expressions of spirituality in cinema. Some find manifestations of the demonic behind much of the world of cinema, while others find intriguing reinterpretations of Christian themes. Art generates a variety of responses, but Christians are still entrusted with the task of discerning good from evil, and this is a challenging responsibility which belies simplistic interpretations. The titles given below are offered as resources for those seeking to define for themselves the proper relationship between Christianity and popular culture as manifest in cinema.

[CIR-010] Baehr, Ted, with Bruce W. Grimes, and Lisa Ann Rice. *Movie and Video Guide: For Christian Families*. Nashville: Thomas Nelson Publishers, 1987. 234 pp.

[CIR-020] Barnett, Leonard P. *A Parson at the Pictures: Talks to a Cinema Audience*. London: Epworth Press, 1949. 56 pp.

[CIR-030] Benfey, Matthias Wilhelm. "Religious Cinema as Virtual Religious Experience: A Theory of Religious Cinema Applied to Werner Herzog's *Herz aus Glas*." Ph.D. Thesis, McGill University, 1987. Ottawa: National Library of Canada, 1988. Bib.

[CIR-040] Billingsley, Lloyd. *The Seductive Image: A Christian Critique of the World of Film*. Westchester, Ill.: Crossway Books, 1989. Bib. pp. 207-221.

[CIR-050] Bird, Michael Shane. "Cinema and the Sacred: An Application of Paul Tillich's Theory of Art to the Film in the Aesthetic Apprehension of the Holy: A Thesis." Ph.D. Thesis, University of Iowa, 1975. Bib. pp. 253-261.

[CIR-060] Burnett, Richard George. *The Cinema for Christ*. 1934. Reprint. London: Religious Tract Society, 1988. 128 pp.

[CIR-070] Butler, Ivan. *Religion in Cinema*. New York: A. S. Barnes and Co.; London: A. Zwemmer, 1969. Bib. p. 204.

[CIR-080] Butler, John. *TV, Movies and Morality: A Guide for Catholics*. Huntington, Ind.: Our Sunday Visitor, 1984. 160 pp.

[CIR-090] Campbell, Richard H., and Michael R. Pitts. *The Bible on Film: A Checklist, 1897-1980*. Metuchen, N.J.: Scarecrow Press, 1981. 224 pp.

[CIR-100] Catholic Church. Pope Pius XII. *Encyclical Letter Concerning the Cinema, Sound Broadcasting, and Television*. London: Catholic Truth Society, 1958. 44 pp.

[CIR-110] *Catholic Film Newsletter*. New York: Division for Film and Broadcasting of the U.S. Catholic Conference, 1935-.

[CIR-120] *Cinema and Audiovisual Throughout the World: OCIC's Activities, 1981-1983*. Brussels: Editions OCIC, 1983. 95 pp. English, French, Spanish.

[CIR-130] Cooper, John C., and Carl Skrade, eds. *Celluloid and Symbols*. Philadelphia: Fortress Press, 1970. 143 pp. Bibs.

[CIR-140] David, C. R. W. *Cinema as Medium of Communication in Tamil Nadu*. Madras: Christian Literature Society, 1983. Bib. pp. 91-93.

[CIR-150] Drew, Donald J. *Images of Man: A Critique of the Contemporary Cinema*. Downers Grove, Ill.: InterVarsity Press, 1974. 121 pp. Bib. refs.

[CIR-160] Fagan, Myron C[oureval]. *The "Christian and Jewish Brotherhood Hoax"*. Hollywood, Calif.: Cinema Educational Guild, 1965. 28 pp.

[CIR-170] Ford, Richard. *Children in the Cinema*. 1939. Reprint. London: G. Allen and Unwin, 1988. 232 pp.

[CIR-180] Geisler, Norman L., and J. Yutaka Amano. *Religion of the Force*. Dallas: Quest Publications, 1983. Bib. refs in notes, pp. 59-61.

[CIR-190] Gibson, Arthur. *The Silence of God: Creative Response to the Films of Ingmar Bergman*. 1969. Reprint. Lewiston, N.Y.: Edwin Mellen Press, 1989. 172 pp.

[CIR-200] Gill, Jerry H. *Ingmar Bergman and the Search for Meaning*. Grand Rapids: William B. Eerdmans Publishing Co., 1969. Bib. p. 45.

104

[CIR-210] Golden, Leon, ed. *Transformations in Literature and Film: Selected Papers from the Sixth Annual Florida State University Conference on Literature and Film*. Tallahassee: University Press of Florida, 1982. 114 pp. Bibs.

[CIR-220] Hadomi, Leah. *The Homecoming Theme in Modern Drama: The Return of the Prodigal*. Lewiston, N.Y.:   Edwin Mellen Press, 1992. 196 pp.

[CIR-230] Hills, Janet. *Are They Safe at the Cinema?: [A Considered Answer to Critics of the Cinema]*. 1900. Reprint. London: British Film Institute, 1954. 24 pp.

[CIR-240] Holloway, Ronald. *Beyond the Image: Approaches to the Religious Dimensions in the Cinema*. Geneva: World Council of Churches with Interfilm, 1977. 215 pp. Bib. pp. 191-195.

[CIR-250] ------. "The Religious Dimension in the Cinema: With Particular Reference to the Films of Carl Theodor Dreyer, Ingmar Bergman and Robert Bresson."   Dissertation, Hamburg, 1972. Bib. pp. 301-304.

[CIR-260] *Index to Religious Periodical Literature*.   Chicago: American Theological Library Association, 1949-. See "Film Reviews."

[CIR-270] International Educational Cinematographic Institute. *The Social Aspects of the Cinema*. Rome: International Educational Cinematographic Institute, 1930. 240 pp.

[CIR-280] Kieser, Ellwood E.   "Cinema as Religious Experience: Five Examples from the Insight Film Series." Thesis, Graduate Theological Union, 1973. Bib. pp. 48-51. 5 sound track film reels, 16 mm.

[CIR-290] Lauder, Robert E. *God, Death and Love: The Philosophical Vision of Ingmar Bergman*. New York: Paulist Press, 1989. Bib. notes pp. 169-186.

[CIR-300] Makau, Nereah. *Cinema Leo Survey: A Study of Viewer Characteristics, Viewing Habits, Preference, and Attitudes*. 2 vols. Nairobi, Kenya: Daystar University College, Research Department, 1988.

[CIR-310] Martin, Thomas M. *Images and the Imageless: A Study in Religious Consciousness and Film*. Lewisburg, Pa.: Buckness University Press; London: Associated University Presses, 1981. Bib. pp. 171-174.

[CIR-320] May, John R., and Michael Bird. *Religion in Film*. Knoxville: University of Tennessee Press, 1982. Bib. pp. 242-244.

[CIR-330] Mitchell, Keith. *The Magic Box and the Silver Screen: A Christian Approach to Television and Cinema*. London: Catholic Truth Society, 1981. 18 pp.

[CIR-340] National Council of Public Morals. Cinema Commission of Inquiry. *The Cinema: Its Present Position and Future Possibilities*. London: Williams and Norgate, 1982. xciii, 372 pp.

[CIR-350] Pavelin, Alan. *Fifty Religious Films*. Chislehurst: A. P. Pavelin, 1990. Bib. p. 108.

[CIR-360] Phillips, Gene D. *Religious Themes in Contemporary Cinema*. Chicago: Meditapes Thomas More Association, 1972. Audio cassette.

[CIR-370] Robson, Emanuel W. *The World is my Cinema*. London: Sidneyan Society, 1947. 205 pp.

[CIR-380] Short, Robert. *The Gospel from Outer Space*. London: Fount, 1983. 96 pp.

[CIR-390] *Une Invention du diable Cinema des premiers temps et religion*. Sainte-Foy, Quebec: Presses de l'Universite Laval, 1992. 383 pp. Bib. refs. French and English.

[CIR-400] Van Deelen, Henry C., et al. The Committee of the Church and the Film Arts. *The Church and the Film Arts*. Grand Rapids: Christian Reformed Publishing House, 1967. 39 pp.

[CIR-410] Wall, James McKendree. *Church and Cinema: A Way of Viewing Film*. 1971. Reprint. Grand Rapids: William B. Eerdmans, 1980. 135 pp.

[CIR-420] White, William H., and Jackie Shelton. "The Culture as Manipulator: The Cinema." Stahlstown, Pa.: Thompson Media, 1970. Audio cassette.

[CIR-430] Yake, John. *Star Wars and the Message of Jesus: An Interpretive Commentary on the Star Wars Trilogy*. Hamilton, Ontario: Image Pub., 1985. 135 pp.

CHAPTER 5

DANCE AND MIME AND CLOWNING

BIBLIOGRAPHIES ON DANCE AND MIME AND CLOWNING

While the volume of literature treating dance is considerable, the number of works examining dance in a scholarly manner is relatively small. Literature covering mime and clowning is even rarer. Of the seventy-seven bibliographies listed below, the most extensive are those produced by the American Alliance for Health, Physical Education, Recreation and Dance [BDM-020 to 040] and the New York Public Library, Dance Collection [BDM-110], [BDM-540], and [BDM-550]. Of the single volume bibliographies, the most current for research purposes is Mary S. Bopp's *Research in Dance: A Guide to Resources* [BDM-120]. For other one volume bibliographies which will prove useful in general research, see the following entries: [BDM-180], [BDM-280], [BDM-320], [BDM-360], [BDM-580], and [BDM-590].

To locate studies treating dance and aesthetics, consult Thomas J. Johnson's *Review and Index to Research in Dance Relevant to Aesthetic Education, 1900-1968* [BDM-380], and Mary H. Kaprelian's *Aesthetics for Dancers: A Selected Annotated Bibliography* [BDM-390]. For locating dissertations and theses treating dance, see [BDM-340] and [BDM-400]. Since much of the recent material on dance can be found in journals, sometimes indexed in general bibliographies, one will also do well to see the following specialized bibliographies: [BDM-080], [BDM-500], [BDM-550], [BDM-580], [BDM-590], and [BDM-620].

Along with the movement toward cultural diversity in university and community programs has come a development of studies treating dance as the product of ethnic groups. For studies analyzing dance from this cultural perspective see the following bibliographies: [BDM-010], [BDM-060], [BDM-130], [BDM-190], [BDM-220], [BDM-250], [BDM-290], [BDM-300], [BDM-320], [BDM-370], [BDM-430], [BDM-490], [BDM-560], [BDM-610], [BDM-640], [BDM-670], [BDM-680], [BDM-690], [BDM-720]. Similarly, several bibliographies analyze dance according to its genre, such as ballet [BDM-150], folk and country dance [BDM-140], [BDM-410], [BDM-520], [BDM-660], and [BDM-750], and operetta [BDM-760]. Many of the sources for studying music in dance overlap with those treating dance by itself, but the following bibliographies will prove especially useful to those studying music as a companion to dance: [BDM-060], [BDM-140], [BDM-200], [BDM-350], [BDM-430], [BDM-470], [BDM-480], [BDM-580], [BDM-610], [BDM-620], [BDM-630], [BDM-640], [BDM-680], [BDM-720], [BDM-750], [BDM-760]. Careful researchers will also do well to note that dance is sometimes classified as a sport and can be found in works such as Ingrid Draayer's eight volume *Sport Bibliography* [BDM-210]. Furthermore, dance is sometimes connected with fitness or physical therapy programs and can therefore be located in bibliographies such as those produced by the American Alliance for Health, Physical Education, Recreation and Dance [BDM-020 to BDM-040], mentioned above, and in Heidi Fledderjohn's and Judith Sewickley's M.A. thesis, "An Annotated Bibliography of Dance/Movement Therapy: 1940-1990" [BDM-270].

Mime and clowning are in many ways related to dance, especially ballet, and are sometimes treated as subsets of dance. Yet mime and clowning are also closely related to drama and may often be found in bibliographies treating theater arts. Unfortunately, no large, specialized bibliography could be located which concentrates on mime and clowning as categories unto themselves. Researchers must be creative and use the bibliographies included in serious studies of these subjects, as given below in Key Works in Mime and

Clowning, or explore various categories of bibliographies treating drama, dance, or music, as identified by the following or related terms: buffoon, ballet, burlesque, clowning, comedy, farce, fool, harlequin, mime, minstrel, mummer, opera, opera bouffe, opera comique, pantomime, and vaudeville.

Finally, for the teaching of dance, several bibliographies will be particularly helpful. Those dealing with dance notation and methods include [BDM-100], [BDM-160], [BDM-260], [BDM-330], [BDM-660], and [BDM-730]. Those treating dance as presented in film and video include [BDM-130], [BDM-450], [BDM-570], [BDM-580], and [BDM-590]. Additional reference texts include the *American Dance Directory* [BDM-050], a concise and useful summary of critical views in *Dance Perspectives* [BDM-170], and a variety of bibliographies treating special collections, such as [BDM-190], [BDM-240], and [BDM-480]. For additional bibliographies, see the bibliographies of bibliographies listed in Chapter 1, or the bibliography section in Chapter 10 on music.

[BDM-010] Adamczyk, Alice J. *Black Dance: An Annotated Bibliography.* Garland Reference Library of the Humanities, vol. 558. New York: Garland Publishing, 1989. 213 pp.

[BDM-020] American Alliance for Health, Physical Education, Recreation and Dance. *Completed Research in Health, Physical Education, Recreation, and Dance.* Reston, Va.: American Alliance for Health, Physical Education, Recreation and Dance, 1958-.

[BDM-030] American Association for Health, Physical Education, and Recreation. Dance Division. *Research in Dance, I.* Washington, D.C.: American Association for Health, Physical Education, and Recreation, 1968. 45 pp. *Research in Dance, II,* 1973. 96 pp. *Research in Dance, III,* Reston, Va.: American Alliance for Health, Physical Education, Recreation, and Dance, 1982. 164 pp. *Research in Dance, IV: 1900-1990,* 1992. 118 pp.

[BDM-040] American Association for Health, Physical Education, and Recreation. National Section on Dance. *Dance Research: Reference Materials with Suggestions for Future Research.* Ed. Virginia Moomaw. [Washington, D.C.]: American Association for Health, Physical Education, and Recreation, 1958. 54 pp.

[BDM-050] *American Dance Directory*. New York: Association of American Dance Companies, 1980-.

[BDM-060] Aning, B. A. *An Annotated Bibliography of Music and Dance in English-Speaking Africa*. 1967? Reprint. Legon: Institute of African Studies, University of Ghana, 1983. 47 pp.

[BDM-070] Beaumont, Cyril W[illiam]. *A Bibliography of Dancing*. 1929. Reprint. New York: n.p., 1963. 228 pp. (500 entries, works in the British Museum)

[BDM-080] Belknap, S. Yancey, comp. *Guide to Dance Periodicals: An Analytical Index of Articles*. New York: Ashville, 1950-1960.

[BDM-090] Bellingham, Susan. *A Catalogue of the Dance Collection in the Doris Lewis Rare Book Room, University of Waterloo Library*. 2nd ed. Waterloo, Ontario: The Library, 1983. 201 p.

[BDM-100] Berry, Irmgard E. *Benesh Movement Notation Score Catalogue: An International Listing of Benesh Movement Notation Scores of Professional Dance Works Recorded, 1955-1985*. London: The Institute, 1986. 94 pp.

[BDM-110] *Bibliographic Guide to Dance*. Bibliographic Guide Series. Boston: G. K. Hall, 1975-.

[BDM-120] Bopp, Mary S. *Research in Dance: A Guide to Resources*. New York: G. K. Hall; Toronto: Maxwell Macmillan Canada; New York: Maxwell Macmillan International, 1993.

[BDM-130] California Institute of the Arts, Library. *World Dance: Bibliography of Books and Films in the CalArts Library*. Valencia, Calif.: California Institute of the Arts Library, 1992. 39 pp.

[BDM-140] Clark, Keith. *Folk Song and Dance*. London: National Book League with English Folk Dance and Song Society, 1972. 48 pp.

[BDM-150] Clarke, Mary, and Clement Crisp. *Ballet Goer's Guide*. London: Michael Joseph, 1981.

[BDM-160] Dance Notation Bureau [New York]. *Notated Theatrical Dances: A Listing of Theatrical Scores at the Dance Notation Bureau*. [2nd ed.] New York: Dance Notation Bureau, 1988. 55 pp.

[BDM-170] *Dance Perspectives*. Brooklyn, N.Y.: Dance Perspectives, 1959-.

[BDM-180] Daniel, Charlie, and James Thomas Jable. *A Research Sourcebook and Bibliography in Aging and Health, Exercise, Recreation and Dance*. 2nd ed. [Reston, Va.]: American Alliance

111

for Health, Physical Education, Recreation and Dance, 1992. 115 pp.

[BDM-190] Detroit Public Library. E. Azalia Hackley Collection. *Catalog of the E. Azalia Hackley Memorial Collection of Negro Music, Dance, and Drama, Detroit Public Library.* Boston: G. K. Hall, 1979. 510 pp.

[BDM-200] De Vita, A. Ray. *Standard Dance Music Guide: A Classified and Alphabetical List of the World's Best and Most Popular Standard Songs with Their Original Keys and Starting Notes, Plus a Handy Fake List and Song Reminder of Top Tunes.* Bayside, N.Y.: A. R. De Vita, 1980. 58 pp.

[BDM-210] Draayer, I[ngrid], ed. *Sport Bibliography.* 8 vols. Ottawa: Sport Information Resource Centre, 1981. English and French. See vol. 3, "Gymnastics and Dance."

[BDM-220] Drewal, Margaret Thompson. *Sources on African and African-Related Dance.* New York: American Dance Guild, 1974. 38 pp.

[BDM-230] Dunin, Elsie Ivancich. *Dance Research: Published or Publicly Presented by Members of the Study Group on Ethnochoreology.* 2nd ed. [Los Angeles]: International Council for Traditional Music, Study Group on Ethnochoreology, 1991. 123 pp. Biennial.

[BDM-240] ------. *Dance Sources, UCLA Libraries and Archives.* Los Angeles: University of California at Los Angeles, Department of Dance, 1991. 465 pp.

[BDM-250] ------. *Yugoslav Dance: An Introduction and List of Sources Available in United States Libraries.* Palo Alto, Calif.: Ragusan Press, 1981. 108 pp.

[BDM-260] Dunin, Elsie Ivancich, and Carol Ann Harrington de Alaiza. *DdA Reference Format for Dance.* Rev. ed. Los Angeles: [Dunin], 1989. 42 pp.

[BDM-270] Fledderjohn, Heidi, and Judith Sewickley. "An Annotated Bibliography of Dance/Movement Therapy: 1940-1990." M.A. Thesis, Goucher College, 1991. 95 pp.

[BDM-280] Forbes, Fred R. *Dance: An Annotated Bibliography, 1965-1982.* Garland Reference Library of the Humanities, vol. 606. New York: Garland Publishing, 1986. 261 pp.

[BDM-290] Garcia, Florencio Oscar. *Tango: A Bibliography: Books, History, People, Words.* Albuquerque: Fog Publications, 1991. 108

pp. English and Spanish.

[BDM-300] Gordon, B., and J. Gordon. *An Introduction to the Dance of India, China, Korea, and Japan.* In *Asia Society Guides,* 1965. Reprint. New York: Arno Press, 1975. 557 pp.

[BDM-310] Hall, Williard. *Bibliography of Social Dancing.* New York: Hastings-on-Hudson, 1940. 105 pp. [1500 entries]

[BDM-320] Hanna, Judith Lynne. *The Anthropology of Dance: A Selected Bibliography.* Rev. ed. College Park, Md.: Hanna, 1980. 19 pp.

[BDM-330] Heaney, Mike. *An Introductory Bibliography of Morris Dancing.* Vaughan Williams Memorial Library Leaflet, no. 19. London: Vaughan Williams Memorial Library: English Folk Dance and Song Society, 1985. 35 pp.

[BDM-340] Herndon, Myrtis E. *Theses and Dissertations Related to Comparative/International Education, Physical Education, Sport, and Dance.* Hiram, Ohio: Department of Physical Education for Women, Hiram College, 1974. 459 pp.

[BDM-350] Hickerson, Joseph C. *A Bibliography of Fiddling, Fiddle Tunes, and Related Dance Tune Collections in North America, Including Representative Materials from the British Isles and Scandinavia.* Washington, D.C.: Archive of Folk Song, 1983. 28 pp.

[BDM-360] Hodgens, Pauline. *Dance: A Selected and Annotated Bibliography of Philosophical Readings in Art, Aesthetics and Criticism.* Guildford: National Resource Centre for Dance, 1985. 68 pp.

[BDM-370] Huerta, Jorge A. *A Bibliography of Chicano and Mexican Dance, Drama and Music.* Oxnard, Calif.: Colegio Quetzalcoat, 1972. 59 pp.

[BDM-380] Johnson, Thomas J. *Review and Index to Research in Dance Relevant to Aesthetic Education, 1900-1968.* [St. Ann, Mo.]: CEMREL, 1970. 157 pp.

[BDM-390] Kaprelian, Mary H. *Aesthetics for Dancers: A Selected Annotated Bibliography.* Washington, D.C.: American Alliance for Health, Physical Education and Recreation, and [National Dance Association], 1976. 87 pp.

[BDM-400] Keighley, J[ohn] S., and L[eo] B[rough] Hendry. *PERDAS: 1950-1980: A List of Theses, Dissertations and Projects on Physical Education, Recreation, Dance, Athletics and Sport,*

Presented at United Kingdom Universities. Lancaster: LISE, 1981. 184 pp.

[BDM-410] Keller, Robert M. *Dance Figures Index: American Country Dances, 1730-1810.* Sandy Hook, Conn.: Hendrickson Group, 1989. Bibs. pp. 8-13.

[BDM-420] Kidson, Frank. *Old English Country Dances, Gathered from Scarce Printed Collections, and from Manuscripts. With Illustrative Notes and a Bibliography of English Country Dance Music.* London: W. Reeves, 1890. 55 pp.

[BDM-430] Kuppuswamy, Gowri. *Indian Dance and Music Literature: A Select Bibliography.* New Delhi: Biblia Impex, 1981. 156 pp.

[BDM-440] Leslie, Serge. *A Bibliography of the Dance Collection of Doris Niles and Serge Leslie, Part IV, A-Z: Mainly 20th Century Publications.* London: Dance Books, Ltd., 1981. 283 pp.

[BDM-450] Levine, Robert. *Guide to Opera and Dance on Videocassette.* Mount Vernon, N.Y.: Consumers Union, 1989. 213 pp.

[BDM-460] Little, Meredith, and Carol G. Marsh. *La Danse Noble: An Inventory of Dances and Sources.* Williamstown, [Mass.]: Broude Brothers, 1992. 173 pp.

[BDM-470] Long, Elizabeth [Baker], and Mary McKee. *A Bibliography of Music for the Dance.* [Austin]: N.p., 1936. 47 pp.

[BDM-480] Luger, Eleanor Rachel. *A Guide to Bibliographic Materials on or Relating to Social Dance as Found in the UCLA Research, Music and Dance Libraries and the Dorathi Bock Pierre Collection at the Beverly Hills Public Library.* [Los Angeles]: Sponsored by President's Undergraduate Program [UCLA], 1975. 112 pp.

[BDM-490] McLean, Mervyn. *Oceanic Music and Dance: An Annotated Bibliography.* Honolulu: University of Hawaii Press, 1977. 252 pp. *Supplement: An Annotated Bibliography of Oceanic Music and Dance,* 1981. 74 pp.

[BDM-500] Magriel, Paul David. *A Bibliography of Dancing: A List of Books and Articles on the Dance and Related Subjects.* New York: [H. N. Wilson?], 1936. 229 pp. Fourth cumulated supplement, 1935-1940, New York: H. N. Wilson, 1941. 104 pp.

[BDM-510] Melcer, Fannie Helen, Charlotte Irey, and Judith Anne Gray. *Research in Dance.* Vols. 1-2, 4. Washington, D.C.: American Association for Health, Physical Education, and Re-

114

creation, 1968. Supplements *Compilation of Dance Research, 1901-1964.*

[BDM-520] Music Department of Minneapolis Public Library. *An Index to Folk Dances and Singing Games.* Chicago: American Library Association, 1936. 202 pp.

[BDM-530] National Dance Association. *Dance Resource Guide.* Reston, Va.: National Dance Association, 1990-.

[BDM-540] New York Public Library. Dance Collection. *Dictionary Catalog of the Dance Collection.* 10 vols. New York: G. K. Hall, 1974. 6,970 pp. Nine supplements, 1976-1984. Also called *Bibliographic Guide to Dance.* Boston: G. K. Hall, 1975-. Annual.

[BDM-550] New York Public Library for the Performing Arts. Dance Collection. *Index to Dance Periodicals.* Boston: G. K. Hall, 1990-. Annual.

[BDM-560] Osterreich, Shelley Anne. *The American Indian Ghost Dance, 1870 and 1890: An Annotated Bibliography.* New York: Greenwood Press, 1991. 96 pp.

[BDM-570] Parker, David L., and Esther Siegel. *Guide to Dance in Films: A Guide to Information Sources.* Performing Arts Information Guide Series, vol. 3. Detroit: Gale Research, 1978. 240 pp.

[BDM-580] Pease, Edward J. *The Historiography of Dance: A Guide to Basic Collections, Bibliographies, Reference Books, Serials, Historical Surveys, Manuals, Special Studies, Films, Addresses, and Other Essentials, with an Appendix, "Researching the Music of Dance".* Bowling Green: Division of Library Services, Western Kentucky University, 1980. 137 pp.

[BDM-590] ------. *Researching Theatrical Dance: A Guide to Basic Collections, Bibliographies, Reference Books, Serials, Historical Surveys, Manuals, Special Studies, Films, Addresses, and Other Essentials, Primarily as Related to Theatrical Dance.* 2 vols. Bowling Green: Western Kentucky University, 1982. 103 pp.

[BDM-600] Peterson, Barbara. "A Bibliographical Essay on the Adult Literature of the Folk Dance of Southern Appalachia." M.S. Thesis, Palmer Graduate Library School of Long Island University, 1972. 119 pp.

[BDM-610] Radet for Folkemusikk og Folkedans. *The Norwegian Council for Folk Music and Folk Dance: Institutions and Organizations in the Council: Norwegian Folk Dance and Folk Music,*

Selected Bibliography. Trondheim: The Council, 1979. 42 pp.

[BDM-620] Robinson, Doris. *Music and Dance Periodicals: An International Directory and Guidebook.* Voorheesville, N.Y.: Peri Press, 1989-. 382 pp.

[BDM-630] Schleman, Hilton R. *Rhythm on Record: A Complete Survey and Register of all the Principal Recorded Dance Music from 1906 to 1936, and a Who's Who of the Artists Concerned in the Making.* London: Melody Maker, 1936. 333 pp.

[BDM-640] Schwartz, Judith L[eah], and Christena L. Schlundt. *French Court Dance and Dance Music: A Guide to Primary Source Writings, 1643-1789.* Stuyvesant, N.Y.: Pendragon Press, 1987. 386 pp.

[BDM-650] Sellars, Jo Anne C., comp. *A Bibliography: "Multi-Disciplinary Approaches to Dance in Elementary Education".* New York: American Dance Guild, 1973. 36 pp.

[BDM-660] Sloanaker, Jack. *Square Dance Chord Book and Tune Locator: Chords to Accompany 500 of the Tunes Commonly Played in New England; Cross-Indexed to Books and Records Containing the Melodies.* 2nd ed. Plymouth, Vt.: F & W Records, 1979. 100 pp.

[BDM-670] Southern, Eileen, and Josephine Wright. *African-American Traditions in Song, Sermon, Tale, and Dance, 1600s-1920: An Annotated Bibliography of Literature, Collections, and Artworks.* Westport, Conn.; London: Greenwood Press, 1990. 416 pp.

[BDM-680] Thompson, Donald, and Annie F[igueroa] Thompson. *Music and Dance in Puerto Rico from the Age of Columbus to Modern Times: An Annotated Bibliography.* Studies in Latin American Music, no. 1. Metuchen, N.J.; London: Metuchen Press, 1991. 339 pp.

[BDM-690] *Union Catalog on Philippine Culture: Dance.* Manila: Cultural Center of the Philippines Library, 1989. 117 pp.

[BDM-700] Universiti Malaya. Perpustakaan. *Literature, Drama, and Dance in Southeast Asia: A Bibliography.* Kuala Lumpur: The Library, 1976. 137 pp.

[BDM-710] Valois, Elaine. *Introduction to Modern Dance.* N.p., 1977. 62 pp.

[BDM-720] Vaughan Williams Memorial Library. *The Vaughan Williams Memorial Library Catalogue of the English Folk Dance and*

Song Society: Acquisitions to the Library of Books, Pamphlets, Periodicals, Sheet Music and Manuscripts, from its Inception to 1971. [London]: Mansell, 1973. 769 pp.

[BDM-730] Warner, Mary Jane, and Frederick E. Warner. *Laban Notation Scores: An International Bibliography.* 2 vols. [N.p.: International Council of Kinetography Laban], 1984. Dist. Dance Notation Bureau, New York.

[BDM-740] Wasserman, Steven R., and Jacqueline W. O'Brien. *The Lively Arts Information Directory.* 2nd ed. Detroit: Gale Research, 1985.

[BDM-750] White, Edward A. *An Index of English Songs Contributed to the Journal of the Folk Song Society, 1899-1931, and its Continuation, the Journal of the English Folk Dance and Song Society, to 1950.* London: English Folk Dance and Song Society, 1951. 58 pp.

[BDM-760] Willis Music Company. *Operetta Music: Children's Action Songs, Musical Recitations, Musical Readings and Music for the Dance Studio.* Reprint. Cincinnati: Willis Music Co., 1974. 72 pp.

[BDM-770] Zirulnik, Ann. *Resource Lists for Children's Dance.* Ed. Jeanette Abeles. East Lansing: Michigan Dance Association, 1985. 62 pp.

KEY WORKS ON DANCE

The following list is offered as a beginning point for those studying dance in its larger context. For current introductions to the topic, consult Jack Anderson's *Ballet and Modern Dance: A Concise History* [DMD-090], Joan Cass's recent work, *Dancing Through History* [DMD-190], and Lincoln Kirstein's *Dance: A Short History of Classic Theatrical Dancing* [DMD-620]. Other reference tools which will be useful for research are [DMD-060], [DMD-650], [DMD-840], and [DMD-870].

The study of dance can be divided by genre, geographical region, historical period, or various topics. For convenience, the list given below is divided alphabetically by topical categories, with the recognition that these categories overlap to some extent. For the study of dance consider the following related topics and categories: aesthetics [DMD-860], [DMD-970], [DMD-

980], [DMD-1090], [DMD-1110]; ballet [DMD-090], [DMD-120], [DMD-130], [DMD-350], [DMD-650], [DMD-730]; belly dancing [DMD-180], [DMD-340], [DMD-530], [DMD-700], [DMD-1190]; cross cultural studies of dance [DMD-020], [DMD-100], [DMD-150], [DMD-160], [DMD-260], [DMD-310], [DMD-420], [DMD-500], [DMD-550], [DMD-600], [DMD-660], [DMD-680], [DMD-780], [DMD-800], [DMD-820], [DMD-1040], [DMD-1160], [DMD-1170], [DMD-1180], [DMD-1200], [DMD-1220]; folk dance [DMD-070], [DMD-110], [DMD-200], [DMD-240], [DMD-360], [DMD-370], [DMD-390], [DMD-430], [DMD-450], [DMD-460], [DMD-580], [DMD-610], [DMD-890], [DMD-940], [DMD-1010]; gymnastics and dance [DMD-470], [DMD-520]; history of dance [DMD-030], [DMD-190], [DMD-250], [DMD-500], [DMD-620], [DMD-830], [DMD-920], [DMD-930], [DMD-1070]; jazz [DMD-050], [DMD-170], [DMD-880], [DMD-1150]; research in miscellaneous categories [DMD-010], [DMD-040], [DMD-080], [DMD-220], [DMD-230], [DMD-330], [DMD-400], [DMD-410], [DMD-540], [DMD-570], [DMD-670], [DMD-740], [DMD-750], [DMD-910], [DMD-1020], [DMD-1030], [DMD-1050], [DMD-1230]; sexuality and dance [DMD-140], [DMD-630], [DMD-690], [DMD-1120], [DMD-1130]; teaching techniques [DMD-590], [DMD-720], [DMD-790], [DMD-950], [DMD-990], [DMD-1000].

Those familiar with the literature of dance will note that most of the popular periodicals on this art form have been omitted. Primarily, only those journals which include scholarly research and book reviews have been presented here, including *Ballet Review* [DMD-130], *Choreography and Dance: An International Journal* [DMD-210], *Dance Magazine* [DMD-270], *Dance Research* [DMD-280], *Dance Research Journal* [DMD-290], *Dance Theatre Journal* [DMD-300], and *Folk Music Journal* [DMD-390]. To locate additional periodicals and their respective articles on dance, see [BDM-080], [BDM-500], [BDM-550], [BDM-580], [BDM-590], and [BDM-620] in the bibliography section of this chapter.

[DMD-010] Adair, Christy. *Women and Dance: Sylphs and Sirens*. London: Macmillan Publishing Co., 1992. Bib. pp. 247-270.

[DMD-020] Adshead, Janet. *Dance, A Multicultural Perspective: Report of the Third Study of Dance Conference, University of Surrey, 5-9*

118

April 1984. 2nd ed. Guildford, Surrey, England: National Resource Centre for Dance, University of Surrey, for Dance Research Unit, 1986. 99 pp. Bibs.

[DMD-030] ------. *Dance History: A Methodology for Study.* London: Dance Books, 1983. Dist. Princeton Book Co., Princeton, N.J. Bib. pp. 208-210.

[DMD-040] Akins, Ann Severance. "Dancing in Dixie's Land: Theatrical Dance in New Orleans, 1860-1870." Ph.D. Thesis, Texas Woman's University, 1991. Bib. pp. 356-363.

[DMD-050] Alford, Marcus R., and Marsha Proser Cohen. *Jazz Danceology: Teaching and Choreographing Jazz Dance.* Marietta, Ga.: Dance Press, 1991. 187 pp.

[DMD-060] Allen, Beverly J. *Dance Directory.* Reston, Va.: National Dance Association, 1990. 104 pp. "Programs of professional preparation in colleges, universities, and performing arts schools in the United States and Canada."

[DMD-070] Allenby Jaffe, Nigel. *Folk Dance of Europe.* Kirby Malham: Folk Dance Enterprises, 1990. Bib. pp. 333-336.

[DMD-080] Alter, Judith B. *Dancing and Mixed Media: Modern Dance in Early Twentieth Century Culture.* New Studies in Aesthetics, vol. 17. New York: Peter Lang, 1993. Bib. refs.

[DMD-090] Anderson, Jack. *Ballet and Modern Dance: A Concise History.* 2nd ed. Princeton: Princeton Book Co., 1992. 287 pp. Bib. refs. pp. 235-246.

[DMD-100] *Anthropological Perspectives on Movement.* Body Movement: Perspectives in Research. New York: Arno Press, 1975. Bibs.

[DMD-110] Armstrong, Lucile, and Diki Gleeson. *A Window on Folk Dance: With Special Reference to the Dances of the Iberian Peninsula.* Huddersfield, West Yorkshire, England: Springfield Books, 1985. Bib. pp. 126-128.

[DMD-120] Austin, Richard. *Ballet and Dance.* London: Macdonald Educational, 1979. Bib. p. 46.

[DMD-130] *Ballet Review.* New York: Dance Research Foundation, Inc., 1965-. Quarterly.

[DMD-140] Banerji, Projesh. *Erotica in Indian Dance.* New Delhi: Cosmo Publications, 1983. 171 pp. Bib. refs.

[DMD-150] Bethe, Monica. *Dance in the No Theater.* 3 vol. Cornell University East Asia Papers, no. 29. Ithaca: China-Japan Program, Cornell University, 1982. Bib., vol. 3, pp. 214-226.

[DMD-160] Bnerji, Sures Chandra. *A Companion to Indian Music and Dance: [Spanning a Period of Over Three Thousand Years and Based Mainly on Sanskrit Sources].* Raga Nrtya Series, no. 4. Delhi: Sri Satguru Publications, 1990. Bib. refs. pp. 250-272.

[DMD-170] Broome, P[aul] J., and Clay Tucker. *The Other Music City: The Dance Bands and Jazz Musicians of Nashville 1920 to 1970.* Nashville, Tenn.: American Press Printing Co., 1990. Bib. refs.

[DMD-180] Buonaventura, Wendy. *Belly Dancing: The Serpent and the Sphinx.* London: Virago, 1983. Bib. pp. 166-167.

[DMD-190] Cass, Joan. *Dancing Through History.* Englewood Cliffs, N.J.: Prentice-Hall Press, 1993. 386 pp. Bib. refs.

[DMD-200] Cauthen, Joyce H. *With Fiddle and Well-Rosined Bow: Old-Time Fiddling in Alabama.* Tuscaloosa: University of Alabama Press, 1989. Bib. pp. 233-269.

[DMD-210] *Choreography and Dance: An International Journal.* London: Harwood Academic Publications, 1988-. Irregular.

[DMD-220] Clark, James M. *The Dance of Death: In the Middle Ages and the Renaissance.* Glasgow: Jackson, Son, and Co., 1950.

[DMD-230] Clarke, Mary. *Dancer: Men in Dance.* London: British Broadcasting Corp., 1984. 207 pp.

[DMD-240] Cooke, Peter. *The Fiddle Tradition of the Shetland Isles.* Cambridge; New York: Cambridge University Press, 1986. Bib. pp. 151-153.

[DMD-250] Copley-Graves, Lynn. *Figure Skating History: The Evolution of Dance on Ice.* Columbus, Ohio: Platoro Press, 1992. Bib. refs. pp. 376-377.

[DMD-260] Cowan, Jane K. *Dance and the Body Politic in Northern Greece.* Princeton: Princeton University Press, 1990. Bib. refs. pp. 235-244.

[DMD-270] *Dance Magazine.* New York: Dance Magazine, Inc., 1926-. Monthly.

[DMD-280] *Dance Research.* Oxford: Oxford University Press, 1983-. Semi-annual.

[DMD-290] *Dance Research Journal*. New York: Congress on Research in Dance, Dance and Dance Education Department, 1967-. Semi-annual.

[DMD-300] *Dance Theatre Journal: The Magazine of Dance and Related Arts*. London: Laban Centre for Movement and Dance, 1983-. Quarterly.

[DMD-310] Davies, Sandra. *The Music of India: Musical Forms, Instruments, Dance, and Folk Traditions*. Vancouver: Pacific Educational Press, 1993. Bib. refs.

[DMD-320] Dearling, Jay. *Technique of Theatre Dance: For Artists, Graduates and Professionals*. New ed. [Brighton]: [IDTA (Sales) Ltd.], 1991. 142 pp.

[DMD-330] Delamater, Jerome. *Dance in the Hollywood Musical*. Studies in Photography and Cinematography, no. 4. Ann Arbor: UMI Research Press, 1992. Bib. pp. 295-301.

[DMD-340] Dhanifu, Alicia. *Bellydance Tips [and] Secrets*. Special Workshop Edition. Pasadena, Calif.: Danifu Productions, 1983. 42 pp.

[DMD-350] Dodd, Craig. *Ballet and Modern Dance*. Oxford: Phaidon Press, 1980. Bib. p. 191.

[DMD-360] Duggan, Anne Schley, Jeanette Schlottmann, and Abbie Rutledge. *Folk Dance Library*. 5 vols. New York: A. S. Barnes, [1948]. Bibs. in each vol.

[DMD-370] Duke, Jerry. "Clog Dance of the Appalachian Mountain Region of the United States of America." Ph.D. Thesis, Texas Woman's University, 1982. Bib. pp. 105-108.

[DMD-380] Empire State Institute for the Performing Arts. *Dance, Resource Workbook*. Albany: Empire State Institute for the Performing Arts, 1982. Bib. pp. 38-39.

[DMD-390] *Folk Music Journal*. London: English Folk Dance and Song Society, 1965-. Annual. Continuation of *The Journal of English Folk Dance*, 1914-1964.

[DMD-400] Foster, Susan Leigh. *Reading Dancing: Bodies and Subjects in Contemporary American Dance*. Berkeley: University of California Press, 1986. xxi, 307 pp. Bib. pp. 263-285.

[DMD-410] Franko, Mark. *Dance as Text: Ideologies of the Baroque Body*.

RES Monographs on Anthropology and Aesthetics. New York: Cambridge University Press, 1993. Bib. refs.

[DMD-420] Frisbie, Charlotte Johnson. *Music and Dance Research of Southwestern United States Indians: Past Trends, Present Activities, and Suggestions for Future Research.* Detroit Studies in Music Bibliography, no. 36. Detroit: Information Coordinators, 1977. Bib. pp. 67-109.

[DMD-430] Garden, John. *A Country Dance Companion: 180 Dances and 120 Tunes.* Civic Square, A.C.T.: Monaro Folk Music Society, 1991. 121 pp. Bib. refs.

[DMD-440] Gilbert, Anne Green. *Creative Dance for all Ages: A Conceptual Approach.* Reston, Va.: American Alliance for Health, Physical Education, Recreation, and Dance, 1992. Bib. pp. 383-386.

[DMD-450] Goss, Gordon, ed. *National Square Dance Directory.* Jackson, Miss.: [The Directory], 1990-. 231 pp. Annual.

[DMD-460] Guillard, Yves, and Roderyk Lange. *Early Scottish Reel Setting Steps and the Influence of the French Quadrille.* Dance Studies, vol. 13. St. Peter, Jersey: Centre for Dance Studies, 1990. 115 pp. Bib. pp. 89-93.

[DMD-470] Gula, Denise, and Terrence J. Gula. *Dance in Gymnastics: A Guide for Coaches and Gymnasts.* Boston: Allyn and Bacon, 1986. 196 pp.

[DMD-480] Hanstein, Penelope. "On the Nature of Art Making in Dance: An Artistic Process Skills Model for the Teaching of Choreography." Ph.D. Thesis, Ohio State University, 1986. Bib. pp. 196-203.

[DMD-490] Haselbach, Barbara, Hilde Zemann, and Margaret Murray. *Improvisation, Dance, Movement.* St. Louis: Magnamusic-Baton, 1981. Bib. p. 125.

[DMD-500] Haskins, James. *Black Dance in America: A History Through its People.* New York: Harper Collins, 1990. Bib. pp. 216-217. Videography, pp. 218-222.

[DMD-510] Hayes, Elizabeth R. *Dance Composition and Production.* 2nd ed. Pennington, N.J.: Princeton Book Co., 1993. Bib. refs.

[DMD-520] Hinman, Mary Wood. *Gymnastic and Folk Dancing.* 5 vols. New York: A. S. Barnes, 1930-1932.

[DMD-530] Hobin, Tina. *Belly Dancing.* London: Duckworth, 1982. 96 pp.

122

[DMD-540] Institute of Contemporary Art. *Art and Dance: Images of the Modern Dialogue, 1890-1980.* Boston: Institute of Contemporary Art, 1982. 119 pp. Bibs.

[DMD-550] Kaposi, Edit, and Erno Pesovar, eds. *The Art of Dance in Hungary.* Trans. *Magyar Tancmuveszet.* [Budapest]: Corvina Kiado, 1985. 249 pp.

[DMD-560] Kelly, Bill, and Dolph Le Moult. *Street Dance.* New York: Charter Books, pub. Berkley, 1987. 280 pp.

[DMD-570] Kendall, Elizabeth. *Where She Danced: The Birth of American Art-Dance.* New York: Alfred A. Knopf, 1979. Reprint. Berkeley: University of California Press, 1984. Bib. pp. 219-221.

[DMD-580] Kennedy, Douglas Neil. *England's Dances: Folk-Dancing To-Day and Yesterday.* London: Bell, 1949. Bib. pp. 154-155.

[DMD-590] Kent Harrison, Mary. *How to Dress Dancers: Costuming Techniques for Dance.* A Dance Horizons Book. Princeton: Princeton Book Co., 1988. 144 pp.

[DMD-600] Khokar, Mohan. *Traditions of Indian Classical Dance.* 2nd ed. London: Books from India, 1984. Bib. pp. 238-239.

[DMD-610] Kidson, Frank, and Mary Neal. *English Folk-Song and Dance.* 1915. Reprint. Totowa, N.J.: Rowman and Littlefield, 1972. Bib. pp. 86-94, 173-176.

[DMD-620] Kirstein, Lincoln. *Dance: A Short History of Classic Theatrical Dancing.* Princeton: Princeton Book Co., 1987. 398 pp. Bib. pp. 359-364.

[DMD-630] Kleinman, Seymour. *Sexuality and the Dance.* Reston, Va.: American Alliance for Health, Physical Education, Recreation and Dance, 1980. 26 pp.

[DMD-640] Knoppers, Yonina. *Street Dance: Body-Popping and Breakdancing.* London: Zomba Books, 1984. 96 pp.

[DMD-650] Koegler, Horst. *The Concise Oxford Dictionary of Ballet.* 2nd ed. New York: Oxford University Press, 1982.

[DMD-660] Kowalska, Jolanta. *Tree of Life Dance: Cultural Universals in Motion.* Library of Polish Ethnography, no. 46. Warsaw: Institute of the History of Material Culture, Polish Academy of Sciences, 1991. Bib. refs. pp. 181-207.

[DMD-670] Kurath, Gertrude Prokosch. *Half a Century of Dance Research:*

Essays. Flagstaff, Ariz.: Cross Cultural Dance Resources, 1986. 436 pp. Bibs. English and Spanish.

[DMD-680] Lawler, Lillian Beatrice. *The Dance in Ancient Greece*. Middletown, Conn.: Wesleyan University Press, 1965. 160 pp. Bib. refs.

[DMD-690] Lazarus, J. A. Abbiechild. "Contemporary Dance and a Feminist Aesthetic." Ph.D. Thesis, Texas Woman's University, 1987. Bib. pp. 186-201.

[DMD-700] Lebwa. *A Belly Dancer's Slim-Down and Shape-Up Secrets*. West Nyack, N.Y.: Parker Publishing Co., 1979. 336 pp.

[DMD-710] Lundahl, Vera. "Compositional Form in Modern Dance and Modern Art." Ph.D. Thesis, Texas Woman's University, 1983. Bib. pp. 193-200.

[DMD-720] McFee, Graham. *The Concept of Dance Education*. London: New York: Routledge, 1993. Bib. refs.

[DMD-730] Mara, Thalia. *The Language of Ballet: A Dictionary*. Princeton: Princeton Book Co., 1987.

[DMD-740] Mather, Betty Bang, and Dean M. Karns. *Dance Rhythms of the French Baroque: A Handbook for Performance*. Bloomington: Indiana University Press, 1987. Bib. pp. 311-322.

[DMD-750] Maynard, Susan Watkins. "Dance in the Arts of the Middle Ages." Ph.D. Thesis, Florida State University, 1992. 273 pp. Bib. refs.

[DMD-760] Mayo, Sandra Marie. *Introduction to Fine Arts: Dance, Music, Theatre, and Visual Art*. 2nd ed. Needham Heights, Mass.: Ginn Press, 1991. Bib. refs. p. 331.

[DMD-770] Mettler-Meibom, Barbara E. *Materials of Dance: As A Creative Art Activity*. Rev. ed. [Tucson, Ariz.]: Mettler Studios, 1979. 418 pp.

[DMD-780] Miettinen, Jukka O. *Classical Dance and Theatre in South-East Asia*. Singapore; New York: Oxford University Press, 1992. Bib. refs. pp. 169-171.

[DMD-790] Minton, Sandra Cerny. *Modern Dance, Body and Mind: A Basic Approach for Beginners*. Englewood, Colo.: Morton, 1991. 123 pp. Bib. refs.

[DMD-800] Osumare, Halifu, and Julinda Lewis-Ferguson. *Black Choreographers Moving: A National Dialogue*. Berkeley: Expansion

Arts Services, 1991. Bib. refs. pp. 105-106.

[DMD-810] Overby, Lynnette Y., and James Harry Humphrey, eds. *Dance: Current Selected Research: Volume 2.* New York: AMS Press, 1990. 296 pp. Bibs.

[DMD-820] Partsch-Gergsohn, Isa. *Modern Dance in Germany and the United States: Cross Currents and Influences.* Choreography and Dance STudies, vol. 4. Chur; Philadelphia: Harwood Academic Publishers, 1993.

[DMD-830] Pask, Edward H. *Enter the Colonies Dancing: A History of Dance in Australia, 1835-1940.* Melbourne; New York: Oxford University Press, 1979. Bib. pp. 174-175.

[DMD-840] Raffe, Walter George, and M. E. Purdon. *Dictionary of the Dance.* New York: A. S. Barnes, [1965]. Bib. pp. 559-565.

[DMD-850] Raphtes, Alkes. *The World of Greek Dance.* Trans. *Ho Kosmos tou Hellenikou chorou.* Athens: Finedawn Publishers, 1987. Bib. pp. 231-238. Discography pp. 211-227.

[DMD-860] Redfern, H[ildred] B[etty]. *Dance, Art, and Aesthetics.* London: Dance Books, 1983. Reprint. London: Dance Books, 1988. Bib. pp. 120-124.

[DMD-870] Robertson, Allen, and Donald Hutera. *The Dance Handbook.* N.p.: Longman Group UK Ltd., 1988. Reprint. Boston: G. K. Hall, 1990. 278 pp. Bib. refs.

[DMD-880] Roe, Cathy. *Jazz Dance Curriculum Guide.* Sante Fe: Cathy Roe Productions, 1993. 211 pp.

[DMD-890] Rogers, Peter. *Country Dance Index: An Index to Sources of English and American Country Dances.* 3rd ed. Berea, Ky.: Christmas Country Dance School; New York: Country Dance and Song Society of America, 1986. 151 pp. Bib. refs. pp. xii-xx. Discography pp. iv-xi.

[DMD-900] Rowe, Patricia A., and Ernestine Stodelle. *Dance Research Collage: A Variety of Subjects Embracing the Abstract and the Practical.* New York: CORD, 1979. 286 pp. Bibs.

[DMD-910] Royce, Anya Peterson. *The Anthropology of Dance.* Bloomington: Indiana University Press, 1977. 256 pp. Bib.

[DMD-920] Sachs, Curt. *World History of the Dance.* Trans. Bessie Schonberg. New York: W. W. Norton and Co., 1937. 469 pp. Bib. refs.

[DMD-930] Sasportes, Jose, and Antonio Pinto Ribeiro. *History of Dance [Portugal]*. Lisbon: Comissariado para a Europalia 91-Portugal: Imprensa Nacional-Casa da Moeda, 1991. Bib. refs. p. 141.

[DMD-940] Senoga-Zake, George W. *Folk Music of Kenya*. Nairobi, Kenya: Uzima Press, 1986. 185 pp.

[DMD-950] Shafranski, Paulette. *Modern Dance: Twelve Creative Problem-Solving Experiments*. Glenview, Ill.: Scott, Foresman, 1985. Bib. pp. 115-118.

[DMD-960] Shaw, Lloyd, Dorothy Shaw, and Milly Riley. *Western Square Dancing: From the Syllabi of the Lloyd Shaw Dance Fellowship, 1955-1970*. Jacksonville, Ill.: M. Riley, 1989. Bib. refs. pp. 311-315.

[DMD-970] Sheets-Johnstone, Maxine, ed. *Illuminating Dance: Philosophical Explorations*. Lewisburg: Bucknell University Press; London: Associated University Presses, 1984 202 pp. Bibs.

[DMD-980] ------. *The Phenomenology of Dance*. 2nd ed. London: Dance Books, 1979. Bib. pp. 153-154.

[DMD-990] Sherbon, Elizabeth, Toni Itravaia, and Joshua Missal. *On the Count of One: Modern Dance Methods*. 3rd ed. Palo Alto, Calif.: Mayfield Publishing Co., 1982. Bib. pp. 262-271, 274. Discography pp. 271-273.

[DMD-1000] Smith-Autard, Jacqueline M[ary]. *Dance Composition: A Practical Guide for Teachers*. 2nd ed. London: A & C Black, 1992. Bib. p. 158.

[DMD-1010] Snider, Marcia Eastman. *Folk Dance: Handbook*. Physical Education Activity Handbook Series. Vancouver, B.C.: Hancock House Publishers, 1980. Bib. p. 73.

[DMD-1020] Sorell, Walter, ed. *The Dance Has Many Faces*. 3rd rev. ed. Chicago, Ill.: A Capella Books, 1992. Bib. refs. pp. 257-263.

[DMD-1030] ------. *The Dance Through the Ages*. New York: Grosset and Dunlap, [1967]. Bib. p. 297.

[DMD-1040] Speck, Frank Gouldsmith, Leonard Broom, and Will West Long. *Cherokee Dance and Drama*. The Civilization of the American Indian Series, vol. 163. Norman: University of Oklahoma Press, 1983. Bib. p. 105.

[DMD-1050] Steiner, Rudolf. *Eurythmy as Visible Speech: Fifteen Lectures Given at Dornach, Switzerland, 24th June to 12th July, 1924*.

Rev. ed. Trans. Vera Compton-Burnett and Judy Compton-Burnett. Trans. *Eurythmie als sichtbare Sprache.* 2nd ed. London: Anthroposophical, 1931. Reprint. London: Steiner, 1984. 287 pp.

[DMD-1060] Steinman, Louise. *The Knowing Body: Elements of Contemporary Performance and Dance.* Boston: Shambhala, 1986. Dist. Random House, New York. Bib. pp. 149-157.

[DMD-1070] *Studies in Dance History.* Pennington, N.J.: Society of Dance History Scholars, 1989. Bi-annual.

[DMD-1080] Symposium on Improvisation in the Performing Arts. *Improvisation in the Performing Arts: A Report of the Symposium on Improvisation in the Performing Arts, Held at the East-West Center, July 10-23, 1983.* Ed. Ricardo D. Trimillos and William Feltz. Honolulu, Hawaii: Institute of Culture and Communication, East-West Center, 1985. 191 pp. Bibs.

[DMD-1090] Taplin, Diana Theodores, ed. *Dance Spectrum: Critical and Philosophical Enquiry.* Monographs in Leisure and Cultural Development, Monograph 2. [Waterloo]: Otium Publications; Dublin: Parsons Press, 1982. 140 pp. Bibs.

[DMD-1100] Terry, Walter, Jack Vartoogian, and Linda Vartoogian. *How to Look at Dance.* New York: Morrow, 1982. Bib. p. 211.

[DMD-1110] Thomas, Carolyn E., ed. *Aesthetics and Dance.* Reston, Va.: National Dance Association, 1980. 30 pp. Bib. refs.

[DMD-1120] Thomas, Helen. *Dance, Gender, and Culture.* New York: St. Martin's Press, 1993.

[DMD-1130] Tomko, Linda Johnston. "Women, Artistic Dance Practices, and Social Change in the United States, 1890-1920." Ph.D. Thesis, UCLA, 1991. Bib. pp. 322-346.

[DMD-1140] Turner, Margery J. *New Dance: Approaches to Nonliteral Choreography.* 1971. Reprint. Pitt Paperback, no. 112. [Pittsburgh]: University of Pittsburgh Press, 1979. Bib. pp. 107-113.

[DMD-1150] Van Gyn, Geraldine, and Donna Van Sant O'Neill. *Jazz Dance.* Champaign, Ill.: Human Kinetics, 1987. Bib. p. 128.

[DMD-1160] Vatsyayan, Kapila. *Dance in Indian Painting.* Atlantic Highlands, N.J.: Humanities Press, 1982. Bib. pp. 193-200.

[DMD-1170] ------. *Traditions of Indian Folk Dance.* 2nd ed. New Delhi: Clarion Books with Hind Pocket Books, 1987. Bib. pp. 384-

388.

[DMD-1180] Whyte, Florence. *The Dance of Death in Spain and Catalonia*. Ph.D. Thesis, Bryn Mawr College, 1931. Reprint. Baltimore: Waverly Press, 1983. Bib. pp. 148-162.

[DMD-1190] Wilson, Serena. *The Belly Dance Book: The Serena Technique for Learning Belly Dancing*. Rev. ed. New York: McGraw-Hill, 1983. 236 pp.

[DMD-1200] Yunesuko Hanguk Wiwonhoe. *Korean Dance, Theater, and Cinema*. Korean Art, no. 4. Seoul, Korea: Si-sa-yong-o-sa Publishers; Arch Cape, Oreg.: Pace International Research, 1983. 205 pp. Bibs.

[DMD-1210] Zerebecky, Bohdan. *Folk Dances of Bukovyna*. Saskatoon, Saskatchewan, Canada: Ukrainian Canadian Committee, Saskatchewan Provincial Council, 1989. 85 pp. Bib. refs.

[DMD-1220] ------. *Ukrainian Dance Resource Booklet*. 2nd rev. ed. 4 vols. Saskatoon, Saskatchewan, Canada: Ukrainian Canadian Committee, Saskatchewan Provincial Council, 1986. Bib. refs.

[DMD-1230] Zimmer, Elizabeth, Mindy N. Levine. *Dance: A Social Study*. 4 vols. New York: Arts Connection; Albany, N.Y.: University of the State of New York, State Education Department, 1984. Bibs.

KEY WORKS ON DANCE AND RELIGION

Of all the art forms to experience a resurgence in the life of the church, dance is in many ways the most surprising. For several centuries the Puritan distrust of dance has kept many churches from acknowledging its potential for use in worship. During the past two decades a revolution of opinions about dance has taken place in churches ranging from the liturgical to the charismatic. As a result, the church body as a whole is renewing its understanding of dance in biblical times and is recognizing the value of involving the whole body in worship. The following section offers a reasonably comprehensive list of works published since 1960 and treating the religious use of dance, although some works date back to 1792 and 1859.

Since many churches during the past several centuries have disapproved of dance in any context, let alone in church, one needs to be familiar with the basic concerns of these protesting groups. For resources treating various arguments against social dancing, see items [DMR-010], [DMR-200], [DMR-260], [DMR-640], [DMR-680], and [DMR-860]. To place dance and the church in a historical framework, consult the following sources: John Gordon Davies' *Liturgical Dance: An Historical, Theological, and Practical Handbook* [DMR-280], G. R. S. Mead's *The Sacred Dance in Christendom* [DMR-580], and Margaret Fisk Taylor's *A Time to Dance: Symbolic Movement in Worship* [DMR-800]. Since Christian dance must often be defined in comparison with, or contrast to, dance in other cultures, several sources have been listed here treating non-Christian forms of religious dance, including [DMR-110], [DMR-210], [DMR-290], [DMR-360], [DMR-380], [DMR-440], [DMR-530], [DMR-550], [DMR-560], [DMR-590], [DMR-620], [DMR-770], and [DMR-870].

Christian or liturgical dance is primarily being promoted by two organizations, the Sacred Dance Guild, whose many resources are listed in [DMR-020], and the Sharing Company, whose numerous publications on dance are typically edited or written by Doug Adams. For individuals or churches concerned about the biblical basis for dance, the following works will be especially useful: [DMR-040], [DMR-050], [DMR-100], [DMR-250], [DMR-400], [DMR-410], [DMR-460], [DMR-510], [DMR-690], [DMR-740], and [DMR-790]. Note especially Doug Adams' and Judith Rock's *Biblical Criteria in Modern Dance: Modern Dance as a Prophetic Form* [DMR-100] as a profitable beginning point in such studies.

One of the clearest signs that dance is being recognized as a valid mode for celebrating the presence of God is the growth of studies treating the use of dance in worship, for congregational involvement as well as that of dance ensembles. The terms used for dance in church are usually carefully chosen disguises, such as interpretive movement or liturgical movement or rhythmic praise, but the presence of dance in church is growing stronger and is gradually becoming meaningful to many congregations. The following list contains a wide variety of texts exploring the role of dance in worship: [DMR-030], [DMR-060], [DMR-070], [DMR-080], [DMR-140], [DMR-150], [DMR-160], [DMR-170], [DMR-220], [DMR-230], [DMR-240], [DMR-300], [DMR-310], [DMR-320], [DMR-330], [DMR-340], [DMR-350], [DMR-370], [DMR-

390], [DMR-400], [DMR-410], [DMR-420], [DMR-430], [DMR-470], [DMR-480], [DMR-490], [DMR-500], [DMR-510], [DMR-520], [DMR-570], [DMR-580], [DMR-610], [DMR-650], [DMR-700], [DMR-710], [DMR-740], [DMR-750], [DMR-760], [DMR-780], [DMR-790], [DMR-820], [DMR-840], [DMR-850].

As this section indicates, dance is rapidly emerging as a significant topic in religious studies. For a thoughtful study of this subject by two of the best known authorities on Christianity and dance, consult Doug Adams' and Diane Apostolos-Cappadona's *Dance as Religious Studies* [DMR-090]. For additional resources on current trends in religious dance, see the *Sacred Dance Guild Journal* [DMR-720] and pertinent works cited in Kay Troxell's recent bibliography, *Resources in Sacred Dance* [DMR-020], also published by the Sacred Dance Guild.

Special Bibliographies

[DMR-010] Magriel, Paul David. *Dancing and Morality: A Bibliography of American Tracts.* In *Bulletin of Bibliography and Dramatic Index*, vol. 17, no. 8 (May-Aug. 1942), pp. 161-162. Boston: F. W. Faxon Co., 1942.

[DMR-020] Troxell, Kay, ed., and Sacred Dance Guild. *Resources in Sacred Dance: Annotated Bibliography from Christian and Jewish Traditions: Books, Booklets and Pamphlets, Articles and Serial Publications, Media, and Reference Sources.* Rev. ed. Peterborough, N.Y.: Sacred Dance Guild, 1991. 55 pp.

[DMR-030] Wolbers, Mary Jane, comp. *Resources in Sacred Dance: A List of Books, Periodical Literature, Unpublished Manuscripts, and Other Suggested Resources in Sacred Dance, Its Use in Worship and Religious Education.* East Stroudsburg, Pa.: N.p., 1964. 18 pp. Supplemented annually in the Sacred Dance Guild newsletter.

Key Works

[DMR-040] Adams, Doug, ed. *The Bible in Dance: Papers Presented at the International Seminar on the Bible in Dance, Jerusalem, August, 1979.* Tel Aviv: Israeli Center of the International Theatre Institute, 1979. c. 350 pp. Bibs.

130

[DMR-050] ------. *Changing Biblical Imagery and Artistic Identity in Twentieth Century Liturgical Dance*. Austin: Sharing Co., 1984. Bib. pp. 12-14.

[DMR-060] ------. *Congregational Dancing in Christian Worship*. Rev. ed. Austin: Sharing Co., 1984.

[DMR-070] ------. *Involving the People in Dancing Worship: Historic and Contemporary Patterns*. Austin: Sharing Co., 1975.

[DMR-080] ------. *Sacred Dance with Senior Citizens*. [Austin: Sharing Co.], 1982. Bib. pp. 12-15.

[DMR-090] Adams, Doug, and Diane Apostolos-Cappadona. *Dance as Religious Studies*. New York: Crossroad, 1990. Bib. pp. 213-221.

[DMR-100] Adams, Doug, and Judith Rock. *Biblical Criteria in Modern Dance: Modern Dance as a Prophetic Form*. Austin: Sharing Co., 1979. 15 pp.

[DMR-110] Andrews, Edward D. "The Dance in Shaker Ritual." *Chronicles of the American Dance*. Ed. Paul Magriel. New York: Henry Holt and Co., 1948.

[DMR-120] Backman, Eugene Louis. *Religious Dances in the Christian Church and in Popular Medicine*. Trans. E. Classen. London: Allen and Unwin, 1952. Bib. pp. 336-354.

[DMR-130] Barboza, Francis Peter. *Christianity in Indian Dance Forms*. Delhi: Sri Satguru Publications, 1990. Bib. refs. pp. 221-223.

[DMR-140] Bellamak, Lu. *Dancing Prayers: Simple Ways to Pray and Dance*. Phoenix: Cybury Graphics, 1982. 82 pp.

[DMR-150] ------. *Non-Judgemental Sacred Dance: Simple Ways to Pray Through Dance*. Austin: Sharing Co., 1984.

[DMR-160] Berry, Madeleine. *Know How to Use Dance in Worship*. London: Scripture Union, 1985. 46 pp.

[DMR-170] Blessin, Ann Marie. *Sacred Dance with Physically and Mentally Handicapped*. Austin: Sharing Co., 1982. Bib. p. 42.

[DMR-180] Blogg, Martin [C.]. *Dance and the Christian Faith: Dance, a Form of Knowing*. London: Hodder and Stoughton, 1985. Bib. pp. 274-279.

[DMR-190] ------. *Time to Dance: 12 Practical Dances for the Non-Dance

Specialist in Education, Church and Community. London: Collins, 1984. Bib. p. 72.

[DMR-200] Brooke, John T. *A Little Thing Great, or, The Dance and the Dancing School: Tested, in a Few Plain Sermons.* New York: R. Carter, 1859. 116 pp.

[DMR-210] Buck, Dorothy. *The Dance of Life.* Patterns of World Spirituality Series. New York: Paragon House, 1987. 151 pp.

[DMR-220] Burrelli, Robert J. "Dance and Related Expressions of Worship." Th.M. Thesis, Dallas Theological Seminary, 1990. Bib. pp. 71-75.

[DMR-230] Challingsworth, Nell. *Liturgical Dance Movement: A Practical Guide.* London: Mowbray, 1982. 32 pp.

[DMR-240] Chew, Joella. *Awakening Sacred Dance Through Spirituals and Scripture.* Ed. Doug Adams. Austin: Sharing Co., 1987. 20 pp.

[DMR-250] Congress on Research in Dance. *Dancing into Marriage: Jewish Wedding Dances.* From *Dance Research Journal*, vol. 17, no. 2 (Fall 1985) and vol. 18, no. 1 (Spring 1986). New York: Congress on Research in Dance, 1986. 104 pp.

[DMR-260] Culpepper, John B. *Your Church is Opposed to Dancing, or, The Dance Shown Up.* Louisville: Pickett, 1900. 64 pp.

[DMR-270] Daniels, Marilyn. *The Dance in Christianity: A History of Religious Dance Through the Ages.* New York: Paulist Press, 1981. 88 pp. Bib. refs. (Largely indebted to [DMR-800])

[DMR-280] Davies, J[ohn] G[ordon]. *Liturgical Dance: An Historical, Theological, and Practical Handbook.* London: SCM Press, 1984. Bib. pp. 243-258.

[DMR-290] ------. *A Shaker Dance Service Reconstructed.* [Birmingham]: Institute for the Study of Worship and Religious Architecture, University of Birmingham, 1984. 15 pp.

[DMR-300] ------, ed. *Worship and Dance.* Birmingham: Institute for the Study of Worship and Religious Architecture, 1975.

[DMR-310] Deiss, Lucien, and Gloria Gabriel Weyman. *Dance as Prayer: Excerpted and Revised from Dance for the Lord.* Chicago: World Library Publications, 1979. 65 pp.

[DMR-320] ------. *Liturgical Dance.* Phoenix: North American Liturgy Resources, 1984. 137 pp. Binder with 1 sound cassette.

132

[DMR-330] Deitering, Carolyn. *Actions, Gestures, and Bodily Attitudes*. Saratoga, Calif.: Resource Publications, 1980.

[DMR-340] ------. *The Liturgy as Dance and the Liturgical Dancer*. New York: Crossroad, 1984. Bib. pp. 143-144.

[DMR-350] DeSola, Carla. *The Spirit Moves: A Handbook of Dance and Prayer*. Washington, D.C.: The Liturgical Conference, 1977. Austin: Sharing Co., 1986. 152 pp.

[DMR-360] Dooling, D. M., Paul Jordan-Smith, and Joseph Bruchae. *I Become Part of It: Sacred Dimensions in Native American Life*. New York: Parabola Books, 1989. 291 pp. Bib. refs.

[DMR-370] Edwards, Brian H[erbert]. *Shall we Dance?: Dance and Drama in Worship*. Welwyn: Evangelical, 1984. 153 pp.

[DMR-380] Fallon, Dennis J., and Mary Jane Wolbers. *Religion and Dance*. Focus on Dance, no. 10. Reston, Va.: American Alliance for Health, Physical Education, Recreation, and Dance, 1982. 90 pp. Bib. refs.

[DMR-390] Fisher, Constance. *Dancing Festivals of the Church Year*. Ed. Doug Adams. Austin: Sharing Co., 1986. 120 pp.

[DMR-400] ------. *Dancing the Old Testament*. Ed. Doug Adams. Austin: Sharing Co., 1980.

[DMR-410] Fisher, Constance, and Doug Adams. *Dancing with Early Christians*. Austin: Sharing Co., 1983. Bib. pp. 171-172.

[DMR-420] Fisher, Constance L. *Music and Dance: In the Worship Program of the Church*. Austin: Sharing Co., 1981.

[DMR-430] Gagne, Ronald, Thomas Kane, and Robert VerEecke. *Introducing Dance in Christian Worship*. Washington, D.C.: The Pastoral Press, 1984. 184 pp.

[DMR-440] Gaston, Anne-Marie. *Siva in Dance: Myth and Iconography*. Oxford University South Asian Studies Series. 1982. Reprint. Delhi; Oxford: Oxford University Press, 1990. Bib. pp. 219-225.

[DMR-450] Grimm, Roberta. *Meditation in Motion*. Buffalo: [R. Grimm], Parkside Printing, 1984. 65 pp.

[DMR-460] Hoeckmann, Olaf. *Dance in Hebrew Poetry*. Austin: Sharing Co., 1987. Bib. p. 22.

[DMR-470] Huff, Joan. *Celebrating Pentecost Through Dance*. Austin: Sharing Co., 1986. Bib. p. 23.

[DMR-480] Jones, Mary. *God's People on the Move: A Manual for Leading Congregations in Dance and Movement.* Broadway, NSW, Australia: Christian Dance Fellowship of Australia, 1988. 339 pp. Bib. refs.

[DMR-490] Knoll, Barbara. *A Time to Dance: An Invitation.* Shippensburg, Pa.: Destiny Image Publishers, 1991. 101 pp.

[DMR-500] Koza-Woodward, Dee. *To Move in Faith: Living the Word Through Dance: A Youth Elect Series Course for Younger and Older Youth.* [New York]: United Church Press, 1983. Bib. pp. 30-32.

[DMR-510] Lamont, Gordon. *Move Yourselves: Exploring the Bible in Movement, Mime and Dance: A Handbook for Churches and Teachers.* Swindon: Bible Society, 1983. Bib. p. 107.

[DMR-520] Lee, Cathy. *Rejoice! Rejoice!: Dance and Mime in Worship.* Blackburn, Victoria, Australia: Dove Communications, 1983. 61 pp.

[DMR-530] Lee, Sun Ock. *Zen Dance: Meditation in Movement.* Seoul, Korea: Seoul International Publishing House, 1985. Bib. p. 108.

[DMR-540] Lewis, Julinda, interviewer. *Dance in Religion and Ritual: Al Carmines, Carla De Sola and Bill Gordh.* Prod. Celia Ipiotis and Jeff Bush. New York: ARC Videodance, 1983. Videocassette, 28 min.

[DMR-550] Lewis, Samuel L. *Spiritual Dance and Walk: An Introduction from the Work of Murshid Samuel L. Lewis.* 2nd rev. ed. 1978. Reprint. San Francisco: Sufi Islamia/Prophecy Publications, 1983. Bib. pp. 61-62. (Sufism, Islamic Mysticism)

[DMR-560] Lonsdale, Steven. *Dance and Ritual Play in Greek Religion.* Baltimore: Johns Hopkins University Press, 1993. Bib. refs.

[DMR-570] MacLeod, Marian B. *Dancing Through Pentecost: Dance Language for Worship from Pentecost to Thanksgiving.* Austin: Sharing Co., 1981. Bib. pp. 33-35.

[DMR-580] Mead, G. R. S. *The Sacred Dance in Christendom.* London: John M. Watkins, 1926.

[DMR-590] Miller, James L. *Measures of Wisdom: The Cosmic Dance in Classical and Christian Antiquity.* Toronto: University of

134

Toronto Press, 1986. 652 pp. Bib. pp. 533-563.

[DMR-600] Neilan, Ruth E. *American Military Movement Relating Sacred Dance*. Austin: Sharing Co., 1985. Bib. p. 16.

[DMR-610] Nelson, Gertrud Mueller. *To Dance with God: Family Ritual and Community Celebration*. New York: Paulist Press, 1986. Bib. pp. 243-245.

[DMR-620] Oesterley, William Oscar Emil. *The Sacred Dance: A Study in Comparative Folklore*. 1923. Reprint. Brooklyn: Dance Horizons, [c. 1968]. 234 pp. Bib. footnotes.

[DMR-630] O'Hanlon, Joseph. *The Dance of the Merrymakers*. N.p.: St. Paul Publications, 1991. 255 pp.

[DMR-640] Olivers, Thomas. *An Answer to Mr. Mark Davis's Thoughts on Dancing: To Which are Added Serious Considerations to Dissuade Christian Parents from Teaching Their Children to Dance*. London: Charles Paramore, 1792. 88 pp.

[DMR-650] Packard, Dane. *The Church Becoming Christ's Body: The Small Church's Manual of Dances for Holy Season*. Ed. Doug Adams. Austin: Sharing Co., 1985. Bib. p. 98.

[DMR-660] Popp, Mary Joan. "A Study of Religious Attitudes as they Related to Modern and Social Dance in the School Curriculum." M.A. Thesis, Ohio State University, 1956. Bib. p. 126.

[DMR-670] Reed, Carlynn. *And We Have Danced: A History of the Sacred Dance Guild: 1958-1978*. Ed. Doug Adams. Austin: Sharing Co., 1979.

[DMR-680] Rice, John R. *What's Wrong with the Dance?* 6th ed. Grand Rapids: Zondervan Press, 1938. 44 pp.

[DMR-690] Roberts, Debbie. *Rejoice: A Biblical Study of the Dance*. Little Rock, Ark.: Revival Press, 1982. 98 pp.

[DMR-700] Rock, Judith. *Theology in the Shape of Dance: Using Dance in Worship and Theological Process*. Austin: Sharing Co., 1977.

[DMR-710] Rock, Judith, and Norman Mealy. *Performer as Priest and Prophet: Restoring the Intuitive in Worship Through Music and Dance*. San Francisco: Harper and Row, 1988. Bib. pp. 133-135.

[DMR-720] *Sacred Dance Guild Journal*. Peterborough, N.H.: Sacred Dance Guild, 1958-. Quarterly.

[DMR-730] Sautter, Cynthia D. *Irish Dance and Spirituality: Relating Folk-dance and Faith*. Austin: Sharing Co., 1986. Bib. pp. 30-31.

[DMR-740] Seaton, Linda K. *Scriptural Choreography: Biblical Dance Forms in Shaping Contemporary Worship*. Austin: Sharing Co., 1979. 21 pp.

[DMR-750] Skidmore, Janet. *Movement in Worship: Communicating the Gospel Through Dance*. Ed. Doug Adams. Austin: Sharing Co., 1987. 15 pp.

[DMR-760] Smagatz-Rawlinson, Diane. *Making the Comparison: A Comparison of Dance in the Concert Versus Worship Setting*. Ed. Doug Adams. Austin: Sharing Co., 1989. 20 pp. Bib. refs.

[DMR-770] Society for the Study of Myth and Tradition. *Sacred Dance*. Parabola, Myth and the Quest for Meaning, vol. 4, no. 2. New York: Society for the Study of Myth and Tradition, 1979. 136 pp.

[DMR-780] Stevenson, Geoffrey. *Steps of Faith: A Practical Introduction to Mime and Dance*. Eastbourne: Kingsway, 1984. Bib. pp. 104-105.

[DMR-790] Taussig, Hal. *New Categories for Dancing the Old Testament*. Austin: Sharing Co., 1981. 27 pp.

[DMR-800] Taylor, Margaret Fisk. *A Time to Dance: Symbolic Movement in Worship*. Austin: Sharing Co., 1980. 192 pp.

[DMR-810] Tucker, JoAnne, and Susan Freeman. *Torah in Motion: Creating Dance Midrash*. Denver: A.R.E. Pub., 1990. Bib. refs. pp. 249-251.

[DMR-820] Verbel, Annyse M. *Dance and Prayer: Meaningful Methods with High School Students and Adults*. Austin: Sharing Co., 1980. Bib. p. 9.

[DMR-830] Wassil, Michael. *Dance of Ecstasy: What you Never Learned in Sunday School*. North Vancouver, British Columbia: Alpha O Press, 1991. Bib. pp. 235-238.

[DMR-840] Winton-Henry, Cynthia. *Dancing God's People into the Year 2000: A Critical Look at Dance Performance in the Church*. Ed. Doug Adams. Austin: Sharing Co., 1985. 22 pp.

[DMR-850] ------. *Leaps of Faith: Improvisational Dance in Worship and Education*. Austin: Sharing Co., 1985. 21 pp.

[DMR-860] Witty, Robert Gee. *Should a Christian Dance?* Orlando, Fla.:

Christ for the World Publishers, 1900. 16 pp.

[DMR-870]   Woisen, Maria-Gabriele. *Sacred Dance: Encounter with the Gods*. Art and Imagination Series. London: Thames and Hudson, 1974. 128 pp.

[DMR-880]   Yates, Martha C. *Financing a Sacred Dance Choir*. [Austin: Sharing Co.], 1981. 55 pp. Bib. refs.

KEY WORKS ON MIME AND CLOWNING

Although mime and clowning have ancient roots, their flowering in the life of the church has been sporadic and belated since the middle ages when morality plays often involved holy fools or sundry forms of pantomime for comic effects. In the twentieth century when comedy has emerged as the most viable medium for conveying weighty truths to a secular audience, mime and clowning have taken on new roles as vehicles for evangelism. Furthermore, the growing role of humor in western church traditions has opened several avenues to mime and clowning as an integral part of Christian worship services. Both inside and outside the church, mime and clowning are achieving new stature as art forms. The following list is the product of repeated searches for literature published since 1960 and treating these two modes of the performing arts. Only a few of these works offer extensive bibliographies since serious study of mime and clowning is a fairly recent enterprise in academic circles, suggesting significant opportunities for those looking for fresh topics to research.

For students of mime, nearly all of the books listed below are useful, but only a few contain serious analyses pointing to other studies. The most useful works for researchers are Kay Hamblin's *Mime: A Playbook of Silent Fantasy* [DMC-120], Claude Kipnis' *The Mime Book* [DMC-200], Joan Lawson's *Mime: The Theory and Practice of Expressive Gesture, with a Description of its Historical Development* [DMC-220], Thomas Leabhart's *Modern and Post-Modern Mime* [DMC-230], Maravene Sheppard Loeschke's *All About Mime: Understanding and Performing the Expressive Silence* [DMC-260], Adrian Pecknold's *Mime: The Step Beyond Words, for the Actors of Dance and Drama* [DMC-350], Bari Rolfe's *Mimes on Miming: An Anthology of Writings on the Art of Mime* [DMC-390], Mark V. Rose's *The Actor and His Double: Mime and Movement for the Theatre of Cruelty* [DMC-400], and Anya Peterson Royce's *Movement and Meaning: Creativity and Interpretation in Ballet and Mime* [DMC-410]. In the world of mime the most prominent figure in the twentieth century is Marcel Marceau, whose insights and work are featured along with that of several other cohorts in Jean Dorcy's book, *The Mime* [DMC-030]. Marceau's work is also analyzed in Ben Martin's *Marcel Marceau: Master of Mime* [DMC-280]. For practical studies of mime as used in church, see Gordon Lamont's *Move Yourselves: Exploring the Bible in Movement, Mime and Dance: A Handbook for Churches and Teachers* [DMC-210] Geoffrey Stevenson's *Steps of Faith: A Practical Introduction to Mime and Dance* [DMC-450], and Susan Kelly Toomey's *Mime Ministry: An Illustrated, Easy-to-Follow Guidebook for Organizing, Programming, and Training a Troupe of Christian Mimes* [DMC-500].

Since books treating clowning typically focus on technical aspects of performance and rarely offer bibliographies for further study, few qualifying works could be located for this section. For those studying clowning as an art form, the following texts will be useful for research: Bruce Fife's *Creative Clowning* [DMC-070], David Ginn's *Clown Magic* [DMC-090], Marvin L. Hardy's *Balloon Magic: Balloon Figure Tying--It's so Easy, It's Magic* [DMC-150], Wes McVicar's *Clown Act Omnibus: Everything you Need to Know about Clowning Plus over 200 Clown Stunts* [DMC-270], William E. Mitchell's *Clowning as Critical Practice: Performance Humor in the South Pacific* [DMC-310], and Jim Roberts's *Complete Guide to Clown Makeup* [DMC-380]. Works treating clowning as related to ministry are becoming increasingly more popular. Those which are especially helpful for research are C. Welton Gaddy's *God's Clowns: Messengers of the Good News* [DMC-080], Mark Liebenow's *Is There Fun After Paul?: A Theology of Clowning* [DMC-240], Janet Litherland's *The Clown Ministry Handbook* [DMC-250], and Stephen P. Perrone's *Send in His Clowns: A Workshop Manual for Training Clown Ministers* [DMC-360]. Other works which are helpful for developing clown ministries are [DMC-130], [DMC-140], [DMC-160], [DMC-170], [DMC-430], [DMC-480], [DMC-490], [DMC-520], and [DMC-540]. One may also find inspiration in Morris West's novel, *The Clowns of God* [DMC-530].

Scholarly periodical literature on mime and clowning is relatively scarce. For a time, the now defunct *Mime Journal* [DMC-300] was most helpful. Now the *Movement Theatre Quarterly* [DMC-320] is the major journal for mime. For additional works on mime and clowning, see suggestions given in the opening section of this chapter.

[DMC-010]   Davis, R. G. *The San Francisco Mime Troupe: The First Ten Years*. Palo Alto, Calif.: Ramparts Press, [1975]. Bib. p. 215.

[DMC-020]   Decroux, Étienne. *Words on Mime*. 2nd ed. Trans. Mark Piper. Trans. *Paroles sur le mime*. Paris: Librairie Theatrale, 1977. Reprint. Claremont, Calif.: Pomona College Theatre Department, 1985. 160 pp.

[DMC-030]   Dorcy, Jean. *The Mime: Essays by Étienne Decroux, Jean-Louis Barrault, and Marcel Marceau*. Trans. Robert Speller, Jr., and Pierre de Fontnouvelle. New York: R. Speller, 1961. xxv, 116 pp.

[DMC-040]   Eastman, Gilbert C., Martin Noretsky, and Sharon Censoplano. *From Mime to Sign*. Silver Spring, Md.: T. J. Publishers, 1989. 183 pp.

[DMC-050]   Enters, Angna. *On Mime*. Hanover, N.H.: Wesleyan University Press, 1965.

[DMC-060]   Felner, Mira. *Apostles of Silence: The Modern French Mimes*. Rutherford, N.J.: Fairleigh Dickinson University Press, 1985. 212 pp.

[DMC-070]   Fife, Bruce. *Creative Clowning*. 2nd ed. Colorado Springs: Piccadilly Books, 1992. Bib. refs. pp. 219-220.

[DMC-080]   Gaddy, C. Welton. *God's Clowns: Messengers of the Good News*. San Francisco: Harper and Row, 1990. Bib. refs. in notes, pp. 131-135.

[DMC-090]   Ginn, David. *Clown Magic*. Colorado Springs: Piccadilly Books, 1993. Bib. refs. pp. 155-159.

[DMC-100]   Gray, Vera, and Rachel Percival. *Music, Movement, and Mime for Children*. New York: Oxford University Press, [1962]. 110 pp. Bibs.

[DMC-110]   *Great Balloon Fun for the Whole Family*. Lincolnwood, Ill.:

Publications International, 1989. 128 pp.

[DMC-120] Hamblin, Kay. *Mime: A Playbook of Silent Fantasy*. Photo. Andrew Fluegelman. Garden City, N.Y.: Dolphin Books, 1978. Bib. pp. 189-190.

[DMC-130] Hansen, Ruth. *The Christian Clown: A Book of Six Christian Clown Sketches in Mime*. Colorado Springs: Contemporary Drama Service, 1985. 28 pp. Bib. refs.

[DMC-140] ------. *The Christian Clown: Production Guide for Six Clown Sketches*. Colorado Springs: Contemporary Drama Service, 1985. Bib. p. 19.

[DMC-150] Hardy, Marvin L. *Balloon Magic: Balloon Figure Tying--It's so Easy, It's Magic*. Wichita, Kansas: Pioneer Balloon Co., 1991. 63 pp.

[DMC-160] Hsu-Flanders, Aaron. *Balloon Hats and Accessories*. Chicago: Contemporary Books, 1989. 136 pp.

[DMC-170] ------. *More Balloon Animals*. Chicago: Contemporary Books, 1990. 133 pp.

[DMC-180] Jetsmark, Torben. *The Dramatic Body: An Introduction to Physical Characterization*. Trans. and ed. Per Brask. Winnipeg: Blizzard Publishing, 1992.

[DMC-190] Keysell, Pat. *Mime Themes and Motifs*. Also entitled *Motives for Mime*. London: Evans Brothers, Ltd., 1975. Reprint. Boston: Plays, Inc., 1980. 80 pp.

[DMC-200] Kipnis, Claude. *The Mime Book*. 2nd ed. Ed. Neil Kleinman. Photo. Edith Chustka. New York: Harper and Row, 1988. Bib. p. 195.

[DMC-210] Lamont, Gordon. *Move Yourselves: Exploring the Bible in Movement, Mime and Dance: A Handbook for Churches and Teachers*. Swindon: Bible Society, 1983. Bib. p. 107.

[DMC-220] Lawson, Joan. *Mime: The Theory and Practice of Expressive Gesture, with a Description of its Historical Development*. Dance Horizons Republication, no. 42. [Brooklyn: Dance Horizons, 1957.] Bib. pp. 161-162.

[DMC-230] Leabhart, Thomas. *Modern and Post-Modern Mime*. New York: St. Martin's Press, 1989. 157 pp. Bib. refs.

[DMC-240] Liebenow, Mark. *Is There Fun After Paul?: A Theology of Clowning*. San Jose, Calif.: Resource Publications, 1987. Bib. pp.

140

87-139.

[DMC-250] Litherland, Janet. *The Clown Ministry Handbook.* 4th ed. Colorado Springs: Meriwether Publishing, 1989. Bib. refs. p. 145.

[DMC-260] Loeschke, Maravene Sheppard. *All About Mime: Understanding and Performing the Expressive Silence.* Englewood Cliffs, N.J.: Prentice-Hall Press, 1982. Bib. pp. 177-178.

[DMC-270] McVicar, Wes. *Clown Act Omnibus: Everything you Need to Know about Clowning Plus over 200 Clown Stunts.* 2nd ed. Colorado Springs: Meriwether Pub., 1987. Bib. pp. 182-184.

[DMC-280] Martin, Ben. *Marcel Marceau: Master of Mime.* New York: Penguin Books, 1979. 158 pp.

[DMC-290] Mayer, David. *Harlequin in his Element: The English Pantomime, 1806-1836.* Cambridge, Mass.: Harvard University Press, 1969. 400 pp.

[DMC-300] *Mime Journal.* Fayetteville, Ark.: Mime School, Department of Speech and Dramatic Art, University of Arkansas, 1974-198?. Semi-annual, irregular. Suspended.

[DMC-310] Mitchell, William E., ed. *Clowning as Critical Practice: Performance Humor in the South Pacific.* ASAO Monograph, no. 13. Pittsburgh: University of Pittsburgh Press, 1992. 227 pp. Bib. refs.

[DMC-320] *Movement Theatre Quarterly.* Portsmouth, N.H.: Nataonal Movement Theatre Association, 1983-. Quarterly. Formerly *Mime News.*

[DMC-330] Nicoll, Allardyce. *Masks, Mimes and Miracles: Studies in the Popular Theatre.* [1931]. Reprint. New York: Cooper Square Publishers, 1963. 407 pp. Bib. footnotes.

[DMC-340] Niedzialkowski, Stefan. *Beyond the Word: The World of Mime.* Troy, Mich.: Momentum Books, 1993.

[DMC-350] Pecknold, Adrian. *Mime: The Step Beyond Words, for the Actors of Dance and Drama.* 2nd ed. Toronto: NC Press, 1989. Bib. p. 144.

[DMC-360] Perrone, Stephen P. *Send in His Clowns: A Workshop Manual for Training Clown Ministers.* [Colorado Springs]: Meriwether Publishing, 1985. Bib. of resources, pp. 63-75.

[DMC-370] Pipkin, Turk. *Be a Clown!: The Complete Guide to Instant Clowning.* New York: Workman Pub., 1989. 112 pp.

[DMC-380] Roberts, Jim. *Complete Guide to Clown Makeup.* Studio City, Calif.: Players Press; Colorado Springs: Piccadilly Books, 1991. Bib. refs. p. 93.

[DMC-390] Rolfe, Bari, ed. *Mimes on Miming: An Anthology of Writings on the Art of Mime.* North Hollywood, Calif.: Panjandrum/Aris Books, [1979]. Bib. pp. 202-232.

[DMC-400] Rose, Mark V. *The Actor and His Double: Mime and Movement for the Theatre of Cruelty.* Chicago: Actor Training and Research Institute Press, 1986. Bib. pp. 52-56.

[DMC-410] Royce, Anya Peterson. *Movement and Meaning: Creativity and Interpretation in Ballet and Mime.* Bloomington: Indiana University Press, 1984. Bib. pp. 214-224.

[DMC-420] Severn, Bill. *Magic Comedy: Tricks, Skits and Clowning.* New York: D. McKay Co., [1968]. 144 pp.

[DMC-430] Shaffer, Floyd. *Clown Ministry Skits for all Seasons.* Loveland, Colo.: Group Books, 1990. 96 pp.

[DMC-440] Shepard, Richmond. *Mime, The Technique of Silence: An Illustrated Workbook.* Illus. E. M. Louise Sandoval. New York: Drama Book Specialists, [1971]. 142 pp.

[DMC-450] Stevenson, Geoffrey. *Steps of Faith: A Practical Introduction to Mime and Dance.* Eastbourne: Kingsway, 1984. Bib. pp. 104-105.

[DMC-460] Stolzenberg, Mark. *Exploring Mime.* Photo. Jim Moore. New York: Sterling Publishing Co., 1991. 128 pp.

[DMC-470] Straub, Cindie, and Matthew Straub. *Mime: Basics for Beginners.* Photo. Jeff Blanton. Boston: Plays, 1984. 152 pp.

[DMC-480] Toomey, Susan Kelly. *Clown Mimes for Christian Ministry: Thematic Skits on a Variety of Christian Ideas.* Colorado Springs: Meriwether Publishing, 1984. 18 pp.

[DMC-490] ------. *Clown Mimes for Christian Ministry II: Thematic Skits on Subjects of Christian Concern.* Colorado Springs: Meriwether Publishing, 1987. 18 pp.

[DMC-500] ------. *Mime Ministry: An Illustrated, Easy-to-Follow Guidebook for Organizing, Programming, and Training a Troupe of Christian Mimes.* Ed. Arthur L. Zapel and Kathy Pijanowski.

142

Colorado Springs: Meriwether Publishing, 1986.   Bib. pp. 163-167.

[DMC-510]   Walker, Kathrine Sorley.   *Eyes on Mime: Language Without Speech*.   New York: John Day Co., [1969].   Bib. pp. 180-181.

[DMC-520]   Watts, Kay, and Paul G. Rigel.   *Bible Story Balloon Sculpture*. Anderson, Ind.:   Warner Press, 1988.   81 pp.

[DMC-530]   West, Morris.   *The Clowns of God*.   New York: William Morrow and Co., Inc., 1981.   370 pp.   Fiction.

[DMC-540]   Wilson, Douglas, and Lori Noelle.   *Balloon Fun: Easy to Follow Step-by-Step Instructions*.   Lincolnwood, Ill.:   Publications International, 1988.

CHAPTER 6

DRAMA AND RHETORIC

BIBLIOGRAPHIES ON DRAMA AND RHETORIC

This chapter presents studies of the spoken arts of drama and rhetoric. Rhetoric, the art of speaking or writing eloquently, is featured here, even though it could be included in several other categories, such as broadcasting in Chapter 7 or literature in Chapter 9. With rare exceptions, effective drama depends on sound rhetoric, and eloquent speech is typically dramatic, thus making these two art forms fitting companions in this chapter. Although preaching is first and foremost a function of worship, preaching too is included here because at times it rises to the level of art. Much of the literature treating preaching, however, has been omitted because of its primarily dogmatic or polemical function. Numerous collections of sermons are available from the early church fathers to the present preachers, but most of these collections illustrate the rhetoric of preaching only indirectly. Furthermore, most books treating techniques of drama or speaking apart from analysis and research have also been left out. This chapter, like the others in this book, includes primarily those works which illustrate the fine arts and offer avenues for continued research in the arts as linked with Christianity.

The bibliographies listed below offer a plethora of options for conducting research in drama and rhetoric. Because the production of drama involves a host of people--including playwrights, directors, set designers, actors, critics, and even audiences--the literature of drama studies can be divided according to any of these categories of participants. Furthermore, drama studies may be divided according to eras of the playwrights, countries or regions of origin, ethnic or cultural origin, genre or style, or content. To begin the research process in drama, consider pertinent categories in the following general bibliographies and guides: [BDR-010], [BDR-070], [BDR-080], [BDR-110], [BDR-160], [BDR-210], [BDR-240], [BDR-570], [BDR-680], [BDR-780], [BDR-820], [BDR-1160]. Furthermore, one can also find many citations to drama and drama criticism in James L. Harner's *Literary Research Guide: A Guide to Reference Sources for the Study of Literatures in English and Related Topics* [BLI-710], listed in Chapter 9 on literature. See Chapter 9 for additional works treating drama as a part of literature studies.

For studies of playwrights, look first at Paul Francis Breed's and Florence M. Sniderman's *Dramatic Criticism Index: A Bibliography of Commentaries on Playwrights from Ibsen to the Avant-Garde* [BDR-140] and *Contemporary Theatre, Film, and Television: A Biographical Guide Featuring Performers, Directors, Writers, Producers, Designers, Managers, Choreographers, Technicians, Composers, Executives, Dancers, and Critics in the United States and Great Britain* [BDR-290], and then see the following bibliographies: [BDR-020], [BDR-040], [BDR-050], [BDR-060], [BDR-190], [BDR-310], [BDR-340], [BDR-420], [BDR-430], [BDR-510], [BDR-580], [BDR-600], [BDR-610], [BDR-620], [BDR-810], [BDR-830], [BDR-840], [BDR-890], [BDR-990]. To find studies of directors, see [BDR-090], and again [BDR-290]. For locating studies of actors, see [BDR-030], [BDR-090], and [BDR-1090 to BDR-1140].

To locate plays in various collections and anthologies, consult the seventh edition of *Ottemiller's Index to Plays in Collections: An Author and Title Index to Plays Appearing in Collections Published Between 1900 and 1985* [BDR-770]. For additional assistance in identifying and locating plays, see the following indexes and bibliographies: [BDR-250], [BDR-260], [BDR-270], [BDR-370], [BDR-470], [BDR-480], [BDR-560], [BDR-590], [BDR-660], [BDR-700], [BDR-720], [BDR-800], [BDR-830], [BDR-840], [BDR-850], [BDR-860], [BDR-870], [BDR-880], [BDR-900], [BDR-930], [BDR-1000],

[BDR-1070], [BDR-1100 to BDR-1140], [BDR-1150]. For bibliographies of criticism on drama, consult the following items: [BDR-010], [BDR-080], [BDR-090], [BDR-100], [BDR-130], [BDR-140], [BDR-170], [BDR-200], [BDR-210], [BDR-240], [BDR-280], [BDR-360], [BDR-410], [BDR-440], [BDR-490], [BDR-620], [BDR-670], [BDR-690], [BDR-790], [BDR-910], [BDR-920]. One can also locate articles on drama in the *Bibliographic Guide to Theatre Arts* [BDR-110] and *Bibliographies and Indexes in the Performing Arts* [BDR-120], as well as in the *MLA Bibliography* [BLI-1250], listed in Chapter 9. To locate studies of the drama critics themselves, see [BDR-290] and [BDR-300]. One will also find below several bibliographies listing studies of puppetry as a form of drama, including [BDR-320] and [BDR-330].

For the study of speech, consult [BDR-150], [BDR-710], [BDR-1040], and [BDR-1060]. To find bibliographies and guides for studying preaching, see the specialized bibliographies listed below in the section entitled Key Works on Drama and Rhetoric and Religion.

[BDR-010] Adelman, Irving, and Rita Dworkin. *Modern Drama: A Checklist of Critical Literature on 20th Century Plays*. Metuchen, N.J.: Scarecrow Press, 1967. 370 pp.

[BDR-020] Arata, Esther S. *More Black American Playwrights: A Bibliography*. Metuchen, N.J.: Scarecrow Press, 1978. 335 pp.

[BDR-030] Archer, Stephen M. *American Actors and Actresses: A Guide to Information Sources*. Performing Arts Information Guide Series 8. Detroit: Gale Research, 1983. 710 pp.

[BDR-040] Backscheider, Paula R., ed. *Restoration and Eighteenth-Century Dramatists: First Series*. Dictionary of Literary Biography, vol. 80. Detroit: Gale Research, 1989. 397 pp. Bibs.

[BDR-050] ------. *Restoration and Eighteenth-Century Dramatists: Second Series*. Dictionary of Literary Biography, vol. 84. Detroit: Gale Research, 1989. 456 pp. Bibs.

[BDR-060] ------. *Restoration and Eighteenth-Century Dramatists: Third Series*. Dictionary of Literary Biography, vol. 89. Detroit: Gale Research, 1989. xxi, 396 pp. Bibs.

[BDR-070] Bailey, Claudia Jean. *A Guide to Reference and Bibliography for Theatre Research*. 2nd ed. Columbus: Ohio State University Libraries, Publications Committee, 1983. 149 pp. Anno-

146

tated.

[BDR-080] Baker, Blanch [Merritt]. *Theatre and Allied Arts: A Guide to Books Dealing with the History, Criticism, and Technic of the Drama and Theatre and Related Arts and Crafts.* New York: B. Blom, [1967]. 536 pp.

[BDR-090] Beacham, Walton, ed. *Research Guide to Biography and Criticism: Drama.* Washington, D.C.: Beacham, 1986.

[BDR-100] Berger, Sidney E. *Medieval English Drama: An Annotated Bibliography of Recent Criticism.* Garland Reference Library of the Humanities. Series no. 956, no. 2. New York: Garland Publishing, 1990. xxii, 500 pp.

[BDR-110] *Bibliographic Guide to Theatre Arts, [1987].* New York Public Library, Theatre and Drama Collection. Boston: G. K. Hall, 1988-. Annual. Irregular.

[BDR-120] *Bibliographies and Indexes in the Performing Arts.* Westport, Conn.: Greenwood Press, Inc., 1984-. Irregular.

[BDR-130] Bonin, Jane F. *Prize-Winning American Drama: A Bibliographical and Descriptive Guide.* Metuchen, N.J.: Scarecrow Press, 1973. 234 pp.

[BDR-140] Breed, Paul Francis, and Florence M. Sniderman. *Dramatic Criticism Index: A Bibliography of Commentaries on Playwrights from Ibsen to the Avant-Garde.* Detroit: Gale Research, [1972]. 1,022 pp.

[BDR-150] Brockett, Oscar G[ross], Samuel L. Becker, and Donald C. Bryant. *A Bibliographical Guide to Research in Speech and Dramatic Art.* Chicago: n.p., [1963]. 118 pp.

[BDR-160] *Bulletin of Bibliography.* [Westwood, Mass.: F. W. Faxon Co., 1978-]. Formerly *Bulletin of Bibliography and Dramatic Index.*

[BDR-170] Burwick, Frederick. *Illusion and the Drama: Critical Theory of the Enlightenment and Romantic Era.* University Park: Penn State University Press, 1991. 326 pp.

[BDR-180] Busfield, Roger M., Jr., ed. *Theatre Arts Publications Available in the United States, 1953-1957: A Five Year Bibliography.* [Evanston?, Ill.]: American Educational Theatre Association, [1964]. 188 pp.

[BDR-190] Bzowski, Frances Diodato. *American Women Playwrights, 1900-1930: A Checklist.* Westport, Conn.: Greenwood Press,

1992. xxiii, 420 pp.

[BDR-200] Carpenter, Charles A., comp. *Modern British Drama*. Goldentree Bibliographies in Language and Literature. Arlington Heights: AHM, 1979. 120 pp.

[BDR-210] ------. *Modern Drama Scholarship and Criticism, 1966-1980: An International Bibliography*. Toronto: University of Toronto Press, 1986. 587 pp. [27,300]

[BDR-220] *Catalog of the Theatre and Drama Collections*. Boston: G. K. Hall, 1967. Supplements.

[BDR-230] Cavanagh, John P. *British Theatre: A Bibliography, 1901 to 1985*. Motley Bibliographies, vol. 1. Mottisfont, Hampshire, England: Motley Press, 1989. 510 pp.

[BDR-240] Cheshire, David F. *Theatre: History, Criticism and Reference*. [Hamden, Conn.]: Archon Books, [1967]. 131 pp.

[BDR-250] Chicorel, Marietta. *Chicorel Theater Index to Plays in Collections, Anthologies, Periodicals, and Discs in England*. New York: Chicorel Library Publishing Corp., [1972]. 466 pp.

[BDR-260] ------. *Chicorel Theater Index to Plays in Periodicals*. New York: Chicorel Library Publishing Corp., 1973. 500 pp.

[BDR-270] ------. *Chicorel Theater Index to Plays in Anthologies, Periodicals, Discs, and Tapes*. 2 vols. New York: Chicorel Library Publishing Co., 1970-1971.

[BDR-280] Coleman, Arthur, and Gary R. Tyler. *Drama Criticism*. Vol. 1: *A Checklist of Interpretation Since 1940 of English and American Plays*. Vol. 2: *A Checklist of Interpretation Since 1940 of Classical and Continental Plays*. Denver: A. Swallow, [1966-1971].

[BDR-290] *Contemporary Theatre, Film, and Television: A Biographical Guide Featuring Performers, Directors, Writers, Producers, Designers, Managers, Choreographers, Technicians, Composers, Executives, Dancers, and Critics in the United States and Great Britain*. Detroit: Gale Research, 1984-. Annual. Expanded continuation of *Who's Who in the Theatre*. Detroit: Gale Research, 1912-1981.

[BDR-300] Comtois, M. E., and Lynn F. Miller. *Contemporary American Theater Critics: A Directory and Anthology of Their Works*. Metuchen, N.J.: Scarecrow Press, 1977. 1,017 pp.

[BDR-310] Coven, Brenda. *American Women Dramatists of the Twentieth*

148

Century: A Bibliography. Metuchen, N.J.: Scarecrow Press, 1982. 244 pp.

[BDR-320] Crothers, J. Frances. *The Puppeteer's Library Guide: The Bibliographic Index to the Literature of the World Puppet Theatre: Vol 1: The Historical Background of Puppetry and its Related Fields*. Metuchen, N.J.: Scarecrow Press, 1971. 474 pp.

[BDR-330] ------. *The Puppeteer's Library Guide: The Bibliographic Index to the Literature of the World Puppet Theatre: Vol 2: The Puppet as an Educator*. Metuchen, N.J.: Scarecrow Press, 1983. 366 pp.

[BDR-340] Davis, Gwenn, and Beverly A. Joyce. *Drama by Women to 1900: A Bibliography of American and British Writers*. Toronto: University of Toronto Press, 1992. xxvi, 189 pp.

[BDR-350] Devlin, Joyce. *Women's Scenes and Monologues: An Annotated Bibliography*. Boston: Baker's Plays, 1989. 244 pp.

[BDR-360] *Drama Criticism*. 2 vols. Denver: Swallow Press, 1970.

[BDR-370] Dramatists Play Service. *Complete Catalogue of Plays, [1990-]*. New York: Dramatists Play Service, 1991-. Annual.

[BDR-380] DuBois, William R. *English and American Stage Productions: An Annotated Checklist of Prompt Books, 1800-1900, from the Nisbet-Snyder Drama Collection, Northern Illinois University Libraries*. Boston: G. K. Hall, 1973. 524 pp.

[BDR-390] Dukore, Bernard F., ed. *A Bibliography of Theatre Arts Publications in English, 1963*. [Evanston?, Ill.]: American Educational Theatre Association, [1965].

[BDR-400] Eberstein, Bernd. *A Selective Guide to Chinese Literature 1900-1949*. Leiden; New York: E. J. Brill, 1990. (Drama.)

[BDR-410] Eddleman, Floyd Eugene, ed. *American Drama Criticism: Interpretations, 1890-1977*. Hamden: Shoe String Press, 1979. 488 pp. *Supplement I*. 1984. 255 pp. *Supplement II*. 1989. 269 pp. *Supplement III*. 1992. 436 pp.

[BDR-420] Elfe, Wolfgang D., James Hardin, eds. *Twentieth-Century German Dramatists, 1889-1918*. Dictionary of Literary Biography, vol. 118. Detroit: Gale Research, 1992. 388 pp.

[BDR-430] ------. *Twentieth-Century German Dramatists, 1919-1992*. Dictionary of Literary Biography, vol. 124. Detroit: Gale Research, 1992. 567 pp.

149

[BDR-440] Evans, James E. *Comedy: An Annotated Bibliography of Theory and Criticism*. Metuchen, N.J.: Scarecrow Press, 1987. 419 pp.

[BDR-450] Faxon, Frederick Winthrop, Mary E. Bates, and Anne C. Sutherland. *Cumulated Dramatic Index, 1900-1949: A Cumulation of the F. W. Faxon Company's Dramatic Index*. 2 vols. Boston: G. K. Hall, 1965.

[BDR-460] Ferguson, Carole, and James F. Hoy, ed. *Bibliography of Medieval Drama, 1977-1980*. Emporia State Research Studies, vol. 37, no. 2. Emporia, Kans.: School of Graduate and Professional Studies of Emporia State University, 1988. 53 pp.

[BDR-470] Fletcher, Steve, Norman Jopling, ed. and comp. *The Book of 1000 Plays*. New York: Facts on File, 1989. 352 pp.

[BDR-480] Firkins, Ina Ten Eyck. *Index to Plays, 1800-1926*. 1927. Reprint. New York: AMS Press, 1971. 307 pp. *Supplement*. New York: H. W. Wilson, 1934. 140 pp.

[BDR-490] Fordyce, Rachel. *Caroline Drama: A Bibliographic History of Criticism*. 2nd ed. New York: G. K. Hall; Toronto: Maxwell Macmillan Canada, 1992. 332 pp.

[BDR-500] Forman, Robert J. *Classical Greek and Roman Drama: An Annotated Bibliography*. Pasadena, Calif.: Salem Press, 1989. 239 pp.

[BDR-510] Gavin, Christy. *American Women Playwrights, 1964-1989: A Research Guide and Annotated Bibliography*. Garland Reference Library of the Humanities, vol. 879. New York: Garland Publishing, 1993. 493 pp.

[BDR-520] Gilder, Rosamond. *A Theatre Library: A Bibliography of One Hundred Books Relating to the Theatre*. New York: Theatre Arts, Inc., 1932. 74 pp.

[BDR-530] Harris, Richard H. *Modern Drama in America and England, 1950-1970: A Guide to Information Sources*. American Literature, English Literature, and World Literatures in English: An Information Guide Series 34. Detroit: Gale Research, 1982. 606 pp.

[BDR-540] Hixon, Don L., and Don A. Hennessee. *Nineteenth-Century American Drama: A Finding Guide*. Metuchen, N.J.: Scarecrow Press, 1977. 581 pp.

[BDR-550] Hochman, Stanley, ed. *McGraw-Hill Encyclopedia of World*

150

Drama: An International Reference Work in 5 Volumes. 2nd ed. 5 vols. New York: McGraw-Hill, 1984.

[BDR-560] Ireland, Norma Olin. Index to Full Length Plays 1944-1964. Boston: F. W. Faxon Co., 1965. 296 pp.

[BDR-570] International Bibliography of Theatre [1982-]. New York: Theatre Research Data Center, Brooklyn College, City University of New York, 1985-. Annual.

[BDR-580] Kaye, Phyllis Johnson. American/Soviet Playwrights Directory. Waterford, Conn.: O'Neill Theater Center, 1988. 140 pp.

[BDR-590] Keller, Dean H[oward]. Index to Plays in Periodicals. Rev. ed. Metuchen, N.J.: Scarecrow Press, 1979. 836 pp. Supplement, Index to Plays in Periodicals: 1977-1987. 1990. 391 pp.

[BDR-600] King, Kimball. Twenty Modern British Playwrights: A Bibliography, 1956-1976. Garland Reference Library of the Humanities, no. 98. New York: Garland Publishing, 1977. 289 pp.

[BDR-610] Kirkpatrick, D. L., and J. Vinson, eds. Contemporary Dramatists. 4th ed. Chicago: St. James Press, 1988. 785 pp.

[BDR-620] Kolin, Philip C., ed. American Playwrights since 1945: A Guide to Scholarship, Criticism, and Performance. New York: Greenwood Press, 1989. 595 pp.

[BDR-630] Larson, Carl F. W. American Regional Theatre History to 1900: A Bibliography. Metuchen, N.J.: Scarecrow Press, 1979. 200 pp.

[BDR-640] Lederer, Herbert. Handbook of East German Drama, 1945-1985. East German Studies, vol. 1. New York: Peter Lang, 1991. 276 pp.

[BDR-650] Leonard, William T. Theatre: Stage to Screen to Television. 2 vols. Metuchen, N.J.: Scarecrow Press, 1981. 1,812 pp.

[BDR-660] Logasa, Hannah, and Winifred Ver Nooy. An Index to One-Act Plays [Since 1900]. Useful Reference Series, no. 30. Boston: F. W. Faxon Co., 1924. 327 pp. Supplement, 1924-1931. 1932. 432 pp. Second Supplement, 1932-1940. 1941. 556 pp. Third Supplement, 1941-1948. 1950. 318 pp. Hannah Logasa, Fourth Supplement, 1948-1957. 1958. 345 pp. Fifth Supplement, 1956-1964. 1966. 260 pp. (For Stage, Radio, and Television.)

[BDR-670] Lopez, Manuel D. Chinese Drama: An Annotated Bibliography of

Commentary, Criticism, and Plays in English Translation. Metuchen, N.J.: Scarecrow Press, 1991. 525 pp.

[BDR-680] Lowe, Claudia Jean. *A Guide to Reference and Bibliography for Theatre Research.* [Columbus]: Office of Educational Services, Ohio State University Libraries, 1971. 137 pp.

[BDR-690] Magill, F. N., ed. *Critical Survey of Drama.* 6 vols. Englewood Cliffs, N.J.: Salem, 1982. Supplement, 1987.

[BDR-700] Mersand, Joseph E. *Index to Plays, with Suggestions for Teaching.* New York: Scarecrow Press, 1966. 114 pp.

[BDR-710] Mitchell, Charity. *Speech Index: An Index to Collections of World Famous Orations and Speeches for Various Occasions.* 4th ed. Supplement 1966-1980. Metuchen, N.J.: Scarecrow Press, 1982. 484 pp.

[BDR-720] NCTE Liaison Committee. *Guide to Play Selection: A Selective Bibliography for Production and Study of Modern Plays.* 3rd ed. Urbana, Ill.: National Council of Teachers of English, 1975.

[BDR-730] New York [City] Public Library. *Catalog of the Theatre and Drama Collections.* 21 vols. Boston: G. K. Hall, 1967.

[BDR-740] Newlyn, Evelyn S. *Cornish Drama of the Middle Ages: A Bibliography.* Cornwall: Institute of Cornish Studies, 1987. 23 pp.

[BDR-750] Norton, Clara Mulliken, et al. *Modern Drama and Opera: Reading Lists on the Works of Various Authors.* 2 vols. Boston: Boston Book Co., 1911-1915.

[BDR-760] *Notable Names in the American Theatre.* Rev. ed. [Ed. Raymond D. McGill.] Clifton: White, 1976. 1,250 pp.

[BDR-770] Ottemiller, John H. *Ottemiller's Index to Plays in Collections: An Author and Title Index to Plays Appearing in Collections Published Between 1900 and 1985.* 7th ed. Rev. Billie M. Connor and Helene G. Mochedlover. Metuchen, N.J.: Scarecrow Press, 1988. 564 pp.

[BDR-780] Packard, William, David Pickering, Charlotte Savidge. *The Facts on File Dictionary of the Theatre.* New York: Facts on File, 1988. 556 pp.

[BDR-790] Palmer, Helen H., and Anne Jane Dyson. *European Drama Criticism, 1900-1975.* 2nd ed. Hamden, Conn.: Shoe String Press, 1977. 653 pp. Supplements, 1970-.

[BDR-800]   Pence, James Harry. *The Magazine and the Drama: An Index.* New York: Dunlap Society, 1896. 190 pp. [4,000].

[BDR-810]   *Performing Arts Biography Master Index.* 2nd ed. Detroit: Gale Research, 1982. Irregular. Formerly *Theatre, Film, and Television Biographies Master Index.*

[BDR-820]   *Performing Arts Resources.* New York: Theatre Library Association, 1974-. Annual.

[BDR-830]   Peterson, Bernard L., Jr. *Contemporary Black American Playwrights and Their Plays: A Biographical Directory and Dramatic Index.* New York: Greenwood Press, 1988. xxvi, 625 pp. Bib. pp. 531-550.

[BDR-840]   ------. *Early Black American Playwrights and Dramatic Writers: A Biographical Directory and Catalog of Plays, Films, and Broadcasting Scripts.* New York: Greenwood Press, 1990. xxviii, 298 pp. Bib. refs.

[BDR-850]   *Plays: A Classified Guide to Play Selection.* Bromley, Kent, England: Stacey Publications, 1951-. Annual.

[BDR-860]   *Play Index.* New York: H. W. Wilson, 1953-. Irregular. Covers since 1949. *Play Index, 1983-1987.* 1988. 522 pp.

[BDR-870]   Richel, Veronica C. *The German Stage, 1767-1890: A Directory of Playwrights and Plays.* New York: Greenwood Press, 1988. 230 pp. Bib. pp. ix-xi.

[BDR-880]   Rossiter, Laurie, David Caron, and Tony Hamill. *Catalogue of Canadian Plays.* Toronto: Playwrights Canada Press, 1991.

[BDR-890]   Roudane, Matthew C., ed. *American Dramatists.* Contemporary Authors: Bibliography Series, Series no. 3. Detroit: Gale Research, 1989. 484 pp. Bibs.

[BDR-900]   Salem, James M. *Drury's Guide to Best Plays.* 4th ed. Metuchen, N.J.: Scarecrow Press, 1987. 488 pp.

[BDR-910]   ------. *A Guide to Critical Reviews.* 4 pts. Metuchen, N.J.: Scarecrow Press, 1971-1984. Pt. 1: *American Drama, 1909-1982.* 3rd ed. 1984. 657 pp. Pt. 2: *The Musical, 1909-1974.* 2nd ed. 1976. 611 pp. Pt. 3: *Foreign Drama, 1909-1977.* 2nd ed. 1979. 420 pp. Pt. 4: *The Screenplay from "The Jazz Singer" to "Dr. Strangelove".* 2 vols. 1971. *Supplement One: 1963-1980.* 1982. 698 pp.

[BDR-920]   Salomon, Brownell. *Critical Analyses in English Renaissance Drama: A Bibliographic Guide.* 3rd ed. Garland Reference

Library of the Humanities, no. 1370. New York: Garland Publishing, 1990. 262 pp.

[BDR-930] Samples, Gordon. *The Drama Scholars' Index to Plays and Film-scripts: A Guide to Plays and Filmscripts in Selected Anthologies, Series, and Periodicals.* 2 vols. Metuchen, N.J.: Scarecrow Press, 1974-1980.

[BDR-940] Skemer, Don C., Mary Y. Osielski, and Laurence Vaschy, comps. *French Theatrical Works, 1650-1803.* Albany, N.Y.: University Libraries, University at Albany, State University of New York, 1990. 45 pp.

[BDR-950] Shaland, Irene. *American Theater and Drama Research: An Annotated Guide to Information Sources, 1945-1990.* Jefferson, N.C.: McFarland, 1991. 157 pp.

[BDR-960] Shuman, R. Baird. *American Drama, 1918-1960: An Annotated Bibliography.* Pasadena, Calif.: Salem Press, 1992. 177 pp.

[BDR-970] ------. *Educational Drama for Today's Schools: With an Annotated Bibliography.* Metuchen, N.J.: Scarecrow Press, 1978. 211 pp.

[BDR-980] Steadman, Susan M. *Dramatic Re-Visions: An Annotated Bibliography of Feminism and Theatre, 1972-1988.* Chicago: American Library Association, 1991. 367 pp.

[BDR-990] Stein, Rita, and Friedhelm Rickert, eds. *Major Modern Dramatists. Vol. I: American, British, Irish, German, Austrian and Swiss Dramatists.* New York: Ungar, 1984. 570 pp.

[BDR-1000] Stilkenboom, Michael. *German Plays in English Translation: A Stock-List of Texts Available in Goethe-Institut Libraries.* 3rd ed. [London]: Goethe-Institut London, 1990. 85 pp.

[BDR-1010] Stratman, Carl Joseph. *Bibliography of Medieval Drama.* 2nd ed. 2 vols. New York: F. Unger Publishing Co., [1972]. 1,035 pp.

[BDR-1020] ------. *Dramatic Play Lists, 1591-1963.* [New York]: New York Public Library, 1966. 44 pp.

[BDR-1030] *Survey and Bibliography of Renaissance Drama, A.* 4 vols. Lincoln: University of Nebraska Press, 1975-1978.

[BDR-1040] Sutton, Roberta Briggs. *Speech Index: An Index to 259 Collections of World Famous Orations and Speeches for Various Occasions.* 4th ed. Metuchen, N.J.: Scarecrow Press, 1966. 947 pp.

154

[BDR-1050] Taylor, Thomas J[ames]. *Restoration Drama: An Annotated Bibliography.* Magill Bibliographies. Pasadena, Calif.: Salem Press, 1989. 156 pp.

[BDR-1060] Thonssen, Lester, Mary Margaret Robb, and Dorothea Thonssen. *Bibliography of Speech Education: Supplement, 1939-1948.* New York: Wilson, 1950. 393 pp.

[BDR-1070] Trefny, Beverly Robin, and Eileen C. Palmer. *Index to Children's Plays in Collections.* 3rd ed. Metuchen, N.J.: Scarecrow Press, 1986. 124 pp.

[BDR-1080] University Microfilms International. *Doctoral Dissertations on Dramatic Arts.* London, Ann Arbor: University Microfilms International, 1977. 46 pp.

[BDR-1090] Wearing, J. P. *American and British Theatrical Biography: A Directory.* Metuchen, N.J.: Scarecrow Press, 1979. 1,012 pp.

[BDR-1100] ------. *The London Stage: 1890-1899: A Calendar of Plays and Players.* 2 vols. Metuchen, N.J.: Scarecrow Press, 1976. 1,242 pp.

[BDR-1110] ------. *The London Stage: 1900-1909: A Calendar of Plays and Players.* 2 vols. Metuchen, N.J.: Scarecrow Press, 1981. 1,202 pp.

[BDR-1120] ------. *The London Stage: 1910-1919: A Calendar of Plays and Players.* 2 vols. Metuchen, N.J.: Scarecrow Press, 1982. 1,370 pp.

[BDR-1130] ------. *The London Stage: 1920-1929: A Calendar of Plays and Players.* 3 vols. Metuchen, N.J.: Scarecrow Press, 1984. 1,808 pp.

[BDR-1140] ------. *The London Stage: 1930-1939: A Calendar of Plays and Players.* 3 vols. Metuchen, N.J.: Scarecrow Press, 1990. 1,999 pp.

[BDR-1150] Wegelin, Oscar. *Early American Plays, 1714-1830.* Ed. John Malone. 1900. Reprint. New York: B. Franklin, [1970]. 113 pp.

[BDR-1160] Whalon, Marion K. *Performing Arts Research: A Guide to Information Sources.* Performing Arts Information Guide Series 1. Detroit: Gale Research, 1976. 280 pp.

[BDR-1170] White, D. Jerry. *Early English Drama: Everyman to 1580: A Reference Guide.* Boston: G. K. Hall, 1986. 289 pp.

[BDR-1180] Wildbihler, Hubert, and Sonja Völklein. *The Musical: An International Annotated Bibliography/Eine internationale annotierte Bibliographie.* Munich: K. G. Saur, 1986. 320 pp.

KEY WORKS ON DRAMA AND RHETORIC

The list of works treating drama and given below is modest when compared with the volume of studies available on this subject. Many such works have been included in Chapter 9 treating literature simply because those studies have overlapped strongly with literature studies of other genres. The works on drama included here focus primarily, if not exclusively, on theater arts.

As an introduction to the study of drama, one will do well to begin with Oscar Gross Brockett's *The Theatre: An Introduction* [DRH-170], Richard Southern's lucid work, *The Seven Ages of the Theatre* [DRH-630], or G. B. Tennyson's *An Introduction to Drama* [DRH-650]. To date, David Bevington's *Medieval Drama* [DRH-110] is the best introduction to the drama of Medieval Europe, and provides an excellent background for studying the work of Shakespeare and later dramatists. Ernest James Burton's *The British Theatre: Its Repertory and Practice, 1100-1900 A.D.* [DRH-220] also provides a useful framework for interpreting English drama. For further assistance in studying the history of drama, consult [DRH-160], or two older works, [DRH-070] and [DRH-510]. One can also find considerable help with history and terminology in any of several current guides to drama, including Martin Banham's *Cambridge Guide to World Theatre* [DRH-060], Eugene Benson's and L. W. Conally's *Oxford Companion to Canadian Theatre* [DRH-090], Gerald Bordman's *The Oxford Companion to American Theatre* [DRH-130], and Phyllis Hartnoll's *The Oxford Companion to the Theatre* [DRH-340]. For additional studies treating world drama, see [DRH-270], [DRH-310], [DRH-330], [DRH-370], and [DRH-480].

One can locate representative criticism of drama readily in Anthony Slide's collections listed below as items [DRH-590 to DRH-620]. One of the best collections of scholarly critiques of drama is Bernard F. Dukore's *Dramatic Theory and Criticism: Greeks to Grotowski* [DRH-290]. For additional criticism also see [DRH-140], [DRH-300], [DRH-390], [DRH-410], [DRH-500], and [DRH-640]. Furthermore, for studies of recent trends in the theater of the absurd, see the exemplary work of Martin Esslin, *Theatre of the Absurd* [DRH-320], and John Raymond Killinger, *World in Collapse: The Vision of Absurd Drama* [DRH-420].

To locate studies focusing on drama performance, see [DRH-010], [DRH-050], [DRH-080], [DRH-250], and [DRH-580]. For the study of musical dramas, see Gerald Bordman's *American Musical Theatre: A Chronicle* [DRH-120], or any of the works listed in bibliographies [BDR-910] and [BDR-1180] given above. Additionally, for studies of puppetry, see [DRH-200], [DRH-490], and [DRH-660].

In the western tradition of studies, rhetoric is typically traced back to Aristotle as the earliest recorded articulator of the art of speaking. Aristotle's *The Poetics* [DRH-040] and various other writings [DRH-030] provide a useful vocabulary and conceptual framework for discussing this subject. For a helpful historical overview of rhetoric, see the sizable collection of readings compiled by Patricia Bizell and Bruce Herzberg, *The Rhetorical Tradition: Readings from Classical Times to the Present* [DRH-150]. A number of fine analyses of rhetoric are available, including the following: [DRH-210], [DRH-230], [DRH-240], [DRH-560], [DRH-700]. Many of the works given below analyze speech as an art form, especially [DRH-020], [DRH-100], [DRH-280], [DRH-360], and [DRH-460].

[DRH-010] Albright, Hardie, and Arnita Albright. *Acting: The Creative Process.* 3rd ed. Belmont, Calif.: Wadsworth Publishing Co., 1980. 393 pp.

[DRH-020] Anderson, Virgil A. *Training the Speaking Voice.* 3rd ed. New York: Oxford University Press, 1977. Bib. pp. 463-465.

[DRH-030] Aristotle. *The Rhetoric of Aristotle.* Trans. Lane Cooper. New York: D. Appleton and Co., 1932. Reprint. Englewood Cliffs, N.J.: Prentice-Hall Press, 1960. Bib. pp. 243-245.

[DRH-040] Aristotle, et al. *The Poetics. . . .* 1932. Reprint. Cambridge, Mass.: Harvard University Press, 1973. 500 pp.

[DRH-050] Balk, H. Wesley. *Performing Power: A New Approach for the*

Singer Actor. Minneapolis: University of Minnesota Press, 1985. Bib. pp. 363-364.

[DRH-060] Banham, Martin, ed. *Cambridge Guide to World Theatre*. Cambridge: Cambridge University Press, 1988. 1,104 pp.

[DRH-070] Bates, Alfred, James P. Boyd, and John P. Lamberton, eds. *The Drama: Its History, Literature and Influence on Civilization*. 22 vols. New York: Historical Publishing Co., 1903-1904. Bib.

[DRH-080] Benedetti, Robert L. *The Actor at Work*. 4th ed. Englewood Cliffs, N.J.: Prentice-Hall Press, 1986. 304 pp.

[DRH-090] Benson, Eugene, and L. W. Conally, ed. *Oxford Companion to Canadian Theatre*. New York: Oxford University Press, 1990. 680 pp.

[DRH-100] Berlo, David K. *The Process of Communication*. New York: Holt, Rinehart and Winston, 1960.

[DRH-110] Bevington, David. *Medieval Drama*. Boston: Houghton Mifflin Co., 1975. Bib. pp. 1071-1073.

[DRH-120] Bordman, Gerald. *American Musical Theatre: A Chronicle*. Expanded ed. New York: Oxford University Press, 1986.

[DRH-130] ------. *The Oxford Companion to American Theatre*. New York: Oxford University Press, 1992. 768 pp.

[DRH-140] Bigsby, C. W. E. *A Critical Introduction to Twentieth-Century American Drama*. 3 vols. Cambridge: Cambridge University Press, 1982-1985.

[DRH-150] Bizell, Patricia, and Bruce Herzberg. *The Rhetorical Tradition: Readings from Classical Times to the Present*. New York: Bedford Books, 1990. 1,282 pp.

[DRH-160] Brockett, Oscar Gross, and Robert R. Findlay. *Century of Innovation: A History of European and American Theatre and Drama Since 1870*. Englewood Cliffs, N.J.: Prentice-Hall Press, [1973]. 826 pp. Bib. pp. 781-802.

[DRH-170] Brockett, Oscar Gross. *The Theatre: An Introduction*. 3rd ed. New York: Holt, Rinehart and Winston, Inc., 1974. Bib. pp. 639-664.

[DRH-180] Bronner, Edwin. *The Encyclopedia of the American Theatre, 1900-1975*. San Diego: Barnes, 1980. 659 pp.

158

[DRH-190] Brownell, Baker. *Art is Action: A Discussion of Nine Arts in a Modern World*. 1939. Reprint. Freeport, N.Y.: Books for Libraries Press, [1969]. 231 pp. Bib. footnotes.

[DRH-200] Burger, Helga. *Fujian Hand Puppets*. [New York: Performing Arts Program of the Asia Society], 1980. 8 pp. (China, Fukien Province.)

[DRH-210] Burke, Kenneth. *A Rhetoric of Motives*. Berkeley: University of California Press, 1969.

[DRH-220] Burton, Ernest James. *The British Theatre: Its Repertory and Practice, 1100-1900 A.D.* 1960. Reprint. Westport, Conn.: Greenwood Press, 1977. Bib. pp. 259-262.

[DRH-230] Campbell, George. *The Philosophy of Rhetoric*. Rev. ed. Boston: Charles Ewer, 1823.

[DRH-240] Corbett, Edward P. J. *Classical Rhetoric for the Modern Student*. 3rd ed. New York: Oxford University Press, 1990. 672 pp.

[DRH-250] Crawford, Jerry L. *Acting in Person & In Style*. 3rd ed. Dubuque, Iowa: William C. Brown Co., 1983. 517 pp. Bibs.

[DRH-260] Dalhaus, Carl, and Sieghart Dohring, eds. *Piper's Enzyklopädie des Musiktheaters*. 8 vols. Munich: R. Piper, 1986-.

[DRH-270] Devlin, Diana. *Mask and Scene: An Introduction to a World View of Theatre*. Metuchen, N.J.: Scarecrow Press, 1989. 227 pp.

[DRH-280] Dixon, John. *How to Speak, Here, There and On the Air: A Guide to Successful Speaking*. New York: Abingdon-Cokesbury Press, [1949]. 249 pp.

[DRH-290] Dukore, Bernard F. *Dramatic Theory and Criticism: Greeks to Grotowski*. New York: Holt, Rinehart and Winston, 1974. Bib. pp. 997-998.

[DRH-300] Eddleman, Floyd Eugene, comp. *American Drama Criticism: Interpretations, 1890-1977*. 2nd ed. Hamden: Shoe String Press, 1979. 488 pp. *Supplement I*. 1984. 255 pp. *Supplement II*. 1989. 269 pp.

[DRH-310] Esslin, Martin, ed. *The Encyclopedia of World Theater*. New York: Charles Scribner's Sons, 1977. 320 pp.

[DRH-320] ------. *The Theatre of the Absurd*. 3rd ed., rev. Harmondsworth, Middlesex, England; New Your: Penguin; [London]: Eyre and Spottiswoode, 1980. Bib. pp. 437-470.

159

[DRH-330] Gassner, John, and Edward Quinn, eds. *The Reader's Encyclopedia of World Drama*. New York: Crowell, 1969. 1,030 pp.

[DRH-340] Hartnoll, Phyllis, ed. *The Oxford Companion to the Theatre*. 4th ed. New York: Oxford University Press, 1984. 934 pp. Bib.

[DRH-350] Hill, Philip G. *The Living Art: An Introduction to Theatre and Drama*. San Francisco: Rinehart Press, [1971]. 578 pp.

[DRH-360] Hilson, Stephen E. *What Do You Say to a Naked Spotlight?* Los Angeles: Tuesday Publishing Co., [1972]. 220 pp.

[DRH-370] Hochman, Stanley, ed. *McGraw-Hill Encyclopedia of World Drama*. 2nd ed. 5 Vols. New York: McGraw-Hill, 1984. Bib.

[DRH-380] Huss, Roy. *The Mindscape of Art: Dimensions of the Psyche in Fiction, Drama and Film*. Cranbury, N.J.: Fairleigh Dickinson University Press, 1985. 224 pp.

[DRH-390] *Journal of Dramatic Theory and Criticism*. Lawrence, Kans.: Hall Center for Humanities, University of Kansas, 1986-. Semi-annual.

[DRH-400] Kawatake, Toshio. *Japan on Stage: Japanese Concepts of Beauty as Shown in the Traditional Theatre*. Trans. *Butai no oku no Nihon*. Tokyo: 3A Corp., 1990. Bib. pp. 291-295.

[DRH-410] Kernan, Alvin B., comp. *The Modern American Theater: A Collection of Critical Essays*. Englewood Cliffs, N.J.: Prentice-Hall Press, 1967. Bib. pp. 181-183.

[DRH-420] Killinger, John Raymond. *World in Collapse: The Vision of Absurd Drama*. [New York: Dell Publishing Co., 1971]. Bib. pp. 172-177.

[DRH-430] Kleinau, Mariion L., and Janet Larsen McHughes. *Theatres for Literature: A Practical Aesthetics for Group Interpretation*. Sherman Oaks, Calif.: Alfred Publishing Co., 1980. 314 pp. Bibs.

[DRH-440] Leiter, Samuel L., ed. *The Encyclopedia of the New York Stage, 1920-1930*. 2 vols. Wesport, Conn.: Greenwood Press, 1985. Additional vols. in progress.

[DRH-450] Locke, Alain Le Roy, and Montgomery Gregory, eds. *Plays of Negro Life: A Source-Book of Native American Drama*. New York: Harper and Row, 1969. Bib. pp. 424-430.

[DRH-460] Machlin, Evangeline. *Speech for the Stage*. New York: Theatre

160

Arts Books, 1980. 254 pp. Bib. p. 221.

[DRH-470] Marx, Milton. *The New Enjoyment of Drama.* New York: F. S. Crafts and Co., 1940. 242 pp. Bib. pp. 221-224. (2nd ed. New York: Irvington Publications, 1961.)

[DRH-480] Matlaw, Myron. *Modern World Drama: An Encyclopedia.* New York: E. P. Dutton and Co., 1972. 960 pp. Bib. p. xi.

[DRH-490] Meschke, Michael, and Margareta Sorenson. *In Search of Aesthetics for the Puppet Theatre.* New Delhi: Indira Gandhi National Centre for the Arts; New York: Sterling Publishers, 1992. 176 pp. (Puppet theater in Sweden.)

[DRH-500] Miller, Tice L. *Bohemians and Critics: The Development of American Theatre Criticism in the Nineteenth Century.* Metuchen, N.J.: Scarecrow Press, 1981. 200 pp.

[DRH-510] Nagler, Alois M[aria]. *A Source Book in Theatrical History.* New York: Dover Publications, 1959. Bib. 593-601.

[DRH-520] *Performing Arts Journal.* Baltimore: Johns Hopkins University Press, 1986-. 3/year.

[DRH-530] Perry, Clarence Arthur. *The Work of the Little Theatres: The Groups they Include, the Plays they Produce, Their Tournaments, and the Handbooks they Use.* New York: Russell Sage Foundation, 1933. 228 pp. Bib. pp. 196-209.

[DRH-540] *Plays and Playwrights.* Miami, Fla.: International Society of Dramatists, 1985-. Biennial.

[DRH-550] Reaske, Christopher Russell. *How to Analyze Drama.* New York: Monarch Press, [1966]. Bib. pp. 105-110.

[DRH-560] Richards, Ivor Armstrong. *The Philosophy of Rhetoric.* New York: Oxford University Press, 1964.

[DRH-570] Rosenberg, Helane S., and Christine Prendergast. *Theatre for Young People: A Sense of Occasion.* New York: Holt, Rinehart, and Winston, 1983. Bib. 357-360.

[DRH-580] Shafer, Gloria. *Performance Power: Winning Ways to Face Your Audience.* Lewiston, N.Y.: Edwin Mellen Press, 1992. 160 pp.

[DRH-590] Slide, Anthony. *Selected Theatre Criticism: Vol. 1: 1900-1919.* Metuchen, N.J.: Scarecrow Press, 1985. 395 pp.

[DRH-600] ------. *Selected Theatre Criticism: Vol. 2: 1920-1930.* Metuchen,

N.J.: Scarecrow Press, 1985. 280 pp.

[DRH-610]   ------. *Selected Theatre Criticism: Vol. 3: 1931-1950*. Metuchen, N.J.: Scarecrow Press, 1986. 297 pp.

[DRH-620]   ------. *Selected Vaudeville Criticism*. Metuchen, N.J.: Scarecrow Press, 1988. 318 pp.

[DRH-630]   Southern, Richard. *The Seven Ages of the Theatre*. New York: Hill and Wang, 1961. 312 pp.

[DRH-640]   Styan, J. L. *Drama, Stage and Audience*. [New York]: Cambridge University Press, [1975]. Bib. pp. 242-245.

[DRH-650]   Tennyson, G. B. *An Introduction to Drama*. New York: Holt, Rinehart and Winston, 1967. Bib. pp. 108-111.

[DRH-660]   Tillis, Steve. *Toward an Aesthetics of the Puppet: Puppetry as a Theatrical Art*. New York; London: Greenwood Press, 1992. 181 pp.

[DRH-670]   Tobey, Frances. *Modern Plays: Some Aspects of Recent Contemporary Drama*. Greeley, Colo.: Colorado State Teachers College, 1926. 29 pp. Bib. p. 29.

[DRH-680]   Trapido, Joel, ed. *An International Dictionary of Theatre Language*. Wesport, Conn.: Greenwood Press, 1985.

[DRH-690]   Virtanen, Keijo. *The Concept of Purification in the Greek and Indian Theories of Drama*. Jyvaskyla Studies in the Arts, 31 0075-4633. Jyvaskyla, Finland: Jyvaskylan Yliopisto, 1988. Bib. pp. 57-62.

[DRH-700]   Whately, Richard. *Elements of Rhetoric*. Carbondale, Ill.: Southern Illinois University Press, 1963.

[DRH-710]   Wilson, Edwin. *The Theater Experience*. 2nd ed. New York: McGraw-Hill, 1980. Bib. pp. 415-417.

KEY WORKS ON DRAMA AND RHETORIC AND RELIGION

During the past several centuries, drama has undergone criticism similar to that lodged against television and cinema today. Disparaging remarks about theater have abounded since at least the seventeenth century when the Puritans began to criticize its excesses and engineer the closing of theaters in England. Some of this legacy of censorship is evident in works such as the 1719 writing of Arthur Bedford [DRR-110]. The more serious result of this censorship has been a tradition of Christian drama which caters to Victorian tastes and opts for the sermonic style in place of the more risky and interesting variety of great drama. In the twentieth century only a few playwrights such as T. S. Eliot, Christopher Fry, Dorothy Sayers, and W. H. Auden have dared to present the Christian message indirectly for an audience outside the church. Considering that Medieval drama began in the church as an illustration of the liturgy, the recent use of drama to portray Christian themes is surprising only in its apologetic posture, as if one had to beg pardon for entertaining people or asking them to think. The gradual reemergence of drama as an art form fit for use in the church has in some ways been matched by a developing sense of drama in the sermon. Radio and television have prompted preachers and evangelists to be far more conscious of the aesthetic and emotional appeal of messages. Even in the 1920s preachers such as Aimee Semple McPherson employed many of the oral and visual theatrics of Hollywood to enhance sermons. Angelus Temple, the church Aimee helped design, is built in the shape of a theater replete with theater seats and a multi-level stage, thus signaling the merging of worship and dramatic performance. More recently, Robert Schuller has built the Crystal Cathedral with elaborate stage machinery for Sunday presentations and seasonal performances of Easter and Christmas pageants including flying angels and a host of live animals. On a more modest scale, St. Peter's Lutheran Church in New York city is built on the lower level of a corporate building such that pedestrians passing by can observe ongoing worship services, as if those worshiping were on stage.

However one interprets the current trends in drama and worship, the merging of theater and preaching is becoming increasingly more common in the twentieth century, and is likely to become more so. This trend is a curious reversal of the secularizing movement of the 1920s and 1930s which sought to replace the church with the theater. For the study of drama as an expression of Christian culture, one will do well to begin with Theodor Herzl Gaster's *Thespis: Ritual, Myth, and Drama in the Ancient Near East* [DRR-420] and Geoffrey Wainwright's *Doxology: The Praise of God in Worship, Doctrine and Life: A Systematic Theology* [DRR-1020] to provide a context for understanding the dramatic practices of early Christians, followed by a survey text such as

O. B. Hardison's masterful text, *Christian Rite and Christian Drama in the Middle Ages: Essays in the Origin and Early History of Modern Drama* [DRR-450], or John Wesley Harris' more recent *Medieval Theatre in Context: An Introduction* [DRR-470]. For studies on expressions of Christian drama after the Middle Ages, see Rudolph Chris Hassel's *Renaissance Drama and the English Church Year* [DRR-500], Ruth Harriett Blackburn's *Biblical Drama Under the Tudors* [DRR-130], Robert Henry Underwood Bloor's *Christianity and the Religious Drama* [DRR-140], Robert Speaight's *Christian Theatre* [DRR-910], Larry D. Bouchard's *Tragic Method and Tragic Theology: Evil in Contemporary Drama and Religious Thought* [DRR-160], and Gordon C. Bennet's *Acting out Faith: Christian Theatre Today* [DRR-120]. Two additional works which offer eloquent interpretations of the modern scene in drama are William V. Spanos' *The Christian Tradition in Modern British Verse Drama: The Poetics of Sacramental Time* [DRR-900] and Eugene Webb's *The Dark Dove: The Sacred and Secular in Modern Literature* [DRR-1030]. Also consult related essays in the works of T. S. Eliot listed in Chapter 9 as [LIC-550] and [LIP-640 to LIP-660].

For additional studies of various eras of drama history, see works listed for the following categories: Ancient and Medieval drama, [DRR-020], [DRR-150], [DRR-180], [DRR-280], [DRR-290], [DRR-300], [DRR-360], [DRR-430], [DRR-520], [DRR-650], [DRR-720], [DRR-770], [DRR-790], [DRR-860], [DRR-990], [DRR-1010], [DRR-1070]; Renaissance and Enlightenment drama, [DRR-220], [DRR-350], [DRR-560], [DRR-710], [DRR-830], [DRR-930], [DRR-1000]; Modern and contemporary drama, [DRR-090], [DRR-330], [DRR-480], [DRR-490], [DRR-540], [DRR-780], and [DRR-1050]; survey, [DRR-040], [DRR-210], [DRR-370], [DRR-510], [DRR-550], [DRR-800]. To assist one in the fine points of production, consult [DRR-190], [DRR-200], [DRR-380], [DRR-440], [DRR-620], [DRR-640], [DRR-680], [DRR-700], [DRR-890], [DRR-950]. One may also find useful two studies on puppetry and ministry, [DRR-460] and [DRR-920].

For locating studies on the art of speaking, especially in preaching, the following bibliographies will prove interesting and useful: [DRR-010], [DRR-020], [DRR-030], [DRR-050], [DRR-060]. To provide one with a historical perspective on preaching, see Clyde E. Fant's and William M. Pinson's thirteen volume set of sermons, *Twenty Centuries of Great Preaching* [DRR-390], and Bill Leonard's *Word of God Across the Ages: Using Christian History in Preaching* [DRR-610]. Other works which help one explore the history of preaching include items [DRR-070], [DRR-100], [DRR-320], [DRR-340], [DRR-730], [DRR-1010], [DRR-1040], [DRR-1060], and [DRR-1070].

The study of homiletics is a complex one, especially when one considers the multitude of ways in which the Holy Spirit leads people in various cultural contexts. Those familiar with the vast body of literature on preaching will find this section curiously brief. The emphasis here is on works which underscore the rhetorical aspects of preaching, although most of the works given here treat exegetical and pastoral concerns as well. Of the numerous texts listed below, a few stand out as solid beginning points, including those by James W. Cox, [DRR-230] and [DRR-240], Fred B. Craddock, [DRR-250] and [DRR-260], and John Raymond Killinger, [DRR-580]. While virtually all of the homiletic works in this section refer to the Bible as the basis for proclamation, a few highlight this indebtedness, including [DRR-410] and [DRR-820]. One of the best classic collections of instructions to young preachers is Charles H. Spurgeon's *Lectures to My Students* [DRR-940]. Other works which will prove useful for research on homiletics are [DRR-170], [DRR-310], [DRR-400], [DRR-530], [DRR-570], [DRR-590], [DRR-600], [DRR-660], [DRR-670], [DRR-690], [DRR-760], [DRR-810], [DRR-840], [DRR-880], [DRR-960], [DRR-980], and [DRR-1090]. Also note a fine and growing series by Michael E. Williams on biblical story telling [DRR-1080]. Finally, one will also find in this list two recent works, Jay Edward Adams' *A Consumer's Guide to Preaching: How to Get the Most out of a Sermon* [DRR-080] and David J. Schlafer's *Surviving the Sermon: A Guide to Preaching for Those who have to Listen* [DRR-850], both of which will help audiences make better use of sermons.

Special Bibliographies

[DRR-010] Blatchly, John. *The Town Library of Ipswich Provided for the use of the Town Preachers in 1599: A History and Catalogue.* Woodbridge, England; Wolfeboro, N.H.: Boydell Press,

1989. 199 pp. Bib. refs.

[DRR-020] Caplan, Harry. *Mediaeval Artes Praedicandi: A Supplementary Hand List.* Cornell Studies in Classical Philology, vol. 25. Ithaca: Cornell University Press; London: H. Milford, Oxford University Press, 1936. 36 pp.

[DRR-030] Herr, Alan Fager. *The Elizabethan Sermon: A Survey and a Bibliography.* 1940. Reprint. New York: Octagon Books, 1969. 169 pp.

[DRR-040] Johnson, Albert. *Best Church Plays: A Bibliography of Religious Drama.* Philadelphia: Pilgrim Press, 1968. 180 pp.

[DRR-050] Toohey, William, William D. Thompson, A. Duane Litfin, and Haddon W. Robinson. *Recent Homiletical Thought: A Bibliography.* 2 vols. Nashville: Abingdon Press, 1967-1983. Vol. 1, 303 pp., covers 1935-1965; vol. 2, 249 pp., covers 1966-1979, annotated.

[DRR-060] Wiersbe, Warren W. *Walking with the Giants: A Minister's Guide to Good Reading and Great Preaching.* Grand Rapids: Baker Book House, 1976. 289 pp. Bibs.

Key Works

[DRR-070] Adams, Henry Hitch. *English Domestic or, Homiletic Tragedy, 1575 to 1642: Being an Account of the Development of the Tragedy of the Common Man Showing its Great Dependence on Religious Morality. . . .* New York: Columbia University Press, 1943. Bib. pp. 207-220.

[DRR-080] Adams, Jay Edward. *A Consumer's Guide to Preaching: How to Get the Most out of a Sermon.* Wheaton, Ill.: Victor Books, 1991. Bib. refs. pp. 157-160.

[DRR-090] Baxter, Kathleen Mary. *Contemporary Theatre and the Christian Faith.* New York: Abingdon Press, [1965]. 112 pp.

[DRR-100] Bayley, Peter. *French Pulpit Oratory, 1598-1650: A Study in Themes and Styles, with a Descriptive Catalogue of Printed Texts.* Cambridge, England; New York: Cambridge University Press, 1980. Bib. pp. 305-316.

[DRR-110] Bedford, Arthur. *A Serious Remonstrance in Behalf of the Christian Religion, Against the Horrid Blasphemies and Impieties which are Still used in the English Play-House. . . .* London: John Darby, 1719. 383 pp. Bib. refs.

166

[DRR-120] Bennet, Gordon C. *Acting out Faith: Christian Theatre Today*. St. Louis: CBP Press, 1986. 192 pp. Bib. pp. 171-179.

[DRR-130] Blackburn, Ruth Harriett. *Biblical Drama Under the Tudors*. The Hague: Mouton, 1971. Bib. pp. 196-201.

[DRR-140] Bloor, Robert Henry Underwood. *Christianity and the Religious Drama*. The Essex Hall Lecture, 1928. 1930. Reprint. [Folcroft, Pa.]: Folcroft Library Editions, 1973. 64 pp. Bib. refs.

[DRR-150] Boitani, Piero, and Anna Torti, eds. *Religion in the Poetry and Drama of the Late Middle Ages in England: The J. A. W. Bennett Memorial Lectures, Perugia, 1988*. Cambridge, [England]: D. S. Brewer, 1990. 239 pp. Bib. refs.

[DRR-160] Bouchard, Larry D. *Tragic Method and Tragic Theology: Evil in Contemporary Drama and Religious Thought*. University Park: Pennsylvania State University Press, 1989. Bib. pp. 252-278.

[DRR-170] Broadus, John A. *On the Preparation and Delivery of Sermons*. 4th ed. Rev. Vernon L. Stanfield. San Francisco: Harper and Row, 1979.

[DRR-180] Carroll, Virginia Schaefer. *The "Noble Gyn" of Comedy in the Middle English Cycle Plays*. New York: Peter Lang, 1989. Bib. pp. 223-237.

[DRR-190] Clausen, Robert Howard, ed. *The Cross and the Cries of Human Need: Drama Selections*. Minneapolis: Augsburg Publishing House, 1973. 64 pp.

[DRR-200] Cole, Richard. *Light Relief: Sketches to Help Explore the Bible Through Drama*. N.p.: Bible Society, 1991. 96 pp.

[DRR-210] Coleman, Edward Davidson. *The Bible in English Drama: An Annotated List of Plays Including Translations from other Languages from the Beginnings to 1931*. With A Survey of Recent Major Plays, 1968, by I. Sheffer. New York: New York Public Library, [1968]. 212 pp.

[DRR-220] Cox, James D. *Shakespeare and the Dramaturgy of Power*. Princeton: Princeton University Press, 1989. 282 pp.

[DRR-230] Cox, James W., ed. *Biblical Preaching: An Expositor's Treasury*. Philadelphia: Westminster Press, 1983.

[DRR-240] ------. *Preaching: A Comprehensive Approach to the Design and Delivery of Sermons*. San Francisco: Harper and Row, 1985.

320 pp. Bib. pp. 287-292.

[DRR-250] Craddock, Fred B. *Preaching.* Nashville: Abingdon Press, 1985. Bib. pp. 223-224.

[DRR-260] ------. *Preaching Through the Christian Year.* Philadelphia: Trinity Press International, 1992.

[DRR-270] Craig, Hardin. *English Religious Drama of the Middle Ages.* Oxford: Clarendon Press, 1955. 421 pp. Bib. pp. 390-401.

[DRR-280] Davidson, Clifford. *Visualizing the Moral Life: Medieval Iconography and the Macro Morality Plays.* New York: AMS Press, 1989. Bib. pp. 131-163.

[DRR-290] Davidson, Clifford, and Ann Eljenholm Nichols. *Iconoclasm vs. Art and Drama.* Kalamazoo, Mich.: Medieval Institute Publications, Western Michigan University, 1989. 210 pp. Bib. refs.

[DRR-300] Davidson, Clifford, and John H. Stroupe, eds. *Iconographic and Comparative Studies in Medieval Drama.* Kalamazoo, Mich.: Medieval Institute Publications, Western Michigan University, 1991. 118 pp. Bib. refs.

[DRR-310] Davis, H. Grady. *Design for Preaching.* Philadelphia: Fortress Press, 1958.

[DRR-320] Demaray, Donald E. *Pulpit Giants: What Made Them Great.* Chicago: Moody Press, 1973. 174 pp.

[DRR-330] Ditsky, John. *The Onstage Christ: Studies in the Persistence of a Theme.* Totowa, N.J.: Barnes and Noble, 1980. 188 pp. Bib. refs.

[DRR-340] Dodd, C. H. *The Apostolic Preaching.* London: Hodder and Stoughton, 1936.

[DRR-350] Dollimore, Jonathan. *Radical Tragedy: Religion, Ideology, and Power in the Drama of Shakespeare and His Contemporaries.* Chicago: University of Chicago Press, 1984. Bib. pp. 290-305.

[DRR-360] Dunn, E[llen] Catherine. *The Gallican Saint's Life and the Late Roman Dramatic Tradition.* Washington, D.C.: Catholic University of America Press, 1989. Bib. pp. 149-159.

[DRR-370] Eastman, Fred. *Christ in the Drama: A Study of the Influence of Christ on the Drama of England and America.* New York: Macmillan Publishing Co., 1947. 174 pp.

168

[DRR-380]   Eastman, Fred, and Louis Wilson. *Drama in the Church: A Manual of Religious Drama Production.* New York: S. French, [1942]. 187 pp.

[DRR-390]   Fant, Clyde E., and William M. Pinson, Jr., eds. *Twenty Centuries of Great Preaching.* 13 vols. Waco, Tex.: Word Books, 1971.

[DRR-400]   Farmer, H. H. *The Servant of the Word.* London: Nisbet and Co., 1941.

[DRR-410]   Fuller, Reginald H. *The Use of the Bible in Preaching.* Philadelphia: Fortress Press, 1981.

[DRR-420]   Gaster, Theodor Herzl. *Thespis: Ritual, Myth, and Drama in the Ancient Near East.* Rev. ed. New York: Gordian Press, 1975. 515 pp. Bib. pp. 473-489.

[DRR-430]   Gibson, Gail McMurray. *The Theater of Devotion: East Anglian Drama and Society in the Late Middle Ages.* Chicago: University of Chicago Press, 1989. Bib. pp. 223-240.

[DRR-440]   Grainger, Roger. *Presenting Drama in Church.* London: Epworth, 1985. 128 pp.

[DRR-450]   Hardison, O. B., Jr. *Christian Rite and Christian Drama in the Middle Ages: Essays in the Origin and Early History of Modern Drama.* Baltimore: Johns Hopkins Press, [1965]. 328 pp. Bib. footnotes.

[DRR-460]   Harp, Grace. *Handbook on Christian Puppetry.* Denver: Accent Books, 1984. Bib. p. 127.

[DRR-470]   Harris, John Wesley. *Medieval Theatre in Context: An Introduction.* London; New York: Routledge, 1992. Bib. refs. pp. 203-205.

[DRR-480]   Harris, Max. *The Dialogical Theatre: Dramatizations of the Conquest of Mexico and the Question of the Other.* New York: St. Martin's Press, 1993. Bib. refs.

[DRR-490]   ------. *Theatre and Incarnation.* New York: St. Martin's Press, 1990. 151 pp. Bib. refs.

[DRR-500]   Hassel, R[udolph] Chris. *Renaissance Drama and the English Church Year.* Lincoln: University of Nebraska Press, 1979. Bib. pp. 205-210.

[DRR-510]   Heilman, Samuel C. *The People of the Book: Drama, Fellowship, and Religion.* Chicago: University of Chicago Press, 1983.

Bib. pp. 323-332.

[DRR-520] Jack, Ronald D. S. *Patterns of Divine Comedy: A Study of Mediaeval English Drama*. Cambridge, England; Wolfeboro, N.H.: D. S. Brewer, 1989. 180 pp. Bib. refs.

[DRR-530] Jasper, David. *Rhetoric, Power and Community: An Exercise in Reserve*. Louisville: Westminster, John Knox Press, 1993. 180 pp. Bib.

[DRR-540] Kari, Daven Michael. *T. S. Eliot's Dramatic Pilgrimage: A Progress in Craft as an Expression of Christian Perspective*. Studies in Art and Religious Interpretation, vol. 13. Lewiston, N.Y.: Edwin Mellen Press, 1990. Bib. pp. 183-191.

[DRR-550] Kelly, Henry Ansgar. *The Devil at Baptism: Ritual, Theology, and Drama*. Ithaca: Cornell University Press, 1985. 301 pp. Bib. refs.

[DRR-560] Kendall, Ritchie D. *The Drama of Dissent: The Radical Poetics of Nonconformity, 1380-1590*. Chapel Hill: University of North Carolina Press, 1986. Bib. pp. 263-274.

[DRR-570] Kennedy, Rodney. *The Creative Power of Metaphor: A Rhetorical Homiletics*. Lanham: University Press of America, 1993. 129 pp. Bib. refs.

[DRR-580] Killinger, John [Raymond]. *Fundamentals of Preaching*. Philadelphia: Fortress Press, 1985. 224 pp.

[DRR-590] Kooienga, William H. *Elements of Style for Preaching*. Grand Rapids: Ministry Resources Library, 1989. Bib. pp. 123-127.

[DRR-600] Lenski, R. C. H. *The Sermon: Its Homiletical Construction*. Columbus, Ohio: Lutheran Book Concern, n.d.

[DRR-610] Leonard, Bill. *Word of God Across the Ages: Using Christian History in Preaching*. Greenville, S.C.: Smyth and Helwys, 1991. 110 pp. Bib. refs.

[DRR-620] Lewis, John, Laura Andrews, Flip Kobler. *The Church Guide to Play Production*. Los Angeles: Morning Star Press, 1992. 422 pp. Bib. refs.

[DRR-630] Litfin, A. Duane. *St. Paul's Theology of Proclamation: I Corinthians 1-4 and Greco-Roman Rhetoric*. Monograph Series/Society for New Testament Studies, vol. 79. Cambridge; New York: Cambridge University Press, 1994. Bib. refs.

170

[DRR-640] Litherland, Janet. *Getting Started in Drama Ministry: A Complete Guide to Christian Drama.* Colorado Springs: Meriwether Publishing, Ltd., 1988. Bib. p. 129.

[DRR-650] Longsworth, Robert. *The Cornish Ordinalia: Religion and Dramaturgy.* Cambridge: Harvard University Press, 1967. 173 pp. Bib. refs.

[DRR-660] Lowry, Eugene L. *The Homiletical Plot: The Sermon as Narrative Art Form.* New York: Crossroad, 1990. 108 pp.

[DRR-670] McLaughlin, Raymond W. *The Ethics of Persuasive Preaching.* Grand Rapids: Baker Book House, 1979. Bib. pp. 195-206.

[DRR-680] Miller, James Hull. *Stagecraft for Christmas and Easter Plays: A Method of Simplified Staging for the Church.* Colorado Springs: Meriwether Pub., 1990. 73 pp.

[DRR-690] Mitchell, Henry H. *The Recovery of Preaching.* San Francisco: Harper and Row, 1977.

[DRR-700] Moynahan, Michael E. *Once upon a Parable: Dramas for Worship and Religious Education.* New York: Paulist Press, 1984. Bib. pp. 239-241.

[DRR-710] Mullany, Peter F. *Religion and the Artifice of Jacobean and Caroline Drama.* Salzburg: Institut fur Englische Sprache und Literatur, Universitat Salzburg, 1977. Bib. pp. 179-184.

[DRR-720] Nagler, A[lois] M[aria]. *The Medieval Religious Stage: Shapes and Phantoms.* [Trans. George C. Schoolfield.] New Haven: Yale University Press, 1976. 108 pp. Bib.

[DRR-730] Nielsen, Alan. *The Great Victorian Sacrilege: Preachers, Politics, and The Passion, 1879-1884.* Jefferson, N.C.: McFarland, 1991. Bib. refs. pp. 281-288.

[DRR-740] Nouwen, Henri J. M. *Creative Ministry.* Garden City, N.Y.: Doubleday, 1971.

[DRR-750] Oberhelman, Steven M. *Rhetoric and Homiletics in Fourth-Century Christian Literature: Prose Rhythm, Oratorical Style, and Preaching in the Works of Ambrose, Jerome, and Augustine.* Atlanta: Scholars Press, 1991. Bib. refs. pp. 127-149.

[DRR-760] Olford, Stephen F. *The Pulpit and the Christian Calendar: Preaching on Significant Days.* Grand Rapids: Baker Book House, 1991.

[DRR-770] Paterno, Salvatore. *The Liturgical Context of Early European*

Drama. Potomac, Md.: Scripta Humanistica, 1989. Bib. pp. 154-158.

[DRR-780] Philomene, Marie. *The Biblical Theme in Modern Drama*. Quezon City: University of the Philippines Press, 1978. Bib. pp. 169-174.

[DRR-790] Prosser, Eleanor. *Drama and Religion in the English Mystery Plays: A Re-Evaluation*. Stanford, Calif.: Stanford University Press, 1961. 229 pp.

[DRR-800] *Religious Drama: 1 (1957)-*. New York: Meridian Books, 1957-.

[DRR-810] *Return to Distinctive Christianity, A*. Seventeenth Annual East Tennessee School of Preaching and Missions Lectureship, 1991. Knoxville: East Tennessee School of Preaching and Missions, 1991. 317 pp. Bib. refs.

[DRR-820] Robertson, Haddon W. *Biblical Preaching*. Grand Rapids: Zondervan Press, 1980.

[DRR-830] Rozett, Martha Tuck. *The Doctrine of Election and the Emergence of Elizabethan Tragedy*. Princeton: Princeton University Press, 1984. Bib. pp. 301-319.

[DRR-840] Sangster, William Edwin. *The Craft of the Sermon*. London: Epworth Press, 1954.

[DRR-850] Schlafer, David J. *Surviving the Sermon: A Guide to Preaching for Those who have to Listen*. Cambridge, Mass.: Cowley Publications, 1992. 132 pp.

[DRR-860] Schnusenberg, Christine [Catharina]. *The Relationship Between the Church Drama and Writings of the Church Fathers and by Liturgical Texts until Amalarius of Metz, 775-852 A.D.* Lanham, Md.: University Press of America, 1988. Bib. pp. 383-426.

[DRR-870] Schweizer, Eduard. *God's Inescapable Nearness*. Trans. and ed. James W. Cox. Waco, Tex.: Word Books, 1971.

[DRR-880] Sider, Robert D[ick]. *The Gospel and Its Proclamation*. Message of the Fathers of the Church, vol. 10. Wilmington, Del.: M. Glazier, 1983. 236 pp. Bibs.

[DRR-890] Smyth, Robert, ed. *Lamb's Players Presents Developing a Drama Group: A Practical Approach for Director, Actor and Designer*. Minneapolis: World Wide Publications, 1989. Bib. refs. pp. 255-261.

172

[DRR-900] Spanos, William V. *The Christian Tradition in Modern British Verse Drama: The Poetics of Sacramental Time.* New Brunswick: Rutgers University Press, 1967.

[DRR-910] Speaight, Robert. *Christian Theatre.* Twentieth Century Encyclopedia of Catholicism, vol. 124. New York: Hawthorn Books, 1960. Bib. p. 141.

[DRR-920] Spence, Rod. *Short Scripts for Puppet Plays.* Cincinnati: Standard Publishing Co., 1988. Bib. p. 128.

[DRR-930] Spivack, Charlotte. *The Comedy of Evil on Shakespeare's Stage.* Rutherford, N.J.: Fairleigh Dickinson University Press, 1978. Bib. pp. 174-180.

[DRR-940] Spurgeon, Charles H. *Lectures to My Students.* London: Passmore and Alabaster, 1875.

[DRR-950] Staeheli, Alice M. *Costuming the Christmas and Easter Play: With Ideas for Other Biblical Dramas.* 3rd ed. Colorado Springs: Meriwether Pub., 1988. Bib. p. 87.

[DRR-960] Stevenson, Dwight E., and Charles F. Diehl. *Reaching People from the Pulpit.* New York: Harper and Row, 1958.

[DRR-970] Stone, Sam E. *The Christian Minister: A Practical Approach to the Preaching Ministry.* Cincinnati: Standard Pub., 1991. Bib. refs. pp. 255-260.

[DRR-980] Tizard, Leslie James. *Preaching: the Art of Communication.* New York: Oxford University Press, 1958.

[DRR-990] Travis, Peter W. *Dramatic Design in the Chester Cycle.* Chicago: University of Chicago Press, 1982. 310 pp.

[DRR-1000] Veevers, Erica. *Images of Love and Religion: Queen Henrietta Maria and Court Entertainments.* New York: Cambridge University Press, 1989. Bib. pp. 228-242.

[DRR-1010] Volk-Birke, Sabine. *Chaucer and Medieval Preaching: Rhetoric for Listeners in Sermons and Poetry.* Tubingen: G. Narr, 1991. Bib. refs. pp. 306-315.

[DRR-1020] Wainwright, Geoffrey. *Doxology: The Praise of God in Worship, Doctrine and Life: A Systematic Theology.* London: Epworth Press, 1980.

[DRR-1030] Webb, Eugene. *The Dark Dove: The Sacred and Secular in Modern Literature.* Seattle: University of Washington Press, 1975. 292 pp.

173

[DRR-1040] Weber, Donald. *Rhetoric and History in Revolutionary New England*. New York: Oxford University Press, 1988. Bib. pp. 157-197.

[DRR-1050] Wellwarth, George E. *Modern Drama and the Death of God.* Madison: University of Wisconsin Press, 1986. Bib. pp. 165-172.

[DRR-1060] Wenzel, Siegfried. *Preachers, Poets, and the Early English Lyric.* Princeton: Princeton University Press, 1986. 272 pp. Bib. refs.

[DRR-1070] ------. *Verses in Sermons: Fasciculus Morum and its Middle English Poems.* Mediaeval Academy of America Publication, no. 87. Cambridge, Mass.: Mediaeval Academy of America, 1978. 234 pp. Bib. refs.

[DRR-1080] Williams, Michael E. *The Storyteller's Companion to the Bible.* 4 vols. Nashville: Abingdon Press, c. 1991-. Old Testament series.

[DRR-1090] Williamson, Clark M. *Interpreting Difficult Texts: Anti-Judaism and Christian Preaching.* London: SCM Press; Philadelphia: Trinity Press, 1989. Bib. refs. pp. 121-129.

CHAPTER 7

ELECTRONIC COMMUNICATIONS: RADIO, TV, VIDEO

BIBLIOGRAPHIES ON ELECTRONIC COMMUNICATIONS

Electronic communications have revolutionized the use of language and images as much as writing altered the use of words in the time of Plato. The current debate over whether one gains or loses when shifting to electronic communications, including computer technology, sounds curiously similar to Plato's argument that writing would destroy people's capacity to memorize. He was right about most people losing their memorizing skills, but he greatly underestimated the gains writing would make for literature, including his own *Republic* which remains available centuries after Plato's civilization faded away. Today, electronic communications are affecting a similar revolution and many educators are concerned that reading skills and disciplined learning as we have known them will be lost in the tide of change. Yet the gains made by these technological advancements are tremendous, greatly reducing the tedium of research, vastly improving the accessibility of most library collections, and quickly widening communications networks to include the entire world. The church has also been profoundly affected by these technological changes as worship services are broadcast live or video taped for home bound members. Electronic communications at their best have become a new art form, transparent as music and enduring as stone sculpture. While radio, television, and video have often been seen as support technologies for other art forms, such as theater and music, these newer media are also developing into new genre's of art. The emergence of the ten second sound bit and the ten minute scene in television programs reflects new understandings of how people respond and learn in a fast paced society. Electronic communications are altering the way people perceive life, and in this sense function as new art forms.

The study of electronic communications could readily involve a wide array of resources ranging from technical manuals for radio broadcasting to aesthetic interpretations of video. The bibliographies listed below offer a beginning point for the study of radio, television, and video. For locating studies of radio communications, see Diane Foxhill Carothers' recent work, *Radio Broadcasting from 1920 to 1990: An Annotated Bibliography* [BEC-080], or Josephine Langham's and Janine Chrichley's *Radio Research: An Annotated Bibliography, 1975-1988* [BEC-340]. For additional bibliographies covering radio, see [BEC-040], [BEC-150], [BEC-390], [BEC-420], [BEC-480], [BEC-510], [BEC-520], and [BEC-530].

For general bibliographies treating television, see Mary B. Cassata's and Thomas Skill's *Television, a Guide to the Literature* [BEC-090], the National Association of Broadcasters' *Broadcasting Bibliography: Guide to the Literature of Radio and Television* [BEC-480], and the National Film Board of Canada's *Books on Film and Television in the Reference Library of the National Film Board of Canada* [BEC-490]. Also see the following more specialized bibliographies and guides: [BEC-120], [BEC-200], [BEC-240], [BEC-350], [BEC-390], [BEC-400], [BEC-420], [BEC-520], [BEC-530], [BEC-540]. To locate studies evaluating cable television, see [BEC-050], [BEC-130], [BEC-140], and [BEC-220]. For identifying studies of television and its effects on viewers, especially children and adolescents, consult [BEC-100], [BEC-110], [BEC-160], [BEC-310], [BEC-450], [BEC-470], and [BEC-630]. For related studies of the effects of advertising on viewers, see [BEC-410] and [BEC-440]. For specialized bibliographies or guides on music and television, see items [BEC-230], [BEC-320], [BEC-500], and [BEC-620]. To locate studies of ethics and television, see [BEC-180]. For ethnic studies and television, see

[BEC-270], [BEC-290], [BEC-300], and [BEC-640]. Finally, for finding periodical literature on television, see Katherine Loughney's *Film, Television, and Video Periodicals: A Comprehensive Annotated List* [BEC-370], and Tracey Thompson's and David H. Chadderdon's *Film and Television Periodicals in English* [BEC-580].

The development of bibliographies and guides for video has been somewhat slow, primarily because video is often treated as just another media format for film. In addition to Laughney's work [BEC-370] mentioned above, researchers of video will be greatly helped by Donald L. McBride's *Doctoral Dissertations about Videotape and Videodisc: A Bibliography* [BEC-380], and items [BEC-320], [BEC-430], [BEC-460], and [BEC-600]. Finally, for those studying in the visual arts, the following bibliographies and guides will be especially useful: [BEC-020], [BEC-190], [BEC-570], and [BEC-650].

[BEC-010] Aimiller, Kurt, Paul Lohr, and Manfred Meyer, comps. *Television and Young People: A Bibliography of International Literature, 1969-1989.* Munich; New York: K. G. Saur, 1989. 225 pp.

[BEC-020] *ArtsAmerica Fine Art Film and Video Source Book.* [Greenwich, Conn.]: ArtsAmerica, Inc., 1987-. Annual.

[BEC-030] Atkin, Charles K., John P. Murray, and Oguz B. Nayman. *Television and Social Behavior: An Annotated Bibliography of Research Focusing on Television's Impact on Children.* Rockville, Md.: National Institute of Mental Health, [1971]. 150 pp.

[BEC-040] Baden, Anne L. *Radio and Radio Broadcasting: A Select List of References.* [Washington, D.C.: U.S. Library of Congress, Division of Bibliography], 1941. 109 pp.

[BEC-050] *BCTV: Bibliography on Cable Television.* San Francisco: Communications Library, 1978-. Annual.

[BEC-060] Bierschenk, Bernhard. *Television as a Technical Aid in Education and in Educational and Psychological Research: A Bibliography.* Malmo, Sweden: Dept of Educational and Psychological Research, School of Education, 1971. 27 pp.

[BEC-070] *British Broadcasting, 1922-1972: A Select Bibliography.* London: BBC, 1972. 49 pp.

178

[BEC-080] Carothers, Diane Foxhill. *Radio Broadcasting from 1920 to 1990: An Annotated Bibliography.* Garland Reference Library of the Humanities, vol. 967. New York: Garland Publishing, 1991. 564 pp.

[BEC-090] Cassata, Mary B., and Thomas Skill. *Television, a Guide to the Literature.* Phoenix: Oryx Press, 1985. 148 pp. Bibs.

[BEC-100] Children's Television Workshop. Research Division. *CTW Research Bibliography: Research Papers Relating to the Children's Television Workshop and its Experimental Educational Series: "Sesame Street" and "The Electric Company"--1968--1976.* New York: Children's Television Worksop, Research Division, [1976]. 20 pp.

[BEC-110] ------. *Sesame Street Research Bibliography: Selected Citations Relating to Sesame Street, 1969-1989.* New York: Research Division, Children's Television Workshop, 1990. 88 pp.

[BEC-120] ------. *Three-Two-One Contact: Research Bibliography.* New York: Research Division, Children's Television Workshop, c. 1990. 43 pp.

[BEC-130] Chin, Felix. *Cable Television: A Comprehensive Bibliography.* New York: IFI/Plenum, 1978. 285 pp.

[BEC-140] ------. *Cable Television: A Selected Bibliography.* Monticello, Ill.: Vance Bibliographies, 1978. 63 pp.

[BEC-150] Columbia Broadcasting System Reference Library. *Radio and Television Bibliography.* 6th ed. N.Y.: The Library, 1942. 96 pp.

[BEC-160] Comstock, George A., and Marilyn Fisher. *Television and Human Behavior: A Guide to the Pertinent Scientific Literature.* Santa Monica, Calif.: Rand, 1975. 344 pp.

[BEC-170] Cooper, Isabella Mitchell. *Bibliography on Educational Broadcasting.* Chicago: University of Chicago Press, [1942]. Reprint. New York: Arno Press and New York Times, 1971. 576 pp.

[BEC-180] Cooper, Thomas W[illiam], Robert Sullivan, Christopher Weir, and Peter Medaglia. *Television and Ethics: A Bibliography.* Boston: G. K. Hall, 1988. 203 pp.

[BEC-190] Covert, Nadine, ed. *Art on Screen: A Directory of Films and Videos About the Visual Arts.* Program for Art on Film: Metropolitan Museum of Art and J. Paul Getty Trust. Boston: G. K. Hall, 1991. 283 pp.

[BEC-200] Einstein, Daniel. *Special Edition: A Guide to Network Television Documentary Series and Special News Reports, 1955-1979.* Metuchen, N.J.: Scarecrow Press, 1987. 1,069 pp.

[BEC-210] Flannery, Gerald V. *Mass Media: Marconi to MTV: 1900-1988. Select Bibliography of New York Times Sunday Magazine Articles on Communication.* Lanham, Md.: University Presses of America, 1989. 342 pp.

[BEC-220] Garay, Ronald. *Cable Television: A Reference Guide to Information.* New York: Greenwood Press, 1988. 177 pp. Bibs.

[BEC-230] Gelfand, Steve. *Television Theme Recordings.* Bronx, N.Y.: Television Music Archives, 1985. 136 pp.

[BEC-240] Gibberman, Susan R. *Star Trek: An Annotated Guide to Resources on the Development, the Phenomenon, the People, the Television Series, the Films, the Novels, and the Recordings.* Jefferson, N.C.: McFarland and Co., 1991. 434 pp.

[BEC-250] Gitter, A. George, and Robert Grunin. *Communication: A Guide to Information Sources.* Detroit: Gale Research, 1980. 157 pp.

[BEC-260] Golter, Bob J. *Bibliography of Theses and Dissertations Relating to Audiovisuals and Broadcasting.* Nashville: Methodist Publishing House, 1958. 185 pp.

[BEC-270] Gray, John, comp. *Blacks in Film and Television: A Pan-African Bibliography of Films, Filmmakers, and Performers.* New York: Greenwood Press, 1990. 496 pp. Bib. refs. pp. 403-425.

[BEC-280] Hall, Doug, and Sally Jo Fifer, eds. *Illuminating Video: An Essential Guide to Video Art.* New York: Aperture with Bay Area Video Coalition, 1990. 566 pp. Bib. refs. pp. 526-546.

[BEC-290] Hill, George, Lorraine Raglin, and Chas Floyd Johnson. *Black Women in Television: An Illustrated History and Bibliography.* Garland Reference Library of the Humanities, no. 1228. New York: Garland Publishing, 1990. 168 pp.

[BEC-300] Hill, George H., and Sylvia Saverson Hill. *Blacks on Television: A Selectively Annotated Bibliography.* Metuchen, N.J.: Scarecrow Press, 1985. 237 pp.

[BEC-310] International Association for Mass Communication Research. *The Effects of Television on Children and Adolescents: An Annotated Bibliography with an Introductory Overview of Research Results.* Ed. Wilbur Schramm. [Paris]: Unesco,

180

[1964]. 54 pp.

[BEC-320] Jakubowski, Masim, and John Tobler. *MTV Music Television: Who's Who in Rock Video*. New York: Quill, 1984. 190 pp.

[BEC-330] Kittross, John M., comp. *A Bibliography of Theses and Dissertations in Broadcasting: 1920-1973*. Washington, D.C.: Broadcast Education Association, 1978. 240 pp.

[BEC-340] Langham, Josephine, and Janine Chrichley, comps. *Radio Research: An Annotated Bibliography, 1975-1988*. 2nd ed. Aldershot, England; Brookfield, USA: Avebury, 1989. 357 pp. Bib. refs. pp. 326-328.

[BEC-350] Lie, Rico, comp. *Television in the Pacific Islands: An Annotated Bibliography*. Honolulu: Institute of Culture and Communication, East-West Center, 1990. 52 pp.

[BEC-360] Lipstein, Benjamin, William James McGuire. *Evaluating Advertising: A Bibliography of the Communications Process*. New York: Advertising Research Foundation, 1978. xxxv, 362 pp.

[BEC-370] Loughney, Katharine. *Film, Television, and Video Periodicals: A Comprehensive Annotated List*. New York: Garland Publishing, 1991. 431 pp.

[BEC-380] McBride, Donald L. *Doctoral Dissertations about Videotape and Videodisc: A Bibliography*. Carbondale: Department of Radio and Television, Southern Illinois University of Carbondale, 1989.

[BEC-390] McCavitt, William E., comp. *Radio and Television, Supplement One: A Selected, Annotated Bibliography: 1977-1981*. Metuchen, N.J.: Scarecrow Press, 1982. 167 pp.

[BEC-400] MacLennan, Donald W., and J. Christopher Reid. *Abstracts of Research on Instructional Television and Film: An Annotated Bibliography*. 2 vols. N.p., [1965].

[BEC-410] McNeal, James U. *A Bibliography of Research and Writings on Marketing and Advertising to Children*. New York: Lexington Books; Toronto: Maxwell Macmillan Canada; New York: Maxwell Macmillan International, 1991. 168 pp.

[BEC-420] *Media Log: A Guide to Film, Television, and Radio Programs Supported by the National Endowment for the Humanities, Division of Public Programs, Humanities Projects in Media*. Washington, D.C.: The Project, c. 1993. Dist. U.S. G.P.O. 127 pp.

[BEC-430] Melton, Hollis. *A Guide to Independent Film and Video.* Bulletin for Film and Video Information, vol. 2, no. 6. New York: Anthology Film Archives, 1976. 87 pp.

[BEC-440] Meringoff, Laurene, ed. *Children and Advertising: An Annotated Bibliography.* New York: Children's Advertising Review Unit, National Advertising Division, Council of Better Business Bureaus, 1980. 87 pp.

[BEC-450] Meyer, Manfred, and Ursula Nissen, comps. *Effects and Functions of Television: Children and Adolescents: A Bibliography of Selected Research Literature, 1970-1978.* Rev. trans. *Wirkungen und Funktionen des Fernsehens, Kinder und Jugendliche.* Munich; New York: K. G. Saur, 1981. 172 pp.

[BEC-460] Moss, Joyce, and George Wilson, eds. *From Page to Screen: Children's and Young Adult Books on Film and Video.* Detroit: Gale Research, 1992. 443 pp.

[BEC-470] Muller, Werner, and Manfred Meyer, comps. *Children and Families Watching Television: A Bibliography of Research on Viewing Processes.* Munich; New York: K. G. Saur, 1985. 159 pp.

[BEC-480] National Association of Broadcasters, Public Affairs Department. *Broadcasting Bibliography: Guide to the Literature of Radio and Television.* Washington, D.C.: National Association of Broadcasters, 1982. 58 pp.

[BEC-490] National Film Board of Canada. Reference Library. *Books on Film and Television in the Reference Library of the National Film Board of Canada.* Montreal: The Library, 1992-. English and French.

[BEC-500] Pattillo, Craig W. *TV Theme Soundtrack Directory and Discography with Cover Versions.* Portland, Oreg.: Braemar Books, 1990. 279 pp.

[BEC-510] Pitts, Michael R. *Radio Soundtracks: A Reference Guide.* 2nd ed. Metuchen, N.J.: Scarecrow Press, 1986. 349 pp.

[BEC-520] Poteet, G. Howard. *Published Radio, Television, and Film Scripts: A Bibliography.* Troy, N.Y.: Whitston Publishing Co., 1975. 245 pp.

[BEC-530] Pringle, Peter K., and Helen E. Clinton. *Radio and Television: Supplement Two: 1982-1986: A Selected, Annotated Bibliography.* Metuchen, N.J.: Scarecrow Press, 1989. 249 pp.

[BEC-540] Saffady, William. *High Definition Television: A Bibliography.*

182

Westport, Conn.: Meckler, 1990. 121 pp.

[BEC-550] Shearer, Benjamin F., and Marilyn Huxford. *Communications and Society: A Bibliography on Communications Technologies and Their Social Impact.* Westport, Conn.: Greenwood Press 1983. 242 pp.

[BEC-560] Source, Inc. *Source Catalog, No. 1: Communications.* [Chicago: Swallow Press, 1971].

[BEC-570] Suhr, Angeline M., and Lois A. Staton, comps. *Films and Video Tapes on Art.* Raleigh, N.C.: State Library of North Carolina, North Carolina Department of Cultural Resources, [1990]. 115 pp.

[BEC-580] Thompson, Tracey, and David H. Chadderdon, comps. *Film and Television Periodicals in English.* [Rev. ed.] Ed. David H. Chadderdon and Odette Salvaggio. Factfile, no. 1. Los Angeles: American Film Institute, Education Services, 1990. 60 pp.

[BEC-590] Voos, Henry. *Organizational Communication: A Bibliography.* New Brunswick: Rutgers University Press, 1967. 251 pp.

[BEC-600] Weber, Olga S., and Deirdre Boyle. *North American Film and Video Directory: A Guide to Media Collections and Services.* New York: R. R. Bowker, 1976. 284 pp.

[BEC-610] Wedell, George, Georg-Michael Luyken, and Rosemary Leonard, eds. *Mass Communications in Western Europe: An Annotated Bibliography.* Manchester: European Institute for the Media, [c. 1985]. 327 pp.

[BEC-620] Wescott, Steven D. *A Comprehensive Bibliography of Music for Film and Television.* Detroit Studies in Music Bibliography, no. 54. Detroit: Information Coordinators, 1985. xxi, 432 pp.

[BEC-630] Wolf, Michelle Andres, and Deanna Morris. *Resources on Children and Television.* Factfile, no. 19. [Los Angeles]: American Film Institute, Education Services, [1989]. 61 pp.

[BEC-640] Woll, Allen L., and Randall M. Miller. *Ethnic and Racial Images in American Film and Television: Historical Essays and Bibliography.* Garland Reference Library of Social Science, vol. 308. New York: Garland Publishing, 1987. 408 pp.

[BEC-650] Zippay, Lori, ed. *Artists' Video: An International Guide/Electronic Arts Intermix.* New York: Cross River Press, 1991. 272 pp. Videographies, pp. 228-247. Bib. refs. pp. 250-251.

KEY WORKS ON ELECTRONIC COMMUNICATIONS

The following selection of works on electronic communications is offered as a brief sampling of works in the discipline and as an update for the bibliographies listed above. For those studying radio broadcasting, only a handful of current books are available. As in other chapters of this book, works of a primarily technical or "how to" nature have been omitted, and works with potential for aiding research in Christianity and the arts have been included. Some of the most substantial research aids for radio include Irving E. Fang's *Television News, Radio News* [ECO-130], Thomas Allen Greenfield's *Radio: A Reference Guide* [ECO-200], and Anthony Slide's *Selected Radio and Television Criticism* [ECO-460]. Other works of a slightly older vintage which will still prove helpful include [ECO-010], [ECO-080], and [ECO-540]. For the study of children's radio programming, see Marilyn L. Boemer's *The Children's Hour: Radio Programs for Children, 1929-1956* [ECO-040]. To locate the latest information about radio broadcasting, see the following periodicals: [ECO-050], [ECO-060], [ECO-120], [ECO-270], [ECO-590].

Studies on television are relatively plentiful. The two works by Fang [ECO-130] and Slide [ECO-460], mentioned above in connection with radio, are also the best beginning points for serious research on television. Several works which are somewhat dated but still useful for research include items [ECO-010], [ECO-030], [ECO-080], [ECO-110], and [ECO-240]. For research into technical matters of production, see [ECO-070], [ECO-350], and [ECO-530]. To identify people involved in various television programs, see [ECO-140 to ECO-180], [ECO-390 to ECO-400], [ECO-430], and [ECO-490]. For analyses of television's impact on various audiences, see [ECO-190], [ECO-210], [ECO-290], and [ECO-320]. Also consult several directories for children's programs, including [ECO-560], [ECO-570], and [ECO-580]. For a fairly recent analysis of television music and how it reflects a postmodern culture, see [ECO-280]. Several periodicals and directories provide current research information on television, including [ECO-120], [ECO-270], [ECO-370], [ECO-480], and [ECO-500].

Some of the recent criticism of video has been particularly probing, including Patricia Marks Greenfield's *Mind and Media: The Effects of Tele-*

184

vision, *Video Games, and Computers* [ECO-190], John G. Hanhardt's *Video Culture: A Critical Investigation* [ECO-220], and Gregory L. Ulmer's *Teletheory: Grammatology in the Age of Video* [ECO-510]. For additional studies which deal primarily with the production and use of video, see [ECO-330], [ECO-340], [ECO-440], and [ECO-550]. To find additional studies of video, as well as radio and television, consult the bibliographies in the works listed below, and see the bibliographies given in the previous section. Also see chapters treating subjects related to electronic communications, such as Chapter 4 on cinema, Chapter 9 on literature, or Chapter 10 on music.

[ECO-010] Abbot, Waldo, and Richard L. Rider. *Handbook of Broadcasting: The Fundamentals of Radio and Television.* 4th ed. New York: McGraw-Hill, 1957. 531 pp.

[ECO-020] Barnouw, Erik, et al., eds. *International Encyclopedia of Communications.* 4 vols. New York: Oxford University Press, 1989.

[ECO-030] Becker, Samuel L., and H. Clay Harshbarger. *Television: Techniques for Planning and Performance.* New York: Holt, [1958]. 182 pp. Bibs.

[ECO-040] Boemer, Marilyn L. *The Children's Hour: Radio Programs for Children, 1929-1956.* Metuchen, N.J.: Scarecrow Press, 1989. 230 pp.

[ECO-050] *Broadcasting: The Fifth Estate.* Washington, D.C.: Broadcasting, Magazine Division, 1931-. Weekly.

[ECO-060] *Broadcasting and the Law.* Miami, Fla.: L & S Publishing Co., 1970-. Bi-weekly.

[ECO-070] Byrne, Terry. *Production Design for Television.* Boston: Focal Press, 1993.

[ECO-080] Chester, Giraud. *Television and Radio, an Introduction.* 2nd ed. New York: Appleton-Century-Crofts, [1956]. 652 pp.

[ECO-090] Connors, Tracy Daniel, ed. *Longman Dictionary of Mass Media and Communication.* New York: Longman, 1982. 255 pp.

[ECO-100] Diamant, Lincoln, ed. *The Broadcast Communications Dictionary.* New York: Hastings House, [1974]. 128 pp.

[ECO-110] Dizard, Wilson P. *Television: A World View.* Syracuse, N.Y.:

Syracuse University Press, [1966]. Bib. pp. 321-333.

[ECO-120] *Electronic Media.* Chicago: Crain Communications, Inc., 1982-. Weekly.

[ECO-130] Fang, Irving E. *Television News, Radio News.* 4th ed. St. Paul: Rada Press, 1985. 418 pp. Bib. pp. 389-398.

[ECO-140] Gianakos, Larry J. *Television Drama Series Programing: A Comprehensive Chronicle: 1947-1959.* Metuchen, N.J.: Scarecrow Press, 1980. 581 pp.

[ECO-150] ------. *Television Drama Series Programing: A Comprehensive Chronicle: 1959-1975.* Metuchen, N.J.: Scarecrow Press, 1978. 806 pp.

[ECO-160] ------. *Television Drama Series Programing: A Comprehensive Chronicle: 1975-1980.* Metuchen, N.J.: Scarecrow Press, 1981. 471 pp.

[ECO-170] ------. *Television Drama Series Programing: A Comprehensive Chronicle: 1980-1982.* Metuchen, N.J.: Scarecrow Press, 1983. 686 pp.

[ECO-180] ------. *Television Drama Series Programing: A Comprehensive Chronicle: 1982-1984.* Metuchen, N.J.: Scarecrow Press, 1987. 838 pp.

[ECO-190] Greenfield, Patricia Marks. *Mind and Media: The Effects of Television, Video Games, and Computers.* Cambridge, Mass.: Harvard University Press, 1984. Bib. pp. 183-204.

[ECO-200] Greenfield, Thomas Allen. *Radio: A Reference Guide.* New York: Greenwood Press, 1989. Bib. refs. p. 161.

[ECO-210] Groombridge, Brian. *Adult Education and Television: A Comparative Study in Canada [by] Lewis Miller, Czechoslovakia [by] Ctibor Tahy, Japan [by] Kanji Hatano.* London: National Institute of Adult Education with UNESCO, 1966. Bib. pp. 142-143.

[ECO-220] Hanhardt, John G., ed. *Video Culture: A Critical Investigation.* Rochester, N.Y.: Visual Studies Workshop Press, 1990. Dist. G. M. Smith/ Peregrine Smith Books, Layton, Utah. Bib. pp. 275-290.

[ECO-230] Harmony, Maureen, ed. *The Arts: ACT's Guide to TV Programming for Children.* Promise and Performance, vol. 2. Cambridge, Mass.: Ballinger Publishing Co., 1979. 216 pp. Bibs.

186

[ECO-240] Hilliard, Robert L. *Understanding Television: An Introduction to Broadcasting*. New York: Hastings House, [1964]. 254 pp. Bibs.

[ECO-250] Hollowell, Mary Louise. *The Cable/Broadband Communications Book*. Vol. 2, 1980-1981. White Plains, N.Y.: Knowledge Industry Publications, 1981. 230 pp. Bib.

[ECO-260] ------. *The Cable/Broadband Communications Book*. Vol. 3, 1982-1983. Washington, D.C.: Broadcasting Publications, Inc., 1983. 167 pp.

[ECO-270] *Journal of Broadcasting and Electronic Media*. Washington, D.C.: Broadcast Education Association, 1956-. Quarterly. (Formerly *Journal of Broadcasting*.)

[ECO-280] Kaplan, E. Ann. *Rocking Around the Clock: Music Television, Postmodernism, and Consumer Culture*. New York: Methuen, 1987. Bib. pp. 181-185.

[ECO-290] Kelley, Michael R. *A Parent's Guide to Television: Making the Most of It*. New York: Wiley, 1983. Bib. pp. 123-124.

[ECO-300] Lanier, Vincent. *The Arts we See: A Simplified Introduction to the Visual Arts*. New York: Teachers College Press, 1982. Bib. pp. 125-128.

[ECO-310] Lawton, Sherman Paxton. *Introduction to Modern Broadcasting: A Manual for Students*. New York: Harper and Row, [1963]. 157 pp. Bibs.

[ECO-320] Madsen, Roy Paul. *The Impact of Film: How Ideas are Communicated Through Cinema and Television*. New York: Macmillan Publishing Co., [1973]. Bib. pp. 535-549.

[ECO-330] Medoff, Norman J., and Tom Tanquary. *Portable Video: ENG and EFP*. White Plains, N.Y.: Knowledge Industry Publications, 1986. Bib. pp. 183-184.

[ECO-340] Miller, Jerome K. *Using Copyrighted Videocassettes in Classrooms, Libraries, and Training Centers*. 2nd ed. Friday Harbor, Wash.: Copyright Information Services, 1987. Bib. pp. 83-87.

[ECO-350] Millerson, Gerald. *The Technique of Television Production*. 6th ed. New York: Hastings House, [1968]. Bib. p. 434.

[ECO-360] Mathison, Stuart L. and Philip M. Walker. *Computer and Telecommunications: Issues in Public Policy*. Englewood Cliffs, N.J.: Prentice-Hall Press, [1970]. Bib. pp. 244-262.

[ECO-370] *NCTV News.* Champaign, Ill.: National Coalition on Television Violence, 1980-. Quarterly.

[ECO-380] *Parents' Choice: A Review of Children's Media.* Newton, Mass.: Parents' Choice Foundation, 1978-. Quarterly. Formerly *It's the Parents' Choice.* (Includes annotated bibliographies.)

[ECO-390] Parish, James Robert, and Vincent Terrace. *The Complete Actors' Television Credits, 1948-1988: Vol. 1: Actors.* 2nd ed. Metuchen, N.J.: Scarecrow Press, 1989. 560 pp.

[ECO-400] ------. *The Complete Actors' Television Credits, 1948-1988: Vol. 2: Actresses.* 2nd ed. Metuchen, N.J.: Scarecrow Press, 1989. 447 pp.

[ECO-410] Pellegrino, Ronald. *The Electronic Arts of Sound and Light.* New York: Van Nostrand Reinhold, 1983. 256 pp. Bibs.

[ECO-420] Pool, Ithiel de Sola, ed. *Handbook of Communication.* Chicago: Rand McNally College Pub. Co., 1973.

[ECO-430] Rainsberry, F. B. *A History of Children's Television in English Canada, 1952-1986.* Metuchen, N.J.: Scarecrow Press, 1988. 320 pp.

[ECO-440] Saffady, William. *Video-based Information Systems: A Guide for Educational, Business, Library, and Home Use.* Chicago: American Library Association, 1985. 240 pp. Bibs.

[ECO-450] Schwartz, Barry N. *Human Connection and the New Media.* Englewood Cliffs, N.J.: Prentice-Hall Press, [1973]. 179 pp. Bib. refs.

[ECO-460] Slide, Anthony, ed. *Selected Radio and Television Criticism.* Metuchen, N.J.: Scarecrow Press, 1987. 213 pp.

[ECO-470] Smith, Anthony. *The Shadow in the Cave: The Broadcaster, His Audience, and the State.* Urbana, Ill.: University of Illinois Press, [1974]. Bib. pp. 313-338.

[ECO-480] *Telemedium.* Madison, Wis.: National Telemedia Council, 1963-. Quarterly. Formerly *Better Broadcast News and Better Broadcast Newsletter.*

[ECO-490] *Television Index: TV Network Program and Production Reporting Service.* Long Island City, N.Y.: Television Index, Inc., 1949-. (Covers three major networks.)

[ECO-500] *Television Quarterly: The Journal of the National Academy of*

Television Arts and Sciences. New York: National Academy of Television Arts and Sciences, 1962-. Quarterly.

[ECO-510] Ulmer, Gregory L. *Teletheory: Grammatology in the Age of Video.* New York: Routledge, 1989. Bib. refs. pp. 244-251.

[ECO-520] Watson, James, and Anne Hill. *A Dictionary of Communication and Media Studies.* London: E. Arnold, 1984. Bib. p. 184.

[ECO-530] Wilkie, Bernard. *Creating Special Effects for TV and Film.* New York: Hastings House, 1977. Bib. p. 153.

[ECO-540] Wimer, Arthur Cecil, and Dale Brix. *Workbook for Radio and TV News Editing and Writing.* Dubuque, Iowa: William. C. Brown, 1975. 280 pp.

[ECO-550] Winston, Brian, and Julia Keydel. *Working with Video: A Comprehensive Guide to the World of Video Production.* New York: AMPHOTO, 1986. 256 pp.

[ECO-560] Woolery, George W. *Animated TV Specials: The Complete Directory to the First Twenty-Five Years, 1962-1987.* Metuchen, N.J.: Scarecrow Press, 1989. 570 pp.

[ECO-570] ------. *Children's Television: The First Thirty-Five Years, 1946-1981: Part 1: Animated Cartoon Series.* Metuchen, N.J.: Scarecrow Press, 1983. 404 pp.

[ECO-580] ------. *Children's Television: The First Thirty-Five Years, 1946-1981: Part 2: Live, Film, and Tape Series.* Metuchen, N.J.: Scarecrow Press, 1985. 820 pp.

[ECO-590] *Worldradio.* Sacramento: Worldradio, Inc., 1971-. Monthly. Formerly *World Radio News.*

KEY WORKS ON ELECTRONIC COMMUNICATIONS

AND RELIGION

Studies on electronic communications and religion tend to fall into three major categories, those which help people sort the good from the bad, those which describe the process of producing religious programing, and those which offer an objective analysis exploring topics such as the nature of belief and how it is affected by electronic communications, or the problem of manipulation through electronic media. Of the books available on radio broadcasting and Christianity, only a few offer bibliographies which lead one to additional research. The most recent works on radio and religion are Howard Dorgan's *The Airwaves of Zion: Radio and Religion in Appalachia* [ECR-180], and James Allen Morgan's doctoral thesis, "Religious Radio Broadcasting in a Town and Country Setting" [ECR-460]. The International Christian Broadcasters' *World Directory of Religious Radio and Television Broadcasting* [ECR-380] is somewhat dated, but at least offers a beginning point for studies of radio broadcasting outside the United States. Other works which are older but still useful are [ECR-070], [ECR-490], and [ECR-500].

Studies of television and religion are more current than those of radio, primarily because television technology is still developing rapidly. The most recent works which represent the best in analyses of television and Christianity are Mary Duckert's *Who Touched the Remote Control?: Television and Christian Choices* [ECR-190], William F. Fore's *Television and Religion: The Shaping of Faith, Values, and Culture* [ECR-290], and Phil Phillips' *Saturday Morning Mind Control* [ECR-520]. Two of the strongest critiques of television as used by evangelicals are Kyong Liong Kim's *Electronic Evangelism: A Mismatch Between Christian Religion and Television* [ECR-420], and Janice Peck's *The Gods of Televangelism: The Crisis of Meaning and the Appeal of Religious Television* [ECR-510]. Additional studies which will prove useful for research of television and Christianity are [ECR-060], [ECR-070], [ECR-100], [ECR-120], [ECR-130], [ECR-300], [ECR-340], [ECR-370], [ECR-380], [ECR-450], [ECR-470], [ECR-500], and [ECR-510].

Since video taping has made a wide variety of television shows, films, and documentaries available as needed, much of the attention of studies treating video and Christianity has fallen on discerning the good from the bad. For example, the following guides serve this sorting purpose: Kenneth George Jackson's *Guide to Christian Video* [ECR-010], the York Religious Education Centre's *Christianity in the Classroom: A Review of Video Material Designed for Educational Use, Prepared for the Chichester Project* [ECR-020], Theodore Baehr's, Bruce W. Grimes's, and Lisa Ann Rice's *The Christian Family's Guide to Movies and Video* [ECR-080], and David Veerman's *Video Movies*

Worth Watching: A Guide for Teens [ECR-600]. For additional resources for research, see [ECR-440] and [ECR-540]. For assistance in the production and use of video, consult [ECR-230], [ECR-260], [ECR-350], [ECR-390], and [ECR-590].

Radio, television, and video overlap considerably, especially the techniques of program production and broadcasting. Most of the studies in this section offer analyses which apply to several of the media of electronic communications and the church. Some of the finest studies available on this subject offer a wide focus which encompasses psychological, sociological and theological concerns. The following works offer a wide variety of perspectives and aids to research, and are well worth consulting: [ECR-030], [ECR-040], [ECR-050], [ECR-090], [ECR-110], [ECR-140], [ECR-150], [ECR-160], [ECR-170], [ECR-200], [ECR-210], [ECR-220], [ECR-250], [ECR-270], [ECR-280], [ECR-310], [ECR-320], [ECR-330], [ECR-360], [ECR-400], [ECR-410], [ECR-420], [ECR-430], [ECR-480], [ECR-530], [ECR-560], [ECR-570], [ECR-580], [ECR-610], [ECR-620], [ECR-630]. Also note *Religion: Communications for Worship* [ECR-550], a bi-monthly, interdenominational publication with a special focus on the use of communications and the other arts to enhance Christian worship. For additional studies of electronic communications and the church, see the bibliographies of the works listed below, consult the relevant categories of the bibliographies listed in the opening of this chapter, and look for related studies given in Chapter 4 on cinema.

Special Bibliographies

[ECR-010] Jackson, K[enneth] G[eorge]. *Guide to Christian Video*. 2nd ed. Hadlow: Jay, 1986. 128 pp.

[ECR-020] York Religious Education Centre. *Christianity in the Classroom: A Review of Video Material Designed for Educational Use, Prepared for the Chichester Project*. York: York Religious Education Centre, 1986. 17 pp.

Key Works

[ECR-030] *Annual Directory of Religious Broadcasting.* Morristown, N.J.: National Religious Broadcasters, 1982-.

[ECR-040] Armstrong, Benjamin Leighton. *The Electronic Church.* Nashville: Thomas Nelson, 1979. 191 pp. Bib.

[ECR-050] Armstrong, Ben. *Religious Broadcasting Sourcebook.* Rev. ed. Morristown, N.J.: National Religious Broadcasters, 1978. 174 pp. Bib. pp. 1-8.

[ECR-060] Bachman, John F. *In the News Tonight: Meditations by a TV News Anchor.* Minneapolis: Augsburg Press, 1990. 64 pp.

[ECR-070] Bachman, John W. *The Church in the World of Radio-Television.* New York: Association Press, [1960]. 191 pp. Bib.

[ECR-080] Baehr, Theodore, Bruce W. Grimes, and Lisa Ann Rice. *The Christian Family's Guide to Movies and Video.* 2nd ed. Brentwood, Tenn.: Wolgemuth and Hyatt, 1989. Bib. refs.

[ECR-090] Barna Research Group. *The Best of Christian Marketing Perspective: Ministry and Marketing.* Glendale, Calif.: Barna Research Group, 1988. 63 pp.

[ECR-100] Bluem, A. William. *Religious Television Programs: A Study of Relevance.* New York: Hastings House, [1969]. 220 pp. Bib.

[ECR-110] British Council of Churches, Commission on Broadcasting. *Christianity and Broadcasting.* London: SCM Press for the British Council of Churches, 1950. 52 pp.

[ECR-120] Bruce, Steve. *Pray TV: Televangelism in America.* London; New York: Routledge, 1990. Bib. pp. 253-268.

[ECR-130] Cardwell, J[erry] D[elmas]. *Mass Media Christianity: Televangelism and the Great Commission.* Lanham, Md.: University Press of America, 1984. 215 pp. Bib. pp. 193-202.

[ECR-140] ------. *A Rumor of Trumpets: The Return of God to Secular Society.* Lanham: University Press of America, 1985. 109 pp. Bib. refs.

[ECR-150] Cook, Coleen. *All that Glitters.* Chicago: Moody Press, 1992. 267 pp. Bib. refs.

192

[ECR-160] Daughters of St. Paul and 2nd Vatican Council, 1962-1965. *Mass Means of Communication*. [Boston]: St. Paul Editions, 1967. 202 pp. Bib. p. 149.

[ECR-170] Dobson, Ed, and Ed Hindson. *The Seduction of Power*. Old Tappan: Fleming H. Revell Co., 1988. Bib. pp. 185-189.

[ECR-180] Dorgan, Howard. *The Airwaves of Zion: Radio and Religion in Appalachia*. Knoxville: University of Tennessee Press, 1993. Bib. refs.

[ECR-190] Duckert, Mary. *Who Touched the Remote Control?: Television and Christian Choices*. New York: Friendship Press, 1990. Bib. refs. p. 63.

[ECR-200] Ellens, J. Harold. *Models of Religious Broadcasting*. Grand Rapids: William B. Eerdmans, [1974]. Bib. pp. 153-163.

[ECR-210] Elvy, Peter. *Buying Time: The Foundations of the Electronic Church*. Great Wakering: McCrimmons, 1986. 159 pp.

[ECR-220] ------. *The Future of Christian Broadcasting Europe*. N.p., Great Britain: McCrimmons for Jerusalem Trust, 1990. Bib. pp. 141-143.

[ECR-230] Emswiler, Thomas Neufer. *A Complete Guide to Making the Most of Video in Religious Settings: How to Produce, Find, Use, and Distribute Video in the Church and Synagogue*. Normal, Ill.: Wesley Foundation, 1985. Bib. pp. 127-128.

[ECR-240] Engel, James F. *Contemporary Christian Communications, Its Theory and Practice*. Nashville: Thomas Nelson, 1979. Bib. pp. 327-333.

[ECR-250] Falconer, Ronald. *Message, Media, Mission*. The Baird Lectures, 1975. Edinburgh: St. Andrew Press, 1977. 138 pp.

[ECR-260] Fassl, Steven. *How to Have an Effective Ministry with Video*. Muskegon, Mich.: Gospel Films, Inc., 1989. 58 pp.

[ECR-270] Fischer, Edward. *Everybody Steals from God: Communication as Worship*. Notre Dame, Ind.: University of Notre Dame Press, 1977. Bib. pp. 165-167.

[ECR-280] Fishwick, Marshall, and Ray B. Browne. *The God Pumpers: Religion in the Electronic Age*. Bowling Green: Bowling Green State University Popular Press, 1987. Bib. pp. 191-196.

[ECR-290] Fore, William F. *Television and Religion: The Shaping of Faith,*

Values, and Culture. Minneapolis: Augsburg Publishing House, 1987. Bib. pp. 206-213.

[ECR-300] Frankl, Razelle. *Televangelism: The Marketing of Popular Religion.* Carbondale: Southern Illinois University Press, 1987. Bib. pp. 181-193.

[ECR-310] Goethals, Gegor T. *The Electronic Golden Calf: Images, Religion, and the Making of Meaning.* Cambridge, Mass.: Cowley Publications, 1990. Bib. refs. pp. 213-217.

[ECR-320] Gow, James D. "America, You're too Young to Die!: The New Christian Right's Rhetoric of Recruitment." Ph.D. Thesis, Pennsylvania State University, 1989. Bib. p. 134-143.

[ECR-330] Griswold, Clayton T., and Charles H. Schmitz. *Broadcasting Religion.* Rev. ed. New York: National Council of the Churches of Christ, Broadcasting and Film Commission, 1954. Bib. p. 102.

[ECR-340] Hadden, Jeffrey K., and Anson Shupe. *Televangelism, Power, and Politics on God's Frontier.* New York: H. Holt, 1988. 325 pp. Bib. pp. 298-312.

[ECR-350] Holland, Daniel W. *Using Nonbroadcasting Video in the Church.* Valley Forge, Pa.: Judson Press, 1980. Bib. pp. 99-105.

[ECR-360] Hoover, Stewart M. *Mass Media Religion: The Social Sources of the Electronic Church.* Newbury Park, Calif.: Sage Publications, 1988. 251 pp. Bibs.

[ECR-370] Horsfield, Peter G. *Religious Television: The American Experience.* New York: Longman, 1984. Bib. pp. 182-193.

[ECR-380] International Christian Broadcasters. *World Directory of Religious Radio and Television Broadcasting.* South Pasadena, Calif.: William Carey Library, 1973. Bib. p. 805.

[ECR-390] Jaberg, Eugene Carl, and Louis G. Wargo, Jr. *The Video Pencil: Cable Communications for Church and Community.* Lanham, Md.: University Press of America, 1980. 147 pp. Bib. refs.

[ECR-400] James, Ross W., and Daniel M. Villa. *Case Studies in Christian Communication in an Asian Context.* Metro Manila, Philippines: OMF Literature, Inc., 1989. Bib. pp. 205-264.

[ECR-410] Kabler, Ciel Dunne. *Telecommunications and the Church.* Virginia Beach: Multi Media Pub., 1979. Bib. pp. 145-148.

194

[ECR-420] Kim, Kyong Liong. *Electronic Evangelism: A Mismatch Between Christian Religion and Television*. [Mount Vernon, Ohio]: Mount Vernon Nazarene College, Department of Communication, 1992. Bib. refs. pp. 156-163.

[ECR-430] Loveless, Wendell Phillips. *Manual of Gospel Broadcasting*. Chicago: Moody Press, [1946]. Bib. pp. 346-348.

[ECR-440] MacDonald, Alan. *Movies in Close-Up: Getting the Most from Film and Video: Love, Sci-Fi, War, Heroes and More*. Downers Grove, Ill.: InterVarsity Press, 1992. 122 pp. Bib. refs.

[ECR-450] McNulty, Edward N. *Television, a Guide for Christians*. Nashville: Abingdon Press, 1976. Bib. pp. 94-96.

[ECR-460] Morgan, James Allen. "Religious Radio Broadcasting in a Town and Country Setting." D.Min. Thesis, Harding Graduate School of Religion, 1990. Bib. refs. pp. 106-113.

[ECR-470] Morris, Colin M. *God-in-a-Box: Christian Strategy in the Television Age*. London: Hodder and Stoughton, 1984. 238 pp. Bib.

[ECR-480] Mosco, Vincent, and Janet Wasco, eds. *Popular Culture and Media Events*. The Critical Communications Review, vol. 3. Norwood, N.J.: Ablex, 1985. 323 pp. Bibs.

[ECR-490] Parker, Everett, Elinor Inman, and Ross Snyder. *Religious Radio: What to do and How*. New York: Harper, 1948. Bib. pp. 257-262.

[ECR-500] Parker, Everett C., David W. Barry, and Dallas W. Smythe. *The Television-Radio Audience and Religion*. New York: Harper, 1955. 464 pp. Bib.

[ECR-510] Peck, Janice. *The Gods of Televangelism: The Crisis of Meaning and the Appeal of Religious Television*. Cresskill, N.J.: Hampton Press, 1992. Bib. refs.

[ECR-520] Phillips, Phil. *Saturday Morning Mind Control*. Nashville: Oliver-Nelson, 1991. Bib. refs. pp. 179-183.

[ECR-530] Poland, Larry W. *The Last Temptation of Hollywood*. Highland, Calif.: Mastermedia International, 1988. Bib. pp. 260-263.

[ECR-540] Pomeroy, Dave. *Video, Violence, and Values: A Workshop on the Impact of Video Violence*. New York: Friendship Press, 1990. Bib. refs. pp. 31-32.

[ECR-550] *Religion: Communications for Worship.* Aurora, Ontario: CRS Communications, 1992-. Bi-monthly.

[ECR-560] Rowe, Lois Farr, and H. Edward Rowe, eds. *Applied Christianity Action Bulletin.* Buena Park, Calif.: Christian Freedom Foundation, 1972-.

[ECR-570] Schultze, Quintin J., ed. *American Evangelicals and the Mass Media: The Business of Popular Religion.* Grand Rapids: Zondervan Press, 1990. 300 pp.

[ECR-580] Swafford, Gary Kenneth. "Leadership Training via Broadcast Media as an Additional Church Development Method for Use by Foreign Missionaries." D.Min., Southeastern Baptist Theological Seminary, 1988. Bib. pp. 139-145.

[ECR-590] Turner, R. Chip. *The Church Video Answerbook.* Nashville: Broadman Press, 1986. Bib. pp. 99-102.

[ECR-600] Veerman, David. *Video Movies Worth Watching: A Guide for Teens.* Grand Rapids, Mich.: Baker Book House, 1992. 291 pp.

[ECR-610] Wheeler, Joe L. *View at Your Own Risk.* Hagerstown, Md.: Review and Herald Pub., 1993.

[ECR-620] Wildmon, Donald E., with Randall Nulton. *Don Wildmon: The Man the Networks Love to Hate.* 2nd ed. Wilmore, Ky.: Bristol Books, 1990. Bib. refs. pp. 216-226.

[ECR-630] Wolfe, Kenneth M. *The Churches and the British Broadcasting Corporation, 1922-1956: The Politics of Broadcast Religion.* London: SCM Press, 1984. 627 pp. Bib. pp. 564-570.

CHAPTER 8

FABRIC ARTS

BIBLIOGRAPHIES ON FABRIC ARTS

Studies of fabric arts typically revolve around techniques and simple descriptions of this art form. Some would prefer to classify fabric arts as crafts, or at best minor arts, but embroidery, wall hangings, tapestries, and quilts have often been used as decorative arts expressing at times the qualities of the great fine arts. The list of fabric arts in this chapter is admittedly limited, including several forms of the fabric arts only in the bibliography section, such as clothing and costume, which are treated as art forms in Chapter 6 on drama. Specialized bibliographies dealing primarily with one of the fabric arts are given below in the relevant sections. For general bibliographies which help one in locating studies of the fabric arts, see Isabel Buschman's recent work, *Handweaving: An Annotated Bibliography* [BRA-040], Kay Salz's *Craft Films: An Index of International Films on Crafts* [BFA-110], and Mary A. Vance's *Arts and Crafts Movement: Monographs* [BFA-130].

For studies of clothing and related arts, see especially [BFA-010] which deals with aesthetics and clothing. Many of the other bibliographies given below are older, offering interesting views from the past. These older bibliographies are best augmented with more recent ones, such as Pegaret Anthony's and Janet Arnold's *Costume: A General Bibliography* [BRA-020], Joanne

Bubolz Eicher's *African Dress: A Select and Annotated Bibliography of Subsaharan Countries* [BFA-060], and James Snowden's *European Folk Dress: A Guide to 555 Books and Other Sources of Illustrations and Information* [BFA-120]. These bibliographies on clothing and costume will be especially helpful to those involved in drama and cinema productions.

[BFA-010]   American Home Economics Association, Textiles and Clothing Section. *Aesthetics and Clothing: An Annotated Bibliography*. Washington, D.C.: American Home Economics Association, 1972. 159 pp.

[BFA-020]   Anthony, Pegaret, and Janet Arnold. *Costume: A General Bibliography*. London: The Victoria and Albert Museum with the Costume Society, 1966. 49 pp.

[BFA-030]   Audsley, George Ashdown. *The Ornamental Arts of Japan*. 2 vols. New York: Charles Scribner's Sons, 1883-1884. Bib. refs.

[BFA-040]   Buschman, Isabel. *Handweaving: An Annotated Bibliography*. Metuchen, N.J.: Scarecrow Press, 1991. 258 pp.

[BFA-050]   *Costume, Dress, and Needlework*. Philadelphia: Drexel Institute, Library Department, 1894. 13 pp. [300].

[BFA-060]   Eicher, Joanne Bubolz. *African Dress: A Select and Annotated Bibliography of Subsaharan Countries*. [East Lansing]: African Studies Center, Michigan State University, 1969. 134 pp.

[BFA-070]   Halevy, Robyne. *Knitting and Crocheting Pattern Index*. Metuchen, N.J.: Scarecrow Press, 1977. 190 pp.

[BFA-080]   Hiler, Hilaire, and Meyer Hiler, comps. *Bibliography of Costume: A Dictionary Catalog of About Eight Thousand Books and Periodicals*. Ed. Helen Grant Cushing and Adah V. Morris. 1939. Reprint. New York: B. Blom, [1967]. 911 pp. [8000].

[BFA-090]   Meyers, Charles Lee. *Bibliography of Colonial Costume*. [New York]: Society of Colonial Wars in the State of New Jersey, [1923]. 36 pp. [750].

[BFA-100]   Morris, Miriam, and Eleanor Kelley. *Dress and Adornment of the Head: An Annotated Bibliography*. [Baton Rouge]: School of Home Economics, Louisiana State University, 1970. 33 pp.

[BFA-110] Salz, Kay, ed. *Craft Films: An Index of International Films on Crafts.* New York: Neal-Schuman Publishers, Inc., 1979. 156 pp.

[BFA-120] Snowden, James. *European Folk Dress: A Guide to 555 Books and Other Sources of Illustrations and Information.* London: Victoria and Albert Museum, Department of Textiles, 1973. 60 pp.

[BFA-130] Vance, Mary A. *Arts and Crafts Movement: Monographs.* Monticello, Ill.: Vance Bibliographies, 1984. 11 pp.

KEY WORKS ON EMBROIDERY

The number of works available on embroidery, and the closely related arts of needlepoint and other needlework, is so vast that the following list can be only a brief introduction to works available on this topic. As in other sections of this book, only those studies which offer a serious analysis of the topic and include leads to other research materials on the arts are included here. Books with a purely descriptive, technical focus are included only if they are substantial in length (forty pages or more) and include a bibliography. For assistance in locating studies of embroidery, see the three works listed as specialized bibliographies, especially [FAE-010] and [FAE-030].

As a beginning point in studying embroidery, one will do well to consult any of several overview texts, such as Nettie Yanoff Brudner's *Painting with a Needle: An Introduction to the Art and Craft of Creative Stitchery* [FAE-160], and Georgiana Brown Harbeson's *American Needlework: The History of Decorative Stitchery and Embroidery from the Late 16th to the 20th Century* [FAE-350]. Also see [FAE-060], [FAE-070], [FAE-460], [FAE-550], and [FAE-740]. For additional information about needle craft in American history, see texts treating folk art, such as Beatrix T. Rumford's and Carolyn J. Weekley's *Treasures of American Folk Art* [VAT-1010], given in Chapter 12. Furthermore, see Jan Messent's *Embroidery and Architecture* [FAE-550] for assistance in relating embroidery to the context in which it is often used.

The study of embroidery could be divided into any number of special styles, subjects, techniques, or geographical and ethnic origins. While researchers can identify most of these divisions (such as Blackwork, Whitework, and embroidery collage) by the titles given below, the following list of geo-graphically or ethnically distinguished studies will be of special interest for those wishing to place embroidery in a global perspective: [FAE-130], [FAE-150], [FAE-370], [FAE-390], [FAE-420], [FAE-440], [FAE-450], [FAE-490], [FAE-520], [FAE-590], [FAE-650], [FAE-780], [FAE-840], [FAE-870]. Note especially Sheila Paine's *Embroidered Textiles: Traditional Patterns from Five Continents: With a Worldwide Guide to Identification* [FAE-600]. For current periodical literature treating embroidery, see [FAE-280] and [FAE-570].

For those interested in how the fabric arts relate to church life, sixteen titles in this section are especially interesting, including [FAE-050], [FAE-140], [FAE-200], [FAE-250], [FAE-260], [FAE-290], [FAE-310], [FAE-330], [FAE-340], [FAE-430], [FAE-470], [FAE-500], [FAE-540], [FAE-640], [FAE-660], and [FAE-760]. Note especially the work of Beryl Dean, [FAE-250] and [FAE-260], for Dean's skillful integration of historical perspective and theo-logical concerns with a fine sense of technical finesse. For additional help with placing embroidery in the church into historical perspective, also see Janet Mayo's *A History of Ecclesiastical Dress* [FAE-540]. Also consult stud-ies of folk art, such as C. Kurt Dewhurst's, Betty MacDowell's, and Marsha MacDowell's *Religious Folk Art in America: Reflections of Faith* [VAR-320], given in Chapter 12.

Special Bibliographies

[FAE-010] Copeland, Sandra K. *Embroidery and Needlepoint: An Informa-tion Sourcebook*. Phoenix, Áriz.: Oryx Press, 1989. 150 pp.

[FAE-020] Nevison, John L. *Catalogue of English Domestic Embroidery of the Sixteenth and Seventeenth Centuries*. Victoria and Albert Museum. London: H. M. Stationery Office, [1950]. 109 pp. Bib. pp. xxv-xxviii.

[FAE-030] Sestay, Catherine. *Needlework: A Selected Bibliography with Special Reference to Embroidery and Needlepoint*. Me-tuchen, N.J.: Scarecrow Press, 1982. 162 pp.

Key Works

[FAE-040] Allen, Sadie. *Creative Embroidery Collage*. London: Bell, 1979. Bib. p. 116.

[FAE-050] Barnet, Peter. *Clothed in Majesty: European Ecclesiastical Textiles from the Detroit Institute of Arts*. Exhibition, 14 September 1991 to 9 February 1992. Detroit: Detroit Institute of Arts, 1991. Bib. refs. pp. 52-53.

[FAE-060] Barton, Julia. *The Art of Embroidery*. London: Merehurst Press, 1989. Dist. Sterling Publishing Co., New York. Bib. refs. p. 141.

[FAE-070] Beaney, Jan. *The Art of the Needle: Designing in Fabric and Thread*. Brookvale, N.S.W.: Simon and Schuster Australia; New York: Pantheon Books, 1988. Reprint. East Roseville, N.S.W.: Simon and Schuster, 1991. Bib. p. 126.

[FAE-080] Beck, Thomasina. *The Embroiderer's Flowers*. Newton Abbot: David and Charles, 1992. Bib. p. 160.

[FAE-090] Behm, Barbara J. *The Business of Computerized Embroidery*. Westminster, Colo.: Melco Industries, 1990. Bib. pp. 271-272

[FAE-100] Benn, Elizabeth, ed. *Treasures from the Embroiderers' Guild Collection*. Devon: David and Charles Craft Book, 1991. 184 pp. Bib. refs.

[FAE-110] Bessac, Susanne L. *Embroidered Hmong Story Cloths*. Missoula, Mont.: Department of Anthropology, University of Montana, 1988. Bib. pp. 65-68. (Hmong = Asian people.)

[FAE-120] Bramley, Sylvia. *Embroidery with Transparent Fabrics*. London: B. T. Batsford, 1989. Bib. refs. p. 142.

[FAE-130] Brij Bhushan, Jamila. *Indian Embroidery*. New Delhi: Publications Division, Ministry of Information and Broadcasting, Government of India, 1990. Bib. refs. pp. 57-58.

[FAE-140] Blum, Dilys. "Ecclesiastical Embroidery [c. 1896, Attrib. to Walter Crane]." *Bulletin [Philadelphia Museum of Art]*, vol. 86 (Spring 1990), pp. 16-21. Bib.

[FAE-150] Brent, Eva. *Oriental Designs in Needlepoint*. New York: Simon and Schuster, 1979. Bib. p. 127.

[FAE-160] Brudner, Nettie Yanoff. *Painting with a Needle: An Introduction to the Art and Craft of Creative Stitchery.* Garden City, N.Y.: Doubleday, 1972. Bib. pp. 188-189.

[FAE-170] Butler, Anne. *The Arco Encyclopedia of Embroidery Stitches.* New York: Arco Publishing, [1979].

[FAE-180] Campbell-Harding, Valerie, and Pamela Watts. *Machine Embroidery: Stitch Techniques.* London: B. T. Batsford, 1989. Bib. refs. p. 142.

[FAE-190] Christie, Grace. *Embroidery and Tapestry Weaving: A Practical Text-Book of Design and Workmanship.* 1915. Reprint. New York: Taplinger Publishing Co., Inc., 1979. 370 pp.

[FAE-200] Chrysostomos, Archimandrite. *Orthodox Liturgical Vesture: An Historical Treatment.* Brooklyn, Mass.: Holy Cross Orthodox, 1981. 76 pp. Bib. refs.

[FAE-210] *Contemporary Embroidery.* Louisville, Ky.: Louisville Art Association, 1989.

[FAE-220] Cool, Kim, and Iona Dettelbach. *Needlepoint from Start to Finish: The Complete Guide for Right and Left Handed Stitchers.* Illus. Heidi Adams Coventry Cool. Frederick, Md.: Fredericktown Press, 1992. Bib. refs. p. 147.

[FAE-230] Coss, Melinda. *Floral Needlepoint.* London: Anaya, 1991. Reprint. Ringwood, Victoria: Greenhouse; New York: Sterling Publishing Co., 1992. Bib. refs. p. 111.

[FAE-240] Dawson, Barbara. *Metal Thread Embroidery.* New York: Taplinger Pub. Co., [1969]. 175 pp. Bib. p. 167.

[FAE-250] Dean, Beryl. *Church Needlework.* New ed. London: B. T. Batsford, 1990. Bib. p. 172.

[FAE-260] ------. *Ecclesiastical Embroidery.* 6th ed. London: B. T. Batsford, Ltd., 1989. Bib. p. 250.

[FAE-270] Edmonds, Mary Jaene. *Geometric Designs in Needlepoint.* New York: Nostrand Reinhold, 1976. Bib. p. 129.

[FAE-280] *Flying Needle, The.* Atlanta: Council of American Embroiderers, 1971-. Quarterly.

[FAE-290] Freeman, Margaret Beam. *The St. Martin Embroideries: A Fifteenth-Century Series Illustrating the Life and Legend of St. Martin of Tours.* [New York]: Metropolitan Museum of Art, [1966]. Bib. pp. 130-132.

[FAE-300] Frost, S[arah] Annie. *The Ladies' Guide to Needle Work: Being A Complete Guide to All Types of Ladies' Fancy Work.* 1877. Reprint. Lopez Island, Wash.: R. L. Shep, 1986. 158 pp.

[FAE-310] Getty Conservation Institute. *The Conservation of Tapestries and Embroideries: Proceedings of Meetings at the Institut royal du Patrimoine artistique, Brussels, Belgium, September 21-24, 1987.* Los Angeles: Getty Conservation Institute, 1989. (Ecclesiastical embroidery.)

[FAE-320] Gostelow, Mary. *Blackwork.* New York: Van Nostrand Reinhold, 1977. Bib. p. 151.

[FAE-330] Hall, Dorothea. *Embroidery in the Church: A Practical Guide to Church Embroidery Containing Many Projects with Clear Step by Step Instructions and Stitch Techniques.* Great Britain: Lyric Books Ltd., 1983. Reprint. Wilton, Conn.: Morehouse-Barlow Co., [1988]. 32 pp.

[FAE-340] Hall, Linda B. *Making Eucharistic Vestments on a Limited Budget.* 2nd ed. Ed. James E. Barrett. N.p.: Hymnary Press, 1985. 48 pp.

[FAE-350] Harbeson, Georgiana [Brown]. *American Needlework: The History of Decorative Stitchery and Embroidery from the Late 16th to the 20th Century.* New York: Bonanza Books, [1938]. 232 pp. Bib. pp. 225-226.

[FAE-360] Harris, Jennifer, and Pennina Barnett. *The Subversive Stitch.* Exhibitions, "Embroidery in Women's Lives, 1300-1900" and "Women and Textiles Today," 1988-1989, Great Britain. Manchester, [England]: Whitworth Art Gallery; Cornerhouse, 1988. 64 pp. Bib. refs.

[FAE-370] Hattox, Ralph S., and Lilo Markrich. *Aegean Crossroads: Greek Island Embroideries in the Textile Museum.* Washington, D.C.: The Museum, 1983. Bib. pp. 147-150.

[FAE-380] Hoskins, Nancy Arthur. *Universal Stitches for Weaving, Embroidery, and Other Fiber Arts.* Eugene, Oreg.: Skein Publications, 1982. 122 pp. Bib. refs.

[FAE-390] Howard, Constance. *Twentieth Century Embroidery in Great Britain.* 3 vols. London: B. T. Batsford, 1982-1985. c. 192 pp. each vol. Bibs.

[FAE-400] Hubbard, Liz. *Thread Painting.* Newton Abbot, Devon: David and Charles Publishers, 1988. Dist. Sterling Publishing Co., New York. Bib. p. 147.

204

[FAE-410]   Huggins, Mabel, and Clarice Blakey. *Stitches on Canvas*. London: B. T. Batsford, 1988. Bib. p. 126.

[FAE-420]   Jalees, Farida. *Glittering Threads: A Socio Economic Study of Women Zari Workers*. Ahmedabad, [India]: Sewa Bharat, 1989. Bib. p. 81. (India.)

[FAE-430]   Jerdee, Rebecca. *Fabrique Applique for Worship: Patterns and Guide for Sewing Banners, Vestments, and Paraments*. Minneapolis: Augsburg Publishing House, 1982. 80 pp.

[FAE-440]   Jessen, Ellen. *Ancient Peruvian Textile Design in Modern Stitchery*. New York: Van Nostrand Reinhold, [1972]. Bib. p. 64.

[FAE-450]   Johnstone, Pauline. *Greek Island Embroidery*. London: A. Tiranti, 1961. 58 pp. Bib. footnotes.

[FAE-460]   Jones, Mary Eirwen. *A History of Western Embroidery*. New York: Watson-Guptill Publications, 1969. Bib. p. 156.

[FAE-470]   Joseph, Elizabeth. *Sewing Church Linens: Convent Hemming and Simple Embroidery*. Harrisburg, Pa.: Morehouse Pub., 1991. 54 pp.

[FAE-480]   Kenyon, Anne. *Embroidery and Design on Patterned Fabric*. Newton Abbot: David and Charles Publishers, 1975. Bib. p. 127.

[FAE-490]   Kozaczka, Grazyna J. *Old World Stitchery for Today: Polish Eyelet Embroidery, Cutwork, Goldwork, Beadwork, Drawn Thread, and Other Techniques*. Radnor, Pa.: Chilton Books Co., 1987. Bib. pp. 226-227.

[FAE-500]   Little, Andrew George, comp. *Franciscan History and Legend in English Mediaeval Art*. 1937. Reprint. Farnborough: Gregg Press, 1966. 118 pp. Bib. refs.

[FAE-510]   Lugg, Vicky, and John Willcocks. *Heraldry for Embroiderers*. London: B. T. Batsford, 1990. Bib. refs. pp. 125-126.

[FAE-520]   MacDowell, Marsha. *Stories in Thread: Hmong Pictorial Embroidery*. [East Lansing, Mich.]: Michigan Traditional Arts Program, Folk Arts Division, Michigan State University Museum, 1989. Bib. pp. 49-50. (Hmong = Asian people.)

[FAE-530]   Markrich, Lilo, and Heinz Edgar Kiewe. *Victorian Fancywork: Nineteenth Century Needlepoint Patterns and Designs*. Chicago: Regnery, [1974]. Bib. pp. 171-172.

[FAE-540]   Mayo, Janet. *A History of Ecclesiastical Dress*. New York:

Holmes and Meier Publishers, 1984. 196 pp. Bib.

[FAE-550] Messent, Jan. *Embroidery and Architecture*. London: B. T. Batsford, 1985. Bib. p. 142.

[FAE-560] Meurant, Georges. *Shoowa Design: African Textiles from the Kingdom of Kuba*. New York: Thames and Hudson, 1986. Bib. p. 202.

[FAE-570] *Needle Arts*. Louisville, Ky.: Embroiderer's Guild of America, Inc., 1970-. Quarterly.

[FAE-580] Nichols, Marion. *Encyclopedia of Embroidery Stitches, Including Crewel*. New York: Dover Publications, 1974. 218 pp.

[FAE-590] Paine, Sheila. *Chikan Embroidery: The Floral Whitework of India*. Shire Ethnography, vol. 12. Aylesbury, Bucks, United Kingdom: Shire Publications, 1989. Bib. refs. p. 59.

[FAE-600] ------. *Embroidered Textiles: Traditional Patterns from Five Continents: With a Worldwide Guide to Identification*. Illus. Imogen Paine. Photo. Dudley Moss. New York: Rizolli International Publications, Inc., 1990. Bib. refs. pp. 179-181.

[FAE-610] Parker, Rozsika. *The Subversive Stitch: Embroidery and the Making of the Feminine*. London: Women's Press, 1984. Reprint. New York: Routledge, 1989. Bib. pp. 233-239.

[FAE-620] Parker, Xenia Ley. *Mosaics in Needlepoint: From Stone to Stitchery*. New York: Charles Scribner's Sons, 1977. Bib. pp. 139-140.

[FAE-630] Pascoe, Margaret. *Blackwork Embroidery: Design and Technique*. London: B. T. Batsford, 1989. Bib. refs. p. 139.

[FAE-640] Piepkorn, Arthur Carl. *The Survival of the Historic Vestments in the Lutheran Church after Fifteen Fifty-Five*. St. Louis: Concordia School of Graduate Studies, 1956. 120 pp.

[FAE-650] Priest, Alan, and Pauline Simmons. *Chinese Textiles: An Introduction to the Study of Their History, Sources, Technique, Symbolism, and Use*. [New York]: Metropolitan Museum of Art, 1931. Bib. pp. 87-88.

[FAE-660] Raynor, Louise A., and Carolyn H. Kerr. *Church Needlepoint: Patterns and Instructions*. 2nd ed. Wilton, Conn.: Morehouse-Barlow, 1989. Bib. refs. p. 68.

[FAE-670] Ring, Betty. *American Needlework Treasures: Samplers and Silk Embroideries from the Collection of Betty Ring*. New York:

E. P. Dutton with the Museum of American Folk Art, 1987. Bib. pp. 107-108.

[FAE-680]   Rivers, Margaret. *Working on Canvas*. Ringwood, Voctoria: Greenhouse; London: B. T. Batsford, 1990. Bib. p. 94.

[FAE-690]   Roberts, Sharee Dawn. *Creative Machine Art*. Paducah, Ky.: American Quilter's Society, 1992. Bib. refs. p. 134.

[FAE-700]   Roth, Ann. *Mosaic Masterpieces in Needlework and Handicraft, Based on Motifs from the Holy Land*. New York: Charles Scribner's Sons, 1975. 63 pp.

[FAE-710]   Russell, Beth. *Traditional Needlepoint*. Pleasantville, N.Y.: Readers' Digest Association, 1992. 128 pp. Bib. refs.

[FAE-720]   Saint-Aubin, Charles Germain de. *Art of the Embroiderer*. (1770) Trans. Nikki Scheuer. Los Angeles: Los Angeles County Museum of Art, 1983. 192 pp. Bib. refs.

[FAE-730]   Schneider, Coleman. *The Art of Embroidery in the 90's*. Tenafly, N.J.: C. Schneider, 1991. 468 pp. Bib. refs. pp. 431-432.

[FAE-740]   Schuette, Marie, and Sigrid Muller-Christensen. *A Pictorial History of Embroidery*. [Trans. Donald King.] New York: Frederick A. Praeger Publishers, [1964]. 336 pp.

[FAE-750]   Schwabe, Alma. *Candlewicking Designs*. Ruffy, Victoria: Ruffy Publishing, 1990. Reprint. South Yarra, Victoria: Greenhouse, 1991. Bib.

[FAE-760]   Scott, Stephen. *Why Do They Dress That Way?* (Church vestments.) Intercourse, Pa.: Good Books, 1986. 160 pp.

[FAE-770]   Siegler, Sus. *Needlework Patterns from the Metropolitan Museum of Art*. Boston: New York Graphic Society, 1976. Bib. p. 184.

[FAE-780]   Singer, Margo, and Mary Spyrou. *Textile Arts: Multicultural Traditions*. Radnor, Pa.: Chilton Book; London: A & C Black, 1989. 128 pp. Bib. refs.

[FAE-790]   Smith, Barbara Lee. *Celebrating the Stitch: Contemporary Embroidery of North America*. Newtown, Conn.: Taunton Press, 1991. Bib. refs. p. 225.

[FAE-800]   Snook, Barbara. *English Embroidery*. London: Mills and Boon, 1974. Bib. pp. 131-132.

[FAE-810]   Staniland, Kay. *Embroiderers*. London: British Museum Press;

Toronto; Buffalo: University of Toronto Press, 1991. Bib. refs. p. 71. (Medieval embroidery.)

[FAE-820] Strite-Kurz, Ann. *The Heart of Blackwork: A Study of Unconventional Blackwork Patterns for Contemporary Use*. Midland, Mich.: A. Strite-Kurz, 1992. Bib. refs. pp. 212-214.

[FAE-830] Swift, Gay. *The Batsford Encyclopaedia of Embroidery Techniques*. London: B. T. Batsford, 1984. Reprint. 1990. Bib. pp. 229-236.

[FAE-840] Takemura, Akihiko. *Fukusa: Japanese Gift Covers*. Tokyo: Iwasaki Bijutsu-sha, 1991. Bib. refs. pp. 293-294. (Edo period, 1600-1868.)

[FAE-850] Taylor, Jacqueline. *Painting and Embroidery on Silk*. London: Cassell, 1992. Dist. Sterling Publishing Co., New York. 128 pp. Bib. refs.

[FAE-860] Taylor, Roderick. *Ottoman Embroidery*. New York: Interlink Books, 1993. Bib. refs.

[FAE-870] *Textiles and Embroideries of India*. Bombay: Marg Publications, [1965]. 72 pp. Bib. refs.

[FAE-880] Thompson, Angela. *Embroidery with Beads*. London: B. T. Batsford, 1987. Reprint. Berkeley: LACIS, 1992. Bib. pp. 113-114.

[FAE-890] Wark, Edna. *Metal Thread Embroidery*. Kenthurst, [N.S.W.]: Kangaroo Press, 1989. Bib. pp. 75-76.

[FAE-900] Washburn, Dorothy Koster. *Style, Classification and Ethnicity: Design Categories on Bakuba Raffia Cloth*. Transactions of the American Philosophical Society, vol. 80, pt. 3. Philadelphia: American Philosophical Society, 1990. 157 pp. Bib. refs. (Embroidery and textile design in Zaire.)

[FAE-910] Williams, R. Anne. *The Batsford Embroidery Course*. London: B. T. Batsford, 1991. Bib. refs. pp. 124-130.

[FAE-920] Wilson, Erica. *Erica Wilson's Embroidery Book*. New York: Charles Scribner's Sons, [1973]. Bib. p. 369.

KEY WORKS ON HANGINGS

The category of hangings is problematic because it overlaps heavily with the other categories of fabric arts, especially tapestries. Yet some objects such as banners and latch hook rugs for walls do not fit neatly into any other category except that of wall hangings. Many of the works listed in this section treat a wide variety of fabric arts, and are included simply because they are some of the few studies which cover wall hangings. Note especially the periodicals--including [FAH-060], [FAH-090], and [FAH-160]--which introduce the latest information about this subject and relate wall hangings to the larger study of textile arts. For a beginning point in studying this art form, see Mildred Constantine's and Jack Lenor Larsen's *Beyond Craft: The Art Fabric* [FAH-050], Michel Thomas', Christine Mainguy's, and Sophie Pommier's *Textile Art* [FAH-170], and David B. Van Dommelen's *Decorative Wall Hangings: Art with Fabric* [FAH-180]. For studying the use of wall hangings in the church, see especially Marion P. Ireland's *Textile Art in the Church: Vestments, Paraments, and Hangings in Contemporary Worship, Art, and Architecture* [FAH-100], along with [FAH-040], [FAH-130], and [FAH-140].

[FAH-010]   Babington, Audrey. *Creative Wall-Hangings and Panels*. New York: Arco Publishing, 1982. 192 pp.

[FAH-020]   Birrell, Verla Leone. *The Textile Arts: A Handbook of Fabric Structure and Design Processes: Ancient and Modern Weaving, Braiding, Printing, and Other Textile Techniques*. New York: Harper, [1959]. 514 pp. Bib.

[FAH-030]   Blumenau, Lili. *Creative Design in Wall Hangings: Weaving Patterns Based on Primitive and Medieval Art*. New York: Crown Publishers, [1967]. 213 pp.

[FAH-040]   Broderick, Virginia, and Judi Bartholomew. *How to Create Banners: For Church, Home, School, Club, Garden--Wherever People Pray*. Northport, N.Y.: Costello, 1977. 75 pp.

[FAH-050]   Constantine, Mildred, and Jack Lenor Larsen. *Beyond Craft: The Art Fabric*. New York: Van Nostrand Reinhold Co., [1972]. Bib. p. 293.

[FAH-060]   *Fiberarts: The Magazine of Textiles*. Asheville, N.C.: Fiberarts

Magazine, 1974-. 5/year. Formerly *Fibercraft Newsletter.*

[FAH-070] Gilfoy, Peggy Stoltz, and Katherine Dolk-Ellis. *Indianapolis Museum of Art: Fabrics in Celebration from the Collection.* Indianapolis: The Museum, 1983. Bib. pp. 376-381.

[FAH-080] Guelzow, Diane. *Banners with Pizazz.* San Jose: Resource Publications, 1992. 108 pp.

[FAH-090] *Handwoven.* Loveland, Colo.: Interweave Press, Inc., 1979-. 5/year. Incorporating *Interweave.*

[FAH-100] Ireland, Marion P. *Textile Art in the Church: Vestments, Paraments, and Hangings in Contemporary Worship, Art, and Architecture.* Nashville: Abingdon Press, 1980. Bib. pp. 271-275.

[FAH-110] Justin, Valerie Sharaf. *Flat-Woven Rugs of the World: Kilim, Soumak, and Brocading.* New York: Van Nostrand Reinhold Co., 1980. 224 pp. Bib. pp. 187-189.

[FAH-120] Laliberte, Norman, and Sterling McIlhany. *Banners and Hangings: Design and Construction.* New York: Reinhold Publishing Corporation, [1966]. 90 pp.

[FAH-130] Lauckner, Edie. *Signs of Celebration: How to Design Church Banners.* St. Louis: Concordia Publishing House, 1978. 32 pp.

[FAH-140] Malden, Richard Henry. *The Hangings in the Quire of Wells Cathedral.* Frome: Butler and Tanner, 1948. 48 pp.

[FAH-150] Phillips, Janet. *The Weaver's Book of Fabric Design.* New York: St. Martin's Press, 1983. Bib. p. 142.

[FAH-160] *Textile History: The Journal of Textile and Costume History and Conservation.* Leeds, England: W. S. Maney and Sons, 1970-. Semi-annual.

[FAH-170] Thomas, Michel, Christine Mainguy, and Sophie Pommier. *Textile Art.* [Trans. Andre Marling]. New York: Rizolli International Publications, Inc., 1985. 279 pp. Bib. pp. 259-263.

[FAH-180] Van Dommelen, David B. *Decorative Wall Hangings: Art with Fabric.* [New York]: Funk and Wagnalls Co., [1962]. Bib. pp. 174-175.

210

KEY WORKS ON TAPESTRIES

Unlike the other fabric arts which are often classified as crafts, tapestries are typically considered one of the fine arts, even if a minor one. Their traditional use to adorn cathedrals and the halls of kings has given tapestries a place of high visibility and considerable financial support which has enabled this craft to flower into one of the finest of the arts involving the talents of artists such as Peter Paul Rubens and Henry Moore. To begin the study of tapestries, one should consult any of several overview texts presenting the history of tapestries and their role in the arts. For example, consider Madeleine Jarry's *World Tapestry: From its Origins to the Present* [FAT-390], Joseph Jobe's *Great Tapestries: The Web of History from the 12th to the 20th Century* [FAT-410], and William George Thomson's *A History of Tapestry from the Earliest Times until the Present Day* [FAT-720]. For additional studies of tapestry from a historical perspective, also see these works dating from 1885 to the present: [FAT-050], [FAT-360], [FAT-490], [FAT-530], [FAT-600], [FAT-700], [FAT-710], [FAT-740], [FAT-760].

Many studies of tapestry revolve around a few famous tapestries, such as the Bayeux Tapestry depicting the Norman Conquest of England in 1066. For studies of this historical masterpiece, see the three bibliographies listed below, including [FAT-010], [FAT-020], [FAT-040]. To introduce one to reasonably current studies of this famous tapestry, read John Bard McNulty's *The Narrative Art of the Bayeux Tapestry Master* [FAT-440], and Lewis G. M. Thorpe's *The Bayeux Tapestry and the Norman Invasion: With an Introduction and a Translation from the Contemporary Account of William of Poitiers* [FAT-730]. Also consult the additional studies listed here: [FAT-080], [FAT-150], [FAT-200], [FAT-400], [FAT-660], [FAT-800], [FAT-810]. For analyses of other famous tapestries, see the large number of works treating collections of tapestries, including the following: [FAT-060], [FAT-070], [FAT-090], [FAT-120], [FAT-140], [FAT-160], [FAT-170], [FAT-190], [FAT-230], [FAT-240], [FAT-260], [FAT-270], [FAT-280], [FAT-290], [FAT-320], [FAT-330], [FAT-340], [FAT-420], [FAT-430], [FAT-450], [FAT-460], [FAT-470], [FAT-480], [FAT-510], [FAT-570], [FAT-610], [FAT-640], [FAT-650], [FAT-680], [FAT-690], [FAT-760], [FAT-770], [FAT-780], [FAT-820], [FAT-830]. For assistance in interpreting these various tapestries, consult Jack Franses' *Tapestries and Their Mythology* [FAT-210].

Several of the texts included below primarily treat the techniques of making tapestries, including [FAT-100], [FAT-110], [FAT-300], [FAT-310], [FAT-350], [FAT-500], [FAT-520], [FAT-540], [FAT-550], [FAT-580], [FAT-740], [FAT-750], and [FAT-830]. For assistance in locating additional books treating various aspects of tapestries, consult Mary A. Vance's *Tapestry: Monographs* [FAT-030]. Also see the various publications entitled the *International Biennial of Tapestry* [FAT-370 and FAT-380] for recent studies on tapestry.

For the study of religion and the arts, the most useful texts listed below are those treating the unicorn tapestries at the Cloisters of the Metropolitan Museum of Art, and a variety of other texts analyzing the use of tapestries in the life of the church. Three of the most recent and substantial studies of the unicorn tapestries are listed below as items [FAT-180], [FAT-220], and [FAT-790]. For other studies of tapestries with religious significance and use, see [FAT-130], [FAT-170], [FAT-250], [FAT-590], [FAT-630], and [FAT-670]. Note especially Charles Scribner's *The Triumph of the Eucharist: Tapestries Designed by Rubens* [FAT-590], John K. G. Shearman's *Raphael's Cartoons in the Collection of Her Majesty the Queen, and the Tapestries for the Sistine Chapel* [FAT-630], and Graham Vivian Sutherland's *Christ in Glory in the Tetramorph: The Genesis of the Great Tapestry in Coventry Cathedral* [FAT-670] for a useful survey of religious tapestries from the Renaissance and the twentieth century.

Special Bibliographies

[FAT-010] Brown, Shirley Ann. *The Bayeux Tapestry: History and Bibliography*. Woodbridge, Suffolk: Boydell Press; Wolfeboro, N.H.: Boydell and Brewer, 1988. 186 pp.

[FAT-020] Cable, Carole. *The Bayeux Tapestry: A Bibliography of Books and Articles About its Architectural, Aesthetic, and Cultural Aspects*. Monticello, Ill.: Vance Bibliographies, 1986. 7 pp.

[FAT-030] Vance, Mary A. *Tapestry: Monographs*. Monticello, Ill.: Vance

212

Bibliographies, 1985. 37 pp.

[FAT-040] Wissolik, Richard David. *The Bayeux Tapestry: A Critical, Annotated Bibliography with Cross-References and Summary Outlines of Scholarship, 1729-1990*. 2nd ed. Rev. Greensburgh, Pa.: Eadmer Press, [1990]. 74 pp.

Key Works

[FAT-050] Ackerman, Phyllis. *Tapestry: The Mirror of Civilization*. New York: Oxford University Press, 1933. Reprint. New York: AMS Press, Inc., [1970]. Bib. pp. 431-433.

[FAT-060] Andrew, Dolores M. *Medieval Tapestry Designs*. Owings Mills, Md.: Stemmer House, 1992. 42 pp.

[FAT-070] Bennet, Anna G. *Five Centuries of Tapestry from the Fine Arts Museums of San Francisco: [Catalogue]*. Rev. ed. San Francisco: Fine Arts Museums of San Francisco; Chronicle Books, 1992. Bib. pp. 322-325.

[FAT-080] Bernstein, David J. *The Mystery of the Bayeux Tapestry*. Chicago: University of Chicago Press, 1986. 272 pp. Bib. pp. 198-229.

[FAT-090] Biriukova, N[ina] I[urevna]. *The Hermitage, Leningrad: Gothic and Renaissance Tapestries*. Photo. W[erner] Forman and B[edlich] Forman. London: Hamlyn, [1965, 1966]. 128 pp. Bib. pp. 31-32.

[FAT-100] Beutlich, Tadek. *The Technique of Woven Tapestry*. New York: Sterling Publishing Co., Inc., 1980. 192 pp. Bib.

[FAT-110] Brostoff, Laya. *Weaving a Tapestry*. Loveland, Colo.: Interweave Press, 1982. Bib. p. 160.

[FAT-120] Cavallo, Adolph S. *Tapestries of Europe and Colonial Peru in the Museum of Fine Arts, Boston*. 2 vols. Boston: Museum of Fine Arts, [1967]. Bib. pp. 211-237.

[FAT-130] *Church Decoration and Furniture: Stained Glass and Arras Tapestry Hangings, Embroideries, etc*. London: Morris and Co., 1906. 56 pp.

[FAT-140] Coss, Melinda. *Bloomsbury Needlepoint: From the Tapestries at Charleston Farmhouse*. Boston: Little, Brown, and Co., 1992. 120 pp. (Designs by Duncan Grant, Vanessa Bell and Roger Fry.)

[FAT-150] Denny, Norman, and Josephine Filmer-Sankey. *The Bayeux Tapestry: The Story of the Norman Conquest, 1066.* Great Britain: N.p., 1966. Reprint. New York: Parkwest, 1988. 72 pp.

[FAT-160] Dominguez Ortiz, Antonio, Concha Herrero Carretero, and Jose A. Godoy. *Resplendence of the Spanish Monarchy: Renaissance Tapestries and Armor from the Patrimonio Nacional.* Exhibition, Metropolitan Museum of Art, 11 October 1991 to 5 January 1992. New York: Metropolitan Museum of Art, 1991. Dist. Harry N. Abrams. Bib. refs. pp. 165-169.

[FAT-170] Dubon, David. *Tapestries from the Samuel H. Kress Collections at the Philadelphia Museum of Art: The History of Constantine the Great, Designed by Peter Paul Rubens and Pietro da Cortona.* [London]: Phaidon Press for Samuel H. Kress Foundation, [1964]. Bib. pp. 147-148. (See [VPRU-220])

[FAT-180] Erlande-Brandenburg, Alain. *The Lady and the Unicorn.* Paris: Éditions de la Réunion des Musées Nationaux, 1979. 78 pp.

[FAT-190] Forman, Werner, Bedrich Forman, and J. Blazkova. *A Book of Tapestries.* Trans. Hedda Vesela-Stranska. London: Spring Books, [1958]. Bib. pp. 66-67.

[FAT-200] Fowke, Frank Rede. *The Bayeux Tapestry: A History and Description.* London: G. Bell, 1913. Reprint. St. Clair Shores, Mich.: Scholarly Press, 1971. ix, lxxix, 139 pp.

[FAT-210] Franses, Jack. *Tapestries and Their Mythology.* New York: Drake, 1975. Bib. p. 145.

[FAT-220] Freeman, Margaret B. *The Unicorn Tapestries.* New York: Metropolitan Museum of Art, 1976. Dist. E. P. Dutton. 244 pp. Bib. refs.

[FAT-230] Friedlander, Paul. *Documents of Dying Paganism: Textiles of Late Antiquity in Washington, New York, and Leningrad.* Berkeley: University of California Press, [1945]. 66 pp. Bib. footnotes.

[FAT-240] Garrould, Ann, and Valerie Power. *Henry Moore Tapestries.* London: Diptych, 1988. 112 pp.

[FAT-250] Gerspach, M. *Coptic Textile Designs.* New York: Dover Publications, 1975. 83 pp.

[FAT-260] Gibson, Katherine. *The Goldsmith of Florence: A Book of Great Craftsmen.* 1929. Reprint. Freeport, N.Y.: Books for Libraries Press, 1967. Bib. pp. 207-209.

214

[FAT-270] Gobel, Heinrich. *Tapestries of the Lowlands*. Trans. Robert West. New York: Hacker Art Books, 1974. 97 pp.

[FAT-280] Gotz, Oswald. *Masterpieces of French Tapestry, Medieval, Renaissance, Modern: Lent by the Cathedrals, Museums and Collectors of France Through the French Government*. Exhibition, Art Institute of Chicago, 17 March to 5 May 1948. Chicago: N.p., 1948. Bib. p. 88.

[FAT-290] Hackenbroch, Yvonne. *English and Other Needlework, Tapestries and Textiles in the Irwin Untermyer Collection*. Irwin Untermyer Collection, vol. 4. Cambridge: Harvard University Press for Metropolitan Museum of Art, 1960. lxxxi, 80 pp.

[FAT-300] Harvey, Nancy. *The Guide to Successful Tapestry Weaving*. Seattle: Pacific Search Press, 1981. Bib. pp. 112-113.

[FAT-310] ------. *Tapestry Weaving: A Comprehensive Study Guide*. Loveland, Colo.: Interweave Press, 1991. Bib. refs. p. 206.

[FAT-320] Hindley, Geoffrey. *The Medieval Establishment, 1200-1500*. New York: G. P. Putnam's Sons, [1970]. Bib. p. 125.

[FAT-330] Hispanic Society of America. *Tapestries and Carpets from the Palace of the Prado, Woven at the Royal Manufactory of Madrid, Loaned by His Majesty the King of Spain for Exhibition by the Hispanic Society of America*. New York: G. P. Putnam's Sons, 1917.

[FAT-340] Hulst, Roger Adolf d'. *Flemish Tapestries, from the Fifteenth to the Eighteenth Century*. Trans. Frances J. Stillman. Trans. *Vlaamse Wandtapijten van de XIVe tot de XVIIIe*. New York: Universe Books, [1967]. 324 pp. Bib. pp. 295-303.

[FAT-350] Hunter, George Leland. *The Practical Book of Tapestries*. Philadelphia; London: J. B. Lippincott Co., 1925. Bib. pp. 281-292.

[FAT-360] ------. *Tapestries: Their Origin, History, and Renaissance*. New York: John Lane Co., 1912. 438 pp. Bib.

[FAT-370] *International Biennial of Tapestry [14th, 1989: Lausanne, Switzerland]*. Lausanne: Centre International de la Tapisserie ancienne et moderne: Musee cantonal des beaux-arts, 1989. 126 pp. (First meeting in c. 1963.)

[FAT-380] *International Biennial of Tapestry [15th, 1992: Lousanne, Switzerland]*. Lausanne: Centre International de la Tapisserie ancienne et moderne: Musee cantonal des beaux-arts, 1992. 186 pp.

[FAT-390] Jarry, Madeleine. *World Tapestry: From its Origins to the Present.* Trans. *La Tapisserie.* New York: G. P. Putnam's Sons, [1969]. Bib. pp. 349-354.

[FAT-400] Jewell, Brian. *Conquest and Overlord: The Story of the Bayeux Tapestry and the Overlord Embroidery.* New York: Arco Publishing, 1981. Bib. p. 96.

[FAT-410] Jobe, Joseph, ed. *Great Tapestries: The Web of History from the 12th to the 20th Century.* Trans. Peggy Rowell Oberson. Trans. *Le grand Livre de la Tapisserie.* Lausanne: Edita, [1965]. Bib. pp. 269-270.

[FAT-420] Kybalova, Ludmila. *Contemporary Tapestries from Czechoslovakia.* Trans. Alga Kuthanova. London: A. Wingate, 1965. Bib. pp. 81-89.

[FAT-430] Lejard, Andre, ed. *French Tapestry.* Trans. *La Tapisserie.* London: P. Elek, [1946]. Paris: Les Editions du Chene, 1947. Bib. p. 107.

[FAT-440] McNulty, J[ohn] Bard. *The Narrative Art of the Bayeux Tapestry Master.* AMS Studies in the Middle Ages, no. 13. New York: AMS Press, 1989. 151 pp. Bib. pp. 78-82.

[FAT-450] Marillier, H[enry] C[urrie]. *English Tapestries of the Eighteenth Century: A Handbook to the Post-Mortlake Productions of English Weavers.* London: Medici Society, 1930. 128 pp.

[FAT-460] *Master Weavers: Tapestry from Dovecot Studios Nineteen-Twelve to Nineteen-Eighty.* Gretna, La.: Pelican Publishing Co., Inc., 1982. 144 pp.

[FAT-470] Metropolitan Museum of Art. *Medieval Tapestries in the Metropolitan Museum of Art.* Ed. Adolfo Salvatore Cavallo. New York: Metropolitan Museum of Art, 1993. Dist. Harry N. Abrams. Bib. refs.

[FAT-480] Mullins, Edwin. *Tapestry: Henry Moore and West Dean.* Alexandria, Va.: International Exhibitions Foundation, 1980. 49 pp.

[FAT-490] Muntz, Eugene. *A Short History of Tapestry: From the Earliest Times to the End of the 18th Century.* Trans. Louisa J. Davis. London; New York: Cassell and Co., Ltd., 1885. 399 pp.

[FAT-500] Pearson, Alec. *Complete Book of Tapestry Weaving.* New York: St. Martin's Press, 1984. 136 pp. Bib. p. 31.

[FAT-510] Pelikan, Jaroslav Jan. *Imago Dei: The Byzantine Apologia for*

Icons. A. W. Mellon Lectures in the Fine Arts, 1987. Bollingen Series, vol. XXXV, no. 36. [Princeton]: Princeton University Press, 1990. Bib. refs. pp. 183-193.

[FAT-520] Petsopoulos, Yanni, and Michael Eanses. *Kilims: Flat Woven Tapestry Rugs.* 1979. Reprint. New York: Rizzoli International Publications, 1982. Bib. pp. 382-386.

[FAT-530] Pianzola, Maurice, and Julien Coffinet. *Tapestry.* Trans. Julian Snelling and Claude Namy. Trans. *La Tapisserie.* Geneva: Editions de Bonvent, [1971]. Bib. p. 121. (History.)

[FAT-540] Rees, Ronald. *Interior Landscapes: Gardens and the Domestic Environment.* Baltimore: Johns Hopkins University Press, 1993. Bib. refs. (Mural painting, wallpaper, tapestry.)

[FAT-550] Rhodes, Mary. *Small Woven Tapestries.* London: B. T. Batsford; Newton Centre, Mass: C. T. Branford, [1973]. Bib. p. 139.

[FAT-560] Rock, Daniel. *Textile Fabrics: A Descriptive Catalogue of the Collection of Church-Vestments, Dresses, Silk Stuffs, Needle-Work and Tapestries, Forming that Section of the [South Kensington] Museum.* London: Chapman and Hall, 1870. 356 pp.

[FAT-570] Rozen, A. *The Art of John Coburn.* Sydney, Australia: URE Smith, 1979. 96 pp. Bib. (Tapestries and paintings, religion and nature.)

[FAT-580] Russell, Carol K. *The Tapestry Handbook: An Illustrated Manual of Traditional Techniques.* Asheville, N.C.: Lark Books, 1990. Bib. refs. p. 174.

[FAT-590] Scribner, Charles, III. *The Triumph of the Eucharist: Tapestries Designed by Rubens.* Ann Arbor, Mich.: UMI Research Press, 1982. Bib. pp. 213-218.

[FAT-600] Sevensma, W. S. *Tapestries.* Trans. Alexim Brown. 1965. Reprint. New York: Universe Books, [1966]. Bib. p. 106. (History.)

[FAT-610] Shaw, Courtney Ann. *American Tapestry Weaving Since the 1930's and its European Roots.* Exhibition, 27 March to 26 April 1989. College Park: Art Gallery, University of Maryland, 1989. Bib. refs. p. 48.

[FAT-620] ------. "The Rise of the Artist/Weaver: Tapestry Weaving in the United States from 1930-1990." 4 vols. Ph.D. Thesis, University of Maryland at College Park, 1992. Bib. refs. pp. 816-869.

[FAT-630] Shearman, John K. G. *Raphael's Cartoons in the Collection of Her Majesty the Queen, and the Tapestries for the Sistine Chapel.* London: Phaidon Press, 1972. 258 pp. Bib. refs.

[FAT-640] Souchal, Genevieve. *Masterpieces of Tapestry from the Fourteenth to the Sixteenth Century: An Exhibition at the Metropolitan Museum of Art.* Trans. Richard A. H. Oxby. Trans. *Chefs-d'oeuvre de la tapisserie du XIVe au XVIe siecle.* [New York: Metropolitan Museum of Art, 1973]. 222 pp. Bibs.

[FAT-650] Standen, Edith Appleton. *European Post-Medieval Tapestries and Related Hangings in the Metropolitan Museum of Art.* 2 vols. New York: Metropolitan Museum of Art, 1986. 848 pp. Bib., vol. 1, p. 12.

[FAT-660] Stenton, F[rank] M[erry]. *The Bayeux Tapestry: A Comprehensive Survey.* 2nd ed. [London]: Phaidon Press, [1965]. 194 pp. Bib. refs.

[FAT-670] Sutherland, Graham Vivian. *Christ in Glory in the Tetramorph: The Genesis of the Great Tapestry in Coventry Cathedral.* Ed. Andrew Revai. Greenwich, Conn.: New York Graphic Society; London: Pallas Gallery; A. Zwemmer, [1964]. 112 pp. New York ed. *The Coventry Tapestry: The Genesis of the Great Tapestry in Coventry Cathedral, "Christ in Glory in the Tetramorph."*

[FAT-680] Szablowski, Jerry, Sophie Schneebalg-Perelman, and Adelbrecht L. J. van de Walle, eds. *The Flemish Tapestries at Wawel Castel in Cracow: Treasures of King Sigismund Augustus Jagiello.* Trans. Haakon Chevalier. Antwerp: Fond Mercator, with Banque de Paris et des Pays-Bas, 1972. Bib. pp. 481-487.

[FAT-690] *Tapestry and Embroidery in the Collection of the National Palace Museum, Taipei.* New York: Abbeville Press, Inc., 1986.

[FAT-700] Thomas, Michel, Christine Mainguy, Sophie Pommier. *Textile Art.* Trans. Andre Marling. Trans. *Histoire d'un art.* Geneva: Skira; New York: Rizolli International Publications, 1985. Bib. pp. 259-263.

[FAT-710] Thomson, F[rancis] P[aul]. *Tapestry: Mirror of History.* New York: Crown Publishers, 1980. 224 pp.

[FAT-720] Thomson, W[illiam] G[eorge]. *A History of Tapestry from the Earliest Times until the Present Day.* 3rd ed. Rev. F[rancis] P[aul] Thomson and E[ster] S[ylvia] Thomson. East Ardsley, [England]: EP Publishing, 1973. xxiv, 596 pp. Bib. pp. 527-534.

[FAT-730] Thorpe, Lewis G. M. *The Bayeux Tapestry and the Norman Invasion: With an Introduction and a Translation from the Contemporary Account of William of Poitiers.* London: Folio Society, 1973. Bib. pp. 109-110.

[FAT-740] Verlet, Pierre. *The Book of Tapestry: History and Technique.* Trans. *La Tapisserie.* New York: Vendome Press, 1978. Dist. Viking Press. Bib. pp. 226-227.

[FAT-750] Verso, Jo. *Picture it in Cross Stitch.* Newton Abbot, England: David and Charles Publishers; Richmond, Victoria: Greenhouse, 1988. Bib. p. 127.

[FAT-760] Viale Ferrero, Mercedes. *Tapestries from the Renaissance to the 19th Century.* Trans. Hamis St. Clair-Erskine and Anthony Rhodes. Trans. *Gli Arazzi.* London: Hamlyn, 1969. Reprint. London: Cassell, 1988. 155 pp.

[FAT-770] Wace, A[lan] J[ohn] B[ayard]. *The Marlborough Tapestries at Blenheim Palace and Their Relation to Other Military Tapestries of the War of the Spanish Succession.* London; New York: Phaidon Press, 1968. Bib. pp. 137-138.

[FAT-780] Weigert, Roger-Armand. *French Tapestry.* Trans. Donald King and Monique King. Trans. *Tapisserie française.* Newton, Mass.: C. T. Branford, [1962]. 214 pp. Bib.

[FAT-790] Williamson, John. *The Oak King, the Holly King, and the Unicorn: The Myths and Symbolism of the Unicorn Tapestries.* New York: Harper and Row, 1986. Bib. pp. 241-252.

[FAT-800] Wilson, David M[ackenzie]. *The Bayeux Tapestry: The Complete Tapestry in Color.* New York: Alfred A. Knopf, 1985. Dist. Random House. Bib. pp. 228-233.

[FAT-810] Wissolik, Richard David. "The Bayeux Tapestry: Its English Connection and Peripheral Narrative." Ph.D. Thesis, Duquesne University, 1988. Bib. pp. 158-214.

[FAT-820] Yates, Frances Amelia. *The Valois Tapestries.* 2nd ed. London: Routledge and Kegan Paul, 1975. xxvii, 150 pp. Bib. refs. pp. 131-143.

[FAT-830] Ysselsteyn, Gerardina Tjebberta van. *Tapestry: The Most Expensive Industry of the XVth and XVIth Centuries: A Renewed Research into Technic, Origin and Iconography.* Brussels: The Hague, 1969. Bib. pp. 204-215.

KEY WORKS ON QUILTS

Studies of quilting abound, but few move beyond technical concerns, and even fewer offer documentation which enables one to conduct scholarly research of the subject. In part this trend is due to the nature of folk art which is passed along primarily in the oral tradition. Some might question the presence of quilting as a subject in a book treating the fine arts, yet quilting constitutes one of the most original examples of domestic art in western history. When carefully executed, quilts qualify as much more than a craft. While quilts have traditionally been used as bedspreads, they have been developed into a form of wall hanging with as much potential for artistic expression as tapestries.

The two best sources for locating books and articles on quilting are Margaret A. Goodrich's *Quilter's Index: Patterns, Subjects, Techniques* [FAQ-010], and Colleen Lahan Makowski's *Quilting 1915-1983: An Annotated Bibliography* [FAQ-020]. Since much of the quilting tradition is conveyed orally, researchers of this subject will do well to contact some of the quilting groups listed in the annual directory of the American Quilter's Society, *Quilt Groups Today: Who they are, Where they Meet, What they do, and How to Contact Them* [FAQ-030]. The major periodical specifically devoted to quilting is *Great American Quilts* [FAQ-170]. Articles on quilting may be found in a wide variety of periodicals, including some of those listed under wall hangings given above.

Quilt making is typically treated as an art form born and bred in the United States and Great Britain, as analyzed in [FAQ-290] and [FAQ-390], but can be found in countries around the world, as indicated in [FAQ-380] and [FAQ-450]. Not surprisingly, the study of quilting is closely related to women's studies, as noted in [FAQ-110] and [FAQ-130]. For the researcher interested in additional studies on the history of quilt making, the following entries will be of special interest: [FAQ-220], [FAQ-240], [FAQ-430], [FAQ-480], and [FAQ-490]. For assistance in identifying the many names for quilts, see Yvonne M. Khin's *The Collector's Dictionary of Quilt Names and Patterns* [FAQ-230].

Most of the other works listed below are largely technical in orientation, of use primarily to those researching the wide variety of patterns developed around the world. The few works which introduce Christian culture as an aspect of quilting are Suzy Lawson's *Amish Patchwork: Full-Size Patterns for 46 Authentic Designs* [FAQ-250], Rachel Thomas Pellman's and Kenneth Pellman's *How to Make an Amish Quilt: More than 80 Beautiful Patterns from the Quilting Heartland of America* [FAQ-370], and Suzanne Schaffhausen's and Judy Rehmel's *Women of the Bible: Quilt Patterns* [FAQ-400]. One can also find in the study of quilting numerous references to biblical motifs or religious symbols, such as the Star of Bethlehem or the Wedding Ring patterns. These religiously oriented patterns deserve further analysis, especially for their theological implications.

Special Bibliographies

[FAQ-010] Goodrich, Margaret A. *Quilter's Index: Patterns, Subjects, Techniques*. Manchester, Mich.: Quilter's Index Co., 1990-. Vol. 1, no. 1, 1980-1984. Vol. 2, no. 1, 1985-1989. Supplements, 1989, 1990-.

[FAQ-020] Makowski, Colleen Lahan. *Quilting 1915-1983: An Annotated Bibliography*. Metuchen, N.J.: Scarecrow Press, 1985. 165 pp.

Key Works

[FAQ-030] American Quilter's Society. *Quilt Groups Today: Who they are, Where they Meet, What they do, and How to Contact Them.* Paducah, Ky.: American Quilter's Society, 1992. 336 pp.

[FAQ-040] Armstrong, Bonnie Barton. *Quilts: How to Plan, Cut, Piece, Applique and Finish a Classic Quilt.* New York: Crescent Books, 1991. Dist. Outlet Book Co. Bib. refs. p. 157.

[FAQ-050] Beyer, Jinny. *Patchwork Portfolio: A Presentation of 165 Original Quilt Designs.* McLean, Va.: EPM Publications, 1989. 248 pp.

[FAQ-060] Brackman, Barbara. *Encyclopedia of Pieced Quilt Patterns.* Paducah, Ky.: American Quilter's Society, 1993. Bib. refs.

[FAQ-070] Coleman, Anne. *Quilting: New Dimensions*. London: B. T. Batsford, 1989. Bib. refs. p. 94.

[FAQ-080] Davis, Mary Kay, and Helen Giammattei. *More Needlepoint from America's Great Quilt Designs*. New York: Workman Pub., 1977. Bib. pp. 207-208.

[FAQ-090] Denton, Susan, and Barbara Macey. *Quiltmaking*. Ringwood, Victoria: Viking O'Neil; New York: Sterling Publishing Co., 1987. Bib. pp. 171-172.

[FAQ-100] Doak, Carol. *Quiltmaker's Guide: Basics and Beyond*. Paducah, Ky.: American Quilter's Society, 1992. 207 pp. Bib. refs.

[FAQ-110] Donnell, Radka. *Quilts as Women's Art: A Quilt Poetics*. North Vancouver, B.C.: Gallerie Publications, 1990. Bib. refs.

[FAQ-120] Duke, D., and D. Harding, eds. *America's Glorious Quilts*. New York: Park Lane, n.d. 320 pp.

[FAQ-130] Ferrero, Pat, Elaine Hedges, and Julie Silber. *Hearts and Hands: The Influence of Women and Quilts on American Society*. San Francisco: Quilt Digest Press, 1987. Bib. pp. 99-103.

[FAQ-140] Gadia-Smitley, Roselyn. *Wearable Quilts: Sewing Timeless Fashions Using Traditional Patterns*. New York: Sterling Publishing Co., 1993. Bib. refs. p. 221.

[FAQ-150] Gardner, Pat Long. *Handkerchief Quilts: Creating Unique Wall Hangings from Collectible Handkerchiefs*. McLean, Va.: EPM Publications, 1993. Bib. refs.

[FAQ-160] Gravatt, Tina M. *Heirloom Miniatures*. Paducah, Ky.: American Quilter's Society, 1990. Bib. refs. p. 59.

[FAQ-170] *Great American Quilts [1987-]*. Birmingham, Ala.: Oxmoor House, 1987-. c. 144 pp. Bib. refs. Annual.

[FAQ-180] Green, Caroline M. *Quilting*. London: Ward Lock, 1990. Bib. refs. p. 66.

[FAQ-190] Guerrier, Katharine. *How to Design and Make your own Quilts*. New York: Mallard Press, 1991. Bib. refs. p. 79.

[FAQ-200] Hargrave, Harriet. *Heirloom Machine Quilting: A Comprehensive Guide to Hand-Quilted Effects using Your Sewing Machine*. Rev. Lafayette, Calif.: C & T Pub., 1990. Bib. refs. p. 127.

[FAQ-210] Hopkins, Judy. *One-of-a-Kind Quilts: Simple Steps to Individual Quilts*. Bothell, Wash.: That Patchwork Place, 1989. Bib.

222

p. 63.

[FAQ-220] Hulbert, Anne, and Sheila Betterton. *Folk Art Quilts*. New York: Meredith Press, 1992. Bib. refs. p. 112.

[FAQ-230] Khin, Yvonne M. *The Collector's Dictionary of Quilt Names and Patterns*. Washington, D.C.: Acropolis Books, 1980. Reprint. New York: Portland House; Washington, D.C.: Acropolis Books, 1988. Dist. Crown Publishers with Acropolis Books. 489 pp. Bib.

[FAQ-240] Lasansky, Jeannette. *In the Heart of Pennsylvania: 19th and 20th Century Quiltmaking Traditions*. Lewisburg, Pa.: Oral Traditions Project of the Union County Historical Society, 1985. Bib. pp. 101-102.

[FAQ-250] Lawson, Suzy. *Amish Patchwork: Full-Size Patterns for 46 Authentic Designs*. Rev. ed. of *Amish Inspirations*. New York: Dover Publications, 1988. Bib. p. 137.

[FAQ-260] McCloskey, Marsha. *Wall Quilts*. Bothell, Wash.: That Patchwork Place, 1983. Reprint. New York: Dover Publications with That Patchwork Place, 1990. Bib. refs. p. 75.

[FAQ-270] McKelvey, Susan Richardson. *Friendship's Offering: Techniques and Inspiration for Writing on Quilts*. Lafayette, Calif.: C & T Pub., 1990. Bib. refs. pp. 90-91.

[FAQ-280] Marston, Gwen, and Joe Cunningham. *American Beauties: Rose and Tulip Quilts*. Paducah, Ky.: American Quilter's Society, 1988. Bib. pp. 93-94.

[FAQ-290] Martin, Nancy J. *Threads of Time*. Bothell, Wash.: That Patchwork Place, 1990. Bib. refs. p. 175. (U.S. History.)

[FAQ-300] Matsunaga, Karen Kim. *Japanese Country Quilting: Sashiko Patterns and Projects for Beginners*. Tokyo; New York: Kodansha International, 1990. Bib. refs. p. 94.

[FAQ-310] Mende, Kazuko, and Reiko Morishige. *Sashiko: Blue and White Quilt Art of Japan*. Tokyo: Shufunotomo, 1991. Dist. Kodansha America through Farrar, Straus and Giroux, New York. Bib. refs. p. 120.

[FAQ-320] Mosey, Caron L. *Contemporary Quilts from Traditional Designs*. New York: E. P. Dutton and Co., 1988. Bib. refs. pp. 98-99.

[FAQ-330] Nadelstern, Paula, and LynNell Hancock. *Quilting Together: How to Organize, Design, and Make Group Quilts*. New York: Crown Publishers, 1988. Bib. p. 230.

[FAQ-340] Olsen, Kirstin. *Southwest by Southwest: Native American and Mexican Designs for Quilters*. New York: Sterling Publishing Co., 1991. Bib. refs. p. 125.

[FAQ-350] Pasquini-Masopust, Katie. *Three Dimensional Design*. Lafayette, Calif.: C & T Pub., 1988. Bib. p. 74.

[FAQ-360] Peaden, Joyce B. *Irish Chain Quilts: A Workbook of Irish Chains and Related Patterns*. Paducah, Ky.: American Quilter's Society, 1988. Bib. p. 93.

[FAQ-370] Pellman, Rachel T[homas], and Kenneth Pellman. *How to Make an Amish Quilt: More than 80 Beautiful Patterns from the Quilting Heartland of America*. Emmaus, Pa.: Rodale Press with Good Books, 1989. Bib. refs. p. 285.

[FAQ-380] Poggioli, Vicki. *Patterns from Paradise: The Art of Tahitian Quilting*. Pittstown, N.J.: Main Street Press, 1988. Bib. pp. 121-122.

[FAQ-390] Rae, Janet. *The Quilts of the British Isles*. New York: E. P. Dutton and Co., 1987. Bib. pp. 122-123.

[FAQ-400] Schaffhausen, Suzanne, and Judy Rehmel. *Women of the Bible: Quilt Patterns*. Minneapolis: Augsburg Fortress, 1991. 32 pp.

[FAQ-410] Seward, Linda. *Successful Quilting: A Step-by-Step Guide to Mastering the Techniques of Piecing, Applique and Quilting*. As *Complete Book of Patchwork, Quilting, and Applique*, New York: Prentice-Hall Press, 1987. Reprint. Emmaus, Pa.: Rodale Press, [1991]. Bib. refs. pp. 178-179.

[FAQ-420] Shirer, Marie. *The Quilters' How-to Dictionary*. Wheatbridge, Colo.: Leman, 1991. Bib. p. 80.

[FAQ-430] Simms, Ami. *Classic Quilts: Patchwork Designs from Ancient Rome*. Flint, Mich.: Mallery Press, 1991. Bib. refs. pp. 141-143.

[FAQ-440] Soltow, Willow Ann. *Designing Your Own Quilts*. Radnor, Pa.: Chilton Book Co., 1993. Bib. refs.

[FAQ-450] ------. *Quilting the World Over*. Radnor, Pa.: Chilton Book Co., 1991. 228 pp. Bib. refs. pp. 188-191.

[FAQ-460] Sturmer, Marie Monteith. *Stenciled Quilts: Techniques, Patterns, and Projects*. As *The Stenciled Quilt*, Dublin, N.H.: Yankee Books, 1986. Reprint. New York: Dover Publications, 1991. Bib. refs. p. 158.

[FAQ-470] Swim, Laurie. *World of Crafts: Quilting*. New York: Mallard Press, 1991. 128 pp. Bib.

[FAQ-480] Webster, Marie D[augherty]. *Quilts: Their Story and How to Make Them*. Garden City: Doubleday, Page, 1915. Reprint. Santa Barbara: Practical Patchwork, 1990. Detroit: Omnigraphics, 1992. Bib. refs. pp. 177-178.

[FAQ-490] Wiss, Audrey, and Douglas Wiss. *Folk Quilts and How to Recreate Them*. New York: Sterling Publishing Co., 1990. Bib. pp. 141-142.

[FAQ-500] Wood, Kaye. *Quilting for the 90's*. West Branch, Mich.: K. Wood Publishing Co., 1991-.

[FAQ-510] ------. *Quilt Like a Pro*. Rev. ed. West Branch, Mich.: K. Wood Publishing Co., 1989. Bib. refs. p. 160.

CHAPTER 9

LITERATURE

BIBLIOGRAPHIES ON LITERATURE

To conduct research on the relationship between Christianity and literature one must be conversant in a wide variety of research tools since many studies making important statements about the role of Christianity in various literary traditions are not identified as such. For example, works on John Donne and John Milton invariably introduce discussions of these authors' religious concerns, but such works are only rarely identified as studies in Christianity and the literary arts. Furthermore, even after one has located the studies by authors such as Leland Ryken and David Lyle Jeffrey showing the connections between Christian culture and literary works, one will still need to trace these analyses to supporting studies as one continues research. As in all of the arts, the more widely read an individual is, the easier time one has in generating analyses integrating faith and literary studies. The number of works which could be listed in this chapter on literature would easily fill a book. Those presented here are offered as useful beginning points in the burgeoning world of literary studies which defies comprehensive study even in narrowly defined specialities. To make the scope of this chapter somewhat reasonable, only non-dramatic studies written in, or translated into, English have been included. A few analyses of literature from non-English speaking countries have been included to provide a beginning point for comparative literature studies, but most of the studies given here treat literature written in English by people originating in Australia, Canada, Great Britain, and the United States.

For the serious researcher of literature, the single best guide is James L. Harner's *Literary Research Guide: A Guide to Reference Sources for the Study of Literatures in English and Related Topics* [BLI-710]. Harner's selections are typically strong, and his annotations and cross references are excellent. Two other research guides which have become standard reference tools for many researchers are Richard D. Altick's and Andrew Wright's *Selective Bibliography for the Study of English and American Literature* [BLI-040], and Margaret C. Patterson's *Literary Research Guide: An Evaluative, Annotated Bibliography of Important Reference Books and Periodicals on English, Irish, Scottish, Welsh, Commonwealth, American, Afro-American, American Indian, Continental, Classical, and World Literature, and Sixty Literature-Related Subject Areas* [BLI-1330]. Other research guides which are helpful for the generalist working in literature include Aliki Lafkidou Dick's *A Student's Guide to British Literature: A Selective Bibliography of 4,128 Titles and Reference Sources from the Anglo-Saxon Period to the Present* [BLI-450], Paul A. Doyle's *Guide to Basic Information Sources in English Literature* [BLI-480], Dorothea Kehler's *Problems in Literary Research: A Guide to Selected Reference Works* [BLI-970], and Michael J. Marcuse's recent and substantial volume, *A Reference Guide for English Studies* [BLI-1150].

Grouped by nationalities and ethnic groups, most of the bibliographies given below fit into one of the following categories: African [BLI-1060]; American [BLI-020], [BLI-040], [BLI-050], [BLI-230], [BLI-260], [BLI-290], [BLI-300], [BLI-320], [BLI-380], [BLI-390], [BLI-400], [BLI-500], [BLI-510], [BLI-530], [BLI-540], [BLI-580], [BLI-590], [BLI-600], [BLI-760], [BLI-780], [BLI-810], [BLI-920], [BLI-930], [BLI-1030], [BLI-1100], [BLI-1110], [BLI-1170], [BLI-1200], [BLI-1270], [BLI-1320], [BLI-1350], [BLI-1360], [BLI-1370], [BLI-1380], [BLI-1390], [BLI-1410], [BLI-1420], [BLI-1470], [BLI-1480], [BLI-1510], [BLI-1630], [BLI-1660]; American Indian [BLI-030], [BLI-130], [BLI-880]; Asian American [BLI-330]; Australian [BLI-150]; Brazilian [BLI-630]; British [BLI-040], [BLI-080], [BLI-140], [BLI-260], [BLI-280],

[BLI-410], [BLI-450], [BLI-480], [BLI-550], [BLI-960], [BLI-1100], [BLI-1150], [BLI-1160], [BLI-1400], [BLI-1470], [BLI-1500], [BLI-1520], [BLI-1530], [BLI-1560], [BLI-1610], [BLI-1670]; Canadian [BLI-650], [BLI-940], [BLI-1040], [BLI-1220], [BLI-1430], [BLI-1550], [BLI-1620]; Caribbean [BLI-430] and [BLI-770]; Chinese [BLI-170]; East Indian [BLI-1280]; European [BLI-120] and [BLI-800]; German [BLI-660]; Icelandic [BLI-1300]; Irish [BLI-550], [BLI-560], [BLI-750], [BLI-960], [BLI-1050]; Japanese [BLI-1140]; Jewish American [BLI-420]; Latin American [BLI-090], [BLI-180], [BLI-610], [BLI-1190], [BLI-1680]; Mexican American [BLI-620] and [BLI-1180]; Polish [BLI-950]; Scottish [BLI-200], [BLI-220], [BLI-700], [BLI-1230]; Spanish [BLI-1490].

For the latest list of articles and books on literature, consult the annual volumes of the *MLA International Bibliography of Books and Articles on the Modern Languages and Literatures* [BLI-1250], and any of the following items: [BLI-050], [BLI-060], [BLI-220], [BLI-520], [BLI-1670]. Also consult the bibliographies given in theses and dissertations, which can be identified in the now monthly volumes of *Dissertation Abstracts International*, and in the following works given below: [BLI-500], [BLI-650], [BLI-670], [BLI-810], [BLI-1100], [BLI-1660]. Researchers will also be helped by directories to the small presses and little magazines--such as [BLI-460], [BLI-830], and [BLI-1460]-- since these publishers often promote minority views and lesser known authors not represented by the larger publishing houses. The small presses have been especially important in promoting the works of new authors establishing new styles and traditions.

Literature studies can be divided according to genres, geographical or ethnic origins, historical periods, subject matter, and even gender studies, all of which are evident in the titles of the works given in this section. Three areas of literature studies are receiving special attention these days, including black, folk, and women's studies. For black studies see items [BLI-190], [BLI-1060], [BLI-1290], [BLI-1420], and [BLI-1510]. For folk studies see items [BLI-010], [BLI-070], [BLI-080], [BLI-500], [BLI-580], [BLI-760], [BLI-850], [BLI-860], [BLI-870], [BLI-900], [BLI-930], [BLI-1090], [BLI-1360], and [BLI-1510]. For women's studies see [BLI-020], [BLI-140], [BLI-240], [BLI-670], [BLI-690], [BLI-820], [BLI-1140], [BLI-1190], [BLI-1370], and [BLI-1380].

One additional work which is likely to prove useful for those tracing pen names is Jennifer Mossman's *Pseudonyms and Nicknames Dictionary* [BLI-1260].

[BLI-010] Aarne, Antti. *The Types of the Folktale: A Classification and Bibliography* (Aarne-Thompson). Trans. and enlarged Stith Thompson. 2nd rev. FF Communications 184. Helsinki: Suomalainen Tiedeakatemia, 1961. 588 pp.

[BLI-020] Addis, Patricia K. *Through a Woman's I: An Annotated Bibliography of American Women's Autobiographical Writings, 1946-1976*. Metuchen, N.J.: Scarecrow Press, 1983. 621 pp.

[BLI-030] Allis, Jeannette B. *West Indian Literature: An Index to Criticism, 1930-1975*. Reference Publication in Latin American Studies. Boston: G. K. Hall, 1981. 353 pp.

[BLI-040] Altick, Richard D., and Andrew Wright, eds. *Selective Bibliography for the Study of English and American Literature*. 6th ed. New York: Macmillan Publishing Co., 1979. 180 pp.

[BLI-050] *American Literary Scholarship: An Annual [1963-]*. Durham, N.C.: Duke University Press, 1965-.

[BLI-060] *Annual Bibliography of Scottish Literature [1969-]*. Edinburgh: Library Association, Scottish Group, Edinburgh University Library, 1970-.

[BLI-070] Azzolina, David S. *Tale Type- and Motif-Indexes: An Annotated Bibliography*. Garland Reference Library of the Humanities, no. 565: Garland Folklore Bibliographies, no. 12. New York: Garland Publishing, 1987. 105 pp.

[BLI-080] Baer, Florence E. *Folklore and Literature of the British Isles: An Annotated Bibliography*. Garland Reference Library of the Humanities, no. 622; Garland Folklore Bibliographies, no. 11. New York: Garland Publishing, 1986. 355 pp.

[BLI-090] Balderston, Daniel, comp. *The Latin American Short Story: An Annotated Guide to Anthologies and Criticism*. Westport, Conn.: Greenwood Press, 1992. 529 pp.

[BLI-100] Barron, Neil, ed. *Fantasy Literature: A Reader's Guide*. Garland Reference Library of the Humanities, no. 874. New York: Garland Publishing, 1990. 586 pp.

[BLI-110] ------. *Horror Literature: A Reader's Guide*. Garland Reference

Library of the Humanities, no. 1220. New York: Garland
Publishing, 1990. 596 pp.

[BLI-120] Bede, Jean-Albert, and William Edgerton. *Columbia Dictionary of
Modern European Literature*. 2nd ed. New York: Columbia
University Press, 1980. 800 pp.

[BLI-130] Beidler, Peter G., and Marion F. Egge. *The American Indian in
Short Fiction: An Annotated Bibliography*. Metuchen, N.J.:
Scarecrow Press, 1979. 215 pp.

[BLI-140] Bell, Maureen, George Parfitt, and Simon Shepherd, eds. *A Biographical Dictionary of English Women Writers, 1580-1720*.
Great Britain; New York: Harvester Wheatsheaf, 1990.
298 pp. Bib. refs. pp. xxi-xxvi.

[BLI-150] Bennett, Bruce, with Peter Cowan, John Hay, and Susan Ashford.
Western Australian Writing: A Bibliography. South Fremantle, Australia: Fremantle Arts Centre Press, 1990. 334 pp.

[BLI-160] Bennett, James R. *A Bibliography of Stylistics and Related Criticism, 1967-1983*. New York: Modern Language Associa-
tion of America, 1986. 405 pp.

[BLI-170] Berry, Margaret. *The Chinese Classic Novels: An Annotated Bibliography of Chiefly English-Language Studies*. Garland Reference Library of the Humanities, no. 775. New York:
Garland Publishing, 1988. 302 pp.

[BLI-180] Bhalia, Alok. *Latin American Writers: A Bibliography with Critical
and Biographical Introductions*. New York: Envoy, 1987.
174 pp.

[BLI-190] *Bibliographic Guide to Black Studies*. New York: G. K. Hall, 1980.
Supplements, 1984, 1986, 1987, 1989.

[BLI-200] *Bibliography of Scotland [1976-]*. Edinburgh: National Library of
Scotland, 1978-. Annual.

[BLI-210] *Bibliophile Dictionary, The: A Biographical Record of the Great
Authors, with Bibliographical Notices of Their Principal Works
from the Beginning of History*. 2 vols. 1904. Reprint.
[Detroit]: Gale Research, 1966.

[BLI-220] *Bibliotheck, The: A Scottish Journal of Bibliography and Allied
Topics*. 1956-. 3/year.

[BLI-230] Blanck, Jacob, comp. *Bibliography of American Literature*. 9 vols.
New Haven: Yale University Press, 1955-1991.

[BLI-240] Boos, Florence, and Lynn Miller, eds. *Bibliography of Women and Literature, I and II. Articles and Books (1974-1978) by and about Women from 600 to 1975; Articles and Books (1979-1981) by and about Women from 600-1975.* New York: Holmes and Meier, 1989. 439 pp.; 342 pp.

[BLI-250] Borck, Jim Springer, ed. *The Eighteenth Century: A Current Bibliography for [1925-].* New York: AMS, 1978-.

[BLI-260] Boswell, Jeanetta. *"Past Ruined Ilion . . .": A Bibliography of English and American Literature Based on Greco-Roman Mythology.* Metuchen, N.J.: Scarecrow Press, 1982. 333 pp.

[BLI-270] British Library, Department of Manuscript Staff. *Index of Manuscripts in the British Library.* 10 vols. Alexandria, Va.: Chadwyck-Healey, 1985.

[BLI-280] *British Writers and Their Works.* 10 vols. Lincoln: University of Nebraska Press, 1964-1970.

[BLI-290] Bruccoli, Matthew J., and Judith S. Baughman, eds. *Bibliography of American Fiction 1919-1988: Vol. 1. James Agee--John P. Marquand; Vol. 2. Peter Matthiesen--Roger Zelanzy.* Facts on File Bibliographies. New York: Facts on File, 1991. 319, 648 pp.

[BLI-300] Bruccoli, Matthew J., Richard Layman, and C. E. Frazer Clark, Jr., eds. *Concise Dictionary of American Literary Bibliography: The Twenties, 1917-1929.* Detroit: Gale Research, 1989. 326 pp.

[BLI-310] Carter, Paul J., and George K. Smart, eds. *Literature and Society, 1961-1965: A Selective Bibliography.* Modern Language Association of America. Coral Gables, Fla.: University of Miami Press, [1967]. 160 pp.

[BLI-320] Caskey, Jefferson D. *Appalachian Authors: A Selective Bibliography.* West Cornwall, Conn.: Locust Hill Press, 1990. 191 pp.

[BLI-330] Cheung, King-Kok, and Stan Yogi, comps. *Asian American Literature: An Annotated Bibliography.* New York: Modern Language Association, 1988. 276 pp.

[BLI-340] Comparative Literature Faculty, Livingston College, Rutgers University. *A Syllabus of Comparative Literature.* Ed. John O. McCormick. Metuchen, N.J.: Scarecrow Press, 1972. 220 pp.

[BLI-350] *Concise Bibliography for Students of English.* 5th ed. Stanford:

Stanford University Press, 1972. 304 pp.

[BLI-360] Connolly, Cyril. *The Modern Movement: One Hundred Key Books from England, France, and America, 1880-1950.* New York: Atheneum, 1966. 148 pp.

[BLI-370] *Contemporary Authors.* Detroit: Gale Research, 1962-.

[BLI-380] *Contemporary Authors: Bibliographical Series.* Detroit: Gale Research, 1986-. Vol. 1: *American Novelists.* Ed. James J. Martine. 1986. 431 pp. Vol. 2: *American Poets.* Ed. Ronald Baughman. 1986. 387 pp.

[BLI-390] Cook, Michael L., Stephen T. Miller. *Mystery, Detective, and Espionage Fiction: A Checklist of Fiction in U.S. Pulp Magazines, 1915-1974, I and II.* Fiction in Pulp Magazines, no. 1. Garland Reference Library of the Humanities, no. 838. New York: Garland Publishing, 1988. 1,183 pp.

[BLI-400] Cripe, Helen, and Diane Campbell, eds. *American Manuscripts, 1763-1815: An Index to Documents Described in Auction Records and Dealer's Catalogues.* Wilmington: Scholarly Resources, 1977. 704 pp.

[BLI-410] Croft, P. J., Theodore Hofmann, and John Horden, eds. *Index of English Literary Manuscripts.* London: Mansell; New York: R. R. Bowker, 1980-.

[BLI-420] Cronin, Gloria L., Blaine H. Hall, and Connie Lamb. *Jewish American Fiction Writers: An Annotated Bibliography.* New York: Garland Publishing, 1991. 1,233 pp.

[BLI-430] Dance, Daryl Cumber, ed. *Fifty Caribbean Writers: A Bio-Bibliographical Critical Sourcebook.* New York: Greenwood Press, 1986. 530 pp.

[BLI-440] Denham, Robert D. *Northrop Frye: An Annotated Bibliography of Primary and Secondary Sources.* Toronto: University of Toronto Press, 1987. 449 pp.

[BLI-450] Dick, Aliki Lafkidou. *A Student's Guide to British Literature: A Selective Bibliography of 4,128 Titles and Reference Sources from the Anglo-Saxon Period to the Present.* Littleton, Colo.: Libraries Unlimited, 1972. 285 pp.

[BLI-460] *Directory of Small Press and Magazine Editors and Publishers.* Paradise, Calif.: Dustbooks, 1971-. Annual.

[BLI-470] Doll, Howard D. *Oral Interpretation of Literature: An Annotated Bibliography with Multimedia Listings.* Metuchen, N.J.:

Scarecrow Press, 1982. 505 pp.

[BLI-480] Doyle, Paul A. *Guide to Basic Information Sources in English Literature.* New York: Wiley, 1976. 143 pp.

[BLI-490] Dudley, Fred Adair, ed. *The Relations of Literature and Science: A Selected Bibliography, 1930-1967.* Ann Arbor, Mich.: University Microfilms, 1968. 137 pp.

[BLI-500] Dundes, Alan, comp. *Folklore Theses and Dissertations in the United States.* Publications of the American Folklore Society: Bibliographical and Special Series 27. Austin: University of Texas Press, for American Folklore Society, 1976. 610 pp. (Covers 1860 to 1968.)

[BLI-510] Eichelberger, Clayton L. *A Guide to Critical Reviews of United States Fiction, 1870-1910: Vol. I.* Metuchen, N.J.: Scarecrow Press, 1971. 415 pp.

[BLI-520] *Essay and General Literature Index.* New York: H. W. Wilson, 1931-. Semi-annual.

[BLI-530] Etulain, R. W., ed. *Bibliographical Guide to the Study of Western American Literature.* Lincoln: University of Nebraska Press, 1982. 317 pp.

[BLI-540] Evans, Charles, ed. *American Bibliography.* 14 vols. Magnolia, Mass.: Peter Smith, 1967.

[BLI-550] Finneran, Richard J., ed. *Anglo-Irish Literature: A Review of Research.* New York: Modern Language Association, 1976. 596 pp.

[BLI-560] ------, ed. *Recent Research on Anglo-Irish Writers: A Supplement to Anglo-Irish Literature: A Review of Research.* 2nd ed. Modern Language Association of America Reviews of Research. New York: Modern Language Association, 1990.

[BLI-570] Fisher, Benjamin Franklin, IV. *The Gothic's Gothic: Study Aids to the Tradition of the Tale of Terror.* Garland Reference Library of the Humanities, no. 567. New York: Garland Publishing, 1988. 485 pp.

[BLI-580] Flanagan, Cathleen C., and John T. Flanagan. *American Folklore: A Bibliography, 1950-1974.* Metuchen, N.J.: Scarecrow Press, 1977. 406 pp.

[BLI-590] Flora, Joseph M., and Robert [A.] Bain, eds. *Fifty Southern Writers after 1900: A Bio-Bibliographical Sourcebook.* Westport,

Conn.: Greenwood Press, 1987. 628 pp.

[BLI-600]   ------. *Contemporary Fiction Writers of the South: A Bio-Biblio-graphical Sourcebook.* Westport, Conn.: Greenwood Press, 1993.

[BLI-610]   Forster, Merlin H. *Vanguardism in Latin American Literature: An Annotated Bibliographical Guide.* New York: Greenwood Press, 1990. 214 pp.

[BLI-620]   Foster, David William. *Mexican Literature: A Bibliography of Secondary Sources.* 2nd ed. Metuchen, N.J.: Scarecrow Press, 1992. 686 pp. Bib. refs. pp. 3-11.

[BLI-630]   Foster, David William, and Walter Rela. *Brazilian Literature: A Research Bibliography.* Garland Reference Library of the Humanities, no. 1162. New York: Garland Publishing, 1990. 426 pp.

[BLI-640]   Frank, Frederick S. *Guide to the Gothic: An Annotated Bibliography of Criticism.* Metuchen, N.J.: Scarecrow Press, 1984. 437 pp.

[BLI-650]   Gabel, Gernot U. *Canadian Literature: An Index to Theses Accepted by Canadian Universities 1925-1980.* Cologne: Gemini, 1984. 157 pp.

[BLI-660]   Gerber, Margy, and Judith Pouget. *Literature of the German Democratic Republic in English Translation: A Bibliography.* Studies in GDR Culture and Society: A Supplementary Volume. Lanham, Md.: University Press of America, 1984. 134 pp.

[BLI-670]   Gilbert, V. F., and D. S. Tatla. *Women's Studies: A Bibliography of Dissertations, 1870-1982.* Oxford: Basil Blackwell Publishing, 1985. 496 pp.

[BLI-680]   *Goldentree Bibliographies in Language and Literature.* Series. Northbrook, Ill.: AHM, 1968-1979.

[BLI-690]   Grimes, Janet, and Diva Daims. *Novels in English by Women, 1891-1920: A Preliminary Checklist.* Garland Reference Library of the Humanities 202. New York: Garland Publishing, 1981. 805 pp.

[BLI-700]   Hancock, P. D., comp. *A Bibliography of Works Relating to Scotland, 1916-1950.* 2 vols. Edinburgh: Edinburgh University Press, 1959-1960.

[BLI-710]   Harner, James L. *Literary Research Guide: A Guide to Reference*

Sources for the Study of Literatures in English and Related Topics. 2nd ed. New York: Modern Language Association, 1993. 766 pp. Annotated.

[BLI-720] Harte, Barbara, and Carolyn Riley, eds. *200 Contemporary Authors: Bio-Bibliographies of Selected Leading Writers of Today with Critical and Personal Sidelights.* Detroit, Mich.: Gale Research, [1969]. 306 pp.

[BLI-730] Havlice, Patricia Pate. *Index to Literary Biography.* 2 vols. Metuchen, N.J.: Scarecrow Press, 1975. 1,308 pp.

[BLI-740] ------. *Index to Literary Biography.* 2 vols. Metuchen, N.J.: Scarecrow Press, 1983. 1,202 pp.

[BLI-750] Hayes, Richard J., ed. *Manuscript Sources for the History of Irish Civilisation.* 11 vols. Boston: G. K. Hall, 1965. *First Supplement, 1965-1975.* 3 vols. 1979.

[BLI-760] Haywood, Charles. *A Bibliography of North American Folklore and Folksong.* 2nd rev. ed. 2 vols. New York: Dover Publications, 1961.

[BLI-770] Herdeck, Donald E., ed. *Caribbean Writers: A Bio-Bibliographical-Critical Encyclopedia.* Washington, D.C.: Three Continents, 1979. 943 pp.

[BLI-780] Hickey, Morgen. *The Bohemian Register: An Annotated Bibliography of the Beat Literary Movement.* Metuchen, N.J.: Scarecrow Press, 1990. 271 pp.

[BLI-790] Holland, Norman N. *A Reader's Guide to Psychoanalytic Psychology and Literature-and-Psychology.* Gainesville: Institute for Psychoanalytic Study of Arts, University of Florida, 1988. 68 pp.

[BLI-800] Hopper, Vincent F., and Bernard D. N. Grebanier. *Bibliography for Essentials of European Literature.* Brooklyn, N.Y.: n.p., 1953. 128 pp. [1,800]

[BLI-810] Howard, Patsy C., comp. *Theses in American Literature, 1896-1971.* Ann Arbor: Pierian, 1973. 307 pp.

[BLI-820] Humm, Maggie. *An Annotated Critical Bibliography of Feminist Criticism.* Harvester Annotated Critical Bibliographies. Boston: G. K. Hall, 1987. 240 pp.

[BLI-830] *International Directory of Little Magazines and Small Presses, The.* Paradise, Calif.: Dustbooks, 1965-. Annual. Formerly *Directory of Little Magazines & Small Presses, 1965-1973.*

28th ed. 932 pp.

[BLI-840]   *IPSA Abstracts and Bibliography in Literature and Psychology*. Gainesville: Institute for Psychological Study of the Arts, Department of English, University of Florida, 1986-. Annual.

[BLI-850]   Ireland, Norma O., comp. *Index to Fairy Tales, 1949--1972: Including Folklore, Legends and Myths in Collections; Third Supplement*. Metuchen, N.J.: Scarecrow Press, 1973. 741 pp.

[BLI-860]   ------, comp. *Index to Fairy Tales, 1973-1977: Including Folklore, Legends and Myths in Collections; Fourth Supplement*. Metuchen, N.J.: Scarecrow Press, 1985. 259 pp.

[BLI-870]   Ireland, Norma O., and Joseph W. Sprug, comps. *Index to Fairy Tales, 1978-1986: Including Folklore, Legends and Myths in Collections; Fifth Supplement*. Metuchen, N.J.: Scarecrow Press, 1989. 585 pp.

[BLI-880]   Jacobson, Angeline. *Contemporary Native American Literature: A Selected and Partially Annotated Bibliography*. Metuchen, N.J.: Scarecrow Press, 1977. 247 pp.

[BLI-890]   Jarrell, Howard R. *International Meditation Bibliography, 1950-1982*. Metuchen, N.J.: Scarecrow Press, 1985. 444 pp.

[BLI-900]   Jobes, Gertrude. *Dictionary of Mythology, Folklore and Symbols*. 3 vols. Metuchen, N.J.: Scarecrow Press, 1961-1962. 2,241 pp.

[BLI-910]   Jobes, Gertrude, and James Jobes. *Outer Space: Myths, Name Meanings, Calendars from the Emergence of History to the Present Day*. Metuchen, N.J.: Scarecrow Press, 1964. 479 pp.

[BLI-920]   Johnson, Thomas H., and Richard M. Ludwig, eds. *Literary History of the United States: Bibliography*. 4th ed. New York: Macillan Publishing Co., 1974. 1,466 pp.

[BLI-930]   Jones, Steven Swann. *Folklore and Literature in the United States: An Annotated Bibliography of Studies of Folklore in American Literature*. Garland Folklore Bibliographies, no. 5. New York: Garland Publishing, 1984. 262 pp.

[BLI-940]   Kandiuk, Mary. *French-Canadian Authors: A Bibliography of Their Works and of English-Language Criticism*. Metuchen, N.J.: Scarecrow Press, 1990. 234 pp.

[BLI-950]   Kanka, August Gerald. *Poland: An Annotated Bibliography of*

Books in English. Garland Reference Library of the Hu-
manties, no. 743. New York: Garland Publishing, 1988.
395 pp.

[BLI-960] Keeble, N. H., ed. *Handbook of English and Celtic Studies in the
United Kingdom and Republic of Ireland.* Stirling: Stirling
University Press, 1988. 379 pp.

[BLI-970] Kehler, Dorothea. *Problems in Literary Research: A Guide to
Selected Reference Works.* 3rd ed. Metuchen, N.J.: Scarecrow Press, 1987. 237 pp.

[BLI-980] Kiell, Norman, ed. *Psychoanalysis, Psychology, and Literature: A
Bibliography.* 2nd ed. 2 vols. Metuchen, N.J.: Scarecrow
Press, 1982. 1,296 pp.

[BLI-990] ------. *Psychoanalysis, Psychology, and Literature, Supplement to the
Second Edition: A Bibliography.* Metuchen, N.J.: Scare-
crow Press, 1990. 599 pp.

[BLI-1000] Koehmstedt, Carol L. *Plot Summary Index.* Metuchen, N.J.:
Scarecrow Press, 1973. 312 pp.

[BLI-1010] Kohl, Benjamin G. *Renaissance Humanism, 1300-1550: A Bibliography of Materials in English.* Garland Reference Library
of the Humanities, no. 570. New York: Garland Publishing,
1985. 354 pp.

[BLI-1020] Krawitz, Henry. *A Post-Symbolist Bibliography.* Metuchen, N.J.:
Scarecrow Press, 1973. 284 pp.

[BLI-1030] Leary, Lewis. *Articles on American Literature, 1900-1950.*
Durham: Duke University Press, 1954. 437 pp. Leary, with
Carolyn Bartholet and Catharine Roth, comps. *1950-1967.*
1970. 751 pp. Leary and John Auchard, comps. *1968-1975.*
1979. 745 pp. (Supplement in progress.)

[BLI-1040] Lecker, Robert, and Jack David, eds. *The Annotated Bibliography
of Canada's Major Authors.* 8 vols. Toronto: ECW, 1979-.

[BLI-1050] Lester, DeeGee, comp. *Irish Research: A Guide to Collections in
North America, Ireland, and Great Britain.* Bibliographies
and Indexes in World History 9. New York: Greenwood
Press, 1987. 348 pp.

[BLI-1060] Lindfors, Bernth. *Black African Literature in English, 1977-1981
Supplement.* New York: Africana, 1986. 382 pp.

[BLI-1070] Lynn, Ruth Nadelman. *Fantasy for Children: An Annotated
Checklist.* New York: R. R. Bowker, 1979. 288 pp.

237

[BLI-1080] McCormick, John O. *A Syllabus of Comparative Literature.* 2nd ed. Metuchen, N.J.: Scarecrow Press, 1972. 233 pp.

[BLI-1090] MacDonald, Margaret Read. *The Storyteller's Sourcebook: A Subject, Title, and Motif Index to Folklore Collections for Children.* Detroit: Neal-Schuman with Gale Research, 1982. 818 pp.

[BLI-1100] McNamee, Lawrence F. *Dissertations in English and American Literature: Theses Accepted by American, British, and German Universities 1865-1964.* New York: R. R. Bowker, 1968.

[BLI-1110] McPheron, William, and Jocelyn Sheppard. *The Bibliography of Contemporary American Fiction, 1945-1988: An Annotated Checklist.* Westport, Conn.: Meckler Corporation; Greenwood Publishing Group, Inc., 1989.

[BLI-1120] Madden, David, and Richard Powers. *Writers' Revisions: An Annotated Bibliography of Articles and Books About Writers' Revisions and Their Comments on the Creative Process.* Metuchen, N.J.: Scarecrow Press, 1981. 254 pp.

[BLI-1130] Magill, F. N., ed. *Critical Survey of Short Fiction.* 7 vols. Englewood Cliffs, N.J.: Salem, 1981. Supplement, 1987.

[BLI-1140] Mamola, Claire Zebroski. *Japanese Women Writers in English Translation: An Annotated Bibliography.* Garland Reference Library of the Humanities, no. 877. New York: Garland Publishing, 1989. 469 pp.

[BLI-1150] Marcuse, Michael J. *A Reference Guide for English Studies.* Berkeley: University of California Press, 1990. 864 pp.

[BLI-1160] Markert, Lawrence W[ayne]. *The Bloomsbury Group: A Reference Guide.* Boston: G. K. Hall, 1990. 325 pp.

[BLI-1170] Marks, Patricia. *American Literary and Drama Reviews: An Index to Late Nineteenth Century Periodicals.* Boston: G. K. Hall, 1984. 313 pp.

[BLI-1180] Martinez, Julio A. *Chicano Scholars and Writers: A Bio-Bibliographical Directory.* Metuchen, N.J.: Scarecrow Press, 1979. 589 pp.

[BLI-1190] Marting, Diane E., ed. *Women Writers of Spanish America: An Annotated Bio-Bibliographical Guide.* New York: Greenwood Press, 1987. 448 pp.

[BLI-1200] Maxwell, Donald W. *Literature of the Great Lakes Region: An*

Annotated Bibliography. New York: Garland Publishing, 1991. 485 pp.

[BLI-1210] Milic, Louis T. *Style and Stylistics: An Analytical Bibliography.* New York: Free Press, 1967.

[BLI-1220] Miska, John. *Ethnic and Native Canadian Literature: A Bibliography.* Toronto: University of Toronto Press, 1990. 445 pp.

[BLI-1230] Mitchell, Arthur, and C. G. Cash. *A Contribution to the Bibliography of Scottish Topography.* 2 vols. Publications of the Scottish History Society 2nd series 14-15. Edinburgh: Edinburgh University Press, for Scottish History Society, 1917.

[BLI-1240] Modern Language Association of America. Bibliography Committee. *A Bibliography on the Relations of Literature and the Other Arts, 1952-1967.* New York: AMS Press, [1968].

[BLI-1250] *MLA International Bibliography of Books and Articles on the Modern Languages and Literatures.* New York: Modern Language Association of America, 1921-present. Annual.

[BLI-1260] Mossman, Jennifer, ed. *Pseudonyms and Nicknames Dictionary: A Guide to 80,000 Aliases, Appellations, Assumed Names, Code Names, Cognomens, Cover Names, Epithets, Initialisms, Nicknames, Noms de Guerre, Noms de Plume, Pen Names, Pseudonyms, Sobriquets, and Stage Names of 55,000 Contemporary and Historical Persons, Including the Subjects' Real Names, Basic Biographical Information, and Citations for the Sources from Which the Entries Were Compiled.* 3rd ed. 2 vols. Detroit: Gale Research, 1987.

[BLI-1270] Myerson, Joel, ed. *Studies in the American Renaissance.* Charlottesville: University Press of Virginia, 1983-1989.

[BLI-1280] Nelson, Emmanuel S[ampath], ed. *Writers of the Indian Diaspora: A Bio-Bibliographical Critical Sourcebook.* Westport, Conn.: Greenwood Press, 1993. Bib. refs.

[BLI-1290] Newby, James Edward. *Black Authors: A Selected Annotated Bibliography.* Garland Reference Library of the Humanities, no. 1260. New York: Garland Publishing, 1991. 720 pp.

[BLI-1300] Ober, Kenneth H. *Bibliography of Modern Icelandic Literature in Translation: Supplement, 1971-1980.* Ithaca: Cornell University Press, 1990. 332 pp.

[BLI-1310] Ocheretianskii, Aleksandr. *Literature and Art of Avant-Garde Russia (1890-1930): Bibliographical Index.* Trans. *Litera-*

turnyi Avangard. Russian Bibliographical Series, no. 7. Newtonville, Mass.: Oriental Research Partners, 1989. Russian with English introduction and index.

[BLI-1320] Parker, Patricia L. *Early American Fiction: A Reference Guide.* Boston: G. K. Hall, 1984. 197 pp.

[BLI-1330] Patterson, Margaret C. *Literary Research Guide: An Evaluative, Annotated Bibliography of Important Reference Books and Periodicals on English, Irish, Scottish, Welsh, Commonwealth, American, Afro-American, American Indian, Continental, Classical, and World Literature, and Sixty Literature-Related Subject Areas.* 2nd ed. New York: Modern Language Association, 1983. 559 pp.

[BLI-1340] Radcliffe, Elsa J. *Gothic Novels of the Twentieth Century: An Annotated Bibliography.* Metuchen, N.J.: Scarecrow Press, 1979. 291 pp.

[BLI-1350] Raimo, John W., ed. *A Guide to Manuscripts Relating to America in Great Britain and Ireland.* Rev. ed. Westport, Conn.: Meckler, for British Association for American Studies, 1979. 467 pp.

[BLI-1360] Randolph, Vance. *Ozark Folklore: A Bibliography.* Bloomington: Indiana University Research Center for the Language Sciences, [1972]. 572 pp.

[BLI-1370] Redfern, Bernice. *Women of Color in the United States: A Guide to the Literature.* Garland Reference Library of Social Science, no. 469. New York: Garland Publishing, 1989. 156 pp.

[BLI-1380] Reisman, Rosemary M. Canfield, and Christopher J. Canfield. *Contemporary Southern Women Fiction Writers: An Annotated Bibliography.* Pasadena, Calif.: Salem Press, 1993.

[BLI-1390] Robbins, J. Albert, et al., eds. *American Literary Manuscripts: A Checklist of Holdings in Academic, Historical, and Public Libraries, Museums, and Authors' Homes in the United States.* 2nd ed. Athens: University of Georgia Press, 1977. 387 pp.

[BLI-1400] *Romantic Movement, The: A Selective and Critical Bibliography for [1964-].* West Cornwall, Conn.: Locust Hill, 1964-. Annual.

[BLI-1410] Rubin, Louis D., Jr. *Bibliographical Guide to the Study of Southern Literature.* Southern Literary Studies Series. Baton Rouge: Louisiana State University Press, 1969. 364 pp.

[BLI-1420] Rush, Theressa Gunnels, Carol Fairbanks Myers, and Esther Spring Arata. *Black American Writers Past and Present: A Biographical and Bibliographical Dictionary.* 2 vols. Metuchen, N.J.: Scarecrow Press, 1975. 865 pp.

[BLI-1430] Ryder, Dorothy E. *Canadian Reference Sources: A Selective Guide.* 2nd ed. Ottawa: Canadian Library Association, 1981. 311 pp.

[BLI-1440] Salisbury, Joyce E. *Medieval Sexuality: A Research Guide.* Garland Reference Library of Social Science (Garland Medieval Bibliographies). Series no. 5, no. 565. New York: Garland Publishing, 1990. 210 pp.

[BLI-1450] Schatzberg, Walter, Ronald A. Waite, and Jonathan K. Johnson, eds. *The Relations of Literature and Science: An Annotated Bibliography of Scholarship, 1880-1980.* New York: Modern Language Association, 1987. 458 pp.

[BLI-1460] *Small Press Record of Books in Print, The.* Paradise, Calif.: Dustbooks, 1972-. Annual. 21st ed. over 1,200 pp.

[BLI-1470] Somer, John L., and Barbara Eck Cooper. *American and British Literature, 1945-1975: An Annotated Bibliography of Contemporary Scholarship.* Lawrence: Regents Press of Kansas, 1980. 326 pp.

[BLI-1480] Spiller, Robert E., et al., eds. *Literary History of the United States.* 4th ed. 2 vols. New York: Macmillan Publishing Co., 1974. Bib. Vol. 2.

[BLI-1490] Stubbings, Hilda U. *Renaissance Spain in its Literary Relations with England and France: A Critical Bibliography.* Nashville: Vanderbilt University Press, [1969].

[BLI-1500] Sullivan, Alvin, ed. *British Literary Magazines.* 4 vols. Historical to the World's Periodicals and Newspapers. Westport, Conn.: Greenwood Press, 1983-1986. Vol. 1: *The Augustan Age and the Age of Johnson, 1698-1788.* 1983. 427 pp. Vol. 2: *The Romantic Age, 1789-1836.* 1983. 491 pp. Vol. 3: *The Victorian and Edwardian Age, 1837-1913.* 1984. 560 pp. Vol. 4: *The Modern Age, 1914-1984.* 1986. 628 pp.

[BLI-1510] Szwed, John F., and Roger D. Abrahams. *Afro-American Folk Culture: An Annotated Bibliography of Materials from North, Central and South America, and the West Indies.* 2 vols. Publications of the American Folklore Society: Bibliographical and Special Series 31-32. Philadelphia: Institute for the Study of Human Issues, 1978.

[BLI-1520] Tajima, Matsuji. *Old and Middle English Language Studies: A Classified Bibliography, 1923-1985.* Amsterdam Studies in the Theory and History of Linguistic Science V: Library and Information Sources in Linguistics, no. 13. Amsterdam: Benjamins, 1988. 391 pp.

[BLI-1530] Tobias, Richard C., and Barbara N. Tobias. *Bibliographies of Studies in Victorian Literature for the Ten Years 1975-1984.* AMS Studies in the Nineteenth Century, no. 11. New York: AMS, 1991. 1130 pp.

[BLI-1540] Trautmann, Joanne, and Carol Pollard. *Literature and Medicine: An Annotated Bibliography.* Rev. ed. Contemporary Community Health Series. Pittsburgh: University of Pittsburgh Press, 1982. 228 pp.

[BLI-1550] Tremaine, Marie. *A Bibliography of Canadian Imprints, 1751-1800.* Toronto: University of Toronto Press, 1952. 705 pp.

[BLI-1560] Vann, J. Don, and Rosemary T. VanArsdel, eds. *Victorian Periodicals: A Guide to Research.* 2 vols. New York: Modern Language Association, 1978, 1989.

[BLI-1570] Vrana, Stan A. *Interviews and Conversations with 20th-Century Authors Writing in English: An Index.* Metuchen, N.J.: Scarecrow Press, 1982. 259 pp.

[BLI-1580] ------. *Interviews and Conversations with 20th-Century Authors Writing in English, Series II: An Index.* Metuchen, N.J.: Scarecrow Press, 1986. 328 pp.

[BLI-1590] ------. *Interviews and Conversations with 20th-Century Authors Writing in English, Series III: An Index.* Metuchen, N.J.: Scarecrow Press, 1990. 467 pp.

[BLI-1600] Walker, Warren S., ed. *Twentieth-Century Short Story Explication: Interpretations, 1900--1975, of Short Fiction Since 1800.* 3rd ed. Hamden, Conn.: Shoe String Press, 1977. 880 pp. Supplements, 1980, 1984, 1987, 1989.

[BLI-1610] Watson, George, and I. R. Willison, eds. *New Cambridge Bibliography of English Literature.* 5 vols. Cambridge: Cambridge University Press, 1969-1977.

[BLI-1620] Watters, Reginald Eyre. *A Checklist of Canadian Literature and Background Materials, 1628-1960.* 2nd ed. Toronto: University of Toronto Press, 1972. 1,085 pp.

[BLI-1630] Wegelin, Oscar. *Bibliography of American Poetry, Sixteen-Fifty to Eighteen-Twenty.* 2 vols. in 1. Magnolia, Mass.: Peter

Smith, n.d.

[BLI-1640] Welch, Jeffrey. *Literature and Film: An Annotated Bibliography,*
1900-1977. New York: Garland Publishing, 1981. 350 pp.

[BLI-1650] ------. *Literature and Film: An Annotated Bibliography, 1978-1988.*
New York: Garland Publishing, 1993. 341 pp.

[BLI-1660] Woodress, James. *Dissertations in American Literature, 1891-*
1966. Rev. ed. Durham: Duke University Press, 1968.
185 pp.

[BLI-1670] *Year's Work in English Studies.* London: Murray; Atlantic Highlands: Humanities for the English Association, 1921-.
Annual.

[BLI-1680] Zubatsky, David. *Latin American Literary Authors: An Annotated*
Guide to Bibliographies. Metuchen, N.J.: Scarecrow Press,
1986. 332 pp.

KEY WORKS ON LITERARY THEORY

Literary theory and criticism are often combined in analyses of literature, but certainly have separate functions, the latter being an application of
the former. To locate studies of critical theory, consult [LIT-010] and [LIT-
020], as well as pertinent sections of the *MLA International Bibliography of*
Books and Articles on the Modern Languages and Literatures [BLI-1250]. For
the most recent articles and reviews of books on this topic, see the journals
listed below, [LIT-670], [LIT-710], and [LIT-720]. For single volume texts
introducing one to the full range of literary theories from Plato to the present,
the two best books are Hazard Adams's *Critical Theory Since Plato* [LIT-050],
and Bernard F. Dukore's *Dramatic Theory and Criticism: Greeks to Grotowski*
[DRH-290] introduced in Chapter 6 on drama. For a more exhaustive treatment of literary theory in recent centuries, see René Wellek's eight volume *A*
History of Modern Criticism, 1750-1850 [LIC-1540], and Joseph Gibaldi's two
collections of essays, [LIC-680] and [LIC-690], also given below in the section
on criticism. Also consult Raman Selden's *A Reader's Guide to Contemporary*
Literary Theory [LIT-800] for a review of recent developments in literary
theory.

During the last half of the twentieth century, schools of literary theorists have subdivided again and again into special interest groups until one is hard pressed to find any school of theorists which represents more than a minority opinion. Literary theory is developing into a rainbow of divergent opinions ranging from the feminist to the ethnic to the third world to the Marxist perspectives. This diversity of theories is reflected well in the works given in this section and can be identified by the titles.

While all of the texts listed below offer useful discussions of literary theory, a few of the authors have provided analyses which have established the vocabulary and trends in criticism. M. H. Abrams is well known for his editing of the *Norton Anthology of English*, but his most impressive work is in his works of literary theory and criticism, especially *The Mirror and the Lamp: Romantic Theory and the Critical Tradition* [LIT-040]. Abrams is also the scholar who is most likely to offer a new synthesis of literary theory to overcome the current trends toward absolute relativism. Wayne C. Booth's works, *A Rhetoric of Irony* [LIT-140] and *The Rhetoric of Fiction* [LIT-150], offer useful interpretations along with numerous illustrations of literary theory and how to apply it. Jonathan Culler's *Structuralist Poetics: Structuralism, Linguistics, and the Study of Literature* [LIT-250] and Robert Detweiler's *Story, Sign, and Self: Phenomenology and Structuralism as Literary Critical Methods* [LIT-270], are considered by many the best reviews of structuralism, although one should note that Detweiler is keenly aware of the tendency for structuralism to disallow Christian belief or values, especially as it is promoted by Culler.

William Empson's *Seven Types of Ambiguity* [LIT-310], E. M. Forster's *Aspects of the Novel* [LIT-340], and Northrop Frye's *Anatomy of Criticism: Four Essays* [LIT-390], have each provided important theoretical bases and useful vocabulary for the discussion of literature. For interpretations of the works by three of the most important theorists of the twentieth century, see studies given below on Jacques Derrida [LIT-080], Mikhail Bakhtin [LIT-640], and Paul Ricoeur [LIT-850]. For the latest developments in reader response theory and beyond, see [LIT-450], [LIT-510], and [LIT-520].

244

Special Bibliographies

[LIT-010] Marshall, Donald G. *Contemporary Critical Theory: A Selective Bibliography*. New York: Modern Language Association, c. 1990.

[LIT-020] New Literary History. *International Bibliography of Literary Theory and Criticism [1984-]*. Baltimore: Johns Hopkins University Press, 1988-. Annual.

[LIT-030] Niles, Susan A. *South American Indian Narrative: Theoretical and Analytical Approaches: An Annotated Bibliography*. New York: Garland Research, 1981. 818 pp.

Key Works

[LIT-040] Abrams, M. H. *The Mirror and the Lamp: Romantic Theory and the Critical Tradition*. New York: Oxford University Press, 1953. Bib. refs. in notes pp. 337-392.

[LIT-050] Adams, Hazard, ed. *Critical Theory Since Plato*. New York: Harcourt, Brace, Jovanovich, Inc., 1971. Bib. pp. 1251-1253.

[LIT-060] Amanuddin, Syed. *Creativity and Reception: Toward a Theory of Third World Criticism*. New York: Peter Lang, 1988. 202 pp.

[LIT-070] Amuta, Chidi. *The Theory of African Literature: Implications for Practical Criticism*. London: Institute for African Alternatives, Zed Books, 1989. 206 pp.

[LIT-080] Attridge, Derek, ed. *Jacques Derrida: Acts of Literature*. London: Routledge, 1992. 456 pp.

[LIT-090] Barricelli, Jean-Pierre, and Joseph Gibaldi, eds. *Interrelations of Literature*. New York: Modern Language Association, 1982. 329 pp. (Interdisciplinary essays, including religion, music, visual arts, and film.)

[LIT-100] Barricelli, Jean-Pierre, Joseph Gibaldi, and Estella Lauter, eds. *Teaching Literature and Other Arts*. New York: Modern Language Association, 1990. 183 pp.

[LIT-110] Barthes, Roland. *Criticism and Truth*. Trans. and ed. Katrine Pilcher Keunemen. Minneapolis: University of Minnesota Press, 1987. 119 pp.

[LIT-120] Belknap, George N. *A Guide to Reading in Aesthetics and Theory of Poetry*. Eugene, Oreg.: University of Oregon, 1934. 91 pp. [poetry: 55]. (See [BAE-050])

[LIT-130] Bennett, Tony. *Formalism and Marxism*. New Accents. New York: Methuen, 1979. 200 pp.

[LIT-140] Booth, Wayne C. *A Rhetoric of Irony*. Chicago: University of Chicago Press, 1974. Bib. pp. 279-284.

[LIT-150] ------. *The Rhetoric of Fiction*. 2nd ed. Chicago: University of Chicago Press, 1983. 552 pp. Bib. pp. 459-520.

[LIT-160] Burke, Kenneth. *The Philosophy of Literary Form: Studies in Symbolic Action*. 3rd ed. Berkeley: University of California Press, 1974. 463 pp.

[LIT-170] Cain, William E. *The Crisis in Criticism: Theory, Literature, and Reform in English Studies*. Baltimore: Johns Hopkins University Press, 1984. 307 pp.

[LIT-180] Caserio, Robert L. *Plot, Story, and the Novel: From Dickens and Poe to the Modern Period*. Princeton: Princeton University Press, 1979. 304 pp. Bib. refs.

[LIT-190] Cassedy, Steven. *Flight from Eden: The Origins of Modern Literary Criticism and Theory*. Berkeley: University of California Press, 1990. 253 pp.

[LIT-200] Clausen, Christopher. *The Moral Imagination: Essays on Literature and Ethics*. Iowa City: University of Iowa Press, 1986. 195 pp.

[LIT-210] Cluysenaar, Anne. *Aspects of Literary Stylistics: A Discussion of Dominant Structures in Verse and Prose*. New York: St. Martin's Press, 1975. 160 pp.

[LIT-220] Collier, Peter, and Helga Geyer-Ryan, eds. *Literary Theory Today*. Ithaca: Cornell University Press, c. 1992. 280 pp.

[LIT-230] Conrad, Peter. *Shandyism: The Character of Romantic Irony*. Oxford: Basil Blackwell Publishing, 1978. 190 pp. Bib. refs.

[LIT-240] Crusius, Timothy W. *Discourse: A Critique and Synthesis of Major Theories*. New York: Modern Language Association, 1989. 167 pp.

[LIT-250] Culler, Jonathan. *Structuralist Poetics: Structuralism, Linguistics, and the Study of Literature*. Ithaca: Cornell University Press, 1975. Bib. pp. 273-293.

246

[LIT-260] Davis, Walter A. *The Act of Interpretation: A Critique of Literary Reason*. Chicago: University of Chicago Press, 1978. 194 pp. Bib. refs.

[LIT-270] Detweiler, Robert. *Story, Sign, and Self: Phenomenology and Structuralism as Literary Critical Methods*. Philadelphia: Fortress Press; Missoula: Scholars Press, 1978. 224 pp. Bib. refs. in notes.

[LIT-280] Dodds, John M. *The Theory and Practice of Text Analysis and Translation Criticism, I*. Udine, Italy: Companotto Editions, 1985. 431 pp.

[LIT-290] Eagleton, Terry. *Literary Theory: An Introduction*. Minneapolis: Minnesota University Press, 1983. 244 pp. Bib. pp. 223-231. (Marxist approach.)

[LIT-300] Eco, Umberto. *The Role of the Reader: Explorations in the Semiotics of Texts*. Bloomington: Indiana University Press, 1979. 288 pp. Bib.

[LIT-310] Empson, William. *Seven Types of Ambiguity*. 3rd ed. New York: New Directions, 1966. 256 pp.

[LIT-320] Eysteinsson, Astradur. *The Concept of Modernism*. Ithaca: Cornell University Press, c. 1990. 280 pp.

[LIT-330] Fokkema, Douwe Wessel, and Elrud Ibsch. *Theories of Literature in the Twentieth Century: Structuralism, Marxism, Aesthetics of Reception, Semiotics*. 3rd impression, corrected. London: C. Hurst; New York: St. Martin's Press, 1986. Bib. pp. 195-214.

[LIT-340] Forster, E. M. *Aspects of the Novel*. New York: Harcourt, Brace, Jovanovich, 1956. 113 pp.

[LIT-350] Fowler, Roger. *Linguistic Criticism*. New York: Oxford University Press, 1986. 190 pp.

[LIT-360] ------, ed. *Style and Structure in Literature: Essays in the New Stylistics*. Ithaca: Cornell University Press, 1975. 257 pp.

[LIT-370] Frank, Francine Wattman, and Paula A. Treichler. *Language, Gender, and Professional Writing: Theoretical Approaches and Guidelines for Nonsexist Usage*. New York: Modern Language Association, 1989. 341 pp. Bib. refs. pp. 281-322.

[LIT-380] Friedman, Norman. *Form and Meaning in Fiction*. Athens: University of Georgia Press, 1975. 420 pp. Bib. refs.

[LIT-390] Frye, Northrop. *Anatomy of Criticism: Four Essays*. Princeton: Princeton University Press, 1957. Bib. notes.

[LIT-400] Halperin, John, ed. *The Theory of the Novel: New Essays*. New York: Oxford University Press, 1974. 396 pp.

[LIT-410] Hayles, N. Katherine. *Chaos Bound: Orderly Disorder in Contemporary Literature and Science*. Ithaca: Cornell University Press, 1991. 296 pp.

[LIT-420] Hirsch, David H. *The Deconstruction of Literature: Criticism After Auschwitz*. Hanover, N.H.: University Press of New England, 1991. 314 pp.

[LIT-430] Hirsch, E[ric] D[onald], Jr. *The Aims of Interpretation*. Chicago: University of Chicago Press, 1976. 177 pp. Bib. refs.

[LIT-440] Hohendahl, Peter Uwe. *Reappraisals: Shifting Alignments in Postwar Critical Theory*. Ithaca: Cornell University Press, c. 1992. 256 pp.

[LIT-450] Holub, Robert C. *Reception Theory: A Critical Introduction*. New Accents. London: Methuen, 1984. 189 pp.

[LIT-460] Hunt, Peter. *Criticism, Theory, and Children's Literature*. Oxford: Basil Blackwell Publishing, 1991. 236 pp.

[LIT-470] Huss, Roy. *The Mindscape of Art: Dimensions of the Psyche in Fiction, Drama and Film*. Cranbury, N.J.: Fairleigh Dickinson University Press, 1985. Bib. pp. 214-220.

[LIT-480] Ingarden, Roman. *The Cognition of the Literary Work of Art*. Trans. Ruth Ann Crowley and Kenneth R. Olson. Evanston: Northwestern University Press, 1973. 436 pp. Bib. refs.

[LIT-490] ------. *The Literary Work of Art*. Trans. George G. Grabowicz. Evanston: Northwestern University Press, 1973. Bib. pp. 397-403.

[LIT-500] Isaak, Jo Anna. *The Ruin of Representation in Modernist Art and Texts*. Ann Arbor, Mich.: UMI Research Press, 1986. Bib. pp. 151-161.

[LIT-510] Iser, Wolfgang. *The Act of Reading: A Theory of Aesthetic Response*. Baltimore: Johns Hopkins University Press, 1978.

[LIT-520] ------. *Prospecting: From Reader Response to Literary Anthropology*. Baltimore: Johns Hopkins University Press, 1989. Bib. pp. 285-308.

248

[LIT-530] Jankowski, Andrzej. *Shakespeare's Idea of Art.* Seria Filologia Angielska, nr. 22. Poznan: Adam Mickiewicz University Press; Delft [Netherlands]: Eburon, 1988. 156 pp.

[LIT-540] Jauss, Hans Robert. *Aesthetic Experience and Literary Hermeneutics.* Trans. *Asthetische Erfahrung und literarische Hermeneutik.* Theory and History of Literature, vol. 3. Minneapolis: University of Minnesota Press, 1982. xl, 357 pp. Bib. pp. 343-348.

[LIT-550] Jefferson, Ann, and David Robey, eds. *Modern Literary Theory: A Comparative Introduction.* 2nd ed. Totowa: Barnes and Noble, 1986. 240 pp.

[LIT-560] Kermode, Frank. *The Sense of an Ending: Studies in the Theory of Fiction.* New York: Oxford University Press, 1967.

[LIT-570] Kirwan, James. *Literature, Rhetoric, Metaphysics: Literary Theory and Literary Aesthetics.* London; New York: Routledge, 1990. Bib. refs. pp. 166-207.

[LIT-580] Lodge, David. *The Modes of Modern Writing: Metaphor, Metonymy, and the Typology of Modern Literature.* 1977. Reprint. Chicago: University of Chicago Press, 1988. 280 pp. Bib.

[LIT-590] Lukacs, Gyorgy. *The Theory of the Novel: A Historical-Philosophical Essay on the Forms of Great Epic Literature.* Trans. Anna Bostock. 1914-1915. Reprint. Cambridge: MIT Press, 1971. 160 pp. Bib. refs.

[LIT-600] Lund, Hans. *Text as Picture: Studies in the Literary Transformation of Pictures.* Lewiston, N.Y.: Edwin Mellen Press, 1992. 226 pp.

[LIT-610] Lundin, Roger. *The Culture of Interpretation: Christian Faith and the Postmodern World.* Grand Rapids: William B. Eerdmans, 1993. 272 pp. Bib. refs. in footnotes.

[LIT-620] Lutze, Lothar. *Hindi Writing in Post-Colonial India: A Study in the Aesthetics of Literary Production.* New Delhi: Manohar, 1985. Bib. pp. 215-224.

[LIT-630] Minnis, A. J., and A. B. Scott, eds. *Medieval Literary Theory and Criticism, c. 1100-c. 1375: The Commentary-Tradition.* New York: Oxford University Press, 1988. Bib. pp. 521-524.

[LIT-640] Morson, Gary Saul, and Caryl Emerson. *Mikhail Bakhtin: Creation of a Prosaics.* Stanford: Stanford University Press, 1990. 530 pp.

[LIT-650] Muecke, Douglas C. *Irony*. New York: Barnes and Noble, 1969. Bib. pp. 83-87.

[LIT-660] Natoli, Joseph, ed. *Tracing Literary Theory*. Urbana: University of Illinois Press, 1987. 371 pp.

[LIT-670] *New Literary History: A Journal of Theory and Interpretation*. Baltimore: Johns Hopkins University Press, 1969-. 3/year.

[LIT-680] Norris, Christopher. *Deconstruction: Theory and Practice*. New Accents. London: Methuen, 1982. 157 pp.

[LIT-690] Palmer, Paulina. *Contemporary Women's Fiction: Narrative Practice and Feminist Theory*. Jackson: University Press of Mississippi, 1989. 192 pp.

[LIT-700] Patterson, David. *Literature and Spirit: Essays on Bakhtin and His Contemporaries*. Lexington: University Press of Kentucky, 1988. 166 pp.

[LIT-710] *Poetics: Journal for Empirical Research on Literature, the Media and the Arts*. Amsterdam: Elsevier Science Publications BV, 1972-. 6/year.

[LIT-720] *Poetics Today: International Journal for Theory and Analysis of Literature and Communication*. Durham, N.C.: Duke University Press, 1979-. Quarterly. Formerly *Poetics Today: Theory and Analysis of Literature and Communication*, 1979-1983.

[LIT-730] Pratt, Mary Louise. *Toward a Speech Act Theory of Literary Discourse*. Bloomington: Indiana University Press, 1977. Bib. p. 224.

[LIT-740] Prince, Gerald. *A Grammar of Stories: An Introduction*. The Hague: Mouton, 1974. Bib. pp. 102-104.

[LIT-750] Reiss, Timothy J. *The Meaning of Literature*. Ithaca: Cornell University Press, c. 1992. 408 pp.

[LIT-760] Rogers, Mary F., and Charles R. Simpson, eds. *Novels, Novelists, and Readers: Toward a Phenomenological Sociology of Literature*. Albany: State University of New York Press, 1991. 324 pp.

[LIT-770] Rosebury, Brian. *Art and Desire: A Study in the Aesthetics of Fiction*. Basingstoke: Macmillan Publishing Co., 1988. 533 pp. Bib.

[LIT-780] Rosenblatt, Louise M. *Literature as Exploration*. 4th ed. New

250

York: Modern Language Association, 1983. 304 pp.

[LIT-790] ------. *The Reader, The Text, The Poem: The Transactional Theory of the Literary Work.* Carbondale: Southern Illinois University Press, 1978. 214 pp. Bib. refs.

[LIT-800] Selden, Raman. *A Reader's Guide to Contemporary Literary Theory.* 2nd ed. Lexington: University Press of Kentucky, 1989. 168 pp.

[LIT-810] Sparks, Elisa K. *Reader's Guide to Contemporary Literary Criticism and Theory.* Boston: G. K. Hall, 1988. 300 pp.

[LIT-820] Striedter, Jurij. *Literary Structure, Evolution, and Value: Russian Formalism and Czech Structuralism Reconsidered.* Harvard Studies in Comparative Literature, no. 38. Cambridge: Harvard University Press, 1989. 317 pp.

[LIT-830] Swingewood, Alan. *Sociological Poetics and Aesthetic Theory.* Houndmills: Macmillan Publishing Co., 1986. Bib. pp. 153-160.

[LIT-840] Traugott, Elizabeth Closs, and Mary Louise Pratt. *Linguistics for Students of Literature.* New York: Harcourt, 1980. 444 pp.

[LIT-850] Valdes, Mario, ed. *A Ricoeur Reader: Reflection and Imagination.* Theory/Culture, no. 2. Toronto: University of Toronto Press, 1991. 516 pp.

[LIT-860] Wilde, Alan. *Horizons of Assent: Modernism, Postmodernism, and the Ironic Imagination.* Philadelphia: University of Pennsylvania Press, 1987. Bib. pp. 189-200.

KEY WORKS ON LITERARY CRITICISM

Those conversant in the literary arts will readily recognize that the following list of criticism on literature is highly selective, offering a mere sampling of the many thousands of works now available in this discipline. Works included here provide a wide scope for research on many authors. Since most research projects in literature begin with a question about a specific author, character, genre, motif, or work, one will usually do well to begin with the special bibliographies listed below, [LIC-010 to LIC-210], which cover criticism of non-dramatic, prose literature. Also note that several of these special bibliographies help one in studying the critics themselves, includ-

Special Bibliographies

[LIC-010] Baker, Nancy L. *A Research Guide for Undergraduate Students: English and American Literature.* 3rd ed. New York: Modern Language Association, 1989. 61 pp.

[LIC-020] Bell, Inglis F., and Donald Baird. *The English Novel, 1578-1956: A Checklist of Twentieth-Century Criticisms.* Denver: Swallow, 1958. 168 pp. Continued by: Helen H. Palmer and Anne Jane Dyson, comps. *English Novel Explication: Criticisms to 1972.* Hamden, Conn.: Shoe String Press, 1973. 329 pp. Peter L. Abernethy, Christian J. W. Kloesel, and Jeffrey R. Smitten, comps. *Supplement I.* 1976. 305 pp. Christian J. W. Kloesel and Jeffrey R. Smitten, comps. *Supplement II.* 1981. Christian J. W. Kloesel, comp. *Supplement III.* 1986. 533 pp. Christian J. W. Kloesel, comp. *Supplement IV.* 1990. 351 pp.

[LIC-030] Borklund, Elmer. *Contemporary Literary Critics.* 2nd ed. Detroit: Gale Research, 1982. 600 pp.

[LIC-040] Brown, Christopher C., and William B. Thesing. *English Prose and Criticism, 1900-1950: A Guide to Information Sources.* Detroit: Gale Research, 1983. 553 pp.

[LIC-050] Bullock, Chris, and David Peck, comps. *Guide to Marxist Literary Criticism.* Bloomington: Indiana University Press, 1980. 176 pp.

[LIC-060] Cohen, Ralph, ed. *New Literary History: International Bibliography of Literary Theory and Criticism.* Baltimore: Johns Hopkins University Press, 1988. 188 pp.

[LIC-070] Coleman, Arthur. *Epic and Romance Criticism: A Checklist of Interpretations, 1940-1972.* New York: Watermill Publishers, 1973-.

[LIC-080] Combs, Richard E. *Authors: Critical and Biographical References: A Guide to 4,700 Critical and Biographical Passages in Books.* Metuchen, N.J.: Scarecrow Press, 1971. 221 pp.

[LIC-090] *Contemporary Literary Criticism.* Detroit: Gale Research, 1973-.

[LIC-100] Fitzgerald, Louise S., and Elizabeth I. Kearney. *The Continental Novel: A Checklist of Criticism in English 1967-1980.* Metuchen, N.J.: Scarecrow Press, 1983. 510 pp.

[LIC-110] Frost, Wendy, and Michele Valiquette. *Feminist Literary Criticism:*

A Bibliography of Journal Articles, 1975-1981. Garland Reference Library of the Humanities, no. 784. New York: Garland Publishing, 1988. xxiv, 867 pp.

[LIC-120] Fuderer, Laura Sue. *The Female Bildungsroman in English: An Annotated Bibliography of Criticism.* New York: Modern Language Association, 1990. 47 pp.

[LIC-130] Gerry, Thomas M. F. *Contemporary Canadian and U.S. Women of Letters: An Annotated Bibliography.* Garland Bibliographies of Modern Critics and Critical Schools, no. 21. Garland Reference Library of the Humanities, no. 1354. New York: Garland, 1993.

[LIC-140] Humm, Maggie. *An Annotated Critical Bibliography of Feminist Criticism.* Harvester Annotated Critical Bibliographies. Boston: G. K. Hall, 1987. 240 pp.

[LIC-150] Meurs, Jos van, and John Kidd. *Jungian Literary Criticism, 1920-1980: An Annotated, Critical Bibliography of Works in English (with a Selection of Titles After 1980).* Metuchen, N.J.: Scarecrow Press, 1988. 353 pp.

[LIC-160] Myerson, Joel, ed. *The Transcendentalists: A Review of Research and Criticism.* New York: Modern Language Association, 1984.

[LIC-170] O'Pecko, Michael T., and Eleanore O. Hofstetter. *The Twentieth-Century German Novel: A Bibliography of English-Language Criticism, 1945-1986.* Metuchen, N.J.: Scarecrow Press, 1989. 816 pp.

[LIC-180] Partridge, Elinore Hughes. *American Prose and Criticism, 1820-1900: A Guide to Information Sources.* Detroit: Gale Research, 1983. 575 pp.

[LIC-190] Ross, Robert L. *Australian Literary Criticism--1945-1988: An Annotated Bibliography.* New York: Garland Publishing, 1989. 375 pp.

[LIC-200] Seidel, Alison P. *Literary Criticism and Authors' Biographies: An Annotated Index.* Metuchen, N.J.: Scarecrow Press, 1978. 215 pp.

[LIC-210] Weiner, Alan R., and Spencer Means. *Literary Criticism Index.* Metuchen, N.J.: Scarecrow Press, 1984. 704 pp.

Key Works

[LIC-220] Abrams, M. H., ed. *The Norton Anthology of English Literature*. 6th ed. 2 vols. New York: W. W. Norton and Co., 1993. Bibs. vol. 1, pp. 2519-2547; vol. 2, pp. 2469-2499.

[LIC-230] Allen, Paula Gunn, ed. *Studies in American Indian Literature: Critical Essays and Course Designs*. New York: Modern Language Association, 1983. 384 pp.

[LIC-240] Altick, Richard Daniel. *The Art of Literary Research*. 3rd ed. Rev. John J. Fenstermaker. New York: W. W. Norton and Co., 1981. 318 pp. Bib. pp. 241-254.

[LIC-250] *American Renaissance Literary Report, I*. Hartford: Transcendental Books, 1987. 263 pp. Bib.

[LIC-260] Battestin, Martin C., ed. *British Novelists, 1660-1800*. 2 pts. Dictionary of Literary Biography, vol. 39. Detroit: Gale Research, 1985.

[LIC-270] Benstock, Gernard, and Thomas F. Staley, eds. *British Mystery Writers, 1860-1919*. Dictionary of Literary Biography, vol. 70. Detroit: Gale Research, 1988. 389 pp.

[LIC-280] Bingham, Jane, and Grayce Scholt. *Fifteen Centuries of Children's Literature: An Annotated Chronology of British and American Works in Historical Context*. Westport, Conn.: Greenwood Press, 1980. 540 pp. Bib.

[LIC-290] Bishop, Rand. *African Literature, African Critics: The Forming of Critical Standards, 1947-1966*. New York: Greenwood Press, 1988. 213 pp.

[LIC-300] Boswell, Jeanetta. *The American Renaissance and the Critics: The Best of a Century in Criticism*. Wakefield, N.H.: Longwood Academic, 1990. 502 pp.

[LIC-310] Bresky, Dushan, Brian Gill, and Miroslav Malik. *Literary Practice, II: Esthetics of Style*. New York: Peter Lang, 1989. 244 pp.

[LIC-320] Bromwich, David, ed. *Romantic Critical Essays*. Cambridge: Cambridge University Press, 1987. 269 pp.

[LIC-330] Bronner, Simon J. *American Folklore Studies: An Intellectual History*. Lawrence: University Press of Kansas, 1986. 213 pp.

[LIC-340] Brunvand, Jan Harold. *Folklore: A Study and Research Guide.* New York: St. Martin's Press, 1976. 144 pp.

[LIC-350] Bufkin, E. C. *The Twentieth Century in English: A Checklist.* 2nd ed. Athens: University of Georgia Press, 1984. 182 pp. Bib.

[LIC-360] Carpenter, Humphrey, and Mari Prichard. *The Oxford Companion to Children's Literature.* Oxford: Oxford University Press, 1984. 587 pp.

[LIC-370] Cech, John, ed. *American Writers for Children, 1900-1969.* Dictionary of Literary Biography, vol. 22. Detroit: Gale Research, 1983. 412 pp.

[LIC-380] Charters, Ann, ed. *The Beats: Literary Bohemians in Postwar America.* 2 pts. Dictionary of Literary Biography, vol. 16. Detroit: Gale Research, 1983. 718 pp.

[LIC-390] Cocchiara, Giuseppe. *The History of Folklore in Europe.* Trans. John N. McDaniel. Translation in Folklore Studies. Philadelphia: Institute for the Study of Human Issues, 1981. 703 pp.

[LIC-400] *Contemporary Literary Criticism: Excerpts from Criticism of the Works of Today's Novelists, Poets, Playwrights, Short Story Writers, Scriptwriters, and Other Creative Writers.* Detroit: Gale Research, 19--?.

[LIC-410] Cowart, David, and Thomas L. Wymer, eds. *Twentieth-Century American Science Fiction Writers.* 2 pts. Dictionary of Literary Biography, vol. 8. Detroit: Gale Research, 1981.

[LIC-420] *Critical Inquiry.* Chicago: University of Chicago Press, 1974-. Quarterly.

[LIC-430] *Critical Survey.* Oxford: Oxford University Press, 1989-. 3/year.

[LIC-440] *Critical Texts: A Review of Theory and Criticism.* New York: Department of English and Comparative Literature, Columbia University, 1982-. 3/year.

[LIC-450] Croce, Benedetto. *Benedetto Croce: Essays on Literature and Literary Criticism.* Ed. M. E. Moss. Albany, N.Y.: State University of New York Press, 1990. Bib. pp. 225-235.

[LIC-460] Daiches, David, and John Flower. *Literary Landscapes of the British Isles: A Narrative Atlas.* New York: Paddington Press Ltd., 1979. Bib. refs. p. 287.

[LIC-470] Davidson, Arnold E., ed. *Studies on Canadian Literature: Introductory and Critical Essays*. New York: Modern Language Association, 1990. 371 pp.

[LIC-480] Davis, Thadious M., and Trudier Harris, eds. *Afro-American Fiction Writers after 1955*. Dictionary of Literary Biography, vol. 33. Detroit: Gale Research, 1984. 350 pp.

[LIC-490] ------, eds. *Afro-American Writers after 1955: Dramatists and Prose Writers*. Dictionary of Literary Biography, vol. 38. Detroit: Gale Research, 1985. 390 pp.

[LIC-500] *Diacritics: A Review of Contemporary Criticism*. Baltimore: Johns Hopkins University Press, 1971-. Quarterly.

[LIC-510] Dorson, Richard M., ed. *Handbook of American Folklore*. Bloomington: Indiana University Press, 1983. 584 pp.

[LIC-520] Drabble, Margaret, ed. *Oxford Companion to English Literature*. 5th ed. New York: Oxford University Press, 1987. 1,168 pp.

[LIC-530] Eagle, Dorothy, and Meic Stephens. *The Oxford Illustrated Literary Guide to Great Britain and Ireland*. 2nd ed. Oxford; New York: Oxford University Press, 1992. Bib. refs. pp. 285-319; Bib. p. 320. (Deceased authors only.)

[LIC-540] Edel, Leon. *The Modern Psychological Novel*. Rev. ed. New York: Grossett and Dunlap, 1964.

[LIC-550] Eliot, T[homas] S[tearns]. *Selected Essays*. New York: Harcourt, Brace and World, 1964. 460 pp.

[LIC-560] Elliott, Emory, ed. *American Colonial Writers, 1606-1734*. Dictionary of Literary Biography, vol. 24. Detroit: Gale Research, 1984. 415 pp.

[LIC-570] ------, ed. *American Colonial Writers, 1735-1781*. Dictionary of Literary Biography, vol. 31. Detroit: Gale Research, 1984. 421 pp.

[LIC-580] ------, ed. *American Writers of the Early Republic*. Dictionary of Literary Biography, vol. 37. Detroit: Gale Research, 1985. 374 pp.

[LIC-590] Estes, Glenn E., ed. *American Writers for Children Before 1900*. Dictionary of Literary Biography, vol. 42. Detroit: Gale Research, 1985. 441 pp.

[LIC-600] ------, ed. *American Writers for Children Since 1960: Fiction*. Dictionary of Literary Biography, vol. 52. Detroit: Gale Research, 1986. 488 pp.

[LIC-610] Fairbanks, Carol. *More Women in Literature: Criticism of the Seventies*. Metuchen, N.J.: Scarecrow Press, 1979. 465 pp.

[LIC-620] Fisher, Dexter, and Robert B. Stepto, eds. *Afro-American Literature: The Reconstruction of Instruction*. New York: Modern Language Association, 1979. 256 pp.

[LIC-630] *Fred Newton Scott Anniversary Papers, The*. 1929. Reprint. Folcroft, Pa.: Folcroft Press; Freeport, N.Y.: Books for Libraries Press, 1968. Bib. pp. 313-319.

[LIC-640] Frye, Northrop. *The Well-Tempered Critic*. Gloucester, Mass.: Peter Smith, 1963. 160 pp.

[LIC-650] Gardner, John. *On Moral Fiction*. New York: Basic Books, Inc., 1977. 214 pp. Bib. refs. in notes.

[LIC-660] Garland, Henry, and Mary Garland, eds. *Oxford Companion to German Literature*. 2nd ed. New York: Oxford University Press, 1986. 1030 pp.

[LIC-670] Gerstenberger, D., and George Hendrick, eds. *American Novel: 1789 to 1968*. Chicago: Swallow Press, 1970.

[LIC-680] Gibaldi, Joseph, ed. *Introduction to Scholarship in Modern Languages and Literatures*. 1st ed. New York: Modern Language Association, 1981. 181 pp. Bibs.

[LIC-690] ------. *Introduction to Scholarship in Modern Languages and Literatures*. 2nd ed. New York: Modern Language Association, 1992. 377 pp. Bibs. (All new essays since 1st ed.)

[LIC-700] Goethe, Johann Wolfgang von. *Essays of Art and Literature*. Ed. John Gearey. Goethe Edition, vol. 3. New York: Suhrkamp Publishers New York, 1986. 268 pp.

[LIC-710] Halio, Jay L., ed. *British Novelists since 1960*. 2 pts. Dictionary of Literary Biography, vol. 14. Detroit: Gale Research, 1983.

[LIC-720] Hall, Vernon. *Literary Criticism: Plato Through Johnson*. New York: Appleton-Century-Crofts, [1970]. 110 pp.

[LIC-730] Hamilton, Robert M., and Dorothy Shields. *The Dictionary of Canadian Quotations and Phrases*. Rev. ed. Toronto: McClelland, 1979. 1,063 pp.

[LIC-740] Hand, Wayland Debs, and Gustave O. Arlt. *Humanoria: Essays in*

Literature, Folklore, Bibliography, Honoring Archer Taylor on his Seventieth Birthday. Locust Valley, N.Y.: J. J. Augustin, 1960. 374 pp.

[LIC-750] Harris, Trudier, and Thadious Davis, eds. *Afro-American Writers Before the Harlem Renaissance.* Dictionary of Literary Biography, vol. 50. Detroit: Gale Research, 1986. 369 pp.

[LIC-760] ------, eds. *Afro-American Writers From the Harlem Renaissance to 1940.* Dictionary of Literary Biography, vol. 51. Detroit: Gale Research, 1987. 386 pp.

[LIC-770] ------, eds. *Afro-American Writers, 1940-1955.* Dictionary of Literary Biography, vol. 76. Detroit: Gale Research, 1988. 389 pp.

[LIC-780] Hart, James D., ed. *Oxford Companion to American Literature.* 5th ed. New York: Oxford University Press, 1983. 896 pp.

[LIC-790] Hart, James D., and Janet E. Heseltine, eds. *Oxford Companion to French Literature.* New York: Oxford University Press, 1959. 771 pp.

[LIC-800] Hazell, Stephen, ed. *The English Novel: Developments in Criticism Since Henry James.* London: Macmillan Publishing Co., 1978.

[LIC-810] Helterman, Jeffrey, and Richard Layman, eds. *American Novelists Since World War II.* Dictionary of Literary Biography, vol. 2. Detroit: Gale Research, 1978. 557 pp.

[LIC-820] Hoffman, Daniel, ed. *Harvard Guide to Contemporary American Writing.* Cambridge: Harvard University Press, 1979. 618 pp.

[LIC-830] Holman, C[larence] Hugh, and William Harmon. *A Handbook to Literature.* 6th ed. New York: Macmillan Publishing Co., 1991. 624 pp.

[LIC-840] Horton, Rod W., and Herbert W. Edwards, eds. *Backgrounds of American Literary Thought.* 3rd ed. Englewood Cliffs, N.J.: Prentice-Hall Press, [1974]. 630 pp. Bib. pp. 605-606.

[LIC-850] Howatson, M. C., ed. *Oxford Companion to Classical Literature.* 2nd ed. New York: Oxford University Press, 1989. 640 pp.

[LIC-860] Hunt, Peter, ed. *Children's Literature: The Development of Criticism.* London: Routledge, 1990. 195 pp.

[LIC-870] JanMohamed, Abdul R. *Manichean Aesthetics: The Politics of*

Literature in Colonial Africa. Amherst, Mass.; London: University of Massachusetts Press, 1983. 328 pp. Bib.

[LIC-880] Jay, Gregory S., ed. *Modern American Critics, 1920-1955.* Dictionary of Literary Biography, vol. 63. Detroit: Gale Research, 1988. 384 pp.

[LIC-890] ------, ed. *Modern American Critics Since 1955.* Dictionary of Literary Biography, vol. 67. Detroit: Gale Research, 1988. 397 pp.

[LIC-900] Jordon, Frank, ed. *The English Romantic Poets: A Review of Research and Criticism.* 4th ed. New York: Modern Language Association, 1985. 765 pp.

[LIC-910] Kane, Richard C[harles]. *Iris Murdoch, Muriel Spark, and John Fowles: Didactic Demons in Modern Fiction.* Rutherford, [N.J.]: Fairleigh Dickinson University Press; London; Cranbury, N.J.: Associated University Presses, 1988. Bib. pp. 158-163.

[LIC-920] Keene, Donald. *The Pleasures of Japanese Literature.* New York: Columbia University Press, 1988. Bib. pp. 123-126.

[LIC-930] Kibler, James E., Jr., ed. *American Novelists Since World War II: Second Series.* Dictionary of Literary Biography, vol. 6. Detroit: Gale Research, 1980.

[LIC-940] Kimbel, Bobby Ellen, ed. *American Short-Story Writers Before 1880.* Dictionary of Literary Biography, vol. 74. Detroit: Gale Research, 1988.

[LIC-950] ------, ed. *American Short-Story Writers, 1880-1910.* Dictionary of Literary Biography, vol. 78. Detroit: Gale Research, 1989.

[LIC-960] Klinck, Carl F., ed. *Literary History of Canada: Canadian Literature in English.* Corrected reprint of 2nd ed. 3 vols. Toronto: University of Toronto Press, 1976-1977. Additional vol. forthcoming.

[LIC-970] Leighton, Lauren Gray, ed. and trans. *Russian Romantic Criticism: An Anthology.* New York: Greenwood Press, 1987. 215 pp.

[LIC-980] Lodge, David. *The Novelist at the Crossroads and Other Essays on Fiction and Criticism.* Ithaca: Cornell University Press, 1971. 297 pp. Bib. refs.

[LIC-990] Lowance, Mason I. *The Language of Canaan: Metaphor and Symbol in New England from the Puritans to the Transcendentalists.* Cambridge: Harvard University Press, 1980. 335

pp. Bib. refs.

[LIC-1000] McArthur, Thomas. *Oxford Companion to the English Language*. New York: Oxford University Press, 1992. 960 pp.

[LIC-1010] McGann, Jerome J., ed. *Historical Studies and Literary Criticism*. Madison: University of Wisconsin Press, 1985. 298 pp. Bib. refs. in notes.

[LIC-1020] McGowan, John. *Postmodernism and Its Critics*. Ithaca: Cornell University Press, c. 1991. 320 pp.

[LIC-1030] Mack, Maynard, et al., eds. *The Norton Anthology of World Masterpieces*. 6th ed. 2 vols. New York: W. W. Norton and Co., 1992. Bibs.

[LIC-1040] Martine, James J., ed. *American Novelists, 1910-1945*. 3 pts. Dictionary of Literary Biography, vol. 9. Detroit: Gale Research, 1981.

[LIC-1050] Medvedev, Pavel Nikolaevich, and M. M. Bakhtin. *The Formal Method in Literary Scholarship: A Critical Introduction to Sociological Poetics*. Trans. Albert J. Wehrle. 1928. Reprint. Baltimore: Johns Hopkins University Press, 1978. 191 pp. Bib. refs.

[LIC-1060] Miller, R[obert] H. *Handbook of Literary Research*. Metuchen, N.J.: Scarecrow Press, 1987. 124 pp.

[LIC-1070] Mueller, Janel M. *The Native Tongue and the Word: Developments in English Prose Style, 1380-1580*. Chicago: University of Chicago Press, 1984. 429 pp. Bib. refs.

[LIC-1080] Murray-Smith, Stephen, ed. *The Dictionary of Australian Quotations*. Richmond: Heinemann, 1984. 464 pp.

[LIC-1090] Myerson, Joel, ed. *The American Renaissance in New England*. Dictionary of Literary Biography, vol. 1. Detroit: Gale Research, 1978. 224 pp.

[LIC-1100] ------, ed. *Antebellum Writers in New York and the South*. Dictionary of Literary Biography, vol. 3. Detroit: Gale Research, 1979. 383 pp.

[LIC-1110] Nadel, Ira B., and William E. Fredeman, eds. *Victorian Novelists After 1885*. Dictionary of Literary Biography, vol. 18. Detroit: Gale Research, 1983. 392 pp.

[LIC-1120] ------, eds. *Victorian Novelists Before 1885*. Dictionary of Literary Biography, vol. 21. Detroit: Gale Research, 1983. 417 pp.

[LIC-1130] New, W. H., ed. *Canadian Writers, 1920-1959: First Series.* Dictionary of Literary Biography, vol. 68. Detroit: Gale Research, 1988. 417 pp.

[LIC-1140] ------, ed. *Canadian Writers Since 1960: First Series.* Dictionary of Literary Biography, vol. 53. Detroit: Gale Research, 1986. 445 pp.

[LIC-1150] ------, ed. *Canadian Writers Since 1960: Second Series.* Dictionary of Literary Biography, vol. 60. Detroit: Gale Research, 1987. 470 pp.

[LIC-1160] Nisbet, Hugh Barr. *German Aesthetic and Literary Criticism.* Cambridge; New York: Cambridge University Press, 1985. Bib. pp. 304-308.

[LIC-1170] Novikov, Vasilii Vasilevich. *Artistic Truth and Dialectics of Creative Work.* Trans. *Khudozhestvennaia pravda i dialektika tvorchestva.* Moscow: Progress Publishers, 1981. 341 pp. Bib. refs.

[LIC-1180] O'Connor, Frank. *The Lonely Voice: A Study of the Short Story.* Cleveland: World, 1963.

[LIC-1190] Oldsey, Bernard, ed. *British Novelists, 1930-1959.* 2 pts. Dictionary of Literary Biography, vol. 15. Detroit: Gale Research, 1983. 713 pp.

[LIC-1200] Parker, Hershel. *Flawed Texts and Verbal Icons: Literary Authority in American Fiction.* Evanston: Northwestern University Press, 1984. 249 pp.

[LIC-1210] Parrinder, Patrick. *Authors and Authority: English and American Criticism 1750-1990.* New York: Columbia University Press, 1991. 392 pp.

[LIC-1220] Patrides, C. A., and Joseph Wittreich, eds. *The Apocalypse in English Renaissance Thought and Literature: Patterns, Antecedents, and Repercussions.* Ithaca: Cornell University Press, 1984. Bib. pp. 369-440.

[LIC-1230] Person, James E., Jr., ed. *Literature Criticism from 1400 to 1800, [1-]: Excerpts from Criticism of the Works of Fifteenth, Sixteenth, Seventeenth, and Eighteenth-Century Novelists, Poets, Playwrights, Philosophers, and Other Creative Writers, from the First Published Critical Appraisals to Current Evaluations.* Detroit: Gale Research, 1985?-. 549 pp.

[LIC-1240] Pierce, Peter, ed. *The Oxford Literary Guide to Australia.* Rev. ed. Melbourne: Oxford University Press, 1992.

263

[LIC-1250] Pizer, Donald, and Earl N. Harbert, eds. *American Realists and Naturalists*. Dictionary of Literary Biography, vol. 12. Detroit: Gale Research, 1982. 486 pp.

[LIC-1260] *PMLA: Publications of the Modern Language Association of America*. New York: Modern Language Association of America, 1886-. 6/year.

[LIC-1270] Poupard, Dennis, Jelena O. Krstovic, and Thomas Ligotti, eds. *Classical and Medieval Literature Criticism, I: Excerpts from Criticism of Works of World Authors from Classical Antiquity Through Fourteenth Century, from First Appraisals to Current Evaluations*. Detroit: Gale Research, 1988. 607 pp.

[LIC-1280] Rathbun, John W., and Monica M. Grecu, eds. *American Literary Critics and Scholars, 1850-1880*. Dictionary of Literary Biography, vol. 64. Detroit: Gale Research, 1988. 352 pp.

[LIC-1290] ------, ed. *American Literary Critics and Scholars, 1880-1900*. Dictionary of Literary Biography, vol. 71. Detroit: Gale Research, 1988. 374 pp. Bib. pp. 307-310.

[LIC-1300] Richards, Ivor A. *Principles of Literary Criticism*. New York: Harcourt, Brace, Jovanovich, 1961. 299 pp.

[LIC-1310] Roberts, Thomas J[ohn]. *An Aesthetics of Junk Fiction*. Athens: University of Georgia Press, 1990. 284 pp. Bib. pp. 251-265.

[LIC-1320] Royle, Trevor. *Companion to Scottish Literature*. Detroit: Gale Research, 1983. 322 pp.

[LIC-1330] Ruoff, A. LaVonne Brown. *American Indian Literatures: An Introduction, Bibliographic Review, and Selected Bibliography*. New York: Modern Language Association, 1990. 200 pp.

[LIC-1340] Ruoff, A. LaVonne Brown, and Jerry W. Ward, Jr., eds. *Redefining American Literary History*. New York: Modern Language Association, 1990. 406 pp.

[LIC-1350] Saltzman, Arthur M. *Designs of Darkness in Contemporary American Fiction*. Philadelphia: University of Pennsylvania Press, 1990. 153 pp.

[LIC-1360] Scott, Wilbur S. *Five Approaches of Literary Criticism: An Arrangement of Contemporary Critical Essays*. New York: Collier Books, 1962. 351 pp.

[LIC-1370] Shattock, Joanne. *The Oxford Guide to British Women Writers*.

Oxford; New York: Oxford University Press, 1993. Bib. refs.

[LIC-1380] Silverman, Hugh J., and Gary E. Aylesworth. *The Textual Sublime: Deconstruction and Its Differences.* Albany, N.Y.: State University of New York Press, 1990. Bib. pp. 253-264.

[LIC-1390] Simpson, David, ed. *German Aesthetic and Literary Criticism: Kant, Fichte, Schelling, Schopenhauer, Hegel.* Cambridge: Cambridge University Press, 1986. 294 pp.

[LIC-1400] Slavens, Thomas P. *The Literary Adviser: Selected Reference Sources in Literature, Speech, Language, Theater, and Film.* Phoenix: Oryx, 1985. 196 pp.

[LIC-1410] Staley, Thomas F., ed. *British Novelists, 1890-1929: Traditionalists.* Dictionary of Literary Biography, vol. 34. Detroit: Gale Research, 1985. 378 pp.

[LIC-1420] ------, ed. *British Novelists, 1890-1929: Modernists.* Dictionary of Literary Biography, vol. 36. Detroit: Gale Research, 1985. 387 pp.

[LIC-1430] Stephens, Meic, ed. *Oxford Companion to the Literature of Wales.* New York: Oxford University Press, 1986. 692 pp.

[LIC-1440] Thesing, William B., ed. *Victorian Prose Writers After 1867.* Dictionary of Literary Biography, vol. 57. Detroit: Gale Research, 1987. 571 pp.

[LIC-1450] ------, ed. *Victorian Prose Writers Before 1867.* Dictionary of Literary Biography, vol. 55. Detroit: Gale Research, 1987. 379 pp.

[LIC-1460] Tillyard, E. M. W. *The Elizabethan World Picture.* New York: Vintage Books, n.d. 116 pp.

[LIC-1470] Toye, William, ed. *Oxford Companion to Canadian Literature.* New York: Oxford University Press, 1983. 843 pp.

[LIC-1480] *Twentieth-Century Literary Criticism, [I-]: Excerpts from Criticism of the Works of Novelists, Poets, Playwrights, Short Story Writers, and Other Creative Writers Who Died Between 1900 and 1960, from the First Published Critical Appraisals to Current Evaluations.* Detroit: Gale Research, 1987-.

[LIC-1490] Unger, Leonard, ed. *American Writers: A Collection of Literary Biographies.* 8 vols. New York: Charles Scribner's Sons, 1979.

[LIC-1500] Walden, Daniel, ed. *Twentieth-Century American-Jewish Fiction Writers.* Dictionary of Literary Biography, vol. 28. Detroit: Gale Research, 1984. 367 pp.

[LIC-1510] Ward, Philip, ed. *Oxford Companion to Spanish Literature.* New York: Oxford University Press, 1978. 629 pp.

[LIC-1520] Watt, Ian. *The Rise of the Novel.* Berkeley; Los Angeles: University of California Press, 1957. 319 pp. Bib. refs.

[LIC-1530] Waynne-Davies, Marion, ed. *Bloomsbury Guide to English Literature.* New York: Prentice-Hall Press, 1992. 1,066 pp. Bib. refs.

[LIC-1540] Wellek, René. *A History of Modern Criticism, 1750-1950.* 8 vols. New Haven: Yale University Press, 1955-1992.

[LIC-1550] Whitlow, Roger. *Black American Literature: A Critical History.* Totowa, N.J.: Littlefield, 1974. 288 pp. Bib. pp. 197-271 [1,520].

[LIC-1560] Wilde, William H., Joy Hooton, and Barry Andrews. *The Oxford Companion to Australian Literature.* Melbourne: Oxford University Press, 1991. 772 pp. Bibs.

[LIC-1570] Wright, Austin M. *The Formal Principle in the Novel.* Ithaca: Cornell University Press, 1982. 320 pp.

KEY WORKS ON NARRATIVE IN LITERATURE

Narrative studies constitute a sub-set of research in literary theory and criticism, but are quickly becoming an important part of literature studies, especially those connected with the Bible and preaching. While all of the works listed in this section are useful for understanding the study of narrative in literature, analyses by the following authors are stellar: Mieke Bal, [LIN-010], Seymour Chatman, [LIN-040] and [LIN-050], Paul Ricoeur, [LIN-170], Cesare Segre, [LIN-190] and [LIN-200], and Meir Sternberg [LIN-230]. To locate additional studies on this topic, see the bibliographical references in the works listed below. For the latest studies in narrative, see the *Journal of Narrative Technique* [LIN-100] and relevant sections of major bibliographies of literary studies, such as the *MLA International Bibliography of Books and Articles on the Modern Languages and Literatures* [BLI-1250]. Also see works on narrative preaching, such as [DRR-1080], given above in Chapter 6.

[LIN-010] Bal, Mieke. *Narratology: Introduction to the Theory of Narrative.* Buffalo: University of Toronto Press, 1985. Bib. pp. 159-162.

[LIN-020] Banfield, Ann. *Unspeakable Sentences: Narration and Representation in the Language of Fiction.* Boston: Routledge and Kegan Paul, 1982. Bib. pp. 320-331.

[LIN-030] Braudy, Leo. *Narrative Form in History and Fiction: Hume, Fielding and Gibbon.* Princeton: Princeton University Press, 1970.

[LIN-040] Chatman, Seymour. *Coming to Terms: The Rhetoric of Narrative in Fiction and Film.* Ithaca: Cornell University Press, c. 1990. 272 pp.

[LIN-050] ------. *Story and Discourse: Narrative Structure in Fiction and Film.* Ithaca: Cornell University Press, 1978. 277 pp.

[LIN-060] Cohn, Dorrit. *Transparent Minds: Narrative Modes for Presenting Consciousness in Fiction.* Princeton: Princeton University Press, 1978.

[LIN-070] El Saffar, Ruth. *Distance and Control in "Don Quixote": A Study in Narrative Technique.* Chapel Hill: University of North Carolina, 1975. Bib.

[LIN-080] Holloway, John. *Narrative and Structure: Exploratory Essays.* New York: Cambridge University Press, 1979. 156 pp.

[LIN-090] Jameson, Fredric. *The Political Unconscious: Narrative as a Socially Symbolic Act.* Ithaca: Cornell University Press, 1981. 305 pp.

[LIN-100] *Journal of Narrative Technique.* Ypsilanti, Mich.: Eastern Michigan University, 1971-. 3/year.

[LIN-110] Kawin, Bruce. *How Movies Work.* New York: Macmillan Publishing Co., 1986. 648 pp.

[LIN-120] ------. *Telling It Again and Again: Repetition in Literature and Film.* Ithaca: Cornell University Press, 1972. Bib. pp. 187-190.

[LIN-130] Kermode, Frank. *The Genesis of Secrecy: On the Interpretation of Narrative.* Cambridge, Mass.: Harvard University Press, 1979. 169 pp. Bib. refs.

267

[LIN-140] Lanser, Susan Sniader. *The Narrative Act: Point of View in Prose Fiction*. Princeton: Princeton University Press, 1981. Bib.

[LIN-150] Leibowitz, Judith. *Narrative Purpose in the Novella*. The Hague: Mouton, 1974. 139 pp.

[LIN-160] Powell, Mark Allan. *What is Narrative Criticism?* Minneapolis: Fortress Press, 1990. Bib. pp. 123-125.

[LIN-170] Ricoeur, Paul. *Time and Narrative*. 3 vols. Trans. Kathleen McLaughlin and David Pellauer. Chicago: University of Chicago Press, 1984-1988. Bib. refs.

[LIN-180] Rimmon-Kenan, Shlomith. *Narrative Fiction*. New York: Methuen, 1983. 173 pp.

[LIN-190] Segre, Cesare. *Introduction to the Analysis of the Literary*. Trans. John Meddemmen. Bloomington: Indiana University Press, 1988. 337 pp. Bibs.

[LIN-200] ------. *Structure and Time: Narration, Poetry, Models*. Trans. John Meddemmen. Chicago: University of Chicago Press, 1979. 271 pp. Bib. refs.

[LIN-210] Stein, Gertrude. *Narration: Four Lectures*. 1935. Reprint. Chicago: University of Chicago Press, 1969.

[LIN-220] Steinberg, Erwin R., ed. *Stream-of-Consciousness Technique in the Modern Novel*. Port Washington, N.Y.: Kennikat Press, 1979. 198 pp. Bib. refs.

[LIN-230] Sternberg, Meir. *Expositional Modes and Temporal Ordering in Fiction*. Baltimore: Johns Hopkins University Press, 1978. 338 pp. Bib. refs.

[LIN-240] Toliver, Harold. *Animate Illusions: Explorations of Narrative Structure*. Lincoln: University of Nebraska Press, 1974. Bib. pp. 393-402.

[LIN-250] Valdes, Mario J., and Owen J. Miller, eds. *Interpretation of Narrative*. Toronto: University of Toronto Press, 1978. Bib. pp. 191-197.

KEY WORKS ON POETRY

Although poetry no longer holds the popular appeal it has had until the early twentieth century, poetry remains one of the most significant genres in literature, and is widely acknowledged as the most refined use of words and music in language. What typically passes for poetry in Christian circles is more correctly called verse, a rhymed sequence of lines lending itself to singing. Some of this verse, such as that by Charles Wesley, contains sound theology and tolerably good poetic techniques. In the list given below, poetry receives the primary emphasis, although verse is also included, especially verse expressing a Christian view.

The list of specialized bibliographies contains a wide variety of research tools, including guides and indexes covering poets, poems, and explications. Works helping one find poets include items [LIP-020], [LIP-050], [LIP-090], [LIP-240], [LIP-250], [LIP-260], [LIP-300], and [LIP-340]. Some of the best resources for helping one find poems are produced by Granger, including the famous *Granger's Index to Poetry* [LIP-040], and the following items: [LIP-020], [LIP-240], [LIP-250], [LIP-260]. Although many of the books given below can assist one in identifying poems, a few additional works which will prove particularly helpful for locating poems are [LIP-050], [LIP-070], [LIP-080], [LIP-120], [LIP-130], and [LIP-230]. Note especially *Hoffman's Index to Poetry: European and Latin American Poetry in Anthologies* [LIP-220] as an augmentation to *Granger's Index to Poetry*. Works which specialize in helping one find criticism of poems include [LIP-010], [LIP-290], [LIP-320], [LIP-370], and [LIP-400]. The bibliographies which are also likely to assist one in locating explications of poems include [LIP-030], [LIP-100], [LIP-150], [LIP-190], [LIP-210], [LIP-270], [LIP-280], [LIP-300], [LIP-310], [LIP-330], [LIP-350], [LIP-360], and [LIP-380]. Finally, the best volume for helping one find current information about publishers of poetry is the annual publication entitled *Directory of Poetry Publishers* [LIP-140]. This work is especially helpful for writers seeking to place their work with small press and little magazine publishers.

Of the key works on poetry which will be particularly helpful for researchers, the most extensive survey works covering the history of poetry are J. W. Courthope's older but as yet unsurpassed six volume work, *A History of English Poetry* [LIP-560], covering through the Romantic era, and David Perkins' very fine two volume work, *A History of Modern Poetry* [LIP-970]. Other works which will help one in developing an understanding of the history and personalities of poetry include a variety of volumes from the *Dictionary of Literary Biography*, including the following: [LIP-680], [LIP-720], [LIP-740], [LIP-750], [LIP-760], [LIP-770], [LIP-1020], [LIP-1030], [LIP-1040], [LIP-1130], [LIP-1140], [LIP-1160], [LIP-1170], [LIP-1180], [LIP-1190]. Two of the strongest anthologies of poetry for the twentieth century are Richard Ellmann's and Robert O'Clair's *The Norton Anthology of Modern Poetry* [LIP-670], and A. Poulin's *Contemporary American Poetry* [LIP-1000]. For useful anthologies containing poetry from previous centuries, see the *Norton Anthology of English Literature* [LIC-220], and *The Norton Anthology of World Masterpieces* [LIC-1030], both listed above.

The two best sets of works offering summaries of criticism on poetry are Frank N. Magill's recent eight volume work, *Critical Survey of Poetry* [LIP-830], and Robyn V. Young's equally new five volume survey, *Poetry Criticism: Excerpts from Criticism of the Works of the Most Significant and Widely Studied Poets of World Literature* [LIP-1290]. For additional assistance in locating and interpreting the criticism of poetry, see items [LIP-470], [LIP-480], [LIP-510], [LIP-580], [LIP-630], [LIP-710], [LIP-930], [LIP-960], [LIP-1010], and [LIP-1060]. The theory of poetry criticism has been shaped by several eloquent masters of criticism in this century, including Owen Barfield in *Poetic Diction: A Study in Meaning* [LIP-430], Cleanth Brooks in *The Well Wrought Urn: Studies in the Structure of Poetry* [LIP-520], Thomas Stearns Eliot in numerous collected essays [LIP-640 to LIP-660], Northrop Frye in *Sound and Poetry* [LIP-690], Ernst Haublein in *The Stanza* [LIP-780], and Jacques Maritain in *Art and Poetry* [LIP-850] and *Art and Scholasticism and the Frontiers of Poetry* [LIP-860]. For the latest studies of poetry, and some of the best poetry being promoted today, see any of the following journals: [LIP-420], [LIP-530], [LIP-790], [LIP-950], [LIP-980], [LIP-990], [LIP-1110], and [LIP-1230]. As with all categories of this chapter, also consult the *MLA International Bibliography* [BLI-1250] for articles and books treating particular poets and poems.

Because analysis of poetry often involves technical terminology and a sophisticated understanding of poetic forms, students of poetry will be greatly helped by the following reference tools: [LIP-590], [LIP-730], [LIP-840], [LIP-910], and [LIP-1120], as well as Holman's and Harmon's *A Handbook to Literature* [LIC-830] mentioned above. For additional help in understanding poetic forms, see [LIP-700], [LIP-1220], and [LIP-1270].

This section also includes a good number of works treating Christian themes in poetry and verse, especially items [LIP-410], [LIP-440], [LIP-500], [LIP-540], [LIP-570], [LIP-620], [LIP-810], [LIP-890], [LIP-900], [LIP-920], [LIP-940], [LIP-1050], [LIP-1070], [LIP-1090], [LIP-1100], [LIP-1200], [LIP-1210], [LIP-1250], [LIP-1260], and [LIP-1280]. Although studies of individual authors are rarely included in this book, several studies on Milton--[LIP-800], [LIP-880], and [LIP-1150]--and one on Byron--[LIP-820]--have been included because of their centrality to the study of the Bible and poetry. One will also want to note that a number of fine studies have been completed treating poetry in the Bible, and these are given in the next section on biblical literature.

Special Bibliographies

[LIP-010] Alexander, Harriet Semmes. *American and British Poetry: A Guide to the Criticism, 1925-1978.* Ed. George Hendrick and Donna Gerstenberger. Athens, Ohio: Swallow Press, 1984. 486 pp.

[LIP-020] *American Poetry Index: An Author, Title, and Subject Index to Poetry by Americans in Single-Author Collections [1981-].* [Great Neck: Granger, 1983-.] Annual.

[LIP-030] Aubrey, Bryan. *English Romantic Poetry: An Annotated Bibliography.* Pasadena, Calif.: Salem Press, 1991. 296 pp.

[LIP-040] Bernhardt, William F., ed. *Granger's Index to Poetry.* 8th ed. New York: Columbia University Press, 1986. 2,014 pp.

[LIP-050] Brewton, John E., and Sara W. Brewton, comps. *Index to Children's Poetry: A Title, Subject, Author, and First Line Index to Poetry in Collections for Children and Youth.* New York: H. W. Wilson, 1942. 965 pp. *First Supplement.* 1957. 405 pp. *Second Supplement.* 1965. 451 pp. *Index to Poetry for Children and Young People, 1964-1969.* Comp. Brewton, Brewton, and G. Meredith Blackburn III. 1972. 574 pp. *1970-1975.* Comp. John E. Brewton, G. Meredith Blackburn III, and Lorraine A. Blackburn. 1978. 472 pp. *1976-1981.* 1984. 317 pp.

[LIP-060] Brogan, T. V. F. *English Versification, 1570-1980: A Reference*

Guide with a Global Appendix. Baltimore: Johns Hopkins University Press, 1981. 794 pp.

[LIP-070] Brown, Carleton [Fairchild]. *A Register of Middle English Religious and Didactic Verse.* Oxford: Bibliographical Society [of London], 1916-1920. 529 and 459 pp. [2723].

[LIP-080] Caskey, Jefferson D., comp. *Index to Poetry in Popular Periodicals, 1955-1959.* Westport, Conn.: Greenwood Publishing Group, Inc., 1984. 269 pp.

[LIP-090] Congdon, Kirby. *Contemporary Poets in American Anthologies 1960-1977.* Metuchen, N.J.: Scarecrow Press, 1978. 236 pp.

[LIP-100] Davis, Gwenn, and Beverly A. Joyce, eds. *Poetry by Women to 1900: A Bibliography of American and British Writers.* Bibliographies of Writings by American and British Women to 1900, vol. 2. London; New York: Mansell; Toronto: University of Toronto Press, 1991. xxiv, 340 pp.

[LIP-110] Davis, Lloyd. *Contemporary American Poetry: A Checklist--Second Series, 1973-1983.* Metuchen, N.J.: Scarecrow Press, 1985. 301 pp.

[LIP-120] Davis, Loyd, and Robert Irwin. *Contemporary American Poetry: A Checklist.* Metuchen, N.J.: Scarecrow Press, 1975. 183 pp.

[LIP-130] Deodene, Frank, and William P. French. *Black American Poetry Since 1944: A Preliminary Checklist.* Chatham, N.J.: Chatham Bookseller, 1971. 41 pp.

[LIP-140] *Directory of Poetry Publishers.* Paradise, Calif.: Dustbooks, 1985-. Annual.

[LIP-150] Dyson, A. E., ed. *English Poetry: Select Bibliographical Guides.* London; New York: Oxford University Press, 1971. 378 pp.

[LIP-160] Friedberg, Ruth C. *American Art Song and American Poetry: Vol. I: America Comes of Age.* Metuchen, N.J.: Scarecrow Press, 1981. 175 pp.

[LIP-170] ------. *American Art Song and American Poetry: Vol. II: Voices of Maturity.* Metuchen, N.J.: Scarecrow Press, 1984. 236 pp.

[LIP-180] ------. *American Art Song and American Poetry: Vol. III: The Century Advances.* Metuchen, N.J.: Scarecrow Press, 1987. 351 pp.

[LIP-190] Gershator, Phillis. *A Bibliographic Guide to the Literature of Contemporary American Poetry, 1970-1975.* Metuchen, N.J.:

Scarecrow Press, 1976. 132 pp.

[LIP-200] Gingerich, Martin E. *Contemporary Poetry in America and England, 1950-1975.* American Literature, English Literature, and World Literatures in English: An Information Guide Series 41. Detroit: Gale Research, 1983. 453 pp.

[LIP-210] Glen, Duncan. *The Poetry of the Scots: An Introduction and Bibliographical Guide to Poetry in Gaelic, Scots, Latin, and English.* Edinburgh: Edinburgh University Press, 1991. xxxi, 149 pp.

[LIP-220] Hoffman, Herbert H. *Hoffman's Index to Poetry: European and Latin American Poetry in Anthologies.* Metuchen, N.J.: Scarecrow Press, 1985. 686 pp.

[LIP-230] *Index of American Periodical Verse: [1971-].* Ed. Rafael Catala, Sander Zulauf, James D. Anderson, et al. Metuchen, N.J.: Scarecrow Press, 1971-1989.

[LIP-240] *Index to Poetry in Periodicals, 1925-1929: An Index of Poets and Poems Published in American Magazines and Newspapers.* Great Neck: Granger, 1984. 265 pp.

[LIP-250] *Index to Poetry in Periodicals, 1920-1924: An Index of Poets and Poems Published in American Magazines and Newspapers.* Great Neck: Granger, 1983. 178 pp.

[LIP-260] *Index to Poetry in Periodicals: American Poetic Renaissance, 1915-1919: An Index of Poets and Poems Published in American Magazines and Newspapers.* Great Neck: Granger, 1981, 1981. 221 pp.

[LIP-270] Jackson, J[ames] R[obert de Jager]. *Romantic Poetry by Women: A Bibliography, 1770-1835.* Oxford: Clarendon Press; New York: Oxford University Press, 1993.

[LIP-280] Jason, Philip K. *Nineteenth Century American Poetry: An Annotated Bibliography.* Pasadena: Salem Press, 1989. 257 pp.

[LIP-290] Kuntz, Joseph Marshall, and Nancy Conrad Martinez. *Poetry Explication: A Checklist of Interpretations Since 1925 of British and American Poems Past and Present.* 3rd ed. Boston: G. K. Hall, 1980.

[LIP-300] McCullough, Kathleen. *Concrete Poetry: An Annotated International Bibliography, with an Index of Poets and Poems.* Troy, N.Y.: Whitston Publishing Co., 1989. 1,010 pp.

[LIP-310] McPheron, William, and Jocelyn Sheppard. *The Bibliography of Contemporary American Poetry, 1945-1985: An Annotated*

Checklist. Wesport, Conn.: Meckler Corporation; Green-wood Publishing Group, Inc., 1986. 72 pp.

[LIP-320] Martinez, Nancy C[onrad], and Joseph G. R. Martinez. *Guide to British Poetry Explication*. 2 vols. Boston: G. K. Hall, 1991. (Vol. 1, Old English, Medieval; Vol. 2, Renaissance.)

[LIP-330] Murray, Sue. *Bibliography of Australian Poetry 1935-1955*. Ed. John Arnold, Sally Batten, and Katie Purvis. Port Melbourne, Victoria: Thorpe with National Centre for Australian Studies, 1991. 274 pp.

[LIP-340] *Poetry Index Annual: A Title, Author, First Line, and Subject Index to Poetry in Anthologies*. Great Neck: Poetry Index, 1982-. Annual.

[LIP-350] Reardon, Joan. *Poetry by American Women, 1975-1989: A Bibliography*. Metuchen, N.J.: Scarecrow Press, 1990. 242 pp. [2,880]

[LIP-360] Reardon, Joan, and Kristine A. Thorsen. *Poetry by American Women, 1900-1975: A Bibliography*. Metuchen, N.J.: Scarecrow Press, 1979. 631 pp. [9,500]

[LIP-370] Ruppert, James, and John R. Leo. *Guide to American Poetry Explication*. 2 vols. Boston: G. K. Hall, 1989.

[LIP-380] Shapiro, Karl. *A Bibliography of Modern Prosody*. Baltimore: n.p., 1948. 36 pp. [75].

[LIP-390] Waggoner, Hyatt H. *American Poetry: From the Puritans to the Present*. Rev. ed. Baton Rouge: Louisiana State University Press, 1984. 656 pp. Bib.

[LIP-400] Wier, John Rex. *Bibliography and Guide to Poetry Interpretation*. Austin: University of Texas, 1966. 44 pp.

Key Works

[LIP-410] Alexander, Pat, ed. *Eerdman's Book of Christian Poetry*. Grand Rapids: William B. Eerdmans, 1981. 128 pp.

[LIP-420] *American Poetry Review* . Philadelphia: American Poetry Review, 1972-. Bi-montly.

[LIP-430] Barfield, Owen. *Poetic Diction: A Study in Meaning*. 3rd ed. Middletown, Conn.: Wesleyan University Press, 1973. 230 pp. Bib. refs.

274

[LIP-440] Barnouw, A[driaan] J[acob]. *Anglo-Saxon Christian Poetry*. Trans. Louise Dudley. 1914. Reprint. [Folcroft, Pa.]: Folcroft Library Editions, 1974.

[LIP-450] Barnstone, Willis, Patricia Terry, Arthur S. Wensinger, Kimon Friar, Sonia Raiziss, Alfredo de Palchi, George Reavey, and Angel Flores, eds. *Modern European Poetry*. New York: Bantam Books, 1978. 614 pp. Bibs.

[LIP-460] Bate, W. Jackson. *The Burden of the Past and the English Poet*. Cambridge, Mass.: Harvard University Press, 1991. 160 pp.

[LIP-470] Bayard, Caroline. *The New Poetics in Canada and Quebec: From Concretism to Post-Modernism*. Toronto; Buffalo: University of Toronto Press, 1989. Bib. refs. pp. 325-361.

[LIP-480] Bellamy, Joe David, ed. *American Poetry Observed: Poets on Their Work*. Urbana: University of Illinois Press, 1984. 313 pp.

[LIP-490] Bloch, Chana. *Spelling the Word: George Herbert and the Bible*. Berkeley: University of California Press, 1985. 375 pp. Bib. refs.

[LIP-500] Bloom, Harold. *Ruin the Sacred Truths: Poetry and Belief from the Bible to the Present*. Charles Eliot Norton Lectures, 1989. Cambridge, Mass.: Harvard University Press, 1991. 216 pp.

[LIP-510] ------, ed. *Pre-Raphaelite Poets*. Modern Critical Views. New York: Chelsea House Publishers, 1986. Bib. pp. 295-299.

[LIP-520] Brooks, Cleanth. *The Well Wrought Urn: Studies in the Structure of Poetry*. New York: Harcourt, Brace and World, 1947. 300 pp.

[LIP-530] *Canadian Poetry: Studies, Documents, Reviews*. London, Ontario: University of Western Ontario, 1977-. Semi-annual.

[LIP-540] Cherniss, Michael D. *Ingeld and Christ: Heroic Conceptions and Values in Old English Christian Poetry*. Studies in English Literature, no. 74. Hawthorne, N.Y.: Mouton de Gruyter, 1972. 267 pp.

[LIP-550] Chevalier, Tracy, ed. *Contemporary Poets*. 5th ed. Chicago: St. James Press, 1991. 1,179 pp. Bib. refs.

[LIP-560] Courthope, W. J. *A History of English Poetry*. 6 vols. New York: Macmillan Publishing Co., 1895-1911. (Covers through Romantic movement.)

[LIP-570] Davie, Donald, ed. *The New Oxford Book of Christian Verse*. New

York: Oxford University Press, 1982. 319 pp. Bib. refs.

[LIP-580] Dennis, John. *The Grounds of Criticism in Poetry.* 1704. Reprint. New York: Garland Publishing, 1971. 127 pp.

[LIP-590] Deutsch, Babette. *Poetry Handbook: A Dictionary of Terms.* 4th ed. Barnes and Noble Books, 1979. 203 pp.

[LIP-600] Donoghue, Denis. *William Butler Yeats.* 1971. Reprint. New York: The Ecco Press, 1988. Bib. pp. 149-152.

[LIP-610] Downes, David A[nthony]. *Hopkins' Sanctifying Imagination.* Lanham, Md.: University Press of America, 1985. Bib. pp. 116-125.

[LIP-620] Eitel, Lorraine, with Jeannine Bohlmeyer. *The Treasury of Christian Poetry.* Old Tappan, N.J.: Fleming H. Revell Co., 1982. 189 pp.

[LIP-630] Elder, John. *Imagining the Earth: Poetry and the Vision of Nature.* Urbana: University of Illinois Press, 1985. Bib. refs. in notes, pp. 217-228.

[LIP-640] Eliot, T[homas] S[tearns]. *On Poetry and Poets.* New York: Farrar, Straus and Cudahy, 1957. Bib. refs.

[LIP-650] ------. *The Sacred Wood.* New York: Alfred A. Knopf, 1921. Bib. refs.

[LIP-660] ------. *The Use of Poetry and the Use of Criticism: Studies in the Relation of Criticism to Poetry in England.* Cambridge: Harvard University Press, 1933. Bib. refs.

[LIP-670] Ellmann, Richard, and Robert O'Clair, eds. *The Norton Anthology of Modern Poetry.* 2nd ed. New York: W. W. Norton and Co., 1988. Bib. pp. 1743-1828.

[LIP-680] Fredeman, William E., and Ira B. Nadel. *Victorian Poets After 1850.* Dictionary of Literary Biography, vol. 35. Detroit: Gale Research, 1985. 437 pp.

[LIP-690] Frye, Northrop. *Sound and Poetry.* New York: Columbia University Press, 1957. 156 pp.

[LIP-700] Fussell, Paul. *Poetic Meter & Poetic Form.* Rev. ed. New York: Random House, 1979. Bib. pp. 181-182.

[LIP-710] Gibson, Donald B., comp. *Modern Black Poets: A Collection of Critical Essays.* Twentieth Century Views, Spectrum Book. Englewood Cliffs, N.J.: Prentice-Hall Press, 1973. Bib. pp.

167-181.

[LIP-720] Greiner, Donald J., ed. *American Poets Since World War II.* 2 pts. Dictionary of Literary Biography, vol. 5. Detroit: Gale Research, 1980. (See R. S. Gwynn for continuation of series.)

[LIP-730] Gross, Harvey. *Sound and Form in Modern Poetry: A Study of Prosody from Thomas Hardy to Robert Lowell.* Ann Arbor: University of Michigan Press, 1964. 334 pp. Bib. refs. in notes.

[LIP-740] Gwynn, R. S., ed. *American Poets Since World War II: Second Series.* Dictionary of Literary Biography, vol. 105. Detroit: Gale Research, 1991. 403 pp. Bib. refs. pp. 323-331.

[LIP-750] ------, ed. *American Poets Since World War II: Third Series.* Dictionary of Literary Biography, vol. 120. Detroit: Gale Research, 1992. 425 pp. Bib. refs.

[LIP-760] Hester, Thomas, ed. *Seventeenth-Century British Nondramatic Poets: First Series.* Dictionary of Literary Biography, vol. 121. Detroit: Gale Research, 1992. xxiii, 414 pp. Bib. refs.

[LIP-770] ------, ed. *Seventeenth-Century British Nondramatic Poets: Second Series.* Dictionary of Literary Biography, vol. 126. Detroit: Gale Research, 1993. Bib. refs.

[LIP-780] Haublein, Ernst. *The Stanza.* London: Methuen and Co., Ltd., 1978. Bib. pp. 117-121.

[LIP-790] *Hudson Review, The.* New York: The Hudson Review, 1948-. Quarterly.

[LIP-800] Lieb, Michael. *Poetics of the Holy: A Reading of Paradise Lost.* Chapel Hill: University of North Carolina Press, 1981. Bib. pp. 389-423.

[LIP-810] Lindskoog, Kathryn Ann. *A Child's Garden of Christian Verses.* Ventura, Calif.: Regal Books, 1983. 160 pp. (Adapted from Robert Louis Stevenson.)

[LIP-820] Looper, Travis. *Byron and the Bible: A Compendium of Biblical Usage in the Poetry of Lord Byron.* Metuchen, N.J.: Scarecrow Press, 1978. 330 pp.

[LIP-830] Magill, Frank N., ed. *Critical Survey of Poetry.* 8 vols. English Language Series. Englewood Cliffs, N.J.: Salem Press, 1992. Bib. refs.

[LIP-840] Malof, Joseph. *A Manual of English Meters.* Bloomington: Indiana University Press, 1970. 236 pp.

[LIP-850] Maritain, Jacques. *Art and Poetry*. Trans. Elva de Pue Matthews. Trans. *Trois peintres, Dialogues, and La Clef des chants*. New York: Philosophical Library, 1943. 104 pp.

[LIP-860] ------. *Art and Scholasticism and the Frontiers of Poetry*. Trans. Joseph W. Evans. 1962. Reprint. Notre Dame: University of Notre Dame Press, 1974. Bib. refs. in notes, pp. 153-229.

[LIP-870] Meeter, Merle, comp. *Country of the Risen King: Anthology of Christian Poetry*. Grand Rapids: Baker Book House, 1978. 446 pp.

[LIP-880] Merrill, Thomas F. *Epic God-Talk: Paradise Lost and The Grammar of Religious Language*. Jefferson, N.C.: McFarland and Co., Inc., 1986. 144 pp. Bib.

[LIP-890] Merton, Thomas. "Poetry and the Contemplative Life, An Essay." In *Figures for an Apocalypse*. Norfolk, Conn.: New Directions, [1948], pp. 93-111.

[LIP-900] Mills, James R., comp. *Poems of Inspiration from the Masters*. Old Tappan, N.J.: Fleming H. Revell Co., 1979. 173 pp.

[LIP-910] Myers, Jack, and Michael Simms. *Longman Dictionary and Handbook of Poetry*. Longman English and Humanities Series. New York: Longman, 1985. 366 pp.

[LIP-920] Noon, William T. *Poetry and Prayer*. New Brunswick: Rutgers University Press, [1967]. Bib. refs. in notes, pp. 311-348.

[LIP-930] Oxley, William. *Distinguishing Poetry: Writings on Poetry*. Salzburg Studies in English Literature. Poetic Drama and Poetic Theory, 70:2. Salzburg, Austria: Institut fur Anglistik und Amerikanistik, Universitat Salzburg, 1989. 245 pp. Bib. refs.

[LIP-940] Pagis, Dan. *Hebrew Poetry of the Middle Ages and the Renaissance*. Berkeley: University of California Press, 1991. 100 pp.

[LIP-950] *Parnassus: Poetry in Review*. New York: Poetry in Review Foundation, 1972-. Semi-annual.

[LIP-960] Patnaik, J. N. *The Aesthetics of New Criticism*. Atlantic Highlands, N.J.: Humanities Press, 1983. Bib. pp. 84-94.

[LIP-970] Perkins, David. *A History of Modern Poetry*. 2 vols. Cambridge: Harvard University Press, 1976, 1987. Vol. 1: *From the 1890s to the High Modernist Mode*. 1976. 617 pp. Vol. 2:

278

Modernism and After. 1987. 712 pp.

[LIP-980] *Poetry*. Chicago: Poetry, 1912-. Monthly.

[LIP-990] *Poetry Review*. London: Poetry Review, 1912-. Quarterly.

[LIP-1000] Poulin, A., Jr., ed. *Contemporary American Poetry*. 3rd ed. Boston: Houghton Mifflin Co., 1980. Bib. in notes and pp. 596-598.

[LIP-1010] Preminger, Alex, ed. *Princeton Encyclopedia of Poetry and Poetics*. Rev. ed. Princeton: Princeton University Press, 1974. 992 pp. (3rd ed. in progress with Preminger and T. V. F. Brogan as editors.)

[LIP-1020] Quartermain, Peter, ed. *American Poets, 1880-1945: First Series*. Dictionary of Literary Biography, vol. 45. Detroit: Gale Research, 1986. 490 pp.

[LIP-1030] ------, ed. *American Poets, 1880-1945: Second Series*. Dictionary of Literary Biography, vol. 48. Detroit: Gale Research, 1986. 510 pp.

[LIP-1040] ------, ed. *American Poets, 1880-1945: Third Series*. 2 pts. Dictionary of Literary Biography, vol. 54. Detroit: Gale Research, 1987.

[LIP-1050] Rivers, Isabel. *Classical and Christian Ideas in English Renaissance Poetry: A Student's Guide*. Boston: G. Allen and Unwin, 1979. Bib. pp. 194-227.

[LIP-1060] Rothenberg, Jerome, and Diane Rothenberg. *Symposium of the Whole: A Range of Discourse Toward an Ethnopoetics*. Berkeley: University of California Press, 1983. Bib. pp. 485-499.

[LIP-1070] Schrand, Gregory J. "The Franciscan and Dominican Aesthetics in Middle English Religious Lyric Poetry." Ph.D. Thesis, Rice University, 1982. Bib. pp. 153-156.

[LIP-1080] Scott, Nathan A., Jr., ed. *Four Ways of Modern Poetry*. Richmond, Va.: John Knox Press, 1965. Bib. pp. 93-95. (Wallace Stevens, Robert Frost, Dylan Thomas, and Wystan Hugh Auden.)

[LIP-1090] ------. *Modern Poetry and the Christian Tradition: A Study in the Relation of Christianity to Culture*. New York: Charles Scribner's Sons, 1952. 287 pp.

[LIP-1100] ------. *The Wild Prayer of Longing: Poetry and the Sacred*. New

Haven: Yale University Press, 1971. 124 pp. Bib. refs.

[LIP-1110] *Sewanee Review*. Sewanee, Tenn.: University of the South, 1892-. Quarterly.

[LIP-1120] Shapiro, Karl, and Robert Beum. *A Prosody Handbook*. New York: Harper, 1965. 214 pp.

[LIP-1130] Sherry, Vincent B., Jr., ed. *Poets of Great Britain and Ireland, 1945-1960*. Dictionary of Literary Biography, vol. 27. Detroit: Gale Research, 1984. 367 pp.

[LIP-1140] ------. *Poets of Great Britain and Ireland Since 1960*. 2 pts. Dictionary of Literary Biography, vol. 40. Detroit: Gale Research, 1985.

[LIP-1150] Sims, James H., and Leland Ryken, eds. *Milton and Scriptural Tradition: The Bible into Poetry*. Columbia: University of Missouri Press, 1984. 212 pp. Bib. refs. in footnotes.

[LIP-1160] Sitter, John, ed. *Eighteenth-Century British Poets: First Series*. Dictionary of Literary Biography, vol. 95. Detroit: Gale Research, 1990. 436 pp. Bib. refs.

[LIP-1170] ------, ed. *Eighteenth-Century British Poets: Second Series*. Dictionary of Literary Biography, vol. 109. Detroit: Gale Research, 1991. 385 pp. Bib. refs. pp. 308-311.

[LIP-1180] Stanford, Donald E., ed. *British Poets, 1880-1914*. Dictionary of Literary Biography, vol. 19. Detroit: Gale Research, 1983. 486 pp.

[LIP-1190] ------, ed. *British Poets, 1914-1945*. Dictionary of Literary Biography, vol. 20. Detroit: Gale Research, 1983. 431 pp.

[LIP-1200] Tennyson, G. B. *Victorian Devotional Poetry: The Tractarian Mode*. Cambridge, Mass.: Harvard University Press, 1980. Bib. refs.

[LIP-1210] Tozer, A. W., ed. *The Christian Book of Mystical Verse*. Rpt. Camp Hill, Pa.: Christian Publications, 1975.

[LIP-1220] Turco, Lewis. *The New Book of Forms: A Handbook of Poetics*. Hanover: University Press of New England, 1986. 280 pp.

[LIP-1230] *Victorian Poetry*. Morgantown, W.V.: West Virginia University, 1963-. Quarterly. (British poetry, 1830-1914.)

[LIP-1240] Warren, Robert Penn. *Democracy and Poetry*. Cambridge, Mass.: Harvard University Press, 1975. 96 pp.

[LIP-1250] Weber, Sarah A. *Theology and Poetry in the Middle English Lyric: A Study of Sacred History and Aesthetic Form.* N.p.: Ohio State University Press, 1969. 310 pp.

[LIP-1260] Whallon, William. *Formula, Character, and Context: Studies in Homeric, Old English, and Old Testament Poetry.* Washington, D.C.: Center for Hellenic Studies, 1969. Reprint. Lanham, Md.: University Press of America, 1986. 244 pp.

[LIP-1270] Williams, Miller. *Patterns of Poetry: An Encyclopedia of Forms.* Baton Rouge: Louisiana State University Press, 1986. 203 pp.

[LIP-1280] Woodhouse, Arthur Sutherland Pigott. *The Poet and His Faith: Religion and Poetry in England from Spenser to Eliot and Auden.* Chicago: University of Chicago Press, [1965]. 304 pp.

[LIP-1290] Young, Robyn V., ed. *Poetry Criticism: Excerpts from Criticism of the Works of the Most Significant and Widely Studied Poets of World Literature.* 5 vols. Detroit: Gale Research, 1991-1992. Bib. refs.

KEY WORKS ON BIBLICAL LITERATURE

For the biblical scholar, the following section will seem very brief since only those works which treat a literary approach to the Bible are included. Nonetheless, many of the research tools used for locating biblical studies as a broader topic have been included here simply because few bibliographies are devoted primarily to the literary study of the Bible. The standard reference tool for finding articles and books in virtually all areas of biblical studies is the *Religion Index* in its various forms, including [LIB-130 to LIB-160]. For additional assistance in locating periodical literature, see [LIB-040], [LIB-080], [LIB-100], and [LIB-110]. The best work published to date for locating books on New Testament studies is Eldon Jay Epp's and George W. MacRae's partly annotated work, *The New Testament and Its Modern Interpreters* [LIB-050], which provides more exhaustive lists than those given in Joseph A. Fitzmyer's foundational volume, *An Introductory Bibliography for the Study of Scripture* [LIB-060]. These bibliographies are nicely augmented by James H. Charlesworth's *The New Testament Apocrypha and Pseudepigrapha: A Guide to Publications, with Excursuses on Apocalypses* [LIB-020].

Students of literary studies on the Bible will be greatly helped by Alice L. Birney's *The Literary Lives of Jesus: An International Bibliography of Poetry, Drama, Fiction, and Criticism* [LIB-010], John H. Gottcent's *The Bible as Literature: A Selective Bibliography* [LIB-070], and Mark Minor's *Literary-Critical Approaches to the Bible: An Annotated Bibliography* [LIB-090]. Since the biblical studies often overlap with the study of worship, and since many art forms are incorporated into worship, Bard Thompson's *A Bibliography of Christian Worship* [LIB-170] will prove a valuable tool for those studying Christianity and the arts. Also note that Heather F. Day's *Protestant Theological Education in America: A Bibliography* [LIB-030] and James D. Purvis' *Jerusalem, The Holy City: A Bibliography* [LIB-120] contain some entries related to the literary study of the Bible.

The bibliographies given in this section refer to articles in numerous journals, many of which offer analyses useful to the literary critic. Since many church organizations and biblical seminaries in the western world produce journals, such as *The Review & Expositor* at Southern Baptist Theological Seminary, which contain literary studies of the Bible only occasionally, these numerous journals have not been listed here. Those journals which are most likely to contain scholarly articles and fine book reviews related to this approach to the Bible include the *Christian Century* [LIB-340], the *Journal of Biblical Literature* [LIB-510], and *Semeia* [LIB-760].

Literary studies of the Bible have come into their own during the past two decades and have provided some of the most refreshing interpretations of Scripture in the twentieth century. The list of key works given below offers a rich sampling of the numerous books now being published on this topic, and provides important clues about who to watch for forthcoming publications. Most of the key works presented below can be fitted into one of four larger categories, each of which has specialized studies within it: biblical studies covering the entire Bible; biblical studies covering the Old Testament; biblical studies covering the New Testament; and studies of the influence of the Bible on literature. For studies of the entire Bible and its literary aspects, the best works are those by James Stokes Ackerman [LIB-180], Edgar V. McKnight [LIB-630], and Leland Ryken [LIB-720]. Other works well worth consulting are given as items [LIB-300], [LIB-440], [LIB-460], [LIB-500], [LIB-570],

[LIB-580], [LIB-610], [LIB-620], [LIB-750], and [LIB-810].

For literary criticism of the Old Testament, the best works are Robert Alter's popularized and lucid analyses, [LIB-200 to LIB-220], Norman K. Gottwald's fine survey text, *The Hebrew Bible: A Socio-Literary Introduction* [LIB-450], Rolf Rendtorff's scholarly and concise book, *The Old Testament: An Introduction* [LIB-700], and Meir Sternberg's dazzling if sometimes obtuse volume, *The Poetics of Biblical Narrative: Ideological Literature and the Drama of Reading* [LIB-780]. Other works worth consulting are [LIB-240], [LIB-250], [LIB-260], [LIB-270], [LIB-330], [LIB-370], [LIB-390], [LIB-400], [LIB-600], [LIB-690], [LIB-740], and [LIB-770].

Most of the literary studies of the New Testament specialize in one book or some aspect of the Bible, such as parables or the gospels. The few texts offering a review of literary studies of the New Testament as a whole include Robert Alter's and Frank Kermode's *The Literary Guide to the Bible* [LIB-230] (covering the Old and New Testaments), William Beardslee's *Literary Criticism of the New Testament* [LIB-280], David Jaspers' *The New Testament and the Literary Imagination* [LIB-490], Donald Juel's, James S. Ackerman's, and Thayer S. Warshaw's *An Introduction to New Testament Literature* [LIB-520], Leland Ryken's *The New Testament in Literary Criticism* [LIB-730], and Amos Wilder's *Early Christian Rhetoric: The Language of the Gospel* [LIB-850]. Literary studies of the gospels are relatively plentiful. For a study of the gospels as a group see Stephen D. Moore's *Literary Criticism and the Gospels: The Theoretical Challenge* [LIB-680]. For a literary analysis of Matthew, see Jack Dean Kingsbury's *Matthew as Story* [LIB-540]. One of the most readable analyses of a gospel is David Rhoads's and Donald Michie's *Mark as Story: An Introduction to the Narrative of a Gospel* [LIB-710]. For studies of Luke, see Luke Timothy Johnson's *The Gospel of Luke* [LIB-480], Robert J. Karris' *Luke: Artist and Theologian: Luke's Passion Account as Literature* [LIB-530], William S. Kurz's *Reading Luke-Acts: Dynamics of Biblical Narrative* [LIB-590], and Charles H. Talbert's *Luke-Acts: New Perspectives from the Society of Biblical Literature Seminar* [LIB-800]. For studies of John, see R. Alan Culpepper's *Anatomy of the Fourth Gospel: A Study in Literary Design* [LIB-360], Paul D. Duke's *Irony in the Fourth Gospel* [LIB-380], George Mlakuzhyil's *The Christocentric Literary Structure of the Fourth Gospel*

[LIB-670]. For those conversant in literary criticism, most of these studies of the gospels are quite basic, yet they offer an important beginning in literary criticism of the Bible.

Some of the best studies of the New Testament are those focusing on the parables of Jesus, including Warren S. Kissinger's survey, *The Parables of Jesus: A History of Interpretation and Bibliography* [LIB-560], Mary Ann Tolbert's fine study, *Perspectives on the Parables: An Approach to Multiple Perspectives* [LIB-820], Dan Otto Via's pioneering work, *The Parables: Their Literary and Existential Dimension* [LIB-840], and Brad H. Young's recent volume, *Jesus and His Jewish Parables: Rediscovering the Roots of Jesus' Teaching* [LIB-870]. For a useful beginning point in studying the Sermon on the Mount, see Warren S. Kissinger's survey, *The Sermon on the Mount: A History of Interpretation and Bibliography* [LIB-550]. Studies of the literary techniques of Paul are not plentiful, but James W. Aageson's *Written Also for Our Sake: Paul and the Art of Biblical Interpretation* [LIB-190] offers an important introduction for such study. Some of the most interesting studies of New Testament literature have been those analyzing Revelation. Three studies offering intriguing literary interpretations are James L. Blevins' interpretation of Revelation as a drama, *Revelation* [LIB-310], John Wick Boman's precurser to Blevins' study, *The First Christian Drama: The Book of Revelation* [LIB-320], and Adela Yarbro Collins' creative and probing interpretation, *Crisis and Catharsis: The Power of the Apocalypse* [LIB-350].

The fourth category of biblical studies realizing significant growth is that treating the influence of the Bible on literature. Although this area of study overlaps heavily with the study of religion and literature, at least four works can be identified as belonging primarily to biblical studies, including David C. Fowler's *The Bible in Early English Literature* [LIB-410], *The Bible in Middle English Literature* [LIB-420], Northrop Frye's commanding work, *The Great Code: The Bible and Literature* [LIB-430], and Terence R. Wright's *Theology and Literature* [LIB-860]. The single reference volume of greatest help for researchers in this area is David Lyle Jeffrey's *A Dictionary of Biblical Tradition in English Literature* [LIR-400], listed below in the literature and religion section because of its primary emphasis on literature. Another study which will prove helpful as a background work is John McManners' *Oxford*

284

Illustrated History of Christianity [LIB-640].

Special Bibliographies

[LIB-010] Birney, Alice L. *The Literary Lives of Jesus: An International Bibliography of Poetry, Drama, Fiction, and Criticism.* Garland Reference Library of the Humanities, vol. 735. New York: Garland Publishing, 1989. 187 pp.

[LIB-020] Charlesworth, James H. *The New Testament Apocrypha and Pseudepigrapha: A Guide to Publications, with Excursuses on Apocalypses.* Metuchen, N.J.: Scarecrow Press, 1987. 468 pp.

[LIB-030] Day, Heather F. *Protestant Theological Education in America: A Bibliography.* Metuchen, N.J.: Scarecrow Press, 1985. 523 pp.

[LIB-040] Dawsey, James. *A Scholar's Guide to Academic Journals in Religion.* Metuchen, N.J.: Scarecrow Press, 1988. 316 pp.

[LIB-050] Epp, Eldon Jay, and George W. MacRae. *The New Testament and Its Modern Interpreters.* Philadelphia: Fortress Press, 1989. 601 pp. [partly annotated].

[LIB-060] Fitzmyer, Joseph A. *An Introductory Bibliography for the Study of Scripture.* 3rd ed. *Subsidia Biblica,* vol. 3. Chicago: Loyola University Press, 1990. 220 pp.

[LIB-070] Gottcent, John H. *The Bible as Literature: A Selective Bibliography.* Boston: G. K. Hall, 1979. 170 pp.

[LIB-080] Hupper, William G., ed., comp. *An Index to English Periodical Literature on the Old Testament and Ancient Near Eastern Studies.* 4 vols. Metuchen, N.J.: Scarecrow Press, 1987-1990.

[LIB-090] Minor, Mark. *Literary-Critical Approaches to the Bible: An Annotated Bibliography.* West Cornwall, Conn.: Locust Hill Press, 1992.

[LIB-100] *New Testament Abstracts: A Record of Current Literature.* Cambridge, Mass.: Weston School of Theology, 1956-. 3/year. Dist. Catholic Biblical Association of America, Washington, D.C.

[LIB-110] *Old Testament Abstracts.* Washington, D.C.: Catholic Biblical

Association of America, 1978-. 3/year.

[LIB-120] Purvis, James D. *Jerusalem, The Holy City: A Bibliography.* Metuchen, N.J.: Scarecrow Press, 1988. 513 pp.

[LIB-130] *Religion Index One: Periodicals.* Chicago: American Theological Library Association, 1952-. 2/year. Formerly: *Index, to Religious Periodical Literature* (1952-1977).

[LIB-140] *Religion Index Two: Multi-Author Works.* 1976-. Annual

[LIB-150] *Religion Index Two: Festschriften, 1960-1969.* Ed. Betty A. O'Brien and Elmer J. O'Brien. 1980. 741 pp.

[LIB-160] *Religion Index Two: Multi-Author Works, 1970-1975.* Ed. G. Fay Dickerson. 2 vols. 1982.

[LIB-170] Thompson, Bard. *A Bibliography of Christian Worship.* Metuchen, N.J.: Scarecrow Press, 1989. 830 pp.

Key Works

[LIB-180] Ackerman, James Stokes. *On Teaching the Bible as Literature: A Guide to Selected Biblical Narratives for Secondary Schools.* Ed. Jane Stouder Hawley. Bloomington: Indiana University Press, [1967]. Bib. pp. 109-112, and bib. refs. in notes, pp. 113-121.

[LIB-190] Aageson, James W. *Written Also for Our Sake: Paul and the Art of Biblical Interpretation.* Louisville: Westminster; John Knox Press, 1993. 160 pp.

[LIB-200] Alter, Robert. *The Art of Biblical Narrative.* New York: Basic Books, Inc., 1981. 195 pp.

[LIB-210] ------. *The Art of Biblical Poetry.* New York: Basic Books, Inc., 1987. 228 pp.

[LIB-220] ------. *The World of Biblical Literature.* New York: Basic Books, Inc., 1992.

[LIB-230] Alter, Robert, and Frank Kermode, eds. *The Literary Guide to the Bible.* Cambridge: Belknap Press; Harvard University Press, 1987. 678 pp. Bib. refs. in notes.

[LIB-240] Aschkenasy, Nehama. *Eve's Journey: Feminine Images in Hebraic Literary Tradition.* Philadelphia: University of Pennyslvania Press, 1986. Bib. pp. 257-262.

[LIB-250] Bal, Mieke. *Lethal Love: Feminist Literary Readings of Biblical Love Stories*. Bloomington: Indiana University Press, 1987. Bib. pp. 133-136.

[LIB-260] ------. *Death and Dissymmetry: The Politics of Coherence in the Book of Judges*. Chicago: University of Chicago Press, 1989.

[LIB-270] Barnstone, Willis. *The Other Bible*. San Francisco: Harper and Row, 1984. Bib. refs. pp. 737-742.

[LIB-280] Beardslee, William. *Literary Criticism of the New Testament*. Philadelphia: Fortress Press, 1970.

[LIB-290] Berlin, Adele. *Biblical Poetry Through Medieval Jewish Eyes*. Bloomington: Indiana University Press, 1991. 224 pp.

[LIB-300] ------. *The Dynamics of Biblical Parallelism*. Bloomington: Indiana University Press, 1985. 192 pp.

[LIB-310] Blevins, James L. *Revelation*. Atlanta: John Knox Press, 1984. 120 pp.

[LIB-320] Boman, John Wick. *The First Christian Drama: The Book of Revelation*. Philadelphia: Westminster Press, [1968]. 159 pp.

[LIB-330] Childs, Brevard S. *Introduction to the Old Testament as Scripture*. Philadelphia: Fortress Press, 1979. 688 pp. Bibs.

[LIB-340] *Christian Century*. Chicago: Christian Century Foundation, 1908-. Weekly.

[LIB-350] Collins, Adela Yarbro. *Crisis and Catharsis: The Power of the Apocalypse*. Philadelphia: Westminster Press, 1984. 179 pp. Bib. refs.

[LIB-360] Culpepper, R. Alan. *Anatomy of the Fourth Gospel: A Study in Literary Design*. Philadelphia: Fortress Press, 1983. Bib. pp. 239-248.

[LIB-370] Damrosch, David. *The Narrative Covenant: Transformations of Genre in the Growth of Biblical Literature*. Ithaca: Cornell University Press, 1991. 352 pp.

[LIB-380] Duke, Paul D. *Irony in the Fourth Gospel*. Atlanta: John Knox Press, 1985. Bib. pp. 197-210.

[LIB-390] Exum, J. Cheryl, and David J. A. Clines. *The New Literary Criticism and the Hebrew Bible*. Valley Forge, Penn.: Trinity Press International, 1993. 240 pp.

[LIB-400] Fisch, Harold. *Poetry with a Purpose: Biblical Poetics and Interpretation*. Bloomington: Indiana University Press, 1988. 218 pp.

[LIB-410] Fowler, David C. *The Bible in Early English Literature*. Seattle: University of Washington Press, 1976. 263 pp.

[LIB-420] ------. *The Bible in Middle English Literature*. Seattle: University of Washington Press, 1984. Bib. pp. 297-314.

[LIB-430] Frye, Northrop. *The Great Code: The Bible and Literature*. New York: Harcourt, Brace, Jovanovich, 1982. 261 pp. Bib. refs. in notes.

[LIB-440] Gabel, John B., and Charles B. Wheeler. *The Bible as Literature: An Introduction*. New York: Oxford University Press, 1986. 278 pp. Bib. refs.

[LIB-450] Gottwald, Norman K. *The Hebrew Bible: A Socio-Literary Introduction*. Philadelphia: Fortress Press, 1985. Bib. pp. 611-665.

[LIB-460] Henn, T[homas] R[ice]. *The Bible as Literature*. New York: Oxford University Press, 1970. Bib. pp. 261-265.

[LIB-470] Johnson, Luke Timothy. *The Acts of the Apostles. Sacra Pagina*. Ed. Daniel J. Harrington. Collegeville, Minn.: The Liturgical Press, 1993? 576 pp.

[LIB-480] ------. *The Gospel of Luke. Sacra Pagina*. Ed. Daniel J. Harrington. Collegeville, Minn.: Liturgical Press, n.d. 480 pp.

[LIB-490] Jaspers, David. *The New Testament and the Literary Imagination*. Atlantic Highlands: Humanities Press, 1987.

[LIB-500] Josipovici, Gabriel. *The Book of God: A Response to the Bible*. London; New Haven: Yale University Press, 1988. Bib. refs. pp. 326-331.

[LIB-510] *Journal of Biblical Literature*. Atlanta: Scholars Press for Society of Biblical Literature, 1881-. Quarterly.

[LIB-520] Juel, Donald, James S. Ackerman, and Thayer S. Warshaw. *An Introduction to New Testament Literature*. Nashville: Abingdon Press, 1978. Bib. pp. 350-358.

[LIB-530] Karris, Robert J. *Luke: Artist and Theologian: Luke's Passion Account as Literature*. New York: Paulist Press, 1985. Bib. pp. 123-125.

[LIB-540] Kingsbury, Jack Dean. *Matthew as Story*. 2nd ed. Philadelphia: Fortress Press, 1988. Bib. pp. 165-171.

[LIB-550] Kissinger, Warren S. *The Sermon on the Mount: A History of Interpretation and Bibliography*. Metuchen, N.J.: Scarecrow Press, 1975. 309 pp.

[LIB-560] ------. *The Parables of Jesus: A History of Interpretation and Bibliography*. Metuchen, N.J.: Scarecrow Press, 1979. 463 pp.

[LIB-570] Kort, Wesley A. *Narrative Elements and Religious Meanings*. Philadelphia: Fortress Press, 1975. 118 pp. Bib. refs.

[LIB-580] ------. *Story, Text & Scripture: Literary Interests in Biblical Narrative*. University Park: Pennsylvania State University Press, 1988. 180 pp. Bib. pp. 147-156.

[LIB-590] Kurz, William S. *Reading Luke-Acts: Dynamics of Biblical Narrative*. Louisville: Westminster; John Knox Press, 1993. 272 pp. Bib.

[LIB-600] McConnell, Frank. *The Bible and the Narrative Tradition*. New York: Oxford University Press, 1986. 152 pp. Bib. refs.

[LIB-610] McEvenue, Sean. *Interpretation and the Bible: Essays on Truth in Literature*. Collegeville, Minn.: The Liturgical Press, 1993. 172 pp.

[LIB-620] McKenzie, Steven L., and Stephen R. Hayes, eds. *To Each Its Own Meaning: An Introduction to Biblical Criticisms and Their Application*. Louisville: Westminster; John Knox Press, 1993. 256 pp.

[LIB-630] McKnight, Edgar V. *The Bible and the Reader: An Introduction to Literary Criticism*. Philadelphia: Fortress Press, 1985. Bib. pp. 134-141.

[LIB-640] McManners, John, ed. *Oxford Illustrated History of Christianity*. New York: Oxford University Press, 1992. 736 pp.

[LIB-650] Mariaselvam, Abraham. *The Song of Songs and Ancient Tamil Love Poems: Poetry and Symbolism*. *Analecta Biblica*, vol. 118. Chicago: Loyola University Press, 1988. 336 pp.

[LIB-660] Mintz, Alan L. *Hurban: Responses to Catastrophe in Hebrew Literature*. New York: Columbia University Press, 1984. Bib. pp. 271-277.

[LIB-670] Mlakuzhyil, George. *The Christocentric Literary Structure of the Fourth Gospel*. *Analecta Biblica*, vol. 117. Chicago: Loyola

University Press, 1987. 372 pp.

[LIB-680] Moore, Stephen D. *Literary Criticism and the Gospels: The Theoretical Challenge.* New Haven: Yale University Press, 1989. Bib.

[LIB-690] Olshen, Barry N., and Yael S. Feldman. *Approaches to Teaching the Hebrew Bible as Literature in Translation.* New York: Modern Language Association of America, 1989. Bib. refs. pp. 137-152.

[LIB-700] Rendtorff, Rolf. *The Old Testament: An Introduction.* Philadelphia: Fortress Press, 1986. 308 pp. Bibs.

[LIB-710] Rhoads, David, and Donald Michie. *Mark as Story: An Introduction to the Narrative of a Gospel.* Philadelphia: Fortress Press, 1982. 159 pp. Bib. refs. in notes.

[LIB-720] Ryken, Leland. *How to Read the Bible as Literature.* Grand Rapids: Academie Books, 1984. Dist. by Zondervan Press. 208 pp.

[LIB-730] ------, ed. *The New Testament in Literary Criticism.* New York: F. Ungar Publishing Co., 1984. 349 pp. Bib. refs. throughout, numerous.

[LIB-740] Sandmel, Samuel. *The Hebrew Scriptures: An Introduction to Their Literature and Religious Ideas.* New York: Alfred A. Knopf, 1963.

[LIB-750] Savran, George W. *Telling and Retelling: Quotation in Biblical Narrative.* Bloomington: Indiana University Press, 1988. 161 pp. Bib. refs.

[LIB-760] *Semeia: An Experimental Journal for Biblical Criticism.* Atlanta: Scholars Press for Society of Biblical Literature, 1974-. Quarterly. English, Greek, and Hebrew.

[LIB-770] Stacey, David. *Prophetic Drama in the Old Testament.* London: Epworth Press, 1990. Bib. refs. pp. 283-302.

[LIB-780] Sternberg, Meir. *The Poetics of Biblical Narrative: Ideological Literature and the Drama of Reading.* Bloomington: Indiana University Press, 1985. 580 pp. Bib. refs. in notes.

[LIB-790] Stowers, Stanley K. *Letter Writing in Greco-Roman Antiquity.* Philadelphia: Westminster Press, 1986. Bib. pp. 177-179.

[LIB-800] Talbert, Charles H., ed. *Luke-Acts: New Perspectives from the Society of Biblical Literature Seminar.* New York: Crossroad, 1984. 244 pp. Bib. refs.

[LIB-810] Thompson, Leonard L. *Introducing Biblical Literature: A More Fantastic Country.* Englewood Cliffs, N.J.: Prentice-Hall Press, 1978. 350 pp. Bib. refs.

[LIB-820] Tolbert, Mary Ann. *Perspectives on the Parables: An Approach to Multiple Perspectives.* Philadelphia: Fortress Press, 1967. 217 pp. Bib. footnotes.

[LIB-830] Tollers, Vincent L., and John R. Maier. *The Bible in Its Literary Milieu: Contemporary Essays.* Grand Rapids: William B. Eerdmans, 1979. 447 pp.

[LIB-840] Via, Dan Otto, Jr. *The Parables: Their Literary and Existential Dimension.* Philadelphia: Fortress Press, 1967. 217 pp. Bib. footnotes.

[LIB-850] Wilder, Amos. *Early Christian Rhetoric: The Language of the Gospel.* Cambridge: Harvard University Press, 1971.

[LIB-860] Wright, T[erence] R. *Theology and Literature.* New York: Basil Blackwell Publishing,, 1988. Bib. pp. 233-237.

[LIB-870] Young, Brad H. *Jesus and His Jewish Parables: Rediscovering the Roots of Jesus' Teaching.* New York: Paulist Press, 1989. 365 pp. Bib. refs. pp. 322-337.

KEY WORKS ON LITERATURE AND RELIGION

The study of literature and religion is distinguished from the study of biblical literature primarily by the former's emphasis on literature and the latter's emphasis on the Bible as the focal point. Most research of literature and religion must be conducted through the standard bibliographies listed in the opening of this chapter since few specialized bibliographies exist for this area of study. The two very useful works given here, [LIR-010] and [LIR-020], offer several suggestions for the kinds of bibliographies which still need to be written. Typically, researchers in this area must begin with studies of authors using religious themes and then follow works identified in the bibliographical references of these studies of authors and their works.

The list of key works given below is offered as one of the few bibliographies available on the topic of religion and literature. Most of the works in this list contain bibliographical references which in turn lead one to other excellent sources. Many of the authors listed below have been stellar literary critics in the twentieth century who have also taken an interest in how the Christian faith is expressed in literature. The most noteworthy critics have been M. H. Abrams [LIR-030], Frank Burch Brown [LIR-100], Robert Detweiler [LIR-180 and LIR-190], Helen Louise Gardner [LIR-290], Giles B. Gunn [LIR-310 and LIR-320], John Killinger [LIR-420 and LIR-430], Leland Ryken [LIR-670 to LIR-700], Nathan A. Scott, Jr., [LIR-720 to LIR-770], and Ralph C. Wood [LIR-870]. A number of these critics--such as Brown, Detweiler, Killinger, Scott, and Wood--bring their fine theological training to bear on literary criticism and thereby produce credible analyses offering keen insights into literature and religion. Also note that T. S. Eliot has contributed significantly to the analysis of faith and literature and his collected essays are listed above as [LIC-550] and [LIP-640 to LIP-660].

One of the most important lines of study in religion and literature is that tracing the influence of the Bible on literature. The best reference tool to date for this topic is David Lyle Jeffrey's *A Dictionary of Biblical Tradition in English Literature* [LIR-400] which lists key biblical characters, motifs, stories, and terms, traces them to biblical passages, and then suggests a wide variety of authors who have used allusions to these passages. Other texts which trace the influence of the Bible on literature and the other arts in the western culture are identified as the following items: [LIR-070], [LIR-260], [LIR-310], [LIR-350], [LIR-450], [LIR-470], [LIR-590].

Some of the best studies of literature and religion involve analyses of individual authors or critics, including critiques of the following writers: Flannery O'Connor [LIR-230], J. R. R. Tolkien [LIR-240], George MacDonald [LIR-360], C. S. Lewis and George MacDonald [LIR-500], and Graham Greene [LIR-780]. Other extended studies of individual authors or sets of them include those numbered as [LIR-080], [LIR-090], [LIR-200], [LIR-210], [LIR-440], [LIR-750], [LIR-870], and [LIR-880]. A great many works have been written by and about the Oxford Christians, a group identified by Clyde Kilby and other scholars associated with Wheaton College as including Owen Barfield, G. K. Chesterton, C. S. Lewis, George MacDonald, Dorothy Sayers, J. R. R. Tolkien, and Charles Williams. These writers, along with W. H.

Auden, T. S. Eliot, and Christopher Fry, to name just a few, have created some of the most profound literature promoting the Christian faith during the past two centuries. Studies of their works invariably involve analyses of the relationship between literature and religion.

While many literary journals treat religious topics from time to time, a few specialize in this blend, including *Christianity and Literature* [LIR-130]--sponsored by the Conference on Christianity and Literature--and *Religion and Literature* [LIR-610]--based at the University of Notre Dame. The *Journal of the American Academy of Religion* [LIR-410] also contains some articles on Christianity and literature. For additional articles, see related titles of articles listed in the *MLA International Bibliography of Books and Articles on the Modern Languages and Literatures* [BLI-1250] and other periodical bibliographies listed in the opening to this chapter.

The balance of works given below treat the historical development of Christian literature in the west, especially during the twentieth century when writers have expressed faith primarily in covert or indirect forms. Also note one additional work, Susan V. Gallagher's and Roger Lundin's *Literature Through the Eyes of Faith* [LIR-280], which provides a very useful set of suggestions for teaching Christianity and literature at the undergraduate level.

Special Bibliographies

[LIR-010] Gainsbrugh, Jonathan, and Jeanette Gainsbrugh. *The Christian Resource Directory*. Old Tappan, N.J.: Fleming H. Revell, 1988. 731 pp.

[LIR-020] Menendez, Albert J. *The Catholic Novel: An Annotated Bibliography*. Garland Reference Library of the Humanities, no. 690. New York: Garland Publishing, 1988. 323 pp.

Key Works

[LIR-030] Abrams, M[eyer] H[oward], ed. *Literature and Belief*. New York: Columbia University Press, 1958. 184 pp. Bibs.

[LIR-040] Anderson, David. *The Tragic Protest: A Christian Study of some Modern Literature*. Richmond, Va.: John Knox Press,

[1969]. 208 pp. Bib. refs.

[LIR-050] Barley, M. W., and R. P. C. Hanson. *Christianity in Britain, 300-700*. Leicester: Leicester University Press; New York: Humanities Press, 1968.

[LIR-060] Bercovitch, Sacvan, ed. *The American Puritan Imagination: Essays in Revaluation*. 1974. Reprint. [London; New York]: Cambridge University Press, 1991. Bib. pp. 241-258.

[LIR-070] Berkowitz, David S., comp. *In Remembrance of Creation: Evolution of Art and Scholarship in the Medieval and Renaissance Bible*. Waltham: Brandeis University Press, 1968. Bib.

[LIR-080] Brantley, Richard E. *Coordinates of Anglo-American Romanticism: Wesley, Edwards, Carlyle, and Emerson*. Gainesville, Fla.: University Press of Florida, 1993. 219 pp. Bib.

[LIR-090] ------. *Locke, Wesley, and the Method of English Romanticism*. Gainesville, Fla.: University Press of Florida, 1984.

[LIR-100] Brown, Frank Burch. *Transfiguration: Poetic Metaphor and the Languages of Religious Belief*. Chapel Hill: University of North Carolina Press, 1983. Bib. pp. 205-222.

[LIR-110] Bryant, James C. *Tudor Drama and Religious Controversy*. Macon, Ga.: Mercer University Press, 1984. 165 pp. Bib. refs.

[LIR-120] Chai, Leon. *Aestheticism: The Religion of Art in Post-Romantic Literature*. New York: Columbia University Press, 1990. Bib. refs. pp. 259-262.

[LIR-130] *Christianity and Literature*. Carrollton, Ga.: West Georgia College, 1950-. Quarterly. Formerly: *Newsletter of the Conference on Christianity and Literature* (1950-1973).

[LIR-140] Coulson, John. *Religion and Imagination: "In Aid of a Grammar of Assent"*. New York: Oxford University Press, 1981. Bib. pp. 170-176.

[LIR-150] Davie, Donald. *Dissentient Voice: Enlightenment and Christian Dissent*. The Ward-Phillips Lectures for 1980 with Some Related Pieces. Notre Dame: University Press of Notre Dame, 1982. 154 pp.

[LIR-160] Dendle, Brian John. *The Spanish Novel of Religious Thesis, 1876-1936*. Princeton: Princeton University, Dept. of Romance Languages, [1968]. Bib. pp. 155-166.

[LIR-170] Dennis, John. *The Advance and Reformation of Modern Poetry: A*

Critical Discourse. 1701. Reprint. New York: Garland Publishing, 1971. 216 pp.

[LIR-180] Detweiler, Robert, ed. *Art/Literature/Religion: Life on the Borders.* Journal of the American Academy of Religion Thematic Studies, vol. 49, no. 2. Chico: Scholars Press, 1983. 201 pp. Bibs.

[LIR-190] ------. *Breaking the Fall: Religious Readings of Contemporary Fiction.* San Francisco: Harper and Row, 1989. Bib. pp. 192-194.

[LIR-200] Evans, James H. *Spiritual Empowerment in Afro-American Literature: Frederick Douglass, Rebecca Jackson, Booker T. Washington, Richard Wright, and Toni Morrison.* Lewiston, N.Y.: Edwin Mellen Press, 1987. 185 pp.

[LIR-210] Ferre, John P. *A Social Gospel for Millions: The Religious Bestsellers of Charles Sheldon, Charles Gordon, and Harold Bell Wright.* Bowling Green, Ohio: Bowling Green State University Popular Press, 1988. 114 pp. Bib. refs.

[LIR-220] Fichter, Andrew. *Poets Historical: Dynastic Epic in the Renaissance.* New Haven: Yale University Press, 1982. 237 pp.

[LIR-230] Fickett, Harold, and Douglas R. Gilbert. *Flannery O'Connor: Images of Grace.* Grand Rapids: William B. Eerdmans, 1986. 151 pp.

[LIR-240] Flieger, Verlyn. *Splintered Light: Logos and Language in Tolkien's World.* Grand Rapids: William B. Eerdmans, 1983. 167 pp.

[LIR-250] Frederick, John Towner. *The Darkened Sky: Nineteenth-Century American Novelists and Religion.* Notre Dame: University of Notre Dame Press, [1969]. Bib. refs. in notes, pp. 254-269.

[LIR-260] Frontain, Raymond-Jean, and Jan Wojcik, eds. *The David Myth in Western Literature.* West Lafayette, Ind.: Purdue University Press, 1980. Bib. refs. in Notes, pp. 179-207.

[LIR-270] Frye, Roland Mushat. *God, Man, and Satan: Patterns of Christian Thought and Life in Paradise Lost, Pilgrim's Progress, and the Great Theologians.* Princeton: Princeton University Press, 1960.

[LIR-280] Gallagher, Susan V., and Roger Lundin. *Literature Through the Eyes of Faith.* San Francisco: Harper San Francisco, 1989. Bib. pp. 181-188.

[LIR-290]   Gardner, Helen Louise. *Religion and Literature*. New York: Oxford University Press, 1971. 194 pp. Bib. refs.

[LIR-300]   Geary, Robert F. *The Supernatural in Gothic Fiction: Horror, Belief, and Literary Change*. Lewiston, N.Y.: Edwin Mellen Press, 1992. 160 pp.

[LIR-310]   Gunn, Giles [B.], ed. *The Bible and American Arts and Letters*. The Bible in American Culture, no. 5. Philadelphia: Fortress Press; Chico: Scholars Press, 1983. 244 pp. Bibs.

[LIR-320]   ------. *The Interpretation of Otherness: Literature, Religion, and the American Imagination*. New York: Oxford University Press, 1979. 250 pp. Bib. refs.

[LIR-330]   Hart, Clive. *Images of Flight*. Berkeley: University of California Press, 1988. 300 pp.

[LIR-340]   Heffernan, Thomas J. *Sacred Biography: Saints and Their Biographers in the Middle Ages*. New York: Oxford University Press, 1989. Bib. pp. 300-318.

[LIR-350]   Henderson, Heather. *The Victorian Self: Autobiography and Biblical Narrative*. Ithaca: Cornell University Press, 1989. 205 pp.

[LIR-360]   Hein, Rolland. *The Harmony Within: The Spiritual Vision of George MacDonald*. Grand Rapids: Christian University Press, 1982. 163 pp.

[LIR-370]   Hoffman, Frederick John. *The Imagination's New Beginning: Theology and Modern Literature*. Notre Dame: University of Notre Dame Press, [1967]. 105 pp. Bib. refs.

[LIR-380]   Hutton, Lewis J. *The Christian Essence of Spanish Literature: An Historical Survey*. Lewiston, N.Y.: Edwin Mellen Press, 1989. 520 pp.

[LIR-390]   Jasper, David, and Colin Crowder. *European Literature and Theology in the Twentieth Century: Ends of Time*. New York: St. Martin's Press, 1990. 191 pp. Bib. refs.

[LIR-400]   Jeffrey, David Lyle, ed. *A Dictionary of Biblical Tradition in English Literature*. Grand Rapids: William B. Eerdmanns, 1992. 960 pp. Bibs.

[LIR-410]   *Journal of the American Academy of Religion*. Atlanta: Scholars Press for American Academy of Religion, 1932-. Quarterly.

[LIR-420]   Killinger, John [Raymond]. *The Failure of Theology in Modern*

Literature. New York: Abingdon Press, 1963. 239 pp. Bib. refs. in footnotes.

[LIR-430] ------. *The Fragile Presence: Transcendence in Modern Literature.* Philadelphia: Fortress Press, 1973. 166 pp. Bib. refs. in footnotes.

[LIR-440] Lang, Amy Schrager. *Prophetic Woman: Anne Hutchinson and the Problem of Dissent in the Literature of New England.* Berkeley: University of California Press, 1987. Bib. pp. 217-231.

[LIR-450] Lass, Abraham H., David Kiremidjian, and Ruth M. Goldstein. *The Facts on File Dictionary of Classical, Biblical and Literary Allusions.* New York: Facts on File, 1987. 240 pp.

[LIR-460] Lawrence, Irene. *Linguistics and Theology: The Significance of Noam Chomsky for Theological Construction.* Metuchen, N.J.: Scarecrow Press, 1980. 214 pp.

[LIR-470] Liptzin, Sol. *Biblical Themes in World Literature.* Hoboken, N.J.: KTAV Publishing House, 1985. 316 pp.

[LIR-480] Lobriolle, Pierre de. *History and Literature of Christianity from Tertullian to Boethius.* Tr. Herbert Wilson. New York: Barnes and Noble, 1968.

[LIR-490] McFague, Sallie. *Literature and the Christian Life.* New Haven: Yale University Press, 1966. Bib. pp. 231-236.

[LIR-500] Marshall, Cynthia, ed. *Essays on C. S. Lewis and George MacDonald: Truth, Fiction, and the Power of Imagination.* Lewiston, N.Y.: Edwin Mellen Press, 1991. 122 pp.

[LIR-510] Mims, Edwin. *Great Writers as Interpreters of Religion.* New York: Abingdon-Cokesbury Press, [1945]. 176 pp.

[LIR-520] Monsarrat, Gilles D. *Light from the Porch: Stoicism and English Renaissance Literature.* Paris: Didier-Erudition, 1984. 301 pp.

[LIR-530] Mulder, John R., ed. "Literature and Religion: The Convergence of Approaches." *Journal of the American Academy of Religion.* Supplement. 47, no. 2 (June 1979): 216-361. Bib. refs.

[LIR-540] Murdock, Kenneth Ballard. *Literature and Theology in Colonial New England.* Cambridge: Harvard University Press, [1949]. Bib. refs. in notes, pp. 211-226.

[LIR-550] North, Richard. *Pagan Words and Christian Meanings.* Amsterdam: Rodopi, 1991. 198 pp.

[LIR-560] Patterson, David. *The Affirming Flame: Religion, Language, Literature*. Norman: University of Oklahoma Press, 1988. Bib. pp. 169-171.

[LIR-570] Pelikan, Jaroslav. *On Searching the Scriptures--Your Own or Someone Else's: A Reader's Guide to* Sacred Writings *and Methods of Studying Them*. N.p.: Sacred Writings, c. 1992. Dist. Book-of-the-Month Club, Camp Hill, Pa.

[LIR-580] ------, ed. *Sacred Writings*. 6 vols. Vol. 1: *Judaism: The Tanakh*. Vol. 2: *Christianity: The Apocrypha and the New Testament*. Vol. 3: *Islam: The Qur'an*. Vol. 4: *Confucianism: The Analects of Confucius*. Vol. 5: *Hinduism: The Rig Veda*. Vol. 6: *Buddhism: The Dhammapada*. N.p.: Sacred Writings, c. 1992. Dist. Book-of-the-Month Club, Camp Hill, Pa.

[LIR-590] Phy, Allene Stuart. *The Bible and Popular Culture in America*. The Bible in American Culture, no. 2. Philadelphia: Fortress Press; Chico, California: Scholars Press, 1985. 248 pp. Bibs.

[LIR-600] Prickett, Stephen. *Romanticism and Religion: The Tradition of Coleridge and Wordsworth in the Victorian Church*. New York: Cambridge University Press, 1976. Bib. pp. 279-288.

[LIR-610] *Religion and Literature*. Notre Dame, Ind.: University of Notre Dame Press, 1960-. 3/year. Formerly: *Notre Dame English Journal: A Journal of Religion in Literature* (1978-1983); *Notre Dame English Journal* (1960-1978). Cumulative index: 1960-1980, comp. Lisa Mary McCartney, 11 (1980): 175-206.

[LIR-620] Rollinson, Philip. *Classical Theories of Allegory and Christian Culture*. Pittsburgh: Duquesne University Press, 1981. 175 pp. Bib. refs.

[LIR-630] Rozett, Martha Tuck. *The Doctrine of Election and the Emergence of Elizabethan Tragedy*. Princeton: Princeton University Press, 1984. Bib. pp. 301-319.

[LIR-640] Ruland, Vernon. *Horizons of Criticism: An Assessment of Religious-Literary Options*. Chicago: American Library Association, 1975. Bib. pp. 229-260.

[LIR-650] Russell, Jeffrey Burton. *The Devil: Perceptions of Evil from Antiquity to Primitive Christianity*. Ithaca: Cornell University Press, 1977. 276 pp.

[LIR-660] ------. *A History of Medieval Christianity: Prophecy and Order*. New York: Crowell, 1968.

298

[LIR-670] Ryken, Leland, ed. *The Christian Imagination: Essays on Literature and the Arts*. Grand Rapids: Baker Book House, 1981. 448 pp. Bib. refs. in footnotes.

[LIR-680] ------. *Culture in Christian Perspective: A Door to Understanding and Enjoying the Arts*. Portland: Multnomah Press, 1986. 283 pp.

[LIR-690] ------. *The Liberated Imagination: Thinking Christianly About the Arts*. Wheaton: Harold Shaw, 1989. 282 pp. (Reprint of [LIR-680].)

[LIR-700] ------. *Windows to the World: Literature in Christian Perspective*. Dallas: Zondervan Press and Prove Ministries International, 1985. Bib. refs. in notes, pp. 177-185.

[LIR-710] Schweitzer, Ivy. "Literature as Sacrament: The Evolution of Puritan Sacramentalism and its Influence on Puritan and Emersonian Aesthetics." Ph.D. Thesis, Brandeis University, 1983. Bib. pp. 375-385.

[LIR-720] Scott, Nathan A., Jr. *The Broken Center: Studies in the Theological Horizon of Modern Literature*. New Haven: Yale University Press, 1966. 237 pp. Bib. refs in footnotes.

[LIR-730] ------, ed. *The Climate of Faith in Modern Literature*. New York: Seabury, 1964. Bib. pp. 235-237.

[LIR-740] ------. *Negative Capability: Studies in the New Literature and the Religious Situation*. New Haven: Yale University Press, 1969. 173 pp. Bib. refs. in footnotes.

[LIR-750] ------. *Rehearsals of Discomposure: Alienation and Reconciliation in Modern Literature: Franz Kafka, Ignazio Silone, D. H. Lawrence, T. S. Eliot*. New York: Kings Crown Press, 1952. Bib. pp. 273-288.

[LIR-760] ------. *Theopoetic: Theology and the Religious Imagination*. Philadelphia: Fortress Press, 1976. 106 pp. Bib. refs.

[LIR-770] ------. *The Tragic Vision and the Christian Faith*. New York: Association Press, 1957. Bib. pp. 330-346.

[LIR-780] Sharrock, Roger. *Saints, Sinners, and Comedians: The Novels of Graham Greene*. Kent, England: Burns and Oates; Notre Dame: University of Notre Dame Press, 1984. 298 pp.

[LIR-790] Sims-Williams, Patrick. *Religion and Literature in Western England 600-800*. Cambridge Studies in Anglo-Saxon England. Cambridge: Cambridge University Press, 1990. 448 pp.

299

[LIR-800] Smithline, Arnold. *Natural Religion in American Literature.* New Haven: College and University Press, [1966]. Bib. pp. 185-188.

[LIR-810] Stevens, William Oliver. *The Cross in the Life and Literature of the Anglo-Saxons.* Yale Studies in English, no. 23. 1900. Reprint. New York: H. Holt and Co., 1967. Bib. pp. 100-105.

[LIR-820] Taylor, Mark C. *Tears.* Albany: State University of New York Press, 1990. 263 pp. Bib. refs.

[LIR-830] Tennyson, G. B., and Edward E. Ericson, Jr., eds. *Religion and Modern Literature: Essays in Theory and Criticism.* Grand Rapids: William B. Eerdmans, [1975]. 424 pp. Bib. refs.

[LIR-840] TeSelle, Sallie McFague. *Literature and the Christian Life.* New Haven and London: Yale University Press, 1966. Bib. pp. 231-236.

[LIR-850] Thickstun, William R. *Visionary Closure in the Modern Novel.* New York: St. Martin's Press, 1988. 208 pp.

[LIR-860] Wellwarth, George E. *Modern Drama and the Death of God.* Madison: University of Wisconsin Press, 1986. Bib. pp. 165-172.

[LIR-870] Wood, Ralph C. *The Comedy of Redemption: Christian Faith and Comic Vision in Four American Novelists.* Notre Dame: University of Notre Dame Press, 1988. Bib. pp. 286-306.

[LIR-880] Woodfield, Malcolm. *R. H. Hutton, Critic and Theologian: The Writings of R. H. Hutton on Newman, Arnold, Tennyson, Wordsworth, and George Eliot.* New York: Oxford University Press, 1986. Bib. pp. 199-225.

CHAPTER 10

MUSIC

BIBLIOGRAPHIES ON MUSIC

Even a simple list of research resources in music could easily fill this entire volume and several more besides. What appears below is a modest list of works which will prove useful to both the novice and the specialist. As with all categories in this volume, one should consult Chapter 1 treating bibliographies of bibliographies which typically include numerous sections on musical topics. For those needing a single, up to date volume offering bibliographical information in many categories of music, the works by William S. Brockman [BMU-120], Phillip Crabtree [BMU-210], Vincent Harris Duckles [BMU-320], Robert Allen Livingston [BMU-710], K. E. Mixter [BMU-810], and Michael Winesanker [BMU-1200] are some of the best options. For locating upcoming bibliographies still in progress, see [BMU-040]. To find the most current list of book and article titles, consult serial publications such as *Bibliographic Guide to Music* [BMU-070], *Music Article Guide* [BMU-830], *The Music Index* [BMU-840], and *RILM Abstracts of Music Literature* [BMU-940], which is also available on-line or on CD ROM disks. For additional assistance in locating periodical literature, also see [BMU-350] and [BMU-780]. To find dissertations in music, see Michael Jay Anderson [BMU-020], *Doctoral Dissertations in Musicology* [BMU-310], and *Music Research Information Network*

Register of Music Research Students in Great Britain and the Republic of Ireland, 19--: With Thesis Titles and General Areas of Study [BMU-850], in addition to *Dissertation Abstracts International* [BBI-270] listed in Chapter 1.

This section includes numerous specialized bibliographies treating topics ranging from folk music to opera to popular music, as well as national music styles and musical eras. Those treating music according to the gender, ethnic identity, or national origin of the composer or performer include the following: African [BMU-690]; American [BMU-100], [BMU-370], [BMU-380], [BMU-390], [BMU-580], [BMU-590], [BMU-660], [BMU-680], [BMU-900], [BMU-910], [BMU-990]; Australian [BMU-030]; Black [BMU-290], [BMU-360], [BMU-600], [BMU-610], [BMU-730], [BMU-1150]; British [BMU-110]; female [BMU-330], [BMU-770], [BMU-1020], [BMU-1150]; Hebrew [BMU-010]; Irish [BMU-1000]; Italian [BMU-700], [BMU-1090]; Latin [BMU-1130]; non-western [BMU-650], [BMU-1040]; Scottish [BMU-080]. The bibliographies concentrating on historical eras include the following: Baroque [BMU-060], [BMU-1080]; Medieval [BMU-630]; Modern or twentieth century [BMU-090], [BMU-140], [BMU-410], [BMU-1030], [BMU-1120], [BMU-1180]; Renaissance [BMU-1080]. Additional works which will prove useful for historical studies include [BMU-400], [BMU-670], [BMU-680], and [BMU-1100]. For bibliographies on musicology and ethnomusicology, see [BMU-230], [BMU-300], [BMU-530], [BMU-920], [BMU-960], and [BMU-1060]. For assistance in studying themes in music, see [BMU-130].

Several of the bibliographies given below treat particular groups of instruments. These specialized works cover the following categories: electronic [BMU-220]; orchestra [BMU-240], [BMU-450], [BMU-610]; organ [BMU-250]; piano [BMU-430], [BMU-550], [BMU-560], [BMU-570], [BMU-600], [BMU-1150]; percussion [BMU-050]. Also see Corliss R. Arnold's 2 volume *Organ Literature: A Comprehensive Survey* [MUT-060]. Several other bibliographies cover genres of music which are primarily, although not exclusively, instrumental: chamber [BMU-930]; general service [BMU-1160]; seasonal [BMU-1170]; symphony [BMU-1070]; twelve tone and serial [BMU-150], [BMU-750], [BMU-1090]; wedding [BMU-460]. Vocal music is covered in a wide variety of bibliographies, including the following genres, some of which also include instrumental music: art song [BMU-370], [BMU-380],

[BMU-390], [BMU-700]; blues [BMU-510]; chamber [BMU-930]; choral [BMU-180], [BMU-260], [BMU-1130], [BMU-1180]; folk [BMU-800]; jazz [BMU-790]; musical [BMU-1190]; opera [BMU-880], [BMU-1050]; popular [BMU-100], [BMU-900], [BMU-910], [BMU-970], [BMU-980], [BMU-990], [BMU-1110]; solo voice [BMU-340]; voice [BMU-440], [BMU-620]; wedding [BMU-460].

For bibliographies treating composers and their works, see the following: [BMU-140], [BMU-170], [BMU-190], [BMU-490], [BMU-500], [BMU-640], [BMU-860], [BMU-870], [BMU-1120]. To locate recordings of music, see [BMU-200] and [BMU-950]. For assistance in locating studies on music education, see [BMU-890] and [BMU-1140], and consult [BMU-520] concerning music therapy. Of particular interest to the researcher are several works on computers and music, including a set by Deta S. Davis [BMU-280], and one by Walter B. Hewlett and Eleanor Selfridge-Field [BMU-530]. Miscellaneous studies of special use to researchers include several bibliographies on anthologies, [BMU-820], music business, [BMU-1010], music libraries, including [BMU-480] and [BMU-720], reference sources, including [BMU-270] and [BMU-740], sets of music, including [BMU-160] and [BMU-540], and two general works not previously mentioned, [BMU-760] and [BMU-1210]. Bibliographies treating music related to Christian themes and worship are listed below in the opening segment of the section entitled Key Works on Music and Religion.

[BMU-010]   Adler, Israel, and Lea Shalem. *Hebrew Notated Manuscripts Sources up to Circa 1840: A Descriptive and Thematic Catalogue with a Checklist of Printed Sources*. 2 vols. International Inventory of Musical Sources, B; 9, 1. Munich: G. Henle Verlag, 1989. lxxix, 899 pp. Bib. refs. pp. 583-600.

[BMU-020]   Anderson, Michael J[ay]. *A Classified Index of American Doctoral Dissertations and Dissertation Projects on Choral Music, Completed or Currently in Progress, Through 1989*. Monograph/American Choral Directors Association, no. 6. Lawton, Okla.: American Choral Directors Association, 1990. 177 pp.

[BMU-030]   Australia Music Centre. *Dramatic Music*. Catalogues of Australian Compositions, no. 5. Sydney: The Centre, 1977.

212 pp.

[BMU-040] Baily, Dee. *A Checklist of Music Bibliographies and Indexes in Progress and Unpublished.* 4th ed. Philadelphia: Music Library Association, 1982. 104 pp.

[BMU-050] Bajzek, Dieter. *Percussion: An Annotated Bibliography, with Special Emphasis on Contemporary Notation and Performance.* Metuchen, N.J.: Scarecrow Press, 1988. 195 pp.

[BMU-060] Baron, John H. *Baroque Music: A Research and Information Guide.* Music Research and Information Guides, vol. 16. New York: Garland Publishing, 1993. 587 pp.

[BMU-070] *Bibliographic Guide to Music.* Boston: G. K. Hall, 1976-. Annual.

[BMU-080] *Bibliography of Scotland [1976-].* Edinburgh: National Library of Scotland, 1978-. Annual.

[BMU-090] Blom, Eric. *A General Index to Modern Musical Literature in the English Language.* 1927. Reprint. New York: Da Capo Press, 1970. 159 pp.

[BMU-100] Booth, Mark W. *American Popular Music: A Reference Guide.* American Popular Culture. Westport, Conn.: Greenwood Press, 1983. 212 pp.

[BMU-110] *British Catalogue of Music, The.* London: British Library Bibliographic Services Division, 1957-present. Semiannual.

[BMU-120] Brockman, William S. *Music: A Guide to the Reference Literature.* Littleton, Colo.: Libraries Unlimited, 1987. 254 pp.

[BMU-130] Brook, Barry S. *Thematic Catalogues in Music: An Annotated Bibliography.* Hillsdale, N.Y.: Pendragon Press, [1972]. 347 pp.

[BMU-140] Bull, Storm. *Index to Biographies of Contemporary Composers.* 3 vols. Metuchen, N.J.: The Scarecrow Press, Inc., [1964], 1974, 1987. [5,800; 8,000; 13,500]

[BMU-150] Carlson, Effie B. *A Bio-Bibliographical Dictionary of Twelve-Tone and Serial Composers.* Metuchen, N.J.: Scarecrow Press, 1970. 233 pp.

[BMU-160] Charles, Sydney Robinson. *A Handbook of Music and Music Literature in Sets and Series.* New York: Free Press, [1972]. 497 pp.

[BMU-170] Chicorel, Marietta, ed. *Chicorel Bibliography to Books on Music and Musicians*. New York: Chicorel Library Publishing Corporation, [1974]. 487 pp.

[BMU-180] *Choral Music for Children: An Annotated List*. Reston, Va.: Music Educators National Conference, 1990. 166 pp.

[BMU-190] *Composers' Collected Editions from Europe*. 6th ed. Special Music Catalog, no. 14. Wiesbaden, Germany: Harrassowitz, 1991. 231 pp.

[BMU-200] Cooper, B. Lee, and Wayne S. Haney. *Response Recordings: An Answer Song Discography, 1950-1990*. Metuchen, N.J.: Scarecrow Press, 1990. 296 pp.

[BMU-210] Crabtree, Phillip. *Sourcebook for Research in Music*. Bloomington: Indiana University Press, 1993.

[BMU-220] Cross, Lowell M., comp. *A Bibliography of Electronic Music*. [Toronto]: University of Toronto Press, [1967]. 126 pp.

[BMU-230] "Current Bibliography, Discography, and Filmography." *Ethnomusicology: Journal of the Society for Ethnomusicology*. 1953-. 3/year. Annual index. Cumulative indexes: vols. 1-10 (Middletown: Wesleyan University Press, 1967, 42 pp.); vols 11-20, comp. Gerard Béhague, Marie Labonville, and Carol Morgan (1977, 78 pp.); and vols 21-30 (1986, 68 pp.).

[BMU-240] Daniels, David. *Orchestral Music: A Source Book*. Metuchen, N.J.: Scarecrow Press, 1972. 301 pp.

[BMU-250] Daugherty, F. Mark, and Walter A. Frankel. *Organ Music in Print*. Music-in-Print Series, 0146-7883, vol. 3s. Philadelphia: Musicdata, 1990. 297 pp. Supplement to *Organ Music in Print*, ed. Walter A. Frankel and Nancy K. Nardone. 2nd ed. 1984.

[BMU-260] Daugherty, F. Mark, and Susan H. Simon. *Secular Choral Music in Print*. Music-in-Print Series, 0146-7883, vol. 2s. Philadelphia: Musicdata, 1991. 188 pp. Updates *Secular Choral Music in Print*, ed. F. Mark Daugherty. 2nd ed. 1987. 128 pp.

[BMU-270] Davies, J. H. *Musicalia: Sources of Information in Music*. 2nd ed. New York: Pergamon Press, [1969]. 184 pp.

[BMU-280] Davis, Deta S. *Computer Applications in Music: A Bibliography*. Madison, Wis.: A-R Editions, 1988. 537 pp. Supplement 1, 1992. 600 pp.

306

[BMU-290] De Lerma, Dominique-Rene. *Bibliography of Black Music.* 4 vols. Westport, Conn.: Greenwood Press, 1981-1984.

[BMU-300] Diamond, Harold J. *Music Analyses: An Annotated Guide to the Literature.* New York; Toronto: Schirmer Books: Maxwell Macmillan International; Collier Macmillan Canada, 1991. 716 pp. Bib. refs.

[BMU-310] *Doctoral Dissertations in Musicology, [December 19-- November 19--].* Philadelphia: American Musicology Society; International Musicology Society, 19--.

[BMU-320] Duckles, Vincent Harris, comp. *Music Reference and Research Materials: An Annotated Bibliography.* 4th ed., rev. New York: Schirmer Books, 1992.

[BMU-330] Ericson, Margaret D. *Women and Music [1989/1990]: A Selective Bibliography on the Collective Subject of Women in Music.* 4th ed. [Ithaca?]: M. Ericson, 1991. 38 pp. 1988/1989, 3rd ed., 1991, 28 pp.

[BMU-340] Espina, Noni. *Repertoire for the Solo Voice: A Fully Annotated Guide to Works for the Solo Voice Published in Modern Editions and Covering Material from the 13th Century to the Present.* 2 vols. Metuchen, N.J.: Scarecrow Press, 1974. 1,341 pp.

[BMU-350] Fidler, Linda M., and Richard S. James. *International Music Journals.* Historical Guides to the World's Periodicals and Newspapers, 0742-5538. New York: Greenwood Press, 1990. 544 pp. Bib. refs. pp. 501-502.

[BMU-360] Floyd, Samuel A. *Black Music Biography: An Annotated Bibliography.* White Plains, N.Y.: Kraus International Publicatiions, 1987. 302 pp.

[BMU-370] Friedberg, Ruth C. *American Art Song and American Poetry: Vol. I: America Comes of Age.* Metuchen, N.J.: Scarecrow Press, 1981. 175 pp.

[BMU-380] ------. *American Art Song and American Poetry: Vol. II: Voices of Maturity.* Metuchen, N.J.: Scarecrow Press, 1984. 236 pp.

[BMU-390] ------. *American Art Song and American Poetry: Vol. III: The Century Advances.* Metuchen, N.J.: Scarecrow Press, 1987. 351 pp.

[BMU-400] Fuld, James J. *The Book of World-Famous Music: Classical, Popular and Folk.* 3rd ed. New York: Dover Publications, 1985. 714 pp. (See [MUT-530])

[BMU-410] *General Index to Modern Musical Literature in the English Language Including Periodicals for the Years 1915-1926.* 1927. Reprint. New York: Da Capo, 1970.

[BMU-420] Gerboth, Walter. *An Index to Musical Festschriften and Similar Publications.* New York: W. W. Norton and Co., [1969]. 188 pp.

[BMU-430] Gillespie, John. *A Bibliography of Nineteenth-Century American Piano Music, With Location Sources and Composer Biography-Index.* Music Reference Collection, 0736-7740, no. 2. Westport, Conn.: Greenwood Press, 1984. 358 pp.

[BMU-440] Goleeke, Thomas. *Literature for Voice: An Index of Songs in Collections and Source Book for Teachers of Singing.* Metuchen, N.J.: Scarecrow Press, 1984. 234 pp.

[BMU-450] Goodenberger, Jennifer. *Subject Guide to Classical Instrumental Music.* Metuchen, N.J.: Scarecrow Press, 1989. 171 pp.

[BMU-460] Goodfellow, William D. *Wedding Music: An Index to Collections.* Metuchen, N.J.: Scarecrow Press, 1992. 197 pp.

[BMU-470] ------. *Where's That Tune? An Index to Songs in Fakebooks.* Metuchen, N.J.: Scarecrow Press, 1990. 457 pp.

[BMU-480] Gottlieb, Jane, Stephen E. Novak, and Taras Pavlovsky, eds. *Guide to the Juilliard School Archives.* New York: Juilliard School, 1992. 113 pp. Bib. refs. pp. 106-107.

[BMU-490] Green, Richard D. *Index to Composer Bibliographies.* Detroit: Information Coordinators, 1985. 76 pp.

[BMU-500] Greene, Frank. *Composers on Record: An Index to Biographical Information on 14,000 Composers Whose Music Has Been Recorded.* Metuchen, N.J.: Scarecrow Press, 1985. 636 pp.

[BMU-510] Hart, Mary L., and Lisa N. Howorth. *The Blues: A Bibliographical Guide.* Music Research and Information Guides, vol. 7. New York: Garland Publishing, 1989. 636 pp.

[BMU-520] Heller, George N. *Historical Research in Music Therapy: A Bibliography.* Lawrence, Ks.: University of Kansas, Department of Art and Music Education and Music Therapy, 1992. 48 pp.

[BMU-530] Hewlett, Walter B., and Eleanor Selfridge-Field, eds. *Computing in Musicology: An International Directory of Applications.* Menlo Park, Calif.: Center for Computer Assisted Research in the Humanities, 1992. 217 pp. Bib. refs.

[BMU-540] Heyer, Anna Harriet, comp. *Historical Sets, Collected Editions, and Monuments of Music: A Guide to Their Contents.* 3rd ed. 2 vols. Chicago: American Library Association, 1980.

[BMU-550] Hinson, Maurice. *Music for Piano and Orchestra: An Annotated Guide.* Bloomington: Indiana University Press, 1993. Bib. refs.

[BMU-560] ------. *The Pianist's Guide to Transcriptions, Arrangements, and Paraphrases.* Bloomington: Indiana University Press, 1990. 159 pp. Bib.

[BMU-570] ------. *The Pianist's Reference Guide: A Bibliographical Survey.* Los Angeles: Alfred Publishing Co., 1987. 336 pp.

[BMU-580] Horn, David. *The Literature of American Music in Books and Folk Music Collections: A Fully Annotated Bibliography.* Metuchen, N.J.: Scarecrow Press, Inc., 1977. 556 pp. [1690]

[BMU-590] Horn, David, with Richard Jackson. *The Literature of American Music in Books and Folk Music Collections, Supplement I: A Fully Annotated Bibliography.* Metuchen, N.J.: Scarecrow Press, 1988. 586 pp.

[BMU-600] Horne, Aaron. *Keyboard Music of Black Composers: A Bibliography.* Music Reference Collection, 0736-7740, no. 37. Westport, Conn.: Greenwood Press, 1992. 331 pp. Bib. refs. Discography, pp. 293-308.

[BMU-610] ------. *String Music of Black Composers: A Bibliography.* Music Reference Collection, no. 33. Westport, Conn.: Greenwood Press, 1992. 352 pp.

[BMU-620] Hovland, Michael A. *Musical Settings of American Poetry: A Bibliography.* Music Reference Collection, 0736-7740, no. 8. Westport, Conn.: Greenwood Press, 1986. xli, 531 pp.

[BMU-630] Hughes, Andrew. *Medieval Music: The Sixth Liberal Art.* Rev. ed. Buffalo: University of Toronto Press, 1980. 360 pp.

[BMU-640] *International Who's Who in Music and Musicians' Directory.* Cambridge, England: Melrose, 1975-.

[BMU-650] Johnson, Sheila J. *Non-Western Music: A Selected Bibliography.* 2nd ed. [Sacramento]: Library, California State University, Sacramento, 1973. 40 pp.

[BMU-660] Krummel, D[onald] W[illiam]. *Bibliographical Handbook of American Music.* Music in American Life. Urbana: University of Illinois Press, 1987. 269 pp.

[BMU-670] ------. *The Literature of Music Bibliography: An Account of the Writings on the History of Music Printing and Publishing.* Berkeley: Fallen Leaf Press, 1992. Bib. refs.

[BMU-680] ------. *Resources of American Music History: A Directory of Source Materials from Colonial Times to World War II.* Urbana: University of Illinois Press, 1981. 463 pp.

[BMU-690] Lems-Dworkin, Carol. *African Music: A Pan-African Annotated Bibliography.* London; New York: Hans Zell, 1991. 382 pp.

[BMU-700] LeVan, Timothy. *Masters of the Italian Art Song: Word-by-Word and Poetic Translations of the Complete Songs for Voice and Piano.* Metuchen, N.J.: Scarecrow Press, 1990. 333 pp.

[BMU-710] Livingston, Robert Allen. *The Music Information and Education Guide.* Cardiff by the Sea, Calif.: GLGLC Music, 1982. 40 pp.

[BMU-720] McColvin, Lionel Roy, and Harold Reeves. *Music Libraries, Including a Comprehensive Bibliography of Music Literature and a Select Bibliography of Music Scores Published Since 1957.* 2 vols. Rev. Jack Dove. [London]: A. Deutsch, [1965].

[BMU-730] Mapp, Edward C. *Directory of Blacks in the Performing Arts.* 2nd ed. Metuchen, N.J.: Scarecrow Press, 1990. 612 pp.

[BMU-740] Marco, Guy A., with Sharon Paugh Ferris. *Information on Music: A Handbook of Reference Sources in European Languages.* Littleton, Colo.: Libraries Unlimited, 1975-.

[BMU-750] Markewich, Reese. *The Definitive Bibliography of Harmonically Sophisticated Tonal Music.* [Riverdale, N.Y.: n.p., 1970]. 55 pp.

[BMU-760] Matthew, James E. *The Literature of Music.* 1896. Reprint. New York: Da Capo Press, 1969. 281 pp.

[BMU-770] Meggett, Joan M. *Keyboard Music by Women Composers: A Catalog and Bibliography.* Westport, Conn.: Greenwood Press, 1981. Bib. pp. 3-19. Discography, pp. 203-210.

[BMU-780] ------. *Music Periodical Literature: An Annotated Bibliography of Indexes and Bibliographies.* Metuchen, N.J.: Scarecrow Press, 1978. 126 pp.

[BMU-790] Merriam, Alan P. *Bibliography of Jazz.* The Roots of Jazz Series.

1954. Reprint. New York: Da Capo Press, Inc., 1970.

[BMU-800] Miller, Terry E. *Folk Music in America: A Reference Guide.* Garland Reference Library to the Humanities, no. 496. New York: Garland Publishing, 1986. 424 pp.

[BMU-810] Mixter, K. E., ed. *General Bibliography for Music Research.* 2nd ed. Detroit: Information Coordinators, 1975. 135 pp.

[BMU-820] Murray, Sterling E. *Anthologies of Music: An Annotated Index.* Detroit Studies in Music Bibliography, no. 68. 2nd ed. Warren, Mich.: Harmonie Park Press, 1992. 215 pp.

[BMU-830] *Music Article Guide.* Detroit: Information Services, Inc., 1966-.

[BMU-840] *Music Index, The.* Detroit: Information Coordinators, Inc., 1949-.

[BMU-850] *Music Research Information Network Register of Music Research Students in Great Britain and the Republic of Ireland, 1991: With Thesis Titles and General Areas of Study.* Oxford: MRIN, 1991. 65 pp.

[BMU-860] Musical America. *International Directory of the Performing Arts.* New York: Musical America, 1960-. Annual.

[BMU-870] *Music-in-Print Master Composer Index, 1988.* Philadelphia: Musicdata, 1989. 824 pp.

[BMU-880] Parsons, Charles H., comp. *The Mellen Opera Reference Index.* 23 vols. Lewiston, N.Y.: Edwin Mellen Press, --1993--. 14 vols. published. Vols. 15-23 forthcoming. Vols. 1-4: *Opera Composers and Their Works*; Vols. 5-6: *Opera Librettists and Their Works*; Vols. 7-8: *Opera Premieres--A Geographical Index*; Vol. 9: *Opera Subjects*; Vols. 10-12: *An Opera Discography in Three Volumes*; Vols. 13-14: *Opera Premieres--An Index of Casts*; Vols. 15-16: *Opera Premieres--Reviews*; Vols. 17-18: *An Opera Bibliography*; Vols. 19-20: *Index of Printed Scores*; Vol. 21: *Opera That is Not Opera*; Vol. 22: *Miscellanea Operatica*; Vol. 23: *Opera and the Librarian.*

[BMU-890] Phelps, Roger P. *A Guide to Research in Music Education.* 3rd ed. Metuchen, N.J.: Scarecrow Press, 1986. 384 pp.

[BMU-900] Pollock, Bruce. *Popular Music: An Annotated Guide to American Popular Songs, Including Introductory Essay, Lyricists and Composers Index, Important Performances Index, Awards Index, and List of Publishers.* Detroit: Gale Research, 1991. 157 pp.

[BMU-910] *Popular Music: An Annotated Index of American Popular Songs.*
6 vols. New York: Adrian, 1964-1973. In progress.

[BMU-920] Pruett, James W., and Thomas P. Slavens. *Research Guide to
Musicology.* Sources of Information in the Humanities, no.
4. Chicago: American Library Association, 1985. 175 pp.

[BMU-930] Rangel-Ribeiro, Victor. *Chamber Music: An International Guide
to Works and Their Instrumentation.* New York: Facts on
File, 1993.

[BMU-940] *RILM Abstracts of Music Literature.* New York: International
Repertory of Music Literature for International Association
of Music Libraries, 1967-.

[BMU-950] Rosenberg, Kenyon C. *A Basic Classical and Operatic Recordings
Collection on Compact Discs for Libraries: A Buying Guide.*
Metuchen, N.J.: Scarecrow Press, 1990. 395 pp.

[BMU-960] Schuursma, Ann Briegleb. *Ethnomusicology Research: A Select
Annotated Bibliography.* Garland Library of Music Ethnolo-
gy, no. 1. New York: Garland Publishing, 1992. 173 pp.

[BMU-970] Shapiro, Nat. *Popular Music, 1920-1979: A Revised Cumulation.*
Detroit: Gale Research, 1985.

[BMU-980] ------. *Popular Music, 1980-1984.* Detroit: Gale Research, 1986.

[BMU-990] Shapiro, Nat, and Bruce Pollock. *Popular Music: An Annotated
Index to American Popular Songs.* Detroit: Gale Research,
1964-.

[BMU-1000] Shields, Hugh. *A Short Bibliography of Irish Folk Song.* Folk
Music Society of Ireland Booklet, no. 2. Dublin: Folk
Music Society of Ireland, 1985. 24 pp.

[BMU-1010] Simpson, Ron. *Mastering the Music Business: The Complete
Annotated Music Industry Bibliography for Songwriters and
Educators.* Salt Lake City: Sound Column Publications,
1989. 99 pp.

[BMU-1020] Skowronski, JoAnn. *Women In American Music: A Bibliography.* Metuchen, N.J.: Scarecrow Press, 1978. 191 pp.

[BMU-1030] Slonimsky, Nicholas. *Supplement to Music Since 1900.* New
York: Charles Scribner's Sons, 1986.

[BMU-1040] Smith, Donna Ridley. *Non-Western Music: A Selected Bibliography.* 3rd ed. Bibliographic Series, no. 10. Sacramento:
Library, California State University, Sacramento, 1982.

45 pp.

[BMU-1050] Sonneck, Oscar George Theodore. *Catalogue of Opera Librettos: Printed Before 1800.* 4 vols. in 3. 1914. Reprint. New York: B. Franklin, [1967].

[BMU-1060] Spiess, Lincoln Bunce. *Historical Musicology: A Reference Manual for Research in Music.* Westport, Conn.: Greenwood Press, 1980. 294 pp.

[BMU-1070] Stedman, Preston. *The Symphony: A Research and Information Guide.* Music Research and Information Guides, vol. 14. New York: Garland Publishing, 1990.

[BMU-1080] Stevenson, Robert Murrell. *Renaissance and Baroque Musical Sources in the Americas.* Washington, D.C.: General Secretariat, Organization of American States, 1970. 346 pp.

[BMU-1090] Stokes, Harvey. *A Selected Annotated Bibliography on Italian Serial Composers.* Lewiston, N.Y.: Edwin Mellen Press, 1990. 80 pp.

[BMU-1100] Strunk, Oliver, ed. *Source Readings in Music History.* 5 vols. New York: W. W. Norton and Co., 1950.

[BMU-1110] Taylor, Paul. *Popular Music Since 1955: A Critical Guide to the Literature.* Boston: G. K. Hall, 1985.

[BMU-1120] Thompson, Kenneth. *A Dictionary of Twentieth-Century Composers (1911-1971).* New York: St. Martin's Press, [1973]. 666 pp.

[BMU-1130] Tiemstra, Suzanne Spicer. *The Choral Music of Latin America: A Guide to Compositions and Research.* Music Reference Collection, 0736-7740, no. 36. New York: Greenwood Press, 1992. 317 pp.

[BMU-1140] *Visual and Performing Arts Framework: A Bibliography of K-8 Books.* [San Diego]: Media Services, San Diego County Office of Education, 1990. 34 pp.

[BMU-1150] Walker-Hill, Helen. *Piano Music by Black Women Composers: A Catalog of Solo and Ensemble Works.* Music Reference Collection, 0736-7740, no. 35. New York: Greenwood Press, 1992. 143 pp. Bib. refs. pp. 127-128. Discography, pp. 129-132.

[BMU-1160] Webb, Marianne. *General Service Music.* [Minneapolis]: Schmitt Music, 1980. 7 pp.

[BMU-1170] ------. *Seasonal Service Music.* [Minneapolis]: Schmitt Music, 1980. 7 pp.

[BMU-1180] White, J. Perry. *Twentieth-Century Choral Music: An Annotated Bibliography of Music Suitable for Use by High School Choirs.* 2nd ed. Metuchen, N.J.: Scarecrow Press, 1990. 226 pp.

[BMU-1190] Wildbihler, Hubert, and Sonja Völklein. *The Musical: An International Annotated Bibliography/Eine internationale annotierte Bibliographie.* Munich: K. G. Saur, 1986. 320 pp. (See [BDR-1180])

[BMU-1200] Winesanker, Michael. *Books on Music: A Classified List.* N.p.: Texas Association of Music Schools, 1979. 166 pp.

[BMU-1210] Yaffe, Michael C. *Annotated Bibliography of Publications, 1934-1976: The National Association of Schools of Music.* Reston, Va.: The Association, 1976. 37 pp.

KEY WORKS ON THEORY AND HISTORY OF MUSIC

Text books explaining the theory and history of music are appearing in increasing numbers, many being informative and interesting. Some of the more readable and lucid standard works are those by Willi Apel, *Harvard Dictionary of Music* [MUT-050], Donald Jay Grout and Claude V. Palisca, *A History of Western Music* [MUT-600], and Percy A. Scholes, *Oxford Companion to Music* [MUT-1150]. For studies of individual musicians, *Baker's Biographical Dictionary of Musicians* [MUT-120] offers a fine beginning point. For more detailed treatments, consult Stanley Sadie's 20 volume *New Grove Dictionary of Music and Musicians* [MUT-1110], Denis Arnold's 2 volume *The New Oxford Companion to Music* [MUT-070], or even Stanley Sadie's and Alison Latham's *The Norton/Grove Concise Encyclopedia of Music* [MUT-1120]. Other works proving helpful in studying individual composers or other musicians include those by Bruce Bahle [MUT-100], Philip James Bone [MUT-210], Gilbert Chase [MUT-260], David Ewen [MUT-420 to 450], John L. Holmes [MUT-650], Wilson Lyle [MUT-880], Sam Morgenstern [MUT-960], John S. Sainsbury [MUT-1130], Kenneth Thompson [MUT-1220], and Oscar Thompson [MUT-1230]. Also keep in mind that entire bibliographies have been written about most musicians and these are listed in the bibliographies of bibliographies given in Chapter 1 as well as in many of the bibliographies listed here in Chapter 10.

For those seeking to understand and appreciate opera, the works of Peter Conrad [MUT-290 and MUT-300] offer inviting and literary interpretations of the highest caliber. Other works which will aid the neophyte as well as the expert include Paul Britten Austin's and Inger Mattsson's *Gustavian Opera: An Interdisciplinary Reader in Swedish Opera, Dance, and Theatre, 1771-1809* [MUT-090], Donald Blair's *Great Opera Singers of the Twentieth Century, 1927-1990* [MUT-180], *The Definitive Kobbe's Opera Book* [MUT-380], David R. Greene's *Listening to Strauss Operas: The Audience's Multiple Standpoints* [MUT-580], Ruth Katz's *Divining the Powers of Music: Aesthetic Theory and the Origins of Opera* [MUT-710], Peter Kivy's *Osmin's Rage: Philosophical Reflections on Opera, Drama, and Text* [MUT-760], Gary Schmidgall's *Literature as Opera* [MUT-1140], Alexander Thomas Simpson's "Opera on Film: A Study of the History and the Aesthetic Principles and Conflicts of a Hybrid Genre" [MUT-1160], and Jeremy Tambling's *Opera, Ideology, and Film* [MUT-1200]. Perhaps the definitive reference tool for studying opera is Charles H. Parsons's 23 volume work, *The Mellen Opera Reference Index* [BMU-880], of which 14 volumes are currently in print and the others are forthcoming soon. The two best periodicals for opera studies are *Opera News* [MUT-1020], covering the New York Metropolitan Opera, and *The Opera Quarterly* [MUT-1030].

Several other works listed below explore the connections between music and literature, including writings by Alex Aronson [MUT-080], Anselm Bayly [MUT-160], Calvin Smith Brown [MUT-230], Joseph Coroniti [MUT-330], James Day [MUT-370], Gretchen Ludke Finney [MUT-480], Northrop Frye [MUT-510], Paula Johnson [MUT-660], Jack Madison Stein [MUT-1180], and Daniel Webb [MUT-1290]. In a similar vein, several other works listed below explore the philosophical and aesthetic dimensions of music, including Warren Dwight Allen's *Philosophies of Music History: A Study of General Histories of Music, 1600-1960* [MUT-020], Carl Dahlhaus' *Analysis and Value Judgement* [MUT-340], and Harold E. Fiske's *Music and Mind: Philosophical Essays on the Cognition and Meaning of Music* [MUT-490]. For the most recent writings on this subject, see the works listed for the following authors: Roland Barthes [MUT-140], Ernst Bloch [MUT-190], Malcolm Budd [MUT-250], Nicholas Cook [MUT-320], Carl Dahlhaus [MUT-360], Enrico Fubini [MUT-520], Eduard Hanslick [MUT-610], Ruth Katz and Carl Dahlhaus [MUT-720], Michael Kraus [MUT-790], Edward A. Lippman [MUT-860 and MUT-870], Robin Maconie [MUT-890], Veikko Rantala ànd others [MUT-1080], and Robert Walker [MUT-1280].

Another category which will be of special interest to the researcher is that connecting music and film. Those listed below include Caryl Flinn's *Strains of Utopia: Gender, Nostalgia, and Hollywood Film Music* [MUT-500], James L. Limbacher's *Film Music: From Violins to Video* [MUT-830] and *Keeping Score: Film Music 1972-1979* [MUT-840]. See Chapter 4 on cinema for additional works on film music and Chapter 6 for works on musical drama.

For the latest scholarly research and book reviews in music, consult the following journals: *American Music: A Quarterly Journal Devoted to all Aspects of American Music and Music in America* [MUT-030], *American Music Teacher: The Official Journal of Music Teachers National Association* [MUT-040], *Early Music* [MUT-390], *Early Music History: Studies in Medieval and Early Modern Music* [MUT-400], *Journal of Ethnomusicology* [MUT-670], *Journal of Music Theory* [MUT-680], *The Journal of Musicology* [MUT-690], *Journal of the American Musicological Society* [MUT-700], *Musical Quarterly* [MUT-970], and *Notes: Quarterly Journal of the Music Library Association* [MUT-1010]. Articles from these journals are typically listed in numerous serial periodical bibliographies, such as *The Music Index* [BMU-840] given in the opening of this chapter, and are abstracted in *RILM Abstracts of Music Literature* [BMU-940]. To locate additional journals treating music, consult Linda M. Fidler's and Richard S. James's bibliography, *International Music Journals* [BMU-350] listed above.

[MUT-010] Adler, Israel. *Hebrew Writings Concerning Music, in Manuscripts and Printed Books from Geonic Times up to 1800.* Munich: G. Henle Verlag, 1975. Bib. pp. 312-330.

[MUT-020] Allen, Warren Dwight. *Philosophies of Music History: A Study of General Histories of Music, 1600-1960.* New York: Dover Publications, [1962]. 382 pp. Bibs.

[MUT-030] *American Music: A Quarterly Journal Devoted to all Aspects of American Music and Music in America.* Champaign, Ill.: University of Illinois Press, 1983-. Quarterly.

[MUT-040] *American Music Teacher: The Official Journal of Music Teachers National Association.* Cincinnati: Music Teachers National Association, 1951-. Bi-monthly.

[MUT-050] Apel, Willi. *Harvard Dictionary of Music.* Rev. ed. Cambridge, Mass.: Harvard University Press, 1969.

[MUT-060] Arnold, Corliss R. *Organ Literature: A Comprehensive Survey.* 2 vols. Metuchen, N.J.: Scarecrow Press, 1984. 940 pp.

[MUT-070] Arnold, Denis, ed. *The New Oxford Companion to Music.* 2 vols. New York: Oxford University Press, 1983. Bibs.

[MUT-080] Aronson, Alex. *Music and the Novel: A Study in Twentieth-Century Fiction.* Totowa, N.J.: Rowman and Littlefield, 1980. Bib. pp. 247-257.

[MUT-090] Austin, Paul Britten, and Inger Mattsson. *Gustavian Opera: An Interdisciplinary Reader in Swedish Opera, Dance, and Theatre, 1771-1809.* [Stockholm; Uppsala: Royal Swedish Academy], 1991. Dist. Almqvist and Wiksell International. 492 pp. Bib. refs.

[MUT-100] Bahle, Bruce, ed. *International Cyclopedia of Music and Musicians.* 11th ed. New York: Dodd, 1985. 2,609 pp.

[MUT-110] Baines, Anthony C. *Oxford Companion to Musical Instruments.* New York: Oxford University Press, 1993. 560 pp.

[MUT-120] *Baker's Biographical Dictionary of Musicians.* Rev. Nicolas Slonimsky. 7th ed. New York: Schirmer Books, 1984. 2,577 pp.

[MUT-130] Barry, Barbara R. *Musical Time: The Sense of Order.* Stuyvesant, N.Y.: Pendragon Press, 1990. Bib. pp. 353-381.

[MUT-140] Barthes, Roland. *The Responsibility of Forms: Critical Essays on Music, Art, and Representation.* Trans. Richard Howard. Berkeley: University of California Press, 1991. 312 pp.

[MUT-150] Bartle, Barton K. *Computer Software in Music and Music Education: A Guide.* Metuchen, N.J.: Scarecrow Press, 1987. 266 pp.

[MUT-160] Bayly, Anselm. *The Alliance of Music, Poetry, and Oratory.* 1789. Reprint. New York: Garland Publishing, 1970. 384 pp.

[MUT-170] Berkowitz, Freda Pastor. *Popular Titles and Subtitles of Musical Compositions*. Metuchen, N.J.: Scarecrow Press, 1975. 217 pp.

[MUT-180] Blair, Donald. *Great Opera Singers of the Twentieth Century, 1927-1990*. Lewiston, N.Y.: Edwin Mellen Press, 1991. 138 pp.

[MUT-190] Bloch, Ernst. *Essays on the Philosophy of Music*. Trans. Peter Palmer. Trans. *Zur philosophie der Musik*. Cambridge: Cambridge University Press, 1985. xlvii, 250 pp.

[MUT-200] Blume, Friedrich, ed. *Die Musik in Geschichte und Gegenwart: Allgemeine Enzyklopädie der Musik*. 14 vols. Kassel: Bärenreiter, 1949-1968. *Supplement*. 2 vols. 1973-1979.

[MUT-210] Bone, Philip James. *The Guitar and Mandolin: Biographies of Celebrated Players and Composers*. 2nd ed. 1954. Reprint. London: Schott and Co., [1972].

[MUT-220] Boyd, Morrison Comegys. *Elizabethan Music and Musical Criticism*. 2nd ed. Philadelphia: University of Pennsylvania Press, [1962]. Bibs. pp. 323-347.

[MUT-230] Brown, Calvin Smith. *Music and Literature: A Comparison of the Arts*. Athens: University of Georgia Press, [1948]. Bib. notes pp. 272-278.

[MUT-240] Bryant, E. T. *Music Librarianship: A Practical Guide*. 2nd ed. Metuchen, N.J.: Scarecrow Press, 1985. 473 pp.

[MUT-250] Budd, Malcolm. *Music and the Emotions: The Philosophical Theories*. 1985. Reprint. London; Boston: Routledge and Kegan Paul, 1992. Bib. pp. 177-188.

[MUT-260] Chase, Gilbert. *The American Composer Speaks: A Historical Anthology, 1770-1965*. [Baton Rouge]: Louisiana State University Press, [1966]. Bib. pp. 307-312.

[MUT-270] Cho, Gene J. *Theories and Practice of Harmonic Analysis*. Lewiston, N.Y.: Edwin Mellen Press, 1992. 132 pp.

[MUT-280] Clifford, Mike. *The Harmony Illustrated Encyclopedia of Rock*. 5th ed. New York: Harmony/Crown Publishers, 1986.

[MUT-290] Conrad, Peter. *A Song of Love and Death: The Meaning of Opera*. New York: Poseidon Press, 1987. 383 pp.

[MUT-300] ------. *Romantic Opera and Literary Form*. Berkeley: University of California Press, 1977. Bib. pp. 179-180.

318

[MUT-310] Cohen, Aaron I. *International Encyclopedia of Women Composers*. New York: R. R. Bowker, 1981.

[MUT-320] Cook, Nicholas. *Music, Imagaination, and Culture*. Oxford; New York: Oxford University Press, 1992. Bib. pp. 244-257.

[MUT-330] Coroniti, Joseph. *Poetry as Text in Twentieth Century Vocal Music: From Stravinsky to Reich*. Lewiston, N.Y.: Edwin Mellen Press, 1992. 112 pp.

[MUT-340] Dahlhaus, Carl. *Analysis and Value Judgement*. Trans. Siegmund Levarie. New York: Pendragon Press, 1983. 87 pp.

[MUT-350] ------. *Esthetics of Music*. Trans. *Musikasthetik*. Cambridge; New York: Cambridge University Press, 1982. Bib. pp. 101-112.

[MUT-360] ------. *The Idea of Absolute Music*. Trans. *Die Idee der absoluten Musik*. Chicago: University of Chicago Press, 1989. Bib. pp. 157-171.

[MUT-370] Day, James. *The Literary Background to Bach's Cantatas*. London: D. Dobson, [1961]. 115 pp.

[MUT-380] *Definitive Kobbe's Opera Book, The*. Ed. and rev. The Earl of Harewood. New York: G. P. Putnam's Sons, 1987.

[MUT-390] *Early Music*. Oxford: Oxford University Press, 1973-. Quarterly.

[MUT-400] *Early Music History: Studies in Medieval and Early Modern Music*. New York: Cambridge University Press, 1982-. Annual.

[MUT-410] Ewen, David. *The Complete Book of 20th Century Music*. Rev. ed. Englewood Cliffs, N.J.: Prentice-Hall Press, 1959. 527 pp.

[MUT-420] ------. *Composers of Yesterday: A Biographical and Critical Guide to the Most Important Composers of the Past*. New York: H. W. Wilson Co., 1937. Bib. pp. 481-486.

[MUT-430] ------. *European Composers Today: A Biographical and Critical Guide*. New York: H. W. Wilson, 1954. Bib. pp. 199-200.

[MUT-440] ------, ed. and comp. *Great Composers: 1300-1900*. New York: H. W. Wilson, 1983.

[MUT-450] ------. *Popular American Composers from Revolutionary Times to the Present: A Biographical and Critical Guide*. New York: H. W. Wilson, 1962. 217 pp.

[MUT-460] Falck, Robert [A.], Timothy Rice, and Mieczyslaw Kolinski.

Cross-Cultural Perspectives on Music. Toronto; Buffalo: University of Toronto Press, 1982. xxiv, 189 pp.

[MUT-470] Feather, Leonard G. *The Encyclopedia of Jazz in the Sixties*. New York: Horizon Press, [1966]. Bib. pp. 311-312. Discography pp. 309-310.

[MUT-480] Finney, Gretchen Ludke. *Musical Backgrounds for English Literature: 1580-1650*. New Brunswick: Rutgers University Press, [1962]. 292 pp. Bib. footnotes.

[MUT-490] Fiske, Harold E. *Music and Mind: Philosophical Essays on the Cognition and Meaning of Music*. Lewiston, N.Y.: Edwin Mellen Press, 1990. 180 pp.

[MUT-500] Flinn, Caryl. *Strains of Utopia: Gender, Nostalgia, and Hollywood Film Music*. Princeton: Princeton University Press, 1992. 224 pp.

[MUT-510] Frye, Northrop. *Sound and Poetry*. New York: Columbia University Press, 1957. 156 pp.

[MUT-520] Fubini, Enrico. *The History of Music Aesthetics*. Trans. *L'estetica musicale*. London: Macmillan Publishing Co., 1990. Bib. pp. 573-593.

[MUT-530] Fuld, James J. *The Book of World-Famous Music: Classical, Popular, and Folk*. 3rd ed. New York: Dover Publications, 1985. 714 pp. Bib. refs. (See [BMU-400])

[MUT-540] Gammond, Peter. *Oxford Companion to Popular Music*. New York: Oxford University Press, 1991. 752 pp.

[MUT-550] Gangwere, Blanche. *Music History from the Late Roman Thru the Gothic Periods, 313-1425: A Documented Chronology*. Westport, Conn.: Greenwood Press, 1986.

[MUT-560] Gioia, Ted. *The Imperfect Art: Reflections on Jazz and Modern Culture*. New York: Oxford University Press, 1988. 152 pp. Bib. refs.

[MUT-570] Goswami, Roshmi. *Man-and-Music in India*. Shimla: Indian Institute of Advanced Study; Delhi: Munshiram Manoharlal Publishers, 1992. 83 pp. Bib. refs.

[MUT-580] Greene, David R. *Listening to Strauss Operas: The Audience's Multiple Standpoints*. New York: Gordon and Breach, 1991. Bib. refs. pp. 182-184.

[MUT-590] Griffiths, Paul. *The Thames and Hudson Encyclopedia of 20th-*

Century Music. London: Thames and Hudson, 1986.

[MUT-600] Grout, Donald Jay, and Claude V. Palisca. *A History of Western Music*. 4th ed. New York: W. W. Norton and Co., 1988. 910 pp. Bibs.

[MUT-610] Hanslick, Eduard. *On the Musically Beautiful: A Contribution Towards the Revision of the Aesthetics of Music*. Trans. Geoffrey Payzant. Trans. *Vom Musikalisch-Schonen*, 8th ed., 1891. Indianapolis: Hackett Publishing Co., 1986. Bib. pp. 103-115.

[MUT-620] Harter, Jim. *Music: A Pictorial Archive of Woodcuts and Engravings: 841 Copyright-Free Illustrations for Artists and Designers*. New York: Dover Publications, 1980. 155 pp.

[MUT-630] Hindley, Geoffrey, ed. *Larousse Encyclopedia of Music*. New York: Hamlyn Publishing Group, Ltd., 1971. Bib. p. 556.

[MUT-640] Hitchcock, H. Wiley, and Stanley Sadie. *The New Grove Dictionary of American Music*. 4 vols. New York: Grove's Dictionaries of Music, 1986. 2,700 pp.

[MUT-650] Holmes, John L. *Composers on Composers*. New York: Greenwood Press, 1990. 189 pp. Bib. refs.

[MUT-660] Johnson, Paula. *Form and Transformation in Music and Poetry of the English Renaissance*. New Haven: Yale University Press, 1972. Bib. pp. 155-162.

[MUT-670] *Journal of Ethnomusicology*. Ann Arbor: Society for Ethnomusicology, 1955-. 3/year. (Formerly *Ethnomusicology*.)

[MUT-680] *Journal of Music Theory*. New Haven: Journal of Music Theory, Department of Music, Yale University, 1957-. Semi-annual.

[MUT-690] *Journal of Musicology, The*. Berkeley: University of California Press Journals, 1982-. Quarterly.

[MUT-700] *Journal of the American Musicological Society*. Philadelphia: American Musicological Society, 1948-. 3/year.

[MUT-710] Katz, Ruth. *Divining the Powers of Music: Aesthetic Theory and the Origins of Opera*. New York: Pendragon Press, 1986. Bib. pp. 199-208.

[MUT-720] Katz, Ruth, and Carl Dahlhaus, eds. *Contemplating Music: Source Readings in the Aesthetics of Music*. 3 vols. New York: Pendragon Press, 1987. Bib. refs.

[MUT-730] Kennedy, Michael. *The Oxford Dictionary of Music*. New York: Oxford University Press, 1985. 810 pp.

[MUT-740] Kernfeld, Barry, ed. *New Grove Dictionary of Jazz*. 2 vols. New York: Grove's Dictionaries of Music, 1988. 1100 pp.

[MUT-750] Kimmey, John A., Jr. *A Critique of Musicology: Clarifying, the Scope, Limits, and Purposes of Musicology*. Lewiston, N.Y.: Edwin Mellen Press, 1989. 328 pp.

[MUT-760] Kivy, Peter. *Osmin's Rage: Philosophical Reflections on Opera, Drama, and Text*. Princeton: Princeton University Press, 1988. Bib. pp. 295-298.

[MUT-770] Koshgarian, Richard. *American Orchestral Music: A Performance Catalog*. Metuchen, N.J.: Scarecrow Press, 1992. Bib. refs. pp. 758-761.

[MUT-780] Kramer, Lawrence. *Music as Cultural Practice, 1800-1900*. Berkeley: University of California Press, 1990. Bib. refs. pp. 219-220.

[MUT-790] Kraus, Michael. *The Interpretation of Music: Philosophical Essays*. Oxford: Clarendon Press; Oxford; New York: Oxford University Press, 1993. 288 pp. Bib. refs.

[MUT-800] Leonard, Neil. *Jazz: Myth and Religion*. New York: Oxford University Press, 1987. 221 pp. Bib. refs.

[MUT-810] LePage, Jane Weiner. *Women Composers, Conductors, and Musicians of the Twentieth Century*. 3 vols. Metuchen, N.J.: Scarecrow Press, 1980, 1983, 1988. 1,023 pp.

[MUT-820] Lightner, Helen. *Class Voice and the American Art Song: A Source Book and Anthology*. Metuchen, N.J.: Scarecrow Press, 1991. 191 pp.

[MUT-830] Limbacher, James L. *Film Music: From Violins to Video*. Metuchen, N.J.: Scarecrow Press, 1974. 835 pp.

[MUT-840] ------. *Keeping Score: Film Music 1972-1979*. Metuchen, N.J.: Scarecrow Press, 1981. 519 pp.

[MUT-850] Ling, Dorothy. *The Original Art of Music*. Lanham, Md.: University Press of America, 1989. 178 pp.

[MUT-860] Lippman, Edward A. *A History of Western Musical Aesthetics*. Lincoln: University of Nebraska Press, 1992. Bib. pp. 519-529.

[MUT-870] ------, ed. *Musical Aesthetics: A Historical Reader.* 2 vols. New York: Pendragon Press, 1986-. In progress.

[MUT-880] Lyle, Wilson. *A Dictionary of Pianists.* New York: Schirmer Books, 1985. 343 pp.

[MUT-890] Maconie, Robin. *The Concept of Music.* Oxford: Clarendon Press; New York: Oxford University Press, 1990. Bib. refs. pp. 181-182.

[MUT-900] Manson, Adele P. *Calendar of Music and Musicians.* Metuchen, N.J.: Scarecrow Press, 1981. 471 pp.

[MUT-910] Marco, Guy A. *Information on Music: A Handbook of Reference Sources in European Languages.* 3 vols. Littleton, Colo.: Libraries Unlimited, 1975-1984.

[MUT-920] Mehta, R[amanlal] C[hotalal], ed. *Studies in Musicology.* Bombay: Indian Musicological Society, 1983. 198 pp. Bib. refs.

[MUT-930] Mender, Mona. *Manuscript Preparation: A Concise Guide.* Metuchen, N.J.: Scarecrow Press, 1991. 222 pp.

[MUT-940] Merriam, Alan P. *The Anthropology of Music.* Evanston, Ill.: Northwestern University Press, 1964.

[MUT-950] Miller, Hugh M. *History of Music.* New York: Barnes and Noble Books, [1972]. 288 pp. Bibs.

[MUT-960] Morgenstern, Sam, ed. *Composers on Music: An Anthology of Composers' Writings from Palestrina to Copland.* [New York]: Pantheon, [1956]. 584 pp. Sources pp. 557-569.

[MUT-970] *Musical Quarterly.* New York: Oxford University Press, 1915-. Quarterly.

[MUT-980] *New Oxford History of Music.* 10 vols. London: Oxford, 1957-present. (In progress.)

[MUT-990] *19th Century Music.* Berkeley: University of California Press, 1977-. 3/year.

[MUT-1000] Norris, Christopher, ed. *Music and the Politics of Culture.* London: Lawrence and Wishart, 1989. 356 pp. Bibs.

[MUT-1010] *Notes: Quarterly Journal of the Music Library Association.* Canton, Mass.: Music Library Association, 1942-. Quarterly.

[MUT-1020] *Opera News.* New York: Metropolitan Opera Guild, Inc.,

1936-. Monthly (May-November), Bi-Weekly (December-April).

[MUT-1030] *Opera Quarterly, The.* Durham, N.C.: Duke University Press, 1983-. Quarterly.

[MUT-1040] Osborne, Charles, ed. *The Dictionary of Composers.* New York: Taplinger Publishing Co., 1978. 380 pp.

[MUT-1050] Pallay, Steven G. *Cross Index Title Guide to Classical Music.* Music Reference Collection, 0736-7740, no. 12. New York: Greenwood Press, 1987. Bib. pp. 205-206.

[MUT-1060] Pettis, Ashley. *Music: Now and Then.* (Biblical roots). New York: Coleman-Ross, [1955]. 118 pp.

[MUT-1070] Randel, Don, ed. *The New Harvard Dictionary of Music.* Cambridge, Mass.: Harvard University Press, 1986. 942 pp. Bibs.

[MUT-1080] Rantala, Veikko, et al. *Essays on the Philosophy of Music.* Acta Philosophica Fennica, vol. 43. Helsinki: Philosophical Society of Finland, 1988. 369 pp. Bibs.

[MUT-1090] Roxon, Lillian. *Rock Encyclopedia.* New York: Grosset and Dunlap, [1969]. 611 pp.

[MUT-1100] Sadie, Stanley, ed. *New Grove Dictionary of Musical Instruments.* 3 vols. New York: Grove's Dictionaries of Music, 1989. Bibs.

[MUT-1110] ------. *New Grove Dictionary of Music and Musicians.* 20 vols. 7th ed. New York: Grove's Dictionaries of Music, 1986. Bibs.

[MUT-1120] Sadie, Stanley, and Alison Latham, eds. *The Norton/Grove Concise Encyclopedia of Music.* New York: W. W. Norton and Co., 1988. 850 pp.

[MUT-1130] Sainsbury, John S., ed. *A Dictionary of Musicians from the Earliest Times.* 2 vols. 1825. Reprint. New York: Da Capo Press, 1966.

[MUT-1140] Schmidgall, Gary. *Literature as Opera.* New York: Oxford University Press, 1977. 431 pp. Bib. refs.

[MUT-1150] Scholes, Percy A. *Oxford Companion to Music.* 10th ed. Ed. John O. Ward. New York: Oxford University Press, 1970. 1248 pp.

324

[MUT-1160] Simpson, Alexander Thomas. "Opera on Film: A Study of the History and the Aesthetic Principles and Conflicts of a Hybrid Genre." Ph.D. Thesis, University of Kentucky, 1990. Bib. pp. 182-193. Filmography, pp. 194-195.

[MUT-1170] Stambler, Irwin, ed. *Encyclopedia of Pop, Rock, and Soul*. Rev. ed. New York: St. Martin's Press, 1989. 881 pp. Bib. refs.

[MUT-1180] Stein, Jack Madison. *Poem and Music in the German Lied from Gluck to Hugo Wolf*. Cambridge, Mass.: Harvard University Press, 1971. Bib. pp. 206-213.

[MUT-1190] Swan, Alfred Julius. *The Music Director's Guide to Musical Literature: For Voices and Instruments*. New York: Prentice-Hall Press, 1941. Bib. pp. 117-164.

[MUT-1200] Tambling, Jeremy. *Opera, Ideology, and Film*. New York: St. Martin's Press, 1987. Bib. pp. 213-216.

[MUT-1210] Taylor, Clifford. *Musical Idea and the Design Aesthetic in Contemporary Music: A Text for Discerning Appraisal of Musical Thought in Western Culture*. Lewiston, N.Y.: Edwin Mellen Press, 1990. 386 pp.

[MUT-1220] Thompson, Kenneth. *A Dictionary of Twentieth Century Composers (1911-1971)*. New York: St. Martin's Press, [1973]. 666 pp.

[MUT-1230] Thompson, Oscar, ed. *The International Cyclopedia of Music and Musicians*. 11th ed. New York: Dodd, Mead, 1985.

[MUT-1240] Thornton, Peter. *Musical Instruments as Works of Art*. 2nd ed. Victoria and Albert Museum. London: H.M.S.O., 1982. 52 pp.

[MUT-1250] Treitler, Leo. *Music and the Historical Imagination*. Cambridge, Mass.; London: Harvard University Press, 1990. Bib. pp. 307-330.

[MUT-1260] van Deusen, Nancy, ed. *The Harp and the Soul: Studies in Early Medieval Music and Its Role in the Intellectual Climate of the Early University*. Lewiston, N.Y.: Edwin Mellen Press, 1989. 456 pp.

[MUT-1270] Vinton, John, ed. *Dictionary of Contemporary Music*. New York: E. P. Dutton and Co., [1974]. 834 pp. Bibs.

[MUT-1280] Walker, Robert. *Musical Beliefs: Psychoacoustic, Mythical, and Educational Perspectives*. New York: Teachers College Press, 1990. Bib. refs. pp. 235-241.

[MUT-1290] Webb, Daniel. *Observations on the Correspondence Between Poetry and Music.* 1769. Reprint. New York: Garland Publishing, 1970. 155 pp.

[MUT-1300] Wenk, Arthur B. *Analyses of Nineteenth- and Twentieth-Century Music, 1940-1985.* Boston: Music Library Association, 1987. 370 pp.

[MUT-1310] Wicke, Peter. *Rock Music: Culture, Aesthetics, and Sociology.* Trans. *Rockmusik.* Cambridge; New York: Cambridge University Press, 1990. Bib. refs. pp. 184-216. Discography, pp. 217-218.

[MUT-1320] Winternitz, Emanuel. *Musical Instruments and Their Symbolism in Western Art.* London: Faber, 1967. 240 pp. Bib. footnotes.

[MUT-1330] *World's Encyclopedia of Recorded Music.* 3 vols. Westport, Conn.: Greenwood Press, n.d.

KEY WORKS ON MUSIC AND RELIGION

The works listed in this section represent the core of concern for this volume, namely to identify the intersection between the fine arts and Christianity. The twenty bibliographies given in the first section offer carefully focused studies of resources treating music and the Christian faith. Two works in this section offer a wide perspective on music in church life and therefore serve as good beginning points for research. These volumes are Ronald Alan Turner's collection of work by seminary students, *Church Music Literature Resource Book* [MUR-180], and Richard C. von Ende's more extensive study, *Church Music: An International Bibliography* [MUR-190]. The other special bibliographies are self explanatory in their respective foci.

For the newcomer to the study of church music, Donald P. Hustad's *Jubilate II: Church Music in Worship and Renewal* [MUR-540] offers a fine overview. Additionally, Robert D. Berglund's *A Philosophy of Church Music* [MUR-240], Harold M. Best's *Music Through the Eyes of Faith* [MUR-250], Edward Foley's *Foundations of Christian Music: The Music of Pre-Constantinian Christianity* [MUR-400], Harold Byron Hannum's *Christian Search for Beauty: A Review of the Relationship of the Arts, Particularly Music, to the Principles of Christianity* [MUR-450], John Harper's *The Forms and Orders of*

Western Liturgy from the Tenth to the Eighteenth Century: A Historical Introduction and Guide for Students and Musicians [MUR-460], and Erik Routley's *Church Music and the Christian Faith* [MUR-830] also offer useful interpretations of the role of music in the life of the church. Note that Best's work is specifically designed to help the teacher and the student integrate questions of faith with the study of music. For two recent studies with a denominational emphasis, see David B. Pass's *Music and the Church* [MUR-780] (from a Southern Baptist perspective), and Larry Penner's *Finding a Voice: A Discussion of Mennonite Music in Mennonite Culture* [MUR-790].

One of the most recent topics of concern in the life of the church is the role of rock music in society and especially in the church. For works treating this delicate topic see John Ankerberg's *Facts on Rock Music* [MUR-230], J. Brent Bill's *Rock and Roll* [MUR-260], Fletcher A. Brothers' *The Rock Report* [MUR-280], Jeff Godwin's *The Devil's Disciples: The Truth About Rock* [MUR-410], Lowell Hart's and Salem Kirban's *Satan's Music Exposed* [MUR-470], Michael K. Haynes's *The God of Rock: A Christian Perspective of Rock Music* [MUR-510], Gary L. Krug's *Rock--The Beat Goes On: A Christian Perspective on Trends in Rock Music* [MUR-630], Bob Larson's *Your Kids and Rock* [MUR-660], David W. Scheer's *PG, A Parental Guide to Rock* [MUR-880], and Beth Whitaker's *The "Calling" of a Rock Star: A Christian Mother's Story* [MUR-1010].

Of special value to the researcher are the numerous titles given below treating sacred music, especially hymns. For example, in researching hymns one would do well to begin with William J. Reynolds and Milburn Price's fine work, *A Survey of Christian Hymnody* [MUR-810]. For more extended research one could consult the reference work by Judy Hunnicutt [MUR-100], as well as the detailed studies by Lionel Adey [MUR-210], Gene Claghorn [MUR-310], Katharine Smith Diehl [MUR-340], Susan Drain [MUR-350], John Julian [MUR-590], Robert F. Klepper [MUR-600 to 620], Robert G. McCutchan [MUR-710], Randle Manwaring [MUR-730], David W. Perry [MUR-800], Erik Routley [MUR-850], and Daniel J. Werning [MUR-990]. Also consult *The Hymn: A Journal of Congregational Song* [MUR-550] and *Sacred Music* [MUR-870]. For other aspects of church music, such as choral music or sacred instrumental music, see titles as given below.

Special Bibliographies

[MUR-010] Berger, Kenneth W. *Christian Choral Music: A Catalog of Catalogs*. 2 vols. Kent, Ohio: Kenneth W. Berger, 1991.

[MUR-020] Britton, Allen Perdue, Irving Lowens, and Richard Crawford. *American Sacred Music Imprints, 1698-1810: A Bibliography*. Worcester: American Antiquarian Society, 1990. 798 pp. Bib. refs. pp. 61-75.

[MUR-030] Daltry, Joseph Samuel. *Religious Perspectives of College Teaching in Music*. New Haven: Edward W. Hazen Foundation, [195-]. 31 pp.

[MUR-040] Daugherty, F. Mark, Susan H. Simon, and Gary S. Eslinger. *Sacred Choral Music in Print*. Music-in-Print Series, 0146-7883; vol. 1t. Philadelphia: Musidcata, 1992. 304 pp. Updates *Sacred Choral Music in Print*, ed. Gary S. Eslinger and F. Mark Daugherty. 2nd ed. 1985, 2 vol., 1,322 pp., 1987 supplement, 137 pp., and 1988 supplement, 277 pp.

[MUR-050] DeVenney, David P. *American Masses and Requiems: A Descriptive Guide*. Fallen Leaf Reference Books in Music, 8755-268X, no. 15. Berkeley: Fallen Leaf Press, 1990. 210 pp. Bib. refs.

[MUR-060] Dovaras, John. *Choral Settings of the Scriptures with English Texts*. Dayton, Ohio: R. Dean Publishing Co., 1988. 62 pp.

[MUR-070] *English Composers of the Twentieth Century; Musical Instruments; Liturgical MSS*. Maggs Brothers Catalogue, no. 1012. London: Maggs Brothers, 1981. 104 pp.

[MUR-080] Espina, Noni. *Vocal Solos for Christian Churches: A Descriptive Reference of Solo Music for the Church Year, Including a Bibliographical Supplement of Choral Works*. 3rd ed. Metuchen, N.J.: Scarecrow Press, 1984. 256 pp.

[MUR-090] *Handbook of Church Music for Weddings*. Rev. ed. Chicago: Liturgy Training Program, Archdiocese of Chicago, 1985. 36 pp.

[MUR-100] Hunnicutt, Judy. *Index of Hymn Tune Accompaniments for Organ*. Fort Worth: Hymn Society of America, 1988. 32 pp.

[MUR-110] Hutcheson, Robert J. *Twentieth-Century Settings of the Passion*. Research Memorandum--American Choral Foundation, no.

129. New York: American Choral Foundation, 1979. 9 pp.

[MUR-120] Lawrence, Joy E. *The Organist's Shortcut to Service Music: A Guide to Finding Intonations, Organ Compositions, and Free Accompaniments Based on Traditional Hymn Tunes. Supplement.* Cleveland, Ohio: Ludwig Music, 1988.

[MUR-130] Liebergen, Patrick M. "Church Music: An Annotated Bibliography and Index of Articles on Choral Music from 1966 to 1978." D.M.A., University of Colorado, Boulder, Colo., 1991. 78 pp.

[MUR-140] Norris, Phil. *Sacred Instrumental Published Music List.* Pentwater, Mich.: Christian Instrumental Directors Association, 1988. 60 pp.

[MUR-150] Ringerwole, Joan. *Bibliography of Organ Music: Based on the Tunes Found in the Psalter Hymnal and Rejoice in the Lord.* N.p.: CRC Publications, 1989. 77 pp.

[MUR-160] Scott, Darwin Floyd. *The Roman Catholic Liturgy and Liturgical Books: A Musical Guide.* 3rd ed. [Los Angeles?]: [UCLA Music Ligrary], 1988. 12 pp.

[MUR-170] Suggs, Julian S[impson]. *Instrumental Music for Churches: A Descriptive Listing.* Nashville: Sunday School Board of the Southern Baptist Convention, 1982. 142 pp.

[MUR-180] Turner, Ronald Alan. *Church Music Literature Resource Book.* [Louisville, Ky.]: Southern Baptist Theological Seminary, 1979. 209 pp.

[MUR-190] von Ende, Richard C. *Church Music: An International Bibliography.* Metuchen, N.J.: Scarecrow Press, 1980. 453 pp.

[MUR-200] Walker, Diane Parr. *German Sacred Polyphonic Vocal Music Between Schutz and Bach: Sources and Critical Editions.* Detroit Studies in Music Bibliography, no. 67. Warren, Mich.: Harmonie Park Press, 1992. 434 pp. Bib. refs. pp. xxi-xxxv.

Key Works

[MUR-210] Adey, Lionel. *Class and Idol in the English Hymn.* Seattle: University of Washington Press, 1989. 355 pp.

[MUR-220] Anderson, Jacqulyn, and Dick Ham. *Developing a Church Music Library.* Nashville: Convention Press, 1989. 36 pp.

[MUR-230] Ankerberg, John. *Facts on Rock Music*. Eugene, Oreg.: Harvest House Publishers, 1992. Bib. refs. pp. 46-48.

[MUR-240] Berglund, Robert D. *A Philosophy of Church Music*. 2nd ed. Saint Paul, Minn.: Bethel Publications, 1985. Bib. p. 103.

[MUR-250] Best, Harold M. *Music Through the Eyes of Faith*. San Francisco: Harper San Francisco, 1993. 225 pp. Bib. refs.

[MUR-260] Bill, J. Brent. *Rock and Roll*. Rev. ed. Old Tappan, N.J.: Fleming H. Revell Co., 1987. 167 pp. Bib. pp. 148-149.

[MUR-270] Blanchard, John. *Pop Goes the Gospel*. Welwyn: Evangelical, 1983. 160 pp.

[MUR-280] Brothers, Fletcher A. *The Rock Report*. Lancaster, Pa.: Starburst, 1987. Bib. p. 144.

[MUR-290] Carroll, J. Robert. *Compendium of Liturgical Music Terms*. Toledo, Ohio: Gregorian Institute of America, 1964. 86 pp.

[MUR-300] Chupungco, Anscar J. *Shaping the Easter Feast*. Washington, D.C.: Pastoral Press, 1992. 106 pp. Bib. refs.

[MUR-310] Claghorn, Gene. *Women Composers and Hymnists: A Concise Biographical Dictionary*. Metuchen, N.J.: Scarecrow Press, 1984. 288 pp.

[MUR-320] *Classified Index to the Bulletin of the Hymn Society of Great Britain and Ireland, A*. Vols. 1-10, 1937-1984.

[MUR-330] Coleman, [Paul] Michael. *Come and Worship*. Old Tappan, N.J.: Chosen Books, 1989. Bib. refs. pp. 155-159.

[MUR-340] Diehl, Katharine Smith. *Hymns and Tunes: An Index*. New York: Scarecrow Press, 1966. Bib. p. 1185.

[MUR-350] Drain, Susan. *The Anglican Church in 19th-Century Britain: Hymns Ancient and Modern (1860-1875)*. Lewiston, N.Y.: Edwin Mellen Press, 1989. 552 pp.

[MUR-360] Edgar, William. *Taking Note of Music*. Third Way Books. London: SPCK, 1986. Bib. pp. 134-141.

[MUR-370] Edson, Jean S. *Organ Preludes: An Index to Compositions on Hymn Tunes, Chorales, Plainsong Melodies, Gregorian Tunes and Carols*. 2 vols. Metuchen, N.J.: Scarecrow Press, 1970. 1,169 pp.

[MUR-380] Eskew, Harry, and Hugh T. McElrath. *Sing with Understanding*.

330

Nashville: Broadman Press, 1980.

[MUR-390] Eversole, Finley, ed. *Christian Faith and the Contemporary Arts*. New York: Abingdon Press, [1962]. 255 pp.

[MUR-400] Foley, Edward. *Foundations of Christian Music: The Music of Pre-Constantinian Christianity*. Bramcote, Nottingham: Grove Books, 1992. 84 pp. Bib. refs.

[MUR-410] Godwin, Jeff. *The Devil's Disciples: The Truth About Rock*. Chino, Calif.: Chick Publications, 1985. 352 pp. Bibs.

[MUR-420] Godwin, Joscelyn. *Harmonies of Heaven and Earth: The Spiritual Dimension of Music from Antiquity to the Avant-Garde*. London: Thames and Hudson, 1987. Bib. pp. 199-205.

[MUR-430] ------. *Music, Mysticism, and Magic: A Sourcebook*. London; New York: Routledge and Kegan Paul, 1986. Bib. pp. 337-342.

[MUR-440] H., E. *Scripture Proof for Singing Hymns and Spiritual Songs, or, An Answer to Several Queries and Objections Frequently Made use of to Stumble and Turn Aside Young Christians from Their duty to God in Singing of Psalms: Gathered out of the Scriptures of Truth, to Which is Added the Testimony of Some Learned Men, to Prove that Scripture-Psalms are Intended by all Those Three Words, Psalms, Hymns, and Songs, Used by the Apostle, Ephesians 5.19, Colosians 3.16*. 1696. Reprint. Ann Arbor: University Microfilms International, 1984. 48 pp. 1 35mm reel.

[MUR-450] Hannum, Harold Byron. *Christian Search for Beauty: A Review of the Relationship of the Arts, Particularly Music, to the Principles of Christianity*. Nashville: Southern Publishing Association, 1975. 160 pp.

[MUR-460] Harper, John. *The Forms and Orders of Western Liturgy from the Tenth to the Eighteenth Century: A Historical Introduction and Guide for Students and Musicians*. Oxford; New York: Clarendon Press; Oxford University Press, 1991. 337 pp. Bib. refs. pp. 276-285.

[MUR-470] Hart, Lowell, and Salem Kirban. *Satan's Music Exposed*. Chattanooga: AMG Publishers, 1981. 187 pp. Bib. refs.

[MUR-480] Hatchett, Marion J. *Music for the Church Year: A Handbook for Clergymen, Organists, and Choir Directors*. New York: The Seabury Press, 1964. 138 pp.

[MUR-490] Haugen, Marty. *Instrumentation and the Liturgical Ensemble*.

Chicago: G.I.A. Publications, 1991. 208 pp. and 2 audio cassettes. Bib. refs.

[MUR-500] Haverluck, Bob. *Love Your Enemies--And Other Neighbours: Workshops for Peace: Meditations, Worship, Art, Music.* Toronto: United Church Publishing House, 1991. Bib. refs. p. 142.

[MUR-510] Haynes, Michael K. *The God of Rock: A Christian Perspective of Rock Music.* Lindale, Tex.: Priority Ministries and Publications, 1984. 216 pp.

[MUR-520] Heskes, Irene. *The Resource Book of Jewish Music: A Bibliographical and Topical Guide to the Book and Journal Literature and Program Materials.* Westport, Conn.: Greenwood Press, 1985. 302 pp.

[MUR-530] Hoffman, Lawrence A., and Janet Roland Walton. *The Sacred Sound and Social Change: Liturgical Music in Jewish and Christian Experience.* Notre Dame: University of Notre Dame Press, 1992. 352 pp. Bib. refs.

[MUR-540] Hustad, Donald P. *Jubilate II: Church Music in Worship and Renewal.* Carol Stream, Ill.: Hope Publishing Co., 1993. Bib. Rev. ed. of *Jubilate: Church Music in the Evangelical Tradition.* Carol Stream, Ill.: Hope Publishing Co., 1981. Bib. pp. 349-361.

[MUR-550] *Hymn, The: A Journal of Congregational Song.* Vol. 1-42, 1949-1991. Quarterly, Hymn Society; indexed annually. *Index to The Hymn.* Vols. 1-32, 1949-1981.

[MUR-560] Irwin, Joyce. *Sacred Sound: Music in Religious Thought and Practice.* Chico, Calif.: Scholars Press, 1983. 172 pp. Bibs.

[MUR-570] Johansson, Calvin M. *Music and Ministry: A Biblical Counterpoint.* Peabody, Mass.: Hendrickson Publishers, 1984. Bib. pp. 129-133.

[MUR-580] Jones, Ivor H. *Music: A Joy For Ever.* London: Epworth, 1989. 176 pp. Bib. refs.

[MUR-590] Julian, John. *A Dictionary of Hymnology, Setting Forth the Origin and History of Christian Hymns of all Ages and Nations.* Rev. ed. 1907. Reprint. New York: Dover Publications, 1957. 1,768 pp.

[MUR-600] Klepper, Robert F., comp. *A Concordance of the Hymnal 1982: According to the Use of the Episcopal Church.* Metuchen, N.J.: Scarecrow Press, 1989. 892 pp.

332

[MUR-610] ------. *A Concordance of the Pilgrim Hymnal*. Metuchen, N.J.: Scarecrow Press, 1989. 790 pp.

[MUR-620] ------. *Methodist Hymnal Concordance*. Metuchen, N.J.: Scarecrow Press, 1987. 800 pp.

[MUR-630] Krug, Gary L. *Rock--The Beat Goes On: A Christian Perspective on Trends in Rock Music*. Milwaukee, Wis.: Northwestern Publishing House, 1987. Bib. pp. 104-106.

[MUR-640] LaCroix, Richard L. *Augustine on Music: An Interdisciplinary Collection of Essays*. Lewiston, N.Y.: Edwin Mellen Press, 1988. 130 pp. Bibs.

[MUR-650] Larrick, Geary. *Musical References and Song Texts in the Bible*. Lewiston, N.Y.: Edwin Mellen Press, 1990. Bib. refs. pp. 148-150.

[MUR-660] Larson, Bob. *Your Kids and Rock*. Wheaton: Tyndale House Publishers, 1988. Bib. pp. 89-92.

[MUR-670] Laster, James. *Catalogue of Choral Music Arranged in Biblical Order*. Metuchen, N.J.: Scarecrow Press, 1983. 269 pp.

[MUR-680] ------. *Catalogue of Vocal Solos and Duets Arranged in Biblical Order*. Metuchen, N.J.: Scarecrow Press, 1984. 212 pp.

[MUR-690] Lewis, Robert C. *The Sacred Word and Its Creative Overtones: Relating Religion and Science Through Music*. Oceanside, Calif.: Rosicrucian Fellowship, 1986. Bib. pp. 157-158.

[MUR-700] Liturgical Conference, The. *Liturgy, Glad Shouts and Songs*. Liturgy/The Liturgical Conference, 0458-063X, vol. 9, no. 1. [Washington, D.C.: The Liturgy Conference], 1990. 104 pp. Bib. refs.

[MUR-710] McCutchan, Robert G. *Hymn Tune Names, Their Sources and Significance*. Nashville: Abingdon Press, [1957]. 206 pp.

[MUR-720] McKinnon, James. *Music in Early Christian Literature*. Cambridge Readings in the Literature of Music. Cambridge: Cambridge University Press, 1987. 357 pp. Bib. pp. 172-177.

[MUR-730] Manwaring, Randle. *A Study of Hymn-Writing and Hymn-Singing in the Christian Church*. Lewiston, N.Y.: Edwin Mellen Press, 1990. 188 pp.

[MUR-740] Nevin, Robert. *Instrumental Music in Christian Worship: A Review, Chiefly in the Way of Reply to Professor Wallace*. 2nd ed. Londonberry: Bible and Colportage Society, 1873. 87 pp.

[MUR-750] Nichols, Timothy Robert. *In Spirit and in Truth.* A review of *Music of the Saints* by Francis Winder. Burlington, W.Va.: Enduring Word Publications, 1992. 108 pp. Bib. refs. in notes.

[MUR-760] Okure, Teresa, and Paul van Thiel. *Thirty-Two Articles Evaluating Inculturation of Christianity in Africa.* Kenya: AMECEA Gaba Publications, 1990. 259 pp.

[MUR-770] Paranjoti, Violet. *The Church and Western Music.* Bombay: Gospel Literature Service, 1972. 104 pp. Bib. refs.

[MUR-780] Pass, David B. *Music and the Church.* Nashville: Broadman Press, 1989. 131 pp. Bibs.

[MUR-790] Penner, Larry. *Finding a Voice: A Discussion of Mennonite Music in Mennonite Culture.* Goshen, Ind.: Pinchpenny Press, 1992. Bib. p. 47.

[MUR-800] Perry, David W. *Hymns and Tunes Indexed by First Lines, Tune Names, and Metres.* Croydon, England: The Hymn Society of Great Britain and Ireland and the Royal School of Church Music, 1980. 310 pp.

[MUR-810] Reynolds, William J., and Milburn Price. *A Survey of Christian Hymnody.* Rev. ed. Carol Stream, Ill.: Hope Publishing Co., 1987. 301 pp. Bib. pp. 121-125.

[MUR-820] Riedel, Jane Rassmussen. *Musical Taste as a Religious Question in Nineteenth-Century America: The Development of Episcopal Church Hymnody.* Lewiston, N.Y.: Edwin Mellen Press, 1986. 632 pp.

[MUR-830] Routley, Erik. *Church Music and the Christian Faith.* Carol Stream, Ill.: Agape, 1978. Bib. pp. 149-150.

[MUR-840] ------. *Music Leadership in the Church.* Carol Stream, Ill.: Agape, 1967. 136 pp.

[MUR-850] ------. *The Music of Christian Hymns.* Chicago: G. I. A. Publications, 1981. 184 pp. plus 605 hymn tunes. Bib. pp. [1]-[6] in back.

[MUR-860] ------. *Twentieth Century Church Music.* Carol Stream, Ill.: Agape, 1964. Bib. pp. 217-239.

[MUR-870] *Sacred Music.* Saint Paul, Minn.: Church Music Association of

334

America, 1874-. Quarterly. (Continuation of *Caecilia* and *The Catholic Choirmaster*.)

[MUR-880] Scheer, David W. *PG, A Parental Guide to Rock*. Camp Hill, Pa.: Christian Publications, 1986. Bib. pp. 205-212.

[MUR-890] Sendrey, Alfred, and Mildred Norton. *David's Harp: The Story of Music in Biblical Times*. [New York: New American Library, [1964]. Bib. pp. 273-276.

[MUR-900] ------. *Music in Ancient Israel*. New York: Philosophical Library, [1969]. 674 pp. Bib. pp. 607-618.

[MUR-910] Serjak, Cynthia. *Music and the Cosmic Dance*. Washington, D.C.: Pastoral Press, 1987. Bib. pp. 171-178.

[MUR-920] Shields, Elizabeth McEwen. *Music in the Religious Growth of Children*. New York; Nashville: Abingdon-Cokesbury Press, 1943. 128 pp. Bib. pp. 38-39.

[MUR-930] Shiloah, Amnon. *The Dimension of Music in Islamic and Jewish Culture*. Collected Studies Series, no. CS393. Aldershot, Hampshire, Great Britain; Brookfield, Vt.: Variorum, 1993.

[MUR-940] Spencer, Jon Michael. *Theological Music: Introduction to Theomusicology*. New York: Greenwood Press, 1991. Bib. refs. pp. 171-174.

[MUR-950] Stainer, John. *The Music of the Bible, with some Account of the Development of Modern Musical Instruments from Ancient Types*. London: Novello and Co., Ltd., [1914]. 230 pp.

[MUR-960] Talbot, John Michael. *The Master Musician*. Grand Rapids: Zondervan, 1992.

[MUR-970] Titon, Jeff Todd. *Powerhouse for God: Speech, Chant, and Song in an Appalachian Baptist Church*. Austin: University of Texas Press, 1988. Bib. pp. 503-512.

[MUR-980] Vitringa, Campegius. *The Synagogue and the Church: Being an Attempt to Show that the Government, Ministeres and Services of the Church were Derived from Those of the Synagogue*. Trans. Joshua Bernard. London: B. Fellowes, 1842. 262 pp.

[MUR-990] Werning, Daniel J. *A Selected Source Index for Hymn and Chorale Tunes in Lutheran Worship Books*. St. Louis: Concordia, 1985-.

[MUR-1000] Westermeyer, Paul. *The Church Musician*. San Francisco:

Harper and Row, 1988. Bib. pp. 119-124, annotated.

[MUR-1010] Whitaker, Beth. *The "Calling" of a Rock Star: A Christian Mother's Story*. Inglewood, Calif.: B. Whitacre/Barren Cross, 1988. Bib. pp. 57-58.

CHAPTER 11

PHOTOGRAPHY

BIBLIOGRAPHIES ON PHOTOGRAPHY

Although once considered primarily a technical craft, photography has, since its birth, steadily gained recognition as an important art form. Beyond shaping the vision of the impressionist painters of the nineteenth century, photography has continued to shape the modern imagination and can be credited with inspiring the cubist movement as well as its more recent counterparts being promoted by David Hockney and others. In addition to conveying information, as in photojournalism, photography has taught people how to see in new ways. Along with its motion picture counterpart, the camera has transformed the modern world into a visually oriented society in which images have become at least as important as words. With the development of digitized cameras offering the capacity to rearrange and enhance photographs, the photographic image has become a medium almost as flexible as a painting and far more efficient for commercial purposes. The difficulty in studying photography in connection with Christianity and the arts is that photography has rarely been interpreted as an expression of religious faith. While some documentary books focus on religious themes, and while many religious organizations wage battles against pornography, little has been written about how photography can express spiritual values and concerns. This lack of material suggests important opportunities for writers seeking new avenues of study in Christianity and the arts.

The bibliographies listed below cover a wide spectrum of topics ranging from the technical to the aesthetic and the ethnic. The most current, general resources for locating books and articles on photography are *The Arts and Photography* [BPH-100], Alexander Davis' *Art Design Photo, 1972-* [BPH-120], Eric Lambrechts' *Photography and Literature: An International Bibliography of Monographs* [BPH-250], Martha Moss's *Photography Books Index: A Subject Guide to Photo Anthologies* [BPH-260] and her *Photography Books Index II* [BPH-270]. One will also do well to consult several other volumes which are somewhat dated but still useful to researchers exploring writings from the middle of the twentieth century, including the following: [BPH-010], [BPH-020], [BPH-030], [BPH-110], [BPH-240], [BPH-300], [BPH-310], and [BPH-340]. For the sake of conducting research of older books on photography, several bibliographies treating early literature have also been included, such as William Burt Gamble's *Color Photography: A List of References in the New York Public Library* [BPH-170], Helmut Gernsheim's *Incunabula of British Photographic Literature: A Bibliography of British Photographic Literature, 1839-75, and British Books Illustrated with Original Photographs* [BPH-180], William Johnson's *Nineteenth-Century Photography: An Annotated Bibliography, 1839-1879* [BPH-220], and Peter E. Palmquist's *A Bibliography of Writings by and About Women in Photography, 1850-1950* [BPH-290].

For resources helping one study the lives of photographers, see Penelope Dixon's *Photographers of the Farm Security Administration: An Annotated Bibliography, 1930-1980* [BPH-130], Gary Edwards' *International Guide to Nineteenth-Century Photographers and Their Works: Based on Catalogues of Auction Houses and Dealers* [BPH-150], Michael Held's, Colin Naylor's, and George Walsh's *Contemporary Photographers* [BPH-190], Colin Naylor's second edition of *Contemporary Photographers* [BPH-280], Robert S. Sennett's *Photography and Photographers to 1900: An Annotated Bibliography* [BPH-350], University of Arizona, Center for Creative Photography's *Researching Photographers* [BPH-360], Deborah Willis-Thomas's *Black Photographers, 1840-1940: An Illustrated Bio-Bibliography* [BPH-400], and her sequel, *An Illustrated Bio-Bibliography of Black Photographers, 1940-1988* [BPH-410]. In this category, also note Palmquist's work [BPH-290] mentioned above. As a support for research of photographers, one will do well to consult bibliographies treating the history of photography, including the following items: [BPH-040], [BPH-050], [BPH-060], [BPH-090], [BPH-210], [BPH-320], and [BPH-330]. Note especially Karen L. Churchill's *Degas and Photography: 'An Annotated Bibliography and List of Published Images* [BPH-090] since it offers a focused study of how photography influenced an important realist painter.

Photography has many applications, one of the most aesthetic and demanding being architectural photography. The following bibliographies are brief but purposeful resources on this subject: Dale E. Casper's *Photography and Architecture: Journal Articles, 1982-1988* [BPH-080], Lamia Doumato's *Architecture and Photography* [BPH-140], Mary A. Vance's *Architectural Photography: A Bibliography* [BPH-370], and Anthony G. White's *Architectural Photography: A Selected Bibliography* [BPH-390]. For bibliographies treating photography and the arts, see items [BPH-100], [BPH-120] (both mentioned above), plus [BPH-230] and [BPH-380]. Also note that [BPH-160], [BPH-200], and [BPH-230] treat resources for using slides, especially in art libraries. For additional bibliographies on photography, consult works listed in Chapter 1.

[BPH-010] Arno Press. *The Literature of Photography*. New York: [Arno] Press, 1974. 18 pp.

[BPH-020] Ars Libri, Ltd. *Photography Books*. Ed. David Stand and Sheppard Ferguson. Catalogue/Ars Libri, Ltd., no. 13. Boston: Ars Libri, Ltd., 1978. 65 pp.

[BPH-030] ------. *Photography, 1839-1975*. Catalogue/Ars Libri, Ltd., no. 8. Boston: Ars Libri, Ltd., 1975. 81 pp.

[BPH-040] Berge, Janet L. *Juvenile Fiction and Photography: A Bibliography*. History of Photography Monograph Series, no. 11. Tempe, Ariz.: School of Art, Arizona State University, 1984. 20 pp.

[BPH-050] Boni, Albert. *Photographic Literature: An International Bibliographic Guide to General and Specialized Literature on Photographic Processes, Techniques, Theory, Chemistry, Physics, Apparatus, Materials and Applications, Industry, History, Biography, Aesthetics*. New York: Morgan and Morgan, 1962. 335 pp.

[BPH-060] ------. *Photographic Literature, 1960-1970: An International Bibliographic Guide.* Hastings-on-Hudson, N.Y.: Morgan and Morgan, 1972. 535 pp.

[BPH-070] Carver, George T. *Photographic Literature.* [Eugene, Oreg.]: School of Journalism, University of Oregon, 1966. 50 pp.

[BPH-080] Casper, Dale E. *Photography and Architecture: Journal Articles, 1982-1988.* Montincello, Ill.: Vance Bibliographies, 1989. 5 pp.

[BPH-090] Churchill, Karen L. *Degas and Photography: An Annotated Bibliography and List of Published Images.* History of Photography Monograph Series, no. 27. Tempe, Ariz.: History of Photography, School of Art, Arizona State University, 1990.

[BPH-100] Collectors' Editions. *The Arts and Photography.* New York: Collectors' Editions, 1984. 28 pp.

[BPH-110] Daum, Timothy. *Photographic Theses and Dissertations, 1942-1972.* [Athens, Ohio]: Duam, 1972. 16 pp.

[BPH-120] Davis, Alexander. *Art Design Photo, 1972-.* 2 vols. Hertfordshire, England; London: Alexander Davis Publications, 1973-. Dist. Idea Books. (Annual bibliography of materials on modern art, graphic design, and photography.)

[BPH-130] Dixon, Penelope. *Photographers of the Farm Security Administration: An Annotated Bibliography, 1930-1980.* New York: Garland Publishing, 1983. 265 pp.

[BPH-140] Doumato, Lamia. *Architecture and Photography.* Monticello, Ill.: Vance Bibliographies, 1987. 12 pp.

[BPH-150] Edwards, Gary. *International Guide to Nineteenth-Century Photographers and Their Works: Based on Catalogues of Auction Houses and Dealers.* Boston: G. K. Hall, 1988. 591 pp.

[BPH-160] Freudenthal, Juan R. *The Slide as a Communication Tool: A Selective Annotated Bibliography.* 2nd rev. ed. Arlington, Va.: Computer Microfilm International Corporation, 1974. 17 pp.

[BPH-170] Gamble, William Burt. *Color Photography: A List of References in the New York Public Library.* New York: [New York City] Library, 1924. 123 pp.

[BPH-180] Gernsheim, Helmut. *Incunabula of British Photographic Literature: A Bibliography of British Photographic Literature, 1839-75, and British Books Illustrated with Original Photographs.*

Berkeley: Scolar Press with Derbyshire College of Higher Education, 1984. 160 pp.

[BPH-190] Held, Michael, Colin Naylor, and George Walsh, eds. *Contemporary Photographers*. New York: St. Martin's Press, 1982. 1,124 pp.

[BPH-200] Hess, Stanley W. *An Annotated Bibliography of Slide Library Literature*. Syracuse, N.Y.: School of Information Studies, Syracuse University, 1978. 47 pp.

[BPH-210] Interlibrum Buchantiquariat. *Sourcebooks in the History of Photography: Theory and Technology of Optics, Light, Colours, Physiology of Colour-Vision: Rare Books from the 16th-19th Centuries*. Vaduz, Lichtenstein: Buchantiquariat Interlibrum, 1988. 197 pp.

[BPH-220] Johnson, William. *Nineteenth-Century Photography: An Annotated Bibliography, 1839-1879*. Boston: G. K. Hall, 1990. 962 pp.

[BPH-230] Kaufman, Peter. *Guide for Art Slide Librarians*. Buffalo: N.p., 1970. 21 pp.

[BPH-240] Kibbey, Ray Anne. *Photography*. 2nd rev. ed. Bibliography Series/Southern Oregon State College Library, vol. 10, no. 3. [Ashland, Oreg.]: Southern Oregon State College Library, 1982. 27 pp.

[BPH-250] Lambrechts, Eric. *Photography and Literature: An International Bibliography of Monographs*. London; New York: Mansell, 1992. 296 pp.

[BPH-260] Moss, Martha. *Photography Books Index: A Subject Guide to Photo Anthologies*. Metuchen, N.J.: Scarecrow Press, 1980. 298 pp.

[BPH-270] ------. *Photography Books Index II*. Metuchen, N.J.: Scarecrow Press, 1985. 276 pp.

[BPH-280] Naylor, Colin, ed. *Contemporary Photographers*. 2nd ed. Chicago: St. James Press, 1988. 1,145 pp. Bibs.

[BPH-290] Palmquist, Peter E. *A Bibliography of Writings by and About Women in Photography, 1850-1950*. Arcata, Calif.: P. E. Palmquist, 1990. 64 pp.

[BPH-300] *Photography*. Modern Art Bibliographical Series, vol. 2. Santa Barbara: Clio Press, 1982. 284 pp.

[BPH-310] *Readers' Guide to Books on Photography*. 3rd ed. [London?]: The Library Asociation, County Libraries Group, 1965. 24 pp.

[BPH-320] Roosens, Laurent. *Books on Photo-History 1*. [Antwerp, Belgium: Provinciaal Museum voor Fotographie Antwerpen, 1990?-].

[BPH-330] ------. *History of Photography: A Bibliography of Books*. New York: Mansell, 1989. 446 pp.

[BPH-340] Saskatchewan Provincial Library, Bibliographic Services. *Photography: A Bibliography*. Regina: N.p., 1973. 28 pp.

[BPH-350] Sennett, Robert S. *Photography and Photographers to 1900: An Annotated Bibliography*. New York: Garland Publishing, 1986. 200 pp.

[BPH-360] University of Arizona, Center for Creative Photography. *Researching Photographers*. Tucson, Ariz.: The Center, 1983. 15 pp.

[BPH-370] Vance, Mary A. *Architectural Photography: A Bibliography*. Architecture Series: Bibliography, 0194-1356, A-418. Monticello, Ill.: Vance Bibliographies, 1981. 5 pp.

[BPH-380] ------. *Artistic Photography: A Bibliography*. Monticello, Ill.: Vance Bibliographies, 1981. 23 pp.

[BPH-390] White, Anthony G. *Architectural Photography: A Selected Bibliography*. Monticello, Ill.: Vance Bibliographies, 1983. 10 pp.

[BPH-400] Willis-Thomas, Deborah. *Black Photographers, 1840-1940: An Illustrated Bio-bibliography*. New York: Garland Publishing, 1985. 141 pp.

[BPH-410] ------. *An Illustrated Bio-Bibliography of Black Photographers, 1940-1988*. New York: Garland Publishing, 1989. Bib. pp. 475-478.

KEY WORKS ON PHOTOGRAPHY

Because photography inevitably involves technical processes, separating its techniques from its aesthetics is very difficult. For example, the work of Ansel Adams set new standards for composition, clarity and definition in black and white photography, essentially redefining the aesthetic potential of this medium, yet his explanations of his work are primarily technical. One must discover Ansel Adams' aesthetic principles in the midst of his mechanical explanations [PHO-010, PHO-020, and PHO-030], especially as connected with his superb photographs. Also note that Ansel Adams' works rarely mention other studies in photography, a pattern all too common in this discipline. For all these reasons, the works listed below do not entirely follow the conventions used in other chapters since doing so does not best facilitate study of this medium which is not often analyzed from a scholarly perspective.

The best works for research in many areas of photography are Eastman Kodak's fourteen volume *Encyclopedia of Practical Photography* [PHO-120], the International Center of Photography's *Encyclopedia of Photography* [PHO-230], Estelle Jussim's *The Eternal Moment: Essays on the Photographic Image* [PHO-240], Max Kozloff's *The Privileged Eye: Essays on Photography* [PHO-260], the eighteen volume *Life Library of Photography* [PHO-290], Barbara London's and John Upton's *Photography: Adapted from the Life Library of Photography* [PHO-300], Luis Nadeau's *Encyclopedia of Printing, Photographic, and Photomechanical Processes* [PHO-330], Bruce Pinkard's *The Photographer's Bible: An Encyclopedia Reference Manual* [PHO-380], Bernard Shaw's collected essays in *Bernard Shaw on Photography* [PHO-470], and Douglas Arthur Spencer's *The Focal Dictionary of Photographic Technologies* [PHO-510]. Three older reference works have been listed below to aid research of photography before 1938, including [PHO-310], [PHO-580], and [PHO-630].

For studying the history of photography, consult the following works: Roy Flukinger's *The Formative Decades: Photography in Great Britain, 1839-1920* [PHO-170], Jonathan Green's *American Photography: A Critical History 1945 to the Present* [PHO-190], Thomas M. Inge's *Handbook of American Popular Culture* [PHO-220], S. Carl King's *The Photographic Impressionists of Spain: A History of the Aesthetics and Technique of Pictorial Photography* [PHO-250], Max Lent's and Tina Lent's *Photography Galleries and Selected Museums: A Survey and International Directory* [PHO-270], Beaumont Newhall's *The Daguerreotype in America* [PHO-340], Christopher Phillips' *Photography in the Modern Era: European Documents and Critical Writings, 1913-1940* [PHO-360], *The Photograph Collectors' Resource Directory* [PHO-370], Floyd Rinhart's and Marion Rinhart's *The American Daguerreotype*

[PHO-400], Richard Rudisill's and Peter E. Palmquist's *Photographers: A Sourcebook for Historical Research* [PHO-420], Martin Sandler's *American Image: 150 Years of Photography* [PHO-430], Grace Seiberling's and Carolyn Bloore's *Amateurs, Photography, and the Mid-Victorian Imagination* [PHO-450], Robert S. Sennett's *The Nineteenth-Century Photographic Press: A Study Guide* [PHO-460], Louis Walton Sipley's *Photography's Great Inventors, Selected by an International Committee for the International Photography Hall of Fame* [PHO-490], Alfred Stieglitz's work in *Alfred Stieglitz* [PHO-520], John Tagg's *Art History, Cultural Politics, and the Discursive Field* [PHO-530], Mike Weaver's *British Photography in the Nineteenth Century: The Fine Art Tradition* [PHO-600], and J. Dustin Wees's and Michael Campbell's *Darkness Visible: The Prints of John Martin* [PHO-610]. For the latest articles on the history of photography, see *History of Photography* [PHO-200].

Other journals which are likely to contain articles of interest to the serious researcher are the following: *Aperture* [PHO-050], *The Archive: Research Series, Center for Creative Photography, University of Arizona* [PHO-060], *Exposure* [PHO-150], *Image* [PHO-210], *Untitled* [PHO-560], and *View Camera: The Journal of Large Format Photography* [PHO-570]. Photography is often linked with the other arts and several of the following works explore this connection, including Sheldan Collins' *How to Photograph Works of Art* [PHO-100], Harvey Edwards' *The Art of Dance* [PHO-130], and John Tagg's *Art History, Cultural Politics, and the Discursive Field* [PHO-530].

The number of works which analyze expressions of the Christian faith in photography are disappointingly few. Most of the works treating Christianity which are listed here are documentary studies presenting religious images but rarely stepping behind the art of photographing. Nonetheless, just as one can discover aesthetic principles in the technical writings of Ansel Adams, so one can find aesthetic concepts operative in works presenting images of faith. However, one must have a well developed sense of aesthetics in the photographic arts as used outside religious circles before one can recognize the aesthetic principles used in these documentary studies. The need for additional research into the theological aesthetics of photography is acute. Those works which will at least provide primary resources for this study include the following: [PHO-080], [PHO-110], [PHO-140], [PHO-180], [PHO-320],

[PHO-350], [PHO-390], [PHO-410], [PHO-440], [PHO-480], [PHO-540], and [PHO-620]. Since much of religious photography involves people, one will also find Keith A. Boas' book, *The Joy of Photographing People* [PHO-090], a helpful resource. Items [PHO-500] and [PHO-590] will also prove useful for those exploring photography for and about children. For additional resources in any of the areas listed above, see the bibliographies in the key works presented below and the bibliographies given in the opening of this chapter.

[PHO-010] Adams, Ansel. *The Camera*. The New Ansel Adams Photography Series, Book 1. Boston: New York Graphic Society, 1980. 203 pp.

[PHO-020] ------. *The Negative*. The New Ansel Adams Photography Series, Book 2. Boston: New York Graphic Society, 1981. 272 pp.

[PHO-030] ------. *The Print*. The New Ansel Adams Photography Series, Book 3. Boston: New York Graphic Society, 1981. 210 pp.

[PHO-040] *American Photography: The Annual of American Editorial, Advertising and Poster, Book, Promotion and Unpublished Photography*. New York: American Photography, 1985-. Annual.

[PHO-050] *Aperture*. New York: Aperture Foundation, 1952-. Quarterly.

[PHO-060] *Archive, The: Research Series, Center for Creative Photography, University of Arizona*. Tucson, Ariz.: Center for Creative Photography, University of Arizona. Semi-annual.

[PHO-070] Bailey, Adrian. *The Illustrated Dictionary of Photography*. New York: Exeter Books, 1987. 192 pp.

[PHO-080] Berlin Photographic Company. *Catalogue of Religious Pictures*. New York: [Berlin Photographic] Co., 1900. 103 pp.

[PHO-090] Boas, Keith A., gen. ed. *The Joy of Photographing People*. N.p.: Eastman Kodak Co. and Addison-Wesley Publishing Co., 1983. Bib. pp. 236-237.

[PHO-100] Collins, Sheldan. *How to Photograph Works of Art*. Nashville: AASLH Press, 1968. Bib. pp. 197-198.

[PHO-110] Curwood, Colin. *Religious Goods, Teas and Refreshments: Ireland's Holy Places*. London: Travelling Light, 1975. 56 pp.

[PHO-120] Eastman Kodak Company, ed. *Encyclopedia of Practical Photog-*

raphy. 14 vols. Garden City, N.Y.: Amphoto, c. 1977-1979. Bib. refs.

[PHO-130] Edwards, Harvey. *The Art of Dance*. Boston: Little, Brown, 1989. 144 pp.

[PHO-140] Engstrom, Barbie. *Faith to See: Reflections and Photographs*. N.p.: Kurios Found, 1979. 64 pp.

[PHO-150] *Exposure*. Boulder, Colo.: Society for Photographic Education, University of Colorado, 1963-. Quarterly.

[PHO-160] Featherstone, David. *Close to Home: Seven Documentary Photographers*. San Francisco: Friends of Photography, 1989. 64 pp.

[PHO-170] Flukinger, Roy. *The Formative Decades: Photography in Great Britain, 1839-1920*. Austin: University of Texas Press, 1985. Bib. pp. 157-160.

[PHO-180] Frith, Francis. *Egypt and the Holy Land in Historic Photographs*. Ed. Jon E. White. Magnolia, Mass.: Peter Smith, [1982].

[PHO-190] Green, Jonathan. *American Photography: A Critical History 1945 to the Present*. New York: Harry N. Abrams, 1984. Bib. pp. 230-237.

[PHO-200] *History of Photography*. London: Taylor and Francis, 1973-. Quarterly.

[PHO-210] *Image*. Rochester, N.Y.: International Museum of Photography, 1952-. Quarterly.

[PHO-220] Inge, M. Thomas, ed. *Handbook of American Popular Culture*. 2 vols. Westport, Conn.: Greenwood Press, 1980.

[PHO-230] International Center of Photography. *Encyclopedia of Photography*. New York: Crown Publishers, 1984. Bib. pp. 600-607.

[PHO-240] Jussim, Estelle. *The Eternal Moment: Essays on the Photographic Image*. New York: Aperture, 1989. Bib. pp. 266-269.

[PHO-250] King, S. Carl. *The Photographic Impressionists of Spain: A History of the Aesthetics and Technique of Pictorial Photography*. Studies in Art and Religious Interpretation, vol. 12. Lewiston, N.Y.: Edwin Mellen Press, 1989. 302 pp. Bib.

[PHO-260] Kozloff, Max. *The Privileged Eye: Essays on Photography*. Albuquerque: University of New Mexico Press, 1987. 307 pp. Bibs.

347

[PHO-270] Lent, Max, and Tina Lent. *Photography Galleries and Selected Museums: A Survey and International Directory.* Venice, Calif.: Garlic Press, 1978. 184 pp. Bib. p. 11.

[PHO-280] Lewis, Steven, James McQuaid, and David Tait. *Photography: Source and Resource: A Source Book for Creative Photography.* [State College, Pa.]: Turnip Press, 1973. Bib. pp. 162-170.

[PHO-290] *Life Library of Photography.* 18 vols. Ed. Time-Life Books. New York: Time-Life Books, 1970-1976. Bibs. Rev. 1981.

[PHO-300] London, Barbara, with John Upton. *Photography: Adapted from the Life Library of Photography.* Glenview, Ill.: Scott, Foresman, 1989. 426 pp. Bib. refs.

[PHO-310] *Modern Encyclopedia of Photography, The: A Standard Work of Reference for Amateur and Professional Photographers.* 2 vols. Ed. S. G. Blaxland, F. J. Mortimer, and Gordon S. Malthouse. Boston: American Photographic Publishing Co., [c. 1938]. Bib. pp. 1,330-1,333.

[PHO-320] Montgomery, Herb, and Mary Montgomery. *Splendor of the Psalms: A Photographic Meditation.* Books to Encourage and Inspire. San Francisco: Harper San Francisco, 1977.

[PHO-330] Nadeau, Luis. *Encyclopedia of Printing, Photographic, and Photomechanical Processes.* 2 vols. New Brunswick, NKC: Atelier Luis Nadeau, 1989-1990. Bib. refs.

[PHO-340] Newhall, Beaumont. *The Daguerreotype in America.* Rev. ed. New York: New York Graphic Society, 1968. Bib. pp. 169-170.

[PHO-350] Nir, Yeshayahu. *The Bible and the Image: The History of Photography in the Holy Land, 1839-1899.* Philadelphia: University of Pennsylvania Press, 1985. 384 pp.

[PHO-360] Phillips, Christopher, ed. *Photography in the Modern Era: European Documents and Critical Writings, 1913-1940.* New York: Metropolitan Museum of Art, Aperture, 1989. Bib. pp. 331-347.

[PHO-370] Photographic Arts Center, The. *The Photograph Collectors' Resource Directory.* New York: [Photographic Arts] Center, 1983-.

[PHO-380] Pinkard, Bruce. *The Photographer's Bible: An Encyclopedia Reference Manual.* N.p.: P-H General Reference and Travel, Arco Test, 1983. 352 pp.

348

[PHO-390] Reilly, C. A., and R. T. Reilly. *Irish Blessing: A Photographic Interpretation.* N.p., England: Pan Books, 1980. 64 pp.

[PHO-400] Rinhart, Floyd, and Marion Rinhart. *The American Daguerreotype.* Athens: University of Georgia Press, 1981. 448 pp. Bib.

[PHO-410] Rubin, Gail, and Michael Graetz. *Psalmist with a Camera: Photographs of a Biblical Safari.* Grantham, England: Grantham Book Services; N.p., U.S.: Abbeville Press, 1979. 116 pp.

[PHO-420] Rudisill, Richard, and Peter E. Palmquist. *Photographers: A Sourcebook for Historical Research.* Brownsville, Calif.: Carl Mautz Pub., 1991. Bib. pp. 52-101.

[PHO-430] Sandler, Martin. *American Image: 150 Years of Photography.* Chicago: Contemporary Books, 1989. 266 pp.

[PHO-440] Schaffer, Ulrich. *Growing into the Blue.* San Francisco: Harper San Francisco, 1984. 96 pp.

[PHO-450] Seiberling, Grace, with Carolyn Bloore. *Amateurs, Photography, and the Mid-Victorian Imagination.* Chicago: University of Chicago Press, 1986. Bib. pp. 177-187.

[PHO-460] Sennett, Robert S. *The Nineteenth-Century Photographic Press: A Study Guide.* New York: Garland Publishing, 1987. Bib.

[PHO-470] Shaw, Bernard. *Bernard Shaw on Photography.* Ed. Bill Jay and Margaret Moore. Salt Lake City: P. Smith Books, 1989. Bib. pp. 137-142.

[PHO-480] Simeone, William E. *The Episcopal Church in Alaska: A Catalog of Photographs from the Archives and Historical Collections of the Episcopal Church.* Alaska Historical Commission Studies in History, no. 19. N.p.: Alaska Historical Commission, 1981. 152 pp.

[PHO-490] Sipley, Louis Walton. *Photography's Great Inventors, Selected by an International Committee for the International Photography Hall of Fame.* Philadelphia: American Museum of Photography, [1965]. 170 pp. Bibs.

[PHO-500] Society of Brothers Staff, eds. *Children in Community: A Photographic Essay.* Rev. ed. N.p.: Plough, 1975. 184 pp.

[PHO-510] Spencer, D[ouglas] A[rthur]. *The Focal Dictionary of Photographic Technologies.* New York: Focal Press, 1973. Bib. pp. 719-725.

[PHO-520] Stieglitz, Alfred. *Alfred Stieglitz*. First Masters of Photography Edition. New York: Aperture Foundation, 1989. Bib. refs. pp. 94-95.

[PHO-530] Tagg, John. *Art History, Cultural Politics, and the Discursive Field*. Minneapolis: University of Minnesota Press, 1992. 288 pp.

[PHO-540] Teiwes, Helga. *Mission San Xacier del Bac: Photographic Essay on the Desert People and Their Church*. Tucson, Ariz.: University of Arizona Press; N.p.: Eurospan, 1973. 32 pp.

[PHO-550] *Two Hundred Ninety-One*. Contemporary Art Series, nos. 1-12. 1916. Reprint. [Salem, N.H.]: Ayer Co. Publications, 1971.

[PHO-560] *Untitled*. San Francisco: Friends of Photography, 1972-. 3/year.

[PHO-570] *View Camera: The Journal of Large Format Photography*. Sacramento: View Camera, 1988-. Bi-monthly.

[PHO-580] Wall, E[dward] J[ohn]. *Wall's Dictionary of Photography: And Reference Book for Amateur and Professional Photographers*. 15th ed. Ed. F. J. Mortimer. Rev. A. L. M. Sowerby. Boston: American Photographic Publishing Co., [1937]. 701 pp. Bib. pp. 70-78.

[PHO-590] Ward, Martha E., and Dorothy A. Marquardt. *Photography in Books for Young People*. Metuchen, N.J.: Scarecrow Press, 1985. 107 pp.

[PHO-600] Weaver, Mike, ed. *British Photography in the Nineteenth Century: The Fine Art Tradition*. New York: Cambridge University Press, 1989. 304 pp. Bib. refs.

[PHO-610] Wees, J. Dustin, and Michael Campbell. *Darkness Visible: The Prints of John Martin*. N.p.: S & F Clark Art, 1986. 88 pp.

[PHO-620] Whitman, Alan. *Christian Occasions: A Photographic Study of Unusual Styles of Religion in American Life*. N.p.: Doubleday, 1979.

[PHO-630] Woodbury, Walter E. *The Encyclopaedic Dictionary of Photography*. 1898. Reprint. New York: Arno Press, 1979. 536 pp. Bib. refs.

CHAPTER 12

VISUAL ARTS I

BIBLIOGRAPHIES ON THE VISUAL ARTS

Of all the chapter headings used in this book, visual arts is the most comprehensive, including thirteen mediums of art in addition to the sections on general theory and religion in the arts. Many of these sections could be subdivided. Lithographs, for example, could be divided from prints and woodcuts, and oil paintings could be divided from frescoes. The following categories, however, are offered as approximate classifications which will inevitably overlap with one another. Because some of the major indexes for the arts are very broad in scope, one will do well to consult works mentioned previously in this volume, such as the New York Public Library's thirty volume *Dictionary Catalog of the Art and Architecture Division* [BAR-470] and its annual supplements in the *Bibliographic Guide to Art and Architecture* [BAR-460]. One will also find that many of the works in Chapter 2 on aesthetics are strongly related to the visual arts and could well be listed below. The works grouped in Chapter 12 and Chapter 13 cover the visual and plastic arts. Only mixed media receives no separate category here since it is in part covered by collage and painting, and since it could--in its widest sense as multimedia--readily involve virtually any combination of the arts, such as music and photography, or posters and dance, thus making this category very difficult to characterize. Beyond consulting Thomas L. Hart's work on *Multi-Media Indexes, Lists, and Review Sources: A Bibliographic Guide* [BVA-310], the many possibilities of mixed media must be left to the artist's and reader's imagination. What one will find in the opening sections of this chapter is a clustering of works which apply to two or more of the visual arts. Specialized bibliographies and key works are given later in specific categories.

For the researcher seeking a reasonably current, single volume bibliography on the visual arts, the following will prove useful during the early stages of study: Brian Allison's *Index of British Studies in Art and Design* [BVA-010], Etta Arntzen's and Robert Rainwater's *Guide to the Literature of Art History* [BVA-040], Christine Bunting's *Reference Tools for Fine Arts Visual Resources Collections* [BVA-160], Donald L. Ehresmann's *Fine Arts: A Bibliographic Guide to Basic Reference Works, Histories, and Handbooks* [BVA-260], Wolfgang M. Freitag's *Art Books: A Basic Bibliography on Artists* [BVA-280], Lois Swan Jones's *Art Information: Research Methods and Resources* [BVA-410], W. Eugene Kleinbauer's and Thomas P. Slavens' *Research Guide to the History of Western Art* [BVA-450], and Elizabeth B. Pollard's *Visual Arts Research: A Handbook* [BVA-570]. To study the works and lives of contemporary artists, see Ann Lee Morgan's *International Contemporary Arts Directory* [BVA-520], and Colin Naylor's *Contemporary Artists* [BVA-530]. For studies involving literature written before 1865 in America, see Janice Gayle Schimmelman's *American Imprints on Art Through 1865: Books and Pamphlets on Drawing, Painting, Sculpture, Aesthetics, Art Criticism, and Instruction: An Annotated Bibliography* [BVA-600].

For extensive research projects, one will need to make use of the many serial bibliographies, directories, and indexes given below. The most prominent of these are *American Art Directory* [BVA-020], *ARTbibliographies Modern* [BVA-050], *Art Books* [BVA-060 to BVA-080], *Art Index* [BVA-100], *Index to Art Periodicals* [BVA-220], *Illustration Index* [BVA-350 to BVA-400], the extensive and readily accessible *RILA: International Repertory of the Literature of Art* [BVA-590], and *Who's Who in American Art* [BVA-670]. The sundry specialized bibliographies given below are included to help augment research into topics such as Canadian native art [BVA-140], design and decorative arts [BVA-030 and BVA-660], east Indian art [BVA-290], folk art

[BVA-150], Latin American art [BVA-120 and BVA-240], and western American artists [BVA-250]. Also note John Castagno's works [BVA-180 and BVA-190] for assistance in the problematic task of identifying enigmatic signatures and monograms. For additional bibliographies, especially those on particular artists, see the works listed in Chapter 1.

[BVA-010] Allison, Brian, ed. *Index of British Studies in Art and Design.* Brookfield, Vt.: Gower Publishing Co., 1986. 688 pp.

[BVA-020] *American Art Directory.* New York: R. R. Bowker, 1952-.

[BVA-030] *Applied and Decorative Arts: A Bibliographic Guide to Basic Reference Works, Histories, and Handbooks.* Littleton: Libraries Unlimited, 1977.

[BVA-040] Arntzen, Etta, and Robert Rainwater. *Guide to the Literature of Art History.* Chicago: American Library Association; London: Art Book, 1980. 616 pp.

[BVA-050] *ARTbibliographies Modern [1969-].* Oxford: Clio, 1969-. 2/year. Formerly *Literature on Modern Art: An Annual Bibliography [1969-1979].*

[BVA-060] *Art Books, 1876-1949.* New York: R. R. Bowker, 1981. 780 pp., annotated.

[BVA-070] *Art Books, 1950-1979.* New York: R. R. Bowker, 1979. 1,500 pp.

[BVA-080] *Art Books, 1980-1984.* New York: R. R. Bowker, 1985.

[BVA-090] *Art Education: A Guide to Information Sources.* Detroit: Gale Research, 1977.

[BVA-100] *Art Index [1929-].* New York: R. R. Bowker, 1930-. Quarterly.

[BVA-110] *Art Reference Books.* New York: New York State College of Ceramics, Publication no. 4, 1950. 70 pp. [1,000].

[BVA-120] Bailey, Joyce Waddell. *Handbook of Latin American Art: A Bibliographic Compilation.* 2 vols. Santa Barbara: ABC-Clio Information Services, 1984.

[BVA-130] Bell, Doris L. *Contemporary Art Trends 1960-1980: A Guide to Sources.* Metuchen, N.J.: Scarecrow Press, 1981. 183 pp.

[BVA-140] Bradley, Ian L. *A Bibliography of Canadian Native Arts: Indian and Eskimo Arts, Craft, Dance and Music.* [Agincourt, Ont.]: GLC Publishers, 1977. 107 pp.

[BVA-150] Bronner, Simon J., ed. *American Folk Art: A Guide to Sources.* New York; London: Garland Publishing, 1984. 313 pp.

[BVA-160] Bunting, Christine, ed. *Reference Tools for Fine Arts Visual Resources Collections.* Tucson, Ariz.: Arts Libraries Society of North America, 1984.

[BVA-170] Carrick, Neville. *How to Find out About the Arts: A Guide to Sources of Information.* New York: Pergamon Press, [1965]. 164 pp.

[BVA-180] Castagno, John. *American Artists: Signatures and Monograms, 1800-1989.* Metuchen, N.J.: Scarecrow Press, 1990. 843 pp.

[BVA-190] ------. *European Artists: Signatures and Monograms, 1800-1990, Including Selected Artists from Other Parts of the World.* Metuchen, N.J.: Scarecrow Press, 1990. 843 pp.

[BVA-200] Cavanagh, Eileen. *Sources of Information on Contemporary Public Art.* [Boston]: Simmons' College, 1975. 18 pp. (Mural Painting, Graffiti, and Municipal Art)

[BVA-210] Chamberlain, Mary W[alls]. *Guide to Art Reference Books.* Chicago: American Library Association: Chicago, 1959. 418 pp. [2,565].

[BVA-220] Chicago Art Institute. Ryerson Library. *Index to Art Periodicals.* 11 vols. Boston: G. K. Hall, 1962. Supplements, 1975-.

[BVA-230] Daly, Peter M., ed. *Index of Emblem Art: Symposium.* Studies in the Emblem Series, no. 6. New York: AMS Press, 1990.

[BVA-240] Davidson, Martha, ed.; Carlota Duarte and Raul Solano Nunez, assoc. eds. *Picture Collections: Mexico: A Guide to Picture Sources in the United Mexican States.* Metuchen, N.J.: Scarecrow Press, 1988. 346 pp.

[BVA-250] Dawdy, Doris Ostrander. *Artists of the American West: A Biographical Dictionary.* 3 vols. Chicago: Sage Books; Chicago: Swallow Press; Athens, Ohio: Swallow Press, 1974-1985. Bib., vol. 1, pp. 261-274; vol. 2, pp. 335-344.

[BVA-260] Ehresmann, Donald L. *Fine Arts: A Bibliographic Guide to Basic Reference Works, Histories, and Handbooks.* 3rd ed. Englewood, Colo.: Libraries Unlimited, 1990. xvii, 373 pp.

[BVA-270] Fehl, Philip P. *A Bibliographical Guide to the Study of the History of Art.* Chapel Hill, N.C.: [University of North Carolina], 1965. 48 pp.

[BVA-280] Freitag, Wolfgang M. *Art Books: A Basic Bibliography on Artists.* Garland Reference Library of the Humanities, vol. 574. New York: Garland Publishing, 1985. xxvii, 351 pp. Bib. pp. xxvii-xxvii.

[BVA-290] Ghose, D. C. *Bibliography of Modern Indian Art.* Lalit Kalaakad: n.p., 1980. 290 pp.

[BVA-300] *Handbook of the S[amuel] P[utman] Avery Collection of Prints and Art Books in the New York Public Library, A.* [New York]: [New York Public Library], 1901. 84 pp. [300].

[BVA-310] Hart, Thomas L., Mary Alice Hunt, and Blanche Woolls. *Multi-Media Indexes, Lists, and Review Sources: A Bibliographic Guide.* New York: Marcel Dekker, 1975. 273 pp.

[BVA-320] Havlice, Patricia P. *Earth Scale Art: A Bibliography, Directory of Artists and Index of Reproductions.* Jefferson, N.C.: McFarland and Co., Inc., 1984. 138 pp.

[BVA-330] ------. *Index to Artistic Biography.* 2 vols. Metuchen, N.J.: Scarecrow Press, 1973. 1,370 pp. Supplement, 1981. 961 pp.

[BVA-340] Held, John, Jr. *Mail Art: An Annotated Bibliography.* Metuchen, N.J.: Scarecrow Press, 1991. 582 pp.

[BVA-350] *Illustration Index I.* Ed. Lucile E. Vance. New York: Scarecrow Press, 1957. 192 pp. Supplement, 1961. 230 pp.

[BVA-360] *Illustration Index II.* Ed. Lucile E. Vance and Esther M. Tracey. New York: Scarecrow Press, 1966. 527 pp.

[BVA-370] *Illustration Index III.* Ed. R. C. Greer. Metuchen, N.J.: Scarecrow Press, 1973. 164 pp.

[BVA-380] *Illustration Index IV.* Ed. Marsha C. Appel. Metuchen, N.J.: Scarecrow Press, 1980. 458 pp.

[BVA-390] *Illustration Index V: 1977-1981.* Ed. Marsha C. Appel. Metuchen, N.J.: Scarecrow Press, 1984. 421 pp.

[BVA-400] *Illustration Index VI: 1982-1986.* Ed. Marsha C. Appel. Metuchen, N.J.: Scarecrow Press, 1988. 541 pp.

[BVA-410] Jones, Lois Swan. *Art Information: Research Methods and Resources.* 3rd ed. Dubuque: Kendall and Hunt Publishing Co., 1990. xxiv, 373 pp. Bib. pp. 107-286.

[BVA-420] Karpel, Bernard, ed. *Arts in America: A Bibliography.* 4 vols. Washington, D.C.: Smithsonian Institution Press for the Archives of American Art, 1979-1980. Vol. 1: Art of the Native Americans, Architecture, Decorative Arts, Design, Sculpture, Art of the West; Vol. 2: Painting and Graphic Arts; Vol. 3: Photography, Film, Theater, Dance, Music, Serials and Periodicals, Dissertations and Theses, Visual Resources; Vol. 4: Index.

[BVA-430] Keaveney, Sydney S. *Contemporary Art Documentation and Fine Arts Libraries.* Metuchen, N.J.: Scarecrow Press, 1986. 181 pp. Bib. pp. 111-119.

[BVA-440] Keen, M. E. *Microfilms in the National Art Library.* London: Victoria and Albert Museum, 1980. 42 pp.

[BVA-450] Kleinbauer, W. Eugene, and Thomas P. Slavens. *Research Guide to the History of Western Art.* Sources of Information in the Humanities, no. 2. Chicago: American Library Association, 1982. 229 pp. Bibs.

[BVA-460] Lekatsas, Barbara. *The Howard L. and Muriel Weingrow Collection of Avant-Garde Art and Literature at Hofstra University: An Annotated Bibliography.* Westport, Conn.: Greenwood Press, 1985. xxv, 322 pp.

[BVA-470] Lerner, Loren R[uth]. *Art and Architecture in Canada: A Bibliography and Guide to the Literature to 1981.* 2 vols. Toronto: University of Toronto Press, 1991. English and French.

[BVA-480] Lindberg, Sten G. *Swedish Books 1280-1967: Illuminated Manuscripts, Illustrated Printed Books and Fine Book Bindings--A Select Guide to Reference Literature on Sweden.* Kungliga Bibliotekets Utstallningskatalog, no. 51. Stockholm: Kungliga Biblioteket, 1968. 111 pp.

[BVA-490] Lucas, Edna Louise. *Art Books: A Basic Bibliography on the Fine Arts.* Greenwich, Conn.: New York Graphic Society, [1968]. 245 pp.

[BVA-500] Mallett, D. T. *Index of Artists, International-Biographical: Including Painters, Sculptors, Illustrators, Engravers and Etchers of the Past and the Present.* New York: R. R. Bowker Co., 1935. Reprint. New York: Peter Smith, 1948. xxxiv, 493 pp. Bib. pp. ix-xxv. Supplement.

[BVA-510] Mitra, Haridas. *Contribution to a Bibliography of Indian Art and Aesthetics.* 2nd ed. Santiniketan: Visva-Bharati Research Publications Co., 1980. 237 pp. Bib. refs. (See [BAE-160])

[BVA-520] Morgan, Ann Lee, ed. *International Contemporary Arts Directory*. New York: St. Martin's Press, 1985. Bib. pp. 371-393, annotated.

[BVA-530] Naylor, Colin, ed. *Contemporary Artists*. 3rd ed. Chicago: St. James Press, 1989. 1,059 pp. Bib. refs.

[BVA-540] Nees, Lawrence. *From Justinian to Charlemagne: European Art, 565-787: An Annotated Bibliography*. Boston: G. K. Hall, 1985. 278 pp.

[BVA-550] Oppelt, Norman T. *Southwestern Pottery: An Annotated Bibliography and List of Types and Wares*. Metuchen, N.J.: Scarecrow Press, 1988. 333 pp.

[BVA-560] Parry, Pamela J. *Contemporary Art and Artists: An Index to Reproductions*. Westport, Conn.: Greenwood Publishing Group, Inc., 1978. 327 pp.

[BVA-570] Pollard, Elizabeth B. *Visual Arts Research: A Handbook*. New York: Greenwood Press, 1986. 165 pp.

[BVA-580] Podszus, Carl O. *Art: A Selected Annotated Art Bibliography*. New York: n.p., 1960. 111 pp. [1,000].

[BVA-590] *RILA: International Repertory of the Literature of Art*. Williamstown: Getty Art History Information Program, 1975-. 2/year.

[BVA-600] Schimmelman, Janice Gayle. *American Imprints on Art Through 1865: Books and Pamphlets on Drawing, Painting, Sculpture, Aesthetics, Art Criticism, and Instruction: An Annotated Bibliography*. Boston: G. K. Hall, 1990. 419 pp.

[BVA-610] Seymour, Nancy N. *An Index-Dictionary of Chinese Artists, Collectors, and Connoisseurs, with Character Identification by Modified Stroke Count--Including over 5,000 Chinese Names and Biographies from the Tang Dynasty through the Modern Period*. Metuchen, N.J.: Scarecrow Press, 1988. 1,004 pp.

[BVA-620] Shipley, Lloyd W., comp. *Information Resources in the Arts: A Directory*. Washington, D.C.: Government Printing Office, 1986.

[BVA-630] Sturgis, Russell, and Henry Edward Krehbiel. *Annotated Bibliography of Fine Arts*. Ed. George Iles. 1897. Reprint. Boston: Longwood Press, 1976.

[BVA-640] Sullivan, Mark W. *The Hudson River School: An Annotated Bibliography*. Metuchen, N.J.: Scarecrow Press, 1991.

231 pp.

[BVA-650] Thompson, Helen (MacPherson). *Manual Arts and Crafts.* San Francisco: Pacific Air Forces, 1965. 188 pp.

[BVA-660] Tinkham, Sandra Shaffer, ed. *Index of American Design: Consolidated Catalog to the Index of American Design.* Cambridge, England: Chadwyck-Healey; Teaneck: Somerset House, 1980. 670 pp. (Architecture to woodcarving.)

[BVA-670] *Who's Who in American Art.* New York: R. R. Bowker, 1935-.

[BVA-680] *Yale University, Art and Architecture Library, Faber Birren Collection of Books on Color: A Bibliography.* New Haven: Yale University Library, 1982. 42 pp.

KEY WORKS ON GENERAL THEORY OF VISUAL ARTS

The books listed below treat two or more of the visual arts and explore the theoretical dimensions of them, including aesthetics. The works in Chapter 2 treating aesthetics approach the arts from a broad perspective, while those listed below typically focus more specifically on the visual arts and the application of aesthetics to them. Nonetheless, some overlap between this section and Chapter 2 is inevitable and one should, therefore, consult both chapters when studying theory of the visual arts. The single best book for analyzing theories behind the visual arts as they are related to the other arts and the flow of middle eastern and western history is William Fleming's *Arts & Ideas* [VAT-340]. Five other volumes of importance in this line of study are Moshe Barasch's recent work, *Modern Theories of Art, 1: From Winckelmann to Baudelaire* [VAT-030], Quentin Bell's *Art* [VAT-060] and *Bad Art* [VAT-070], Francis Edward Sparshott's *Theory of the Arts* [VAT-1100], and Warren E. Steinkraus' *Philosophy of Art* [VAT-1110]. For more specialized studies of art theory, see items [VAT-010], [VAT-110], [VAT-230], [VAT-350], [VAT-370], [VAT-420], [VAT-440], [VAT-450], [VAT-540], [VAT-580], [VAT-620], [VAT-630], [VAT-830], [VAT-870], [VAT-1020], [VAT-1030], [VAT-1050], [VAT-1180], [VAT-1190], [VAT-1250], and [VAT-1260].

Because art studies often involve using technical terminology which can confuse all but the most proficient, several reference tools will prove particularly helpful to nearly all students of art. Hans Biedermann's recent work, *Dictionary of Symbolism: Cultural Icons and the Meanings Behind Them* [VAT-080], is excellent for helping one identify obscure symbols and their origin. Also see Jaynie Anderson's *The Eloquence of Symbols: Studies in Humanist Art* [VAT-020], Jean C. Cooper's *An Illustrated Encyclopedia of Traditional Symbols* [VAT-220], and James Hall's *Dictionary of Subjects and Symbols in Art* [VAT-460]. One additional reference work which will be useful for newcomers to the study of art is Thomasine Kimbrough Kushner's *The Anatomy of Art: Problems in the Description and Evaluation of Works of Art* [VAT-590].

The most popular and substantial single volume anthologies treating the arts are Horst Woldermar Janson's *History of Art* [VAT-520], sometimes used as the authoritative text for organizing art libraries, and Horst de la Croix's and Richard G. Tansey's *Gardner's Art Through the Ages* [VAT-600], which also includes a large section on non-western arts. Also consider two recent encyclopedias, Hohn J. Norwich's *Oxford Illustrated Encyclopedia, Vol. 5: The Arts* [VAT-780], and M. Rugoff's *Britannica Encyclopedia of America Art* [VAT-1000]. For more extensive study of the arts, see the fifteen volume *Encyclopedia of World Art* [VAT-310] with its several supplements. One will also find considerable help in the various Oxford companions to art, including [VAT-800], [VAT-810], and [VAT-820], and in Kenneth McLeish's *Penguin Companion to the Arts in the Twentieth Century* [VAT-690], John Fleming's and Hugh Honour's *The Penguin Dictionary of Decorative Arts* [VAT-330], and the still growing series, *The Pelican History of Art* [VAT-890].

For specialized studies in art history, one can choose from nearly sixty additional texts given here. The titles of most of these texts are self explanatory, but the following categories of art studies will be of special interest to researchers: African [VAT-1180]; American [VAT-120], [VAT-720], [VAT-920], [VAT-1000], [VAT-1200]; avant garde [VAT-560], [VAT-790]; British [VAT-150], [VAT-190], [VAT-860], [VAT-870], [VAT-1120]; collaborative [VAT-670]; cubist [VAT-410]; east Asian [VAT-1060]; European [VAT-300], [VAT-470], [VAT-1080], [VAT-1090]; fantastic [VAT-570]; folk [VAT-1010]; French [VAT-040], [VAT-130], [VAT-160], [VAT-170], [VAT-260]; general [VAT-240], [VAT-750], [VAT-780], [VAT-930], [VAT-1160]; German [VAT-

1150], [VAT-1220]; Greek [VAT-970]; Italian [VAT-490]; Japanese [VAT-640]; jewelry [VAT-1140]; literature and visual arts [VAT-980], [VAT-990]; Modern [VAT-840]; Persian [VAT-320]; popular [VAT-270]; Primitive [VAT-390], [VAT-950]; Roman [VAT-500]; Russian [VAT-090]; Symbolist [VAT-650]; Victorian [VAT-150], [VAT-290]; women's studies [VAT-150], [VAT-760], [VAT-900], [VAT-940]; western [VAT-550], [VAT-1230]; world [VAT-700], [VAT-1040].

One of the most serious challenges facing Christians seeking to work in the visual arts is the use of the human body, especially in the nude form. This issue is problematic not only in the visual arts, but also in dance, drama, photography, television and video, and even the literary arts as they describe the body. Finding a balance point between, on the one hand, appreciating the body as being pure and beautiful because it in some sense bears the *imago Dei*, and, on the other hand, respecting the privacy and sacredness of the body because it houses a unique and precious person is not easy in a world prone to sacrilegious treatment of both God and sexuality. Probably the greater part of the discomfort of Christians and others with the use of the body in art stems from an incomplete view of the body, a view lacking the ancient Hebraic insights into the body as being one with the soul. Although the following studies do not often address theological concerns connected with nudity in art, they do offer instructive studies which will prove helpful for those seeking to formulate their own theology of the body in art. Some of the best, serious studies of this subject are Kenneth M. Clark's now classic study, *The Nude: A Study in Ideal Form* [VAT-210], Virginius De Saltinbene's *Thoughts in Contemplation of the Feminine Nude in the Realm of Art* [VAT-280], Michael Gill's *Image of the Body: Aspects of the Nude* [VAT-360], Edward Lucie-Smith's *The Body: Images of the Nude in Art* [VAT-660], Pavel Machotka's *The Nude: Perception and Personality* [VAT-680], Rudolph Parravicini's *The Most Famous Nudes Painted by the Greatest Italian Masters of the Renaissance* [VAT-850], Morse Peckham's *Art and Pornography: An Experiment in Explanation* [VAT-880], Amy Richlin's *Pornography and Representation in Greece and Rome* [VAT-960], Marina Warner's *Monuments and Maidens: The Allegory of the Female Form* [VAT-1210], and Ruth Karola Westheimer's *The Art of Arousal* [VAT-1240]. For additional studies in any of the above categories, see the bibliographies listed in the opening of this chapter.

[VAT-010] Aagaard-Mogensen, Lars, ed. *The Idea of the Museum: Philosophical, Artistic, and Political Questions.* Lewiston, N.Y.: Edwin Mellen Press, 1989. 248 pp.

[VAT-020] Anderson, Jaynie, ed. *The Eloquence of Symbols: Studies in Humanist Art.* New York: Oxford University Press; Oxford: Clarendon Press, 1983. xxxvi and 135 pp. Bibs. on art historian Edgar Wind.

[VAT-030] Barasch, Moshe. *Modern Theories of Art, 1: From Winckelmann to Baudelaire.* New York: New York University Press, 1990. 420 pp. Bib. refs.

[VAT-040] Baudelaire, Charles. *Art in Paris: 1845-1862: Salons and Exhibitions.* Trans. and ed. Jonathan Mayne. London: Phaidon Press, 1965. Bib. pp. xiii-xiv. 241 pp.

[VAT-050] Beaney, Jan, Audrey Brockbank, and Alan Wysman. *Buildings in Picture, Collage and Design.* London: Pelham, 1976. Bib. p. 48.

[VAT-060] Bell, Quentin. *Art.* 1949. Reprint. Oxford; New York: Oxford University Press, 1987.

[VAT-070] ------. *Bad Art.* Chicago: University of Chicago Press, 1989. Bib. pp. 232-237.

[VAT-080] Biedermann, Hans. *Dictionary of Symbolism: Cultural Icons and the Meanings Behind Them.* Trans. James Hulbert. New York: Facts on File, 1992. 465 pp. Bib. pp. 397-400.

[VAT-090] Bowlt, John E. *A New Spirit: Explorations in Early 20th Century Russian Art: Andreenko, Bogomazov, Chashnik, Khidekel, Kliun, Kogan, Larionov, Sofronova, Suetin.* New York: Barry Friedman, Ltd., 1987. Bib. p. 44.

[VAT-100] Brincard, Marie-Therese. *Beauty by Design: The Aesthetics of African Adornment: The African-American Institute, New York, September 19, 1984--January 5, 1985, Center for the Fine Arts, Miami, February 2, 1985--March 17, 1985.* Trans. Thomas Repensek. New York: The Institute, 1984. 136 pp. Bibs.

[VAT-110] Buettner, Stewart. *American Art Theory, 1945-1970.* Studies in Fine Arts. Art Theory, no. 1. Ann Arbor, Mich.: University Microfilms, International, 1981. Bib. pp. 187-203.

362

[VAT-120] Burke, Doreen Golger, et al. *In Pursuit of Beauty: Americans and the Aesthetic Movement.* New York: Metropolitan Museum of Art, Rizzoli International Publications, 1986. Bib. pp. 488-502.

[VAT-130] Caisse nationale des Monuments historiques et des Sites (France). *Fine and Decorative Arts in France.* 8 vols. London: Mindata, 1984. 1,014 microfiches.

[VAT-140] Calas, Nicolas, and Elena Calas. *Icons and Images of the Sixties.* New York: E. P. Dutton and Co., 1971. Bib. refs. in footnotes. 347 pp.

[VAT-150] Casteras, Susan P. *Images of Victorian Womanhood in English Art.* Rutherford, [N.J.]: Fairleigh Dickinson University Press; London; Cranbury, N.J.: Associated University Presses, 1987. Bib. pp. 186-189.

[VAT-160] Cate, Phillip Dennis. *The Graphic Arts and French Society, 1871-1914.* New Brunswick, [N.J.]: Rutgers University Press, Jane Voorhees Zimmerli Art Museum, 1988. Bib. pp. 185-187.

[VAT-170] Caws, Mary Ann, and Rudolf E. Kuenzli. *Duchamp Centennial.* Dada Surrealism, no. 16. Iowa City: University of Iowa, 1987. 256 pp. Bib.

[VAT-180] Chaet, Bernard. *The Art of Drawing.* New York: Holt, Rinehart and Winston, 1970. 288 pp.

[VAT-190] Cheney, Liana De Girolami, ed. *Pre-Raphaelitism and Medievalism in the Arts.* Lewiston, N.Y.: Edwin Mellen Press, 1993. 328 pp.

[VAT-200] Chilvers, Ian, ed. *The Concise Dictionary of Art and Artists.* New York: Oxford University Press, 1990. 517 pp.

[VAT-210] Clark, Kenneth M. *The Nude: A Study in Ideal Form.* Bollingen Series, no. 35. Princeton: Princeton University Press, 1972. 458 pp. Bib. pp. 415-421.

[VAT-220] Cooper, J[ean] C. *An Illustrated Encyclopedia of Traditional Symbols.* London: Thames and Hudson, 1978. Bib. pp. 203-207.

[VAT-230] Coote, Jeremy, and Anthony Shelton. *Anthropology, Art and Aesthetics.* Oxford: Clarendon Press; New York: Oxford University Press, 1992. 281 pp. Bib. refs.

[VAT-240] Copplestone, Trewin, ed. *Art in Society: A Guide to the Visual*

Arts. Englewood Cliffs, N.J.: Prentice-Hall Press, 1984. 384 pp. Bib. p. 6.

[VAT-250] Courtney, Richard. *The Quest: Research and Inquiry in Arts Education.* Lanham, Md.: University Press of America, 1987. Bib. pp. 113-124.

[VAT-260] Dayot, Armand Pierre Marie. *The Salon of 1890: One Hundred Plates in Photogravure and Etchings by Goupil and Co.* * Boston: Estes and Lauriat, [1890]. 104 pp.

[VAT-270] Deer, Irving, comp. *The Popular Arts: A Critical Reader.* New York: Charles Scribner's Sons, 1967. Bib. pp. 351-356. (Art, Cinema, Comedy, Literature, Music, Tragedy, TV, Pornography.)

[VAT-280] De Saltinbene, Virginius. *Thoughts in Contemplation of the Feminine Nude in the Realm of Art.* Albuquerque: American Classical College Press, 1984. 117 pp.

[VAT-290] Denvir, Bernard. *The Late Victorians: Art, Design, and Society, 1852-1910.* London; New York: Longman, 1986. 269 pp. Bib. refs. Biographical index, pp. 249-263.

[VAT-300] Dickens, A. G. *Reformation and Society in Sixteenth-Century Europe.* New York: Harcourt, Brace, and World, 1966.

[VAT-310] *Encyclopedia of World Art.* 15 vols. Palatine, Ill.: Publishers Guild, 1959-1968. Supplements, New York: McGraw-Hill, 1983 and 1987.

[VAT-320] Ferrier, R[onald] W., ed. *The Arts of Persia.* New Haven: Yale University Press, 1989. Bib. pp. 315-331.

[VAT-330] Fleming, John, and Hugh Honour. *The Penguin Dictionary of Decorative Arts.* New ed. New York: Viking, 1989. 935 pp.

[VAT-340] Fleming, William. *Arts & Ideas.* 8th ed. New York: Holt, Rinehart and Winston, 1991. 642 pp.

[VAT-350] Frascina, Francis, and Jonathan Harris. *Art in Modern Culture: An Anthology of Critical Texts.* Icon Editions. New York: Harper Collins, 1992. 341 pp. Bib. refs.

[VAT-360] Gill, Michael. *Image of the Body: Aspects of the Nude.* New York: Doubleday, 1989. 476 pp. Bib. pp. 441-450.

[VAT-370] Glusberg, Jorge. *Rhetoric of Art.* Milan, Italy: Giancarlo Politi Editore, 1986. Bib. pp. 92-93.

364

[VAT-380] Goldman, Bernard. *Reading and Writing in the Arts: A Handbook*. Detroit: Wayne State University Press, 1972. 163 pp.

[VAT-390] Goldwater, Robert. *Primitivism in Modern Art*. Rev. ed. New York: Vintage Books, 1967. Bib. refs. in notes. 289 pp.

[VAT-400] Gombrich, E. H. *The Story of Art*. 15th ed. Englewood Cliffs, N.J.: Prentice-Hall Press, 1990. Bib. pp. 510-518.

[VAT-410] Green, Christopher. *Cubism and Its Enemies: Modern Movements and Reaction in French Art, 1916-1928*. New Haven: Yale University Press, 1987. Bib. pp. 301-320.

[VAT-420] Grieder, Terence. *Artist and Audience*. Fort Worth: Holt, Rinehart and Winston, 1990. Bib. refs. in notes. 480 pp.

[VAT-430] Grim, William, ed. *A Yearbook of Interdisciplinary Studies in the Fine Arts*. Lewiston, N.Y.: Edwin Mellen Press, 19--. Annual.

[VAT-440] Ground, Ian. *Art or Bunk?* New York: St. Martin's Press, 1989. Bib. pp. 145-146.

[VAT-450] Hale, Nathan Cabot. *Abstraction in Art and Nature*. New York: Watson-Guptill Publications, 1972. Reprint. New York: Dover Publications, 1993. Bib. refs. p. 273.

[VAT-460] Hall, James. *Dictionary of Subjects and Symbols in Art*. 2nd ed. New York: Harper and Row, 1979. 349 pp. Bib. pp. xxv-xxix.

[VAT-470] Hamilton, George Heard. *Painting and Sculpture in Europe 1880-1940*. New York: Penguin Books, 1981. Bib. pp. 550-581.

[VAT-480] Hardin, James N., and American Folklife Center. *Folklife Annual 90: A Publication of the American Folklife Center at the Library of Congress*. Washington, D.C.: Library of Congress, 1991. 176 pp. Bib. refs.

[VAT-490] Hartt, Frederich. *History of Italian Renaissance Art*. 4th ed. Englewood Cliff, N.J.: Prentice-Hall Press; New York: Harry N. Abrams, 1993. Bib. refs.

[VAT-500] Heintze, Helga Freifrau von. *Roman Art*. New York: Universe Books, 1990. Bib. refs. pp. 193-195.

[VAT-510] *J. Paul Getty Museum Journal*. Santa Monica, Calif.: J. Paul Getty Museum, 1974-. Annual.

[VAT-520] Janson, H[orst] W[oldemar]. *History of Art*. 4th ed. Rev. Anthony F. Janson. Englewood Cliffs, N.J.: Prentice-Hall Press, 1991. Bib. pp. 820-826.

[VAT-530] Jarnow, Jill. *(Re)do it Yourself: A Guide to Decoration and Renovation with Stencil, Folk Art Painting, Decoupage, Collage, and Mosaic.* New York: Dial Press, 1977. Bib. pp. 171-172.

[VAT-540] Kaelin, Eugene Francis. *An Aesthetics for Art Educators.* New York: Teachers College Press, 1989. Bib. pp. 217-222.

[VAT-550] Kleinbauer, W. Eugene, ed. *Modern Perspectives in Western Art History: An Anthology of Twentieth-Century Writings on the Visual Arts.* Toronto: University of Toronto Press with Medieval Academy of America, 1989. 528 pp.

[VAT-560] Kostelanetz, Richard. *The Dictionary of the Avant-Gardes.* Pennington, N.J.: A Cappella Books, 1993. Bib. refs.

[VAT-570] Krichbaum, Jorg, and Rein Zondergeld. *Dictionary of Fantastic Art.* Trans. Donna Pedini Simpson. Woodbury, N.Y.: Barron's, 1985. Bib.

[VAT-580] Kuchler, Susanne, and Walter S. Melion, eds. *Images of Memory: On Remembering and Representation.* Washington, D.C.: Smithsonian Institution Press, 1991. Bib. refs. pp. 247-257.

[VAT-590] Kushner, Thomasine Kimbrough. *The Anatomy of Art: Problems in the Description and Evaluation of Works of Art.* St. Louis: W. H. Green, 1983. 181 pp. Bib. refs.

[VAT-600] la Croix, Horst de, and Richard G. Tansey. *Gardner's Art Through the Ages.* 8th ed. San Diego: Harcourt Brace Jovanovich, 1986. Bib. pp. 984-991.

[VAT-610] Land, Norman. *The Viewer as Poet: The Renaissance Response to Art.* University Park, Pa.: Pennsylvania State University Press, 1994. Bib. refs.

[VAT-620] Lang, Berel, ed. *The Death of Art.* Art and Philosophy, vol. 2. New York: Haven, 1984. 275 pp. Bibs.

[VAT-630] Layton, Robert. *The Anthropology of Art.* 2nd ed. Cambridge: Cambridge University Press, 1991.

[VAT-640] Link, Howard A., and Sanna Saks Deutsch. *The Feminine Image: Women of Japan.* Exhibition, Honolulu Academy of Arts, fall 1985. [Honolulu, Hawaii]: Honolulu Academy of Arts, 1985. Bib. pp. 144-146.

366

[VAT-650] Lucie-Smith, Edward. *Symbolist Art*. New York: Oxford University Press; New York: Frederick A. Praeger Publishers, 1972. Bib. p. 209.

[VAT-660] ------. *The Body: Images of the Nude in Art*. London: Thames and Hudson, 1981. 176 pp.

[VAT-670] McCabe, Cynthia Jaffee. *Artistic Collaboration in the Twentieth Century*. Washington, D.C.: Smithsonian Institution Press, 1984. Bib. pp. 217-224.

[VAT-680] Machotka, Pavel. *The Nude: Perception and Personality*. New York: Irvington Publications, 1982. 352 pp.

[VAT-690] McLeish, Kenneth. *Penguin Companion to the Arts in the Twentieth Century*. New York: Penguin, 1986. 608 pp.

[VAT-700] Marks, Claude. *World Artists, 1950-1980*. New York: H. W. Wilson, 1984.

[VAT-710] Mayer, Ralph. *The Artist's Handbook of Materials and Techniques*. 5th ed. New York: Viking, 1991. 761 pp. Bib. pp. 675-711.

[VAT-720] Mendelowitz, Daniel M. *A History of American Art*. 2nd ed. New York: Holt, Rinehart and Winston, 1970. Bib. pp. 510-512.

[VAT-730] *Metropolitan Museum Journal*. New York: Metropolitan Museum of Art, 1968-. Annual.

[VAT-740] *Metropolitan Museum of Art. Bulletin*. New York: Metropolitan Museum of Art, 1942-. Quarterly.

[VAT-750] Myers, Bernard S., ed. *McGraw-Hill Dictionary of Art*. 5 vols. New York: McGraw, 1969. [15,000]

[VAT-760] Navaretta, Cynthia. *Guide to Women's Art Organizations: Groups, Activities, Networks, Publications: Painting, Sculpture, Drawing, Photography, Architecture, Design, Film and Video, Dance, Music, Theatre, Writing, with a Bibliography and Resource List*. New York: Midmarch Associates, 1979. Bib. pp. 65-76.

[VAT-770] Newman, Jay Hartley. *Wire Art: Metals, Techniques, Sculpture, Collage, Jewelry, Mixed Media*. New York: Crown Publishers, 1975. Bib. p. 239.

[VAT-780] Norwich, Hohn J., ed. *Oxford Illustrated Encyclopedia, Vol. 5: The Arts*. New York: Oxford University Press, 1990. 512 pp.

367

[VAT-790] Olson, Arlene R[ita]. *Art Critics and the Avant-Garde, New York, 1900-1913*. Studies in the Fine Arts. Criticism, no. 3. Ann Arbor, Mich.: UMI Research Press, 1980. Bib. pp. 109-115.

[VAT-800] Osborne, Harold, ed. *Oxford Companion to Art*. New York: Oxford University Press, 1970. Bib. pp. 1232-1277.

[VAT-810] ------, ed. *Oxford Companion to the Decorative Arts*. New York: Oxford University Press, 1985. 865 pp.

[VAT-820] ------, ed. *Oxford Companion to Twentieth-Century Art*. New York: Oxford University Press, 1988. 800 pp.

[VAT-830] Otten, Charlotte M., ed. *Anthropology and Art: Readings in Cross-Cultural Aesthetics*. Garden City, N.Y.: National History Press, 1971. Reprint. Austin: University of Texas Press, 1990. 440 pp. Bib. refs.

[VAT-840] Ozenfant, Amedee. *Foundations of Modern Art*. Trans. John Rodker. New York: Dover Publications, [1952]. 348 pp.

[VAT-850] Parravicini, Rudolph. *The Most Famous Nudes Painted by the Greatest Italian Masters of the Renaissance*. The Art Library of the Great Masters of History. Albuquerque: American Classical College Press, 1983. 122 pp.

[VAT-860] Parry, Graham. *The Golden Age Restor'd: The Culture of the Stuart Court, 1603-42*. Manchester: Manchester University Press; New York: St. Martin's Press, 1981. 276 pp. Bib. (All arts.)

[VAT-870] Paulson, Ronald. *Breaking and Remaking: Aesthetic Practice in England, 1700-1820*. New Brunswick: Rutgers University Press, 1989. Bib. pp. 3331-356.

[VAT-880] Peckham, Morse. *Art and Pornography: An Experiment in Explanation*. Sex and Society Series. New York: Harper and Row, [1971]. 306 pp.

[VAT-890] *Pelican History of Art, The*. Projected 50 vols. East Rutherford: Penguin, 1953-.

[VAT-900] Petteys, Chris, with Hazel Gustow, Ferris Olin, and Verna Ritchie. *Dictionary of Women Artists: An International Dictionary of Women Artists Born Before 1900*. Boston: G. K. Hall, 1985. Bib. pp. 781-851.

[VAT-910] Piccolomini, Manfredi. *Changing Modes of Originality in Art*. Wakefield, N.H.: Longwood Academic, 1991. Reprint. Wakefield, N.H.: Hollowbrook Publishing, 1992. Bib. refs.

pp. 181-192.

[VAT-920] Pincus-Witten, Robert. *Postminimalism into Maximalism: American Art, 1966-1986.* Studies in the Fine Arts. Criticism, no. 22. Ann Arbor, Mich.: UMI Research Press, 1987. 429 pp. Bibs.

[VAT-930] Piper, David, ed. *The Random House Library of Painting and Sculpture.* 4 vols. New York: Beazley; Random House, 1981.

[VAT-940] Prather-Moses, Alice Irma. *The International Dictionary of Women Workers in the Decorative Arts: A Historical Survey from the Distant Past to the Early Decades of the Twentieth Century.* Metuchen, N.J.: Scarecrow Press, 1981. 218 pp.

[VAT-950] Price, Sally. *Primitive Art in Civilized Places.* Chicago: University of Chicago Press, 1989. Bib. pp. 137-145.

[VAT-960] Richlin, Amy, ed. *Pornography and Representation in Greece and Rome.* New York: Oxford University Press, 1992. Bib. refs. pp. 285-311.

[VAT-970] Richter, Gisela Marie Augusta. *A Handbook of Greek Art: Architecture, Sculpture, Gems, Coins, Jewelry, Metalwork, Pottery and Vase Painting, Glass, Furniture, Textiles, Paintings and Mosaics.* 4th ed., rev. [London]: Phaidon Publishers, 1965. Dist. New York Graphic Society. 424 pp. Bib. pp. 389-401.

[VAT-980] Roston, Murray. *Changing Perspectives in Literature and the Visual Arts, 1650-1820.* Princeton: Princeton University Press, 1993. 469 pp. 123 illus.

[VAT-990] ------. *Renaissance Perspectives in Literature and the Visual Arts.* Princeton: Princeton University Press, 1987. 448 pp. 80 illus.

[VAT-1000] Rugoff, M., ed. *Britannica Encyclopedia of America Art.* Chicago: Encyclopedia Britannica, 1973.

[VAT-1010] Rumford, Beatrix T., and Carolyn J. Weekley. *Treasures of American Folk Art: From the Folk Art Center at Colonial Williamsburg.* Boston: Little, Brown, with Colonial Williamsburg Foundation, 1989. Bib. pp. 220-221.

[VAT-1020] Ruskin, John. *The Lamp of Beauty: Writings on Art.* Ed. Joan Evans. London: Phaidon Press, [1959]. 342 pp.

[VAT-1030] Russell, John. *The Meanings of Modern Art.* New York: Museum of Modern Art, New York, and Harper and Row, 1981.

Bib. pp. 406-416.

[VAT-1040] Russell, Stella Pandell. *Art in the World*. 3rd ed. Fort Worth: Holt, Rinehart and Winston, 1989. Bib. pp. 446-450.

[VAT-1050] Schwarz, Ira P. *Arts and Humanity: An Introduction to Applied Aesthetics: A Basic Text and Source Book*. Danville, Ill.: Interstate Printers and Publishers, 1986. Bib. pp. 478-492.

[VAT-1060] Scott, Rosemary E., Graham Hutt, and William Watson. *Style in the East Asian Tradition*. London: School of Oriental and African Studies, University of London, 1987. 227 pp. Bibs.

[VAT-1070] Smith, Ralph Alexander. *The Sense of Art: A Study in Aesthetic Education*. New York: Routledge, 1989. Bib. pp. 253-274.

[VAT-1080] Snyder, James. *Medieval Art: Painting, Sculpture, Architecture: 4th-14th Century*. New York: Harry N. Abrams, 1989. Bib. pp. 487-493.

[VAT-1090] ------. *Northern Renaissance Art: Painting, Sculpture, Architecture from 1350-1575*. Englewood Cliffs, N.J.: Prentice-Hall Press, 1985. Bib. pp. 534-537.

[VAT-1100] Sparshott, Francis Edward. *Theory of the Arts*. Princeton: Princeton University Press, 1982. Bib. pp. 685-671.

[VAT-1110] Steinkraus, Warren E. *Philosophy of Art*. Rev. ed. Lanham, Md.: University Press of America, 1984. Bib. pp. 233-238.

[VAT-1120] Sutherland, Guilland, ed. *British Art, 1740-1820: Essays in Honor of Robert R. Wark*. San Marino, Calif.: Huntington Library, 1992. 239 pp. Bib. refs.

[VAT-1130] Sypher, Wylie. *Rococo to Cubism in Art and Literature: Transformations in Style, in Art and Literature from the 18th to the 20th Century*. New York: Vintage Books, 1960. Bib. pp. 337-342.

[VAT-1140] Tait, Hugh, ed. *Jewelry, 7,000 Years: An International History and Illustrated Survey from the Collections of the British Museum*. New York: Harry N. Abrams, 1991. Bib. p. 251.

[VAT-1150] Taylor, Brandon, and Wilfried van der Will. *The Nazification of Art: Art, Design, Music, Architecture, and Film in the Third Reich*. Winchester, Hampshire: Winchester Press, Winchester School of Art, 1990. Bib. refs. pp. 265-272.

[VAT-1160] *Time-Life Library of Art*. c. 31 vols. New York: Time-Life Books, 1966-1977. Bibs.

370

[VAT-1170]   Urdang, Laurence, ed. *Fine and Applied Arts Terms Index.*
             Detroit: Gale Research, 1983.

[VAT-1180]   Van Damme, Wilfried. *A Comparative Analysis Concerning
             Beauty and Ugliness in Sub-Saharan African.* Africana
             Gandensia, no. 4. Ghent: Rijksuniversiteit, 1987. Bib. refs.
             pp. 81-97.

[VAT-1190]   Varnedoe, Kirk, and Adam Gopnik. *High and Low: Modern Art
             and Popular Culture.* New York: Museum of Modern Art,
             New York, 1991. Bib. pp. 429-449, comp. Matthew Arm-
             strong and Fereshteh Daftari.

[VAT-1200]   Vermeule, Cornelius Clarkson. *Philatelic Art in America: Aes-
             thetics of the United States Postage and Revenue Stamps.*
             Weston, Mass.: Cardinal Spellman Philatelic Museum,
             1987. 145 pp. Bib. refs.

[VAT-1210]   Warner, Marina. *Monuments and Maidens: The Allegory of the
             Female Form.* London: Pan Books, 1985. Bib. pp. 377-400.

[VAT-1220]   Weinstein, Joan. *The End of Expressionism: Art and the Novem-
             ber Revolution in Germany, 1918-19.* Chicago: University of
             Chicago Press, 1990. Bib. pp. 307-323.

[VAT-1230]   Weisberg, Gabriel P. *Beyond Impressionism: The Naturalist
             Impulse.* New York: Harry N. Abrams, 1992. Bib. pp. 290-
             294.

[VAT-1240]   Westheimer, Ruth K[arola]. *The Art of Arousal.* New York:
             Abbeville Press, 1993. 180 pp.

[VAT-1250]   Weyl, Hermann. *Symmetry.* Princeton Science Library. 1980.
             Reprint. Princeton: Princeton University Press, 1989. 168
             pp. Bib. refs.

[VAT-1260]   Wind, Edgar. *Art and Anarchy.* 3rd ed. London: Duckworth,
             1985. 160 pp.

KEY WORKS ON THEORY OF VISUAL ARTS AND RELIGION

The revival of the arts in the church has gradually engendered a resurgence of studies about them. While fine studies have been written throughout
the twentieth century, the number of them has increased dramatically during
the past twenty years. Unfortunately, bibliographies have rarely kept pace
with this growth in religious art studies. The two bibliographies listed below

are the only ones which could be found of this variety, and they are both somewhat limited in scope. Linda B. Parshall's and Peter W. Parshall's work, *Art and the Reformation: An Annotated Bibliography* [VAR-010], is very useful, but covers just one phase of Christian history and the arts. Diane Peters' volume, *Christianity and the Visual Arts: A Bibliography* [VAR-020], is nicely focused, but relatively small and brief in scope since it is based on the holdings of only one university's library. Most of the bibliographies which will aid one in research of Christianity and the arts must be found within sundry studies of the arts, like those listed below. This initial section contains studies which treat two or more of the arts and religion. Religious studies focusing on one of the arts will be found in the pertinent sections given later.

Readers will do well to start religion and arts studies with Jane Dillenberger's *Style and Content in Christian Art* [VAR-360] because of her finesse in explaining the intricacies of art studies in lucid terms. Along with this volume, readers will also do well to explore several collections of essays, including Doug Adams' and Diane Apostolos-Cappadona's *Art as Religious Studies* [VAR-050], and Diane Apostolos-Cappadona's earlier anthology, *Art, Creativity, and the Sacred* [VAR-070], both of which contain excellent essays and solid bibliographical references. Nearly all of the authors whose works are contained in these anthologies have written a wide variety of other essays and books which are also well worth reading.

Since religious art typically includes complex symbolism, one will do well to consult any of several handbooks on this subject, the two best works being George Ferguson's *Signs and Symbols in Christian Art* [VAR-450], especially in its initial large format, and F. R. Webber's older but still irreplaceable volume, *Church Symbolism: An Explanation of the more Important Symbols of the Old and New Testament, The Primitive, The Mediaeval and the Modern Church* [VAR-1200]. Other handbooks on symbolism which will prove helpful, in addition to Hans Biedermann's excellent work [VAT-080] mentioned above, are J. E. Cirlot's *A Dictionary of Symbols* [VAR-230], and Edward Hulme's *Symbolism in Christian Art* [VAR-630]. For more exhaustive study of symbols adopted by Christians in the first few centuries, see Erwin R. Goodenough's thirteen volume work, *Jewish Symbols in the Greco-Roman Period* [VAR-500]. Although Goodenough argues that Christian symbolism is entirely derivative, at least he does help alert readers to the wide variety of symbols in use since ancient times. Another intriguing but debatable study which connects Christian symbolism with that from other religions is Roger Cook's *The Tree of Life: Image for the Cosmos* [VAR-250]. Two other studies on symbolism which will prove helpful in this discussion are André Grabar's *Christian Iconography: A Study of Its Origins* [VAR-530], and Albert C. Moore's *Iconography of World Religions: An Introduction* [VAR-850]. For a carefully formulated philosophical interpretation of religious symbolism, see Mircea Eliade writings in *Symbolism, the Sacred and the Arts* [AER-230], cited in Chapter 2.

One of the most important developments in the study of religion and the arts has been the formulation of a Christian theological aesthetic. The leading works in this area are John Dillenberger's lucid and comprehensive text, *A Theology of Artistic Sensibilities: The Visual Arts and the Church* [AER-160], cited in Chapter 2, James Alfred Martin's intriguing study, *Beauty and Holiness: The Dialogue Between Aesthetics and Religion* [AER-530], also cited in Chapter 2, Margaret R. Miles' provocative reinterpretation of the role of religious images in history, *Image as Insight: Visual Understanding in Western Christianity and Secular Culture* [VAR-830], and, for a sound theological perspective to undergird the study of aesthetics, Rudolf Otto's *The Idea of the Holy* [VAR-910]. For additional insights into the theological approach to the arts, also consider Aiden Nichols' *The Art of God Incarnate: Theology and Symbol from Genesis to the Twentieth Century* [VAR-890].

A related topic of great importance to the study of religion and the arts is the use of the imagination. The best studies on this subject are John W. Dixon's *Art and the Theological Imagination* [AER-170], cited in Chapter 2, Madeleine L'Engle's *Walking on Water: Reflections on Faith and Art* [VAR-710], Leland Ryken's selection of essays, *The Christian Imagination: Essays on Literature and the Arts* [VAR-1000], and Timothy Verdan's and John Henderson's *Christianity and the Renaissance: Images and Religious Imagination in the Quattrocento* [VAR-1160].

The other works given below cover a wide spectrum of topics related to the study of religion and the arts. While the titles are typically self-explanatory, the following subject guide will help in locating related works on art:

American [VAR-380], [VAR-400], [VAR-480]; angels [VAR-120]; Baroque [VAR-1240]; British [VAR-090], [VAR-310], [VAR-900]; Byzantine [VAR-540], [VAR-1180]; contemporary [VAR-430], [VAR-610], [VAR-1120]; decorative [VAR-470]; French [VAR-420], [VAR-620], [VAR-740 to VAR-760]; folk [VAR-320]; life of Jesus Christ [VAR-030], [VAR-170], [VAR-280], [VAR-680], [VAR-690], [VAR-930], [VAR-1090]; Jewish [VAR-410], [VAR-500], [VAR-550], [VAR-560], [VAR-570], [VAR-580]; church history and art, general [VAR-040], [VAR-100], [VAR-200], [VAR-270], [VAR-390], [VAR-460], [VAR-600], [VAR-710], [VAR-720], [VAR-820], [VAR-860], [VAR-880], [VAR-970], [VAR-1010], [VAR-1130], [VAR-1170], [VAR-1220]; church history and art, early [VAR-220], [VAR-440], [VAR-520], [VAR-730], [VAR-770], [VAR-840], [VAR-860], [VAR-880], [VAR-940], [VAR-1110], [VAR-1140], [VAR-1210]; cross [VAR-110], [VAR-650]; eastern versus western [VAR-180], [VAR-190]; iconography [VAR-420], [VAR-530], [VAR-1030], [VAR-1050], [VAR-1180]; icons [VAR-330], [VAR-1070]; Italy [VAR-1230]; Medieval [VAR-620], [VAR-740 to VAR-760], [VAR-900], [VAR-920], [VAR-1100]; Modern [VAR-300], [VAR-370], [VAR-610], [VAR-980], [VAR-990]; New Testament [VAR-260], [VAR-780], [VAR-790], [VAR-810], [VAR-1020], [VAR-1060], [VAR-1150], [VAR-1190]; Old Testament [VAR-240], [VAR-260], [VAR-800], [VAR-1020]; primitive [VAR-060], [VAR-660]; Reformation [VAR-210], [VAR-510], [VAR-590]; Renaissance [VAR-870], [VAR-950], [VAR-1080], [VAR-1160]; Russian [VAR-150]; sacred versus secular [VAR-340], [VAR-350]; worship and ministry [VAR-140], [VAR-160], [VAR-200], [VAR-290], [VAR-670], [VAR-700].

Although many of the authors whose works are listed here have much to offer, a few are worthy of recognition for almost anything they write, especially the works given below. These stellar authors not already singled out are André Grabar [VAR-520 to VAR-540], Joseph Gutmann [VAR-550 to VAR-570], Madeleine L'Engle [VAR-710], Emile Mâle [VAR-740 to VAR-760], and Leo Steinberg [VAR-1090]. One other author whose tastes are not as discerning as one would hope, but whose reference works are nonetheless interesting and informative for studies of Christianity and the arts is Cynthia Pearl Maus [VAR-790 to VAR-820].

Journals treating Christianity and the visual arts are not numerous, but the following new periodicals promise to be some of the best publications to date: *Arts: The Arts in Religious and Theological Studies* [VAR-080] which includes articles and news items treating some of the most authoritative personalities in the profession; *Bible Review* [VAR-130], which does not specialize in the visual arts, but often includes articles about them; *To His Glory* or *Glory* [VAR-490], which often includes treatments of the visual arts from a largely Lutheran perspective; and *Image: A Journal of the Arts and Religion* [VAR-640], which promises to be a very scholarly and substantial publication. For additional studies related to Christianity and the visual arts, see the aesthetics and religion section of Chapter 2, and pertinent titles linked to specific categories of the visual arts given after this section.

Special Bibliographies

[VAR-010] Parshall, Linda B., and Peter W. Parshall. *Art and the Reformation: An Annotated Bibliography*. Boston: G. K. Hall, 1986. xlvi and 282 pp.

[VAR-020] Peters, Diane. *Christianity and the Visual Arts: A Bibliography*. 2nd ed. [Waterloo, Ontario]: The Library, Wilfrid Laurier University, 1990. 113 pp.

Key Works

[VAR-030] Abrams, Richard I., and Warner A. Hutchinson. *An Illustrated Life of Jesus: From the National Gallery of Art Collection*. New York: Bell Publishing Co., 1988. 159 pp.

[VAR-040] Abulafia, David, M[ichael] J. Franklin, and Miri Rubin, eds. *Church and City, 1000-1500: Essays in Honour of Christopher Brooke*. Cambridge, England; New York: Cambridge University Press, 1992. Bib. pp. 333-339.

[VAR-050] Adams, Doug, and Diane Apostolos-Cappadona, eds. *Art as Religious Studies*. New York: Crossroad, 1987. Bib. pp. 217-237, partly annotated.

[VAR-060] Anderson, Richard L. *Art in Primitive Societies*. Englewood Cliffs, N.J.: Prentice-Hall Press, 1979. Bib. pp. 205-222.

[VAR-070] Apostolos-Cappadona, Diane, ed. *Art, Creativity, and the Sacred.* New York: Crossroad, 1984. Bib. pp. 321-335.

[VAR-080] *Arts: The Arts in Religious and Theological Studies.* New Brighton, Minn.: Religion and Arts Program, United Theological Seminary, 1988-. Quarterly.

[VAR-090] Aston, Margaret. *England's Iconoclasts.* New York: Oxford University Press, 1988. Bib., vol. 1, pp. 481-524.

[VAR-100] Barraclough, Geoffrey. *The Christian World: A Social and Cultural History of Christianity.* New York: Harry N. Abrams, Inc., 1981. Bib.

[VAR-110] Benson, George Willard. *The Cross: Its History and Symbolism.* Buffalo, N.Y.: N.p., 1934. 197 pp.

[VAR-120] Berefelt, Gunnar. *A Study on the Winged Angel: The Origin of a Motif.* Stockholm, Sweden: Almqvist and Wiksell, 1968. Bib. pp. 112-118.

[VAR-130] *Bible Review.* Washington, D.C.: Biblical Archaeology Society, 1985-. Quarterly.

[VAR-140] Bowlam, David W., and James L. Henderson. *Art and Belief.* New York: Schocken Books, 1970. 206 pp. Bibs.

[VAR-150] Brumfield, William Craft, and Milos Velimirovic, eds. *Christianity and the Arts in Russia.* Cambridge, [England]; New York: Cambridge University Press, 1991. 172 pp. Bib. refs.

[VAR-160] Bryans, Nena. *Full Circle: A Proposal to the Church for an Arts Ministry.* San Carlos, Calif.: Schuyler Institute for Worship and the Arts, 1988. Dist. Thomas House Publications. Bib. pp. 71-79.

[VAR-170] Buechner, Frederick. *The Faces of Jesus.* Photo. Lee Boltin. New York: Riverwood Publishers Ltd. and Simon and Schuster, 1974. 256 pp.

[VAR-180] Burckhardt, Titus. *Sacred Art in East and West.* London: Perennial, 1967.

[VAR-190] Butler, John F. *Christianity in Asia and America: After A.D. 1500.* Iconography of Religions, Section 24: Christianity. Leiden, Netherlands: E. J. Brill, 1979. 45 pp. and 68 plates. Bib. pp. ix-xxiv.

[VAR-200] Caemmerer, Richard R., Jr. *Visual Art in the Life of the Church: Encouraging Creative Worship and Witness in the Congrega-*

tion. Minneapolis: Augsburg Publishing House, 1983. Bib. pp. 92-94.

[VAR-210] Christensen, Carl G. *Art and the Reformation in Germany.* Detroit: Wayne State University Press, 1979. Bib. pp. 255-262.

[VAR-220] Christie, Yves, et al. *Art of the Christian World, A.D. 200-1500: A Handbook of Styles and Forms.* Trans. French. New York: Rizzoli International Publications, 1982. 504 pp. Bibs.

[VAR-230] Cirlot, J. E. *A Dictionary of Symbols.* New York: Philosophical Library, 1972.

[VAR-240] Coen, Rena Neumann. *The Old Testament in Art.* Fine Art Books for Young People. Minneapolis: Lerner Publications Co., 1970. 72 pp.

[VAR-250] Cook, Roger. *The Tree of Life: Image for the Cosmos.* New York; London: Thames and Hudson, 1974. c. 125 pp. Bib. refs.

[VAR-260] Cope, Gilbert. *Symbolism in the Bible and the Church.* New York: Philosophical Library, 1959.

[VAR-270] Crawford, Alexander Crawford Lindsay, Earl of. *Sketches of the History of Christian Art.* 3 vols. London: J. Murray, 1847.

[VAR-280] de Unamuno, Miguel. *The Christ of Velasquez.* Trans. Eleanor L. Turnbull. Baltimore: Johns Hopkins Press, 1951.

[VAR-290] De Vito, Albert Conrad. *Art at the Service of Faith: Art, Painting, Architecture, Symbols, Local Customs, Music, and Dance at the Service of the Church, as Visualized by the Fathers of the II Vatican Ecumenical Council Outside the Council Hall.* Lucknow: St. Joseph's Cathedral, 1963. 124 pp.

[VAR-300] Davies, Horton, and Hugh Davies. *Sacred Art in the Secular Century.* Collegeville: Liturgical Press, 1980.

[VAR-310] Day, Michael. *Modern Art in English Churches.* London; Oxford: Mowbray, 1984. 91 pp.

[VAR-320] Dewhurst, C. Kurt, Betty MacDowell, and Marsha MacDowell. *Religious Folk Art in America: Reflections of Faith.* New York: E. P. Dutton and Co., 1984. Bib. pp. 155-159.

[VAR-330] Didron, Adolphe Napoleon. *Christian Iconography: The History of Christian Art in the Middle Ages.* 2 vols. Trans. E. J. Millington. New York: F. Ungar Publishing Co., [1965].

Bib. footnotes.

[VAR-340] Dillenberger, Jane. *Image and Spirit in Sacred and Secular Art*. New York: Crossroad, 1990. Bib. refs. in Notes, pp. 191-204. Bib. pp. 205-206.

[VAR-350] ------. *Secular Art with Sacred Themes*. Nashville: Abingdon Press, 1969. Bib. pp. 131-137, annotated.

[VAR-360] ------. *Style and Content in Christian Art*. 2nd ed. New York: Crossroad, 1988. Bib. pp. 229-234, annotated.

[VAR-370] Dillenberger, Jane, and John Dillenberger. *Perceptions of the Spirit in Twentieth Century American Art*. Indianapolis: Indianapolis Museum of Art, 1977.

[VAR-380] Dillenberger, Jane, and Joshua C. Taylor. *The Hand and the Spirit: Religious Art in America, 1700-1900*. Exhibition. Berkeley: University Art Museum, 1972.

[VAR-390] Dillenberger, John. *Contours of Faith: Changing Forms of Christian Thought*. Nashville: Abingdon Press, 1969. Bib. pp. 166-168.

[VAR-400] ------. *The Visual Arts and Christianity in America: From the Colonial Period to the Present*. New York: Crossroad, 1989. 290 pp. Bib. refs. in notes.

[VAR-410] *Encyclopaedia Judaica*. 16 vols. Jerusalem: Encyclopaedia Judaica; New York: Macmillan Publishing Co., 1971-1972. *Decennial Book, 1973-1982*, n.d. *Yearbook, 1983/5*, 1985.

[VAR-420] Evans, Joan. *Monastic Iconography in France from the Renaissance to the Revolution*. Cambridge, England: Cambridge University Press, 1970. Bib. pp. 57-59.

[VAR-430] Eversole, Finley. *The Christian Faith and the Contemporary Arts*. New York: Abingdon Press, 1962. Bib. pp. 239-248.

[VAR-440] Ferguson, Everett, David Scholar, and Paul Corby Finney, eds. *Art, Archaeology, and Architecture of Early Christianity*. Vol. 18 in *Studies in Early Christianity*. New York; Hamden, Conn.: Garland Publishing, 1993. 443 pp. Bib. refs.

[VAR-450] Ferguson, George. *Signs and Symbols in Christian Art*. New York: Oxford University Press, 1954. Bib. pp. 343-346.

[VAR-460] Frere-Cook, Gervis. *Art and Architecture of Christianity*. Cleveland: Press of Case Western Reserve University, 1972. 296 pp.

[VAR-470] ------. *The Decorative Arts of the Christian Church*. London: Cassell and Co., 1972. 296 pp.

[VAR-480] Gambone, Robert L. *Art and Popular Religion in Evangelical America, 1915-1940*. Knoxville: University of Tennessee Press, 1989. 278 pp. Bib. refs.

[VAR-490] *Glory, To His*. Milwaukee, Wis.: Glory, 1991-. Quarterly.

[VAR-500] Goodenough, Erwin R. *Jewish Symbols in the Greco-Roman Period*. 13 vols. New York: Pantheon Books, 1953-1968. Bib. footnotes.

[VAR-510] Garside, Charles. *Zwingli and the Arts*. New Haven: Yale University Press, 1966. Bib. pp. 185-186.

[VAR-520] Grabar, André. *The Beginnings of Christian Art: 200-395*. Trans. Stuart Gilbert and James Emmons. Ed. Andre Malraux and Georges Salles. [London]: Thames and Hudson, 1967.

[VAR-530] ------. *Christian Iconography: A Study of Its Origins*. Trans. Terry Grabar. The A. W. Mellon Lectures in the Fine Arts, 1961. Bollingen Series, no. 35. Princeton: Princeton University Press, [1968]. Bib. pp. 149-158.

[VAR-540] ------. *L'Empereur dans L'Art Byzantin: Recherches sur L'Art Officiel de L'Empire d'Orient*. Paris: Les Belles Lettres, 1936. 296 pp. Bib. footnotes.

[VAR-550] Gutmann, Joseph. *Beauty in Holiness: Studies in Jewish Customs and Ceremonial Art*. New York: KTAV Publishing House, 1970.

[VAR-560] ------. *Jewish Ceremonial Art*. New York: Thomas Yoseloff, 1964.

[VAR-570] ------. *No Graven Images: Studies in Art and the Hebrew Bible*. New York: KTAV Publishing House, 1971.

[VAR-580] Haftmann, W. *Marc Chagall*. Trans. H. Baumann, and A. Brown. London: Thames and Hudson, 1985. 128 pp.

[VAR-590] Harbison, Craig. *The Last Judgment in Sixteenth Century Northern Europe: A Study of the Relation Between Art and the Reformation*. New York: Garland Publishing, 1976. 441 pp. Bib. pp. 267-306.

[VAR-600] Healy, Edith. *On Christian Art*. New York: Benziger, 1892. 114 pp.

[VAR-610] Heyer, George S. *Signs of Our Times: Theological Essays on Art in the Twentieth Century*. Grand Rapids: William B. Eerdmanns, 1980.

[VAR-620] Hufgard, M. Kilian. *Saint Bernard of Clairvaux: A Theory of Art Formed from His Writings*. Lewiston, N.Y.: Edwin Mellen Press, 1990. 196 pp.

[VAR-630] Hulme, Edward. *Symbolism in Christian Art*. Rev. ed. 1891. Reprint. Poole, Dorset: Blandford Press, 1976.

[VAR-640] *Image: A Journal of the Arts and Religion*. Berkeley: Graduate Theological Union and Center for Arts, Religion and Education, 1992-.

[VAR-650] Jakob, Sepp, and P. Donatus M. Leicher. *Schrift and Symbol: in Stein Holz und Metall*. Munich: Brend'amour, Simhart and Co., 1977.

[VAR-660] Jopling, Carol F., ed. *Art and Aesthetics in Primitive Societies*. New York: E. P. Dutton and Co., 1971.

[VAR-670] Kandinsky, Wassily. *Concerning the Spiritual in Art*. New York: Dover Publications, 1977. 57 pp. Bib. refs.

[VAR-680] Kaplan, Paul H[enry] D[aniel]. *The Rise of the Black Magus in Western Art*. Studies in the Fine Arts, Iconography, no. 9. Ann Arbor, Mich.: UMI Research Press, 1985. Bib. pp. 283-303.

[VAR-690] Kartsonis, Anna D. *Anastasis: The Making of an Image*. Princeton: Princeton University Press, 1986. Bib. pp. 237-255.

[VAR-700] Krier, Catherine H. *Symbols for all Seasons: Environmental Planning for Cycles A, B, and C*. San Jose, Calif.: Resource Publications, 1988. Bib. pp. 174-175. (Catholic Church Liturgy.)

[VAR-710] L'Engle, Madeleine. *Walking on Water: Reflections on Faith and Art*. Wheaton, Ill.: Harold Shaw Publications, 1980. 198 pp.

[VAR-720] Laeuchli, Samuel. *Religion and Art in Conflict: Introduction to a Cross-Disciplinary Task*. Philadelphia: Fortress Press, 1980. Bib. pp. 189-193.

[VAR-730] Lowrie, Walter. *Art in the Early Church*. 1947. Reprint. New York: Norton Classics, 1969.

[VAR-740] Mâle, Emile. *Religious Art in France: The Late Middle Ages: A Study of Medieval Iconography and Its Sources*. Trans.

380

Marthiel Mathews. Ed. Harry Bober. Princeton: Princeton University Press, 1986. Bib. pp. 549-573.

[VAR-750] ------. *Religious Art in France: The Thirteenth Century: A Study of Medieval Iconography and Its Sources.* Trans. Marthiel Mathews. Ed. Harry Bober. Princeton: Princeton University Press, 1984. Bib. pp. 501-524.

[VAR-760] ------. *Religious Art in France: The Twelfth Century: A Study of the Origins of Medieval Iconography.* Trans. Marthiel Mathews. Ed. Harry Bober. Princeton: Princeton University Press, 1978. Bib. pp. 517-540.

[VAR-770] Mancinelli, Fabrizio. *Catacombs and Basilicas: The Early Christians in Rome.* Scala, Firenze: Conti Tipocolor, 1989. Bib. p. 64.

[VAR-780] Marrow, James H. *Passion Iconography in Northern European Art of the Late Middle Ages and Early Renaissance: A Study of the Transformation of Sacred Metaphor into Descriptive Narrative.* Kortrijk, Belgium: Van Ghemmert Pub., Co., 1979. Bib. pp. 339-350.

[VAR-790] Maus, Cynthia Pearl. *Christ and The Fine Arts.* Rev. ed. New York: Harper and Brothers Publishers, 1959. 813 pp.

[VAR-800] ------. *The Old Testament and The Fine Arts.* New York: Harper and Brothers Publishers, 1954. 826 pp.

[VAR-810] ------. *The World's Great Madonnas.* New York: Harper and Brothers Publishers, [1947]. 789 pp.

[VAR-820] Maus, Cynthia Pearl, with John P. Cavarnos, Jean Louise Smith, Ronald E. Osborn, and Alfred T. Degroot. *The Church and The Fine Arts.* New York: Harper and Brothers Publishers, 1960. 902 pp.

[VAR-830] Miles, Margaret R. *Image as Insight: Visual Understanding in Western Christianity and Secular Culture.* Boston: Beacon Press, 1985. Bib. pp. 193-196.

[VAR-840] Milburn, Robert. *Early Christian Art and Architecture.* Berkeley: University of California Press, 1988. Bib. pp. 306-312.

[VAR-850] Moore, Albert C. *Iconography of World Religions: An Introduction.* Philadelphia: Fortress Press, 1977. Bib. pp. 323-325.

[VAR-860] Morey, Charles Rufus. *Early Christian Art: An Outline of the Evolution of Style and Iconography in Sculpture and Painting from Antiquity to the Eighth Century.* Princeton: Princeton

University Press, 1942. 282 pp.

[VAR-870] Murray, Peter, and Linda Murray. *The Art of the Renaissance.* New York: Oxford University Press, 1963.

[VAR-880] Newton, Eric, and William Neil. *2000 Years of Christian Art.* New York: Harper and Row, 1966.

[VAR-890] Nichols, Aiden. *The Art of God Incarnate: Theology and Symbol from Genesis to the Twentieth Century.* New York: Paulist Press, 1980.

[VAR-900] Norton, Christopher, and David Park, eds. *Cistercian Art and Architecture in the British Isles.* New York: Cambridge University Press, 1986. Bib. pp. 402-430.

[VAR-910] Otto, Rudolf. *The Idea of the Holy.* London: Oxford University Press, 1958.

[VAR-920] Parker, Elizabeth C., and Mary B. Shepard. *The Cloisters: Studies in Honor of the Fiftieth Anniversary.* New York: Metropolitan Museum of Art: International Center of Medieval Art, 1992. 459 pp. Bib. refs.

[VAR-930] Pelikan, Jaroslav. *Jesus Through The Centuries: His Place in the History of Culture.* New York: Harper and Row, 1985. 270 pp. Bib. refs. in notes.

[VAR-940] Perkins, Ann. *The Art of Dura-Europos.* New York: Oxford University Press, 1973.

[VAR-950] Petersson, Robert T. *The Art of Ecstasy: Teresa, Bernini and Crashaw.* New York: Atheneum, 1970.

[VAR-960] *Religious Art of Today: Paintings, Sculpture, Drawings, Liturgical Objects, Architecture.* Dayton, Ohio: Dayton Art Institute, 1944. 53 pp.

[VAR-970] Rookmaaker, H[endrik] R[oelof]. *Art Needs no Justification.* Downers Grove, Ill.: Inter-Varsity Press, 1978. Bib. refs. in notes, p. 63.

[VAR-980] ------. *Modern Art and the Death of a Culture.* Downers Grove, Ill.: Inter-Varsity Press, 1970. Bib. pp. 253-254.

[VAR-990] Rubin, William S. *Modern Sacred Art and the Church of Assy.* New York: Columbia University Press, 1961.

[VAR-1000] Ryken, Leland, ed. *The Christian Imagination: Essays on Literature and the Arts.* Grand Rapids: Baker Book House, 1981.

448 pp. Bib. refs. in footnotes.

[VAR-1010] ------. *Culture in Christian Perspective: A Door to Understanding and Enjoying the Arts*. Portland, Oreg.: Multnomah Press, 1986. 283 pp. Bibs.

[VAR-1020] Schaeffer, Francis A. *Art and the Bible*. Downers Grove, Ill.: Inter-Varsity Press, 1973. 64 pp.

[VAR-1030] Schiller, Gertrud. *Iconography of Christian Art*. 2 vols. Trans. Janet Seligman. Greenwich, Conn.: New York Graphic Society, 1971-1972. Bib. Vol. 1, pp. 467-470.

[VAR-1040] Scully, Vincent. *The Earth, the Temple and the Gods*. New Haven: Yale University Press, 1982.

[VAR-1050] Sherrard, Philip. *Constantinople: Iconography of a Sacred City*. New York: Oxford University Press, 1965. Bib. pp. 135-136.

[VAR-1060] Shissler, Barbara Johnson. *The New Testament in Art*. Fine Arts Books for Young People. Minneapolis: Lerner Publications Co., 1970. 68 pp.

[VAR-1070] Sinding-Larson, Staale. *Iconography and Ritual: A Study of Analytical Perspectives*. N.p.: Universitetsfarlaget, 1984. Bib. pp. 196-203.

[VAR-1080] Steckow, Wolfgang. *Northern Renaissance Art 1400-1600*. Englewood Cliffs, N.J.: Prentice-Hall Press, 1966.

[VAR-1090] Steinberg, Leo. *The Sexuality of Christ in Renaissance Art and in Modern Oblivion*. New York: Pantheon Books, 1983. Bib. pp. 204-205.

[VAR-1100] Stoddard, Whitney S. *Art and Architecture, Sculpture, Stained Glass, Manuscripts, the Art of the Church Treasuries*. Rev. of *Monastery and Cathedral in France*, 1966. New York: Harper and Row, 1972. 412 pp.

[VAR-1110] Syndicus, Edward. *Early Christian Art*. N.p.: Hawthorne Books, 1962.

[VAR-1120] Taylor, Mark C. *Disfiguring: Art, Architecture, Religion*. Religion and Postmodernism Series. Chicago: University of Chicago Press, 1992. Bib. refs. pp. 321-340.

[VAR-1130] Tillich, Paul. *On Art and Architecture*. Ed. John Dillenberger and Jane Dillenberger. New York: Crossroad, 1987. 275 pp. Bib. refs.

[VAR-1140] van der Meer, Frederik. *Atlas of the Early Christian World*. N.p.: Nelson, 1958. Bib.

[VAR-1150] Van Dyke, Henry. *The Christ-Child in Art: A Study of Interpretation*. New York: Harper and Brothers Publishers, 1894. 236 pp.

[VAR-1160] Verdan, Timothy, and John Henderson, eds. *Christianity and the Renaissance: Images and Religious Imagination in the Quattrocento*. Syracuse, N.Y.: Syracuse University Press, 1990. 611 pp. Bib. refs in notes.

[VAR-1170] Waddell, James, and Frederick William Dillistone. *Art and Religion as Communication*. Atlanta: John Knox Press, 1974. Bib. pp. 245-252.

[VAR-1180] Walter, Christopher. *Studies in Byzantine Iconography*. London: Variorum Reprints, 1977. 283 pp. Bib. refs.

[VAR-1190] Warner, Marina. *Alone of All Her Sex: The Myth and the Cult of the Virgin Mary*. New York: Alfred A. Knopf, 1976. Bib. pp. 395-400.

[VAR-1200] Webber, F. R. *Church Symbolism: An Explanation of the more Important Symbols of the Old and New Testament, The Primitive, The Mediaeval and the Modern Church*. Cleveland: J. H. Jansen, 1938. Bib. pp. 389-394.

[VAR-1210] Weitzmann, Kurt. *The Age of Spirituality: Late Antique and Early Christian Art, Third to Seventh Centuries*. Exhibition, 1977 to 1978. New York: Metropolitan Museum of Art, 1979.

[VAR-1220] ------. *Studies in the Arts at Sinai: Essays*. Princeton: Princeton University Press, 1982. 449 pp. Bib. refs.

[VAR-1230] Wittkower, Rudolf. *Art and Architecture in Italy, 1600-1750*. 3rd ed. Baltimore: Penguin, 1973. 458 pp. Bib. pp. 415-452.

[VAR-1240] Wittkower, Rudolf, and Irma Jaffe. *Baroque Art: The Jesuit Contribution*. New York: Fordham University Press, 1972.

KEY WORKS ON CALLIGRAPHY

Calligraphy, the art of beautiful writing, has a history almost as long as that of writing itself. Although this form of handwriting has been in part displaced initially by the printing press and more recently by computers and printers capable of mechanically reproducing almost any style of writing, interest in the craft of handwriting has realized a renaissance along with other handicrafts. When well executed, calligraphy can become an art form as exacting and intricate as painting, as illustrated well in the section on illuminated manuscripts given below. Calligraphy has been especially important in cultures such as the Hebraic and Islamic which eschew making images of the created world. The non-representational writing in these cultures has grown into a highly ornate art form. In the Chinese culture, calligraphy has developed as an integral part of the pictorial and poetic arts, making calligraphy as important to the visual arts as it is to the verbal arts. For researchers wishing to study calligraphy in connection with Christian beliefs, illuminated manuscripts from the Middle Ages will provide the best examples.

Of the works listed below, most will provide good primary sources for research, but few will offer scholarly analyses of this art form. The only two bibliographies which specialize in calligraphy are *The Book Arts Directory* [VCA-010], which is largely technical in orientation, and Cecil H. Uyehara's more substantial volume, *Japanese Calligraphy: A Bibliography Study* [VCA-020]. The most substantial general works for researchers are Martin Andersch's *Symbols, Signs, Letters* [VCA-040], Donald M. Anderson's *Calligraphy: The Art of Written Forms* [VCA-050], Marc Drogin's *Medieval Calligraphy, Its History and Technique* [VCA-220], Joyce Irene Whalley's *The Art of Calligraphy: Western Europe and America* [VCA-640], and Hermann Zapf's collected writings, *Hermann Zapf and His Design Philosophy* [VCA-700].

For those primarily interested in the techniques of calligraphy, the most useful texts are Marie Angel's *The Art of Calligraphy: A Practical Guide* [VCA-060] and her *Painting for Calligraphers* [VCA-070], Heather Child's *The Calligrapher's Handbook* [VCA-160], Jinnie Y. Davis' and John V. Richardson's *Calligraphy: A Sourcebook* [VCA-200], Lewis Foreman Day's *Alphabets Old and New, for the Use of Craftsmen, with an Introductory Essay on Art in the Alphabet* [VCA-210], Rose Folsom's *The Calligraphers' Dictionary* [VCA-280], Peter Halliday's and Thomas Ingmire's *Calligraphy Masterclass* [VCA-320], David Harris' *Calligraphy: Inspiration, Innovation, Communication* [VCA-330], Christopher Jarman's *Illumination: A Source Book for Modern Calligraphers* [VCA-360], John Nash's *Practical Calligraphy* [VCA-490], Margaret

385

Shepherd's *Borders for Calligraphy: How to Design a Decorated Page* [VCA-540] and her *Calligraphy Now: New Light on Traditional Letters* [VCA-550], Jacqueline Svaren's *Written Letters: 33 Alphabets for Calligraphers* [VCA-590], Peter E. Taylor's *A Manual of Calligraphy* [VCA-600], Eleanor Winters' *Mastering Copperplate: A Step-by-Step Manual for Calligraphers* [VCA-670], and Frederick Wong's *The Complete Calligrapher* [VCA-680].

The books on calligraphy listed in this section represent a variety of cultures, eras, and styles, as follows: ambegrams [VCA-410]; American [VCA-500]; Celtic [VCA-450]; Chinese [VCA-100], [VCA-150], [VCA-250], [VCA-290], [VCA-300], [VCA-390], [VCA-430], [VCA-480]; contemporary [VCA-180], [VCA-550]; eastern [VCA-470], [VCA-580]; Egyptian [VCA-260]; English [VCA-110]; Hebrew [VCA-190], [VCA-440], [VCA-610]; historical and general [VCA-090], [VCA-310], [VCA-420], [VCA-570], [VCA-630], [VCA-690]; Islamic [VCA-270], [VCA-520], [VCA-530], [VCA-560], [VCA-710]; Italic [VCA-080], [VCA-230], [VCA-380], [VCA-510]; Japanese [VCA-030], [VCA-240], [VCA-390]; Medieval [VCA-220], [VCA-400]; modern [VCA-170], [VCA-340], [VCA-460]; penmanship [VCA-370], [VCA-500], [VCA-620]; serif [VCA-140]; western [VCA-640], [VCA-650], [VCA-660].

Although calligraphy was associated with Christianity during the Middle Ages, the affiliation of these two today is tangential. Most texts connecting the two usually are illustrated books of psalms or prayers and contain little or no analysis of the theological aesthetics involved. One such work, Timothy R. Botts's *Windsongs* [VCA-120], illustrates this trend well. The primary journal for calligraphy news and book reviews is *Calligraphy Review* [VCA-130]. For additional studies of calligraphy, see the bibliographies in the opening of this chapter.

Special Bibliographies

[VCA-010] *Book Arts Directory, The: A Sourcebook for: Papermakers, Calligraphers, Printmakers, Book Designers, Fine Printers, Bookbinders and Their Suppliers*. [Portland, Oreg.]: Page Two, Inc., 1992. 39 pp.

[VCA-020] Uyehara, Cecil H. *Japanese Calligraphy: A Bibliography Study*.

386

Lanham, Md.: University Press of America, 1991. 364 pp.

Key Works

[VCA-030] Addiss, Stephen. *The Art of Zen: Paintings and Calligraphy by Japanese Monks, 1600-1925*. New York: Harry N. Abrams, 1989. Bib. pp. 214-218.

[VCA-040] Andersch, Martin. *Symbols, Signs, Letters*. New York: Design Press, 1989. Bib. pp. 251-254.

[VCA-050] Anderson, Donald M. *Calligraphy: The Art of Written Forms*. New York: Holt, Rinehart and Winston, [1992]. Notes and Bib. pp. 329-344.

[VCA-060] Angel, Marie. *The Art of Calligraphy: A Practical Guide*. New York: Charles Scribner's Sons, 1977. 120 pp.

[VCA-070] ------. *Painting for Calligraphers*. Woodstock, N.Y.: Overlook Press, 1984. Bib. p. 123.

[VCA-080] Atkins, Kathryn A. *Masters of the Italic Letter: Twenty-Two Exemplars from the Sixteenth Century*. Boston: David R. Godine, 1988. 192 pp. Bibs. London: Allen Lane, 1988. 183 pp. Bib. pp. 179-183.

[VCA-090] Baker, Arthur. *Arthur Baker's Historic Calligraphic Alphabets*. New York: Dover Publications, 1980. 89 pp.

[VCA-100] Billeter, Jean François. *The Chinese Art of Writing*. Trans. New York: Skira/Rizzoli, 1990. 319 pp. Bib. pp. 294-297.

[VCA-110] Bishop, Terence Alan Martyn. *English Caroline Minuscule*. Oxford: Clarendon Press, 1971. xxx, 26 pp.

[VCA-120] Botts, Timothy R. *Windsongs*. Wheaton: Tyndale House Publishing, 1989. (Calligraphy, Christian literature, and Illustrations.)

[VCA-130] *Calligraphy Review*. Norman, Okla.: Calligraphy Review, Inc., 1982-. Quarterly. Formerly *Calligraphy Idea Exchange*.

[VCA-140] Catich, Edward M. *The Origin of the Serif: Brush Writing and Roman Letters*. 2nd ed. Ed. Mary W. Gilroy. Davenport, Iowa: Catich Gallery, St. Ambrose University, 1991. 310 pp. Bib. refs.

[VCA-150] Chiang, Yee. *Chinese Calligraphy: An Introduction to Its Beauty and Technique*. 1938. Reprint. Singapore: Brash, 1990. Bib. refs. pp. 221-222.

[VCA-160] Child, Heather. *The Calligrapher's Handbook*. 2nd ed. New York: Taplinger Publishing Co., 1986. Bib. pp. 249-252.

[VCA-170] ------. *Calligraphy Today: Twentieth-Century Tradition and Practice*. [3rd ed.] New York: Taplinger Publishing Co., 1988. Bib. pp. 124-127.

[VCA-180] *Contemporary Calligraphy: Modern Scribes and Lettering Artists II*. Boston: David R. Godine, 1990. 168 pp. See *Modern Scribes and Lettering Artists* [VCA-460].

[VCA-190] David, Ismar. *Hebrew Letter: Calligraphic Variations*. Northvale, N.J.: J. Aronson, Inc., 1990. Bib. refs. pp. 85-86.

[VCA-200] Davis, Jinnie Y., and John V. Richardson, Jr. *Calligraphy: A Sourcebook*. Littleton, Colo.: Libraries Unlimited, Inc., 1982. 222 pp.

[VCA-210] Day, Lewis Foreman. *Alphabets Old and New, for the Use of Craftsmen, with an Introductory Essay on Art in the Alphabet*. Detroit: Gale Research, 1968. 256 pp.

[VCA-220] Drogin, Marc. *Medieval Calligraphy, Its History and Technique*. Montclair, N.J.: Allanheld and Schram, 1980. Bib. pp. 183-186.

[VCA-230] Dubay, Inga. *Italic Letters: Calligraphy and Handwriting*. Rev. ed. Portland, Oreg.: Portland State University, Continuing Education Press, 1992. Bib. pp. 123-124.

[VCA-240] Earnshaw, C. *Sho: Japanese Calligraphy*. Rutland, Vt.; Tokyo, Japan: Tuttle, 1989. 173 pp. Bib. refs.

[VCA-250] Farrer, Anne. *The Brush Dances and The Ink Sings: Chinese Paintings and Calligraphy from the British Museum*. London: South Bank Centre, Hayward Gallery, 1990. Bib. refs. pp. 140-141.

[VCA-260] Fischer, Henry George. *Ancient Egyptian Calligraphy: A Beginner's Guide to Writing Hieroglyphs*. 3rd ed. New York: Metropolitan Museum of Art, 1988. Bib. pp. 59-68.

[VCA-270] Fisher, Carrol Garret. *Brocade of the Pen: The Art of Islamic Writing*. East Lansing, Mich.: Kresge Art Museum, Michigan State University, 1991. 100 pp. Bib. refs. pp. 77-79.

[VCA-280] Folsom, Rose. *The Calligraphers' Dictionary*. New York: Thames

388

and Hudson, 1990. Bib. refs. pp. 142-143.

[VCA-290] Fong, Wen C. *Beyond Representation: Chinese Paintings and Calligraphy, 8th-14th Century.* Princeton Monographs in Art and Archaeology, no. 48. New York; New Haven; London: Metropolitan Museum of Art; Yale University Press, 1992. 549 pp. Bib. refs.

[VCA-300] Fong, Wen C., et al. *Images of the Mind: Selections from the Edward L. Elliott Family and John B. Elliott Collections of Chinese Calligraphy and Painting at The Art Museum, Princeton University.* Princeton: The Art Museum, Princeton University with Princeton University Press, 1984. Bib. pp. 491-493.

[VCA-310] Gray, Nicolete. *A History of Lettering: Creative Experiment and Letter Identity.* Boston: David R. Godine, 1986. 256 pp.

[VCA-320] Halliday, Peter, and Thomas Ingmire. *Calligraphy Masterclass.* Woodstock, N.Y.: Overlook Press, 1990. Bib. refs. p. 128.

[VCA-330] Harris, David. *Calligraphy: Inspiration, Innovation, Communication.* London: Anaya, 1991. Bib. pp. 125-126.

[VCA-340] ------. *Calligraphy: Modern Masters--Art, Inspiration, and Technique.* New York: Crescent Books, 1991. Bib. pp. 125-126.

[VCA-350] Harvey, Michael. *Calligraphy in the Graphic Arts.* London: Bodley Head, 1988. 64 pp. Bib.

[VCA-360] Jarman, Christopher. *Illumination: A Source Book for Modern Calligraphers.* London: Dryad, 1988. Bib. p. 134.

[VCA-370] Johnston, Edward, Heather Child, and Justin Howes. *Lessons in Formal Writing.* London: Lund Humphries, 1986. Bib. pp. 239-243.

[VCA-380] Knudsen, Carolyn. *An Italic Calligraphic Handbook.* Owings Mills, Md.: Stemmer House Publishers, 1985. Bib. p. 95.

[VCA-390] Komatsu, Shigemi, Kwan S. Wong, Heinz Gotze. *Chinese and Japanese Calligraphy Spanning two Thousand Years: The Heinz Gotze Collection, Heidelberg.* Munich: Prestel, 1989. 198 pp. Bib. refs.

[VCA-400] Lancaster, John. *Writing Medieval Scripts.* London: Dryad Press, 1988. Bib. p. 75.

[VCA-410] Langdon, John. *Wordplay: Ambigrams and Reflections on the Art of Ambigrams.* New York: Harcourt Brace Jovanovich,

1992. xlv, 172 pp. Bib. refs. p. 172.

[VCA-420] Larcher, Jean. *Calligraphies: Approaches*. Paris: Quentette, 1984. Bib. pp. 124-125.

[VCA-430] Lu, Ya. *Lee Kong Chian Art Museum: Collection of Chinese Ceramics, Bronze, Archaic Jade, Painting and Calligraphy in the Light of Recent Archaeological Discoveries*. Singapore: Singapore University Press, 1990. 440 pp.

[VCA-440] Marks, Cara Goldberg. *The Handbook of Hebrew Calligraphy*. Northvale, N.J.: J. Aronson, 1990. Bib. refs. pp. 183-184.

[VCA-450] Meehan, Aidan. *Celtic Design: Illuminated Letters*. New York: Thames and Hudson, 1992. 160 pp. Bib. refs.

[VCA-460] *Modern Scribes and Lettering Artists*. Boston: David R. Godine, 1991. 160 pp.

[VCA-470] Mote, Frederick W., and Hung-lam Chu. *Calligraphy and the East Asian Book*. Princeton: Trustees of Princeton University; Boston: Shambhala, 1988. Bib. pp. 233-238.

[VCA-480] Murck, Alfreda, and Wen Fong, eds. *Words and Images: Chinese Poetry, Calligraphy, and Painting*. New York: Metropolitan Museum of Art; Princeton: Princeton University Press, 1991. 589 pp. Bib. refs.

[VCA-490] Nash, John. *Practical Calligraphy*. London: Hamlyn, 1992. Bib. pp. 142-144.

[VCA-500] Nash, Ray. *American Penmanship, 1800-1850: A History of Writing and a Bibliography of Copybooks from Jenkins to Spencer*. Worcester: American Antiquarian Society, 1969. 303 pp. Bib.

[VCA-510] Nemoy, Maury. *Calligraphy: The Study of Letterforms--Italic*. New York: Collier Books, 1985. Bib. pp. 155-156.

[VCA-520] Rahman, A[bdur], ed. *The Proceedings of the Hijra Celebration Symposium on Islamic Art, Calligraphy, Architecture and Archaeology: March 1-6, 1981*. 3 vols. Peshawar: Department of Archaeology, University of Peshawar, 1987. Bib. refs.

[VCA-530] Schimmel, Annemarie. *Calligraphy and Islamic Culture*. New York: New York University Press, 1990. 264 pp. Bib. refs. pp. 209-231.

[VCA-540] Shepherd, Margaret. *Borders for Calligraphy: How to Design a*

Decorated Page. New York: Collier Books, 1980. 109 pp.

[VCA-550] ------. *Calligraphy Now: New Light on Traditional Letters.* New York: G. P. Putnam's Sons, 1984. 191 pp.

[VCA-560] Siddiqui, Atiq R. *The Story of Islamic Calligraphy.* Delhi: Sarita Book House, 1990. Bib. refs. pp. 111-115.

[VCA-570] Sprotte, Siegward, and Herbert Edward Read. *Coloured Calligraphy/Farbige Kalligraphie.* Munich; New York: Hirmer, 1988. Dist. in USA by Falkenstern Fine Art. 211 pp. Bib. refs.

[VCA-580] Stevens, John, and Alice Rae Yelen. *Zenga: Brushstrokes of Enlightenment.* New Orleans: New Orleans Museum of Art, 1990. Bib. refs. p. 197.

[VCA-590] Svaren, Jacqueline. *Written Letters: 33 Alphabets for Calligraphers.* 2nd ed. New York: Taplinger Pub. Co., 1986. Bib. p. 74.

[VCA-600] Taylor, Peter E. *The Australian Manual of Calligraphy.* Sydney: Allen and Unwin, 1987. *A Manual of Calligraphy.* London: Unwin Hyman, 1988. Bib. pp. 206-207.

[VCA-610] Toby, L[udwig] F[ritz], and Emanuel Grau Rothschild-Lippmann. *The Art of Hebrew Lettering: With 26 Calligraphic, Typographic and Historical Tablets.* Tel Aviv: Rolf Schuster; Spring Valley, N.Y.: Philipp Feldheim, 1987. 48 pp.

[VCA-620] Trudgill, Anne. *Traditional Penmanship.* New York: Watson-Guptill Publications, 1989. Bib. refs. p. 80.

[VCA-630] Tschichold, Jan, ed. *Treasury of Calligraphy: 219 Great Examples, 1522-1840.* New York: Dover Publications, 1984. 200 pp. Bib. xi-xiii.

[VCA-640] Whalley, Joyce Irene. *The Art of Calligraphy: Western Europe and America.* London: Bloomsbury Books, 1980. Bib. pp. 395-397.

[VCA-650] ------. *The Student's Guide to Western Calligraphy: An Illustrated Survey.* Boulder, Colo.: Shambhala, 1984. Bib. p. 183.

[VCA-660] Whalley, Joyce Irene, and Vera C. Kaden. *The Universal Penman: A Survey of Western Calligraphy from the Roman Period to 1980: Catalogue of an Exhibition held at the Victoria and Albert Museum, London, July--September, 1980.* London: H. M. Stationery Office, 1980. 152 pp.

[VCA-670] Winters, Eleanor. *Mastering Copperplate: A Step-by-Step Manual for Calligraphers.* New York: Watson-Guptill Publications, 1989. Bib. p. 190.

[VCA-680] Wong, Frederick. *The Complete Calligrapher.* New York: Watson-Guptill Publications, 1980. Bib. p. 181.

[VCA-690] Young, Caroline. *Calligraphy.* Tulsa, Okla.: EDC Publications; London: Usborne, 1990. Bib. p. 47.

[VCA-700] Zapf, Hermann. *Hermann Zapf and His Design Philosophy: Selected Articles and Lectures on Calligraphy and Contemporary Developments in Type Design, with Illustrations and Bibliographical notes, and a Complete List of his Typefaces.* Chicago: Society of Typographic Arts, 1987. Bib. pp. 113-124.

[VCA-710] Ziauddin, M. *A Monograph on Moslem Calligraphy: With 168 Illustrations of its Various Styles and Ornamental Designs.* Calcutta: Visva-Bharati Book-Shop, 1936. Bib. pp. 71-78.

KEY WORKS ON COLLAGE

Collage, the arranging of seemingly unrelated objects and materials in a symbolic form, has gained special recognition as an art form because of the Cubist and Dada movements. Artists such as Pablo Picasso, Marcel Duchamp, and, more recently, Louise Nevelson have demonstrated well that collage can enhance the viewer's awareness at least as well as painting and sculpture, both of which have contributed significantly to collage. One of the best and most recent studies of the history of collage is Christine Poggi's *In Defiance of Painting: Cubism, Futurism, and the Invention of Collage* [VCO-400], which also includes an excellent bibliography. Other serious studies worth consulting as introductions to the study of collage include Katherine Hoffman's *Collage: Critical Views* [VCO-270], George Myers's *Alphabets Sublime: Contemporary Artists on Collage and Visual Literature* [VCO-380], and Diane Waldman's *Collage, Assemblage, and the Found Object* [VCO-480]. Several of the works given below treat artists, exhibitions, and the history of making collage, including [VCO-090], [VCO-120], [VCO-180], [VCO-250], [VCO-260], [VCO-280], [VCO-310], [VCO-330], [VCO-350], [VCO-360], [VCO-370], [VCO-380], [VCO-470], and [VCO-500].

For technical assistance in designing collage from various materials, consult Anne Brigadier's *Collage: A Complete Guide for Artists* [VCO-040], John Digby's and Joan Digby's *The Collage Handbook* [VCO-140], and Oscar Liebman's *Collage Fundamentals: Two- and Three-Dimensional Techniques for Illustration and Advertising* [VCO-320]. The balance of works not already mentioned, constituting over half of the volumes listed below, deal with the craft of collage. Such works are included here simply because few other sources exist for the serious study of collage.

One of the most important works listed below for studies of religion and the arts is Ken Grist's *Batik, Collage and All that Graffiti: Ideas for Art in Religious Education* [VCO-230]. As an aid to education, also consider Judy Loeb's *Feminist Collage: Educating Women in the Visual Arts* [VCO-330]. For additional works on collage, see the bibliographies given in the opening of this chapter. As one can see, the paucity of works treating collage from a Christian perspective suggests additional needs for serious research in this aspect of the arts.

[VCO-010] Ballarian, Anna. *Fabric Collage: Contemporary Stitchery and Applique*. Worchester, Mass.: Davis Publications, 1976. Bib. p. 77.

[VCO-020] Beaney, Jan. *Fun with Collage*. [New ed.]. London; New Rochelle, N.Y.: Kaye and Ward, 1979. Dist. Sportshelf. Bib. p. 64.

[VCO-030] Bissett, Bill. *Rezoning: Collage and Assemblage*. Exhibition, Vancouver Art Gallery, 19 October 1989 to 1 January 1990. Vancouver, B.C., Canada: Vancouver Art Gallery, 1989. 60 pp. Bib. refs.

[VCO-040] Brigadier, Anne. *Collage: A Complete Guide for Artists*. New York: Watson-Guptill Publications; London: Pitman, 1978. 192 pp.

[VCO-050] Brommer, Gerald F. *The Art of Collage*. Ed. George F. Horn and Sarita Rainey. Worchester, Mass.: Davis Publications, 1978. Bib. p. 172.

[VCO-060] ------. *Watercolor and Collage Workshop*. New York: Watson-Guptill Publications, 1986. Bib. p. 142.

[VCO-070] Capon, Robin. *Making Three-Dimensional Pictures*. London: B. T. Batsford, 1976. Bib. p. 93.

[VCO-080] ------. *Paper Collage*. Newton, Mass.: C. T. Branford, 1975. Bib. p. 96.

[VCO-090] Cathcart, Linda L. *The Americans: The Collage: Contemporary Arts Museum, Houston, Texas, July 11--October 3, 1982*. Houston: The Museum, 1982. Bib. pp. 138-140.

[VCO-100] Connor, Margaret. *Introducing Fabric Collage*. London: B. T. Batsford; New York: Watson-Guptill Publications, 1969. Bib. p. 92.

[VCO-110] *Contemporary Drawings, Watercolors and Collages: The Properties of Hirshhorn Museum and Sculpture Garden*. New York: Christie, Manson and Woods International, Inc., 1989. 162 pp. Bib. refs.

[VCO-120] Craig, Betty Jean, ed. *Relativism in the Arts*. Athens: University of Georgia Press, 1983. 203 pp.

[VCO-130] D'Arbeloff, Natalie. *Creating in Collage*. New York: Watson-Guptill Publications, [1967]. Bib. p. 101.

[VCO-140] Digby, John, and Joan Digby. *The Collage Handbook*. New York: Thames and Hudson, 1985. Bib. pp. 234-237.

[VCO-150] Edlich, Stephen. *Stephen Edlich: Collage as Carving: September 22--October 21, 1978*. New York: Marlborough, 1978. 72 pp. Bib. refs. in footnotes.

[VCO-160] Farnworth, Warren. *Approaches to Collage*. New York: Taplinger, 1976. Bib. p. 95.

[VCO-170] Foster, Maureen. *Making Animal and Bird Collages: With Grasses, Leaves, Seedheads and Cones*. London: Pelham, 1980. Bib. p. 88.

[VCO-180] Fox, Howard N. *Collages, Selections from the Hirshhorn Museum and Sculpture Garden*. Washington, D.C.: Smithsonian Institution Traveling Exhibition Service, 1981. Bib. pp. 39-40.

[VCO-190] French, Brian. *Principles of Collage*. Buchanan, N.Y.: Emerson Books, 1978. Bib. pp. 117-118.

[VCO-200] French, Brian, and Anne Butler. *Practice of Collage*. Levittown, N.Y.: Transatlantic Arts, 1976. 87 pp. London: Mills and Boon, 1976. Bib. p. 86

[VCO-210] Geary, Ida. *Plant Prints and Collages*. New York: Viking Press, 1978. Bib. pp. 95-97.

[VCO-220] Gillon, Edmund V., Jr. *Picture Sourcebook for Collage and Decoupage*. New York: Dover Publications, 1974. 144 pp. Bib. p. xx.

[VCO-230] Grist, Ken. *Batik, Collage and All that Graffiti: Ideas for Art in Religious Education*. Leigh-on-Sea: Mayhew, 1978. 80 pp.

[VCO-240] Haley, Ivy. *Creative Collage*. London: B. T. Batsford; Newton Centre, Mass.: C. T. Branford, 1971. Bib. p. 78.

[VCO-250] Hanson, Anne Coffin. *The Futurist Imagination: Word + Image in Italian Futurist Painting, Drawing, Collage and Free-Word Poetry: Exhibition*. Exhibition, Yale University Art Gallery, 13 April to 26 June 1983. New Haven: Yale University Art Gallery, 1983. 118 pp. Bib. p. vi.

[VCO-260] Hiller, Karol, Jane Beckett, and Andrei Nakov. *Collages and Reliefs, 1910-1945*. Exhibition, Annely Juda Fine Art, London, 30 June to 2 October 1982. London: Annely Juda Fine Art, 1982. 119 pp. Bib. refs.

[VCO-270] Hoffman, Katherine. *Collage: Critical Views*. Ann Arbor: UMI Research Press, 1989. Bib. pp. 419-423.

[VCO-280] Janis, Harriet Grossman, and Rudi Blesh. *Collage: Personalities, Concepts [and] Techniques*. Rev. ed. Philadelphia: Chilton Book Co., [1967]. 342 pp. Bib. footnotes.

[VCO-290] Kalamazoo Institute of Arts. *The Cutting Edge: New Directions in Handmade Paper: An Exhibition*. Kalamazoo, Mich.: The Institute, 1988. Bib. p. 37.

[VCO-300] Kay, Frances. *Starting Fabric Collage*. London: Studio Vista; New York: Watson-Guptill Publications, 1969. Bib. p. 102.

[VCO-310] Laliberte, Norman. *Collage, Montage, Assemblage: History and Contemporary Techniques*. New York: Van Nostrand Reinhold Co., [1971]. 80 pp.

[VCO-320] Liebman, Oscar. *Collage Fundamentals: Two- and Three-Dimensional Techniques for Illustration and Advertising*. New York: Stravon Educational Press, 1979. 108 pp.

[VCO-330] Loeb, Judy, ed. *Feminist Collage: Educating Women in the Visual Arts*. New York: Teachers College, Columbia University, 1979. 317 pp. Bib. refs.

[VCO-340] Low, Josephine. *Collage*. Newton Abbot: David and Charles; New York: Arco Publishing, 1975. Bib. p. 102.

[VCO-350] McIntyre, Arthur. *Contemporary Australian Collage and Its Origins*. Roseville, NSW, Australia: Craftsman House, 1990. Bib. refs. p. 217.

[VCO-360] Meilach, Dona Zweigoron, and Elvie Ten Hoor. *Collage and Assemblage: Trends and Techniques*. New York: Crown Publishers; London: Allen and Unwin, 1973. 246 pp.

[VCO-370] *Mississippi Museum of Art Presents, The: Collage and Assemblage*. Jackson, Miss.: The Museum, 1981. 85 pp. Bib. refs.

[VCO-380] Myers, George. *Alphabets Sublime: Contemporary Artists on Collage and Visual Literature*. Washington, D.C.: Paycock Press, 1986. Bib. pp. 151-171.

[VCO-390] Plottel, Jeanine Parisier. *Collage*. New York: New York Literary Forum, 1983. Bib. pp. 229-233.

[VCO-400] Poggi, Christine. *In Defiance of Painting: Cubism, Futurism, and the Invention of Collage*. New Haven; London: Yale University Press, 1992. Bib. pp. 292-305.

[VCO-410] Portchmouth, John. *Working in Collage*. London: Studio Vista, 1973. Bib. p. 124.

[VCO-420] Rodari, Florian. *Collage: Pasted, Cut, and Torn Papers*. Geneva: Skira; New York: Rizzoli International Publications, 1988. Bib. refs. pp. 171-172.

[VCO-430] Romano, Clare, and John Ross. *The Complete Collagraph: The Art and Technique of Printmaking from Collage Plates*. New York: Macmillan Publishing Co., 1980.

[VCO-440] Scott, Margaret Kennedy. *Pressed Flowers and Flower Pictures*. London: B. T. Batsford, 1988. Bib. p. 115.

[VCO-450] Seyd, Mary. *Designing with String*. London: B. T. Batsford; New York: Watson-Guptill Publications, 1969. 96 pp. Bib. p. 19.

[VCO-460] Sorman, Steven. *Collage Prints and Monoprints*. Bedford Village, N.Y.: Tyler Graphics, Ltd., 1985. 23 pp.

[VCO-470] Spies, Werner. *Max Ernst, Collages: The Invention of the Surrealist Landscape*. Trans. Exhibition, Kunsthalle Tubingen, the Kunstmuseum Bern, and the Kunstsammlung Nordrhein-Westfalen, Dusseldorf, 1988-1989. New York: Harry N. Abrams, 1991. 540 pp. Bib. pp. 283-284.

[VCO-480]   Waldman, Diane. *Collage, Assemblage, and the Found Object.* New York: Harry N. Abrams, 1992. Bib. refs. pp. 324-331.

[VCO-490]   Wescher, Herta. *Collage.* New York: Harry N. Abrams, 1971. 417 pp.

[VCO-500]   Wolfram, Eddie. *History of Collage: An Anthology of Collage, Assemblage, and Event Structures.* London: Studio Vista, 1975. Bib. p. 187.

KEY WORKS ON GLASS PAINTING OR STAINED GLASS

The discovery of glass can be traced to 3000 B.C. in Egypt, and the art of using glass in decorative windows can be traced to Roman times. Glass painting, or the making of stained glass windows, dates at least from the ninth century, and has long been one of the most important distinctives in Christian architecture. Although research of stained glass windows is still problematic since the names and intentions of the artists making them have typically gone unrecorded or have been lost, even in the twentieth century, resources for studying windows are second only in quantity to those for painting and of equal stature in quality. Of the bibliographies listed below, Darlene A. Brady's and William Serban's *Stained Glass: A Guide to Information Sources* [VGP-010], Madeline Harrison Caviness' and Evelyn Ruth Staudinger's *Stained Glass Before 1540: An Annotated Bibliography* [VGP-050], Davie Evans' *A Bibliography of Stained Glass* [VGP-060], and Mary A. Vance's *Stained and Painted Glass: Monographs* [VGP-100], are the most substantial of recent works. Other reference tools of note are the index to articles in the journal *Stained Glass* [VGP-020], the several directories by the British Society of Master Glass Painters [VGP-030 and VGP-040], the Vance Bibliography on uses of stained glass in architecture [VGP-070], L. L. Hench's *A Bibliography of Ceramics and Glass* [VGP-080], and Melanie S. Mayo's *Directory of Stained Glass Books and Patterns* [VGP-090], which is especially useful for those making windows.

For studying stained glass windows, the single best book for neophytes and specialists alike is Lawrence Lee's, George Seddon's, and Francis Stephens' *Stained Glass* [VGP-730]. The numerous color plates and sundry short chapters in this book are visually pleasing as well as highly informative. Two other works which are also excellent for students of stained glass are Catherine Brisac's scholarly work, *A Thousand Years of Stained Glass* [VGP-230], Sarah Brown's recent and substantial volume, *Stained Glass: An Illustrated History* [VGP-240], and Louis Grodecki's and Catherine Brisac's authoritative text covering the height of glass painting, *Gothic Stained Glass, 1200-1300* [VGP-540]. Lawrence Lee has also written *The Appreciation of Stained Glass* [VGP-720], a short but pithy volume on the nature of aesthetics in the design of stained glass windows. The more recent volume by Patrick Reyntiens, *The Beauty of Stained Glass* [VGP-1020], is also highly valuable for the study of aesthetics since Reyntiens perfected his understanding of stained glass window design with John Piper. As a team, Piper and Reyntiens have produced some of the finest and most innovative windows in the twentieth century, including the baptistry window at the new Coventry Cathedral, and the crown of windows representing the Trinity on top of the Metropolitan Cathedral of Christ the King in Liverpool, England.

The books on stained glass given below can be divided according to the eras they cover, the artists they include, or the countries best represented by the individual studies. For convenience, all three categories are used for grouping the following works, with most works being classified according to the current geographical location of the windows. For various eras, see the following given in chronological order: comprehensive works covering history, religious motifs, and techniques [VGP-230], [VGP-240], [VGP-400], [VGP-410], [VGP-430], [VGP-510], [VGP-560], [VGP-570], [VGP-680], [VGP-730], [VGP-880], [VGP-890], [VGP-900], [VGP-1080], [VGP-1170], [VGP-1180]; Romanesque [VGP-550]; Gothic [VGP-160], [VGP-420], [VGP-500], [VGP-520], [VGP-540], [VGP-620], [VGP-650], [VGP-970], [VGP-1090], [VGP-1150], [VGP-1240]; Renaissance [VGP-350], [VGP-420], [VGP-990]; Victorian and nineteenth century [VGP-460], [VGP-480], [VGP-590], [VGP-700], [VGP-930]; twentieth century [VGP-370], [VGP-870], [VGP-950].

For studies concentrating on stained glass made or now residing in specific countries, see the following: America [VGP-190], [VGP-310], [VGP-320], [VGP-330], [VGP-440], [VGP-460], [VGP-480], [VGP-490], [VGP-640], [VGP-700], [VGP-710], [VGP-780], [VGP-790], [VGP-800], [VGP-810],

[VGP-820], [VGP-850], [VGP-930], [VGP-1010], [VGP-1140], [VGP-1160]; Australia [VGP-1060], [VGP-1290]; Canada [VGP-1040]; England [VGP-110], [VGP-130], [VGP-140], [VGP-170], [VGP-180], [VGP-200], [VGP-270], [VGP-280], [VGP-290], [VGP-350], [VGP-360], [VGP-370], [VGP-420], [VGP-450], [VGP-500], [VGP-600], [VGP-610], [VGP-620], [VGP-840], [VGP-910], [VGP-1000], [VGP-1070], [VGP-1090], [VGP-1120], [VGP-1150], [VGP-1190], [VGP-1200], [VGP-1210], [VGP-1220], [VGP-1250], [VGP-1270], [VGP-1280]; France [VGP-150], [VGP-160], [VGP-520], [VGP-750], [VGP-760], [VGP-770], [VGP-920], [VGP-1260]; Germany [VGP-1230]; Great Britain [VGP-120], [VGP-390], [VGP-660]; Ireland [VGP-210], [VGP-220], [VGP-530]; Italy [VGP-830]; Switzerland [VGP-1130]; Wales [VGP-740].

Although works treating individual artists are not typically included in this book, a few artists have been so prominent in the design and production of stained glass windows that one cannot hope to understand the trends in this art form during the nineteenth and twentieth centuries without knowing something about these artists. In alphabetical order these artists are as follows: Marc Chagall [VGP-850]; John Piper [VGP-370]; Patrick Reyntiens [VGP-1020], [VGP-1030]; and Louis Comfort Tiffany [VGP-460], [VGP-480], [VGP-700], [VGP-930]. For additional works focusing on painters and designers of stained glass windows, see [VGP-250] and [VGP-800]. Also consult any of the several strong journals listed below, including [VGP-660], [VGP-670], [VGP-960], and [VGP-1100]. Finally, note that some studies of stained glass are linked with the study of architecture, as indicated in bibliography [VGP-070] given above, and in [VGP-340] and [VGP-870]. See Chapter 3 on architecture for additional works linking these two art forms.

Special Bibliographies

[VGP-010] Brady, Darlene A., and William Serban. *Stained Glass: A Guide to Information Sources*. Art and Architecture Information Guide Series, vol. 10. Detroit: Gale Research, 1980. 572 pp.

[VGP-020] ------. *Stained Glass Index, 1906-1977*. St. Louis: Stained Glass

399

Association of America, 1979. 172 pp.

[VGP-030] British Society of Master Glass Painters. *A Directory of Stained Glass Windows*. London: British Society of Master Glass-Painters, 1952. 113 pp. 1966. 113 pp.

[VGP-040] ------. *A Directory of Stained Glass Painters, Executed Within the Past Twenty Years*. [London]: N.p., 1955. 109 pp.

[VGP-050] Caviness, Madeline Harrison, and Evelyn Ruth Staudinger. *Stained Glass Before 1540: An Annotated Bibliography*. Boston: G. K. Hall, 1983. 304 pp.

[VGP-060] Evans, David. *A Bibliography of Stained Glass*. Cambridge, [Cambridgeshire]: D. S. Brewer; Totowa, N.J.: Biblio Distribution Services, 1982. 200 pp.

[VGP-070] Harmon, Robert B[artlett]. *The Uses of Stained Glass in Architecture: A Selected Bibliography*. Architecture Series--Bibliography, 0194-1356; A-788. Monticello, Ill.: Vance Bibliographies, 1982. 13 pp.

[VGP-080] Hench, L. L., ed. *A Bibliography of Ceramics and Glass*. Gainesville, Fla.: n.p., 1967. 85 pp.

[VGP-090] Mayo, Melanie S., comp. and ed. *Directory of Stained Glass Books and Patterns*. 3rd. ed. San Carlos, Calif.: Stained Glass Images, 1992.

[VGP-100] Vance, Mary A. *Stained and Painted Glass: Monographs*. Monticello, Ill.: Vance Bibliographies, 1984. 100 pp.

Key Works

[VGP-110] Addleshaw, G[eorge] W[illiam] O[utram]. *Chester Cathedral: The Stained Glass Windows, Mosaics, Monuments and Some of its Other Treasures*. 4th ed. Gloucester: British Publishing Co., 1974. 40 pp.

[VGP-120] Angus, Mark. *Modern Stained Glass in British Churches*. London: Mowbray, 1984. Bib. pp. 119-120.

[VGP-130] Archer, Michael. *An Introduction to English Stained Glass*. Victoria and Albert Introductions to the Decorative Arts. London: H.M.S.O.; Owings Mills, Md.: Stemmer House, 1985. Bib. p. 48.

[VGP-140] ------. *English Heritage in Stained Glass: Oxford*. Oxford; New

York: TAI, 1988. Bib. p. 79.

[VGP-150] Aschokke, Fridtjor. *Die Romanischen Glasgemalde des Strass-burger Münsters.* Basel: B. Schwabe and Co., 1942. Bib. pp. 212-213.

[VGP-160] Aubert, Marcel. *French Cathedral Windows of the Twelfth and Thirteenth Centuries.* New York: Oxford University Press, 1947. 14 pp.

[VGP-170] Baker, John. *English Stained Glass.* London: Thames and Hudson, 1960. Bib. pp. 242-243.

[VGP-180] ------. *English Stained Glass of the Medieval Period.* Photo. Alfred Lammer. London: Thames and Hudson, 1978. [96] pp.

[VGP-190] Bayless, John Hocking, Nancy S. Montgomery, and Marcia P. Johnson. *Jewels of Light: The Stained Glass and Mosaics of Washington Cathedral.* Rev. ed. Washington, D.C.: Cathedral Church of Saint Peter and Saint Paul, 1984. 72 pp.

[VGP-200] Beaumont, John. *The Stained Glass of Southwell Minster: A Brief Guide to the Stained and Painted Glass at the Parish Church and Cathedral of St. Mary, Southwell, Commonly Known as Southwell Minster.* Southwell: J. Beaumont, 1988. Bib. p. 46.

[VGP-210] Bowe, Nicola Gordon. *The Life and Work of Harry Clarke.* Dublin: Irish Academic Press, 1989. Bib. pp. 279-285.

[VGP-220] Bowe, Nicola Gordon, David Caron, and Michael Wynne. *Gazetteer of Irish Stained Glass: The Works of Harry Clarke and the Artists of an tur gloine (The Tower of Glass), 1903-1963.* Dublin: Irish Academic Press, 1988. Bib. refs. pp. 110-112.

[VGP-230] Brisac, Catherine. *A Thousand Years of Stained Glass.* Trans. Geoffrey Culverwell. Trans. *Vitrail.* Garden City, N.Y.: Doubleday, 1986. Bib. pp. 195-198.

[VGP-240] Brown, Sarah. *Stained Glass: An Illustrated History.* Avenel, N.J.: Crescent Books, 1992. Bib. pp. 174-175.

[VGP-250] Brown, Sarah, and David O'Connor. *Glass-Painters.* London: British Museum, 1991. Bib.

[VGP-260] Cannon, Linda. *Stained Glass in the Burrell Collection.* Edinburgh: Chambers, 1991. Bib. pp. 93-94.

[VGP-270] Caviness, Madeline Harrison. *Corpus vitrearum Medii Aevi.* Vol. 1, *Christ Church Cathedral, Canterbury: The Windows of*

Christ Church Cathedral Canterbury. London: Oxford University Press for the British Academy, 1981. 352 pp. 224 pp. of plates.

[VGP-280] ------. *The Early Stained Glass of Canterbury Cathedral, c. 1175-1220*. Princeton: Princeton University Press, 1977. Bib. pp. 179-184.

[VGP-290] ------. "Fifteenth Century Stained Glass from the Chapel of Hampton Court, Herefordshire: The Apostles' Creed and Other Subjects." *The Forty-Second Volume of the Walpole Society, 1968-1970*. Glasgow: Robert MacLehose and Co., University Press for Walpole Society, 1970. pp. 35-60, 13 pp. of plates. Bib. refs.

[VGP-300] ------. *Sumptuous Arts and the Royal Abbeys in Reims and Braine*. Princeton; Oxford: Princeton University Press, 1990. 401 pp. Bib. pp. 157-162.

[VGP-310] Caviness, Madeline Harrison, and Busch-Reisinger Museum. *Medieval and Renaissance Stained Glass from New England Collections*. Exhibition, Busch-Reisinger Museum, Harvard University, 25 April to 10 June 1978. Medford, Mass.: Tufts University, 1978. Bib. refs. pp. 92-96.

[VGP-320] Caviness, Madeline Harrison, et al. *Stained Glass Before 1700 in American Collections: Corpus Vitrearum Checklist*. 4 vols. Studies in the History of Art, vols. 15, 23, 28, 39, Monograph Series, 1. Washington, D.C.: National Gallery of Art, 1985-1991. Dist. Hanover, [N.H.]: University Press of New England. Bibs. Vol. 1: *New England and New York*. Vol. 2: *Mid-Atlantic and Southeastern Seaboard States*. Vol. 3: *Midwestern and Western States*. Vol. 4: *Silver-Stained Roundels and Unipartite Panels*.

[VGP-330] Clark, Willene B. *The Stained Glass Art of William Jay Bolton*. Syracuse, N.Y.: Syracuse University Press, 1992. 242 pp. Bib. refs. pp. 145-152.

[VGP-340] Clarke, Brian, ed. *Architectural Stained Glass*. London: John Murray; New York: Architectural Record Books, 1979. Bib. pp. 230-232.

[VGP-350] Coe, Brian. *Stained Glass in England, 1150-1550*. London: W. H. Allen, 1981. Bib. pp. 132-134.

[VGP-360] Colchester, L. S. *Stained Glass in Wells Cathedral*. 5th ed. [Wells, England]: Friends of Wells Cathedral, 1977. 35 pp. Bib. refs.

[VGP-370] Compton, Ann. *John Piper, Painting in Coloured Light: An Exhibition of Stained Glass and Related Works*. Cambridge: The Gallery, 1982. 35 pp.

[VGP-380] *Conservation and Restoration of Stained Glass: An Owner's Guide*. [New York]: Census of Stained Glass Windows in America, 1988. 40 pp. Bib. refs.

[VGP-390] Cowen, Painton. *A Guide to Stained Glass in Britain*. London: M. Joseph, 1985. 280 pp. Bib. p. 258.

[VGP-400] ------. *Rose Windows*. San Francisco: Chronicle Books, 1979. Bib. p. 142.

[VGP-410] Cox, Van Loren. "Growth and Progression in Stained Glass: A Conceptual Interpretation of the Basic Christian Iconographic Theme of the Jesse Window in a Contemporary Idiom." M.F.A. Thesis, Louisiana State University, Baton Rouge, 1979. Bib. pp. 42-43.

[VGP-420] Crewe, Sarah, and Royal Commission on Historical Monuments. *Stained Glass in England c. 1180-1540*. London: H.M.S.O., 1987. Bib. pp. 99-101.

[VGP-430] Dean, Ann S. *A William Morris Christmas Book: The Christmas Story in Stained Glass by William Morris and Burne-Jones, and in Verses by Morris and Others*. Malvern: Heritage Press, 1990. Bib.

[VGP-440] Dennison, Antonette. "The Stained Glass Windows in Four Palm Beaches Churches, 1889-1984: The Religions and Social Context of Their Styles and Programs." Florida State University, 1988. Bib. pp. 415-437.

[VGP-450] Drake, Maurice. *A History of English Glass-Painting, with some Remarks upon the Swiss Glass Miniatures of the Sixteenth and Seventeenth Centuries*. New York: McBride, 1913. 226 pp.

[VGP-460] Duncan, Alastair. *Tiffany Windows*. New York: Simon and Schuster, 1980. Bib. pp. 196-199.

[VGP-470] Elskus, Albinas. *The Art of Painting on Glass: Techniques and Designs for Stained Glass*. New York: Charles Scribner's Sons, 1980. Bib. p. 140.

[VGP-480] Feldman, Joan Sharp. "Louis Comfort Tiffany: Artist and Innovator in Ecclesiastical Stained Glass." M.A. Thesis, University of Maryland, College Park, 1989. 97 pp. Bib. refs.

[VGP-490] Frelinghuysen, Alice Cooney. "A New Renaissance: Stained

Glass in the Aesthetic Period." *In Pursuit of Beauty: Americans and the Aesthetic Movement*. New York: Metropolitan Museum of Art, Rizzoli International Publications, 1986. pp. 176-197. Bib. refs. pp. 196-197.

[VGP-500] French, Thomas [W.], and David Elgar O'Connor. *York Minster: A Catalogue of Medieval Stained Glass*. Corpus vitrearum Medii Aevi, Great Britain, vol. 3. Oxford; New York: Oxford University Press for the British Academy, 1987. Bib. vol. 1, pp. xvii-xviii.

[VGP-510] Frohbieter-Mueller, Jo. *Practical Stained Glass Craft*. Newton Abbot: David and Charles, 1984. Bib. p. 171.

[VGP-520] Gobillot, Rene. *The Cathedral of Chartres: Its Influence on the Art of Glass*. Trans. Anne-Gaby Young. N.p.: Helio-Cachan, 1962. 49 pp.

[VGP-530] Gordon Bowe, Nicola, David Caron, and Michael Wynne. *A Gazeteer of Irish Stained Glass*. Dublin: n.p., 1988.

[VGP-540] Grodecki, Louis, and Catherine Brisac. *Gothic Stained Glass, 1200-1300*. Trans. Barbara Drake Boehm. *Le vitrail gothique au XIIIe siecle*. Ithaca: Cornell University Press; London: Thames and Hudson, 1985. Bib. pp. 269-270.

[VGP-550] Grodecki, Louis, Catherine Brisac, and Claudine Lautier. *Le Vitrail Roman*. Fribourg, Switzerland: Office du livre, 1977. Bib. p. 299.

[VGP-560] Halliday, Sonia. *The Christmas Story in Stained Glass*. Tring: Lion Publishing, 1980. 32 pp.

[VGP-570] Halliday, Sonia, Laura Lushington, and Tim Dowley. *The Bible in Stained Glass*. Swindon: Bible Society, 1990. 160 pp.

[VGP-580] Harries, John. *Discovering Stained Glass*. 2nd ed. Aylesbury, Bucks: Shire Publications, 1980. Bib. p. 56.

[VGP-590] Harrison, Martin. *Victorian Stained Glass*. London: Barrie and Jenkins, 1980. Bib. pp. 86-89.

[VGP-600] Haward, Birkin. *Nineteenth Century Norfolk Stained Glass: Gazetteer, Directory: An Account of Norfolk Stained Glass Painters*. Norwich, England: Geo Books; Centre of East Anglican Studies, 1984. Bib. pp. 293-298.

[VGP-610] ------. *Nineteenth Century Suffolk Stained Glass: Gazetteer, Directory, An Account of Suffolk Stained Glass Painters*. Woodbridge: Boydell, 1989. 256 pp.

[VGP-620] Hill, D. Ingram. *The Stained Glass of Canterbury Cathedral*. Canterbury: Friends of Canterbury Cathedral, 1975. 36 pp.

[VGP-630] Hillman, Bill. *Religious Stained Glass for Today*. N.p.: CKE Publications, 1990. 60 pp.

[VGP-640] Husband, Timothy B., and Madeline Harrison Caviness. *Stained Glass before 1700 in American Collections: Silver-Stained Roundels and Unipartite Panels (Corpus Vitrearum Checklist IV)*. Studies in the History of Art (Washington, D.C.), Monograph Series 1. Washington, D.C.: National Gallery of Art, 1991. Dist. University Press of New England, Hanover, N.H. Bib. refs. pp. 256-258.

[VGP-650] Hutter, Heribert. *Medieval Stained Glass*. Trans. *Glasmalerei im Mittelalter*. London: Methuen, 1964. 62 pp. Bib. p. 15.

[VGP-660] *Journal of the British Society of Master Glass-Painters*. Also called *The Journal of Stained Glass*. London: The Society, 1924-1982. Bib. refs.

[VGP-670] *Journal of Glass Studies*. Corning, N.Y.: Corning Museum of Glass, 1959-. Annual.

[VGP-680] Judson, Walter W. *Living Light: A Stained Glass Manual and History*. San Diego: A. S. Barnes, 1983. Dist. Oak Tree Publications.

[VGP-690] Kari, Daven Michael. "Finding a Face for the Triune God: Christian Iconography in Stained Glass." Ph.D. Thesis, Southern Baptist Theological Seminary, 1991. Bib. pp. 319-331.

[VGP-700] Koch, Robert. "The Stained Glass Decades: A Study of Louis Comfort Tiffany (1848-1933) and the Art Nouveau in America." 3 vols. Ph.D. Thesis, Yale University, 1957.

[VGP-710] Kockakian, Garbed. *Armenian Portraits of Faith: Stained Glass Windows, St. Mesrob Church*. Racine, Wis.: E. J. Hill, 1989. Bib. refs. p. 69.

[VGP-720] Lee, Lawrence. *The Appreciation of Stained Glass*. New York: Oxford University Press, 1977. 117 pp. Bib. refs.

[VGP-730] Lee, Lawrence, George Seddon, and Francis Stephens. *Stained Glass*. Photo. Sonia Halliday and Laura Lushington. New York: Crown Publishers, 1976. Reprint. London: Artists House, 1982. Reprint. Secaucus, N.J.: Chartwell Books; London: Spring, 1989. Bib. p. 207.

[VGP-740] Lewis, Mostyn. *Stained Glass in North Wales up to 1850*. Altrincham: Sherratt, 1970. 173 pp. Bib. pp. xix-xxi.

[VGP-750] Lillich, Meredith P. *The Armor of Light: Stained Glass in Western France, 1250-1325.* California Studies in the History of Art, vol. 23. Berkeley: University of California Press, 1993. Bib. refs.

[VGP-760] ------. *Rainbow like an Emerald: Stained Glass in Lorraine in the Thirteenth and Early Fourteenth Centuries.* Monographs on the Fine Arts, vol. 47. University Park: Pennsylvania State University Press for College Art Association, 1991. Bib. refs. pp. 109-153.

[VGP-770] ------. *The Stained Glass of Saint-Pere de Chartres.* Middletown, Conn.: Wesleyan University Press, 1978. Bib. pp. 197-201.

[VGP-780] Lloyd, John Gilbert. *Stained Glass in America.* Jenkintown, Pa.: Foundation Books, 1963. Bib. pp. 143-145.

[VGP-790] Loring, Bronwyn Evans. *St. John's Stained Glass.* [Beverly Farms, Mass.]: St. John's Episcopal Church, 1985. Bib. pp. 59-60.

[VGP-800] MacDowell, Betty Ann. "American Women Stained Glass Artists, 1870S [sic] to 1930S [sic]: Their World and Their Windows." Ph.D. Thesis, Michigan State University, 1986. Bib. pp. 331-357.

[VGP-810] Maddy, Dorothy L., Barbra E. Krueger, and Richard L. Hoover. *SGAA [Stained Glass Association of America] Reference and Technical Manual: A Comprehensive Guide to Stained Glass.* 2nd ed. Lee's Summit, Mo.: The Association, 1992. 785 pp. Bib. refs.

[VGP-820] Manning, Martha Lewis. *Stained Glass at Trinity.* Morgantown, W. Va.: Trinity Episcopal Church, 1987. Bib. pp. 37-38.

[VGP-830] Marchini, Giusseppe. *Italian Stained Glass Windows.* Trans. *Le vetrate Italiane.* New York: Harry N. Abrams, Inc., 1956. Bib. refs. in Notes, pp. 233-255. Bib. p. 256.

[VGP-840] Marks, Richard. *The Stained Glass of the Collegiate of the Holy Trinity, Tattershall (Lincolnshire).* Outstanding Theses from the Courtauld Institute of Art. New York; London: Garland Publishing, 1984. Bib. pp. 328-351.

[VGP-850] Marteau, Robert. *The Stained-Glass Windows of Chagall: 1957-1970.* Trans. New York: Tudor Pub. Co., [1973]. 159 pp.

[VGP-860] Mayo, Melanie S. *Stained Glass Images, Inc. Presents: The Directory of Stained Glass Books and Patterns.* San Carlos, Calif.:

Stained Glass Images, Inc., 1988.

[VGP-870] Moor, Andrew. *Contemporary Stained Glass: A Guide to the Potential of Modern Stained Glass in Architecture*. London: Mitchell Beazley, 1990. 144 pp.

[VGP-880] Moore, Peter Clement. *Crown in Glory: A Celebration of Craftsmanship: Studies in Stained Glass*. Norwich: Jarrold and Sons, 1982. 80 pp. Bib. refs.

[VGP-890] Newton, R[oy] G. *The Deterioration and Conservation of Painted Glass: A Critical Bibliography and Three Research Papers*. London: Oxford University Press, 1974. 93 pp.

[VGP-900] Newton, Roy, and Peter Gison. *Caring for Stained Glass*. London: Ecclesiastical Architects' and Surveyors' Association, 1987. Bib. refs. pp. 24-26.

[VGP-910] Osbourne, June. *Stained Glass in England*. Dover, N.H.: Alan Sutton, 1993. Bib. refs.

[VGP-920] Papanicolaou, Linda Morey. "Stained Glass Windows of the Choir of the Cathedral of Tours." 2 vols. Ph.D. Thesis, New York University, Graduate School of Arts and Science, 1979. Bib. pp. 259-269.

[VGP-930] *Partial List of Windows, A: Designed and Executed by Tiffany Studios*. 3rd ed. New York: Tiffany Press, 1979. 119 pp.

[VGP-940] Pastan, Elizabeth Carson. "The Early Stained Glass of Troyes Cathedral: The Ambulatory Chapel Glazing c. 1200-1240." Ph.D. Thesis, Brown University, 1986. Bib. pp. 184-195.

[VGP-950] Piper, John. *Stained Glass: Art or Anti-Art*. New York: Reinhold Book Corporation, 1968. 95 pp.

[VGP-960] *Professional Stained Glass*. [New York: Edge Publishing Group, 1981-].

[VGP-970] Rackham, Bernard. *The Ancient Glass of Canterbury Cathedral*. London: Lund Humphries, 1949. Bib. pp. 185-186.

[VGP-980] Raguin, Virginia Chieffo. *Stained Glass in Thirteenth-Century Burgundy*. Princeton: Princeton University Press, 1982. Bib. pp. 175-178.

[VGP-990] Raguin, Virginia Chieffo, Eckhard Bernstein, Timothy Husband, and Ellen Konowitz. *Northern Renaissance Stained Glass: Continuity and Transformations*. Exhibition, 2 February to 8 March 1987. Worcester, Mass.: Iris and B. Gerald Cantor

Art Gallery, College of the Holy Cross, 1987. 85 pp. Bib. refs.

[VGP-1000] Read, Herbert Edward. *English Stained Glass*. New York: G. P. Putnam's Sons, [1926]. Bib. pp. 250-253.

[VGP-1010] Reed, Cleota. *Henry Keck Stained Glass Studio, 1913-1974*. Syracuse, N.Y.: Syracuse University Press, 1985. 159 pp. Bib. refs.

[VGP-1020] Reyntiens, Patrick. *The Beauty of Stained Glass*. Boston: Bullfinch Press Book, 1990. Bib. refs. pp. 219-220.

[VGP-1030] ------. *The Technique of Stained Glass*. New York: Watson-Guptill Publications, 1967. Bib. pp. 179-182.

[VGP-1040] Russ, Joel. *Contemporary Stained Glass: A Portfolio of Canadian Work*. Toronto: Doubleday Canada Ltd.; Garden City, N.Y.: Doubleday, 1985. 192 pp.

[VGP-1050] San Casciani, Paul. *The Technique of Decorative Stained Glass*. London: B. T. Batsford, 1985. Reprint. New York: Dover Publications, 1989. Bib. p. 116.

[VGP-1060] Sherry, Beverley. *Australia's Historic Stained Glass*. Sydney: Murray Child, 1991. Bib. pp. 122-125.

[VGP-1070] Smith, M. Q. *The Stained Glass of Bristol Cathedral*. Bristol: Redcliffe, 1983. 96 pp. Bib. refs.

[VGP-1080] Sowers, Robert. *The Language of Stained Glass*. Forest Grove, Oreg.: Timber Press, 1981. 206 pp. Bib. refs.

[VGP-1090] Spring, Roy Orland Charles. *The Stained Glass of Salisbury Cathedral*. 2nd ed. Salisbury: Friends of Salisbury Cathedral, 1979. Bib. p. 32.

[VGP-1100] *Stained Glass Quarterly*. [Saint Louis]: Stained Glass Association of America, 1906-. Quarterly. Continues *Stained Glass*, 1906-1986.

[VGP-1110] *Stained Glass Window Manufacturing*. Irvine, Calif.: Entrepreneur Inc., American Entrepreneurs Association, 1988. Bib. pp. 146-147.

[VGP-1120] Stavridi, Margaret. *Master of Glass: Charles Eamer Kempe, 1837-1907 and the Work of his Firm in Stained Glass and Church Decoration*. Hatfield Herts, Stevenage Herts: J. Taylor Book Ventures for the Kempe Society, 1988. Dist. Spa Books. Bib. refs. pp. 157-158.

[VGP-1130] Stettler, Michael. *Old Stained Glass in Switzerland.* Zurich: Swiss National Tourist Office, 1953. Bib. p. 47.

[VGP-1140] Sturm, James L. *Stained Glass from Medieval Times to the Present: Treasures to be Seen in New York.* Photo. James Chotas. New York: E. P. Dutton and Co., 1982. Bib. pp. 145-148.

[VGP-1150] Toy, John. *A Guide and Index to the Windows of York Minster.* [York]: Dean and Chapter of York, 1985. 55 pp.

[VGP-1160] Tutag, Nola Huse, and Lucy Hamilton. *Discovering Stained Glass in Detroit.* Detroit: Wayne State University Press, 1987. Bib. p. 163.

[VGP-1170] Voigt, Robert J. *Symbols in Stained Glass.* St. John's Seminary, Collegeville, Minnesota. St. Paul: North Central Publishing Co., 1957. 55 pp. Bib.

[VGP-1180] Walker, Samuel S., Sonia Halliday, Laura Lushington. *The Life of Christ in Stained Glass: With Text from the Bible.* New York: Walker and Co., 1978. 155 pp.

[VGP-1190] Wayment, Hilary. *King's College Chapel, Cambridge: The Great Windows, Introduction and Guide.* Cambridge: Provost and Scholars of King's College, 1982. Bib. p. 64.

[VGP-1200] ------. *King's College Chapel Cambridge: The Side-Chapel Glass.* Cambridge: Cambridge Antiquarian Society and the Provost and Scholars of King's College, Cambridge, 1991. Bib. pp. 213-215.

[VGP-1210] ------. *The Stained Glass of the Church of St. Mary, Fairford, Gloucestershire.* Occasional Paper (New Series)/Society of Antiquaries of London, no. 5. London: Society of Antiquaries of London, 1984. 115 pp.

[VGP-1220] Welander, David. *The Stained Glass of Gloucester Cathedral.* N.p.: David Welander, 1985. Bib. pp. 136-142.

[VGP-1230] Wentzel, Hans. *Meisterwerke der Glasmalerei.* Berlin: Deutscher Verein für Kunstwissenschaft, 1954. Bib. p. 85.

[VGP-1240] Wilson, Christopher. *The Gothic Cathedral.* London: n.p., 1990.

[VGP-1250] Winston, Charles. *An Inquiry into the Difference of Style Observable in Ancient Glass Paintings, Especially in England: With Hints on Glass Painting, by an Amateur.* 2 vols. Oxford: J. H. Parker, 1847.

[VGP-1260] Witzleben, Elisabeth von. *French Stained Glass*. Trans. *Licht und Farbe aus Frankreichs Kathedralen*. New York: Reynal; London: Thames and Hudson, 1968. Bib. pp. 260-261.

[VGP-1270] Woodforde, Christopher. *English Stained and Painted Glass*. Oxford: Clarendon Press, 1954. Bib. pp. 67-69.

[VGP-1280] ------. *The Norwich School of Glass-Painting in the Fifteenth Century*. London: Oxford University Press, 1950. 233 pp. Bib. refs in footnotes.

[VGP-1290] Zimmer, Jenny. *Stained Glass in Australia*. Melbourne; Oxford: Oxford University Press, 1984. Bib. pp. 168-170.

KEY WORKS ON GRAFFITI

Graffiti, the practice of writing on walls and other public objects, is ancient in usage, but has primarily been recognized as an art form only in the twentieth century. The slight number of works available on this subject betrays a suspicion of graffiti as being more of a nuisance to society than a creative expression of culture. But the extensive use of graffiti in the subways of New York and London, on the Berlin Wall, and in major cities throughout the western world has caused analysts of art to recognize in graffiti a popular and typically anonymous expression of folk art. The best research on this subject is being produced in Germany, as revealed in the substantial bibliography by Axel Thiel and Reinhold Aman [VGR-020], and in the six volumes of research compiled by Axel Thiel [VGR-230]. For conducting research, one will also find some assistance in Dlaine J. Epstein's short but seminal work, *American Graffiti: A Bibliography, with Library of Congress Call Numbers* [VGR-010].

Of the following works which discuss graffiti, the most recent and substantial are John Bushnell's *Moscow Graffiti: Language and Subculture* [VGR-070], Leland Rice's *Up Against It: Photographs of the Berlin Wall* [VGR-200], David Robinson's *Soho Walls: Beyond Graffiti* [VGR-210], and Jack Stewart's dissertation, "Subway Graffiti: An Aesthetic Study of Graffiti on the Subway System of New York City, 1970-1978" [VGR-220]. For one of the oldest accounts of graffiti in its two versions, see *The Merry-Thought, or, The Glass-Window and Bog-House Miscellany: Part 1 (1731)* [VGR-120] and

[VGR-160]. For reference texts offering useful surveys of this topic, see [VGR-050], [VGR-180], and [VGR-190]. The balance of works in this section treat graffiti from Medieval times-- [VGR-060] and [VGR-170]--to the twentieth century, including all the works not yet mentioned. Of special note for researchers is Ernest L. Abel's and Barbara E. Buckley's work, *The Handwriting on the Wall: Toward a Sociology and Psychology of Graffiti* [VGR-030], which attempts to analyze the sources of cultural influence on graffiti. None of the works written to date on graffiti appears to introduce a Christian perspective on this form of folk art, thus suggesting yet another topic for researchers exploring Christianity and the arts.

Special Bibliographies

[VGR-010] Epstein, Dlaine J. *American Graffiti: A Bibliography, with Library of Congress Call Numbers*. Washington, D.C.: Library of Congress, Archive of Folk Song, 1979. 7 pp.

[VGR-020] Thiel, Axel, and Reinhold Aman. *Graffitti-Bibliographie/Graffiti-Bibliography: International Work-Group on Graffiti-Research, German Work-Group on Graffiti-Research*. 3rd. ed. Kassel: AT Verlag, 1986. 105 pp.

Key Works

[VGR-030] Abel, Ernest L., and Barbara E. Buckley. *The Handwriting on the Wall: Toward a Sociology and Psychology of Graffiti*. Westport, Conn.: Greenwood Press, 1977. Bib. pp. 147-151.

[VGR-040] *Aesthetics of Graffiti: April 28--July 2, 1978*. San Francisco: Museum of Modern Art, 1978. [104] pp.

[VGR-050] Barclay, Bob. *A Dictionary of Graffiti*. New York: State Mutual Books, 1984.

[VGR-060] Blindheim, Martin. *Graffiti in Norwegian Stave Churches, c. 1150-c. 1350*. Oslo: Universitetsforlaget; Irvington-on-Hudson, N.Y.: Columbia University Press, 1985. Bib. pp. 72-74.

[VGR-070] Bushnell, John. *Moscow Graffiti: Language and Subculture*. Boston: Unwin Hyman, 1990. Bib. pp. 243-256.

[VGR-080]   Castleman, Craig. *Getting Up: Subway Graffiti in New York.* Cambridge: MIT Press, 1982. Bib. pp. 185-191.

[VGR-090]   Cooper, Martha, and Henry Chalfant. *Subway Art.* New York: Holt, Rinehart and Winston, 1984. 104 pp.

[VGR-100]   Erickson, Paul A. *Graffiti Halifax Style.* Hantsport, Novia Scotia: Lancelot Press, 1987. 56 pp. Bib. refs.

[VGR-110]   Hager, Steven. *Hip Hop: The Illustrated History of Break Dancing, Rap Music, and Graffiti.* New York: St. Martin's Press, 1984.

[VGR-120]   Hurlothrumbo. *The Merry-Thought, or, The Glass-Window and Boghouse Miscellany.* 4 vols. in 2. 1731. Reprint. Los Angeles: William Andrews Clark Memorial Library, University of California, 1982-1983. Bib. refs. (See [VGR-160])

[VGR-130]   Kohl, Herbert R. *Golden Boy as Anthony Cool: A Photo Essay on Naming and Graffiti.* Photo. James Hinton. New York: Dial Press, 1972. 177 pp.

[VGR-140]   Lang, Mabel. *Graffiti in the Athenian Agora.* American School of Classical Studies at Athens. Princeton: The School, 1974. [36] pp.

[VGR-150]   Levitt, Helen. *Chalk Drawings and Messages, New York City, 1938-1948.* Durham, N.C.: Duke University Press, 1987. 105 pp.

[VGR-160]   *Merry-Thought, or, The Glass-Window and Bog-House Miscellany, The: Part 1 (1731).* 1731. Reprint. Los Angeles: William Andrews Clark Memorial Library, University of California, Los Angeles, 1982. 32 pp. Bib. pp. vii-x. (See [VGR-120])

[VGR-170]   Pritchard, Violet. *English Medieval Graffiti.* Cambridge: Cambridge University Press, 1967. Bib. pp. 184-189.

[VGR-180]   Reisner, Robert George. *Graffiti: Two Thousand Years of Wall Writing.* Chicago: H. Regnery, [1971]. 204 pp.

[VGR-190]   Reisner, Robert George, and Lorraine Wechsler. *Encyclopedia of Graffiti.* New York: Galahad Books, 1980. Bib. p. 403.

[VGR-200]   Rice, Leland. *Up Against It: Photographs of the Berlin Wall.* Albuquerque: University of New Mexico Press, 1991. Bib. refs. pp. 117-127.

[VGR-210]   Robinson, David. *Soho Walls: Beyond Graffiti.* New York: Thames and Hudson, 1990. 96 pp. Bib. refs. p. 15.

[VGR-220] Stewart, Jack. "Subway Graffiti: An Aesthetic Study of Graffiti
on the Subway System of New York City, 1970-1978." Ph.D.
Thesis, New York University, 1990. 604 pp. Bib. refs.

[VGR-230] Thiel, Axel. *Einfuhrung in die Graffitti-Forschung/Introduction to
Graffiti-Research.* 6 vols. Kassel: A. Thiel, 1983.

KEY WORKS ON ICONS

Icons, images of Jesus or Mary or the venerated saints, have played a
prominent role in worship by the Eastern Orthodox Church since its earliest
days. While the exact date of origin for icons as elements in worship is difficult to ascertain, the presence of images in places of Christian worship can be
traced at least to the fourth century A.D., and very possibly as far back as the
second. The function of these earliest images in worship services is debatable,
especially since the catacombs where so many of these early images have been
found are no longer thought to have been places of worship for the early
Christians. What is certain is that by the eighth century the use of icons in
worship was so wide spread that a wave of often violent iconoclasm broke out
in the Byzantine empire and was not entirely settled until well into the next
century. Such persecution drove many painters of icons to Rome where their
influence blended with western traditions. While the Roman Catholic Church
does not often use the term icon, it does in fact make use of many icons, albeit
in a more natural style than that in the east. Officially, an icon is designed to
present to the eye the inner light of meditation and holiness. Realistic representation is intentionally limited to clarify the spiritual meaning.

Of the works listed below, the best studies seem to be those written by
Leonid Ouspensky, who worked with Vladimir Lossky for his major study of
icons, *The Meaning of Icons* [VIC-210 and VIC-220]. This particular study is
presented in both the first and second editions because the former has an
extensive bibliography not retained in the second edition. For a careful exploration of theological aesthetics as applied to icons, see Ouspensky's work
Theology of the Icon [VIC-200], along with John Baggley's *Doors of Perception:
Icons and Their Spiritual Significances* [VIC-010], Egon Sendler's *The Icon,
Image of the Invisible: Elements of Theology, Aesthetics, and Technique* [VIC-

290], and Eugene N. Trubetskoi's *Icons: Theology in Color* [VIC-340].

The other volumes listed below tend to treat regional developments of icons, including the following: American [VIC-100]; Byzantine [VIC-160]; Celtic [VIC-170]; Czechoslovakian [VIC-300]; Greek [VIC-050], [VIC-090], [VIC-230], [VIC-270], [VIC-320]; Palestinian [VIC-020]; Romanian [VIC-150]; Russian [VIC-080], [VIC-140], [VIC-180], [VIC-310], [VIC-320], [VIC-350]. For comprehensive surveys of icons and their history, see the works of Kurt Weitzmann, including *The Icon: Holy Images--Sixth to Fourteenth Century* [VIC-360], and *The Icon* [VIC-370]. For other useful studies treating a wide variety of icons and their development through history, see [VIC-030], [VIC-040], [VIC-070], [VIC-110], [VIC-120], [VIC-130], [VIC-190], [VIC-240], [VIC-250], [VIC-260], [VIC-330], and [VIC-380].

[VIC-010] Baggley, John. *Doors of Perception: Icons and Their Spiritual Significances*. Crestwood, N.Y.: St. Vladimir's Seminary Press, 1987. 160 pp. Bib. refs.

[VIC-020] Beneshevich, V. N., and Saint Catherine Monastery, Mount Sinai. *Pamiatniki Sinaia, Arkheologicheskie I Paleograficheskie*. 2 vols. Leningrad: Izd. Rossiiskoi Akademii Nauk, 1912.

[VIC-030] Bosilkov [sic], Svetlin. *Arbanassi: Iconostases and Religious Easel Art, 15th-18th and 19th Centuries*. Sofia: Svyat Publishers, 1989. Bib. refs. pp. 376-388.

[VIC-040] Bossilkov [sic], Svetlin. *Arbanassi: Icons and Religious Art, 15th-18th Century*. London: Alpine Fine Arts; N.p., U.S.: Alpine Fine Arts Collection, 1991. 400 pp.

[VIC-050] Chatzedakes, Manoles. *Icons of Patmos: Questions of Byzantine and Post-Byzantine Painting*. Trans. Thetis Xanthaki. [Athens]: National Bank of Greece, 1985. 205 pp. Bib. pp. 13-16.

[VIC-060] Evdokimou, Paul. *L'Art de L'Icône: Théologie de la Beauté*. N.p.: Desclée de Brouwer, 1970. Bib. p. 301.

[VIC-070] Fabricius, Ulrich. *Icons: Portrayals of Christ*. Trans. Hans Hermann Rosenwald. Recklinghausen: Aurel Bongers, 1967; dist. Taplinger Publishing Co. 82 pp.

[VIC-080] Farbman, Michael S. *Masterpieces of Russian Painting: Twenty Colour Plates and Forty-Three Monochrome Reproductions of*

414

Russian Icons and Frescoes from the XI to the XVIII Centuries. London: Zwemmer, [1930]. Bib. p. 125.

[VIC-090] Feast Day Icons: 15th-17th Century. Exhibition, New Grecian Gallery, November 1973 to January 1974. London: Lund Humphries, n.d. 52 illustrations with bib. refs.

[VIC-100] Galavaris, George. Icons from The Elvehjem Art Center. [Madison, Wis.]: The Elvehjem Art Center, University of Wisconsin-Madison, 1973. 127 pp. Bib. pp. xv-xxii.

[VIC-110] ------. The Icon in the Life of the Church: Doctrine, Liturgy, Devotion. Leiden: E. J. Brill, 1981. Bib. pp. xiii-xv.

[VIC-120] Gerhard, H. P. The World of Icons. Trans. New York: Harper and Row, 1971. Bib. pp. 222-224.

[VIC-130] Giraud, Marie-Françoise. Approches des Icones. Paris: Mediaspaul; Montreal: Editions Paulines, 1987. Bib. p. 90.

[VIC-140] Hnatenko, Stefaniia. Treasures of Early Ukrainian Art: Religious Art of the 16th-18th Centuries. New York: Ukrainian Museum, 1989. 44 pp. Bib. refs.

[VIC-150] Irimie, Cornel, and Marcela Focsa. Romanian Icons Painted on Glass. New York: W. W. Norton and Co., 1970. 35 pp. and 149 illus. Bib. pp. 23-26.

[VIC-160] Mathew, Gervase. Byzantine Aesthetics. 1969. Reprint. N.p.: John Murray, 1981.

[VIC-170] Meehan, Aidan. Celtic Design: Illuminated Letters. New York: Thames and Hudson, 1992. 160 pp. Bib. refs.

[VIC-180] Millenium of the Holy Baptism of the Kievan Rus', The: 988-1988. Leuven: Ukrainian House, 1987. 202 pp.

[VIC-190] Onasch, Konrad. Icons. Trans. Marianne von Herzfeld. New York: Barnes, 1963. Bib. pp. 409-413.

[VIC-200] Ouspensky, Leonid. Theology of the Icon. Crestwood, N.Y.: St. Vladimir's Seminary Press, 1978.

[VIC-210] Ouspensky, Leonid, and Vladimir Lossky. The Meaning of Icons. Trans. G. E. H. Palmer and E. Kadloubovsky. Boston: Boston Book and Art Shop, [1969]. Bib. pp. 147-216.

[VIC-220] ------. The Meaning of Icons. Rev. ed. Trans. G. E. H. Palmer and E. Kadloubovsky. Crestwood, N.Y.: St. Vladimir's Seminary, 1982. Bib. p. 221.

[VIC-230] Papastratou, Dore. *Paper Icons: Greek Orthodox Religious Engravings, 1665-1899.* Trans. of *Chartines Eikones.* 2 vols. Athens: Papastratos; Recklinghausen: A. Bongers, 1990.

[VIC-240] Pramod, Kumar. *Folk Icons and Rituals in Tribal Life.* New Delhi: Abhinav, 1984. Bib. pp. 84-85.

[VIC-250] Ramos-Poqui, Guillem. *The Technique of Icon Painting.* Harrisburg, Pa.: Morehouse Publishing, 1990. Bib. p. 78.

[VIC-260] Rice, David, and Tamara Talbot Rice. *Icons and Their History.* Woodstock, N.Y.: The Overlook Press, 1974. 192 pp. Bib. p. 6.

[VIC-270] Rice, D. Talbot, Rupert Gunnis, and Tamara Talbot Rice. *The Icons of Cyprus.* London: George Allen and Unwin, Ltd., 1937. 192 pp. and 153 illustrations. Bib.

[VIC-280] Sahas, Daniel J. *Icon and Logos: Sources in Eighth-Century Iconoclasm: An Annotated Translation of the Sixth Session of the Seventh Ecumenical Council (Nicea, 787).* Toronto: University of Toronto Press, 1986.

[VIC-290] Sendler, Egon. *The Icon, Image of the Invisible: Elements of Theology, Aesthetics, and Technique.* Trans. Steven Bigham. Redondo Beach, Calif.: Oakwood Publications, 1988. Bib. pp. 281-282.

[VIC-300] Skrobucha, Heinz. *Icons in Czechoslovakia.* Photo Ladislav Neubert. London; New York: Hamlyn Publishing Group, Ltd., 1971. xxxiv, 131 pp. Unpaginated text, Bib. pp. 125-127.

[VIC-310] Stockley, Francine Jenna. "The Meaning and Religious Significance of Russian Orthodox Icons." M.A. Thesis, University of Georgia, 1973. 116 pp.

[VIC-320] Temple, D., and J. Stuart. *Russian and Greek Icons.* San Francisco: Van Doren Gallery, 1981. 80 pp. Bib.

[VIC-330] Temple, Richard [C. C.]. *Icons and the Mystical Origins of Christianity.* Shaftesbury; Rockport, Mass.: Element, 1990, 1992. 198 pp. Bib. refs.

[VIC-340] Trubetskoi, Eugene N. *Icons: Theology in Color.* 1973. Reprint. Crestwood, N.Y.: St. Vladimir's Seminary Press, 1980.

[VIC-350] Trubetskoi, E[vgenii] N[ikolaevich]. *Tri Ocherka O Russkoi Ikone: Umozrenie V Kraskakh, Dva Mira V Drevne-Russkoi Ikonopisi, Rossiia V Ee Ikone.* Paris: YMCA-Press, 1965. 161 pp.

[VIC-360] Weitzmann, Kurt. *The Icon: Holy Images--Sixth to Fourteenth Century.* New York: George Braziller, 1978. 134 pp. Bib. p. 34.

[VIC-370] Weitzmann, Kurt, et al. *The Icon.* Trans. *Le Icone.* New York: Alfred A. Knopf, 1982. Dist. Random House. Bib. pp. 413-415.

[VIC-380] Wunderle, Georg. *Um die Seele der heiligen Ikonen: Eine religionspsychologische Betrachtung.* Das östliche Christenteum Neue Folge, Heft 5. Dritte, erweiterte Auflage. Würzburg: Augustinus-Verlag, 1947. 83 pp. Bib. refs.

KEY WORKS ON ILLUMINATED MANUSCRIPTS

Illuminated manuscripts can be traced as far back as ancient Egypt. By the Middle Ages this art form had been developed significantly in the monasteries of Ireland, England, and continental Europe. Often devoted to religious materials, illuminated manuscripts typically combine the arts of calligraphy and painting to produce an illustrated text. Research on illuminated manuscripts is usually done best in the major libraries which house the rare originals of these costly books, such as the Bodleian Library, the British Library, or the National Library of Greece. However, one can conduct considerable research through the fine reproductions of these manuscripts, many of which are listed below. The best and most current bibliographies on illuminated manuscripts have been produced by Thomas H. Ohlgren [VIL-040 to VIL-060] and several other prominent writers [VIL-010 to VIL-030]. While these bibliographies do not begin to list all of the fine illuminated manuscripts available in Europe, especially those in French and German and other non-English languages, the bibliographies given here do help readers identify many of the major texts in English, and hence accessible to those not versed in Old French or Old German or other archaic forms of the modern languages. For the latest reviews of research on illuminated manuscripts, see the semi-annual journal, the *International Review of Manuscript Studies* [VIL-940], written in both French and English.

Of the key works listed below, several are particularly helpful as reasonably current and scholarly introductions to the study of illustrated manuscripts, including the following: Janet Backhouse' *Books of Hours* [VIL-180], David Bland's *A History of Book Illustration: The Illuminated Manuscript and the Printed Book* [VIL-260], Robert G. Calkins' *Illuminated Books of the Middle Ages* [VIL-320], Christopher De Hamel's *A History of Illuminated Manuscripts* [VIL-340], David Diringer's *The Illuminated Book: Its History and Production* [VIL-370], John P. Harthan's *An Introduction to Illuminated Manuscripts* [VIL-510], and Thomas Kren's, Janet Backhouse', Mark Evans', and Myra Orth's *Renaissance Painting in Manuscripts: Treasures of the British Library* [VIL-620]. Some of the major writers worth noting in this area of research are Jonathan James Graham Alexander [VIL-070 to VIL-110, VIL-720, and VIL-850], Robert Gary Babcock [VIL-170], Lucy Freeman Sandler [VIL-900 to VIL-920], Kurt Weitzmann [VIL-1110 to VIL-1140], and Roger S. Wieck [VIL-1160 to VIL-1180].

The study of illuminated manuscripts, like that of most of the arts, can be divided according to author, time, place of origin, or place of current residence. Since calligraphers and illustrators are only rarely known for these manuscripts, using the creators of the manuscripts as a dividing principle is problematic. Even the authors of these texts are not often known, so they are often identified by their place of origin or by their original recipient or sponsor. For the sake of simplifying this classification system, the following works are grouped according to their place of origin: America [VIL-960]; Armenia [VIL-810]; Belgium [VIL-830], [VIL-910]; British Isles, excluding Ireland [VIL-100], [VIL-110], [VIL-150], [VIL-210], [VIL-220], [VIL-380], [VIL-490], [VIL-530], [VIL-760], [VIL-780], [VIL-820], [VIL-850], [VIL-1010], [VIL-1040], [VIL-1050], [VIL-1200]; Byzantium [VIL-330], [VIL-660], [VIL-990], [VIL-1110]; Flanders [VIL-480]; France [VIL-160], [VIL-200], [VIL-280], [VIL-400], [VIL-520], [VIL-830], [VIL-870], [VIL-880], [VIL-1030], [VIL-1090], [VIL-1220]; Germany [VIL-480]; Greece [VIL-860], [VIL-980], [VIL-1080]; Hungary [VIL-230], [VIL-240]; Ireland [VIL-300], [VIL-540], [VIL-970], [VIL-1000]; Italy [VIL-090], [VIL-130], [VIL-140], [VIL-440], [VIL-460], [VIL-500], [VIL-560], [VIL-610], [VIL-700]; Netherlands [VIL-550], [VIL-1020]; Palestine [VIL-1140]; Persia [VIL-1060]; Spain [VIL-710], [VIL-1190]; Syria [VIL-1130]; Thailand [VIL-420]; Turkey [VIL-120].

418

Some studies of illuminated manuscripts have a wide focus and include evaluations of works from many times and places, including the following valuable works: [VIL-070], [VIL-080], [VIL-100], [VIL-110], [VIL-170], [VIL-190], [VIL-210], [VIL-230], [VIL-270], [VIL-310], [VIL-430], [VIL-450], [VIL-460], [VIL-570], [VIL-600], [VIL-650], [VIL-680], [VIL-690], [VIL-770], [VIL-840], [VIL-850], [VIL-890], [VIL-900], [VIL-1210]. For studies of specific sacred works, consult the following categories: Books of Hours [VIL-180], [VIL-380], [VIL-400], [VIL-410], [VIL-720], [VIL-730], [VIL-1040], [VIL-1090], [VIL-1170], [VIL-1220]; Christian Bibles [VIL-820], [VIL-1150]; Hebrew Bibles and sacred texts [VIL-030], [VIL-470], [VIL-560], [VIL-640], [VIL-750], [VIL-790], [VIL-800], [VIL-950], [VIL-1100]; Korans or Qurans [VIL-350], [VIL-580], [VIL-590]. For additional studies of illuminated manuscripts, consult the bibliographies listed below.

Special Bibliographies

[VIL-010] Hionides, Harry, and Brian De Jongh. *Catalogue of the Illuminated Byzantine Manuscripts of the National Library of Greece.* Trans. *Katalogos mikrographion Vyzantinon cheirographon tes Ethnikes Vivliothekes tes Hellados.* Athens: Publications Bureau, Academy of Athens, 1978. Vol. 1, "Manuscripts of the New Testament Texts 10th-12th Century." Bib. refs.

[VIL-020] Horst, K[oert] van der. *Illuminated and Decorated Medieval Manuscripts in the University Library, Utrecht: An Illustrated Catalogue.* Cambridge: Cambridge University Press, 1989. Bib. pp. 72-75.

[VIL-030] Narkiss, Bezalel, with Aliza Cohen-Mushlin and Anat Tcherikover. *Hebrew Illuminated Manuscripts in the British Isles: A Catalogue Raisonne.* 2 vols. Oxford; New York: Oxford University Press for the Israel Academy of Sciences and Humanities and the British Academy, 1982. Bib. vol. 1, pt. 1, pp. 185-189.

[VIL-040] Ohlgren, Thomas H. *Illuminated Manuscripts: An Index to Selected Bodleian Library Color Reproductions.* Garland Reference Library of the Humanities, vol. 89. New York: Garland Publishing, 1977. 646 pp.

[VIL-050] ------. *Illuminated Manuscripts and Books in the Bodleian Library: A Supplemental Index.* Garland Reference Library of the

Humanities, vol. 123. New York: Garland Publishing, 1978. 583 pp.

[VIL-060] ------, ed. *Insular and Anglo-Saxon Illuminated Manuscripts: An Iconographic Catalogue, c. A.D. 625 to 1100.* Garland Reference Library of the Humanities, vol. 631. New York: Garland Publishing, 1986. xxvii, 400 pp. Bib. pp. xxi-xxvii.

Key Works

[VIL-070] Alexander, J[onathan] J[ames] G[raham]. *The Decorated Letter.* London: Thames and Hudson, 1978. 119 pp. Bib. pp. 31-34.

[VIL-080] ------. *Insular Manuscripts: 6th to the 9th Century.* London: Harvey Miller, 1978. 219 pp. Bib. refs.

[VIL-090] ------. *Italian Renaissance Illuminations.* London: Chatto and Windus, 1978. 119 pp. Bib. pp. 29-34.

[VIL-100] ------. *A Survey of Manuscripts Illuminated in the British Isles.* 4 vols. London: Henry Miller, 1975. Vol. 1: J[onathan] J[ames] G[raham] Alexander, *Insular Manuscripts, 6th to 9th Century.* Vol. 2: Elzbieta Temple, *Anglo-Saxon Manuscripts, 900-1066.* Vol. 3: C. M. Kauffmann, *Romanesque Manuscripts, 1066-1190.* Vol. 4: Nigel Morgan, *Early Gothic Manuscripts [I], 1190-1250.* (Also listed separately.)

[VIL-110] Alexander, J[onathan] J[ames] G[raham], and Elzbieta Temple. *Illuminated Manuscripts in the Oxford College Libraries, the University Archives, and the Taylor Institution.* New York: Oxford University Press, 1985. 142 pp.

[VIL-120] And, Metin. *Turkish Miniature Painting.* Ankara: Dost yay nlar, 1978. 142 pp.

[VIL-130] Armstrong, Lilian. *Opus Petri: Renaissance Illuminated Books from Venice and Rome.* Berkeley: University of California Press, 1990. [385]-412 pp. Bib. refs.

[VIL-140] ------. *Renaissance Miniature Painters and Classical Imagery: The Master of the Putti and his Venetian Workshop.* London; Philadelphia: Harvey Miller, 1981. Dist. Heyden. 223 pp. Bib. pp. 139-148.

[VIL-150] Auerbach, Erna. *Tudor Artists: A Study of Painters in the Royal Service and of Portraiture on Illuminated Documents from the Accession of Henry VIII to the Death of Elizabeth I.* [London]: University of London, Athlone Press, 1954. Bib. pp. 204-211.

[VIL-160] Avril, François. *Manuscript Painting at the Court of France: The Fourteenth Century, 1310-1380.* Trans. Ursule Molinaro and Bruce Benderson. New York: George Braziller, 1978. 118 pp. Bib. pp. 31-33.

[VIL-170] Babcock, Robert Gary, ed. *Beinecke Studies in Early Manuscripts.* The Yale University Library gazette, Supplement, vol. 66. New Haven: Yale University Library, 1991. pp. 101-241. Bib. refs.

[VIL-180] Backhouse, Janet. *Books of Hours.* London; Dover, N.H.: British Library, 1985. Bib. p. 80.

[VIL-190] ------. *The Illuminated Manuscript.* Oxford: Phaidon Press, 1976. Reprint. Oxford: Phaidon Press; N.p.: Marboro Books, 1986. 80 pp. Bib. p. 6.

[VIL-200] ------. *The Luttrell Psalter.* London: British Library, 1990. Bib. p. 64.

[VIL-210] Basing, Patricia. *Trades and Crafts in Medieval Manuscripts.* London: British Library, 1990. 112 pp. Bib.

[VIL-220] Beckwith, Alice H. R. H. *Victorian Bibliomania: The Illuminated Book in 19th-Century Britain.* Providence, R.I.: Museum of Art, Rhode Island School of Design, 1987. Bib. pp. 79-80.

[VIL-230] Berkovits, Ilona. *Illuminated Manuscripts from the Library of Matthias Corvinus.* Trans. *A Magyarorszagi Corvinak.* Budapest: Corvina Press, 1964. 147 pp. Bib. refs. in notes, pp. 105-117.

[VIL-240] ------. *Illuminated Manuscripts in Hungary, XI-XVI Centuries.* Rev. Alick West. Trans. *Magyar kodexek a XI-XVI szazadban.* Shannon: Irish University Press; New York: Frederick A. Praeger Publishers, 1969. Bib. pp. 97-100.

[VIL-250] Bise, Gabriel. *Tristan and Isolde: From a Manuscript of The Romance of Tristan (15th Century).* Fribourg: Productions Liber, 1978. 123 pp. Bib. p. 22.

[VIL-260] Bland, David. *A History of Book Illustration: The Illuminated Manuscript and the Printed Book.* 2nd ed. Berkeley: University of California Press, 1969. Bib. pp. 437-441.

[VIL-270] Bologna, Giulia. *Illuminated Manuscripts: The Book Before Gutenberg.* Trans. *Manoscritti e miniature.* London: Thames and Hudson; New York: Weidenfeld and Nicolson, 1988. Bib. p. 193.

[VIL-280] Branner, Robert. *Manuscript Painting in Paris During the Reign of Saint Louis: A Study of Styles.* Berkeley: University of California Press, 1977. 270 pp. Bib.

[VIL-290] Brieger, Peter H., Millard Meiss, and Charles S. Singleton. *Illuminated Mansucripts of the Divine Comedy.* 2 vols. Princeton: Princeton University Press, [1969]. Bib. vol. 1, pp. 343-350. London: Routledge and Kegan Paul, 1969. Bib. vol. 1, pp. 341-350.

[VIL-300] Brown, Peter, ed. *The Book of Kells: Forty-Eight Pages and Details in Colour from the Manuscript in Trinity College, Dublin.* London: Thames and Hudson, 1980. Bib. p. 96.

[VIL-310] Buchthal, Hugo. *A Hand List of Illuminated Oriental Christian Manuscripts.* London; Nendeln: The Warburg Institute; Nendeln: Kraus Reprint, 1968. Bib. pp. 110-116.

[VIL-320] Calkins, Robert G. *Illuminated Books of the Middle Ages.* Ithaca: Cornell University Press; [London]: Thames and Hudson, 1983. Bib. pp. 324-334.

[VIL-330] Cutler, Anthony. *Imagery and Ideology in Byzantine Art.* Hampshire, Great Britain: Variorum; Brookfield, Vt.: Ashgate Publishing Co., 1992. Bib. refs.

[VIL-340] De Hamel, Christopher. *A History of Illuminated Manuscripts.* Boston: David R. Godine, 1986. Bib. pp. 245-249.

[VIL-350] Deroche, François, and Nasser D. Khalili Collection of Islamic Art. *The Abbasid Tradition: Qur'ans of the 8th to the 10th Centuries AD.* [London]: Nour Foundation in association with Azmimuth and Oxford University Press, 1992. Bib. pp. 187-190.

[VIL-360] Dewald, Ernest Theodore. *The Illustrations of the Utrecht Psalter.* Princeton: Princeton University Press, 1932. Reprint. Ann Arbor: University Microfilms, 1970. Bib. p. 73.

[VIL-370] Diringer, David. *The Illuminated Book: Its History and Production.* Rev. with Reinhold Regensburger. New York: Frederick A. Praeger Publishers, [1967]. 514 pp. Bib. pp. 464-469.

[VIL-380] Donovan, Claire. *The de Brailes Hours: Shaping the Book of Hours in 13th-Century Oxford.* London: British Library, 1991. 216 pp.

422

[VIL-390] Erdman, David V. *The Illuminated Blake*. London: Oxford University Press, 1975. 416 pp.

[VIL-400] Fouquet, Jean. *The Hours of Étienne Chevalier*. Trans. *Les heures d'Étienne Chevalier*. London: Thames and Hudson, 1972. Bib. pp. 126-127.

[VIL-410] François, Maitre. *The Wharncliffe Hours: A Fifteenth-Century Illuminated Prayerbook in the Collection of the National Gallery of Victoria, Australia*. Ed. Margaret M. Manion. London: Thames and Hudson, 1981. Bib. p. 96.

[VIL-420] Ginsburg, Henry. *Thai Manuscript Painting*. London: British Library, 1989. 112 pp. Bib.

[VIL-430] Glaister, Geoffrey Ashall. *Glaister's Glossary of the Book: Terms used in Papermaking, Printing, Bookbinding and Publishing with Notes on Illuminated Manuscripts and Private Presses*. 2nd ed. Berkeley: University of California Press, 1979. Bib. pp. 547-551.

[VIL-440] Goff, Frederick Richmond, and Annmary Brown Memorial, Providence, R.I. *Illuminated Woodcut Borders and Initials in Early Venetian Books (1469-1475)*. N.p., 1962. Bib. p. 389.

[VIL-450] *Gothic and Renaissance Illuminated Manuscripts from Texas Collections. [Exhibition] 23 April--23 June 1971*. Austin: Miriam Lutcher Stark Library, University of Texas, 1971. Bib. pp. 46-47.

[VIL-460] Grafton, Anthony, ed. *Rome Reborn: The Vatican Library and Renaissance Culture*. Washington, D.C.: Library of Congress; London; New Haven: Yale University Press; Vatican City: Biblioteca Apostolica Vaticana, 1993. Bib. refs. pp. 305-312.

[VIL-470] Gutmann, Joseph. *Hebrew Manuscript Painting*. New York: George Brazilier, 1978.

[VIL-480] Hamburger, Jeffrey F. *The Rothschild Canticles: Art and Mysticism in Flanders and the Rhineland circa 1300*. New Haven; London: Yale University Press, 1990. 462 pp. Bib. refs. pp. 307-324.

[VIL-490] Haney, Kristine Edmondson. *The Winchester Psalter: An Iconographic Study*. [Leicester]: Leicester University Press; Atlantic Highlands, N.J.: Humanities Press, 1986. Bib. pp. 168-171.

[VIL-500] Harrsen, Meta, and George K. Boyce, comp. *Italian Manuscripts in the Pierpont Morgan Library: Descriptive Survey of the Principal Illuminated Manuscripts of the Sixth to Sixteenth Centuries, With a Selection of Important Letters and Documents.* New York: Pierpont Morgan Library, 1953. 79 pp. Bib. refs.

[VIL-510] Harthan, John P., and Victoria and Albert Museum. *An Introduction to Illuminated Manuscripts.* London: H.M.S.O., 1983. Bib. p. 48.

[VIL-520] Hedeman, Anne D[awson]. *The Royal Image: Illustrations of the Grandes chroniques de France, 1274-1422.* Berkeley; Oxford: University of California Press, 1991. Bib. pp. 321-328.

[VIL-530] Henry, Avril. *The Eton Roundels: Eton College MS 177 ("Figurae Bibliorum"): A Colour Facsimile with Transcription, Translation and Commentary.* Aldershot: Scolar Press, 1990. 224 pp. Bib.

[VIL-540] Henry, Françoise. *The Book of Kells: Reproductions from the Manuscript in Trinity College, Dublin.* London: Thames and Hudson, 1974. 230 pp. Bib. refs.

[VIL-550] Horst, Koert van der, and Johann-Christian Klamt, eds. *Masters and Miniatures: Proceedings of the Congress on Medieval Manuscript Illumination in Northern Netherlands (Utrecht, 10-13 December 1989).* Doornspijk, Netherlands: Davaco, 1991. 475 pp. Bib. refs.

[VIL-560] Irblich, Eva, and Gabriel Bise. *The Illuminated Naples Bible (Old Testament): 14th-Century Manuscript.* [New York]: Crescent Books, 1979. 124 pp.

[VIL-570] Jaeger, Jerome Thomas. *How to Detect Art Swindles in Classical and Renaissance Paintings, Illuminated Manuscripts, Drawings, Printings and Sculptures.* 2 vols. [Albuquerque]: Gloucester Art Press, 1979. Bib. refs.

[VIL-580] James, David, and Nasser D. Khalili Collection of Islamic Art. *After Timur: Qur'ans of the 15th and 16th Centuries.* [London]: Nour Foundation with Azmimuth and Oxford University Press, 1992. Bib. pp. 253-254.

[VIL-590] ------. *Qurans of the Mamluks.* London: Alexandria with Thames and Hudson, 1988. Bib. pp. 261-265.

[VIL-600] Kauffmann, C[laus] M[ichael]. *Romanesque Manuscripts, 1066-1190.* A Survey of Manuscripts Illuminated in the British Isles, vol. 3. London: Henry Miller, 1975. 235 pp. Bib. refs.

[VIL-610]   Kirsch, Edith W. *Five Illuminated Manuscripts of Giangaleazzo Visconti.* Monographs on the Fine Arts, vol. 46. University Park, Pa.: Pennsylvania State University Press for College Art Association, 1991. 169 pp. Bib. refs. pp. 105-109.

[VIL-620]   Kren, Thomas, Janet Backhouse, Mark Evans, and Myra Orth. *Renaissance Painting in Manuscripts: Treasures from the British Library.* New York: Hudson Hills Press, 1983. Bib. pp. 196-204.

[VIL-630]   Lewis, Suzanne. *The Art of Matthew Paris in the Chronica Majora.* Aldershot: Scolar Press with Corpus Christi College, Cambridge, 1983. 553 pp. Bib. pp. 513-520.

[VIL-640]   Loewe, Raphael. *The Rylands Haggadah: A Medieval Sephardi Masterpiece in Facsimile: An Illuminated Passover Compendium from Mid-14th-Century Catalonia in the Collections of the John Rylands University Library of Manchester, with a Commentary and a Cycle of Poems.* Tel-Aviv: Steimatzky, 1988. 114 pp. Bib. pp. 23-24.

[VIL-650]   Loomis, Roger Sherman. *Arthurian Legends in Medieval Art.* London: Oxford University Press, 1939. Bib. footnotes, pp. 87-88.

[VIL-660]   Lowden, John. *Illuminated Prophet Books: A Study of Byzantine Manuscripts of the Major and Minor Prophets.* University Park: Pennsylvania State University Press, 1989. 176 pp. Bib. refs.

[VIL-670]   Maimonides, Moses. *Codex Maimuni: Moses Maimonides' Code of Law: The Illuminated Pages of the Kaufmann Mishneh Torah.* Trans. *A Majmuni Kodex.* Ed. Sandor Scheiber and Gabrielle Sed-Rajna. [Budapest]: Corvina, 1984. 171 pp. Bib. p. 40.

[VIL-680]   Manion, Margaret M., and Vera F. Vines. *Medieval and Renaissance Illuminated Manuscripts in Australian Collections.* Melbourne; New York: Thames and Hudson, 1984. Bib. pp. 232-234.

[VIL-690]   ------. *Medieval and Renaissance Manuscripts in New Zealand Collections.* Melbourne; New York: Thames and Hudson, 1989. Bib. refs. pp. 193-194.

[VIL-700]   Mann, Vivian B., ed. *Gardens and Ghettos: The Art of Jewish Life in Italy.* Berkeley: University of California Press, 1989. Bib. pp. 345-352.

[VIL-710]   Mann, Vivian B., Jerrilynn Denise Dodds, and Thomas F. Glick, eds. *Convivencia: Jews, Muslims, and Christians in Medieval Spain.* New York: George Braziller in association with the Jewish Museum, 1992. 263 pp.

[VIL-720] Master of Mary of Burgundy. *A Book of Hours for Engelbert of Nassau.* Ed. J[onathan] J[ames] G[raham] Alexander. London: Phaidon Press, 1970. 193 pp. Bib. pp. 32-33.

[VIL-730] Meiss, Millard, and Edith Weisbord Kirsch. *The Visconti Hours.* London: Thames and Hudson, 1972. Bib. p. 262.

[VIL-740] Mellini, Gian Lorenzo. *The Brimani Breviary, Reproduced from the Illuminated Manuscript Belonging to the Biblioteca Marciana, Venice.* Woodstock, N.Y.: Overlook Press, 1972. Bib. pp. 271-276.

[VIL-750] Metzger, Therese. *Jewish Life in the Middle Ages: Illuminated Hebrew Manuscripts of the Thirteenth to the Sixteenth Centuries.* Trans. *La vie juive au Moyen Age.* Secaucus, N.J.: Chartwell Books; New York: Alpine Fine Arts Collection, 1982. Bib. pp. 311-313.

[VIL-760] Mitchell, W. J. Thomas. *Blake's Composite Art: A Study of the Illuminated Poetry.* Princeton: Princeton University Press, 1978. 230 pp. Bib. refs.

[VIL-770] Morgan, Nigel J[ohn]. *Early Gothic Manuscripts [I], 1190-1250.* 2 vols. New York: Harvey Miller Publishers; Oxford University Press, 1982. Bib. refs.

[VIL-780] Morgan, Nigel John, and Michelle P. Brown. *The Lambeth Apocalypse: Manuscript 209 in Lambeth Palace Library: A Critical Study.* London: Harvey Miller, 1990. 383 pp. Bib.

[VIL-790] Narkiss, Bezalel. *The Golden Haggadah: A Fourteenth-Century Illuminated Hebrew Manuscript in the British Museum.* London: Eugrammia Press, 1970. 86 pp. Bib. refs.

[VIL-800] ------. *Illuminated Hebrew Manuscripts.* Jerusalem: Encyclopaedia Judaica; New York: L. Amiel; Macmillan Publishing Co., 1969. Reprint. New York: Alpine Fine Arts Collections, 1983. Bib. pp. 170-172.

[VIL-810] Nersessian, Vrej. *Armenian Illuminated Gospel-Books.* London; Wolfeboro, N.H.: British Library, 1987. 100 pp. Bibs.

[VIL-820] Oakeshott, Walter Fraser. *The two Winchester Bibles.* Oxford: Clarendon Press; New York: Oxford University Press, 1981. 149 pp. Bib. refs.

426

[VIL-830] Oliver, Judith [H.] *Gothic Manuscript Illumination in the Diocese of Liege (c. 1250-c. 1330).* 2 vols. Leuven, [Belgium]: Uitgeverij Peeters, 1988. Bib. refs.

[VIL-840] Pacht, Otto. *Book Illumination in the Middle Ages: An Introduction.* Trans. *Buchmalerei des Mittelalters.* London: Harvey Miller Publishers; Oxford and New York: Oxford University Press, 1986. 221 pp. Bibs.

[VIL-850] Pacht, Otto, and J. J. G. Alexander, comps. *Illuminated Manuscripts in the Bodleian Library, Oxford.* 3 vols. Oxford: Clarendon Press, 1966-1973.

[VIL-860] Patriarchikon Hidryma Paterikon Meleton. *The Treasures of Mount Athos: Illuminated Manuscripts, Miniatures--Headpieces--Initial Letters.* Trans. *Hoi thesauroi tou Hagiou Orous.* Ed. Stylianos M. Pelekanides. Athens: Ekdotike Athenon, 1974. Bib. vol. 1, p. 489.

[VIL-870] Plummer, John, and Gregory Clark. *The Last Flowering: French Painting in Manuscripts, 1420-1530: From American Collections.* New York: Pierpont Morgan Library; Oxford University Press, 1982. Bib. pp. 119-123.

[VIL-880] Porcher, Jean. *Medieval French Miniatures: From Illuminated Manuscripts.* Trans. Julian Brown. London: Collins, 1960. 275 pp. Bib. pp. 85-94.

[VIL-890] Robb, David Metheny. *The Art of the Illuminated Manuscript.* [Philadelphia]: Philadelphia Art Alliance; South Brunswick: A. S. Barnes, 1973. Bib. pp. 337-345.

[VIL-900] Sandler, Lucy Freeman. *Gothic Manuscripts: 1285-1385.* 2 vols. London: Harvey Miller; New York: Oxford University Press, 1986. Bib.

[VIL-910] ------. *The Peterborough Psalter in Brussels and Other Fenland Manuscripts.* London: Harvey Miller, 1975. Bib. pp. 169-170.

[VIL-920] ------. *The Psalter of Robert de Lisle in the British Library.* London: Harvey Miller; New York: Oxford University Press, 1983. Bib. pp. 140-142.

[VIL-930] Schapiro, Meyer. *The Parma Ildefonsus: A Romanesque Illuminated Manuscript from Cluny, and Related Works.* [New York?]: College Art Association of America, 1964. 85 pp. Bib. footnotes.

[VIL-940] *Scriptorium: Revue internationale des etudes relatives aux manu-*

scrits/*International Review of Manuscript Studies*. Brussels, Belgium: Centre d'Etudes des Manuscrits, 1946-. Semi-annual. French and English.

[VIL-950] Sed-Rajna, Gabrielle. *The Hebrew Bible in Medieval Illuminated Manuscripts*. Trans. Josephine Bacon. New York: Rizzoli International Publications, 1987. Bib. pp. 165-167.

[VIL-960] Shelley, Donald A. *The Fraktur-Writings or Illuminated Manuscripts of the Pennsylvania Germans*. Allentown: Pennsylvania German Folklore Society, 1961. 375 pp. Bib. pp. 187-219.

[VIL-970] Simms, George Otto. *Exploring The Book of Kells*. Dublin: O'Brien Press, 1988. 72 pp.

[VIL-980] Spatharakis, Iohannis. *Corpus of Dated Illuminated Greek Manuscripts: To the Year 1453*. 2 vols. Leiden: E. J. Brill, 1981. Bib. vol. 1, pp. ix-xv.

[VIL-990] ------. *The Portrait in Byzantine Illuminated Manuscripts*. Leiden: E. J. Brill, 1976. 287 pp. Bib. refs.

[VIL-1000] Sullivan, Edward, and J[ohan] A[dolf]. *The Book of Kells*. 1920; reprint, London: Studio Editions, 1986. 138 pp.

[VIL-1010] Temple, Elzbieta. *Anglo-Saxon Manuscripts, 900-1066*. London: Harvey Miller, 1976. 243 pp. Bib. refs.

[VIL-1020] Testa, Judith Anne. *The Beatty Rosarium: A Manuscript with Miniatures by Simon Bening*. Doornspijk, Netherlands: Davaco Publishers, 1986. 184 pp. Bib. refs. and Bib.

[VIL-1030] Thomas, Marcel, Victoria Benedict, and Benita Eisler. *Les Grandes heures de Jean Duc de Berry*. London: Thames and Hudson, 1971. Bib. p. 183.

[VIL-1040] Thomas, Marcel, and Katherine W. Carson. *The Rohan Book of Hours*. London: Thames and Hudson; New York: George Braziller, 1973. Bib. pp. 246-247.

[VIL-1050] Thomson, Rodney M. *Manuscripts from St. Albans Abbey, 1066-1235*. 2 vols. Woodbridge; Totowa, N.J.: D. S. Brewer for the University of Tasmania, 1982. Bib. refs.

[VIL-1060] Titley, Norah M. *Persian Miniature Painting and its Influence on the Arts of Turkey and India: The British Library Collections*. London: British Library, 1983. Bib. pp. 259-261.

[VIL-1070] Trapp, J[oseph] B[urney], ed. *Manuscripts in the Fifty Years After*

428

the *Invention of Printing: Some Papers Read at a Colloquium at the Warburg Institute on 12-13 March 1982*. London: Warburg Institute, University of London, 1983. 112 pp. Bibs.

[VIL-1080] Vikan, Gary, ed. *Illuminated Greek Manuscripts from American Collections: An Exhibition in Honor of Kurt Weitzmann*. [Princeton]: Art Museum, Princeton University, 1973. Dist. Princeton University Press. 231 pp. Bibs.

[VIL-1090] Watson, Rowan. *The Playfair Hours: A Late Fifteenth Century Illuminated Manuscript from Rouen*. [London]: Victoria and Albert Museum, 1984. Bib. pp. 121-127.

[VIL-1100] Weinstein, Myron M., ed. *The Washington Haggadah: A Facsimile Edition of an Illuminated Fifteenth-Century Hebrew Manuscript at the Library of Congress*. Joel ben Simeon, 15th century. Vol. 1: facsimile; Vol. 2: commentary. Washington, D.C.: Library of Congress, 1990. Bib. refs.

[VIL-1110] Weitzmann, Kurt. *Byzantine Book Illumination and Ivories*. Brookfield, Vt.: Gower Publishing Co., 1980. 328 pp.

[VIL-1120] ------. *Late Antique and Early Christian Book Illumination*. New York: George Braziller, 1977.

[VIL-1130] ------. *The Miniatures of the 'Sacra parallela': Parisinus Graecus 923*. John of Damascus. Princeton; Guildford: Princeton University Press for Department of Art and Archaeology, Princeton University, 1980. Bib. pp. 265-266.

[VIL-1140] ------. *The Monastery of Saint Catherine at Mount Sinai: The Illuminated Greek Manuscripts*. Princeton: Princeton University Press, 1990. Bib. refs.

[VIL-1150] Westwood, J[ohn] O[badiah]. *The Art of Illuminated Manuscripts: Illustrated Sacred Writings: Being a Series of Illustrations of the Ancient Versions of the Bible, Copied from Illuminated Manuscripts, Executed Between the Fourth and Sixteenth Centuries*. 1843-1845, *Palaeographia Sacra Pictoria*. Reprint. London: Blacken Books, 1988. Bib. refs.

[VIL-1160] Wieck, Roger S. *European Illuminated Manuscripts*. [Turin]: U. Allemandi, 1985. 48 pp. Bib. refs.

[VIL-1170] Wieck, Roger S., Lawrence R. Poos, Virginia Reinberg, and John Plummer. *Time Sanctified: Book of Hours in Medieval Art and Life*. New York: George Braziller with Walters Art Gallery, Baltimore, 1988. Bib. pp. 228-229. Also titled *Books of Hours in Medieval Art and Life*. London: Sotheby's, 1988. Bib. pp. 228-230.

[VIL-1180] ------. *Late Medieval and Renaissance Illuminated Manuscripts, 1350-1525, in the Houghton Library.* Cambridge, Mass.: Department of Print and Graphic Arts, Harvard College Library, 1983. Bib. p. 175.

[VIL-1190] Williams, John. *Early Spanish Manuscript Illumination.* London: Chatto and Windus, 1978. 119 pp. Bib. pp. 33-34.

[VIL-1200] Wormald, Francis. *The Miniatures in the Gospels of St. Augustine: Corpus Christi College Manuscript 286.* Sandars Lectures in Bibliography Series, 1948. 1954. Reprint. N.p.: Books by Demand, 1984.

[VIL-1210] Yapp, W[illiam] B[runsdon]. *Birds in Medieval Manuscripts.* London: British Library, 1981. Bib. pp. 177-180.

[VIL-1220] Zolotova, Yekaterina. *Books of Hours: Fifteenth-Century French Illuminated Manuscripts in Moscow Collections, the Lenin Library, the Historical Museum, the Pushkin Museum of Fine Arts, the Gorky Library of Moscow University, the Arkhangels-koye Estate-Museum.* Leningrad: Aurora Art Publishers, 1991. Unpaginated. Bib.

KEY WORKS ON LITHOGRAPHS

The works included in this category primarily treat lithographs, but sometimes overlap with studies of aquatints, drypoints, engravings, etchings, linoleum cuts, monotypes, serigraphs or silk-screen prints, and woodcuts. Some of these sundry forms of printing can be traced back at least as far as the Renaissance, while others were invented during the past two centuries. For the sake of simplifying this bibliography, lithographs have been chosen as the primary focus, recognizing that many of the works listed below and many of those given in the opening sections of this chapter also include treatments of the other print forms.

Lithographs are made from etchings in stones or metal plates and use a printing process invented by Aloys Senefelder in about 1796. During the nineteenth century lithography gained status as an art form as well known artists such as Goya, Delacroix, and Degas perfected the use of this process. Because studies of lithography typically rotate around key personalities, this section of necessity presents numerous works treating a single artist, a pattern not followed in most sections of this bibliography. As one can ascertain from reviewing the following list, serious studies of lithography are none too plentiful, and lengthy bibliographies to guide the researcher have begun to emerge only during the past decade. The three bibliographies listed below offer at least a beginning point for the study of lithographs.

For those seeking a recent, comprehensive work treating lithographs, see Elizabeth Broun's *Images on Stone: Two Centuries of Artists' Lithographs* [VLI-170], Felix H. Man's *Artists' Lithographs: A World History from Senefelder to the Present Day* [VLI-660], John Muench's *The Painter's Guide to Lithography* [VLI-810], Domenico Porzio's *Lithography: 200 Years of Art, History, and Technique* [VLI-900], and Mary Ann Wenniger's *Lithography: A Complete Guide* [VLI-1150]. Also see items numbered [VLI-160], [VLI-230], [VLI-300], [VLI-330], [VLI-420], [VLI-540], [VLI-620], [VLI-650], [VLI-680], [VLI-710], [VLI-890], [VLI-1040], and, for the modern era, [VLI-1170]. For the more technical aspects of printing lithographs, see Abrahim Lavi's and George W. Jorgensen's *Lithographic Pressman's Handbook* [VLI-520], A. S. Porter's *Lithographic Presswork* [VLI-890], John Ross's and Clare Romano's *The Complete Printmaker* [VLI-980], and Donald Saff's and Deli Sacilotto's *Printmaking: History and Process* [VLI-990]. For a pricing guide, see [VLI-220]. Although not directly related to lithography, woodcuts constitute a forerunner to this later form of printing and can be studied in [VLI-300], [VLI-370], [VLI-470], and [VLI-850]. Studies of woodcuts are often included with reviews of the works by individual artists, such as Lyonel Feininger [VLI-910], Henri Matisse [VLI-920], Edvard Munch [VLI-580 and VLI-1180], Pablo Picasso [VLI-610], John Piper [VLI-840], and Albrecht Dürer as covered below in the section on painting.

Several of the following studies focus on national expressions of art in lithography, such as the following: American [VLI-050], [VLI-470], [VLI-560], [VLI-690], [VLI-870], [VLI-940], [VLI-950], [VLI-960], [VLI-970]; French [VLI-270]. A number of the studies listed below treat special topics, including the following: Pennsylvania Prints [VLI-350]; San Francisco [VLI-120]; Saul and David [VLI-460]; Stamps [VLI-1030]; Vanity Fair [VLI-1020].

For studies of the works by specific lithographers, see the following item numbers: Albert Belleroche [VLI-140]; George Bellows [VLI-150], [VLI-340], [VLI-700], [VLI-820]; Thomas Hart Benton [VLI-280]; Pierre-Nolasque Bergeret [VLI-110]; Georges Braque [VLI-630], [VLI-1130]; Bolton Brown [VLI-060]; Walter Lawry Buller [VLI-1110]; Marc Chagall [VLI-790], [VLI-1050], [VLI-1060], [VLI-1070]; Samuel Chamberlain [VLI-190]; Thomas Sidney Cooper [VLI-1160]; Ralston Crawford [VLI-290]; Currier and Ives [VLI-430], [VLI-860], [VLI-1120], [VLI-1140]; Ken Danby [VLI-260]; Edgar Degas [VLI-090]; Dominique Vivant Denon [VLI-200]; Honoré Daumier [VLI-440], [VLI-770], [VLI-930]; Lyonel Feininger [VLI-910]; Gavarni [VLI-830]; Rudolph Carl Gorman [VLI-760]; Francisco Goya [VLI-360], [VLI-480], [VLI-1000]; Eugene von Guerard [VLI-180], [VLI-1100]; Childe Hassam [VLI-320]; David Hockney [VLI-390], [VLI-590]; Edward Lear [VLI-410]; Reginald Marsh [VLI-1010]; Henri Matisse [VLI-490], [VLI-500], [VLI-640], [VLI-720], [VLI-730], [VLI-920]; Francisco Messina [VLI-740]; Joan Miró [VLI-750]; Robert Motherwell [VLI-780]; Edvard Munch [VLI-580], [VLI-1180]; LeRoy Neiman [VLI-530]; Philip Pearlstein [VLI-510]; Pablo Picasso [VLI-550], [VLI-610], [VLI-800], [VLI-880]; John Piper [VLI-840]; Lloyd Rees [VLI-450]; Robert Riggs [VLI-130]; David Roberts [VLI-210]; Aloys Senefelder [VLI-670]; Fritz Scholder [VLI-070]; Charles Shannon [VLI-240]; Jakob Steinhardt [VLI-100]; Henri Toulouse-Lautrec [VLI-080], [VLI-250], [VLI-710]; Stow Wengenroth [VLI-1080], [VLI-1090]; James Abbott McNeill Whistler [VLI-380], [VLI-400], [VLI-570], [VLI-600].

Special Bibliographies

[VLI-010] Brown, J. H. U. *A Guide to Collecting Fine Prints*. Metuchen, N.J.: Scarecrow Press, 1989. 192 pp.

[VLI-020] Parry, Pamela J., and Kathe Chipman, comps. *Print Index: A Guide to Reproductions*. Westport, Conn.: Greenwood Press, 1983.

[VLI-030] Wilson, Raymond L. *Index of American Print Exhibitions, 1882-1940*. Metuchen, N.J.: Scarecrow Press, 1988. 920 pp.

432

Key Works

[VLI-040] Abbey, John Roland. *Travel in Aquatint and Lithography, 1770-1860, from the Library of J. R. Abbey: A Bibliographical Catalogue.* 2 vols. Folkestone: Dawsons of Pall Mall, 1972.

[VLI-050] Adams, Clinton. *American Lithographers, 1900-1960: Their Artists and Their Printers.* Albuquerque: University of New Mexico Press, 1983. 344 pp. Bib.

[VLI-060] ------. *Crayonstone: The Life and Work of Bolton Brown with a Catalogue of his Lithographs.* Albuquerque: University of New Mexico Press, 1993. Bib. refs.

[VLI-070] ------. *Fritz Scholder: Lithographs.* Boston: New York Graphic Society, 1975. Bib. pp. 150-153.

[VLI-080] Adhemar, Jean, ed. *Toulouse-Lautrec: His Complete Lithographs and Drypoints.* Trans. Marianne Alexandre. New York: Harry N. Abrams; London: Thames and Hudson, 1965. Reprint. Secaucus, N.J.: Wellfleet Press, 1980. London: Alpine Fine Arts Collection, Ltd., 1987. 370 pp. Bib. p. xxxviii.

[VLI-090] Adhemar, Jean, and Françoise Cachin. *Degas: The Complete Etchings, Lithographs and Monotypes.* Trans. Jane Brenton. Trans. *Edgar Degas: Gravures et Monotypes.* London: Thames and Hudson; Secaucus, N.J.: Chartwell Books; New York: Viking Press, 1974. Bib. p. 289.

[VLI-100] Amishai-Maisels, Ziva. *Jakob Steinhardt: Etchings and Lithographs.* Tel-Aviv: Dvir, 1981. Bib. pp. 138-139.

[VLI-110] Art Institute (Dayton, Ohio). *The Lithographs of Pierre-Nolasque Bergeret.* Dayton, Ohio: Art Institute, 1982. Bib.

[VLI-120] Baird, Joseph Armstrong, and Edwin Clyve Evans. *Historic Lithographs of San Francisco.* San Francisco: S. A. Waterson for Burger-Evans, 1972. Bib. pp. 39-40.

[VLI-130] Bassham, Ben L. *The Lithographs of Robert Riggs: With a Catalogue Raisonne.* Philadelphia: Art Alliance Press; London: Associated University Presses, 1986. Bib. pp. 99-100.

[VLI-140] Belleroche, Albert de. *Selected Lithographs of Albert Belleroche.* Chicago: Richard Reed Armstrong, 1989. Bib. refs.

[VLI-150] Bellows, George, Lauris Mason, and Joan Ludman. *The Litho-

graphs of George Bellows: A Catalogue Raisonne. Rev. ed.
San Francisco: Alan Wofsy Fine Arts, 1992. 300 pp. Bib.
refs. pp. 271-273.

[VLI-160] Boyd, Arthur. *Etchings and Lithographs*. London: Lund Humphries for Maltzahn Gallery, 1971. 142 pp. Bib. p. 17.

[VLI-170] Broun, Elizabeth. *Images on Stone: Two Centuries of Artists'
Lithographs*. Houston: University of Houston, 1987. Bib.
pp. 141-143.

[VLI-180] Carroll, Alison, and John Tregenza. *Eugene von Guerard's South
Australia: Drawings, Paintings, and Lithographs from Jour-
neys in South Australia in 1855 and 1857*. Adelaide: Art
Gallery Board of South Australia with History Trust of
South Australia, 1986. 98 pp. Bib. refs.

[VLI-190] Chamberlain, Narcissa G., and Jane Field Kingsland. *The Prints of
Samuel Chamberlain, N.A.: Drypoints, Etchings, Litho-
graphs*. [Boston, Mass]: Boston Public Library, 1984. Bib.
pp. 344-346.

[VLI-200] Chu, Petra ten-Doesschate. *French Masters of the Nineteenth
Century: Dominique Vivant Denon*. 2 vols. New York:
Abaris Books, 1985.

[VLI-210] Culliford, Barbara, ed. *David Roberts: A Victorian Artist in Egypt
and the Holy Land*. London: Barrie and Jenkins, 1987. 192
pp. Bib.

[VLI-220] Davenport, R[ay] J. *Ray's Art Price Guide: Paintings, Sculpture,
Watercolors, Drawings, Lithographs: Prices on over 30,000
Artists*. [Ventura, Calif.]: R. J. Davenport, 1984. c. 600 pp.
Bib.

[VLI-230] Dean, Sonia. *The Artist and the Printer: Lithographs, 1966-1981: A
Collection of Printers' Proofs*. Exhibition, works by Fred
Genis. [Victoria]: National Gallery of Victoria, 1982. Bib.
p. 63.

[VLI-240] Delaney, Paul. *The Lithographs of Charles Shannon: Catalogue*.
London: Taranman, 1978. Bib. pp. 52-54.

[VLI-250] Donson, Theodore B., and Marvel M. Griepp. *Great Lithographs
by Toulouse-Lautrec*. New York: Dover Publications, 1982.
79 pp. Bib. p. vi.

[VLI-260] Duval, Paul. *Ken Danby: The New Decade*. Toronto; New York:
Stoddart, 1984. 196 pp. Bib. p. 174. (Sports in art; complete catalogue of lithographs and serigraphs.)

434

[VLI-270] Farwell, Beatrice. *French Popular Lithographic Imagery, 1815-1870*. 12 vols. Chicago: University of Chicago Press, 1981.

[VLI-280] Fath, Creekmore, ed. *The Lithographs of Thomas Hart Benton*. Austin: University of Texas Press, 1969. Chronology and Bib., pp. 183-193.

[VLI-290] Freeman, Richard B., ed. *The Lithographs of Ralston Crawford*. [Lexington]: University of Kentucky Press, 1962. Reprint. [Lexington]: University of Kentucky Press, 1980. Bib. p. 73.

[VLI-300] Getlein, Frank, and Dorothy Getlein. *The Bite of the Print: Satire and Irony in Woodcuts, Engravings, Etchings, Lithographs and Serigraphs*. New York: Bramhall House, 1963. Bib. pp. 268-270. New York: C. N. Potter, 1963. London: H. Jenkins, 1964. Bib. pp. 269-272. (See [WHU-380])

[VLI-310] Gilmour, Pat. *Artists at Curwen: A Celebration of the Gift of Artists' Prints from the Curwen Studio*. Woodbury, N.Y.: Barron's, 1977. 167 pp. Bib. refs.

[VLI-320] Griffith, Fuller. *The Lithographs of Childe Hassam: A Catalog*. New York: Martin Gordon, 1980. 66 pp. Bib. p. 2.

[VLI-330] Grolier Club, New York. *Catalogue of an Exhibition Illustrative of a Centenary of Artistic Lithography, 1796-1896; With 244 Examples by 160 Different Artists*. New York: The Grolier Club, 1896. 83 pp.

[VLI-340] H. V. Allison Galleries. *George Bellows (1822-1925): A Selection of Paintings, Drawings and Lithographs: Oct. 17--Nov. 27, 1985*. New York: The Galleries, 1985. 44 pp. Bib. refs.

[VLI-350] Hansen, Judith W. *Pennsylvania Prints from the Collection of John C. O'Connor and Ralph M. Yeager: Lithographs, Engravings, Aquatints, and Watercolors from the Tavern Restaurant, January 13--March 30, 1980: Catalog*. University Park: Museum of Art, Pennsylvania State University, 1980. Dist. Pennsylvania State University Press. c. 200 pp. Bib.

[VLI-360] Harris, Tomas. *Goya: Engravings and Lithographs*. 2 vols. Oxford: B. Cassirer, 1964. Reprint. San Francisco: Alan Wofsy Fine Arts, 1983. Bib. Vol. 2, pp. xii-xiii.

[VLI-370] Hind, Arthur M. *An Introduction to a History of Woodcut*. 2 vols. New York: Dover Publications, 1935. 838 pp. Bibs.

[VLI-380] Hobbs, Susan, with Nesta R. Spink. *Lithographs of James McNeill Whistler: From the Collection of Steven Louis Block*. Washington, D.C.: Smithsonian Institution Traveling Exhibition Service, 1982. Bib. pp. 77-78.

[VLI-390] Hockney, David, and Marco Livingstone. *David Hockney: Etch-ings and Lithographs, 1961-1986: A Retrospective Exhibition of Original Prints, 26 October-19 November 1988, Wadding-ton Graphics.* [London]: Thames and Hudson; Wadding-ton, 1988. 26 pp. and 98 pp. of plates. Bib. refs.

[VLI-400] Hom Gallery. *James Abbott McNeill Whistler: A Retrospective Exhibition of the Artist's Lithographs.* Washington, D.C.: Hom Gallery, 1980. Bib. p. 40.

[VLI-410] Hyman, Susan. *Edward Lear's Birds.* London: Weidenfeld and Nicolson, 1980. Bib. pp. 9-93.

[VLI-420] Keller, Judith. *El Taller de Grafica Popular: Block Prints and Lithographs by Artists of the TGP from the Archer M. Hunt-ington Art Gallery, March 7--April 21, 1985.* Austin: Archer M. Huntington Art Gallery, College of Fine Arts, University of Texas at Austin, 1985. Bib. p. 48.

[VLI-430] Kipp, Robert. *Currier's Price Guide to Currier and Ives Prints: Current Average Retail Prices of over 6000 Original Litho-graphs of the Currier and Ives Firm.* 2nd ed. Brockton, Mass.: Currier Publications, 1991. Bib. refs. pp. 269-270.

[VLI-440] Kist, J. R., and Mary Charles. *Daumier, Eyewitness of an Epoch.* Trans. *Daumier, verslaggever van zijn tijd, 1832-1872.* (Utrecht: Bruna, 1971.) London: Victoria and Albert Museum, 1976. 125 pp. Bib. p. 23.

[VLI-450] Kolenberg, Hendrik. *Lloyd Rees, Etchings and Lithographs: A Catalogue Raisonne.* Sydney, N.S.W.: Beagle Press, 1986. 112 pp. Bib. p. 14.

[VLI-460] Kokoschka, Oskar. *Lithographs for Saul and David.* New York: G. P. Putnam's Sons, 1973. Also titled *Saul and David: With 41 Lithographs.* London: Thames and Hudson, 1973. 215 pp. (Bible, Old Testament.)

[VLI-470] Kraeft, June, and Norman Kraeft. *Great American Prints, 1900-1950: 138 Lithographs, Etchings, and Woodcuts.* New York: Dover Publications, 1984. xxi, 149 pp. Bib. pp. 147-149.

[VLI-480] Lafuente Ferrari, Enrique. *Goya: His Complete Etchings, Aquat-ints, and Lithographs.* 3rd ed. London: Thames and Hudson, 1968. xxxiii, 288 pp.

[VLI-490] Lambert, Susan. *Matisse: Lithographs.* New York: Universe Books, 1982. 50 pp. Bib. p. 20.

436

[VLI-500] ------. *Matisse: Lithographs: [Catalogue of an Exhibition Organized by the] Victoria and Albert Museum*. London: Her Majesty's Stationery Office, 1981. 71 pp. Bib. p. 20.

[VLI-510] Landwehr, William C., and Richard S. Field. *The Lithographs and Etchings of Philip Pearlstein: February 25 Through March 26, 1978, Springfield Art Museum, Springfield, Missouri*. Springfield, Mo.: Springfield Art Museum, 1978. Bib. pp. 70-73.

[VLI-520] Lavi, Abrahim, and George W. Jorgensen. *Lithographic Pressman's Handbook*. 2nd ed. Pittsburgh, Pa.: Graphic Arts Technical Foundation, 1977. 168 pp.

[VLI-530] Leibovitz, Maury, and F. Lanier Graham. *The Prints of LeRoy Neiman: A Catalogue Raisonne of Serigraphs, Lithographs, and Etchings*. New York: Knoedler Pub., 1980. 632 pp. Bib. pp. 346-347.

[VLI-540] Lenky, Susan V., comp., and Stanford University, Libraries, Dept. of Special Collections. *Portraits: A Catalog of the Engravings, Etchings, Mezzotints, and Lithographs*. [Stanford, Calif.]: Stanford University, 1972. 373 pp.

[VLI-550] Leonhard, Kurt, and Hans Bolliger. *Picasso: Recent Etchings, Lithographs, and Linoleum Cuts*. New York: Harry N. Abrams, 1967. xxxiv, 144 pp. Bib. pp. 133-139.

[VLI-560] Levy, Lester S. *Picture the Songs: Lithographs from the Sheet Music of Nineteenth-Century America*. Baltimore: Johns Hopkins University Press, 1976. London: Johns Hopkins University Press, 1977. Bib. pp. 206-211.

[VLI-570] Levy, Mervyn. *Whistler Lithographs: An Illustrated Catalogue Raisonne*. London: Jupiter Books, 1975. 150 pp. Bib. p. 23.

[VLI-580] Lieberman, William Slattery. *Edvard Munch, Lithographs, Etchings, Woodcuts: Los Angeles County Museum of Art, January 28--March 9, 1969*. [Los Angeles: The Museum], 1969. Bib. pp. 117-118.

[VLI-590] Livingstone, Marco. *David Hockney: Etchings and Lithographs*. London: Thames and Hudson; Waddington Graphics, 1988. Bib. p. 107.

[VLI-600] Lochnan, Katharine A. *Whistler and His Circle: Etchings and Lithographs from the Collection of the Art Gallery of Ontario*. [Toronto]: The Gallery, 1986. 84 pp. Bib. refs.

[VLI-610] Los Angeles County Museum of Art. *Picasso: Sixty Years of*

Graphic Works: Aquatints, Dry Points, Engravings, Etchings, Linoleum Cuts, Lithographs, Woodcuts. [Los Angeles: Los Angeles County Museum of Art], 1967. Bib. pp. 167-168.

[VLI-620] Lovejoy, Margot. *Surface Printing in the 1980s: Lithographs, Screenprints, and Monotypes from the Rutgers Archives for Printmaking Studios: Essay.* New Brunswick: Jane Voorhees Zimmerli Art Museum, Rutgers, the State University of New Jersey, 1989. 61 pp. Bib. refs.

[VLI-630] Lumley Cazalet, Ltd. *Georges Braque: Important Lithographs, 1921-1963: [Exhibition: Lumley Cazalet Ltd., 27 October-- 25 November, 1972.* London: Lumley Cazalet, Ltd., 1972. 24 pp. Bib. refs.

[VLI-640] ------. *Henry Matisse: Fifty Fine Prints, Lithographs, Etchings, Aquatints, Linocuts, 1903-1950.* London: Lumley Cazalet, Ltd., 1984. Bib.

[VLI-650] McCauley, Lois B., and Maryland Historical Society. *A. Hoen on Stone: Lithographs of E. Weber and Co. and A. Hoen and Co., Baltimore, 1835-1969.* [Baltimore: Maryland Historical Society], 1969. Bib. pp. 51-52.

[VLI-660] Man, Felix H. *Artists' Lithographs: A World History from Senefelder to the Present Day.* London: Studio Vista; New York: G. P. Putnam's Sons, 1970. Bib. pp. 208-212.

[VLI-670] ------. *Homage to Senefelder: Artists' Lithographs from the Felix H. Man Collection.* Exhibition, the Victoria and Albert Museum, November 1971 to January 1972. London: Victoria and Albert Museum, 1971. Bib. pp. 38-39.

[VLI-680] ------. *150 Years of Artists' Lithographs, 1803-1953.* London: Heinemann, [1954]. Bib. pp. liv-lvii.

[VLI-690] Marzio, Peter C. *The Democratic Art: Chromolithography, 1840-1900: Pictures for a 19th-Century America.* Boston: David R. Godine, 1979. Reprint. London: Scolar Press for Amon Carter Museum of Western Art, Fort Worth, 1980. 357 pp. Bib. pp. 265-276.

[VLI-700] Mason, Lauris, and Joan Ludman. *The Lithographs of George Bellows: A Catalogue Raisonne.* Millwood, N.Y.: KTO Press, 1977. Bib. pp. 241-243.

[VLI-710] *Masterwork Treasury of Great Prints and Printmakers, The: A Remarkable Compendium of World-Renowned Masters: Daumier, Goya, Cassatt, Toulouse-Lautrec, Corot, Piranesi.* Collector's ed. *Print Collector's Quarterly,* 1911-1922. New

York: Collector's Guild, 1960. 204 pp.

[VLI-720] Matisse, Henri. *Henri Matisse: Etchings, Lithographs, Linocuts, Aquatints and Livres Illustres: A Retrospective Exhibition of Original Prints 1900-1952.* London: Waddington Graphics, 1988. 88 pp. Bib. refs.

[VLI-730] ------. *The Lithographs, 1913-1930.* London: Waddington Graphics, 1990. Bib. refs. p. 55.

[VLI-740] Messina, Francesco. *Francesco Messina, Graphic Works: Drawings, Pastels and Lithographs from 1930 to 1973.* Livorno: Graphis Arete Editore, 1973. Dist. Rizzoli International Publications, in U.S. 117 pp. Bib. pp. xvi-xvii.

[VLI-750] Miró, Joan. *Miró Lithographs.* Art Library. New York: Dover Publications, 1983. 48 pp.

[VLI-760] Monthan, Doris Born. *R[udolph] C[arl] Gorman: the Lithographs.* Flagstaff: Northland Press, 1978. 170 pp. Bibs.

[VLI-770] Morrissey, Ann. *Daumier on Women, the Lithographs: University Art Galleries, University of Southern California, September 12--October 23, 1982.* [Los Angeles]: The Galleries, 1982. 30 pp. bib. p. 23.

[VLI-780] Motherwell, Robert. *Robert Motherwell: Etchings, Lithographs, Livres Illustres, 1986-1989.* London: Waddington Graphics, 1989. Bib. pp. 53-55.

[VLI-790] Mourlot, Fernand. *The Lithographs of Chagall.* 4 vols. Monte Carlo: A. Sauret; New York: George Braziller, 1963.

[VLI-800] ------. *Picasso Lithographs.* [Boston]: Boston Book and Art Publisher, 1970. 299 pp.

[VLI-810] Muench, John. *The Painter's Guide to Lithography.* New York: North Light Books, 1983. 125 pp.

[VLI-820] Myers, Jane. *George Bellows: The Artist and his Lithographs, 1916-1924.* Fort Worth, Tex.: Amon Carter Museum, 1988. Bib. pp. 196-198.

[VLI-830] Olson, Nancy. *Gavarni: The Carnival Lithographs.* [New Haven]: Yale University Art Gallery, 1979. 46 pp. Bib. p. 28.

[VLI-840] Orde, Levinson, ed. and comp. *John Piper: The Complete Graphic Works: A Catalogue Raisonne 1923-1983: Etchings and Aquatints, Wood Engravings, Lithographs and Screenprints Compiled and Edited by Orde Levinson.* London: Faber,

1987. 141 pp.

[VLI-850] Passeron, Roger. *Impressionist Prints: Lithographs, Etchings, Drypoints, Aquatints, Woodcuts*. Trans. *La Gravure impressionniste: Origines et rayonnement*. London: Phaidon Press, 1974. 222 pp.

[VLI-860] Peters, Harry T[wyford]. *Currier and Ives: Printmakers to the American People*. 2 vols. 1929. Reprint. New York: Arno Press, 1976.

[VLI-870] ------. *America on Stone: The Other Printmakers to the American People*. 1931. Reprint. New York: Arno Press, 1976. Bib.

[VLI-880] Picasso, Pablo. *Picasso: Graphics from the Marina Picasso Collection: Linoleum Cuts, Etchings, Lithographs, Aquatints: November 1985--January 1986*. San Francisco: Erika Meyerovich Gallery, 1985. 48 pp. Bib. p. 4.

[VLI-890] Porter, A. S. *Lithographic Presswork*. Pittsburgh, Pa.: Graphic Arts Technical Foundation, 1980. 320 pp.

[VLI-900] Porzio, Domenico, ed. *Lithography: 200 Years of Art, History, and Technique*. Trans. Geoffrey Culverwell. New York: Harry N. Abrams, 1983. Bib. p. 271.

[VLI-910] Prasse, Leona E. *Lyonel Feininger: A Definitive Catalogue of his Graphic Work: Etchings, Lithographs, Woodcuts*. Trans. *Das graphische Werk: Radierungen, Lithographien, Holzschnitte*. [Cleveland]: Cleveland Museum of Art, 1972. Bib. pp. 285-286.

[VLI-920] R. S. Johnson International. *Master of Graphic Art, Henri Matisse, 1869-1954: Wood-Cuts and Lithographs 1904-29: A Retrospective Exhibition*. Chicago: R. S. Johnson International Gallery, 1972. Bib. p. 47.

[VLI-930] Ramus, Charles F. *Daumier: 120 Great Lithographs*. New York: Dover Publications, 1978. Bib. pp. 137-138.

[VLI-940] Reps, John William. *Cities on Stone: Nineteenth Century Lithograph Images of the Urban West*. Fortworth, Tex.: Amon Carter Museum, 1976. 100 pp. Bib. pp. 36-38.

[VLI-950] ------. *Panoramas of Promise: Pacific Northwest Cities and Towns on Nineteenth-Century Lithographs*. Pullman, Wash.: Washington State University Press, 1984. Bib. p. 93.

[VLI-960] ------. *Saint Louis Illustrated: Nineteenth-Century Engravings and Lithographs of a Mississippi River Metropolis*. Columbia,

Mo.; London: University of Missouri Press, 1989. 208 pp. Bib.

[VLI-970] ------. *Views and Viewmakers of Urban America: Lithographs of Towns and Cities in the United States and Canada, Notes on the Artists and Publishers, and a Union Catalog of Their Work, 1825-1925.* Columbia: University of Missouri Press, 1984. 570 pp. Bib. pp. 87-94.

[VLI-980] Ross, John, and Clare Romano. *The Complete Printmaker: The Art and Technique of the Relief Print, the Intaglio Print, the Collograph, the Lithograph, the Screen Print, the Dimensional Print, Photographic Prints, Children's Prints, Collecting Prints.* New York: Free Press, [1972]. Bib. pp. 295-297.

[VLI-990] Saff, Donald, and Deli Sacilotto. *Printmaking: History and Process.* New York: Holt, Rinehart and Winston, 1978. Bib. pp. 422-424.

[VLI-1000] Salas, Xavier de. *Goya: Drawings from the Prado Museum and the Lazaro Galdiano Museum, Madrid: Etchings from the Lazaro Galdiano Museum and the Collection of Tomas Harris: Lithographs from the Lazaro Galdiano Museum: 12 June-15 July 1954.* London: Arts Council, 1954. Bib. pp. 27-28.

[VLI-1010] Sasowsky, Norman. *The Prints of Reginald Marsh: An Essay and Definitive Catalog of his Linoleum Cuts, Etchings, Engravings, and Lithographs.* New York: C. N. Potter, 1976. Dist. Crown Publishers. Bib. pp. 282-284.

[VLI-1020] Savory, Jerold. *The Vanity Fair Lithographs: An Illustrated Checklist.* Photo. Tom Poland. New York: Garland Publishing, 1978. 146 pp. Bib. pp. xviii-xix.

[VLI-1030] Sherwood, William, Bernard Seckler, and Francine Stewart. *Paintings on Stamps: An Encyclopedic Handbook Arranged by Artist and Covering All Paintings, Drawings, Watercolors, Lithographs, Sketches, Engravings, Etchings, and Similar Works on Postage Stamps.* 4 vols. Temple, Pa.: Fine Arts Philatelists, 1984.

[VLI-1040] Sloan, John, and Peter T. Morse. *Prints: A Catalogue Raisonne of the Etchings, Lithographs, and Posters.* [New Haven]: Yale University Press, 1969. Bib. pp. 393-394.

[VLI-1050] Sorlier, Charles. *Chagall Lithographs: 1974-1979.* Trans. *Chagall Lithographe.* New York: Crown Publishers, 1984. 250 pp.

[VLI-1060] ------. *Chagall Lithographs: 1980-1985.* Trans. *Chagall Litho-*

graphe. New York: Crown Publishers, 1986. 224 pp.

[VLI-1070] Sorlier, Charles, and Fernand Mourlot. *The Lithographs of Chagall, 1969-1973.* Vol. 4, 1969-1973. New York: Crown Publishers, 1974. 180 pp.

[VLI-1080] Stuckey, Ronald, and Joan Stuckey. *The Lithographs of Stow Wengenroth, 1931-1972.* [Boston]; [New York]: Boston Public Library, 1974. Dist. Crown Publishers. Bib. p. 290.

[VLI-1090] ------. *Stow Wegnenroth's Lithographs: A Supplement.* Huntington, N.Y.: Black Oak Publications, 1982. 117 pp. Bib. p. 87.

[VLI-1100] Tipping, Marjorie. *Eugene von Guerard's Australian Landscapes.* Melbourne: Hamel and Ferguson, 1867. Reprint. Melbourne: Lansdowne Press, 1975. Bib. pp. 116-118.

[VLI-1110] Turbott, Evan Graham, ed. *Buller's Birds of New Zealand: A New Edition of Sir Walter Lawry Buller's A History of the Birds of New Zealand, Reproducing in Six-Colour Offset the 48 Stone-Plate Lithographs by J[ohn] G[errard] Keulemans, from the 2nd Edition, 1888.* London: Macdonald, 1967. 261 pp.

[VLI-1120] United States Naval Academy Museum. *Currier and Ives Navy: Lithographs from the Beverly R. Robinson Collection.* Annapolis, Md.: U.S. Nval Academy Museum, 1983. Bib. p. 97.

[VLI-1130] Waddington Galleries. *Georges Braque: Engravings and Lithographs, 1911-1963: [Exhibition, Waddington Galleries] 3 April--4 May 1985.* London: Waddington Graphics, 1985. Bib. p. 43.

[VLI-1140] Weaver, Warren A. *Lithographs of N. Currier and Currier and Ives.* New York: Holport Publishing Co., [1925]. 159 pp.

[VLI-1150] Wenniger, Mary Ann. *Lithography: A Complete Guide.* Photo. Mace Wenniger. Englewood Cliffs, N.J.: Prentice-Hall Press, 1983. Bib. p. 205.

[VLI-1160] Westwood, Kenneth J. *Thomas Sidney Cooper: His Life and Work.* Master of Lithography, vol. 1. Gillingham, Dorset: Wilson Hunt, 1991. 165 pp.

[VLI-1170] William Weston Gallery. *Etchings and Lithographs by Modern Masters.* London: William Weston Gallery, 1984. Bib.

[VLI-1180] Woll, Gerd. *Edvard Munch: Death and Desire: Etchings, Litho-*

442

graphs and Woodcuts from the Munch Museum, Oslo. Adelaide: Art Gallery of South Australia, 1986. Bib. pp. 78-79.

CHAPTER 13

VISUAL ARTS II

KEY WORKS ON MOSAICS

Mosaics are pictures or images made from pieces of colored marble, glass, tile, or stones. Pictures composed in this way constitute a mode of painting and may at times be created with painted tiles. Mosaics are typically associated with the era of the Byzantine Empire when this art form came to fruition in the Eastern Orthodox churches, but can be found much earlier in the era of the Roman Empire and, in some forms, in ancient far eastern cultures. The best single volume bibliographies on mosaics are Denise Chafer's and Hugh Pagan's *The Arts Applied: A Catalogue of Books* [VMO-020] and Mary A. Vance's short but slightly more current work, *Mosaic Decoration: A List of Books* [VMO-030]. For a list of the most recent writings on mosaics one must consult the French serial publication *Bulletin d'information de l'association internationale pour l'étude de la Mosaïque antique* [VMO-010]. Furthermore, the *Dumbarton Oaks Papers, [Nos. 1-45]* [VMO-390] provide current studies as well as references to the latest works appearing elsewhere.

Those looking for the latest single volume study on the aesthetics and history of mosaics will do well to consult Carlo Bertelli's and Xavier Barral i Altet's *Mosaics* [VMO-110]. Also consider Edgar Waterman Anthony's older but substantial work, *A History of Mosaics* [VMO-050], Larry Argior's somewhat dated but helpful study, *Mosaic Art Today* [VMO-060], Michael Avi-Yonah's short but useful volume, *The Art of Mosaics* [VMO-070], J. Mellentin Haswell's *The Thames and Hudson Manual of Mosaic* [VMO-560], and Hans Peter L'Orange's *Mosaics* [VMO-710]. For studies that focus on the technical aspects of mosaics, see Peter Fischer's *Mosaic: History and Technique* [VMO-430], Arthur Goodwin's and Elaine M. Goodwin's recent volume, *The Technique of Mosaic* [VMO-490], Helen Hutton's *Mosaic Making Techniques* [VMO-580], Janice Lovoos' *Modern Mosaic Techniques* [VMO-720], and Ferdinando Rossi's *Mosaics: A Survey of Their History and Techniques* [VMO-970].

Although many fine mosaics exist, the Hagia Sophia in Istanbul is generally agreed to be the stellar example of mosaics in church buildings. For studies of this church see [VMO-610] and [VMO-760]. See the more recent general studies identified above and related articles in the *Dumbarton Oaks Papers* for additional discoveries regarding the mosaics in the Hagia Sophia.

Since mosaics are typically built into the architecture of the buildings they decorate, they are rarely portable and usually linked solidly with their original location. Studies of mosaics typically treat specific sites, but some explore mosaics of a given era, such as the Roman Empire or Byzantine Empire, rather than concentrate on a particular country or century. The following works are grouped alphabetically according to their geographic placement, with distinctions about their eras being added when useful to clarify whether the works treated are ancient, Medieval, or Modern: America [VMO-360], [VMO-370]; Balkans [VMO-670], [VMO-770]; Byzantine Empire [VMO-320], [VMO-510], [VMO-530], [VMO-630], [VMO-750], [VMO-830], [VMO-900], [VMO-1130]; Cyprus [VMO-300], [VMO-310], [VMO-420], [VMO-450], [VMO-780], [VMO-790]; Egypt [VMO-150], [VMO-290]; England, Medieval [VMO-410], [VMO-440]; England, Modern [VMO-880]; Great Britain, Roman [VMO-280], [VMO-590], [VMO-810], [VMO-820], [VMO-990], [VMO-1080]; Greece [VMO-210], [VMO-540], [VMO-680], [VMO-800], [VMO-840], [VMO-920], [VMO-940], [VMO-1060], [VMO-1070]; Hungary [VMO-620]; Israel and Palestine [VMO-480], [VMO-640], [VMO-870], [VMO-950], [VMO-980]; Italy [VMO-120], [VMO-130], [VMO-140], [VMO-160], [VMO-190], [VMO-200], [VMO-220], [VMO-240],

[VMO-250], [VMO-330], [VMO-340], [VMO-350], [VMO-600], [VMO-650], [VMO-660], [VMO-740], [VMO-850], [VMO-890], [VMO-930], [VMO-1010], [VMO-1040], [VMO-1120]; Libya [VMO-040]; Mediterranean [VMO-100]; North Africa [VMO-400], [VMO-910]; Roman Empire [VMO-380], [VMO-730], [VMO-1030], [VMO-1070]; Russia [VMO-270], [690]; Syria [VMO-170], [VMO-700]; Tunisia [VMO-1050], [VMO-1090]; Turkey [VMO-080], [VMO-090], [VMO-180], [VMO-230], [VMO-550], [VMO-610], [VMO-760], [VMO-960], [VMO-1000], [VMO-1100], [VMO-1140]. For studies which treat themes or specialized applications appearing in a wide variety of places, see [VMO-260], [VMO-460], [VMO-470], [VMO-500], [VMO-520], [VMO-570], [VMO-860], [VMO-1020], and [VMO-1110]. For additional studies of mosaics, see the bibliographies and works on the general theory of the arts listed in the opening sections of Chapter 12.

Special Bibliographies

[VMO-010] *Bulletin d'information de l'association internationale pour l'étude de la Mosaïque antique.* Association Internationale pour l'étude de la Mosaïque antique: Paris, 1968-.

[VMO-020] Chafer, Denise, and Hugh Pagan. *The Arts Applied: A Catalogue of Books: Furniture, Interior Design, Murals, Mosaics, Ceilings, Exhibitions, Ceramics, Metalwork, Jewelry, Textiles, Vases, Ornament; Some Original Drawings.* London: B. Weinreb Architectural Books Lted., 1975. 319 pp.

[VMO-030] Vance, Mary A. *Mosaic Decoration: A List of Books.* Monticello, Ill.: Vance Bibliographies, 1980. 14 pp.

Key Works

[VMO-040] Alfoldi-Rosenbaum, Elisabeth. *Justinianic Mosaic Pavements in Cyrenaican Churches.* Monografie di archeologia libica, no. 14. Rome: "L'Erma" di Bretschneider, 1980. 158 pp. Bib. pp. xi-xv.

[VMO-050] Anthony, Edgar Waterman. *A History of Mosaics.* Boston: P. Sargent, [1935]. Bib. pp. 297-314.

[VMO-060] Argior, Larry. *Mosaic Art Today.* Scranton: International Textbook Co., [1961]. 242 pp. Bib.

[VMO-070] Avi-Yonah, Michael. *The Art of Mosaics*. Minneapolis: Lerner Publications, 1975. 96 pp.

[VMO-080] Ayyildiz, Ugur. *The Kariye Museum: Art Historian and Profesional Guide*. 7th ed. Istanbul: NET, 1990. 52 pp.

[VMO-090] Belting, Hans, Cyril A. Mango, and Doula Mouriki. *The Mosaics and Frescoes of St. Mary Pammakaristos [Fethiye Camii] at Istanbul*. [Washington, D.C.]; Locust Valley, N.Y.: Dumbarton Oaks Center for Byzantine Studies, 1978. Dist. J. J. Augustin. 118 pp. Bib. refs.

[VMO-100] Benarde, Anita. *Mediterranean Mosaic Designs*. International Design Library. Owings Mills, Md.: Stemmer House Publications, Inc., 1984.

[VMO-110] Bertelli, Carlo, and Xavier Barral i Altet. *Mosaics*. Trans. *Il Mosaico*. New York: Gallery Books, 1989. *The Art of Mosaic*. London: Cassell, 1989. Bib. pp. 353-355.

[VMO-120] Bertoli, Bruno, and Antonio Niero. *The Mosaics of St. Mark's: A Biblical Itinerary*. Trans. *Mosaici di San Marco*. Milan: Electa, 1987. 83 pp. Bibs.

[VMO-130] Borsook, Eve. *Messages in Mosaic: The Royal Programmes of Norman Sicily (1130-1187)*. Clarendon Studies in the History of Art. Oxford: Clarendon, 1990. Bib. pp. 87-101.

[VMO-140] Bovini, Giuseppi. *Ravenna Mosaics: The Mausaleum of Galla Placidia, the Cathedral Baptistery, the Archiepiscopal Chapel, the Baptistery of the Arians, the Basilica of Sant' Appolinare Nuova, the Church of San Vitale, the Basilica of Sant' Appolinare in Classe*. New York: New York Graphic Society, 1956. Reprint. Oxford: Phaidon Press; New York: E. P. Dutton and Co., 1978. Bib. pp. 56-57.

[VMO-150] Brown, Blanche R. *Ptolemaic Paintings and Mosaics and the Alexandrian Style*. Monographs on Archaeology and Fine Arts, no. 6. N.p.: Archaeological Institute of America, 1957. 108 pp. Bib. pp. xv-xvii.

[VMO-160] Bustacchini, Gianfranco. *Ravenna: Capital of Mosaic*. Revenna: Salbaroli Publications, 1988. Reprint. Bologna, Italy: Italcards, 1990. 159 pp.

[VMO-170] Campbell, Sheila D. *The Mosaics of Antioch*. The Corpus of Mosaic Pavements in Turkey, Subsidia Mediaevalia, no. 15. Toronto: Pontifical Institute of Mediaeval Studies, 1988.

Bib. refs. pp. 101-103.

[VMO-180] ------. *The Mosaics of Aphrodisias in Caria*. Corpus of Mosaic Pavements in Turkey, Subsidia Mediaevalia, no. 18. Toronto: Pontifical Institute of Mediaeval Studies, 1991. Bib. refs.

[VMO-190] Capizzi, Carmelo. *Piazza Armerina: The Mosaics and Morgantina*. Bologna, Italy: Italcards; Piazza Armerina: N. Mantese, 1990. Bib. refs. p. 96.

[VMO-200] Carandini, Andrea, Andreina Ricci, and Mariette De Vos. *Filosofiana, the Villa of Piazza: The Image of a Roman Aristocrat at the Time of Constantine*. 2 vols. Trans. Marie Christine Keith. Palermo: S. F. Flaccovio, 1982. Bib., vol. 1, pp. 393-403.

[VMO-210] Chatzedakes, Manoles, Nicos Drandakis, and Nikos Zias. *Naxos*. Trans. *Naxos*. Athens: "Melissa" Publishing House, 1989. 104 pp. Bib. refs.

[VMO-220] Chierichetti, Sandro. *The Cathedral of Monreale [Italy]*. Palermo: Perna Cartoleria, 1979. Bib. p. 91.

[VMO-230] Cimok, Fatih, and Erdem Yucel. *Chora: Mosaics and Frescoes*. Tesvikiye, Istanbul: A Turizm Yayinlari Ltd., 1987. Bib. refs. p. 118.

[VMO-240] Clarke, John R. *The Houses of Roman Italy, 100 B.C.-A.D. 250: Ritual, Space, and Decorations*. Berkeley: University of California Press, 1991. Bib. refs. pp. 379-396.

[VMO-250] ------. *Roman Black-and-White Figural Mosaics*. New York: New York University Press, 1979. 147 pp. Bib. refs. in notes.

[VMO-260] Cohen, Ada. "Studies in Large-Scale Painting and Mosaic in the Late Classical and Early Hellenistic Periods: Battles, Hunts, Abductions." 2 vols. Ph.D. Thesis, Harvard University, 1990. Bib. refs.

[VMO-270] Collet's Holdings Limited Staff, ed. *Early Russian Painting 11th to Early 13th Centuries: Mosaics, Frescoes and Icons*. New York: State Mutual Book and Periodical Service, 1982. 308 pp.

[VMO-280] Cookson, Neil Andrew. *Romano-British Mosaics: A Reasessment and Critique of Some Notable Stylistic Affinities*. BAR British Series, no. 135. Oxford: BAR, 1984. Bib. pp. 139-158.

[VMO-290] Daszewski, Wiktor Andrzej. *Corpus of Mosaics from Egypt*.

448

Aegyptiaca Treverensia, Bd. 3. Mainz am Rhein: P. von Zabern, 1985. Bib. refs.

[VMO-300] Daszewski, Wiktor Andrzej, and Demetres Michaelides. *Guide to the Paphos Mosaics*. [Cyprus]: Bank of Cyprus Cultural Foundation with Department of Antiquities, 1988. Bib. refs. pp. 72-73.

[VMO-310] ------. *Mosaic Floors in Cyprus*. Biblioteca di "Felix Ravenna," no. 3. Ravenna, Italy: Mario Lapucci, Edizioni del Girasole, 1988. 166 pp. Bib. refs.

[VMO-320] Demus, Otto. *Byzantine Mosaic Decoration: Aspects of Monumental Art in Byzantium*. Boston: Boston Book and Art Shop, [1955].

[VMO-330] ------. *The Mosaics of Norman Sicily*. Routledge and Kegan Paul, 1949. Reprint. Ann Arbor: University Microfilms International, 1979. 478 pp. Bib. refs.

[VMO-340] ------. *The Mosaics of San Marco in Venice*. 4 vols. Chicago: University of Chicago Press, 1986. Bibs.

[VMO-350] Demus, Otto, and Herbert L. Kessler. *The Mosaic Decoration of San Marco, Venice*. Chicago: University of Chicago Press, 1988. 207 pp.

[VMO-360] DiFederico, Frank R. *The Mosaics of Saint Peter's: Decorating the New Basilica*. University Park: Pennsylvania State University Press, 1983. Bib. pp. 153-156.

[VMO-370] ------. *The Mosaics of the National Shrine of the Immaculate Conception*. Washington, D.C.: Decatur House Press, 1980. 80 pp. Bib. refs.

[VMO-380] Dorigo, Wladimiro. *Late Roman Painting*. Trans. James Cleugh and John Warrington. Trans. *Pittura tardoromana*. New York: Frederick A. Praeger Publishers, [1970]; London: J. M. Dent, 1971; Bib. pp. 308-321.

[VMO-390] *Dumbarton Oaks Papers, [Nos. 1-45]*. Washington, D.C.: Dumbarton Oaks Research Library and Collection, Center for Byzantine Studies, -1991. Bib. refs.

[VMO-400] Dunbabin, Katherine M. D. *The Mosaics of Roman North Africa: Studies in Iconography and Patronage*. Oxford: Clarendon Press, 1978. Bib. pp. 280-289.

[VMO-410] Eames, Elizabeth S. *English Medieval Tiles*. British Museum Series. Cambridge, Mass.: Harvard University Press, 1985.

Bib. p. 71.

[VMO-420] Eliades, Georgios S. *The House of Dionysus: The Villa of the Mosaics in New Paphos*. 3rd ed. Trans. *Oikos tou Dionysou*. Paphos, Cyprus: G. S. Eliades, 1985. Bib. pp. 60-61.

[VMO-430] Fischer, Peter. *Mosaic: History and Technique*. London: Thames and Hudson, 1971. Bib. pp. 149-150.

[VMO-440] Foster, Richard. *Patterns of Thought: The Hidden Meaning of the Great Pavement of Westminster Abbey*. London: Jonathan Cape, 1991. Bib. refs. pp. 168-174.

[VMO-450] Getty Conservation Institute and the Department of Antiquities of Cyprus. *The Conservation of the Orpheus Mosaic at Paphos, Cyprus*. [Marina del Rey, Calif.]: Getty Conservation Institute, 1991. 69 pp. Bib. refs.

[VMO-460] Giusti, Anna Maria. *Pietre dure: Hardstone in Furniture and Decorations*. London: Philip Wilson, 1992. Bib. refs. pp. 301-308.

[VMO-470] Glass, Dorothy F. *Studies on Cosmatesque Pavements*. BAR International Series, no. 82. Oxford: BAR, 1980. Bib. pp. 235-242.

[VMO-480] Goldman, Bernard. *The Sacred Portal: A Primary Symbol in Ancient Judaic Art*. [Detroit]: Wayne State University Press, 1966. Bib. pp. 191-206.

[VMO-490] Goodwin, Arthur, and E[laine] M. Goodwin. *The Technique of Mosaic*. London: B. T. Batsford, 1985. Bib. p. 157.

[VMO-500] Goodwin, E[laine] M. *Decorative Mosaics*. Sydney: Doubleday, 1992. Bib.

[VMO-510] Grabar, André. *Byzantine Painting: Historical and Critical Study*. [Trans. Stuart Gilbert]. New York: Rizzoli International Publications, 1979. Bib. p. 194.

[VMO-520] ------. *Early Medieval Painting from the Fourth to the Eleventh Century: Mosaics and Mural Painting*. The Great Centuries of Painting. [New York]: Skira, 1967. Bib. pp. 223-225.

[VMO-530] Gravgaard, Anne-Mette. *Inscriptions of Old Testament Prophecies in Byzantine Churches: A Catalogue*. Copenhagen: Museum Tusculanum, 1979. Bib. pp. 110-112.

[VMO-540] *Greece: Byzantine Mosaics*. [Greenwich, Conn.]: New York Graphic Society with UNESCO, [1959]. Bib. p. 22.

450

[VMO-550] Gulersoy, Celik, and Ernst Reidl. *Kariye [Choral]*. Istanbul: Istanbul Kitapligi, 1976. 61 pp. Bib. refs.

[VMO-560] Haswell, J. Mellentin. *The Thames and Hudson Manual of Mosaic*. London: Thames and Hudson, 1973. Bib. pp. 231-232.

[VMO-570] Herbert, Michael, and Grahame Herbert. *Daphni: A Guide to the Mosaics and Their Inscriptions*. [London]: Pindy Books, 1978. 41 pp.

[VMO-580] Hutton, Helen. *Mosaic Making Techniques*. New ed. New York: Charles Scribner's Sons, 1977. Bib. p. 133.

[VMO-590] Johnson, Peter. *Romano-British Mosaics*. 2nd ed. Princes Risborough: Shire, 1987. Bib. pp. 68-70.

[VMO-600] Joyce, Hetty. *The Decoration of Walls, Ceilings, and Floors in Italy in the Second and Third Centuries A.D.* Rome: G. Bretschneider, 1981. 129 pp. Bib. refs.

[VMO-610] Kahler, Heinz. *Hagia Sophia*. London: A. Zwemmer, 1967. 74 pp. Bib.

[VMO-620] Kiss, Akos. *Roman Mosaics in Hungary*. Budapest: Akademiai Kiado, 1973. 72 pp. Bib. refs.

[VMO-630] Kitzinger, Ernst. *The Art of Byzantium and the Medieval West: Selected Studies*. Bloomington: Indiana University Press, 1976. 419 pp. Bib. refs.

[VMO-640] ------. *Israeli Mosaics of the Byzantine Period*. [London]: Collins with UNESCO, [1965]. Bib. p. 25.

[VMO-650] ------. *Mosaics of Monreale, [Italy]*. Palermo: S. F. Flaccovio, 1960. Bib. refs. in notes, pp. 123-132.

[VMO-660] ------. *The Mosaics of St. Mary's of the Admiral in Palermo*. Dumbarton Oaks Studies, no. 27. Washington, D.C.: Dumbarton Oaks Research Library and Collection, 1990. 480 pp. Bib. refs.

[VMO-670] Kolarik, Ruth Ellen. "The Floor Mosaics of Stobi and Their Balkan Context." Ph.D. Thesis, Harvard University, 1981. Bib. pp. 555-584.

[VMO-680] Kollias, Elias. *Patmos*. Trans. Greek. Athens: "Melissa" Publishing House, 1986. 40 pp. Bib. refs.

[VMO-690] Lazarev, Viktor Nikitich. *Old Russian Murals and Mosaics:*

451

From the 11th to the 16th Century. Trans. Boris Roniger and Nancy Dunn. London: Phaidon Press, 1966. Bib. pp. 271-177.

[VMO-700] Levi, Doro. *Antioch Mosaic Pavements.* 2 vols. Princeton: Princeton University Press, 1947. Bib.

[VMO-710] L'Orange, Hans Peter. *Mosaics.* Methuen Handbooks of Archaeology. London: Methuen, 1966. Bib. pp. 82-83.

[VMO-720] Lovoos, Janice. *Modern Mosaic Techniques.* New York: Watson-Guptill Publications, 1967. Bib. pp. 163-164.

[VMO-730] McKeon, Carolyn Hessenbruch. "Iconology of the Gorgon Medusa in Roman Mosaic." 3 vols. Ph.D. Thesis, University of Michigan, 1983. Bib. refs.

[VMO-740] Macmillan, Hugh. *Roman Mosaics, or Studies in Rome and Its Neighborhood.* Salem, N.H.: Ayer Co. Publications, n.d.

[VMO-750] Maguire, Henry. *Earth and Ocean: The Terrestrial World in Early Byzantine Art.* Monographs on the Fine Art, no. 43. University Park: Pennsylvania State University Press for the College Art Association of America, 1987. Bib. pp. 101-103.

[VMO-760] Mango, Cyril A. *Materials for the Study of the Mosaics of St. Sophia at Istanbul.* Dumbarton Oaks Studies, no. 8. Washington, D.C.: Dumbarton Oaks Research Library and Collection, 1962. 145 pp. Bib. footnotes.

[VMO-770] Mauropoulou-Tsioume, Chrysanthe. *The Church of St. Nicholas Orphanos.* Trans. *Ho Hagios Nikolaos ho Orphanos.* Guides of the Institute for Balkan Studies (I.M.X.A.), no. 3. Thessalonica: Institute for Balkan Studies, 1986. Bib. p. 47.

[VMO-780] Megaw, Arthur H. S., and Ernest J. W. Hawkins. *The Church of the Panagia Kanakaria at Lythrankomi in Cyprus: Its Mosaics and Frescoes.* Washington, D.C.; Locust Valley, N.Y.: Dumbarton Oaks Center for Byzantine Studies, Trustees for Harvard University, 1977. Dist. J. J. Augustin. 173 pp. Bib. pp. xvii-xx.

[VMO-790] Michaelides, D., and Vassos Karageorghis. *Cypriot Mosaics.* Nicosia: Department of Antiquities, Cyprus, and Nicosia Printing Works Chr. Nicolaou and Sons, 1987. 57 pp. Bibs.

[VMO-800] Mouriki, Doula. *The Mosaics of Nea Moni on Chios.* 2 vols. Fourth Series, Byzantine Monuments. Trans. *Psephidota tes Neas Mones Chiou.* Athens: Commercial Bank of Greece, 1985. Bib. pp. 13-18.

452

[VMO-810] Munby, Julian, and Martin Henig. *Roman Life and Art in Britain: A Celebration in Honour of the Eightieth Birthday of Jocelyn Toynbee.* 2 vols. Oxford: British Archaeological Reports, 1977. Bib. pp. 437-460. (Architecture, Carpets, Gemstones, Mosaics Numismatics, Painting, Sculpture)

[VMO-820] Neal, David S. *Roman Mosaics in Britain: An Introduction to Their Schemes and Catalogue of Paintings.* Britannia Monograph Series, no. 1. London: Society for the Promotion of Roman Studies, 1981. 127 pp. Bib. pp. 9-15.

[VMO-830] Neumayer, Heinrich. *Byzantine Mosaics.* New York: Crown Publishers, 1964. 62 pp. Bib. p. 15.

[VMO-840] Nikonanos, Nikos. *The Church of the Holy Apostles in Thessaloniki.* Trans. *Hoi Hagioi Apostoloi Thessalonikes.* Guides of the Institute for Balkan Studies (I.M.X.A.), no. 4. Thessalonica: Institute for Balkan Studies, 1986. Bib. pp. 67-69.

[VMO-850] Oakeshott, Walter Fraser. *The Mosaics of Rome, from the Third to the Fourteenth Centuries.* Greenwich, Conn.: New York Graphic Society; London: Thames and Hudson, 1967. Bib. pp. 380-385.

[VMO-860] Ovadiah, Asher. *Geometric and Floral Patterns in Ancient Mosaics: A Study of Their Origin in the Mosaics from the Classical Period to the Age of Augustus.* Rome: "L'Erma" di Bretschneider, 1980. 205 pp. Bib. pp. 11-16.

[VMO-870] Ovadiah, Ruth. *Hellenistic, Roman and Early Byzantine Mosaic Pavements in Israel.* Bibliotheca Archaeologica, no. 6. Rome: "L'erma" di Bretschneider, 1987. 276 pp. Bib. pp. 189-199.

[VMO-880] Paolozzi, Eduardo, Richard Cork. *Eduardo Paolozzi Underground: [Exhibition at the] Royal Academy of Arts, London.* London: The Academy with Weidenfeld and Nicolson, 1986. Bib. p. 48.

[VMO-890] Paolucci, Antonio, and Simon Dally. *Ravenna.* Trans. *Ravenna.* Firenze: Edizione Salbaroli, 1983. 126 pp.

[VMO-900] Papadakes, Theodoros. *Hosios Lukas and its Byzantine Mosaics.* Trans. *Hosios Lukas und seine byzantinischen Mosaiken.* Munich: Schnell and Steiner, 1969. xv, 32 pp. Bib. p. ii.

[VMO-910] Parrish, David. *Season Mosaics of Roman North Africa.* Rome: Giorgio Bretschneider Editore, 1984. 272 pp. Bibs.

[VMO-920] Pelekanides, Stylianos M., and Manoles Chatzedakes. *Kastoria.*

Trans. *Kastoria*. Athens: "Melissa" Publishing House, 1985. 119 pp. Bibs.

[VMO-930]   *Piazza Armerina: The Imperial Villa of Casale: Morgantium.* Palermo: Mistretta, 1988. 62 pp. Bib. refs.

[VMO-940]   Prokopiou, Angelos G. *The Macedonian Question in Byzantine Painting.* Trans. *Makedoniko zetema ste Vyzantine zographike.* Athens: A. Procopiou, 1962. Bib. pp. 49-50.

[VMO-950]   Rappel, Joel, and Meir Ben-Dov. *Mosaics in the Holy Land.* Trans. Shmuel Himmelstein. New York: Adama Publications, Inc., 1986. 96 pp.

[VMO-960]   Rice, David Talbot. *The Great Palace of the Byzantine Emperors, Second Report.* Edinburgh: University Press, [1958]. 203 pp. Bib. footnotes.

[VMO-970]   Rossi, Ferdinando. *Mosaics: A Survey of Their History and Techniques.* Trans. *Il Mosaico.* New York: Frederick A. Praeger Publishers, 1970. Bib. pp. 194-195.

[VMO-980]   Roussin, Lucille Alice. "The Iconography of the Figural Pavements of Early Byzantine Palestine." Ph.D. Thesis, Columbia University, 1985. Bib. pp. 375-406.

[VMO-990]   Rule, Margaret. *Floor Mosaics in Roman Britain.* London: Macmillan Publishing Co. for the Sussex Archaeological Trust, 1974. Bib. p. 41.

[VMO-1000]   Russell, James. *The Mosaic Inscriptions of Anemurium.* Denkschriften/Osterreichische Akademie der Wissenschaften, Philosophisch-Historische Klasse, Erganzungsbande zu den tituli Asiae Minoris, nr. 13. Vienna: Verlag der Osterreichischen Akademie der Wissenschaften, 1987. 92 pp. Bib. refs.

[VMO-1010]   *San Marco: Patriarchal Basilica in Venice.* 2 vols. Milan: Fabbri, 1990. Vol. 2, New York: Rizzoli International Publications, 1990. Bib. vol. 2, p. 251.

[VMO-1020]   Saycell, K. J., ed. *Papers of the Second Conference of the UNISA Medieval Association held on 18 September 1985.* UNISA Medieval Studies, vol. 2. Pretoria: University of South Africa, 1985. 106 pp. Bibs.

[VMO-1030]   Sear, Frank B. *Roman Wall and Vault Mosaics.* Heidelberg: F. H. Kerle, 1977. 202 pp. Bib. refs.

[VMO-1040]   Selvig, Forrest. *Mosaics, No. 1: Deterioration and Conservation,*

Rome, November 1977. Rome: International Centre for the Study of the Preservation and the Restoration of Cultural Property, 1978. 103 pp. Bib. refs.

[VMO-1050] Smith, Claudia Gwen. "Black and White Mosaic Pavements at Utica." 2 vols. Ph.D. Thesis, University of Minnesota, 1985. Bib. pp. 305-324.

[VMO-1060] Spiro, Marie. *Critical Corpus of the Mosaic Pavements on the Greek Mainland, Fourth/Sixth Centuries, with Architectural Surveys*. 2 vols. New York: Garland Publishing, 1978. Bib. vol. 1, pp. 665-684.

[VMO-1070] Stern, Henri, and Marcel Le Glay. *La Mosaique greco-romaine II: [actes du] IIe Colloque international pour l'etude de la Mosaique antique, Vienne, 30 aout--4 september 1971*. Paris: A. & J. Picard, 1975. 446 pp. Bib. refs. English, French, German, Italian, or Spanish.

[VMO-1080] Stevens-Cox, James. "A Catalogue of Roman Mosaics in Ilchester." *Roman Mosaics in Ilchester*. Ilchester and District Occasional Papers, 0306-6010, no. 62. Guernsey: Toucan Press, 1985.

[VMO-1090] *Tunisia: Ancient Mosaics*. [Greenwich, Conn.]: New York Graphic Society with UNESCO, [1962]. Bib. p. 22.

[VMO-1100] Underwood, Paul Atkins. *The Kariye Djami*. Bollingen Series 70, 4 vols. [Princeton]: Princeton University Press, 1966. Bib. vol. 1, pp. 313-315; vol. 4, pp. 159-160.

[VMO-1110] Vermeule, Cornelius Clarkson, Norman Neuerburg, and Helen Lattimore. *Catalogue of the Ancient Art in the J. Paul Getty Museum: The Larger Statuary, Wall Paintings and Mosaics*. [Malibu, Calif.: The Museum], 1973. 60 pp. Bib. refs.

[VMO-1120] Volbach, Wolfgang Friedrich. *Early Christian Mosaics, from the Fourth to the Seventh Centuries: Rome, Naples, Milan, Ravenna*. New York: Oxford University Press, 1946. 13 pp.

[VMO-1130] Winfield, June, and David Winfield. *Proportion and Structure of the Human Figure in Byzantine Wall-Painting and Mosaic*. BAR International Series, no. 154. Oxford: BAR, 1982. Bib. pp. 200-203.

[VMO-1140] Yucel, Erdem. *The Great Palace Mosaic Museum*. Istanbul: A Turizm Yayinlari, 1987. Bib. p. 40.

KEY WORKS ON MURALS

Murals differ from other forms of painting primarily in size and function. Murals are typically large and are painted directly on or attached to walls or ceilings. The form of paint used for such paintings has varied through the centuries, including charcoal, egg tempera, fresco, oil base, and photographic processes, to name just a few. Murals qualify as one of the oldest art forms since the mural cave paintings of Lascaux and Niaux are some of the earliest records of civilization. Murals may also be distinguished from other forms of painting by function since murals often serve a public or community purpose rather than simply a private one. This distinction is especially evident in the church frescoes of Medieval Italy and in twentieth century revivals of mural art in Mexico and southern California where such paintings beside freeways and on buildings portray ethnic and community spirit. For those interested in murals used by the early Christians, note especially studies of Dura Europos in Syria [VMU-860] and studies of the catacombs [VMU-050] and [VMU-830].

Like mosaics, murals are typically rooted to a particular place and are rarely portable. For this reason, studies of murals are usually linked to the sites and countries in which they reside. The following list is, therefore, organized according to countries. America [VMU-020], [VMU-060], [VMU-070], [VMU-080], [VMU-090], [VMU-100], [VMU-150], [VMU-160], [VMU-190], [VMU-210], [VMU-240], [VMU-310], [VMU-320], [VMU-330], [VMU-350], [VMU-410], [VMU-510], [VMU-540], [VMU-580], [VMU-660], [VMU-680], [VMU-770], [VMU-800], [VMU-850], [VMU-880]; Brazil [VMU-030]; Bulgaria [VMU-550], [VMU-620]; Burma [VMU-870]; Canada [VMU-810]; China [VMU-360]; Crete [VMU-440]; Cyprus [VMU-200]; Denmark [VMU-520]; England [VMU-220], [VMU-230], [VMU-560], [VMU-650], [VMU-700], [VMU-710]; France [VMU-600], [VMU-780]; Greece [VMU-180], [VMU-290], [VMU-500]; Hungary [VMU-670]; India [VMU-010], [VMU-380]; Ireland [VMU-720]; Italy [VMU-040], [VMU-050], [VMU-130], [VMU-140], [VMU-280], [VMU-390], [VMU-400], [VMU-420], [VMU-430], [VMU-460], [VMU-480], [VMU-490], [VMU-610], [VMU-730], [VMU-740], [VMU-750], [VMU-790], [VMU-820], [VMU-830]; Mexico [VMU-110], [VMU-260],

[VMU-340], [VMU-570], [VMU-630], [VMU-640]; Peru [VMU-120]; Rumania [VMU-300]; Russia [VMU-470], [VMU-840]; Sweden [VMU-450]; Syria [VMU-860]; Taiwan [VMU-370]; Thailand [VMU-690]; Turkey [VMU-250]; Vatican [VMU-270]; Yugoslavia [VMU-590]. For a brief study treating murals in general, see [VMU-170]. To learn about the techniques of making frescoes and murals, see [VMU-530] and [VMU-760].

For additional studies of murals, see the sections on bibliographies and art history books given in the opening of Chapter 12. Note especially the studies of early Christian art in *Gardner's Art Through the Ages* [VAT-600] and Janson's *History of Art* [VAT-520]. Furthermore, the section given below on painting also includes studies of frescoes and other forms of murals, particularly Pierre du Bourguet's *Early Christian Painting* [VPA-310].

Key Works

[VMU-010] Agarawala, R[am] A[vatar]. *Marwar Murals*. Delhi; New Delhi: Agam Prakashan, 1977. Dist. D. K. Publishers' Distributors. Bib. pp. 111-119.

[VMU-020] Allen, Edward D. *Early American Wall Paintings: 1710-1850*. Ed. Serry Wood. Visual Art Classic Series. 1926. Reprint. Watkins Glen, N.Y.: Century House, [1969]. 110 pp.

[VMU-030] *Artistas do Muralismo Brasileiro/Brazilian Mural Artists*. [Sao Paulo?]: Volkswagen do Brasil, 1988. 216 pp. English, German, and Portuguese.

[VMU-040] Baldini, Umberto, and Ornella Casazza. *The Brancacci Chapel Frescoes*. London: Thames and Hudson, 1992. Bib. pp. 365-373.

[VMU-050] Bargebuhr, Frederick Perez. *The Paintings of the "New" Catacomb of the Via Latina and the Struggle of Christianity Against Paganism*. Ed. Joachim Utz. Abhandlungen der Heidelberger Akademie der Wissenschaften, Philosophisch-Historische Klass. Jahg. 1991, 2. Heidelberg: Winter, 1991. 107 pp. Bibs. English.

[VMU-060] Barnett, Alan W. *Community Murals*. Cranbury, N.J.: Association of University Presses, 1984. 520 pp. *Community Murals: The People's Art*. Philadelphia: Art Alliance Press; New York: Cornwall Books, 1984. 516 pp. Bib. pp. 497-

503.

[VMU-070] ------. *Murals of Protest.* Cranbury, N.J.: Art Alliance Press, 1984. 520 pp.

[VMU-080] Barthelmeh, Valker. *Street Murals.* New York: Alfred A. Knopf, 1982.

[VMU-090] Beckham, Sue Bridwell. *Depression Post Office Murals and Southern Culture: A Gentle Reconstruction.* Baton Rouge: Louisiana State University Press, 1989. 228 pp.

[VMU-100] Berman, Greta. *The Last Years: Mural Painting in New York City Under the Works Progress Administration's Federal Art Project: 1935-1943.* Outstanding Dissertations in the Fine Arts Series. New York: Garland Publishing, 1978. 436 pp. Bib.

[VMU-110] Berrin, Kathleen, and Clara Millon. *Feathered Serpents and Flowering Trees: Reconstructing the Murals of Teotihuacan.* [San Francisco]; Seattle: Fine Arts Museums of San Francisco, 1988. Dist. University of Washington Press. 238 pp. Bibs.

[VMU-120] Bonavia, Duccio. *Mural Painting in Ancient Peru.* Trans. Patricia J. Lyon. Bloomington: Indiana University Press, 1985. 240 pp. Bib.

[VMU-130] Borsook, Eve. *Fra Filippo Lippi and the Murals for Prato Cathedral.* [Firenze, Italy: Kunsthistorisches Institut], 1975. 148 pp. Bib. refs.

[VMU-140] ------. *The Mural Painters of Tuscany: From Cimbue to Aandrea Del Sarto.* 2nd ed. New York: Oxford University Press, 1979. Bib.

[VMU-150] Bowman, Ruth, cur. *Murals Without Walls: Arshile Gorky's Aviation Murals Rediscovered.* Newark, N.J.: Newark Museum, 1978. Bib. pp. 93-95.

[VMU-160] Boyens, Charles William. "The WPA Mural Projects: The Effects of Constraints on Artistic Freedom." Ed.D. Thesis, Columbia University, 1984. Bib. pp. 212-225.

[VMU-170] Brisbane, Cameron, Rick Rogers, and Judith Stone. *The Murals Book.* [London]: Hammersmith and Fulham Amenity Trust, 1985. Bib. p. 40.

[VMU-180] *Byzantine Murals and Icons: [Exhibition] National Gallery, September--December 1976.* Athens: Archaeological Service, 1976. 78 pp. Bib. pp. 16-17.

458

[VMU-190] Calcagno, Nicholas A. *New Deal Murals in Oklahoma: A Bicentennial Project.* Miami, Okla.: Pioneer Printing, 1976. Bib. p. 52.

[VMU-200] Carr, Annemarie Weyl, Laurence J. Morrocco. *A Byzantine Masterpiece Recovered, the Thirteenth-Century Murals of Lysi, Cyprus.* Austin: University of Texas Press with the Menil Foundation, 1991. 157 pp. Bib. refs.

[VMU-210] Cass, Caroline. *Modern Murals: Grand Illusions in Interior Decoration.* Photo. Tom Leighton. New York: Witney Library of Design, 1988. Bib. p. 159.

[VMU-220] Cather, Sharon, David Park, and Paul Williamson, eds. *Early Medieval Wall Paintings and Painted Sculpture in England: Based on the Proceedings of a Symposium at the Courtauld Institute of Art, February, 1985.* Oxford: BAR, 1990. 262 pp. Bib. refs.

[VMU-230] Christian, John. *The Oxford Union Murals.* Chicago: University of Chicago Press, 1981. Bib. pp. 71-72. (Dante Gabriel Rossetti, et al.)

[VMU-240] Cohn, Marjorie B., ed. *Mark Rothko's Harvard Murals.* Cambridge, Mass.: Center for Conservation and Technical Studies, Harvard University Art Museums, 1988. 62 pp. Bibs.

[VMU-250] Connor, Carolyn L[oessel]. *Art and Miracles in Medieval Byzantium: The Crypt of Hosios Loukas and its Frescoes.* Princeton: Princeton University Press, 1991. Bib. refs. pp. 125-128.

[VMU-260] Crosby, Harry. *The Cave Paintings of Baja California: The Great Murals of an Unknown People.* [La Jolla, Calif.]: Copley Books, 1975. Bib. pp. 170-171.

[VMU-270] Davidson, Bernice F. *Raphael's Bible: A Study of the Vatican Logge.* College Art Association Monographs, vol. 39. University Park, Pa.: Pennsylvania State University Press, 1985. Bib. pp. 97-104.

[VMU-280] Di Francesco, Carla. *Pomposa: History and Art of the Abbey.* Bologna, Italy: Italcards, 1988. 95 pp.

[VMU-290] Douma, C[hristos]. *The Wall-Paintings of Thera.* Athens; London: Thera Foundation, 1992. Bib. pp. 189-190.

[VMU-300] Dragut, Vasile, and Petre Lupan. *Moldavian Murals: From the 15th to the 16th Century.* Trans. Andreea Gheorghitoiu.

Bucharest: Meridane Publishing House, 1982. 47 pp. and 132 pp. of plates. Bib. pp. 47-48.

[VMU-310] Drescher, Tim. *San Francisco Murals: Community Creates its Muse, 1914-1990.* St. Paul: Pogo Press, 1991. Bib. p. 104.

[VMU-320] Dunitz, Robin J. *Street Gallery: Guide to 1000 Los Angeles Murals.* Los Angeles: RJD Enterprises, 1993. 468 pp. Bib. refs. pp. 412-418.

[VMU-330] Dutton, Bertha Pauline. *Sun Father's Way: The Kiva Mural of Kuaua: A Pueblo Ruin, Coronado State Monument, New Mexico.* Albuquerque: University of New Mexico Press, [1963]. Bib. pp. 221-228.

[VMU-340] Edwards, Emily. *Painted Walls of Mexico: From Prehistoric Times Until Today.* Austin: University of Texas Press, 1966. 330 pp.

[VMU-350] Environmental Communication. *Big Art: A Visual Document of American Wall Art, Murals, and Supergraphics.* Ed. David Greenberg, Kathryn Smith, and Stuart Teacher. Philadelphia: Running Press Book Publications, 1977.

[VMU-360] Fairbank, Wilma. *Adventures in Retrieval: Han Murals and Shang Bronze Molds.* Harvard-Yenching Institute Studies, no. 28. Cambridge, Mass.: Harvard University Press, 1972. 187 pp. Bib. refs.

[VMU-370] Fontein, Jan, and Tung Wu. *Han and Tang Murals: Discovered in Tombs in the People's Republic of China and Copied by Contemporary Chinese Painters.* Boston: Museum of Fine Arts, 1976. Bib. pp. 127-131.

[VMU-380] Goepper, Roger, Barbara Lutterbeck, and Jaroslav Poncar. *Alchi: Buddhas, Goddesses, Mandalas: Murals in a Monastery of the Western Himalaya.* Koln: DuMont, 1984. 110 pp. Bib. refs. pp. 46-47.

[VMU-390] Guillaud, Jacqueline, and Maurice Guillaud. *Fra Angelico: The Light of the Soul: Painting Panels and Frescoes from the Convent of San Marco, Florence.* Paris: Guillaud Editions; New York: Clarkson N. Potter, 1986. Dist. Crown Publishers. Bib. p. 397.

[VMU-400] Guillaud, Jacqueline, Maurice Guillaud, and Margherita Lenzini Moriondo. *Piero della Francesca, Poet of Form: The Frescos of San Francesco di Arezzo.* New York: C. N. Potter; Paris; New York: Guillaud Editions, 1988. Bib. pp. 304-305.

460

[VMU-410] Harris, Moira F. *Museum of the Streets: Minnesota's Contemporary Outdoor Murals*. St. Paul: Pogo Press, 1987. Bib. pp. 128-130.

[VMU-420] Hills, Paul. *The Light of Early Italian Painting*. New Haven: Yale University Press, 1987. Bib. pp. 148-158.

[VMU-430] Howe, Eunice D. *The Hospital of Sante Spirito and Pope Sixtus IV*. Outstanding Dissertations in the Fine Arts Series. New York: Garland Publishing, 1978. 444 pp. Bib.

[VMU-440] Kalokyris, Konstantin. *The Byzantine Wall Paintings of Crete*. Ed. Harry Hionides. Trans. Leonidas Contos. New York: Red Dust, 1973. 186 pp.

[VMU-450] Langaard, Johan H[enrik], and Reidar Revold. *Edvard Munch: The University Murals, Graphic Art and Paintings*. Oslo: Forlaget Norsk Kunstreproduksjon, 1960. Bib. p. 99.

[VMU-460] Lavin, Marilyn Aronberg. *The Place of Narrative: Mural Decoration in Italian Churches, 431-1600*. Chicago: University of Chicago Press, 1990. Bib. refs. pp. 373-394.

[VMU-470] Lazarev, Viktor Nikitich. *Old Russian Murals and Mosaics: From the 11th to the 16th Century*. London: Phaidon Press, 1966. Bib. pp. 271-277.

[VMU-480] Ling, Roger. *Roman Painting*. Cambridge, England; New York: Cambridge University Press, 1991. Bib. refs. pp. 225-235.

[VMU-490] Little, Alan. *Roman Bridal Drama*. Ossining, N.Y.: Moretus Press, Inc., 1978.

[VMU-500] Marinatos, Nanno. *Art and Religion in Thera: Reconstructing a Bronze Age Society*. Athens: D. & I. Mathioulakis, 1984. 128 pp.

[VMU-510] Marling, Karal Ann. *Wall-to-Wall America: A Cultural History of Post-Office Murals in the Great Depression*. Minneapolis: University of Minnesota Press, 1982. 348 pp. Bib. refs.

[VMU-520] Mellon, James, ed. *A Danish Gospel: The Life of our Lord Jesus Christ*. [Vivy, Denmark]: Centrum, 1986. 111 pp. English. (Mural painting.)

[VMU-530] Merrifield, Mary. *The Art of Fresco Painting*. Albuquerque: Transatlantic Arts, Inc., 1971.

[VMU-540] Metzger, Robert P[aul]. *Franz Kline: The Jazz Murals*. Lewisburg, Pa.: Center Gallery of Bucknell University, 1989. Bib.

p. 62.

[VMU-550] Miiatev, Krustiu. *The Boyana Murals*. Dresden: Verlag der Kunst, 1961. Bib. p. 88. (Boyana, Bulgaria)

[VMU-560] Miles, Malcolm, ed. *Art for Public Places: Critical Essays*. Winchester, Hampshire: Winchester School of Art Press, 1989. Bib. refs. pp. 222-234.

[VMU-570] Miller, Mary Ellen. *The Murals of Bonampak [Mexico]*. Princeton: Princeton University Press, 1986. Bib. pp. 163-169.

[VMU-580] Mueller, Mary K., and Ted G. Pollack. *Murals: Creating an Environment*. Worcester, Mass.: Davis Publications, 1979. 87 pp.

[VMU-590] Muller, Paul Johannes. *Famous Frescoes*. Photo. Miodrag Djordjevic. Belgrade, [Yugoslavia]: Jugoslovenska Revija, 1986. Bib. refs. p. 168.

[VMU-600] Muntfanu, Voichita. *The Cycle of Frescoes of the Chapel of Le Liget*. Outstanding Dissertations in the Fine Arts Series. New York: Garland Publishing, 1978. 270 pp.

[VMU-610] Osborne, John. *Early Medieval Wall-Painting in the Lower Church of San Clemente, Rome*. Theses from the Courtland Institute of Art Series. New York: Garland Publishing, 1984. 350 pp. Bib.

[VMU-620] Panayotova, Dora. *Bulgarian Mural Paintings of the 14th Century*. Trans. Marguerite Alexieva and Theodora Athanassova. New York: Irvington Publications, n.d.

[VMU-630] Pasztory, Esther. *The Murals of Tepantitla, Teotihuacan [Mexico]*. New York: Garland Publishing, 1976. 392 pp. Bib. pp. 260-275. (Art, religion, and mythology.)

[VMU-640] Peterson, Jeanette Favrot. *The Paradise Garden Murals of Malinolco: Utopia and Empire in Sixteenth-Century Mexico*. Austin: University of Texas Press, 1993. Bib. refs.

[VMU-650] Philp, Brian, and Joanna Bird. *The Roman House with Bacchic Murals at Dover*. Research Report in the Kent Monograph Series, 0141-2264, no. 5. Kent: Kent Archaeological Rescue Unit, CIB Headquarters, Dover Castle, 1989. Bib. refs. pp. 285-288.

[VMU-660] Plagin, V. *Frescoes of St. Demetrius' Cathedral*. New York: State Mutual Book and Periodical Services, Ltd., 1974. 44 pp.

462

[VMU-670] Prokopp, Maria. *Italian Trecento Influence on Murals in East Central Europe, Particularly Hungary.* [Trans. Agnes Simon]. Budapest: Akademiai Kiado, 1983. 198 pp. Bibs.

[VMU-680] Randall, Arne W. *Murals for Schools: Sharing Creative Experiences.* Worcester, Mass.: Davis, [1956]. 104 pp.

[VMU-690] Ringis, Rita. *Thai Temples and Temple Murals.* Singapore; Oxford: Oxford University Press, 1990. 208 pp. Bib.

[VMU-700] Roberts, Eileen. *A Guide to the Medieval Murals in St. Albans Abbey.* [St. Albans]: Fraternity of the Friends of St. Albans Abbey, 1971. Bib. p. 45.

[VMU-710] Rochfort, Desmond, and Julia Engelhardt. *The Murals of Diego Rivera.* London: South Bank Board with Journeyman, 1987. Bib. pp. 98-99.

[VMU-720] Rolston, Bill. *Politics and Painting: Murals and Conflict in Northern Ireland.* Rutherford; London: Fairleigh Dickinson University Press; Cranbury, N.J.: Associated University Presses, 1991. Bib. pp. 128-131.

[VMU-730] Sandstrom, Sven. *Levels of Unreality: Studies in Structure and Construction in Italian Mural Painting During the Renaissance.* Philadelphia: Coronet Books, 1963. 260 pp.

[VMU-740] Schulz, Juergen. *Venetian Painted Ceilings of the Renaissance.* California Studies in the History of Art, no. 9. Berkeley: University of California Press, 1968.

[VMU-750] Scott, John Beldon. *Images of Nepotism: The Painted Ceilings of Palazzo Barberini.* Princeton: Princeton University Press, 1991. Bib. refs. pp. 221-234.

[VMU-760] Seligman, Patricia. *Painting Murals: Images, Ideas, and Techniques.* Cincinnati: North Light Books, 1988. Bib. p. 163.

[VMU-770] Sheppard, Carl D. *The Saint Francis Murals of Santa Fe: The Commission and the Artists.* Santa Fe: Sunstone Press, 1989. Bib. refs. p. 95.

[VMU-780] Spector, Jack J. *The Murals of Eugene Delacroix at Saint-Sulpice [Church].* Monographs on Archaeology and Fine Arts, no. 16. New York: College Art Association of America, 1967. 171 pp. Bib. refs.

[VMU-790] Stubblebine, James H. *Giotto: The Arena Chapel.* New York: W. W. Norton and Co., 1969.

[VMU-800] Sugg, Redding S., Jr. *A Painter's Psalm: The Mural in Walter Anderson's Cottage*. N.p.: Memphis State University Press, 1978.

[VMU-810] Thom, Ian M[acEwan]. *Murals from a Great Canadian Train/De l'art dans un grand train canadien*. [Montreal]: Art Global and Via Rail Canada, 1986. Bib. pp. 187-188.

[VMU-820] Tintori, Leonette, and Millard Meiss. *The Painting of the Life of St. Francis in Assisi, with Notes on the Arena Chapel*. 1962. Reprint. Ann Arbor, Mich.: Books on Demand UMI, 1984.

[VMU-830] Tronzo, William. *The Via Latina Catacomb: Imitation and Discontinuity in Fourth-Century Roman Painting*. University Park: Pennsylvania State University Press for the College Art Association of America, 1986. 141 pp. Bib.

[VMU-840] Vzdornov, G. *The Frescoes of Theophanes the Greek in the Church of the Transfiguration in Novgorod*. New York: State Mutual Book and Periodical Services, Ltd., 1976. 292 pp.

[VMU-850] Webster, Sara B[eyer]. "The Albany Murals of William Morris Hunt." 2 vols. Ph.D. Thesis, City University of New York, 1985. Bib. pp. 407-428.

[VMU-860] Weitzmann, Kurt, and Herbert L. Kessler. *The Frescoes of the Dura Synagogue and Christian Art*. Dumbarton Oaks Studies, no. 28. Washington, D.C.: Dumbarton Oaks Research Library and Collection, 1990. Bib. pp. 185-195.

[VMU-870] Wenk, Klaus, and U. Tin Lwin. *Murals in Burma*. Trans. Jane K. Bunjes and Werner E. Bunjes. Zurich: Verlag Inigo von Oppersdorff, 1977. Bib. pp. 259-261.

[VMU-880] Wyeth, N[ewell] C[onvers], and Douglas Allen. *N. C. Wyeth: The Collected Paintings, Illustrations, and Murals*. New York: Bonanza Books, 1972. Dist. Crown Publishers. Bib. pp. 193-317.

KEY WORKS ON NUMISMATICS

Numismatics is popularly thought to treat coins alone, but also includes medals, paper money, scarabs, seals, and tokens. Some may find numismatics an unusual topic in a bibliography on Christianity and the arts, but the artistry used in designing coins and related objects, along with the religious symbolism often involved, have many times produced items of keen interest to those studying the arts. In particular, several eras have produced many coins reflecting Judeo-Christian values and concerns, namely those of the nation of Israel during the Old and New Testament periods, the Byzantine Empire, and the Holy Roman Empire. Coins and other numismatic items have often served a political and economic function, but have also promoted religious concerns, especially as they have been linked to the state. One need only look at coins and paper currency from the United States to realize that statements such as "In God we trust" and symbols such as the pyramid with the eye at the top reveal a strong religious heritage even in a country seeking to keep a clear separation of church and state. Those interested in Christianity and the arts cannot afford to overlook these statements of faith in the art of currency, even if numismatics is classified by some as a minor art.

The number of bibliographies available on numismatics is substantial, alerting readers to a vast body of literature available on this topic. The bibliographies listed below range from older, substantial works to periodicals commenting on the latest writings on numismatics. One of the most helpful publications in this latter category is Dennis Kroh's series of "Reference Reviews" printed in *The Celator: Journal of Ancient and Medieval Art and Artifacts* [VNU-190]. Using a five star ranking system, Kroh's reviews identify the strengths and weaknesses of the many volumes available on numismatics, and thereby provide for the neophyte crucial guidance in building a solid working library. *Numismatic Literature* [VNU-250] also provides useful reviews of current literature. The major numismatic organizations and their respective bibliographies are as follows: the American Numismatic Association [VNU-020] and [VNU-030], the American Numismatic Society [VNU-250], the Canadian Numismatic Research Society [VNU-050], and the International Numismatic Commission [VNU-170]. Three other major organizations are not represented by bibliographies, but their catalogs and other publications are nonetheless very important to researchers of numismatics. The first of these, the British Museum, houses major collections of coins and produces important catalogs of them, such as [VNU-430], [VNU-440], [VNU-460], [VNU-690], [VNU-1080], and [VNU-1090]. The British Museum also publishes the *Numismatic Chronicle and Journal* [VNU-810], an old and well established periodical of the Royal Numismatic Society. Second, the British

Numismatic Society produces a major annual periodical, *British Numismatic Journal* [VNU-450], which researchers should also consult for current studies and references to the latest findings in numismatics. Third, the Dumbarton Oaks Center for Byzantine Studies has produced numerous fine books on the Byzantine era, including [VNU-370], [VNU-550], [VNU-600], [VNU-830], [VNU-840], and [VNU-850].

Most of the other twenty-four bibliographies given below are specialized works treating the following countries and regions: America [VNU-110], [VNU-130], [VNU-290]; Byzantine Empire [VNU-200]; Canada [VNU-050]; Egypt [VNU-220]; Far East [VNU-040], [VNU-090], [VNU-100]; Great Britain [VNU-210]; Greece [VNU-140], [VNU-300], [VNU-310]; India [VNU-150], [VNU-270]; Latin America [VNU-010]; Moslem world [VNU-240]; Palestine and Jewish world [VNU-180], [VNU-230], [VNU-280]; Roman Empire [VNU-300]. For more widely focused studies, see bibliographies by the the following authors: Gregory G. Brunk [VNU-060] and [VNU-070]; Elvira Eliza Clain-Stefanelli [VNU-080]; C. E. Dekesel [VNU-120]; George Francis Hill [VNU-160]; Phares O. Sigler [VNU-260].

The key works listed below include several major categories which are likely to contribute to the study of Christianity and the arts. Grouped by countries and regions, these works are as follows: Byzantine Empire [VNU-350], [VNU-370], [VNU-380], [VNU-400], [VNU-430], [VNU-440], [VNU-550], [VNU-560], [VNU-580], [VNU-600], [VNU-610], [VNU-620], [VNU-730], [VNU-830], [VNU-840], [VNU-850], [VNU-910], [VNU-1070], [VNU-1080], [VNU-1090], the most authoritative one volume works being Philip Grierson's *Byzantine Coins* [VNU-580], and David R. Sear's *Byzantine Coins and Their Values* [VNU-930], while the best multi-volume work is Alfred R. Bellinger's and Philip Grierson's *Catalogue of the Byzantine Coins in the Dumbarton Oaks Collection and in the Whittemore Collection* [VNU-370]; Crete and Greece [VNU-630], [VNU-660], [VNU-800], [VNU-940], [VNU-1000]; Egypt [VNU-530]; Israel and Near East [VNU-700], [VNU-710], [VNU-750], [VNU-760], [VNU-770], [VNU-780], [VNU-790], [VNU-990]; Roman Empire [VNU-390], [VNU-410], [VNU-460], [VNU-510], [VNU-520], [VNU-570], [VNU-630], [VNU-650], [VNU-680], [VNU-690], [VNU-720], [VNU-880], [VNU-890], [VNU-900], [VNU-950], [VNU-1010], [VNU-1030], the most concise and authoritative single volume work being David Sear's *Roman Coins and Their Values* [VNU-950], and the most authoritative multi-volume work being *The Roman Imperial Coinage* [VNU-900]; United States [VNU-320], [VNU-420], [VNU-960], [VNU-1040]; Venice [VNU-540]; World or general [VNU-740], [VNU-980]. To study the techniques of coin making from ancient times to the present, see the following works: [VNU-360], [VNU-500], [VNU-1050].

For those intent on studying coins related to the Bible, take special note of the works already listed under studies of Israel and the Near East, especially the excellent works by Ya'akov Meshorer--[VNU-750], [VNU-760], [VNU-770], and [VNU-780]--and Leo Mildenberg [VNU-790]. For studies linked with the early Christian era, the following works will be particularly helpful: *Ancient Coins Associated with Christianity* [VNU-340], David Hendin's excellent volume, *Guide to Biblical Coins with Values by Herbert Kreindler* [VNU-590], Kenneth A. Jacob's recent study, *Coins and Christianity* [VNU-640], James Edward Jennings' M.A. thesis, "The Witness of Roman Coinage to Christianity, A.D. 313-395" [VNU-650], and Othmar Keel's and Adolphe Gutbug's German work on seal art in the Old Testament [VNU-670].

To locate the latest studies on numismatics, consult the sundry journals given below, including the following: the American Numismatic Society's annual periodical *American Journal of Numismatics, Series 2* [VNU-330], the British Numismatic Society's annual periodical *British Numismatic Journal* [VNU-450], a major monthly *The Celator: Journal of Ancient and Medieval Art and Artifacts* [VNU-470], *Coin News* [VNU-480], *Coin World: The News Weekly for the Entire Numismatic Field* [VNU-490], *Numismatic Chronicle and Journal* [VNU-810], *Numismatist: For Collectors of Coins, Medals, Tokens and Paper Money* [VNU-820], *SAN: Journal of the Society for Ancient Numismatics* [VNU-920], and *The U.S. Coin Collector: The Official Journal of the National Coin Collectors Association* [VNU-1020]. While numerous other works have been printed on numismatics, the few mentioned here will allow the serious student of art at least to begin investigating this pervasive yet often overlooked realm of art studies.

Special Bibliographies

[VNU-010]   Almanzar, Alcedo. *Latin American Numismatic Bibliography [Including the Caribbean]*. San Antonio, Tex.: Almanzar's Coins of the World, 1972. 42 pp.

[VNU-020]   American Numismatic Association. *Dictionary Catalogue of the Library of the American Numismatic Society*. 7 vols. Boston: G. K. Hall, 1962. *Dictionary and Auction Catalogues of the Library of the American Numismatic Society. First Supplement, 1962-1967*. Boston: G. K. Hall, 1967. *Second Supplement, 1968-1972*, 1973. *Third Supplement, 1973-1977*. 2 vols. Boston: G. K. Hall, 1978.

[VNU-030]   ------. *Library Catalogue of the American Numismatic Association*. 2nd ed. Ed. Geneva Karlson. Colorado Springs: American Numismatic Association, 1977. 768 pp. *Supplement 1977-1984*. Ed. Nancy W. Green. Colorado Springs: American Numismatic Association, 1985. 113 pp.

[VNU-040]   Bowker, Howard Franklin. *A Numismatic Bibliography of the Far East: A Check List of Titles in European Languages*. Numismatic Notes and Monographs, no. 101. New York: American Numismatic Society, 1943. 144 pp.

[VNU-050]   Bowman, Frederick. *Canadian Numismatic Research Index*. N.p.: Canadian Numismatic Research Society, 1969. Bib. pp. 69-176.

[VNU-060]   Brunk, Gregory G. *A Bibliography of Numismatic Literature on Countermarked Coins*. Waterloo, Iowa: [G. G. Brunk?], 1975. 122 pp.

[VNU-070]   ------. *Identifying Coins, Medals and Tokens: Late Antiquity to Modern Times: A Bibliographical Survey of Useful Articles*. Nashua, N.H.: Laurion Numismatics, 1991. 145 pp.

[VNU-080]   Clain-Stefanelli, Elvira E[liza]. *Numismatic Bibliography*. Munich: Battenberg; New York: K. G. Saur, 1985. 1,848 pp. English, French, and German.

[VNU-090]   Coole, Arthur Braddan. *A Bibliography on Far Eastern Numismatics and an Union Index of the Currency, Charms and Amulets of the Far East*. Peking: California College in China, College of Chinese Studies, 1940. 421 pp.

[VNU-100]   Coole, Arthur Braddan, Hitoshi Kozono, and Howard Franklin Bowker. *A Bibliography of Far Eastern Numismatology and a Coin Index*. An Encyclopedia of Chinese Coins, vol. 1. Denver: N.p., 1967. 581 pp.

[VNU-110] Davis, Charles E. *American Numismatic Literature: An Annotated Survey of Auction Sales, 1980-1991*. Lincoln, Mass.: Quarterman Publications, 1992. 218 pp.

[VNU-120] Dekesel, C. E. *Twelve Highlights from the Numismatic Book Collection in the Herzog August Bibliothek [Augusteer] in Wolfenbuttel [BDR]*. XIth International Numismatic Congress, Brussels, 8-12th September 1991. Gandavum Flandrorum: Bibliotheca Numismatica Siliciana, 1991. 106 pp.

[VNU-130] Durst, Lorraine S. *United States Numismatic Auction Catalogs: A Bibliography*. New York: S. J. Durst, 1981. 87 pp.

[VNU-140] Fowler, Harold North. *Greek Coins*. Chicago: Obol International; Bolchazy-Carducci Publishers, 1981. 94 pp.

[VNU-150] Gupta, Parmeshwari Lal. *Bibliography of Indian Numismatics*. 2 vols. Varanasi: Numismatic Society of India, 1977. Supplement to C. R. Singhal's *Bibliography of Indian Coins*.

[VNU-160] Hill, George Francis. *Coins and Medals*. [London]: W. Dawson, 1969. 62 pp.

[VNU-170] International Numismatic Commission. *A Survey of Numismatic Research, 1966-1971*. 3 vols. New York: International Numismatic Commission, 1973. *A Survey of Numismatic Research, 1972-1977*. c. 1979. *A Survey of Numismatic Research, 1978-1984*. 3 vols. Ed. Martin Price. Special Publication/International Association of Professional Numismatists, no. 9. London: International Numismatic Commission, International Association of Professional Numismatists, 1986. *A Survey of Numismatic Research, 1985-1990*. 2 vols. Ed. Tony Hackens. Brussels: International Numismatic Commission, 1991. 896 pp. Bib. refs.

[VNU-180] Kindler, A[rie], and Alla Stein. *A Bibliography of the City Coinage of Palestine: From the 2nd Century B.C. to the 3rd Century A.D.* BAR International Series, no. 374. Oxford: BAR, 1987. 261 pp.

[VNU-190] Kroh, Dennis. "Reference Reviews." *The Celator: Journal of Ancient and Medieval Art and Artifacts*. Lodi, Wis.: Clio's Cabinet, 1991-. 2-4 pp. per monthly issue.

[VNU-200] Malter, Joel L. *Byzantine Numismatic Bibliography, 1950-1965*. Chicago; Argonaut, 1968. 59 pp.

469

[VNU-210] Manville, Harrington E. *British Numismatic Auction Catalogues, 1710-1984. Encyclopaedia of British Numismatics*, vol. 1. [London]: A. H. Baldwin; Spink and Son, 1986. 420 pp.

[VNU-220] Martin, Geoffrey Thorndike. *Scarabs, Cylinders, and Other Ancient Egyptian Seals: A Checklist of Publications*. Warminster, Wilts, England: Aris and Phillips, 1985. 61 pp.

[VNU-230] Mayer, L[eo] A[ry]. *A Bibliography of Jewish Numismatics*. Jerusalem: Magnes Press, Hebrew University, 1966. 78 pp.

[VNU-240] ------. *A Bibliography of Moslem Numismatics, India Excepted*. 2nd ed. Oriental Translation Fund, vol. 35. London: Royal Asiatic Society, 1954. 283 pp.

[VNU-250] *Numismatic Literature*. New York: American Numismatic Society, 1947-1949, quarterly. 1976-, semi-annual.

[VNU-260] Sigler, Phares O. *Numismatic Bibliography*. Dearborn, Mich.: Dearborn Press, 1951. 189 pp.

[VNU-270] Singhal, C. R., comp. *Bibliography of Indian Coins*. Ed. Anant Sadashiv Altekar. 2 vols. Bombay: Numismatic Society of India, 1950.

[VNU-280] Suder, Robert W. *Hebrew Inscriptions: A Classified Bibliography*. Selinsgrove: Susquehanna University Press, 1984. 170 pp.

[VNU-290] Thomas, Harold Edward. *United States Numismatic Bibliography: A Bibliography of Books, Periodicals, Pamphlets, Auction Catalogs, and Articles Related to United States Coins, Paper Currency, Tokens, Medals, Exonumia, Etc.*. [Lehigh Acres, Fla.]: H. E. Thomas, 1992. Unpaginated.

[VNU-300] Vermeule, Cornelius Clarkson. *A Bibliography of Applied Numismatics in the Fields of Greek and Roman Archaeology and the Fine Arts*. London: Spink and Son, 1956. 172 pp.

[VNU-310] Younger, John G[rimes]. *A Bibliography for Aegean Glyptic in the Bronze Age*. Berlin: Mann, 1991. 118 pp.

Key Works

[VNU-320] Adams, John W. *United States Numismatic Literature*. Mission Viejo, Calif.: G. F. Kolbe Publications, 1982. Bib. p. 245.

[VNU-330] *American Journal of Numismatics. Series 2*. New York: American Numismatic Society, 1989-. Annual. Continuation of

Museum Notes.

[VNU-340] *Ancient Coins Associated with Christianity*. [3rd ed.] [Philadelphia]: Philadelphia Transportation Co., 1951. 13 pp.

[VNU-350] Bates, George Eugene. *Byzantine Coins*. Archaeological Exploration of Sardis (1958-), Monograph vol. 1. Cambridge: Harvard University Press, 1971. 159 pp.

[VNU-360] Becker, Thomas W. *The Coin Makers: The Development of Coinage from Earliest Times*. Garden City, N.Y.: Doubleday, 1970. 178 pp.

[VNU-370] Bellinger, Alfred R. and Philip Grierson, eds. *Catalogue of the Byzantine Coins in the Dumbarton Oaks Collection and in the Whittemore Collection*. 3 vols. Washington, D.C.: Dumbarton Oaks Center for Byzantine Studies, Trustees for Harvard University, 1966-1973. Dist. J. J. Augustin, Locust Valley, N.Y. Bib., vol. 1, pp. xxii-xxvi. (Vols. 4 and 5 forthcoming.)

[VNU-380] Bendall, S. *The Billon Trachea of Michael VIII Palaeologus, 1258-1282*. London: A. H. Baldwin, 1974. 47 pp. Bib. pp. xvii-xviii. (Byzantine Empire)

[VNU-390] Berk, Harlan J. *Roman Gold Coins of the Medieval World, 383-1453 A.D.* Joliet, Ill.: Professional Numistmatists Guild, 1986. 88 pp. Bib. p. 1.

[VNU-400] Boyd, Ernest C. "The Imperial Foundations of Byzantine Iconoclasm: The Numismatic Evidence." M.A. Thesis, University of Oregon, 1987. Bib. pp. 76-77.

[VNU-410] Boyne, William. *A Manual of Roman Coins*. London, 1865. Rev. ed., Chicago: Ammon Press, 1968. 86 pp.

[VNU-420] Bressett, Kenneth E. with American Numismatic Association. *Collectible American Coins*. New York: Crescent Books, 1991. Dist. Outlet Book Co., Inc., Random House, New York. 320 pp.

[VNU-430] British Museum, Department of Coins and Metals. *Catalogue of the Imperial Byzantine Coins in the British Museum*. 2 vols. Ed. Warwick William Wroth. London: British Museum, 1908.

[VNU-440] ------. *Western and Provincial Byzantine Coins of the Vandals, Ostrogoths, and Lombards, and of the Empires of Thessalonica, Nicaea, and Trebizond, in the British Museum*. 1911. Reprint. Chicago: Argonaut, 1966. 344 pp. (See [VNU-1090])

[VNU-450] *British Numismatic Journal*. Edgeware, Middlesex, England: British Numismatic Society, 1905-. Annual.

[VNU-460] Carson, Robert Andrew Glindinning. *Principal Coins of the Romans*. 3 vols. London: British Museum Publications, 1978-1981. Bib., vol. 1, p. 84. Also see *Coins of the Roman Empire in the British Museum*, 6 vols. to 1975, ed. Harold Mattingly, R. A. G. Carson, Philip V. Hill, et al.

[VNU-470] *Celator, The: Journal of Ancient and Medieval Art and Artifacts*. Lodi, Wis.: Clio's Cabinet, 1987-. Monthly. Incorporating *Roman Coins and Culture*.

[VNU-480] *Coin News*. Honiton, Devon, England: Token Publishing, Ltd., 1979-. Monthly. Formerly *Coin and Medal News*.

[VNU-490] *Coin World: The News Weekly for the Entire Numismatic Field*. Sidney, Ohio: Amos Press, 1960-. Weekly. Formerly *Numismatic Scrapbook*; *World Coins*.

[VNU-500] Cooper, Denis R. *The Art and Craft of Coinmaking: A History of Minting Technology*. London: Spink and Son, 1988. 264 pp.

[VNU-510] Crawford, Michael H. *Coinage and Money Under the Roman Republic*. London: Methuen, 1985. xxv, 355 pp.

[VNU-520] ------. *Roman Republican Coinage*. 2 vols. London; New York: Cambridge University Press, 1974.

[VNU-530] Curriers, Douglas D. "Scarabs: Their Implications on Israelite History." M. A. Thesis, Trinity Evangelical Divinity School, 1988. Bib. pp. 157-173.

[VNU-540] Dal Gian, Maria-Luisa. *Il Leone di S. Marco sulle monete e sulle oselle della Serenissima*. La Bala d'oro, no. 5. Venice: Edizioni della Fortuna, 1958. Bib. pp. 55-56.

[VNU-550] Dumbarton Oaks. *Catalogue of Byzantine Seals at Dumbarton Oaks and in the Fogg Museum of Art*. Washington, D.C.: Dumbarton Oaks Research Library and Collection, 1991. Bib. refs.

[VNU-560] Goodacre, Hugh George. *A Handbook of the Coinage of the Byzantine Empire*. 3 vols. London: Spink and Son, 1928. Reprint. 1 vol. London: Spink and Son, 1957, 1960, 1964, 1965, 1967. 361 pp.

[VNU-570] Grant, Michael. *Roman History from Coins: Some Uses of the Imperial Coinage to the Historian*. Cambridge: Cambridge University Press, [1958]. Reprint. Cambridge: Cambridge

472

University Press, 1968. Bib. pp. 90-91.

[VNU-580] Grierson, Philip. *Byzantine Coins*. London: Methuen; Berkeley: University of California Press, 1982. 411 pp. Bib. pp. 347-348.

[VNU-590] Hendin, David. *Guide to Biblical Coins with Values by Herbert Kreindler*. Nyack, N.Y.: Amphora, 1987. 224 pp.

[VNU-600] Hendy, Michael F. *Coinage and Money in the Byzantine Empire, 1081-1261*. Dumbarton Oaks Studies, no. 12. Washington, D.C.: Dumbarton Oaks Center for Byzantine Studies, 1969. 453 pp. Bib. pp. xii-xvii.

[VNU-610] ------. *The Economy, Fiscal Administration, and Coinage of Byzantium*. Northampton: Variorum Reprints, 1989. Bib. refs.

[VNU-620] ------. *Studies in the Byzantine Monetary Economy, c. 300-1450*. Cambridge; New York: Cambridge University Press, 1985. 773 pp. Bib. pp. 670-709.

[VNU-630] Hill, George F. *A Handbook of Greek and Roman Coins*. London, 1899. Reprint. Chicago: Argonaut, 1964. 295 pp.

[VNU-640] Jacob, Kenneth A. *Coins and Christianity*. 2nd ed. London: B. A. Seaby, Ltd., 1985. Dist. B. T. Batsford, Essex, England. Bib. pp. 92-95.

[VNU-650] Jennings, James Edward. "The Witness of Roman Coinage to Christianity, A.D. 313-395." M.A. Thesis, Wheaton College, 1963. Bib. pp. 95-100.

[VNU-660] Jones, M. J. *A Dictionary of Ancient Greek Coins*. London: Seabys, 1986.

[VNU-670] Keel, Othmar, and Adolphe Gutbug. *Jahwe-Visionen und Siegelkunst: Eine neue Deutung der Majestatsschilderungen in Jes 6, Ex 1 und 10 und Sach 4*. Stuttgart: Verlag Katholisches Bibelwerk, 1977. 410 pp. Bib. pp. 361-383.

[VNU-680] Kent, J[ohn] P. C. *Roman Coins*. Rev. ed. Trans. *Die römische Münze*. New York: Harry N. Abrams, 1978. Bib. pp. 360-361.

[VNU-690] Kent, J[ohn] P. C., and K. S. Painter, eds. *Wealth of the Roman World: AD 300-700*. Exhibition catalog. London: British Museum Publications, 1977. Bib. pp. 189-190.

[VNU-700] Kindler, Arie. *The Coinage of Bostra*. England: Aris and Phillips; Bloomington, Ind.: David Brown, 1983. 160 pp.

[VNU-710] Kouymjian, Dickran, ed. *Near Eastern Numismatics, Iconography, Epigraphy, and History: Studies in Honor of George C. Miles.* Beirut: American University of Beirut, 1974. 478 pp. Bib. pp. xvii-xxv, and bib. refs.

[VNU-720] Lhotka, John F. *Introduction to East Roman Coinage.* N.p., 1954. 112 pp. Bibs.

[VNU-730] Lowick, N. M. *The Mardin [Turkey] Hoard: Islamic Counter-marks on Byzantine Folles.* [London]: A. H. Baldwin and Sons, Ltd., 1977. 79 pp. Bib. refs.

[VNU-740] Macdonald, G. *Coin Types: Their Origin and Development.* 1905. Reprint. Chicago: Argonaut Inc. Publishers, 1969.

[VNU-750] Meshorer, Ya'akov. *Ancient Jewish Coinage.* 2 vols. Cleveland: American School of Oriental Research, 1982. 184 and 295 pp.

[VNU-760] ------. *Jewish Coins of the Second Temple Period.* Trans. I. H. Levine. Trans. *Matbe'ot ha-Yehudim bi-yeme Bayit sheni.* Tel Aviv: Am Hassefer, [1967]. 184 pp. Bib. refs. in notes, pp. 110-112.

[VNU-770] ------. *Nabataean Coins.* Trans. I. H. Levine. [Jerusalem]: Institute of Archaeology, Hebrew University of Jerusalem, 1975. Dist. Israel Exploration Society. 111 pp. Bib. refs.

[VNU-780] ------. *Sylloge Nummorum Graecorum: The Collection of the American Numismatic Society. Part 6, Jewish Coins.* New York: American Numismatic Society, 1981. 108 pp.

[VNU-790] Mildenberg, Leo. *The Coinage of the Bar Kokhba War.* Los Angeles: Numismatic Fine Arts, 1984. c. 400 pp.

[VNU-800] Murphy, Penny S. "The Depiction of Religious Shrines on Minoan and Mycenaean Sealstones." M.A. Thesis, State University of New York at Albany, 1982. 99 pp. Bib. pp. 65-70.

[VNU-810] *Numismatic Chronicle and Journal.* London: Royal Numismatic Society, British Museum, 1839-.

[VNU-820] *Numismatist: For Collectors of Coins, Medals, Tokens and Paper Money.* Colorado Springs: American Numismatic Association, 1888-. Monthly.

[VNU-830] Oikonomides, Nicolas. *A Collection of Dated Byzantine Lead*

474

Seals. Washington, D.C.: Dumbarton Oaks Research Library and Collection, 1986. 175 pp.

[VNU-840] ------, ed. *Studies in Byzantine Sigillography.* Washington, D.C.: Dumbarton Oaks Research Library and Collection, 1987. 119 pp. Bib. refs. English, French, and German.

[VNU-850] ------, ed. *Studies in Byzantine Sigillography, 2.* Washington, D.C.: Dumbarton Oaks Research Library and Collection, 1990. 321 pp. Bib. refs. English, French, German, and Greek.

[VNU-860] Pemsel, Johann Nepomuk. *Antike Munzen zur Heilsgeschichte.* Kataloge und Schriften/Bischofliches Zentralarchiv und Bischofliche Zentralbibliothek Regensburg, Bd. 4. Munich: Schnell und Steiner, 1989. 181 pp. Bib. refs. pp. 136-138.

[VNU-870] Price, Martin Jessop, and Bluma L. Trell. *Coins and Their Cities: Architecture on the Ancient Coins of Greece, Rome, and Palestine.* London: Vecchi, 1977. 298 pp. Bib. pp. 229-238.

[VNU-880] Robertson, Anne S. *Roman Imperial Coins in the Hunter Coin Cabinet, University of Glasgow.* 5 vols. London: Oxford University Press for University of Glasgow, 1962-1982.

[VNU-890] *Roman Coins and Culture.* West Germany, vols. 1-3, 1985-1987. Ann Arbor, Mich., vols. 4-, 1989-.

[VNU-900] *Roman Imperial Coinage, The.* 9 vols. in 12. Ed. Harold Mattingly, et al. London: Spink and Son, 1923-1981. Vol. 1 revised by C. H. V. Sutherland and R. A. G. Carson, 1984. Other revisions forthcoming.

[VNU-910] Rynearson, Paul F. *Byzantine Coin Values: A Guide.* [2nd ed.] San Clemente, Calif.: Malter-Westerfield, 1971. Bib. pp. 107-108.

[VNU-920] *SAN: Journal of the Society for Ancient Numismatics.* Los Angeles, Calif., 1969-. (Vol. 20, 1993) Quarterly.

[VNU-930] Sear, David R. *Byzantine Coins and Their Values.* 2nd ed. London: B. A. Seaby; Los Angeles: Numismatic Fine Arts, 1987. 528 pp.

[VNU-940] ------. *Greek Coins and Their Values.* 2 vols. London: B. A. Seaby, 1978-1979. Bib., vol. 1, pp. xxxvii-xxxviii; vol. 2, pp. xxxix-xl.

[VNU-950] ------. *Roman Coins and Their Values.* 4th ed. Los Angeles: Numismatic Fine Arts, 1988.

[VNU-960] Shankle, George Earlie. *State Names, Flags, Seals, Songs, Birds, Flowers, and Other Symbols: A Study Based on Historical Documents Giving the Origin and Significance of the State Names, Nicknames, Mottoes, Seals, Flags, Flowers, Birds, Songs, and Descriptive Comments on the Capitol Buildings and on Some of the Leading State Histories.* Rev. ed. 1938. Reprint. Westport, Conn.: Greenwood Press, 1973. 522 pp. Bib. pp. 427-479.

[VNU-970] Shearer, Benjamin F. *State Names, Seals, Flags, and Symbols: A Historical Guide.* New York: Greenwood Press, 1987. Bib. pp. 205-218.

[VNU-980] *Standard Catalog of World Coins.* 18th ed. Iola, Wis.: Kraus Publications, Inc., n.d.

[VNU-990] Spijkerman, Augustus. *The Coins of the Decapolis and Provincia Arabia.* N.p.: Jerusalem, 1978. 404 pp. Bib., solid.

[VNU-1000] Sutherland, C[arol] H[umphrey] V[ivian]. *Art in Coinage: The Aesthetics of Money from Greece to the Present Day.* London: B. T. Batsford, [1955]. New York: Philosophical Library, [1956]. Bib. pp. 210-212.

[VNU-1010] ------. *Coinage in Roman Imperial Policy 31 B.C.--A.D. 68.* London: Methuen, [1951]. Reprint. New York: Barnes and Noble, [1971]. 220 pp. Bib. refs. in footnotes.

[VNU-1020] *U.S. Coin Collector, The: The Official Journal of the National Coin Collectors Association.* Murphysboro, Ill.: National Coin Collectors Association, 1990-. Bi-monthly.

[VNU-1030] Van Meter, David. *Handbook of Roman Imperial Coins: A Complete Guide to the History, Types and Values of Roman Imperial Coinage.* Nashua, N.H.: Laurion Numismatics, 1991. 334 pp.

[VNU-1040] Vermeule, Cornelius Clarkson. *Numismatic Art in America: Aesthetics of the United States Coinage.* Cambridge, Mass.: Belknap Press of Harvard University Press, 1971. Bib. pp. 229-231.

[VNU-1050] ------. *Some Notes on Ancient Dies and Coining Methods.* London: Spink and Son, 1954. Update by William Malkmus, "Addenda to Vermeule's Catalog of Ancient Coin Dies," *SAN: Journal of the Society for Ancient Numismatics* 17, no. 4 (September 1989), 18, no. 1 (1991), pp. 16-22; 18, no. 2 (May 1991), pp. 40-49.

[VNU-1060] Walsh, R[obert]. *An Essay on Ancient Coins, Medals, and Gems:*

As Illustrating the Progress of Christianity in the Early Ages.
3rd ed. London: F. Westley and A. H. Davis, 1830. 140 pp.

[VNU-1070] Whitting, Philip D. *Byzantine Coins.* The World of Numismatics. New York: G. P. Putnam's Sons; London: Barrie and
Jenkins, 1973. 311 pp.

[VNU-1080] Wroth, Warwick. *Imperial Byzantine Coins in the British
Museum.* 2 vols. in 1. Formerly *Catalogue of the Imperial
Byzantine Coins in the British Museum,* 1908. Reprint.
Chicago: Argonaut, 1966. cxii, 683 pp.

[VNU-1090] ------. *Western and Provincial Byzantine Coins of the Vandals,
Ostrogoths, and Lombards, and of the Empires of Thessaloni-
ca, Nicaea, and Trebizond, in the British Museum.* Formerly
*Catalogue of the Coins of the Vandals, Ostrogoths, and
Lombards, and of the Empires of Thessalonica, Nicaea, and
Trebizond in the British Museum,* 1911. Reprint. Chicago:
Argonaut, 1966. xciv, 344 pp. (See [VNU-440])

[VNU-1100] Zimmerman, Jeremiah. *Religious Character of Ancient Coins.*
London: Spink and Son, 1908. 14 pp.

KEY WORKS ON PAINTING

Painting is covered extensively in most books treating the visual arts,
especially when one considers the sundry forms of painting in collage, glass
painting, frescoes, icons, illuminated manuscripts, and murals, to name just a
few related categories. Although diverse in application, painting is a discipline unto itself and deserves singular attention. Works listed below primarily
treat painting in the narrower sense of using paint on canvas, silk, or wood.
Furthermore, the following section specializes in works exploring the relationship between Christianity and painting, from the early centuries of the Christian era to the present.

In studying painting, one will be greatly aided by several major indexes
and bibliographies, such as Patricia P. Havilice's *World Painting Index* [VPA-
020] and its first supplement [VPA-030], along with Eugene L. Huddleston's
and Douglas A. Noverr's *The Relationship of Painting and Literature: A Guide
to Information Sources* [VPA-040]. Two specialized bibliographies are also
listed below, including Jessie Croft Ellis' *Nature Index* [VPA-010] and Helene
E. Roberts' *Iconographic Index to Old Testament Paintings Represented in*

Photographs and Slides of Paintings in the Visual Collections, Fine Arts Library, Harvard University [VPA-050]. These five bibliographies should be used to supplement those given in the opening section of Chapter 12, many of which also treat painting.

Several of the following key works serve best as supplements to the more comprehensive and current volumes listed in the second section of Chapter 12 treating general theory of the visual arts. These augmenting works on the general study of painting include the following volumes: Richard D. Altick's excellent guide to literary sources for paintings, *Paintings from Books: Art and Literature in Britain, 1760-1900* [VPA-060], Joachim Fernau's somewhat dated but still useful volume, *The Praeger Encyclopedia of Old Masters* [VPA-350], Carlton Lake's and Robert Maillard's older but still helpful work, *A Dictionary of Modern Painting* [VPA-540], a useful recent directory, *Larousse Dictionary of Painters* [VPA-570], and two older indexes by Isabel Stevenson Monro and Kate M. Monro, *Index to Reproductions of European Paintings: A Guide to Pictures in More than Three Hundred Books* [VPA-710], *Index to Reproductions of American Paintings: First Supplement* [VPA-720]. Of the works listed in Chapter 12 which will be most useful in connection with studying painting, several are worthy of note. The most popular and substantial single volume anthologies treating the arts are Horst Woldermar Janson's *History of Art* [VAT-520], sometimes used as the authoritative text for organizing art libraries, and Horst de la Croix's and Richard G. Tansey's *Gardner's Art Through the Ages* [VAT-600], which also includes a large section on non-western arts. Also consider two recent encyclopedias, Hohn J. Norwich's *Oxford Illustrated Encyclopedia, Vol. 5: The Arts* [VAT-780], and M. Rugoff's *Britannica Encyclopedia of America Art* [VAT-1000]. For more extensive study of the arts, see the fifteen volume *Encyclopedia of World Art* [VAT-310] with its several supplements. One will also find considerable help in the various Oxford companions to art, including [VAT-800], [VAT-810], and [VAT-820], and in Kenneth McLeish's *Penguin Companion to the Arts in the Twentieth Century* [VAT-690], and the still growing series, *The Pelican History of Art* [VAT-890].

The remainder of works listed below can be divided roughly into two categories, the general, largely secular studies, and the religious studies, often including treatments of individual artists. In the former category, the following sub-categories of painting studies may be found: American [VPA-890], [VPA-1170]; Dutch [VPA-210], [VPA-750], [VPA-820]; English [VPA-230], [VPA-250], [VPA-850]; French [VPA-630], [VPA-660]; Hungarian [VPA-680]; Impressionism [VPA-1040]; Italian [VPA-620], [VPA-640], [VPA-670]; National Gallery of London [VPA-080], [VPA-600], [VPA-760]; Navaho [VPA-830]; Pre-Raphaelite [VPA-480], [VPA-1020], [VPA-1060]; Renaissance [VPA-730], [VPA-1100]; Renaissance of Italy [VPA-330], [VPA-420], [VPA-950], [VPA-1070], [VPA-1080], [VPA-1150]; Renaissance of Northern Europe [VPA-130], [VPA-260], [VPA-1000]; Soviet [VPA-170]; Spanish [VPA-650], [VPA-1030]; technique [VPA-470]; theory [VPA-110], [VPA-190], [VPA-280], [VPA-460]; Tibetan [VPA-800]; twentieth century [VPA-410]; western [VPA-200], [VPA-610], [VPA-880], [VPA-910], [VPA-970]; world [VPA-490], [VPA-740], [VPA-880].

The second major category of key works listed below treats religious themes, primarily Christian. The following categories and subjects are treated primarily for their religious emphases in painting: Adam and Eve [VPA-980]; America [VPA-120], [VPA-240], [VPA-370], [VPA-1160]; Apocalyptic [VPA-810]; Bali [VPA-900]; Bestiary of St. Jerome [VPA-360]; Bible [VPA-140], [VPA-220], [VPA-270], [VPA-590], [VPA-690], [VPA-870]; Celtic [VPA-400]; Christian, early [VPA-310]; France [VPA-960]; Italy [VPA-700], [VPA-780], [VPA-860], [VPA-990]; Jesus Christ [VPA-100], [VPA-1120]; Jews [VPA-1140]; Mexico [VPA-380]; myth and symbols [VPA-150], [VPA-270], [VPA-1180]; Nesterov religious community [VPA-320]; religious painting, general [VPA-180], [VPA-430], [VPA-550], [VPA-920], [VPA-930], [VPA-940], [VPA-1130]; Saint Peters and Vatican [VPA-440]; Shaker [VPA-840]; Sikh Court [VPA-390]; Sistine Chapel [VPA-340], [VPA-450]; Spain [VPA-770]; technique [VPA-550]; Vatican [VPA-1090]; Westminster [VPA-160]. The following painters have made prominent use of religious themes and the works listed below explore these artists' use of biblical and religious motifs: Michel Ciry [VPA-300], James Ensor [VPA-580], Paul Gauguin [VPA-070], Theophile Hamel [VPA-1110], William Holman Hunt [VPA-560], Charles Huot [VPA-790], Deni Ponty [VPA-530], Raphael Santi [VPA-500], Victor Sparre [VPA-1010], Jan Steen [VPA-510], Graham Sutherland [VPA-1050],

Giambattista Tiepolo [VPA-090], Vincent Van Gogh [VPA-520], and Benjamin West [VPA-290]. For extended bibliographies of works treating some of the acknowledged masters of religious art, see the section on selected painters given below.

Of the key works listed below, several are outstanding examples of the study of painting and will prove useful for any serious student of this medium. The three most prominent art historians are Otto Benesch [VPA-130], Michael Levey [VPA-600 to VPA-640], and Erwin Panofsky [VPA-820]. Also note the work of Jacques Derrida [VPA-280] for its probing aesthetic treatment of painting. For additional works treating painting, see the opening three sections of Chapter 12.

Special Bibliographies

[VPA-010] Ellis, Jessie [Croft]. *Nature Index: 5000 Selected References to Nature Forms and Illustrations of Nature in Design, Painting and Sculpture.* Useful Reference Series, no. 41. Boston: F. W. Faxon Co., 1930. 319 pp.

[VPA-020] Havilice, Patricia P. *World Painting Index.* 2 vols. Metuchen, N.J.: Scarecrow Press, 1977. 2,136 pp. Bib. pp. 1-65.

[VPA-030] ------. *World Painting Index--First Supplement 1973-1980.* 2 vols. Metuchen, N.J.: Scarecrow Press, 1982. 1,233 pp.

[VPA-040] Huddleston, Eugene L., and Douglas A. Noverr. *The Relationship of Painting and Literature: A Guide to Information Sources.* American Studies Information Guide Series, vol. 4. Detroit: Gale Research, 1978. xxiii, 184 pp.

[VPA-050] Roberts, Helene E. *Iconographic Index to Old Testament Paintings Represented in Photographs and Slides of Paintings in the Visual Collections, Fine Arts Library, Harvard University.* Garland Reference Library of the Humanities, vol. 1154. New York: Garland Publishing, 1990. 224 pp.

Key Works

[VPA-060] Altick, Richard D. *Paintings from Books: Art and Literature in Britain, 1760-1900.* Columbus: Ohio State University Press, 1985. 527 pp.

[VPA-070] Amishai-Maisels, Z. *Gauguin's Religious Themes.* New York; London: Garland Publishing, 1985. 670 pp. Bib.

[VPA-080] Anzil, Marina. *The National Gallery of London and its Paintings.* New York: Arco Publishing, 1974. 104 pp.

[VPA-090] Barcham, William L. *Religious Paintings of Giambattista Tiepolo: Piety and Tradition in Eighteenth-Century Venice.* Oxford: Oxford University Press, 1990. 272 pp.

[VPA-100] Barraud, Marc, and Georges Haldas. *The Life of Christ: Paintings of the 11th-15th Centuries: With Passages from the Gospels.* London: Zwemmer, 1967. 156 pp.

[VPA-110] Barron, John N. *The Language of Painting: An Informal Dictionary.* Cleveland: World Pub. Co., [1967]. Bib. pp. 205-207.

[VPA-120] Bauer, Fred, and Norman Rockwell. *The Faith of America.* New York: Abbeville Press, 1980. 160 pp.

[VPA-130] Benesch, Otto. *The Art of the Renaissance in Northern Europe.* Cambridge, Mass.: Harvard University Press, 1967.

[VPA-140] Bernard, Bruce. *The Bible and its Painters.* N.p.: Orbis Pub., 1983. Reprint. London: Macdonald and Co., Ltd., 1988. Bib. p. 299.

[VPA-150] Bernen, Satia, and Robert Bernen. *Myth and Religion in European Painting, 1270-1700: The Stories as the Artists Knew Them.* New York: George Braziller; N.p., England: Constable, 1973. 288 pp.

[VPA-160] Binski, Paul. *The Painted Chamber at Westminster.* Occasional Paper [Society of Antiquaries of London], no. 9. London: Society of Antiquaries of London, 1986. 166 pp. Bib. (Religious themes.)

[VPA-170] Bown, Matthew Cullerne, and Brandon Taylor. *Art of the Soviets: Painting, Sculpture, and Architecture in a One-Party State, 1917-1992.* Manchester; New York: Manchester University Press, 1993. Dist. St. Martin's Press, U.S.A. and Canada.

[VPA-180] Brown, Stephanie. *Religious Painting.* Mayflower Gallery Series. N.p.: Smithmark, 1979.

[VPA-190] Brownell, Baker. *Art is Action: A Discussion of Nine Arts in a Modern World.* 1939. Reprint. Freeport, N.Y.: Books for Libraries Press, [1969]. 231 pp. Bib. footnotes.

[VPA-200] Byron, Robert, and Talbot Rice. *The Birth of Western Painting: A*

History of Colour, Form, and Iconography, Illustrated from the Paintings of Mistras and Mount Athos, of Giotto and Duccio, and of El Greco. New York: Alfred A. Knopf, 1931. Bib. pp. 220-226.

[VPA-210] Chatelet, Albert. *Early Dutch Painting: Painting in the Northern Netherlands in the Fifteenth Century.* Trans. Christopher Brown and Anthony Turner. Oxford: Phaidon Press; New York: Rizzoli International Publications, 1981. 264 pp. Bib.

[VPA-220] Cockerell, Sydney C., and John Plummer. *Old Testament Miniatures.* New York: George Braziller, 1969. 216 pp. Bib.

[VPA-230] Cohen, Michael. *Engaging English Art: Entering the Work in Two Centuries of English Painting and Poetry.* University, Ala.: University of Alabama Press, 1987. Bib. pp. 211-221.

[VPA-240] Craven, Wayne. *Colonial American Portraiture: The Economic, Religious, Social, Cultural, Philosophical, Scientific, and Aesthetic Foundations.* Cambridge: Cambridge University Press, 1986. 459 pp. Bib. (John Calvin's influence.)

[VPA-250] Cust, Lionel. *Notes on Pictures in the Royal Collections.* London: Chatto and Windus, 1911. 91 pp. Bib. refs.

[VPA-260] Cuttler, Charles D. *Northern Painting from Pucelle to Bruegel: Fourteenth, Fifteenth, and Sixteenth Centuries.* New York: Holt, Rinehart and Winston, 1968. Bib. pp. 486-491.

[VPA-270] Daniel, Howard. *Encyclopedia of Themes and Subjects in Painting: Mythological, Biblical, Historical, Literary, Allegorical and Topical.* New York: Harry N. Abrams, 1971. 252 pp.

[VPA-280] Derrida, Jacques. *The Truth in Painting.* Trans. *La Vérité en Peinture.* Chicago: University of Chicago Press, 1987. 386 pp.

[VPA-290] Dillenberger, John. *Benjamin West: The Context of His Life's Work with Particular Attention to Paintings with Religious Subject Matter.* San Antonio: Trinity University Press, 1977. 239 pp.

[VPA-300] Droit, Michel, ed. *Michel Ciry.* Neuchatel, Switzerland: Ides et Calendes, 1977. 236 pp. Bib. French. (Painting, drawing, and religion.)

[VPA-310] du Bourguet, Pierre. *Early Christian Painting.* Trans. Simon Watson Taylor. New York: Viking Press, 1965. Bib. pp. 53-54.

[VPA-320] Durylin, S. N. *Nesterov in Life and Art*. 2nd ed. Moscow: Molodaja Gvardija, 1976. 464 pp. Bib. (Treats Nesterov and his association with the religious community and artists near Moscow, such as Vasilij Dmitrievic Polenov, Elena Dmitrievna Polenova, Ilja Efimovic Repin, Apollinarij Mihajlovic Vasnecov, and Viktor Mihajlovic Vasnecov.)

[VPA-330] Edgerton, Samuel Y., Jr. *Pictures and Punishment: Art and Criminal Prosecution During the Florentine Renaissance*. Ithaca: Cornell University Press, 1985. 243 pp.

[VPA-340] Ettlinger, Leopold David, and H. Otto Fein. *The Sistine Chapel before Michelangelo: Religious Imagery and Papal Primacy*. Oxford: Clarendon Press, 1965. 128 pp.

[VPA-350] Fernau, Joachim. *The Praeger Encyclopedia of Old Masters*. Trans. James Cleugh and Monica Brooksbank. New York: Frederick A. Praeger Publishers, [1959]. Bib. p. 335.

[VPA-360] Friedmann, Herbert. *A Bestiary for St. Jerome: Animal Symbolism in European Religious Art*. Washington, D.C.: Smithsonian Institute, 1980. 378 pp.

[VPA-370] Gambone, Robert L. *Art and Popular Religion in Evangelical America, 1915-1940*. Knoxville: University of Tennessee Press, 1989. 304 pp. Bib. pp. 257-263.

[VPA-380] Giffords, G. K. *Mexican Folk Retablos: Masterpieces on Tin*. Tucson, Ariz.: University of Arizona Press, 1974. 160 pp. Bib.

[VPA-390] Goswamy, Brijinder N. *Painters at the Sikh Court*. [Philadelphia]: Coronet Books, 1975. 135 pp.

[VPA-400] Green, Miranda J. *Symbol and Image in Celtic Religious Art*. London: Routledge and Kegan Paul, 1992. 296 pp.

[VPA-410] Haftmann, Werner. *Painting in the Twentieth Century: An Analysis of the Artists and Their Work*. 2 vols. New York: Frederick A. Praeger Publishers, 1961. Bib., Vol. I, pp. 379-425. Vol. II, 418 pp.

[VPA-420] Hartt, Frederick. *History of Italian Renaissance Art: Painting, Sculpture, Architecture*. 4th ed. Ed. David G. Wilkins. Englewood Cliff, N.J.: Prentice-Hall Press; New York: Harry N. Abrams, 1993. Bib. refs.

[VPA-430] Healy, Norbert H. *An Anthology of the Great Religious Painters of the Western World*. N.p.: Gloucester Art, 1989. 147 pp.

[VPA-440] Hersey, George L. *High Renaissance Art in St. Peter's and the Vatican: An Interpretive Guide.* Chicago: University of Chicago Press, 1993. 344 pp.

[VPA-450] Heusinger, Lutz, and Fabrizio Mancinelli. *The Sistine Chapel.* Ed. Francesco Papafava. Florence: Lito Terrazzi, 1989. Bib. p. 96.

[VPA-460] Homer, William I. *Seurat and the Science of Painting.* 1964. Reprint. N.p.: Hacker, 1985. 327 pp.

[VPA-470] Howard, Rob. *Illustrators Bible.* New York: Watson-Guptill Publications; N.p., England: Phaidon Press, 1993. 176 pp.

[VPA-480] Ironside, Robin. *Pre-Raphaelite Painting.* London: Phaidon Press, 1948.

[VPA-490] Jaffé, Hans L. C. *20,000 Years of World Painting.* New York: Crown Publishers, 1967. Reprint. New York: Greenwich House, 1983.

[VPA-500] Jones, Roger, and Nicholas Penny. *Raphael.* New Haven; London: Yale University Press, 1983. 256 pp. Bib. (Painting and architecture.)

[VPA-510] Kirschenbaum, Baruch D. *The Religious and Historical Paintings of Jan Steen.* New York: Allanheld and Schram, 1977. 261 pp. Bib.

[VPA-520] Kodera, Tsukasa. *Vincent Van Gogh: Christianity Versus Nature.* Amsterdam; Philadelphia: John Benjamins Publishing Co., 1990. 284 pp. Bib.

[VPA-530] Koslow, David. *Intimate Angel: Paintings and Drawings by Deni Ponty.* London: Editions Aubrey Walter/GMP, 1990. 72 pp. Bib.

[VPA-540] Lake, Carlton, and Robert Maillard. *A Dictionary of Modern Painting.* Trans. Lawrence Samuelson, et al. New York: Tudor Pub. Co., [1956].

[VPA-550] Landa, Robin. *Inspired by Faith: A How-to Guide to Religious Oil Painting.* Old Tappan, N.J.: Fleming H. Revell Co., 1988. Bib. p. 167.

[VPA-560] Landow, G. P. *William Holman Hunt and Typological Symbolism.* New Haven, Conn.; London: Yale University Press for Paul Mellon Center for Studies in British Art, 1979. 208 pp. Bib.

[VPA-570] *Larousse Dictionary of Painters.* New York: BDD Promotional

Book Co., Inc., 1990. 467 pp.

[VPA-580] Lesko, Diane. *James Ensor: The Creative Years*. Princeton: Princeton University Press, 1985. 174 pp. Bib. (Religion and literature and his art.)

[VPA-590] Leveen, Jacob. *The Hebrew Bible in Art*. The Schweich Lectures of the British Academy, 1939. 1944. Reprint. New York: Hermon Press, 1974. Bib. pp. 129-135.

[VPA-600] Levey, Michael. *A Room-by-Room Guide to the National Gallery*. London: National Gallery [Great Britain], 1969. 121 pp.

[VPA-610] ------. *From Giotto to Cezanne: A Concise History of Painting*. World of Art Series. New York: Thames and Hudson, 1985. 324 pp.

[VPA-620] ------. *The Eighteenth Century Italian Schools*. London: National Gallery [Great Britain], 1956.

[VPA-630] ------. *Painting and Sculpture in France 1700-1789*. Yale University Press Pelican History of Art. New Haven; London: Yale University Press, 1993. 318 pp. Bib. refs.

[VPA-640] ------. *Painting in Eighteenth-Century Venice*. Rev. ed. Ithaca: Cornell University Press, 1980. 264 pp.

[VPA-650] Licht, F. *Goya: The Origins of the Modern Temper in Art*. London: John Murray, 1980. 288 pp. Bib.

[VPA-660] Lichtenstein, Jacqueline. *The Eloquence of Color: Rhetoric and Painting in the French Classical Age*. Trans. *Couleur eloquente*. New Historicism: Studies in Cultural Poetics, no. 18. Berkeley: University of California Press, 1993. 269 pp. Bib. refs.

[VPA-670] Lloyd, Christopher, comp. *A Catalogue of the Earlier Italian Paintings in the Ashmolean Museum*. Oxford: Clarendon Press, 1977. 222 pp. Bib. pp. xi-xii.

[VPA-680] Mansbach, Steven A., and Richard V. West. *Standing in the Tempest: Painters of the Hungarian Avant-Garde, 1908-1930*. Santa Barbara: Santa Barbara Museum of Art; Cambridge: MIT Press, 1991. 240 pp. Bib.

[VPA-690] *Masterpieces of Biblical Art*. Saint Paul, Minn.: Catholic Digest Edition, College of St. Thomas, 1973. xvi and 95 illustrations.

[VPA-700] Meiss, Millard. *Painting in Florence and Siena After the Black*

Death: The Arts, Religion and Society in the Mid-Fourteenth-Century. Princeton: Princeton University Press, 1976.

[VPA-710] Monro, Isabel Stevenson, and Kate M. Monro. *Index to Reproductions of European Paintings: A Guide to Pictures in More than Three Hundred Books.* New York: H. W. Wilson, 1956.

[VPA-720] ------. *Index to Reproductions of American Paintings: First Supplement.* New York: H. W. Wilson, 1964. 480 pp.

[VPA-730] Murray, Peter, and Linda Murray. *The Art of the Renaissance.* 1963. Reprint. New York: Thames and Hudson, 1985. 286 pp.

[VPA-740] Myers, Bernard S., ed. *Encyclopedia of Painting: Painters and Painting of the World from Prehistoric Times to the Present Day.* New York: Crown Publishers, 1955. 511 pp.

[VPA-750] Nash, John Malcolm. *The Age of Rembrandt and Vermeer: Dutch Painting in the Seventeenth Century.* 2nd ed. London: Phaidon Press, 1979. Bib. p. 265.

[VPA-760] *National Gallery of Pictures by the Great Masters, The: Presented by Individuals, or Purchased by Grant of Parliament.* 2 vols. London: Jones and Co., [1840].

[VPA-770] Oakeshott, Walter. *Sigena: Romanesque Paintings in Spain and the Artists of the Winchester Bible Artists.* London: Harvey Miller and Medcalf; New York: New York Graphic Society, 1972. 144 pp. Bib.

[VPA-780] Os, Henk van, and Kees van der Ploeg. *Sienese Altarpieces, 1215-1460: Form, Content, Function: Vol. 1: 1215-1344.* Trans. Michael Hoyle. Mediaevalia Groningana 4. Groningen: Bouma's Boekhuis, 1984. 163 pp. Bib.

[VPA-790] Ostiguy, J.-R. *Charles Huot.* Canadian Artists Series, no. 7. Ottawa: National Gallery of Canada, 1979. 94 pp. Bib.

[VPA-800] Pal, Pratapaditya. *Art of Tibet.* Los Angeles: Los Angeles County Museum of Art with Mapin Publishing, Ahmedabad, India, 1990. Dist. Harry N. Abrams, New York. 343 pp. Bib. (Painting, sculpture, and ritual objects in their religious context.)

[VPA-810] Paley, Morton D. *The Apocalyptic Sublime.* New Haven; London: Yale University Press, 1986. 196 pp. Bib.

[VPA-820] Panofsky, Erwin. *Early Netherlandish Painting: Its Origins and Character.* 2 vols. The Charles Eliot Norton Lectures 1947-

1948. Cambridge: Harvard University Press, 1953. Bib. refs. in notes, vol. 1, pp. 359-511. Bib., vol. 1, pp. 513-535.

[VPA-830] Parezo, Nancy J. *Navaho Sand Paintings: From Religious Act to Commercial Art.* Tucson, Ariz.: University of Arizona Press; N.p., England: Eurospan, 1983. 251 pp.

[VPA-840] Patterson, Daniel W. *Gift Drawing and Gift Song: A Study of Two Forms of Shaker Inspiration.* Sabbathday Lake: United Society of Shakers, 1983. 126 pp. Bib. (Painting and religious iconography.)

[VPA-850] Paulson, Ronald. *Book and Painting: Shakespeare, Milton, and the Bible--Literary Texts and the Emergence of English Painting.* Hodges Lectures Series. Knoxville: University of Tennessee Press, 1983. 236 pp. Bib.

[VPA-860] Pepper, Stephen. *Bob Jones University Collection of Religious Art: Italian Paintings.* Greenville, S.C.: Bob Jones University Press, 1984. 336 pp.

[VPA-870] Pigrem, Sheila. *Help I Can't Draw: Pictorial Workbook of the Bible.* London: Church Pastoral Aid Society; N.p.: Kingsway Publications, 1991. 48 pp.

[VPA-880] Piper, David. *Looking at Art: An Introduction to Enjoying the Great Paintings of the World.* New York: Random House, 1984. 256 pp.

[VPA-890] Prown, Jules David. *American Painting: From Its Beginning to the Armory Show.* New York: Rizzoli International Publications, 1980. Bib. pp. 135-139.

[VPA-900] Pucci, Idanna. *Bhima Swarga: The Balinese Journey of the Soul.* N.p.: Bulfinch Press, 1992. 200 pp.

[VPA-910] Read, Herbert. *A Concise History of Modern Painting.* New York: Frederick A. Praeger Publishers, 1959. Bib. pp. 347-349.

[VPA-920] Ringbom, Sixten. *Icon to Narrative: The Rise of the Dramatic Close-up in Fifteenth-Century Devotional Painting.* 2nd ed. Netherlands: Davaco, 1984. Bib. pp. 220-227.

[VPA-930] Robinson, Jeremy. *Glorification: Religious Abstraction in Renaissance and 20th Century Painting.* Kidderminster, England: Crescent Moon, 1990. 229 pp.

[VPA-940] Rogers, Peter. *A Painter's Quest: Art As a Way of Revelation.* 2nd ed. N.p.: Bear and Co., 1988. 160 pp.

[VPA-950] Rosand, David. *Painting in Cinquecento Venice: Titian, Veronese, Tintoretto*. New Haven: Yale University Press, 1982. 346 pp. Bib.

[VPA-960] Rosenthal, Donald A. *La Grande Maniere: Religious and Historical Painting in France, 1700-1800*. N.p.: University of Washington Press, 1987. 200 pp.

[VPA-970] Ruskin, John. *Modern Painters*. 2nd ed. 6 vols. London: G. Allen, 1900. Bib., vol. 6.

[VPA-980] Portal Gallery [London]. *Adam and Eve/Willie Rushton and the Artists of the Portal Gallery*. London: Bell and Hyman, 1985. 62 pp.

[VPA-990] Staale, Sinding-Larsen, and Annette Kuhn. *Christ in the Council Hall: Studies in the Religious Iconography of the Venetian Republic*. Rome: L'erma di Bretschneider, 1974. xli, 314 pp. Bib. pp. xv-xxxvi.

[VPA-1000] Steckow, Wolfgang. *Northern Renaissance Art 1400-1600*. Englewood Cliffs, N.J.: Prentice-Hall Press, 1966.

[VPA-1010] Stubberud, Tore. *Victor Sparre*. Oslo, Norway: Aventura, 1984. 143 pp. Norwegian with summary in English. (Painting and stained glass, Christianity and aesthetics.)

[VPA-1020] Sussman, H. L. *Fact into Figure: Typology in Carlyle, Ruskin, and the Pre-Raphaelite Brotherhood*. Columbus: Ohio State University Press, 1979. 158 pp. Bib.

[VPA-1030] Szekely, Andras. *Spanish Painting*. Trans. Lily Halapy and Elisabeth West. Budapest: Kossuth Printing House, 1989. 31 pp. and 48 plates. Bib. p. 29.

[VPA-1040] Thomson, Belinda, and Michael Howard. *Impressionism*. New York: Exeter Books, 1988. 192 pp.

[VPA-1050] Thuillier, R. *Graham Sutherland: Inspirations*. Guildford, England: Lutterworth Press, 1982. 128 pp. Bib.

[VPA-1060] Treuherz, Julian. *Pre-Raphaelite Paintings from the Manchester City Art Gallery*. London: L. Humphries, 1980. 151 pp. Bib.

[VPA-1070] Vasari, Giorgio. *The Great Masters: Giotto, Botticelli, Leonardo, Raphael, Michelangelo, Titian*. Trans. Gaston Du C. de Vere. New York: Hugh Lauter Levin Associates, 1986. 388 pp.

[VPA-1080] ------. *Lives of Seventy of the most Eminent Painters, Sculptors, and Architects.* 4 vols. Trans. Mrs. Jonathan Foster. Ed. E. H. Blashfield, E. W. Blashfield, and A. A. Hopkins. London: George Bell and Sons, 1896. Bib. Vol. 4, pp. 333-387.

[VPA-1090] *Vatican Collections, The: The Papacy and Art.* New York: Metropolitan Museum of Art and Harry N. Abrams, Inc., 1982. 256 pp.

[VPA-1100] Venturi, Lionello. *Renaissance Painting.* 2 vols. Geneva: Skira; New York: Rizzoli International Publications, 1979.

[VPA-1110] Vezina, Raymond. *Theophile Hamel, National Painter (1817-1870).* 2 vols. Montreal: Elysee, 1975-1976. Bib. and bib. refs. (Includes treatment of his religious paintings.)

[VPA-1120] Wheeler, Marion, ed. *His Face: Images of Christ in Art [with] Selections from the King James Version of the Bible.* New York: Chameleon Books, 1988. 128 pp.

[VPA-1130] Wilcox, Michael. *The Wilcox Guide to the Best Watercolor Paints.* N.p.: North Light Books, 1991. 285 pp. (Monasticism and religious orders for women.)

[VPA-1140] Wischnitzer, Rachel. *From Dura to Rembrandt: Studies in the History of Art.* Milwaukee: Aldrich; Vienna: IRSA Verlag; Jerusalem: Center for Jewish Art, 1990. Bib. pp. 180-187. Bib. refs. pp. 189-206.

[VPA-1150] Wittkower, Rudolf, and Margot Wittkower. *Idea and Image: Studies in the Italian Renaissance.* London: Thames and Hudson, 1978. 255 pp. Bib.

[VPA-1160] Wroth, William. *Christian Images in Hispanic New Mexico: The Taylor Museum Collection of Santos.* Colorado Springs: Fine Arts Center, Taylor Museum, 1982. 215 pp. Bib. (Jose Rafael Aragon, et al.)

[VPA-1170] Yale University Art Gallery, John and Mable Ringling Museum of Art, and Nelson-Atkins Museum of Art. *A Taste for Angels: Neapolitan Painting in North America, 1650-1750.* New Haven: Yale University Art Gallery, 1987. Bib. pp. 331-355.

[VPA-1180] Yoder, Don, ed. *Picture Bible of Ludwig Denig: Pennsylvania German Emblem Book.* 2 vols. N.p., U.S.: Hudson Hills Press; London: T. Heneage, 1990. 192 pp.

KEY WORKS ON SELECTED PAINTERS

In contrast to the organizational principle of the rest of this bibliography, the following painters have been singled out because of their representative work in religious painting and other media. Unlike the world of music in which the great composers such as Johann Sebastian Bach, Wolfgang Amadeus Mozart, and Ludwig van Beethoven redefined their respective eras as much as they represented them, the following painters epitomized aesthetic and religious ideals of their day. Albrecht Dürer (1471-1528), best known for his fine woodcuts and illustrated altars, helped adapt the principles of the art of the Italian Renaissance to the northern European mind set on the eve of the Protestant Reformation. The paintings of El Greco (1541-1614) represent well the Catholic Reformation or Counter Reformation in Spain, his religious paintings proving influential for generations to come. The work of Matthias Grünewald (1475-1528), best known for painting the Isenheim Altar, represents the German expression of Renaissance religious art with its somber style and profound sense of grief over sin and the death of Christ. The paintings of Michelangelo Buonarroti (1475-1564) represent the High Renaissance in Italy and the development of Mannerist and Baroque art styles in the Roman Catholic tradition. The drawings and paintings of Rembrandt Harmenszoon van Rijn (1606-1669) epitomize Dutch portraiture, but also embody the Protestant ideals in some of the greatest religious art ever created. Finally, the thematically diverse paintings of Peter Paul Rubens (1577-1640) represent a curious blend of Flemish, Italian, and Spanish heritage while he portrayed both pagan joy in life as well as deeply religious ideals. Two of Rubens' best known religious paintings are his *Raising of the Cross* and *Descent from the Cross*. His Aristocratic Baroque style represents in many ways a culmination of the use of vibrant color, dynamic lines, and unbounded energy. While many other painters could be listed below as creators of religious art, those given here represent the most thoughtful and prolific of the Christian artists of the late Renaissance and Reformation, eras rich with religious concerns.

Albrecht Dürer

Books treating the works of Albrecht Dürer are not especially plentiful in English, at least when compared to the volume of studies on the other major artists. The large, although somewhat dated, bibliography by Matthias Mende [VPAD-010] is the most recent, major bibliography available on Dürer. For more current bibliographies, see two respectable, recent studies, Jane Campbell Hutchinson's *Albrecht Dürer: A Biography* [VPAD-180], and Joseph Leo Koerner's *The Moment of Self-Portraiture in German Renaissance Art* [VPAD-200]. The most complete collections of Dürer's works can be found in volumes compiled and written by Andre Deguer and Monika Heffels [VPAD-090], Karl-Adolf Knappe [VPAD-190], Horst Michael [VPAD-300], Angela Ottino Della Chiesa [VPAD-360], Walter L. Straus [VPAD-490 to VPAD-540], Peter Strieder [VPAD-560], and Peter Strieder and Hano Johannesen [VPAD-590]. To date, the most authoritative study of Dürer's work is Erwin Panofsky's [VPAD-370 to VPAD-380], listed here in two editions to represent different bibliographies, the earlier one being more comprehensive. Other important studies of Dürer have been completed fairly recently by Fedja Anzelewsky [VPAD-040], Jan Bialostocki [VPAD-050], Astrid von Geyso [VPAD-150], Fritz Koreny [VPAD-210], Simon Monneret [VPAD-310], James S. Patty [VPAD-390], and Christopher White [VPAD-630]. For studies which place Dürer in the context of his time, see *The Northern Renaissance: Albrecht Dürer, Lucas Cranach, Hans Holbein, Pieter Bruegel* [VPAD-340], Theodore K. Rabb's *Renaissance Lives: Portraits of an Age* [VPAD-400], Julian Raby's *Venice, Dürer, and the Oriental Mode* [VPAD-410], John Rowlands's *The Age of Dürer and Holbein: German Drawings 1400-1550* [VPAD-420], Robert Walter Hans Peter Scheller's *The Graphic Art of Albrecht Dürer, Hans Dürer, and The Dürer School* [VPAD-450], and Kenneth Albert Strand's *Woodcuts to the Apocalypse in Dürer's Time: Albrecht Dürer's Woodcuts plus Five Other Sets from the 15th and 16th Centuries* [VPAD-480].

491

Special Bibliographies

[VPAD-010] Mende, Matthias. *Dürer--Bibliographie*. Wiesbaden: Harrassowitz, 1971. 707 pp.

Key Works

[VPAD-020] Anzelewsky, Fedja. *The Drawings and Graphic Works of Dürer*. London; New York: Hamlyn, 1970. Bib. p. 51.

[VPAD-030] ------. *Dürer and his Time: An Exhibition from the Collection of the Print Room, State Museum, Berlin, Stiftung Preussischer Kulturbesitz*. Washington, D.C.: Smithsonian Press, 1967. Reprint. 1983. 252 pp. Bib. pp. 31-33.

[VPAD-040] ------. *Dürer: His Art and Life*. Trans. Heide Grieve. Trans. *Dürer: Werk und Wirkung*. Seacaucus, N.J.: Chartwell Books; New York: Alpine Fine Arts Collection, 1980. Reprint. London: Gordon Fraser, 1982. Bib. pp. 257-267.

[VPAD-050] Bialostocki, Jan. *Dürer and His Critics, 1500-1971: Chapters in the History of Ideas, Including a Collection of Texts*. Baden-Baden: V. Koerner, 1986. 471 pp. Bib. pp. 403-451.

[VPAD-060] Boon, Karel G., and Robert Walter Hans Peter Scheller, eds. *Albrecht and Hans Dürer*. Hollstein's German Engravings, Etchings, and Woodcuts, vol. 7, 1962. Amsterdam: Menno Hertzberger, c. 1965. 279 pp.

[VPAD-070] Brion, Marcel. *Dürer: His Life and Work*. New York: Tudor, 1960. Reprint. N.p.: Thames and Hudson, 1965. 320 pp.

[VPAD-080] Chadraba, Rudolf. *Dürer's Apokalypse, eine ikonologische Deutung*. Prague: Verlag der Tschechoslowkischen Akademie der Wissenschaften, 1964. 210 pp.

[VPAD-090] Deguer, Andre, and Monika Heffels. *Albrecht Dürer: The Complete Woodcuts*. Trans. Lilian Stephany. Masterpieces in the Art of Woodcutting. Bristol, Avon, England: Artline Editions, 1990. 251 pp.

[VPAD-100] Descargues, Pierre. *Dürer*. London: W. Heinemann, 1954. 64 pp. Bib. pp. xxix-xxx.

[VPAD-110] Dornik-Eger, Hanna. *Albrecht Dürer und die Graphik der Reformationszeit*. Vienna: Osterreichisches Museum für

492

Angewandte Kunst, 1969.

[VPAD-120] Dürer, Albrecht, with Benedictus Chelidonius. *The Little Passion.* Also *Passio Christi* or *Kleine Passion.* Verona: [Officina Bodoni, 1971]. English and Latin.

[VPAD-130] Eisler, Colin T. *Dürer's Animals.* Washington, D.C.: Smithsonian Institution Press, 1991. Bib. pp. 361-363.

[VPAD-140] Fenyo, Ivan. *Albrecht Dürer.* Budapest: Corvina, 1956. Bib. pp. 75-77.

[VPAD-150] Geyso, Astrid von, with Willi Bongard and Matthias Mende. *Dürer Today.* 2nd ed. Trans. *Dürer Heute.* Bonn-Bad Godesberg: Inter Nationes, 1978. Bib. p. 108.

[VPAD-160] Grote, Ludwig. *Dürer: Biographical and Critical Study.* Taste of our Time, vol. 43. [Geneva]: Skira, 1965. Dist. World Publishing Co., Cleveland. Bib. pp. 131-132.

[VPAD-170] Howett, John. *Woodcuts by Albrecht Dürer: An Exhibition of Print Connoisseurship.* Exhibition, Emory University Museum of Art and Archaeology, 4 April to 7 June 1986. Atlanta: The Museum, 1986. 60 pp. Bib. p. 14.

[VPAD-180] Hutchinson, Jane Campbell. *Albrecht Dürer: A Biography.* Princeton: Princeton University Press, 1990. Bib. pp. 223-232.

[VPAD-190] Knappe, Karl-Adolf. *Dürer: The Complete Engravings, Etchings and Woodcuts.* Syracuse, N.J.: Wellfleet Press, 1964. Reprint. London: Alpine Fine Arts Collection (U.K.), Ltd., 1980. Reprint. 1989. lviii, 385 pp. Bib. p. 11.

[VPAD-200] Koerner, Joseph Leo. *The Moment of Self-Portraiture in German Renaissance Art.* Chicago: University of Chicago Press, 1993. Bib. refs. pp. 449-528. (Albrecht Dürer and Hans Baldung.)

[VPAD-210] Koreny, Fritz. *Albrecht Dürer and the Animal and Plant Studies of the Renaissance.* Trans. Pamela Marwood and Yehuda Shapiro. Trans. *Albrecht Dürer und die Tier-und Pflanzenstudien der Renaissance.* Boston: Little, Brown and Co., for New York Graphic Society Books, 1989. Bib. pp. 268-270.

[VPAD-220] Koschatzky, Walter. *Albrecht Dürer: The Landscape Water-Colours.* Trans. Philippa McDermott. Trans. *Albrecht Dürer: Die Landschaftsaquarelle.* London: Academy Editions; New York: St. Martin's Press, 1973. Bib. pp. 107-109.

[VPAD-230] Koschatzky, Walter, and Alice Strobl. *Dürer Drawings in the Albertina*. Trans. *Dürerzeichnungen der Albertina*. London: Secker and Warburg; Greenwich, Conn.: New York Graphic Society, 1972. Bib. pp. 335-365.

[VPAD-240] Levey, Michael. *Dürer*. London: Weidenfeld and Nicolson, 1964. Bib. p. 132.

[VPAD-250] Levey, Michael, and C[harles] R[eginald], eds. *Essays on Dürer*. Manchester Studies in the History of Art, no. 2. Manchester, England; Toronto; Buffalo: Manchester University Press, University of Toronto Press, 1973. 154 pp. Bib. refs.

[VPAD-260] Livie, R. Bruce. *Auch Kleine Dinge: Dürer and the Decorative Tradition*. Exhibition, 4 March to 3 April 1971. [Cambridge]: Busch-Reisinger Museum, Harvard University, 1971. Bib. pp. 169-174.

[VPAD-270] Ludecke, Heinz. *Albrecht Dürer*. Leipzig: VEB E. A. Seeman, 1970. Bib. pp. 171-173. New York: G. P. Putnam's Sons, 1972. Bib. p. 168.

[VPAD-280] Marazov, Ivan. *Albrecht Dürer: Forty-Eight Metal Engravings*. [London]: MacDonald Orbis, 1988.

[VPAD-290] Mende, Matthias, and Chester Beatty Library. *Dürer in Dublin: Engravings and Woodcuts of Albrecht Dürer from the Chester Beatty Library*. Trans. Janet C. L. Craig. Nurnberg: H. Carl, 1983. xxii, 201 pp. Bib. pp. 195-199.

[VPAD-300] Michael, Horst. *Albrecht Dürer: The Complete Engravings*. Thornbury, England: Artline Editions, 1987. 206 pp.

[VPAD-310] Monneret, Simon. *Dürer*. New York: Excalibur Books, 1979. Dist. Bookthrift. Bib. p. 143.

[VPAD-320] Museum of Fine Arts, Boston. *Albrecht Dürer: Master Printmaker*. Exhibition, Museum of Fine Arts, Boston, 17 November 1971 to 16 January 1972. New York: Hacker Art Books, 1971. Reprint. 1988. Bib. p. 282.

[VPAD-330] Musper, H[einrich] Theodor. *Albrecht Dürer*. Library of Great Painters. New York: Harry N. Abrams; London: Thames and Hudson, 1960. Reprint. 1966, 1969. Bib. p. 142.

[VPAD-340] *Northern Renaissance, The: Albrecht Dürer, Lucas Cranach, Hans Holbein, Pieter Bruegel*. Great Artists of the Western World II, vol. 2. London; New York: Marshall Cavendish, 1988. Bib. p. 139.

494

[VPAD-350] Olds, Clifton C., Egon Verheyen, and Warren David Tresidder. *Dürer's Cities: Nuremberg and Venice.* Ann Arbor: University of Michigan Museum of Art, 1971. 63 pp.

[VPAD-360] Ottino Della Chiesa, Angela. *The Complete Paintings of Dürer.* Penguin Classics of World Art. Middlesex, England; New York: Penguin, 1986. 120 pp. Bib. p. 82.

[VPAD-370] Panofsky, Erwin. *Albrecht Dürer.* 3rd ed. 2 vols. Princeton: Princeton University Press, 1948. Bib. Vol. 1, pp. 285-296.

[VPAD-380] ------. *The Life and Art of Albrecht Dürer.* 4th ed. Princeton: Princeton University Press, 1955. Reprint. 1967, 1971. Bib. pp. 287-296.

[VPAD-390] Patty, James S. *Dürer in French Letters.* Paris: Champion-Slatkine, 1989. 357 pp. Bib. pp. 304-336.

[VPAD-400] Rabb, Theodore K. *Renaissance Lives: Portraits of an Age.* New York: Pantheon Books, 1993. 262 pp.

[VPAD-410] Raby, Julian. *Venice, Dürer, and the Oriental Mode.* The Hans Huth Memorial Studies, no. 1. Totowa, N.J.: Islamic Art Publications, 1982. Dist. Sotheby Publications. Bib. pp. 97-98.

[VPAD-420] Rowlands, John. *The Age of Dürer and Holbein: German Drawings 1400-1550.* Exhibition, British Museum. Cambridge; New York: Cambridge University Press, 1988. Bib. pp. 253-259.

[VPAD-430] Ruggeri, Ugo. *Dürer.* American ed. Woodbury, N.Y.: Barron's, 1979. Bib. p. 143.

[VPAD-440] Russell, Francis. *The World of Dürer, 1471-1528.* New York: Time, 1967. Reprint. New York: Time, 1975, 1981. Bib. p. 177.

[VPAD-450] Scheller, Robert Walter Hans Peter. *The Graphic Art of Albrecht Dürer, Hans Dürer, and The Dürer School.* Originally *Hollstein's German Engravings, Etchings, and Woodcuts,* vol. 7, 1962. Amsterdam: Van Gendt and Co., 1971. 279 pp. Bib. pp. 2-3.

[VPAD-460] Steckow, Wolfgang. *Dürer and America.* Washington, D.C.: National Gallery of Art, 1971. Bib. refs.

[VPAD-470] Sterling and Francine Clark Art Institute, Williams College. *Dürer Through other Eyes: His Graphic Work Mirrored in Copies and Forgeries of Three Centuries: An Exhibition*

Prepared by Studies in the Williams College--Clark Art Institute Graduate Program in Art History, March 14 to June 15, 1975. Williamstown, Mass.: Sterling and Francine Clark Art Institute, 1975. 99 pp. Bib. pp. 68-73.

[VPAD-480] Strand, Kenneth Albert. *Woodcuts to the Apocalypse in Dürer's Time: Albrecht Dürer's Woodcuts plus Five Other Sets from the 15th and 16th Centuries.* [Ann Arbor, Mich.]: Ann Arbor Publishers, 1968. 86 pp.

[VPAD-490] Strauss, Walter L. *Albrecht Dürer Woodcuts and Wood Blocks.* New York: Abaris Books, 1979. Bib. pp. 732-753.

[VPAD-500] ------. *The Complete Drawings of Albrecht Dürer.* 6 vols. New York: Abaris Books, 1974. Bib. pp. 3295-3318. Supplement, 1977. Bib. vol. 1, p. 15.

[VPAD-510] ------. *The Complete Engravings, Etchings, and Drypoints of Albrecht Dürer.* 2nd ed. New York: Dover Publications, 1973. Bib. refs. pp. 229-232.

[VPAD-520] ------, ed. *The Human Figure: The Complete "Dresden Sketchbook."* New York: Dover Publications, 1972. Bib. pp. 345-347.

[VPAD-530] ------, ed. *The Intaglio Prints of Albrecht Dürer: Engravings, Etchings and Drypoints.* 3rd ed. New York: Kennedy Galleries and Abaris Books, 1981. Bib. pp. 342-343.

[VPAD-540] ------. *The Painter's Manual: A Manual of Measurement of Lines, Areas, and Solids by Means of Compass and Ruler Assembled by Albrecth Dürer for the use of all Lovers of Art with Appropriate Illustrations Arranged to be Printed in the Year MDXXV.* Trans. *Unterweisung der Messung.* New York: Abaris Books, 1977. Bib. pp. 469-472. German and English.

[VPAD-550] ------, ed. *Sixteenth Century German Artists: Albrecht Dürer [Commentary].* Illustrated Bartsch, vol. 10. New York: Abaris Books, 1981. 615 pp.

[VPAD-560] Strieder, Peter. *Albrecht Dürer: Paintings, Prints, Drawings.* Trans. Nancy M. Gordon and Walter L. Strauss. Trans. *Albrecht Dürer.* London: Frederick Muller; New York: Abaris Books, 1982. Reprint. 1989. 400 pp. Bib. pp. 374-378.

[VPAD-570] ------. *Dürer.* The Hidden Masters. Danbury, Conn.: MasterWorks Press, 1978. Reprint. 1984. Bib. pp. 188-189.

[VPAD-580]   ------. *The Hidden Dürer*. Trans. *Albrecht Dürer*. Chicago: Rand McNally Co., 1978. Oxford: Phaidon Press, 1978. Bib. p. 189.

[VPAD-590]   Strieder, Peter, and Hano Johannesen. *Dürer: The Complete Paintings*. Trans. *Dürer*, Milan: Rizzoli International Publications, 1979. London: Granada, 1980. Bib. p. 96.

[VPAD-600]   Strieder, Peter, and David Piper. *Dürer*. New York: Rizzoli International Publications, 1980. Bib. p. 94.

[VPAD-610]   Talbot, Charles W., Gaillard F. Ravenel, and Jay A. Leverson. *Dürer in America: His Graphic Work*. Exhibition, National Gallery of Art, 25 April to 6 June 1971. New York: Macmillan Publishing Co. for National Gallery of Art, Washington, D.C.; London: Collier-Macmillan, 1971. Reprint. 1979. Bib. pp. 358-360.

[VPAD-620]   Troutman, Philip. *Albrecht Dürer: Sketchbook of his Journey to the Netherlands 1520-21*. Trans. *Niederlandisches Reiseskizzenbuch, 1520-21*. New York: Frederick A. Praeger Publishers, 1971. 104 pp.

[VPAD-630]   White, Christopher. *Dürer: The Artist and His Drawings*. New York: Watson-Guptill Publications; London: Phaidon Press, 1971. Reprint. Oxford: Phaidon Press, 1981. Bib. p. 225.

[VPAD-640]   Whitworth Art Gallery. *Engravings and Woodcuts by Albrecht Dürer, 1471-1528: 22 October to December 1971, Whitworth Art Gallery, University of Manchester*. N.p.: Richmond Press, 1971. 67 pp. Bib. refs.

[VPAD-650]   Wolfflin, Heinrich. *The Art of Albrecht Dürer*. Trans. Alastair Ian and Heide Grieve. Trans. *Die Kunst Albrecht Dürers*, Munich: Bruckmann, 1963. New York: Phaidon Press, [1971]. Bib. p. 303.

[VPAD-660]   Wolfflin, Heinrich, and Stanley Appelbaum. *Drawings of Albrecht Dürer*. Trans. *Albrecht Dürer: Handzeichnungen*, Munich: R. Piper, 1923. New York: Dover Publications; London: Constable, 1970. Bib. pp. xi-xii.

El Greco (Domenikos Theotokopoulos)

Studies of El Greco in English are also not plentiful, but those given below will be more than adequate as an introduction to this artist. The most complete collections of his work may be found in volumes edited by Edi Baccheschi and Ellis Kirkham Waterhouse [VPEG-040], and Jose Gudiol [VPEG-150]. Also consult the several volumes of documentary items edited by Nicos Hadjinicolaou [VPEG-180 to VPEG-200]. For studies placing El Greco in the context of his time, see the several volumes edited by Jonathan Brown and others [VPEG-070 to VPEG-090], a serious study by Enriqueta Harris Frankfort and Philip Troutman [VPEG-130], an interesting and recent study by Nina A. Mallory [VPEG-280], and an older but substantial two volume study by Harold Edwin Wethey [VPEG-410]. For several skillful interpretations of El Greco's paintings, see a collection of the Paine Lectures in Religion as delivered by Thomas F. Mathews, John Wesley Cook, and Jonathan Brown [VPEG-310]. Also note that Stefan Paul Andres' fictional work, *El Greco Paints the Grand Inquisitor* [VPEG-030], has been included as a creative interpretation of El Greco's dramatic biography.

[VPEG-010]   Acheimastou-Potamianou, Myrtale. *From Byzantium to El Greco: Greek Frescoes and Icons.* Exhibition, Royal Academy of Arts, London, 27 March to 21 June 1987. [Athens]: Greek Ministry of Culture, Byzantine Museum of Athens, 1987. Bib. pp. 201-205.

[VPEG-020]   Allen, George R. *El Greco: Two Studies.* Philadelphia: J. F. Warren, 1984. 62 pp. Bib. refs.

[VPEG-030]   Andres, Stefan Paul. *El Greco Paints the Grand Inquisitor.* Trans. *El Greco Malt den Grossinquisitor.* Austin: Dimension Press, 1989. 78 pp. Fiction.

[VPEG-040]   Baccheschi, Edi, and Ellis Kirkham Waterhouse, comps. *El Greco: The Complete Paintings.* Trans. Jane Carroll. London: Granada; New York: Rizzoli International Publications, 1980. Bib. p. 96.

[VPEG-050]   Braham, Allan. *El Greco to Goya: The Taste for Spanish Paintings in Britain and Ireland.* 2nd ed. Exhibition, National Gallery, 16 September to 29 November 1981. London: Publications Department, National Gallery, 1981. Bib. pp. 117-119.

[VPEG-060]   Bronstein, Leo. *El Greco.* Masters of Art Series. 1966. Reprint. New York: Harry N. Abrams, 1990. London: Thames and Hudson, 1991. 128 pp.

498

[VPEG-070] Brown, Jonathan, ed. *Figures of Thought: El Greco as Interpreter of History, Tradition, and Ideas.* Studies in the History of Art [Washington, D.C.], vol. 11. Washington, D.C.: National Gallery of Art, 1982. 91 pp. Bib. refs.

[VPEG-080] Brown, Jonathan, and Jose Manuel Pita Andrade, eds. *El Greco--Italy and Spain.* Studies in the History of Art [Washington, D.C.], vol. 13. Washington, D.C.: National Gallery of Art, 1984. Dist. University Press of New England, Hanover. 188 pp. Bib. refs.

[VPEG-090] Brown, Jonathan, and Toledo Museum of Art. *El Greco of Toledo.* Boston: Little, Brown and Co., 1982. 275 pp.

[VPEG-100] Bruno de Jesus-Marie, ed. *Three Mystics: El Greco, St. John of the Cross, St. Teresa of Avila.* London: Sheed and Ward, 1952. 187 pp.

[VPEG-110] Dabell, Frank. *Venetian Paintings: From Titian to El Greco.* Exhibition, Piero Corsini Gallery, New York, 10 October to 8 November 1991. New York: Piero Corsini Gallery, 1991. Bib. refs. pp. 131-141.

[VPEG-120] *El Greaco: Works in Spain.* Rethymno: Crete University Press, 1990.

[VPEG-130] Frankfort, Enriqueta Harris, and Philip Troutman. *The Golden Age of Spanish Art: From El Greco to Murillo and Valdes Leal: Paintings and Drawings from British Collections.* Exhibition, Nottingham University Art Gallery, 11 February to 29 March 1980. Nottingham: Nottingham University Art Gallery, 1980. Bib. p. 48.

[VPEG-140] Goldscheider, Ludwig. *El Greco: Paintings, Drawings, and Sculptures.* 3rd ed. New York: Phaidon Publishers, 1954. Dist. Garden City Books. Bib. p. 219.

[VPEG-150] Gudiol, Jose. *The Complete Paintings of El Greco, 1541--1614.* Trans. Kenneth Lyons. Trans. *Domenikos Theotokopoulos.* New York: Greenwich House, 1983. Dist. Crown Publishers. Bib. pp. 361-364.

[VPEG-160] ------. *El Greco: 1541--1614.* Trans. *Domenikos Theotokopoulos, El Greco, 1541--1614.* London: Secker and Warburg, 1973. Reprint. London: Alpine Fine Arts Collections, 1987. Bib. pp. 363-364.

[VPEG-170] Guinard, Paul. *El Greco: Biographical and Critical Study.* Trans. James Emmons. Taste of our Time, vol. 15. Lausanne: Skira, 1956. Bib. pp. 131-133.

[VPEG-180] Hadjinicolaou, Nicos, ed. *El Greco: Byzantium and Italy*. Literary Sources of Art History. Rethymno: Crete University Press, 1990. Dist. Orpheus, New Rochelle, N.Y. 479 pp. Bib. refs. English, French, German, Greek, Italian, and Spanish.

[VPEG-190] ------, ed. *El Greco: Documents on His Life and Work*. Literary Sources of Art History. Rethymno: Crete University Press, 1990. 416 pp. Bib. refs. English, French, Greek, Italian, and Spanish.

[VPEG-200] ------. *El Greco: Works in Spain*. Literary Sources of Art History. Rethymno: Crete University Press, 1990. 490 pp. Bib. refs. English, French, German, Greek, Italian, and Spanish.

[VPEG-210] Kelemen, P. *El Greco Revisited--Candia--Venice--Toledo*. New York: n.p., 1961.

[VPEG-220] Konstantinou, Ioanna, and Nicos Hadjinicolaou. *Sta ichne tou Dominikou Theotokopoulou: Katalogos ektheses tekmerkon gia te zoe kai to ergo tou: Aithousa "Theotokopoulos," 1 Septemvriou--10 Oktovriou.* Heraklion, Crete: Demos Herakliou-Vikelaia Vivliotheke, 1990. 92 pp. Bib. refs. Greek and English.

[VPEG-230] Lafuente Ferrari, Enrique, and Jose Manuel Pita Andrade. *El Greco: The Expressionism of His Final Years*. Trans. *Il Greco di Toledo e il suo espressionismo estremo*. New York: Harry N. Abrams, 1969. Reprint. 1975. Bib. pp. 163-164.

[VPEG-240] Larsen, Erik. *El Greco and the Spanish Golden Age*. New York: Tudor Publishing Co., 1969. 40 pp. Bib. p. 18.

[VPEG-250] Lassaigne, Jacques, and Jane Brenton. *El Greco*. Trans. *El Greco*, Paris: Aimery Somogy, 1973. London: Thames and Hudson, 1974. 264 pp.

[VPEG-260] Legendre, M., and A. Hartmann. *El Greco*. 1937. Reprint. N.p.: Norwood Editions, 1984. 512 pp.

[VPEG-270] Legendre, Maurice. *El Greco*. New York: Hyperion Press, 1947. Bib. pp. 69-70.

[VPEG-280] Mallory, Nina A. *El Greco to Murillo: Spanish Painting in the Golden Age, 1556-1700*. Icon Editions. New York: HarperCollins, 1990. Bib. refs. pp. 295-304.

[VPEG-290] Mann, Richard G[eorge]. *El Greco and His Patrons: Three Major Projects*. Cambridge Studies in the History of Art.

Cambridge: Cambridge University Press, 1986. Bib. pp. 151-158.

[VPEG-300] Marias, Fernando. *El Greco*. New York: n.p., 1991. Bib. refs. p. 99.

[VPEG-310] Mathews, Thomas F., John Wesley Cook, and Jonathan Brown. *Art and Religion: Faith, Form and Reform*. Paine Lectures in Religion, 1984. [Columbia, Mo.]: University of Missouri-Columbia, 1986. 66 pp. Bib. refs.

[VPEG-320] Matthews, John F. *El Greco (1541-1614): [Domenicos Theoto-copoulos]*. Fontana Pocket Library of Great Art. New York: Harry N. Abrams with Pocket Books, 1953. Bib. p. 74. [London]: Collins, 1953. Bib. p. 80.

[VPEG-330] National Gallery of Art. *El Greco: Italy and Spain*. Ed. Jonathan Brown and Jose M. Andrade. Hanover, N.H.: University Press of New England, 1984. 188 pp.

[VPEG-340] National Gallery of Scotland. *El Greco: Mystery and Illumination*. Exhibition, National Gallery of Scotland, Edinburgh, 29 July to 15 October 1989. Edinburgh: Trustees of the National Galleries of Scotland, 1989. 96 pp. Bib. refs.

[VPEG-350] Preston, Stuart. *El Greco*. New York: Beechhurst Press, 1960. 61 pp. Bib. refs.

[VPEG-360] Puppi, Lionello. *El Greco: The Life and Work of the Artist*. London: Thames and Hudson, 1967. 118 pp. Bib. refs.

[VPEG-370] Pye, Patrick. *The Time Gatherer: A Study of El Greco's Treatment of the Sacred Theme*. Dublin: Four Courts Press, 1991. 125 pp.

[VPEG-380] Trapier, Elizabeth. *El Greco: Early Years in Toledo*. Hispanic Notes and Monographs; Essays, Studies, and Brief Biographies. New York: Interbook, Inc.; Hispanic Society of America, 1958. Bib. refs. in notes, pp. 38-40.

[VPEG-390] Vallentin, Antonina. *El Greco*. Garden City, N.Y.: Doubleday, 1954. Bib. pp. 297-301.

[VPEG-400] Waterhouse, Ellis Kirkham. *El Greco*. Vol. 9. *The Great Artists: A Library of Their Lives, Times and Paintings*. 25 vols. New York: Funk and Wagnalls Co., 1978. 35 pp.

[VPEG-410] Wethey, Harold E[dwin]. *El Greco and His School*. 2 vols. Princeton: Princeton University Press, 1962. Bib. refs.

Matthias Grünewald

Studies in English about Matthias Grünewald and his paintings are relatively scarce, in part because interest in his work has emerged almost exclusively in the twentieth century. Most of the studies concern his Isenheim Altar, including those by the following writers: Christian Baur [VPMA-020], Arthur Burkhard [VPMA-030], Emmie Donadio [VPMA-070], Andree Hayum [VPMA-120], Martyria Madauss [VPMA-130], Ruth Mellinkoff [VPMA-140], Eugene Monick [VPMA-150], Linda Nochlin [VPMA-160], Karen Barbara Roberts [VPMA-200], and Georg Scheja [VPMA-210]. Jane Dillenberger [VPMA-060] has also written a fine analysis of the Isenheim Altar in contrast to Michelangelo's work in the Sistine Chapel as an illustration of the differences between the northern and southern aesthetic sensibilities during the late Renaissance. For collections and studies treating other works by Grünewald, see Drysdale Alsfeld's *The Perplexing Art by Matthias Grünewald and His Most Impressive Paintings* [VPMA-010], and Grünewald's works as edited by Guido Schoenberger in *The Drawings of Mathis Gothart Nithert, Called Grünewald* [VPMA-090]. The balance of books listed below includes biographies ranging from the 1911 work of Hans Wolfgang Singer, *Stories of the German Artists* [VPMA-220], to the 1992 volume by Berta Reichenauer, *Grünewald* [VPMA-180]. Perhaps the most substantial recent biography is that by Wilhelm Fraenger, Gustel Fraenger, and Ingeborg Baier-Fraenger, *Matthias Grünewald* [VPMA-080]. For additional studies treating Grünewald, see the bibliographies given in the books listed below and consult works given in the opening three sections of Chapter 12.

[VPMA-010] Alsfeld, Drysdale. *The Perplexing Art by Matthias Grünewald and His Most Impressive Paintings*. Art Library of the Great Masters of the World. Albuquerque: Gloucester Art Press, 1983. 117 pp.

[VPMA-020] Baur, Christian. *Grünewald: The Isenheim Altar*. Millwood, N.Y.: Kraus Reprint and Periodicals, 1983.

[VPMA-030] Burkhard, Arthur. "The Isenheim Altar of Matthias Grünewald." *Speculum* 9 (1934): 56-69. Reprint. Arthur Burkhard. *The Isenheim Altar of Matthias Grünewald*. Vol. 1.

Seven German Altars. 7 vols. Cambridge, Mass.: Dorothea Moore Burkhard, 1965. Bib. refs.

[VPMA-040] ------. *Matthias Grünewald: Personality and Accomplishment.* Cambridge: Harvard University Press, 1936. Bib. pp. 93-111.

[VPMA-050] Collinson, Howard Creel. "Three Paintings by Mathis Gothart-Neithart, called Grünewald: The Transcendent Narrative as Devotional Image." Ph.D. Thesis, Yale University, 1986. 391 pp. Bib. refs.

[VPMA-060] Dillenberger, Jane. "Northern and Southern Sensibilities in Art on the Eve of the Reformation." In *Image and Spirit in Sacred and Secular Art.* Ed. Diane Apostolos-Cappadona, 108-131. New York: Crossroad, 1990.

[VPMA-070] Donadio, Emmie. "Painting for Patients: Grünewald's 'Isenheim Altarpiece'." *Medical Heritage* 1, no. 6 (Nov./Dec. 1985): 448-455.

[VPMA-080] Fraenger, Wilhelm, Gustel Fraenger, and Ingeborg Baier-Fraenger. *Matthias Grünewald.* Sonderausgabe 1988. Munich: Verlag C. H. Beck, 1988. 354 pp. Bib. refs.

[VPMA-090] Grünewald, Mathais. *The Drawings of Mathis Gothart Nithert, Called Grünewald.* Ed. Guido Schoenberger. New York: Bittner, 1948. Reprint. New York: AMS Press, Inc., n.d.

[VPMA-100] Hagen, Oscar Frank Leonard. *Matthias Grünewald.* Munich: R. Piper, 1919. Bib. pp. 224-225.

[VPMA-110] Haug, Hans. *Grünewald (Mathis Nithart): ca. 1455-1528.* Paris: Braun, 1950. 86 pp.

[VPMA-120] Hayum, Andree. *The Isenheim Altarpiece: God's Medicine and the Painter's Vision.* Princeton: Princeton University Press, 1989. Bib. refs. pp. 151-194.

[VPMA-130] Madauss, Martyria. *Jesus, A Portrait of Love: A Meditation on Matthias Grünewald's Isenheim Altar.* Rev. ed. Trans. *Jesus vor augen gemalt,* 1972. Damstadt: Evangelical Sisterhood of Mary, 1977. 57 pp.

[VPMA-140] Mellinkoff, Ruth. *The Devil at Isenheim: Reflections of Popular Belief in Grünewald's Altarpiece.* Berkeley: University of California Press, 1988. Bib. pp. 103-106.

[VPMA-150] Monick, Eugene. *Evil, Sexuality, and Disease in Grünewald's Body of Christ.* Dallas: Spring Publications, 1993. Bib. refs.

[VPMA-160]   Nochlin, Linda. *Mathis at Colmar: A Visual Confrontation.* New York: Red Dust, Inc., 1963.

[VPMA-170]   Pevsner, Nikolaus, and Michael Meier. *Grünewald.* London: Thames and Hudson, 1958. 42 pp. Bib. p. 29.

[VPMA-180]   Reichenauer, Berta. *Grünewald.* Thaur; Munich: Kulturverlag, 1992. 224 pp. Bib. refs.

[VPMA-190]   Rieckenberg, Hans Jurgen. *Matthias Grünewald.* Epochen, Künstler, Meisterwerke. Herrsching: Pawlak, 1976. Bib. p. 80.

[VPMA-200]   Roberts, Karen Barbara. "The Influence of the Rosary Devotion on Grünewald's Isenheim Altarpiece." Ph.D. Thesis, State University of New York at Binghamton, 1985. Bib. pp. 178-194.

[VPMA-210]   Scheja, Georg. *The Isenheim Altarpiece.* Photo. Bert Kock. [Trans. Robert Erich Wolf]. Trans. *Der Isenheimer Altar des Matthias Grünewald.* New York: Harry N. Abrams, 1969. 80 pp. Bib. refs.

[VPMA-220]   Singer, Hans Wolfgang. *Stories of the German Artists.* New York: Duffield, 1911. Bib. p. 309.

[VPMA-230]   Weixlgartner, Arpad. *Grünewald.* Neue Sammlung Schroll, 3 Bd. Vienna: A. Schroll, 1962. Bib. pp. 139-140. List of artist's works, pp. 141-148.

Michelangelo Buonarroti

Studies of the art works of Michelangelo Buonarroti are so numerous that even the lengthy list given below can be only a representative sample. The bibliographies given here by Laura S. Kline [VPMB-010] and Luitpold Dussler [VPMB-020] offer a little fuller review of the literature written about Michelangelo, but even these works are far from being exhaustive or current. At least the works given here will give one important clues about who the major scholars have been and are in research on Michelangelo.

The three most prolific and prominent scholars studying Michelangelo and his work are Robert John Clements [VPMB-190 to VPMB-210], Charles de Tolnay [VPMB-260 to VPMB-340], and Frederick Hartt [VPMB-510 to VPMB-530]. The biographies on Michelangelo range from the sixteenth century, eye witness account by Giorgio Vasari [VPMB-1070], to John Addington Symonds' early biography of 1893 [VPMB-1040], to a plethora of new biographies which have emerged since 1990, including [VPMB-040], [VPMB-080], [VPMB-220], [VPMB-350], and [VPMB-620]. Other biographies worth consulting are [VPMB-110], [VPMB-130], [VPMB-150], [VPMB-230], [VPMB-430], [VPMB-570], [VPMB-600], [VPMB-610], [VPMB-690], [VPMB-700], [VPMB-730], [VPMB-740], [VPMB-810], [VPMB-1080], and a fine novel by Irving Stone [VPMB-1020], who also edited with his wife an excellent selection of autobiographical letters by Michelangelo [VPMB-780]. For works which place him in the context of his time, see [VPMB-050], [VPMB-240], [VPMB-410], [VPMB-470], [VPMB-560], [VPMB-1060], and [VPMB-1100].

The study of Michelangelo's work is typically divided into the mediums in which he worked, although a few studies attempt to cover all of his visual art works, including [VPMB-090], [VPMB-440], and [VPMB-930]. For studies of his architecture, see [VPMB-030], [VPMB-040], [VPMB-560], and [VPMB-800]. For works treating his drawings, see [VPMB-140], [VPMB-510], [VPMB-630], [VPMB-640], [VPMB-710], [VPMB-770], [VPMB-870], [VPMB-990], and [VPMB-1090]. For analyses of his paintings, see [VPMB-070], [VPMB-170], [VPMB-180], [VPMB-320], [VPMB-420], [VPMB-460], [VPMB-480], [VPMB-550], [VPMB-580], [VPMB-590], [VPMB-650], [VPMB-660], [VPMB-850], [VPMB-880], [VPMB-890], [VPMB-900], [VPMB-910], [VPMB-970], [VPMB-1010], and [VPMB-1120]. For collections and discussions of his poetry, see [VPMB-160], [VPMB-210], [VPMB-490], [VPMB-750], [VPMB-760], and [VPMB-790]. For interpretations of his sculpture, see [VPMB-060], [VPMB-120], [VPMB-250], [VPMB-270], [VPMB-290], [VPMB-330], [VPMB-370], [VPMB-450], [VPMB-520], [VPMB-530], [VPMB-540], [VPMB-680], [VPMB-720], [VPMB-920], [VPMB-960], [VPMB-1050], and [VPMB-1060]. For discussions of his theories of art, see [VPMB-200], [VPMB-260], and [VPMB-1030]. The balance of books listed below and not yet mentioned offer general discussions of various works by Michelangelo. The best of these general works include Charles de Tolnay's authoritative five volume study [VPMB-300] and single general volume [VPMB-310], Bernard Lamarche-Vadel's lavishly illustrated and highly readable work [VPMB-670], and Walter Pater's nineteenth century essays which are models of clarity and stylistic finesse [VPMB-860]. Also see Creighton Gilbert's collection of writings by poets responding to the art work of the Renaissance, including interpretations of Michelangelo's works [VPMB-400].

Specialized Bibliographies

[VPMB-010] Kline, Laura S. *Michelangelo's Architecture: A Selected Bibliography.* Monticello, Ill.: Vance Bibliographies, 1983. 26 pp.

[VPMB-020] Dussler, Luitpold. *Michelangelo--Bibliographie, 1927-1970.* Wiesbaden: Harrassowitz, 1974.

Key Works

[VPMB-030] Ackerman, James Sloss. *The Architecture of Michelangelo.* 2nd ed. 2 vols. London: Zwemmer, 1964. Bib. Vol. 1, pp. 143-151. Reprint. Harmondsworth: Penguin, 1970. Bib. pp. 351-365. Reprint. Chicago: University of Chicago Press; Harmondsworth; New York: Penguin, 1986. Bib. pp. 337-355.

[VPMB-040] Argan, Giulio Carlo. *Michelangelo Architect.* New York: Harry N. Abrams, 1993. Bib. refs.

[VPMB-050] Arthos, John. *Dante, Michelangelo, and Milton.* New York: Humanities Press, 1963. 124 pp. Bib. footnotes.

[VPMB-060] Baldini, Umberto. *The Sculpture of Michelangelo.* Photo. Liberto Perugi. [Trans. Clare Coope.] Trans. *Michelangelo Scultore.* New York: Rizzoli International Publications, 1982. Bib. pp. 295-298.

[VPMB-070] Barnes, Bernadine Ann. "The Invention of Michelangelo's Last Judgment." Ph.D. Thesis, University of Virginia, 1986. Bib. pp. 268-278.

[VPMB-080] Barolsky, Paul. *Michelangelo's Nose: A Myth and its Maker.* University Park: Pennsylvania State University Press, 1990. Bib. refs. pp. 163-166.

[VPMB-090] Berti, Luciano. *All the Works of Michelangelo.* Trans. Susan

Glasspool. Trans. *Michelangelo*. Italia Artistica, no. 14. Firenze: Bonechi, 1969. 95 pp.

[VPMB-100] Bertram, Anthony. *Michelangelo*. London: Studio Vista, 1964. 160 pp. Bib. p. 4.

[VPMB-110] Besdine, Matthew. *The Unknown Michelangelo*. Ed. Marilyn Eisenberg. Garden City, N.Y.: Adelphi University Press, 1985. Bib. pp. 112-114.

[VPMB-120] Bissonnette, Denise L., Maurizia Binda. *The Genius of the Sculptor in Michelangelo's Work*. Exhibition, Montreal Museum of Fine Arts, 12 June to 13 September 1992. Montreal: Montreal Museum of Fine Arts, 1992. Bib. refs. pp. 505-518.

[VPMB-130] Brandes, Georg Morris Cohen. *Michelangelo: His Life, His Times, His Era*. [2nd ed., rev.] New York: Ungar, 1967. 434 pp. Bib. refs.

[VPMB-140] British Museum. *Drawings by Michelangelo, from the British Museum*. Exhibition, Pierpont Morgan Library, 24 April to 28 July 1979. New York: Pierpont Morgan Library, 1979. Bib. pp. 109-111.

[VPMB-150] Bull, George Anthony, and Peter Porter. *Michelangelo, Life, Letters, and Poetry*. Oxford; New York: Oxford University Press, 1987. xxiv, 182 pp. Bib. pp. xviii-xix.

[VPMB-160] Cambon, Glauco. *Michelangelo's Poetry: Fury of Form*. Princeton: Princeton University Press, 1985. Bib. pp. 203-211.

[VPMB-170] Camesasca, Ettore. *The Complete Paintings of Michelangelo*. Classics of World Art. New York: Harry N. Abrams, 1966. Bib. p. 82.

[VPMB-180] Cartocci, Sergio. *The Sistine Chapel and the Rooms of Raphael*. Rome: OTO, 1974. 70 pp.

[VPMB-190] Clements, Robert John. *Michelangelo's Self-Portrait: A Sourcebook*. Rev. ed. New York: New York University Press, 1979. 193 pp. Bib. refs.

[VPMB-200] ------. *Michelangelo's Theory of Art*. New York: Gramercy Publishing Co.; Zurich: Buehler Buchdruck, 1961. London: Routledge and Kegan Paul, 1963. xxxiii, 471 pp. Bib. refs. in notes, pp. 421-457. Bib. p. 458.

[VPMB-210] ------. *The Poetry of Michelangelo*. London: Peter Owen, 1965. 368 pp. Bib. pp. 343-347.

507

[VPMB-220] Collinge, Lucinda Hawkins, and Annabel Ricketts. *Michelange-lo*. [Greenwich, Conn.]: Brompton; New York: Mallard Press, 1991. Bib. p. 237.

[VPMB-230] Condivi, Ascanio. *The Life of Michelangelo*. Trans. Alice Sedgwick Wohl. Trans. *Vita di Michelangelo Buonarroti*. Baton Rouge: Louisiana State University Press, 1976. Bib. pp. 149-151.

[VPMB-240] Coughlan, Robert. *The World of Michelangelo, 1475-1564*. Amsterdam: Time-Life Books, 1962. Reprint. 1982. Bib. pp. 198-199.

[VPMB-250] Davila, Juan, and Paul Foss. *The Mutilated Pieta*. Surry Hills, NSW: Artspace, 1985. 47 pp. Bib. refs.

[VPMB-260] de Tolnay, Charles. *The Art and Thought of Michelangelo*. New York: Pantheon Books, 1964.

[VPMB-270] ------. *Casa Buonarroti: The Sculptures of Michelangelo and the Family Collection*. Trans. *La Casa Buonarroti. Le Sculture di Michelangelo e le Collezioni della Famiglia*. Firenze: Arnaud, 1984. 130 pp. Bib. pp. 21-22.

[VPMB-280] ------. *The Final Period: Last Judgment, Frescoes of the Pauline Chapel, Last Pietas*. Vol. 5. Princeton: Princeton University Press, 1960. Bib. pp. 231-236.

[VPMB-290] ------. *The Medici Chapel*. Vol. 3. Princeton: Princeton University Press, 1948. 275 pp. Bib. refs. pp. 245-247.

[VPMB-300] ------. *Michelangelo*. 2nd ed. rev. 5 vols. 1947. Reprint. Princeton: Princeton University Press, 1969.

[VPMB-310] ------. *Michelangelo: Sculptor, Painter, Architect*. Trans. *Michel-Ange*. Princeton: Princeton University Press, 1975. 283 pp. Bib. pp. 235-248.

[VPMB-320] ------. *The Sistine Ceiling*. Vol. 2. Princeton: Princeton University Press, 1969. 285 pp. Bib. pp. 250-253.

[VPMB-330] ------. *The Tomb of Julius II*. Vol. 4. Princeton: Princeton University Press, 1970. 200 pp. Bib. abbreviations pp. 163-166.

[VPMB-340] ------. *The Youth of Michelangelo*. Vol. 1. Princeton: Princeton University Press, 1969. 296 pp. Bib. abbreviations, pp. 257-262.

[VPMB-350] De Vecchi, Pierluigi. *Michelangelo*. New York: H. Holt, 1992.

508

Bib. refs. p. 160.

[VPMB-360] Einem, Herbert von. *Michelangelo.* Rev. trans. from German ed., 1959. London: Methuen, 1976. 329 pp. Bib. pp. 266-270.

[VPMB-370] Finn, David, and Frederick Hartt. *Michelangelo's Three Pietas.* New York: Harry N. Abrams, 1975. Reprint. [London]: [Thames and Hudson], 1976. Bib. p. 201.

[VPMB-380] Furse, John. *Michelangelo and His Art.* London; New York: Hamlyn, 1975. Bib. p. 126.

[VPMB-390] Gatti, Enzo., and Guilia Conte Micheli. *The Crucifix of Michelangelo Re-Discovered.* Trans. *Il Crocefisso di Michelangelo ritrovato.* S. Massimo/Verona: G. Grazia, 1969. Bib. p. 87.

[VPMB-400] Gilbert, Creighton. *Poets Seeing Artists' Work: Instances in the Italian Renaissance.* Saggi di "Lettere Italiane," vol. 42. Firenze: Leo S. Olschki, 1991. 293 pp. Bib. refs.

[VPMB-410] Gilbert, Sarah Joan. "A Study of Some Influences on the Creativeness of Da Vinci and Michelangelo During Their Early Years by the Culture and Society of that Period." Ed.D. Thesis, Indiana University, 1962. Bib. pp. 218-235.

[VPMB-420] Gitay, Tzfira Zarchi. "The Meaning of the Ten Medallions in Michelangelo's Program for the Sistine Ceiling." Ph.D. Thesis, Emory University, 1980. Bib. refs. pp. 198-214.

[VPMB-430] Giunta, Jacopo. *The Divine Michelangelo: The Florentine Academy's Homage on his Death in 1564.* Trans. and ed. Rudolf Wittkower and Margot Wittkower. [London]: Phaidon Press, 1964. Dist. New York Graphic Society, Greenwich, Conn. 170 pp. Bib. pp. 137-140.

[VPMB-440] Goldscheider, Ludwig. *Michelangelo: Paintings, Sculpture, Architecture.* 5th ed. London: Phaidon Press, 1975. Bib. pp. 25-26. Reprint. New York: Harrison House, 1986. Dist. Crown Publishers. 264 pp. Bib. pp. 24-25.

[VPMB-450] ------. *A Survey of Michelangelo's Models in Wax and Clay.* London: Phaidon Press, 1962. Unpaged. Bib.

[VPMB-460] Gould, Cecil Hilton Monk, Enio Sindona, Jane Carroll, and David Piper. *Michelangelo: The Complete Paintings.* London; New York: Granada, 1980. Bib. p. 96.

[VPMB-470] Hager, Serafina, ed. *Leonardo, Michelangelo, and Raphael in Renaissance Florence from 1500 to 1508.* Symposium papers, 14 June 1989. Washington, D.C.: Georgetown University Press, 1992. 120 pp. Bib. refs. English and Italian.

[VPMB-480] Hall, Marcia B. *Michelangelo: The Sistine Ceiling Restored.* New York: Rizzoli International Publications, 1993. Bib. refs.

[VPMB-490] Hallock, Ann Hayes. *Michelangelo the Poet: The Man Behind the Myth.* Monterey, Calif.: Page-Ficklin Publications, 1978. Bib. pp. 391-397.

[VPMB-500] Hardy, Camille. *Michelangelo and the Pauline Modello: Art, Document and Odyssey.* New York: Eagle I, 1992. Bib. refs. pp. 78-79.

[VPMB-510] Hartt, Frederick. *Michelangelo Drawings.* New York: Harry N. Abrams, 1970. Bib. pp. 403-404.

[VPMB-520] ------. *Michelangelo's Three Pietas.* New York: Harry N. Abrams, [1975]. Bib. p. 201.

[VPMB-530] ------. *Michelangelo: The Complete Sculpture.* Rev. ed. New York: Harry N. Abrams, 1976. Bib. pp. 309-310.

[VPMB-540] Hartt, Frederick, and David Finn. *David by the Hand of Michelangelo: The Original Model Discovered.* New York: Abbeville Press; London: Thames and Hudson, 1987. Bib. pp. 139-141.

[VPMB-550] Hartt, Frederick, and Takashi Okamura. *The Sistine Chapel.* 2 vols. London: Barrie and Jenkins with Nippon Network Television, 1991. Bib. vol. 1, p. 371, and vol. 2, p. 375.

[VPMB-560] Hersey, George L. *High Renaissance Art in St. Peter's and the Vatican: An Interpretive Guide.* Chicago: University of Chicago Press, 1993. 334 pp. Bib. refs.

[VPMB-570] Heusinger, Lutz. *Michelangelo: Life and Works in Chronological Order.* Firenze: Innocenti, 1978. Bib. p. 96. Reprint. Firenze: Scala Books, 1982. Reprint. Firenze: Becocci, 1986. 91 pp. Bib. Reprint. Antella [Florence]: Scala, 1989. Bib. p. 80.

[VPMB-580] Heusinger, Lutz, and Fabrizio Mancinelli. *All the Frescoes of the Sistine Chapel.* Firenze: Zincografia Fiorentina; Firenze: Coop. Officine Grafiche, 1973. Bib. p. 96.

[VPMB-590] Heusinger, Lutz, Fabrizio Mancinelli, and Francesco Papafava. *The Sistine Chapel.* Florence: Scala, Instituto Fotografico Editoriale, 1986. Bib. p. 96.

510

[VPMB-600] Hibbard, Howard. *Michelangelo*. 2nd ed. Harmondsworth: Penguin; Cambridge, Mass.: Harper and Row, 1985. 347 pp. Bib. pp. 321-325.

[VPMB-610] ------. *Michelangelo: Painter, Sculptor, Architect*. [New ed.] Secaucus, N.J.: Chartwell Books, 1978. Bib. pp. 209-212. Reprint. London: Octopus Books, 1979. Bib. pp. 211-212.

[VPMB-620] *High Renaissance, The: Leonardo da Vinci, Michelangelo, Raphael, Titian*. Ref. ed. Great Artists of the Western World, vol. 2. London: London; New York: Marshall Cavendish, 1990. Bib. p. 139.

[VPMB-630] Hirst, Michael. *Michelangelo and His Drawings*. London; New Haven: Yale University Press, 1988. [256 pp.] Bib. pp. 119-123.

[VPMB-640] ------. *Michelangelo Draftsman*. Exhibition, National Gallery of Art, Washington, D.C., 9 October to 11 December 1988. Milan: Olivetti, 1988. Bib. pp. 165-168.

[VPMB-650] Januszczak, Waldemar. *Sayonara, Michelangelo: The Sistine Chapel Restored and Repackaged*. Reading, Mass.: Addison-Wesley, 1990. 207 pp.

[VPMB-660] Jeffery, David. "The Sistine Restoration: A Renaissance for Michelangelo." *National Geographic* 176, no. 6 (Dec. 1989): 688-713.

[VPMB-670] Lamarche-Vadel, Bernard. *Michelangelo*. Trans. Anni Gandon Heminway and Patricia Allen-Browne. Secaucus, N.J.: Chartwell Books; New York: Konecky and Konecky; [New York; London]: Alpine Fine Arts Collection, 1986. Bib. p. 190.

[VPMB-680] LeBrooy, Paul James. *Michelangelo Models Formerly in the Paul von Praun Collection*. Vancouver: Creelman and Drummond Publishers, 1972. Bib. pp. 148-149.

[VPMB-690] Leites, Nathan Constantin. *Art and Life: Aspects of Michelangelo*. Psychoanalytic Crosscurrents. New York: New York University Press, 1986. Bib. pp. 117-120.

[VPMB-700] Liebert, Robert S. *Michelangelo: A Psychoanalytic Study of his Life and Images*. New Haven; London: Yale University Press, 1983. xxii, 447 pp. Bib. pp. 429-435.

[VPMB-710] Maffei, Fernanda de'. *Michelangelo's Lost St. John: The Story of a Discovery*. London: Faber and Faber, 1964. Bib. refs. pp. 38-40.

[VPMB-720] Mancusi-Ungaro, Harold R. *Michelangelo: The Bruges Madonna and the Piccolomini Altar.* New Haven: Yale University Press, 1971. Bib. pp. 179-183. Italian and English.

[VPMB-730] Mariani, Valerio. *Michelangelo the Painter.* New York: Harry N. Abrams; Milano: Arti Grafiche Ricordi, 1964. Reprint. New York: Harry N. Abrams, 1973. Reprint. New York: Harrison House, 1987. Bib. pp. 150-151. 86 large plates.

[VPMB-740] Martellucci, Nils. *Life and Works of Michelangelo in Florence.* Florence: Bonechi, 1966. Bib. p. 65.

[VPMB-750] Michelangelo Buonarroti. *The Complete Poems and Selected Letters of Michelangelo.* 3rd ed. Trans. Gilbert Creighton and Robert Newton Linscott. Princeton: Princeton University Press, 1980. lvii, 317 pp.

[VPMB-760] ------. *The Complete Poems of Michelangelo.* Trans. Joseph Tusiani. London: Peter Owen, 1960. Dist. Dufour Editions, Chester Springs, Penn. Reprint. New York: Humanities Press, 1970. 217 pp.

[VPMB-770] ------. *Drawings by Michelangelo in the Collection of Her Majesty the Queen at Windsor Castle, the Ashmolean Museum, the British Museum and Other English Collections: An Exhibition held in the Department of Prints and Drawings in the British Museum, 6th February to 27th April 1975.* London: British Museums Publications Ltd., 1975. 160 pp. Bib. refs.

[VPMB-780] ------. *I, Michelangelo, Sculptor: An Autobiography Through Letters.* Ed. Irving Stone and Jean Stone. New York: New American Library, 1962. 256 pp.

[VPMB-790] ------. *The Sonnets of Michelangelo.* Trans. Elizabeth Jennings. [New ed.] London: Allison and Busby, 1969. 100 pp.

[VPMB-800] Millon, Henry A., and Craig Hugh Smyth. *Michelangelo Architect: The Facade of San Lorenzo and the Drum and Dome of St. Peter's.* Exhibition, National Gallery of Art, Washington, D.C., 9 October to 11 December 1988. Milan: Olivetti, 1988. Bib. pp. 189-196.

[VPMB-810] Morgan, Charles Hill. *The Life of Michelangelo.* New York: Reynal, 1960. 253 pp. Bib.

[VPMB-820] Murray, Linda. *Michelangelo.* World of Art Library. New York: Thames and Hudson; New York: Oxford University Press, 1979. London: Thames and Hudson, 1980. Bib. p. 208.

512

[VPMB-830] ------. *Michelangelo: His Life, Work and Times.* London; New York: Thames and Hudson, 1984. Bib. pp. 233-234.

[VPMB-840] Nardini, Bruno. *Michelangelo: His Life and Works.* Trans. *Incontro con Michelangiolo.* [London]: Collins, 1977. Bib. p. 214.

[VPMB-850] Oremland, Jerome D. *Michelangelo's Sistine Ceiling: A Psychoanalytic Study of Creativity.* Applied Psychoanalysis Series, Monograph 2. Madison, Conn.: International Universities Press, 1989. Bib. p. 287-292.

[VPMB-860] Pater, Walter. *Michelangelo.* This Beautiful World, vol. 6. Tokyo; Palo Alto, Calif.: Kodansha International Ltd., 1968. 138 pp.

[VPMB-870] Perrig, Alexander. *Michelangelo's Drawings: The Science of Attribution.* New Haven: Yale University Press, 1991. Bib. refs. pp. 135-161.

[VPMB-880] Pietrangeli, Carlo. *The Sistine Chapel: A New Light on Michelangelo: The Art, the History, and the Restoration.* New York: Harmony Books, 1986.

[VPMB-890] Redig de Campos, D[eoclecio]. *Michelangelo the Last Judgment.* Trans. *Il Giudizio universale di Michelangelo.* Garden City, N.Y.: Doubleday, 1978. 106 pp., 64 leaves of plates. Bib.

[VPMB-900] Richmond, Robin. *Michelangelo and the Creation of the Sistine Chapel.* London: Barrie and Jenkins, 1992. 160 pp.

[VPMB-910] Roberts, Jane. *A Dictionary of Michelangelo's Watermarks.* Milan: Olivetti, 1988. 49 pp. Bib. refs.

[VPMB-920] Russoli, Franco. *All the Sculpture of Michelangelo.* Complete Library of World Art, vol. 11. [London]: Oldbourne, 1963. 77 pp., 132 plates. Bib. pp. 76-77.

[VPMB-930] Salmi, Mario, ed. *The Complete Work of Michelangelo.* Artabras Book. New York: Reynal and Co. with William Morrow and Co., 1965. Bib. pp. 585-593.

[VPMB-940] Salvini, Roberto. *Michelangelo.* Trans. *Michelangelo.* The Hidden Masters. New York: Mayflower; Danbury, Conn.: MasterWorks Press, 1978. Bib. pp. 188-189. Also titled *The Hidden Michelangelo.* Chicago: Rand McNally, 1978.

[VPMB-950] Schott, Rudolf. *Michelangelo.* London: Thames and Hudson, 1963. Bib. p. 248.

513

[VPMB-960] Seymour, Charles. *Michelangelo's David: A Search for Identity.* A. W. Mellon Studies in the Humanities. [Pittsburgh]: University of Pittsburgh Press, 1967. xxi, 194 pp. Bib. refs.

[VPMB-970] ------. *Michelangelo, The Sistine Chapel Ceiling: Illustrations, Introductory Essay, Backgrounds and Sources, Critical Essays.* New York: Norton, 1972. Bib. pp. 239-243.

[VPMB-980] Sindona, Enio. *Michelangelo.* New York: Rizzoli International Publications, 1980. Bib. p. 96.

[VPMB-990] Smyth, Craig Hugh, and Ann Gilkerson, eds. *Michelangelo Drawings.* Studies in the History of Art, no. 33. Symposium Papers. Washington, D.C.: National Gallery of Art, 1992. Dist. University Press of New England, Hanover. Bib. refs. pp. 281-283.

[VPMB-1000] Stearns, Monroe. *Michelangelo.* Immortals of Art. New York: F. Watts, 1970. Bib. pp. 237-239.

[VPMB-1010] Steinberg, Leo. *Michelangelo's Last Paintings: The Conversion of St. Paul and the Crucifixion of St. Peter in the Cappella Paolina, Vatican Palace.* London: Phaidon Press; New York: Oxford University Press, 1975. Bib. p. 56.

[VPMB-1020] Stone, Irving. *The Agony and the Ecstasy: A Novel of Michelangelo.* Garden City, N.Y.: Doubleday, 1961. Bib. pp. 693-700. Reprint. Garden City, N.Y.: Doubleday, 1963. Bib. pp. 705-713.

[VPMB-1030] Summers, David. *Michelangelo and the Language of Art.* Princeton: Princeton University Press, 1981. Bib. pp. 585-607.

[VPMB-1040] Symonds, John Addington. *The Life of Michelangelo.* London: n.p., 1893.

[VPMB-1050] Theberge, Pierre. *The Genius of the Sculptor in Michelangelo's Work.* Exhibition, Montreal Museum of Fine Arts, 12 June to 13 September 1992. Montreal: Montreal Museum of Fine Arts, 1992. Bib. refs. pp. 505-518.

[VPMB-1060] Tselos, Dimitri. *The Pieta: Its Byzantine Iconographic Origins and its Western Titular Diversity.* Chronika Aisthetikes, vols. 25-26 (1986-1987). [Athens]: Hellenike Hetaireia Aisthetikes, 1986. Bib. refs. pp. 82-87.

[VPMB-1070] Vasari, Giorgio. *Life of Michelangelo Buonarroti.* Trans. George Anthony Bull. London: Folio Society, 1971. 158 pp., 31 plates.

[VPMB-1080]   Weinberger, Martin. *Michelangelo, The Sculptor.* 2 vols. London: Routledge and Kegan Paul; New York: Columbia University Press, 1967. Bib. Vol. 1, pp. ix-x.

[VPMB-1090]   Whistler, Catherine. *Drawings by Michelangelo and Raphael.* Oxford: Ashmolean Museum, 1990. Reprint. *Michelangelo and Raphael Drawings.* Oxford: Phaidon-Christie's, 1991. Bib. refs. p. 80.

[VPMB-1100]   Wilde, Johannes. *Michelangelo and His Studio.* Trans. from German. London: British Museum Publications for the Trustees of the British Museum, 1953. Reprint. 1975. 142 pp. Bib. refs. pp. xvii-xx.

[VPMB-1110]   Wilde, Johannes, John K. G. Shearman, and Michael Hirst. *Michelangelo: Six Lectures.* Oxford Studies in the History of Art and Architecture. Oxford: Clarendon Press; New York: Oxford University Press, 1978. 194 pp.

[VPMB-1120]   Wind, Edgar. *Michelangelo's Prophets and Sibyls.* London: Oxford University Press, 1965. 84 pp. Bib. refs.

Rembrandt Harmenszoon van Rijn

Studies of the life and work of Rembrandt Harmenszoon van Rijn are plentiful and reasonably current. The first two critical tools listed below, [VPRE-010] and [VPRE-020], provide a brief introduction to research on Rembrandt and his work. The two most prolific and authoritative writers treating the life and works of Rembrandt are Otto Benesch [VPRE-100 to VPRE-150] and Christopher White [VPRE-1170 to VPRE-1180], who also worked with other critics [VPRE-1190 to VPRE-1200].

While most of the books treating the works of Rembrandt also include some biographical elements, the following studies are especially helpful in examining his life: [VPRE-040], [VPRE-060], [VPRE-090], [VPRE-140], [VPRE-240], [VPRE-410], [VPRE-460], [VPRE-510], [VPRE-520], [VPRE-760], [VPRE-900], [VPRE-920], [VPRE-990], [VPRE-1180]. Note especially Ludwig Goldscheider's review of three early biographies [VPRE-460]. To locate primary documents by and about Rembrandt, see [VPRE-1070]. For studies which help place Rembrandt in his larger context, see the following works: [VPRE-050], [VPRE-110], [VPRE-340], [VPRE-370], [VPRE-390],

[VPRE-400], [VPRE-420], [VPRE-450], [VPRE-650], [VPRE-660], [VPRE-670], [VPRE-740], [VPRE-780], [VPRE-790], [VPRE-1010], [VPRE-1060], [VPRE-1150], and [VPRE-1190]. Note particularly studies of his school which produced several works attributed to him but recently discovered to have been painted or drawn by his students, as noted for an exhibition at Purdue University [VPRE-860] and as discussed in the following works: [VPRE-170], [VPRE-450], [VPRE-650], [VPRE-1020]. In the exploration of how to authenticate the work of Rembrandt, one will be helped by a special study documented by Maryan Wynn Ainsworth, *Art and Autoradiography: Insights into the Genesis of Paintings by Rembrandt, Van Dyck, and Vermeer* [VPRE-030]. For studies which trace the influence of Rembrandt on subsequent generations, see [VPRE-190] and [VPRE-660]. For works treating the responses of critics to Rembrandt's work, see [VPRE-070], [VPRE-080], [VPRE-1030], and [VPRE-1140].

The study of Rembrandt's works is usually divided into media, including drawings, etchings, and paintings. The studies which attempt to cover all three media include the following: [VPRE-300], [VPRE-460], [VPRE-510], [VPRE-520], [VPRE-600], [VPRE-820], [VPRE-920], [VPRE-1130], [VPRE-1160], [VPRE-1220]. For works treating his drawings, see [VPRE-130], [VPRE-150], [VPRE-370], [VPRE-450], [VPRE-500], [VPRE-880], [VPRE-930], [VPRE-950], [VPRE-960], and [VPRE-1020]. The most complete studies of Rembrandt's etchings are Karel G. Boon's *Rembrandt: The Complete Etchings* [VPRE-270], Arthur Mayger Hind's *A Catalogue of Rembrandt's Etchings, Chronologically Arranged and Completely Illustrated* [VPRE-620], and Gary Schwartz's *Rembrandt: All the Etchings Reproduced in True Size* [VPRE-980]. Other important works on his etchings include [VPRE-160], [VPRE-180], [VPRE-420], [VPRE-480], [VPRE-730], [VPRE-840], [VPRE-1040], [VPRE-1080], [VPRE-1180], [VPRE-1200], and [VPRE-1210]. Of the many works treating Rembrandt's paintings, three attempt to be comprehensive, including [VPRE-280], [VPRE-290], and [VPRE-720], with the second one [VPRE-290] by Christopher Brown and David Piper being the most recent. The following works treat one or more of Rembrandt's paintings, including his numerous self-portraits: [VPRE-210], [VPRE-240], [VPRE-250], [VPRE-310], [VPRE-320], [VPRE-360], [VPRE-440], [VPRE-

530], [VPRE-560], [VPRE-570], [VPRE-580], [VPRE-590], [VPRE-610], [VPRE-800], [VPRE-810], [VPRE-870], [VPRE-890], [VPRE-970], [VPRE-1230]. One of the most significant categories of Rembrandt's works is that group treating the Bible, this category being analyzed in the following studies: [VPRE-550], [VPRE-630], [VPRE-700], [VPRE-750], [VPRE-840], [VPRE-940], [VPRE-1100], [VPRE-1110].

The balance of books listed below are general studies ranging from solid introductions, like that by Kenneth Clark [VPRE-330], to recent studies including the latest research findings, such as Michael Bockemuhl's *Rembrandt, 1606-1669: The Mystery of the Revealed Form* [VPRE-200], and Pascal Bonafoux's *Rembrandt: Substance and Shadow* [VPRE-260]. Other valuable general works given below include [VPRE-100], [VPRE-120], [VPRE-220], [VPRE-230], [VPRE-350], [VPRE-380], [VPRE-430], [VPRE-490], [VPRE-640], [VPRE-680], [VPRE-690], [VPRE-710], [VPRE-850], [VPRE-770], [VPRE-830], [VPRE-910], [VPRE-1000], [VPRE-1050], [VPRE-1090], [VPRE-1120], and [VPRE-1170]. For additional studies treating Rembrandt, see the opening three sections of Chapter 12, and the general section above on painting.

Special Bibliographies

[VPRE-010] Walker, John Alan. *A Bibliography of 238 Items Relating to Rembrandt Hermensz van Rijn, 1606-1669*. Big Pine, Calif.: Avenues to Art Editions, 1988. 24 pp.

[VPRE-020] Broos, B. P. J. *Index to the Formal Sources of Rembrandt's Art*. Maarssen: Schwartz, 1977. 142 pp. Bib. pp. 13-34.

Key Works

[VPRE-030] Ainsworth, Maryan Wynn. *Art and Autoradiography: Insights into the Genesis of Paintings by Rembrandt, Van Dyck, and Vermeer*. New York: Metropolitan Museum of Art, 1982. Reprint. 1987. 112 pp. Bib. refs.

[VPRE-040] Alpers, Svetlana. *Rembrandt's Enterprise: The Studio and the Market*. Chicago: University of Chicago Press; London:

Thames and Hudson, 1988. 160 pp., 134 pp. of plates. Bib. pp. 123-155.

[VPRE-050] Aronson, Alex. *Shakespeare and Rembrandt: Metaphorical Representation in Poetry and the Visual Arts.* Essen: Verlag die blaue Eule, 1987. Bib. pp. 143-147.

[VPRE-060] Bailey, Anthony. *Rembrandt's House.* Boston: Houghton Mifflin; London: J. M. Dent, 1978. Bib. pp. 237-240.

[VPRE-070] ------. *Responses to Rembrandt.* New York: Timken Publishers, 1993. Bib. refs.

[VPRE-080] Bal, Mieke. *Reading Rembrandt: Beyond the Word-Image Opposition: The Northrop Frye Lectures in Literary Theory.* Cambridge New Art History and Criticism Series. Cambridge: Cambridge University Press, 1991. Bib. refs. pp. 399-480.

[VPRE-090] Baudiquey, Paul. *The Life and Work of Rembrandt.* Trans. *La vie et louvre de Rembrandt.* Secaucus, N.J.: Chartwell Books, 1984. Bib. p. 255.

[VPRE-100] Benesch, Otto. *Rembrandt.* Vol. 1. *Collected Writings.* 4 vols. Trans. Gillian Mullins. [London]; [New York]: Phaidon Press, 1970. 456 pp. Bibs.

[VPRE-110] ------. *From an Art Historian's Workshop: Rembrandt, Dutch and Flemish Masters, Velasquez, Frederik Van Valckenborch.* Ed. Eva Benesch. New York: Hacker Art Books, 1979. 187 pp.

[VPRE-120] ------. *Rembrandt.* New York: Skira, 1957. Reprint. Geneva: Skira; New York: Rizzoli International Publications, 1990. 140 pp.

[VPRE-130] ------. *Rembrandt as a Draughtsman: An Essay.* New York: Phaidon Press, 1960. Dist. Doubleday, Garden City, N.Y. 163 pp. Bib. p. 142.

[VPRE-140] ------. *Rembrandt: Biographical and Critical Study.* Taste of Our Time, vol. 22. Geneva: Skira, 1957. Dist. World Publishing Co., Cleveland. Bib. pp. 138-142. [New York]: Skira, 1957. Bib. pp. 137-141.

[VPRE-150] ------. *The Drawings of Rembrandt.* 6 vols. London: Phaidon Press, 1954-1957. Enlarged and Ed. Eva Benesch. [New York]: Phaidon Press, 1973. xxiv, 394 pp. Bib.

[VPRE-160] Bevers, Holm, and Barbara Welzel. *Rembrandt: The Master and His Workshop: Etchings.* New Haven; London: Yale

University Press with National Gallery Publications, London, 1991. Bib. pp. 132-136.

[VPRE-170]   Bevers, Holm, Peter Schatborn, and Barbara Welzel. *Rembrandt: The Master and His Workshop: Drawings and Etchings*. Exhibition, Kupferstichkabinett SMPK at the Altes Museum, Berlin, 12 September 1991 to 27 October 1991; Rijksmuseum, Amsterdam, 4 December 1991 to 19 January 1992; The National Gallery, London, 26 March 1992 to 24 May 1992. New Haven; London: Yale University Press with National Gallery Publications, 1991. Bib. pp. 284-286.

[VPRE-180]   Biorklund, George. *Rembrandt's Etchings: True and False*. 2nd ed. New York: Hacker Art Books, 1988. 199 pp.

[VPRE-190]   Blankert, Albert. *The Impact of a Genius: Rembrandt, His Pupils and Followers in the Seventeenth Century: Paintings from Museum and Private Collections*. Trans. *Ina Rike*. Exhibition, Waterman Gallery and Gronniger Museum. Amsterdam: K. and V. Waterman, 1983. Bib. pp. 233-234.

[VPRE-200]   Bockemuhl, Michael. *Rembrandt, 1606-1669: The Mystery of the Revealed Form*. Trans. *Rembrandt, 1606-1669*. Koln: Benedikt Taschen, 1992. Bib. refs. pp. 166-171.

[VPRE-210]   Bolten, J[aap], ed. *Rembrandt and the Incredulity of Thomas: Papers on a Rediscovered Painting from the Seventeenth Century*. Leiden: Aliotta and Manhart, 1981. 54 pp. Bib. pp. 31-34.

[VPRE-220]   Bolten, Jaap, and Jelleke Bolten-Rempt. *The Hidden Rembrandt*. Trans. Danielle Adkinson. Chicago: Rand McNally, 1977. Also titled *Rembrandt*. Sydney: Bay Books, 1977. Reprint. New York: Mayflower Books, 1981. Reprint. Danbury, Conn.: MasterWorks Press, 1984. Bib. p. 206.

[VPRE-230]   Bomford, David. *Rembrandt*. Art in the Making. Exhibition, National Gallery, London, 12 October 1988 to 17 January 1989. [London]: National Gallery Publications, 1988. Bib. pp. 150-153.

[VPRE-240]   Bonafoux, Pascal. *Rembrandt: A Self-Portrait*. Trans. *Rembrandt: Autoportrait*. Geneva: Skira; New York: Rizzoli International Publications; London: Weidenfeld and Nicolson, 1985. Bib. p. 158.

[VPRE-250]   ------. *Rembrandt: Master of the Portrait*. New York: Harry N. Abrams, 1992. 175 pp. Bib. refs.

[VPRE-260]   ------. *Rembrandt: Substance and Shadow*. New Horizons.

London: Thames and Hudson, 1992. Bib. p. 168.

[VPRE-270] Boon, Karel G. *Rembrandt: The Complete Etchings*. Rev. ed. Trans. *Rembrandt de etser*. New York: Harry N. Abrams, 1978. Reprint. London: Alpine Fine Arts Collection, 1987. c. 300 pp. Bib.

[VPRE-280] Bredius, Abraham, and H[orst] Gerson. *Rembrandt: The Complete Edition of the Paintings*. Trans. *Rembrandt schilderijen*. 4th ed. London: Phaidon Press, 1971. 636 pp.

[VPRE-290] Brown, Christopher, and David Piper. *Rembrandt: The Complete Paintings, 1-2*. 2 vols. London; New York: Granada, 1980. Bib. Also titled *Rembrandt*. 2 vols. New York: Rizzoli International Publications, 1980. Bib.

[VPRE-300] Brown, Christopher, and Sally Salvesen, eds. *Rembrandt: The Master and His Workshop*. 2 vols. Exhibition, Gemaldegalerie SMPK at the Altes Museum, Berlin, 12 September 1991 to 10 November 1991; Rijksmuseum, Amsterdam, 4 December 1991 to 1 March 1992; The National Gallery, London, 25 March to 24 May 1992. New Haven: Yale University Press; London: National Gallery Publications, 1991. Vol. 1: *Paintings*. Ed. Christopher Brown, Jan Kelch, and Pieter van Thiel. Vol. 2: *Drawings and Etchings*. Ed. Holm Bevers, Peter Schatborn, and Barbara Welzel. Bib. pp. 391-394.

[VPRE-310] Bruyn, J., and Stichting Foundation Rembrandt Research Project. *A Corpus of Rembrandt Paintings*. Dordrecht; London: Nijhoff, 1989. 803 pp.

[VPRE-320] Chapman, H. Perry. *Rembrandt's Self-Portraits: A Study in Seventeenth-Century Identity*. Princeton: Princeton University Press, 1990. Bib. pp. 171-176.

[VPRE-330] Clark, Kenneth. *An Introduction to Rembrandt*. New York: Harper and Row, 1978. 153 pp.

[VPRE-340] ------. *Rembrandt and the Italian Renaissance*. Wrightsman Lectures, 1964. New York: W. W. Norton and Co.; New York: New York University Press; London: Murray, 1966. Reprint. Norton Library, no. 424. New York: W. W. Norton and Co., 1968. 225 pp., 181 plates. Bib. p. 210.

[VPRE-350] Copplestone, Trewin. *Rembrandt*. Rev. Reprint. London: Spring Books, 1961. 136 pp. Bib. refs.

[VPRE-360] Dulwich Picture Gallery. *Rembrandt van Rijn: Girl at a Window*. Paintings and Their Context, no. 4. London: Dulwich

520

Picture Gallery, 1993. Bib. pp. 68-69.

[VPRE-370]   Duparc, Frederik J. *Landscape in Perspective: Drawings by Rembrandt and His Contemporaries*. Exhibition, Arthur M. Sackler Museum, Harvard University, Cambridge, 20 February to 3 April 1988, Montreal Museum of Arts, 15 April to 29 May 1988. Montreal: Montreal Museum of Fine Arts, 1988. Bib. pp. 239-243.

[VPRE-380]   Esteban, Claude, Jean Rudel, and Simon Monneret. *Rembrandt*. Trans. from French. New York: Excalibur Books, 1978. Dist. Bookthrift. Bib. p. 141.

[VPRE-390]   Fitzwilliam Museum. *Rembrandt and His Circle*. Exhibition, Fitzwilliam Museum, Cambridge, February to June 1966. Cambridge: Fitzwilliam Museum, 1966. 72 pp. Bib. pp. 8-11.

[VPRE-400] Fleischer, Roland E., and Susan Scott Munshower, eds. *The Age of Rembrandt: Studies in Seventeenth-Century Dutch Painting*. Papers in Art History from the Pennsylvania State University, vol. 3. [University Park, Pa.]: Pennsylvania State University, 1988. 245 pp. Bibs.

[VPRE-410]   Fowkes, Charles. *The Life of Rembrandt*. London; New York: Hamlyn, 1978. Bib. p. 140.

[VPRE-420]   Fredericksen, Burton B., and Richard Kubiak. *Etchings of Rembrandt and His Followers: A Selection from the Robert Engel Family Collection: Catalogue*. Exhibition, Santa Barbara Museum of Art, 1 September to 5 October 1977. [Malibu, Calif.]: J. Paul Getty Museum, 1977. Bib. pp. 51-52.

[VPRE-430]   Fuchs, Rudolf Herman. *Rembrandt in Amsterdam*. Greenwich, Conn.: New York Graphic Society, 1968. 80 pp. Bib. refs.

[VPRE-440]   Gerson, H[orst]. *Rembrandt Paintings*. Trans. *Rembrandt Gemalde*. London: Weidenfeld and Nicolson; New York: Harrison House; New York: Reynal and Co., 1968. Bib. pp. 505-509.

[VPRE-450]   Giltaij, Jeroen. *The Drawings by Rembrandt and His School in the Museum Boymansvan Beuningen, Rotterdam, 1988*. Trans. *Tekeningen van Rembrandt en zijn School*. Rotterdam: Museum Boymansvan Beuningen, 1988. Dist. Thames and Hudson, London. Bib. refs. pp. 332-345.

[VPRE-460]   Goldscheider, Ludwig. *Rembrandt: Paintings, Drawings and Etchings: The Three Early Biographies*. 2nd ed. London:

Phaidon Press, 1964. 207 pp. Bib. refs.

[VPRE-470] Gregory, John, and Irena Zdanowicz. *Rembrandt in the Collections of the National Gallery of Victoria.* Robert Raynor Publications in Prints and Drawings, no. 2. Melbourne: National Gallery of Victoria, 1988. Bib. refs. pp. 155-156.

[VPRE-480] Grigsby, Thea. *Rembrandt, Master Etcher: Selections from Texas Collections.* Austin: The Art Museum, University of Texas at Austin, 1979. 96 pp. Bib. refs.

[VPRE-490] Guillaud, Maurice, and Jacqueline Guillaud. *Rembrandt: The Human Form and Spirit.* New York: C. N. Potter, 1986. Bib. p. 676.

[VPRE-500] Haak, B. *Rembrandt Drawings.* Trans. *Rembrandt.* Woodstock: Overlook Press; London: Thames and Hudson, 1976. Bib. pp. 222-223.

[VPRE-510] ------. *Rembrandt: His Life, His Work, His Time.* [Trans. Elizabeth Willems-Treeman]. Trans. *Rembrandt, Zijn Leven, Zijn Werk, Zijn Tijd.* New York: Harry N. Abrams, [1969]. Bib. pp. 337-340. Also titled *Rembrandt: His Life, Work and Times.* London: Thames and Hudson, 1969. Bib. pp. 337-338.

[VPRE-520] ------. *Rembrandt, Life and Work.* Trans. *Rembrandt, Leben und Werk.* Woodbury, N.Y.: Barron's Educational Series, Inc., 1981. Bib. pp. 106-107.

[VPRE-530] Haeger, Barbara Joan. "The Religious Significance of Rembrandt's Return of the Prodigal Son: An Examination of the Picture in the Context of the Visual and Iconographic Tradition." Ph.D. Thesis, University of Michigan, 1983. Bib. refs. pp. 254-262.

[VPRE-540] Halewood, William H. *Six Subjects of Reformation Art: A Preface to Rembrandt.* Toronto; Buffalo: University of Toronto Press, 1982. 153 pp. Bib. refs.

[VPRE-550] Harcourt, Glenn Robert. "The Representation of Religious Knowledge in the Work of Rembrandt and His Pupil Gerard Dou." Ph.D. Thesis, University of California, Berkeley, May 1990. Bib. pp. 308-316.

[VPRE-560] Haverkamp Begemann, Egbert. *Rembrandt, The Nightwatch.* Princeton: Princeton University Press, 1982. Bib. pp. 115-132.

[VPRE-570] Heckscher, William S. *Rembrandt's Anatomy of Dr. Nicolaas*

522

Tulp: An Iconological Study. [New York]: New York University Press, 1958. 283 pp. Bib. pp. 193-217.

[VPRE-580] Held, Julius Samuel. *Rembrandt and the Book of Tobit.* [Northampton, Mass.]: Gehenna Press, 1964. 33 pp.

[VPRE-590] ------. *Rembrandt's Aristotle, and Other Rembrandt Studies.* Princeton: Princeton University Press, 1969. 155 pp. Bib. footnotes.

[VPRE-600] ------. *Rembrandt Studies.* Princeton: Princeton University Press, 1990. 211 pp. Bib. refs.

[VPRE-610] Hijmans, Willem, Luitsen Kuiper, and Annemarie Vels Heijn. *Rembrandt's Nightwatch: The History of a Painting.* Trans. *Rembrandt's Nachtwacht.* Alphen aan den Rijn: A. W. Sijthoff, 1978. Bib. p. 124.

[VPRE-620] Hind, Arthur Mayger. *A Catalogue of Rembrandt's Etchings, Chronologically Arranged and Completely Illustrated.* 2 vols. New York: Da Capo Press, 1967. Bib. Vol. 1, pp. 3-10.

[VPRE-630] Hoekstra, Hidde, ed. *Rembrandt and the Bible: Stories from the Old and New Testament, Illustrated by Rembrandt in Paintings, Etchings and Drawings.* Trans. T. Langham and P. Peters. [Weert, Netherlands]: Magna Books, 1990. 480 pp. Bib. p. 446. Also listed by shorter title, *Rembrandt and the Bible*.

[VPRE-640] Hoppenbrouwers, René. *Rembrandt.* New York: Arch Cape Press, 1990. 99 pp. Bib. refs.

[VPRE-650] Huys Janssen, Paul, and Werner Sumowski. *The Hoogsteder Exhibition of Rembrandt's Academy.* Exhibition, 4 February to 2 May 1992. [Brussels]: The Hague, Hoogsteder and Hoogsteder; Zwolle: Waanders Publishers, 1992. Bib. refs. p. 29.

[VPRE-660] Judson, J[ay] Richard, and Egbert Haverkamp Begemann. *Rembrandt After Three Hundred Years: An Exhibition of Rembrandt and His Followers.* [Chicago]: Art Institute of Chicago, 1969. 280 pp. Bib. refs.

[VPRE-670] Kahr, Madlyn Millner. *Dutch Painting in the Seventeenth Century.* 2nd ed. New York: IconEditions, 1993. Bib. refs. pp. 309-314.

[VPRE-680] Kanba, Nobuyuki, and Tatsuji Omori. *In Darkness and Light: A Rembrandt in Tokyo Reconsidered.* Tokyo: Bridgestone Museum of Art, Ishibashi Foundation, 1989. 159 pp. Bib.

pp. 99-121.

[VPRE-690] Kitson, Michael. *Rembrandt*. 3rd ed. Oxford: Phaidon Press, 1982. Bib. p. 97. London: Phaidon Press, 1992. 126 pp. Bib. p. 27.

[VPRE-700] Landsberger, Franz. *Rembrandt, the Jews and the Bible*. 2nd ed. Philadelphia: Jewish Publications Society of America, 1962. Reprint. 1967. 190 pp. Bib. pp. 183-187.

[VPRE-710] Le Bot, Marc. *Rembrandt*. Vaduz, Liechtenstein: Bonfini Press, 1980. Reprint. New York: Crown Publishers, 1990. Bib. refs. pp. 92-94.

[VPRE-720] Lecaldano, Paolo, and Gregory Martin, eds. *The Complete Paintings of Rembrandt*. Classics of World Art. Trans. *L'opera pittorica completa di Rembrandt*. New York: Harry N. Abrams, 1969. Reprint. London: Weidenfeld and Nicolson, 1973. 143 pp. Bib. p. 82.

[VPRE-730] Levitin, E[vgenii] S[emenovich]. *Rembrandt: Etchings*. Pushkin Museum of Fine Arts, Moscow. Rev. ed. Leningrad: Aurora Art Publishers, 1985. Bib. p. 239.

[VPRE-740] Ludwig, Emil. *Three Titans*. (Michelangelo, Rembrandt, and Beethoven). New York: G. P. Putnam's Sons, 1930. 363 pp.

[VPRE-750] Mayor, A. Hyatt. *Rembrandt and the Bible*. New York: Metropolitan Museum of Art, 1979. 52 pp.

[VPRE-760] Mee, Charles L., Jr. *Rembrandt's Portrait: A Biography*. New York: Simon and Schuster, 1988. Bib. pp. 314-317.

[VPRE-770] Muller, Joseph-Emile. *Rembrandt*. World of Art Library. New York: Harry N. Abrams; London: Thames and Hudson, 1968. Reprint. London: Thames and Hudson, 1975. Bib. p. 271.

[VPRE-780] Murray, John Joseph. *Amsterdam in the Age of Rembrandt*. Centers of Civilization Series, no. 21. Norman: University of Oklahoma Press, 1967. Reprint. Newton Abbot: David and Charles, 1972. 194 pp. Bib. refs. pp. 176-177.

[VPRE-790] Nash, John Malcolm. *The Age of Rembrandt and Vermeer: Dutch Painting in the Seventeenth Century*. 2nd ed. Oxford: Phaidon Press, 1979. Dist. E. P. Dutton and Co., New York. Bib. refs. p. 265.

[VPRE-800] Nordenfalk, Carl Adam Johan. *The Batavians' Oath of Alle-*

524

giance: *Rembrandt's Only Monumental Painting.* Stockholm: Nationalmuseum, 1982. Bib. pp. 53-55.

[VPRE-810] Nouwen, Henri J. *Return of the Prodigal Son.* N.p.: Doubleday, 1992.

[VPRE-820] Ornstein-Van Slooten, E[va], Marijke Holtrop, and Peter Schatborn. *The Rembrandt House: The Prints, Drawings, and Paintings.* Zwolle: Waanders Publishers; Amsterdam: Museum Het Rembrandthuis, 1991. Bib. refs. pp. 175-176.

[VPRE-830] Partsch, Susanna. *Rembrandt.* Trans. from German. London: Weidenfeld and Nicolson, 1991. Bib. pp. 196-197.

[VPRE-840] Perlove, Shelley, and Robert Baldwin. *Impressions of Faith: Rembrandt's Biblical Etchings.* Exhibition. Dearborn, Mich.: University of Michigan, Dearborn, Mardigian Library, 1989. Bib. pp. 79-80.

[VPRE-850] Puppi, Lionello, and Pearl Sanders. *Rembrandt.* 1969. Reprint. New York: Thames and Hudson, 1989. 119 pp. Bib. pp. 31-35.

[VPRE-860] Purdue University Galleries. *Old Students and Old Masters: The School of Rembrandt: Selections from the Bader Collection: Union Gallery, Purdue University, West Lafayette, Indiana, October 9-30, 1980.* West Lafayette, Ind.: Purdue University Galleries, 1980. 47 pp. Bib. refs.

[VPRE-870] Rand, Richard, and Joseph Fronek. *The Raising of Lazarus by Rembrandt.* Exhibition, Los Angeles County Museum of Art, 17 October 1991 to 12 January 1992. Los Angeles: Los Angeles County Museum of Art, 1991. Bib. p. 39.

[VPRE-880] Rembrandt Harmenszoon van Rijn. *Rembrandt Bible Drawings: 60 Works.* New York: Dover Publications, 1979. 62 pp.

[VPRE-890] *Rembrandt Harmensz van Rijn: Paintings from Soviet Museums.* 5th ed. Leningrad: Arora Art Publishers, 1987. 76 pp. Bibs. refs.

[VPRE-900] Ripley, Elizabeth. *Rembrandt: A Biography.* New York: H. Z. Walck, 1955. Bib. p. 71.

[VPRE-910] Roger-Marx, Claude. *Rembrandt.* New York: Universe Books, 1960. Reprint. 1972. Bib. refs. pp. 353-356.

[VPRE-920] Rosenberg, Jakob. *Rembrandt: Life and Work.* 4th ed. Oxford: Phaidon Press, 1980. Bib. pp. 367-381. Rev. ed. Ithaca: Cornell University Press, 1989. Bib. pp. 367-369.

[VPRE-930] Royalton-Kisch, Martin. *Drawings by Rembrandt and His Circle in the British Museum*. Exhibition, British Museum, 26 March to 4 August 1992. London: British Museum Press, 1992. Bib. refs. pp. 230-238.

[VPRE-940] Rubinstein, Michael. *Rembrandt and Angels*. Tunbridge Wells, Kent, England: Institute for Cultural Research, 1982. 47 pp. Bib. refs.

[VPRE-950] Scheidig, Walther, and Margaret Playle. *Rembrandt's Drawings*. Boston: Boston Book and Art Shop, 1965. Bib. pp. 277-278.

[VPRE-960] Schneider, Cynthia P. *Rembrandt's Landscapes: Drawings and Prints*. Exhibition, National Gallery of Art, 11 March to 20 May 1990. Washington, D.C.: National Gallery of Art, 1990. Dist. Bulfinch Press, Boston. Bib. pp. 283-300. New Haven: Yale University Press, 1990. Bib. pp. 255-276.

[VPRE-970] Schupbach, William. *The Paradox of Rembrandt's "Anatomy of Dr. Tulp"*. London: Wellcome Institute for the History of Medicine, 1982. 131 pp. Bib. refs.

[VPRE-980] Schwartz, Gary. *Rembrandt: All the Etchings Reproduced in True Size*. Netherlands: Maarssen, 1977. 19 pp., 101 leaves of plates.

[VPRE-990] ------. *Rembrandt: His Life, His Paintings: A New Biography with all Accessible Paintings Illustrated in Colour*. Trans. *Rembrandt; Zijn Leven, Zijn Schilderijen*. New York: Viking, 1985. Reprint. London; New York: Penguin Books, 1991. Bib. 372-374.

[VPRE-1000] Silver, Larry. *Rembrandt*. [New York]: Rizzoli International Publications, 1992. Bib. refs.

[VPRE-1010] Slatkes, Leonard J. *Rembrandt and Persia*. New Horizon Series. New York: Abaris Books, 1983. Bib. pp. 148-158.

[VPRE-1020] Slive, Seymour. *Drawings of Rembrandt: With a Selection of Drawings by his Pupils and Followers*. New York: Dover Publications, 1965. xxvii, 300 pp. Bib. refs. pp. xvii-xviii.

[VPRE-1030] ------. *Rembrandt and His Critics, 1630-1730*. The Hague: M. Nijhoff, 1953. Reprint. New York: Hacker Art Books, 1988. 240 pp., 32 pp. of plates. Bib. refs.

[VPRE-1040] Snite Museum of Art. *Rembrandt Etchings from a Private Collection: Biblical Subjects, the Old and the New Testaments: January 18 to March 29 [1981]*. South Bend, Ind.:

Snite Museum of Art, University of Notre Dame, 1981. 49 pp. Bib. refs.

[VPRE-1050] Starcky, Emmanuel. *Rembrandt*. Trans. from French. New York: Portland House; London: Studio Editions, 1990. Bib. p. 144.

[VPRE-1060] Stearns, Monroe. *Rembrandt and His World*. New York: F. Watts, 1967. Bib. pp. 206-209.

[VPRE-1070] Strauss, Walter L., and Marjon van der Meulen. *The Rembrandt Documents*. New York: Abaris Books, 1979. Bib. pp. 633-652.

[VPRE-1080] Theodore B. Donson, Ltd. *Rembrandt, Fifty Exceptional Etchings: [Proofs Printed by the Master]: Fall Exhibition November 11--December 31, 1981, Theodore B. Donson Ltd.* New York: Theodore B. Donson, Ltd., 1981. 84 pp. Bib. refs.

[VPRE-1090] Tumpel, Christian, and Astrid Tumpel. *Rembrandt*. Trans. Antwerp: Fonds Mercator, 1986. Bib. pp. 387-396.

[VPRE-1100] Van Rijn, Rembrandt. *Rembrandt Bible Drawings*. Fine Art Library. [New York?]: Dover Publications, 1980. 64 pp.

[VPRE-1110] Visser't Hooft, Willem Adolph. *Rembrandt and the Gospel*. Trans. K. Gregor Smith. Trans. *Rembrandts Weg zum Evangelium*. Philadelphia: Westminster Press, 1958. Reprint. New York: Meridian Books, 1960. 192 pp.

[VPRE-1120] Vries, A[ry] B[ob] de. *Rembrandt*. Baarn, Holland: World's Window, 1956. Bib. p. 77.

[VPRE-1130] Vries, A[ry] B[ob], Magdi Toth-Ubbens, and W. Froentjes. *Rembrandt in the Mauritshuis [The Hague, Netherlands]: An Interdisciplinary Study*. Alphen aan den Rijn: Sijthoff and Noordhoff, 1978. 223 pp. Bib. refs.

[VPRE-1140] Waal, H[enri] van de, and Rudolf Herman Fuchs, eds. *Steps Towards Rembrandt: Collected Articles 1937-1972*. Amsterdam: North-Holland, 1974. 292 pp. Bib. refs.

[VPRE-1150] Wallace, Robert. *The World of Rembrandt, 1606-1669*. Rev. ed. New York: Time-Life Books, 1979. Bib. p. 183.

[VPRE-1160] Walsh, Jean, H. Perry Chapman, Halla Beloff, and Michael Franken. *Rembrandt by Himself*. Exhibition. Glasgow: Glasgow Museums and Art Galleries, 1990. Bib. p. 47.

[VPRE-1170]   White, Christopher. *Rembrandt.* New York: Thames and Hudson, 1984. Bib. pp. 213-214.

[VPRE-1180]   ------. *Rembrandt as an Etcher: A Study of the Artist at Work.* 2 vols. University Park: Pennsylvania State University Press; London: A. Zwemmer, Ltd., 1969. Bib. refs. in footnotes.

[VPRE-1190]   White, Christopher, David S. Alexander, and Ellen D'Oench. *Rembrandt in Eighteenth Century England.* Exhibition. [New Haven]: Yale Center for British Art, 1983. 181 pp. Bib. refs.

[VPRE-1200]   White, Christopher, and Karel G. Boon. *Rembrandt's Etchings: An Illustrated Critical Catalogue.* 2 vols. Amsterdam: Van Gendt; New York: Abner Schram, 1969.

[VPRE-1210]   Williams, Gloria. *Rembrandt Etchings in the Norton Simon Museum.* Exhibition, Norton Simon Museum, 30 January to 6 September 1992. Pasadena, Calif.: Norton Simon Museum, 1991. Bib. refs. p. 57.

[VPRE-1220]   Wright, Christopher. *Rembrandt and His Art.* London; New York: Hamlyn; Northbrook, Ill.: Book Value International, 1975. Bib. p. 128.

[VPRE-1230]   ------. *Rembrandt: Self-Portraits.* London: G. Fraser, 1982. Bib. p. 133.

Peter Paul Rubens

Aside from being the most prominent and prolific Flemish painter of the seventeenth century, Peter Paul Rubens was also a prominent artist of religious subjects. Many of his paintings, drawings, and tapestries remain as some of the best art yet produced on Christian themes. Research into Rubens' work is greatly helped by two bibliographies, the most recent being produced by RILA [VPRU-010], and the next most recent being compiled by Margit Hoffman [VPRU-020]. Aside from these sources, one will also find assistance in the bibliographies and general works listed in the opening three sections of Chapter 12.

Studies of Rubens' life include a variety of biographies and historical works treating his era. Christopher White's biography, *Peter Paul Rubens: Man and Artist* [VPRU-740], is the most recent study of Rubens' life by a major art critic. Other helpful biographies include [VPRU-090], [VPRU-230], [VPRU-420], [VPRU-430], [VPRU-480], and [VPRU-700]. For studies which help place Rubens in the context of his time and era, see [VPRU-080] about his patron, [VPRU-280] about his involvement in the Counter Reformation, and the following works treating his circle of colleagues and his historical significance: [VPRU-050], [VPRU-340], [VPRU-370], [VPRU-390], [VPRU-500], [VPRU-520], [VPRU-590], [VPRU-620], [VPRU-630], [VPRU-710], [VPRU-720].

Rubens' works can be divided into three major categories: drawings and illustrations, paintings (including the oil sketches), and tapestries. For the study of his drawings and book illustrations, see [VPRU-140], [VPRU-320], [VPRU-330], [VPRU-400], [VPRU-530], [VPRU-570], [VPRU-580], and [VPRU-730]. To study his paintings, see [VPRU-100], [VPRU-170], [VPRU-290], [VPRU-300], [VPRU-310], [VPRU-350], [VPRU-380], [VPRU-410], [VPRU-640], [VPRU-650], [VPRU-660], and [VPRU-680]. Among his paintings also note studies of the subcategories of Bacchanals [VPRU-060] and [VPRU-160]; costume [VPRU-110]; decorations [VPRU-040] and [VPRU-440]; gems and coins and other antiques [VPRU-180], [VPRU-470], and [VPRU-510]; hunting [VPRU-070]; landscapes [VPRU-030] and [VPRU-670]; and women [VPRU-210]. For specialized studies of his religious subjects, also note the following topics treated below: altars [VPRU-450], Christ [VPRU-270], Old Testament [VPRU-360], and saints [VPRU-690]. For studies of Rubens' tapestries, see [VPRU-220], [VPRU-540], [VPRU-550], and [VPRU-610].

The remainder of texts listed below consist of a variety of general texts treating a wide range of topics related to Rubens and his work. One of the most noteworthy of these is Charles Scribner's study, *Peter Paul Rubens* [VPRU-600]. The following general works are also helpful: [VPRU-120], [VPRU-130], [VPRU-150], [VPRU-190], [VPRU-200], [VPRU-240], [VPRU-250], [VPRU-260], [VPRU-460], and [VPRU-560]. Finally, note a collection of symposium papers [VPRU-750] which will prove useful in rounding out one's studies of Rubens and his work. For additional information on Rubens, see the general category on painting given above.

Special Bibliographies

[VPRU-010]   DIALOG Information Services. *Peter Paul Rubens: A Bibliography, 1975-1986.* N.p.: RILA, 1987. 125 pp.

[VPRU-020]   Hoffman, Margit. *The Rubens Year 1977: A Bibliography.* Stockholm: Society of History of Art, 1979. 45 pp. Supplement to *Konsthistorisk Tidskrift,* 1979:2, Art Review.

Key Works

[VPRU-030]   Adler, Wolfgang. *Landscapes.* Corpus Rubenianum Ludwig Burchard, part 18, vol. 1. London: Harvey Miller; New York: Oxford University Press, 1982. 376 pp. Bib. refs.

[VPRU-040]   Alpers, Svetlana. *The Decoration of the Torre de la Parada.* Corpus Rubeninum Ludwig Burchard, part 9. Brussels: Arcade Press; London; New York: Phaidon Press, 1971. Dist. Frederick A. Praeger Publishers. 386 pp. Bib. refs. pp. 11-15.

[VPRU-050]   Avermaete, Roger. *Rubens and His Times.* Trans. *Rubens et son temps.* South Brunswick: A. S. Barnes; London: Allen and Unwin, 1968. 218 pp.

[VPRU-060]   *Bacchanals by Titian and Rubens, The.* Exhibition, Nationalmuseum, 18 March to 17 May 1987. Stockholm: Nationalmuseum, 1987. 114 pp. Bib. refs.

[VPRU-070]   Balis, Arnout. *Rubens Hunting Scenes.* Trans. from Dutch. Corpus Rubenianum Ludwig Burchard, part 18, vol. 2. London: Harvey Miller, 1985. 406 pp.

[VPRU-080]   Baudouin, Frans. *Nicolaas Rockox, Friend and Patron of Peter Paul Rubens.* 2nd ed. Antwerp: KB, 1984. Bib. pp. 47-48.

[VPRU-090]   ------. *Pietro Pauolo Rubens.* New York: Harry N. Abrams; Antwerp: Mercatorfonds, 1977. Reprint. New York: Portland House, 1989. 405 pp. Bib. refs. pp. 365-385.

[VPRU-100]   Baumstark, Reinhold. *Peter Paul Rubens: The Decius Mus Cycle.* Collections of the Prince of Liechtenstein. [New York]: Metropolitan Museum of Art, 1985. 63 pp. Bib. p. 12.

[VPRU-110]   Belkin, Kristin Lohse. *The Costume Book.* Corpus Rubenianum Ludwig Burchard, part 24. Brussels: Arcade, 1980. 208 pp., 120 pp. of plates. Bib. pp. 15-20.

[VPRU-120] Braham, Allan. *Rubens*. Themes and Painters in the National Gallery, no. 8. London: National Gallery, 1972. 52 pp. Bib. refs.

[VPRU-130] Brown University, Department of Art. *Rubenism: An Exhibition by the Department of Art, Brown University, and the Museum of Art, Rhode Island School of Design, Bell Gallery, List Art Building, Brown University, Providence, Rhode Island, January 30 Through February 23, 1975*. Providence, R.I.: Department of Art, Brown University, 1975. Bib. pp. 274-275.

[VPRU-140] Burchard, Ludwig, and Roger Adolf d' Hulst. *Rubens Drawings*. 2 vols. Brussels: Arcade Press, 1963.

[VPRU-150] Cabanne, Pierre. *Rubens*. World of Art Library. London: Thames and Hudson; New York: Tudor Publishing Co., 1967. Bib. refs. pp. 274-276.

[VPRU-160] Cavalli-Bjorkman, Gorel. *Bacchanals by Titian and Rubens: Papers given at a Symposium in Nationalmuseum, Stockholm, March 18-19, 1987*. Nationalmusei Skriftserie, no. 10. Stockholm: Nationalmusuem, 1987. 166 pp. Bib. refs.

[VPRU-170] Daugherty, Frances P. "The Self-Portraits of Peter Paul Rubens: Some Problems in Iconography." Thesis, University of North Carolina at Chapel Hill, 1976. 565 pp. Bib. pp. 354-384.

[VPRU-180] De Grummond, Nancy Thomson. "Rubens and Antique Coins and Gems." Thesis, University of North Carolina, Chapel Hill, 1968. Bib. pp. 258-264.

[VPRU-190] Dobrzycka, Anna. *Rubens*. Warszawa: Arkady, 1960. 66 pp. Bib.

[VPRU-200] Downes, Kerry. *Rubens*. London: Jupiter Books, 1980. Bib. pp. 167-169.

[VPRU-210] Druker, Lisa Rosenthal. "Seduction and its Consequences: The Representation of Gender in the Early Work of Peter Paul Rubens." Ph.D. Thesis, University of California, Berkeley, 1990. Bib. refs. pp. 257-280. (See [FAT-170])

[VPRU-220] Dudon, David T. *Tapestries from the Samuel H. Kress Collections at the Philadelphia Museum of Art; The History of Constantine the Great, Designed by Peter Paul Rubens and*

Pietro da Cortona. Catalog. [London]: Phaidon Press for Samuel H. Kress Foundation, 1964. Bib. pp. 147-148.

[VPRU-230] Edwards, Samuel. *Peter Paul Rubens: A Biography of a Giant*. New York: D. McKay Co., 1973. Bib. p. 240.

[VPRU-240] Farmer, John David, and Birmingham Museum of Art. *Rubens and Humanism: Birmingham Museum of Art, April 15--May 28, 1978*. [Birmingham, Ala.]: The Museum, 1978. 68 pp. Bib. refs.

[VPRU-250] Fletcher, Jennifer. *Peter Paul Rubens*. London; New York: Phaidon Press, 1969. 90 pp. Bib. p. 29.

[VPRU-260] ------. *Rubens*. Great Artists Collection, vol. 10. London: Encyclopaedia Britannica, 1968. Reprint. 1971. 48 pp. Bib. p. 21.

[VPRU-270] Freedberg, David. *Rubens: The Life of Christ after the Passion*. Corpus Rubenianum Ludwig Burchard, part 7. London: H. Miller; New York: Oxford University Press, 1984. 425 pp. Bib. refs.

[VPRU-280] Glen, Thomas L. *Rubens and the Counter Reformation: Studies in His Religious Paintings Between 1609-1620*. Outstanding Dissertations in the Fine Arts Series. New York: Garland Publishing, 1977. Bib. pp. 294-308.

[VPRU-290] Goodman, Elise. *Rubens: The Garden of Love as Conversatie a la mode*. Oculi, vol. 4. Amsterdam; Philadelphia: Benjamins Publishing Co., 1992. 199 pp., 66 pp. of plates. Bib. pp. 113-120.

[VPRU-300] Haverkamp Begemann, Egbert. *The Achilles Series*. Corpus Rubenianum Ludwig Burchard, part 10. London: Phaidon Press; Brussels: Arcade Press, 1975. 157 pp., 87 pp. of plates. Bib. pp. 7-11.

[VPRU-310] Held, Julius Samuel. *The Oil Sketches of Peter Paul Rubens: A Critical Catalogue*. 2 vols. Princeton: Princeton University Press, 1980. Bib. vol. 1, pp. 649-672.

[VPRU-320] ------. *Rubens and the Book: Title Pages by Peter Paul Rubens: An Exhibition at Chapin Library, Stetson Hall, May 2-31, 1977*. Williamstown, Mass.: Williams College, 1977. 307 pp. Bib. refs.

[VPRU-330] ------. *Rubens--Selected Drawings*. Rev. ed. Mt. Kisco, N.Y.: Moyer Bell Ltd., 1986. Bib. p. 284.

532

[VPRU-340] Held, Julius Samuel, Anne W. Lowenthal, David Rosand, and John Walsh. *Rubens and His Circle: Studies*. Princeton: Princeton University Press, 1982. xxiv, 207 pp., 36 leaves of plates. Bib. refs.

[VPRU-350] Huemer, Frances. *Portraits*.   Corpus Rubenianum Ludwig Burchard, part 19, vol. 1.   New York: Phaidon Press; London: H. Miller, 1977. Dist. Frederick A. Praeger Publishers. Bib. refs.

[VPRU-360] Hulst, Roger Adolf d', and M. Vandenven. *Rubens: The Old Testament*. Corpus Rubenianum Ludwig Burchard, pt. 3. H. Miller; Oxford University Press, 1989. 402 pp. Bib. refs. pp. 10-17.

[VPRU-370] Jaffe, David. *Esso Presents Rubens and the Italian Renaissance: Exhibition*. Canberra: Australian National Gallery, 1992. Bib. pp. 195-198.

[VPRU-380] ------. *Rubens' Self-Portrait in Focus: 13 August--30 October 1988, Australian National Gallery, Canberra*.   Brisbane: Boolarong, 1988. 63 pp. Bibs.

[VPRU-390] Jaffe, Michael. *Rubens and Italy*. Ithaca: Cornell University Press; Oxford: Phaidon Press, 1977. Bib. pp. 121-123.

[VPRU-400] Judson, J[ay] Richard, and C[arl] van de Velde. *Book Illustrations and Title-Pages*. 2 vols. Corpus Rubenianum Ludwig Burchard, part 21. Brussels: Arcade Press, 1977. Dist. Heyden, Philadelphia. Bib. refs.

[VPRU-410] Koninklijk Museum voor Schone Kunsten (Belgium). *P. P. Rubens: Catalogue, Paintings, Oil Sketches*. Antwerp: Blonde Artprinting International, 1990. Bib. refs. p. 102.

[VPRU-420] Lepore, Mario. *The Life and Times of Rubens*. Feltham; New York: Hamlyn, 1970. 75 pp.

[VPRU-430] Lescourret, Marie-Anne. *Rubens: A Double Life*. Chicago: I. R. Dee, 1993. Bib. refs.

[VPRU-440] Martin, James Rupert. *The Decorations for the Pompa Introitus Ferdinanadi*. Corpus Rubenianum Ludwig Burchard, pt. 16. Brussels: Arcade Press; London; New York: Phaidon Press, 1972. 278 pp. Bib. refs.

[VPRU-450] Martin, John Rupert. *Rubens: The Antwerp Altarpieces: The Raising of the Cross and the Descent from the Cross*. Critical Studies in Art History. London: Thames and Hudson, 1969. Norton Critical Studies in Art History. New York:

W. W. Norton Co., 1969. Bib. pp. 131-132.

[VPRU-460]   ------, ed. *Rubens Before 1620.* [Princeton]: Art Museum, Princeton University, 1972. Dist. Princeton University Press. 186 pp. Bib. refs.

[VPRU-470]   Meulen, Jarjon van der. *Petrus Paulus Rubens Antiquarius: Collector and Copyist of Antique Gems.* Alphen aan den Rijn: Vis-Druk; Canaletto, 1975. Bib. pp. 188-196.

[VPRU-480]   Micheletti, Emma. *Rubens: The Life and Work of the Artist Illustrated with 80 Colour Plates.* Trans. Firmin O'Sullivan. New York: Thames and Hudson, 1968. Reprint. 1989. 39 pp., 80 pp. of plates. Bib. refs.

[VPRU-490]   Millen, Ronald, and Robert Erich Wolf. *Heroic Deeds and Mystic Figures: A New Reading of Rubens' Life of Maria de' Medici.* Princeton: Princeton University Press, 1989. Bib. pp. 244-248.

[VPRU-500]   Morford, Mark P. O. *Stoics and Neostoics: Rubens and the Circle of Lipsius.* Princeton: Princeton University Press, 1991. Bib. refs. pp. 225-235.

[VPRU-510]   Muller, Jeffrey M. *Rubens: The Artist as Collector.* Princeton: Princeton University Press, 1989. 185 pp., 136 pp. of plates. Bib. pp. 157-169.

[VPRU-520]   *Old Masters, The: Peter Paul Rubens, Frans Hals, Rembrandt van Rijn, Johannes Vermeer.* Ref. ed. Great Artists of the Western World, vol. 3. London; New York: Marshall Cavendish, 1990. Bib. p. 139.

[VPRU-530]   P. & D. Colnaghi and Co. *Rubens and His Engravers: An Exhibition November 22--December 10, 1977.* London: P. & D. Colnaghi and Co., 1977. 88 pp. Bib. p. 3.

[VPRU-540]   Philadelphia Museum of Art. *Catalogue of the Exhibition: Constantine the Great: First Public Exhibition of all Major Panels of the Tapestries from the Barberini Palace, Rome, given to the Philadelphia Museum of Art by the Samuel H. Kress Foundation, the Designs by Peter Paul Rubens and Pietro da Cortona, Lent by European and American Collections.* Philadelphia: The Museum, 1964. 99 pp. Bib. refs.

[VPRU-550]   Poorter, Nora de. *The Eucharist Series.* 2 vols. Corpus Rubenianum Ludwig Burchard, part 2. London: Harvey Miller; Philadelphia: Heyden, 1978. Bib. vol. 1, pp. 13-19.

[VPRU-560]   Puyvelde, Leo van. *Rubens.* Brusseles: Meddens, 1977. Bib. p.

534

178.

[VPRU-570] Rowlands, John. *Rubens: Drawings and Sketches: Catalogue of an Exhibition at the Department of Prints and Drawings in the British Museum, 1977.* London: British Museum Publications, Ltd., 1977. 173 pp. Bib. p. 19.

[VPRU-580] Royal Museum of Fine Arts (Amsterdam). *P. P. Rubens: Paintings--Oilsketches--Drawings, 29th June--30th September 1977.* Antwerp: Royal Museum of Fine Arts, 1977. xxiv, 388 pp. Bib. refs.

[VPRU-590] Saward, Susan. *The Golden Age of Marie de' Medici.* Studies in Baroque Art History, no. 2. Epping: R. R. Bowker, 1982. Bib. pp. 297-301.

[VPRU-600] Scribner, Charles. *Peter Paul Rubens.* New York: Harry N. Abrams, 1989. Bib. refs. p. 128.

[VPRU-610] ------. *The Triumph of the Eucharist: Tapestries Designed by Rubens.* Studies in Baroque Art History. Ann Arbor: UMI Research Press, 1982. Bib. pp. 213-218.

[VPRU-620] Stampfle, Felice, and Pierpont Morgan Library. *Rubens and Rembrandt in Their Century: Flemish and Dutch Drawings of the 17th Century from the Pierpont Morgan Library.* New York: The Library, 1978. 298 pp.

[VPRU-630] Stella, Frank. *Working Space.* Charles Eliot Norton Lectures: 1983-1984. Cambridge, Mass.: Harvard University Press, 1986. 177 pp.

[VPRU-640] Strong, Roy C. *Britannia Triumphans: Inigo Jones, Rubens, and Whitehall Palace.* Walter Neurath Memorial Lectures, no. 12. New York; [London]: Thames and Hudson, 1980. 72 pp. Bib. refs.

[VPRU-650] Thuillier, Jacques, and Jacques Foucart. *Rubens' Life of Marie de Medici.* Trans. *Le storie di Maria de' Medici di Rubens al Lussemburgo.* New York: Harry N. Abrams, 1967. Bib. pp. 155-156.

[VPRU-660] Varshavskaia, M. Ia., and K[seniia] S[ergeevna] Egorova. *Peter Paul Rubens: Paintings from Soviet Museums.* Trans. from Russian. Leningrad: Aurora Art Publishers, 1989. 206 pp. Bib. refs.

[VPRU-670] Vergara, Lisa. *Rubens and the Poetics of Landscape.* New Haven: Yale University Press, 1982. Bib. pp. 197-203.

[VPRU-680]   Vlieghe, Hans. *Rubens Portraits of Identified Sitters Painted in Antwerp.* Trans. *De schilder Rubens.* Corpus Rubenianum Ludwig Burchard, part 19, vol. 2. London: Harvey Miller, 1987. 400 pp. Bib.

[VPRU-690]   ------. *Saints.* 2 vols. Corpus Rubenianium Ludwig Burchard, part 8. Brussels: Arcade Press, 1972. Bib. refs.

[VPRU-700]   Warnke, Martin. *Peter Paul Rubens: Life and Work.* Woodbury, N.Y.:   Barron's Educational Series,(1980.   022 pp. Bib. pp. 187-190.

[VPRU-710]   Wedgwood, C[icely] V[eronica]. *The Political Career of Peter Paul Rubens.* Walter Neurath Memorial Lectures, no. 7. London: Thames and Hudson, 1975. Bib. p. 62.

[VPRU-720]   ------. *The World of Rubens, 1577-1640.* Rev. ed. Alexandria, Va.: Time-Life Books, 1981. Reprint. Amsterdam: Time-Life Books, 1982. Bib. p. 187.

[VPRU-730]   Whistler, Catherine, Jeremy Wood, and James Byam Shaw. *Rubens in Oxford: An Exhibition of Drawings from Christ Church and the Ashmolean Museum: The Picture Gallery, Christ Church, Oxford, 25th April--20th May 1988 . . . P. & D. Colnaghi and Co. Ltd. London, 26th May--18th June 1988.* London: P. & D. Colnaghi and Co., 1988. Bib. pp. 99-100.

[VPRU-740]   White, Christopher. *Peter Paul Rubens: Man and Artist.* New Haven: Yale University Press, 1987. Bib. pp. 302-306.

[VPRU-750]   Wilson, William Harry, Wendy McFarland, Frances Huemer, Kristi Ann Nelson, and Nancy Thomson De Grummond, eds. *Papers Presented at the International Rubens Symposium: April 14-16, 1982, the John and Mable Ringling Museum of Art, the State Art Museum of Florida.* Ringling Museum of Art Journal, 1983. Sarasota, Fla.: John and Mable Ringling Museum of Art Foundation, 1983.

KEY WORKS ON POSTERS

The study of posters has emerged as a serious aspect of research in the visual arts primarily during the past few decades, although posters have been used prominently since the beginning of printing, and particularly since the development in 1796 of lithography, a category covered above in the last section of Chapter 12. As a popular mode of advertising, posters have been prominent since the 1870s and have been designed by such major artists as Honoré Daumier, Édouard Manet, Alphonse Mucha, Henri de Toulouse-Lautrec, Pablo Picasso, and, in America and Canada, Charles Dana Gibson, Maxfield Parrish, Ben Shahn, and Norman Rockwell. For those studying posters, only a few research resources are available, including Brian Dalton Copland's somewhat dated but interesting study, *A Review of Poster Research* [VPO-140], Alan Maxwell Fern's fairly recent and valuable work, *Off the Wall: Research into the Art of the Poster* [VPO-270], Tony Fusco's recent guide for collectors, *The Official Identification and Price Guide to Posters* [VPO-310], Martin B. Pedersen's annual catalog, *Graphis Poster 92: The International Annual of Poster Art* [VPO-550], and Vicki Wray's commercially oriented book, *The Poster Catalogue* [VPO-750]. Aside from these specialized works, one can also find many studies on lithographs which treat posters.

The most current and comprehensive historical survey of posters is Alain Weill's *The Poster: A Worldwide History and Survey* [VPO-730]. John Barnicoat's *Concise History of Posters* [VPO-060] is now over twenty years old, but is still a substantial resource for the study of posters in the modern and post-World War II eras. Ervine Metzl's survey *The Poster: Its History and Its Art* [VPO-520] is over thirty years old, but still provides a useful early study of posters as an art form worthy of 'serious research. Edward McKnight Kauffer's *The Art of the Poster, Its Origin, Evolution and Purpose* [VPO-400] is quite old, but does offer an interesting and useful perspective from the 1920s. Also note Max Gallo's and Arturo Carlo Quintavalle's recent study, *The Poster in History* [VPO-320] which helps place posters in their larger historical context.

Many of the works listed below treat special eras of the history of posters, or treat specific subjects, including the following categories of posters: advertising [VPO-380]; art [VPO-530], [VPO-680]; Art Deco [VPO-190]; Art Nouveau [VPO-370], [VPO-410], [VPO-450]; Avant Garde [VPO-020]; cinema [VPO-230], [VPO-240], [VPO-460], [VPO-470], [VPO-580], [VPO-710]; Classic [VPO-030]; general [VPO-510]; Golden Age [VPO-100]; modern [VPO-760]; railway [VPO-110]; rock [VPO-350]; theater [VPO-250]; war [VPO-160], [VPO-170], [VPO-540], [VPO-600].

Some of the following studies are organized according to the nationalities of the artists, including the following: American [VPO-200], [VPO-210],

[VPO-330], [VPO-390], [VPO-490], [VPO-500]; Australian [VPO-670]; Belgian [VPO-080]; Canadian [VPO-650]; Chinese [VPO-290], [VPO-420]; Dutch [VPO-220]; English [VPO-160], [VPO-170], [VPO-340]; French [VPO-010], [VPO-120], [VPO-610], [VPO-640], [VPO-700], [VPO-720]; German [VPO-570], [VPO-660]; Russian [VPO-050], [VPO-070], [VPO-280], [VPO-740]; Swiss [VPO-440]. For studies of the posters by specific artists, see the following: Marc Chagall [VPO-630]; John Farleigh [VPO-560]; Rick Griffin [VPO-480]; David Hockney [VPO-360]; Joan Miró [VPO-150]; Alphonse Mucha [VPO-590]; James Pryde and William Nicholson [VPO-090]; Pablo Picasso [VPO-130]; John Sloan [VPO-620]; Henri de Toulouse-Lautrec [VPO-040], [VPO-260], [VPO-690].

Finally, for those interested in creating and publishing posters, consult two recently published works by Harold Davis, *Publishing Your Art as Cards and Posters: The Complete Guide to Creating, Designing and Marketing* [VPO-180], and Roger Lethbridge, *Techniques for Successful Seminars and Poster Presentations* [VPO-430]. Numerous works have been produced about posters, but few contain bibliographies which make them useful for serious research. The works given below offer a sampling of the most scholarly of poster books which definitely move beyond the picture book category.

[VPO-010] Abdy, Jane. *The French Poster: Cheret to Cappiello.* [New York]: C. N. Potter, 1970. Dist. Crown Publishers. Bib. p. 173.

[VPO-020] Ades, Dawn, Robert K. Brown, and Mildred S. Friedman. *The 20th-Century Poster: Design of the Avant-Garde.* 2nd ed. New York: Abbeville Press, 1990. Bib. pp. 218-219.

[VPO-030] Alejandro, Reynaldo G. *Classic Poster Design: A Collection of Historic Posters from the Collection at the New York Public Library.* Glen Cove, N.Y.: PBC International, 1989.

[VPO-040] Ash, Russell. *Toulouse-Lautrec: The Complete Posters.* London: Pavilion, 1991. 74 pp. Bib. refs.

[VPO-050] Baburina, N[ina] I[vanovna]. *The Soviet Arts Poster: Theatre, Cinema, Ballet, Circus 1917-1987: From the USSR Lenin Library Collection.* Trans. *Sovetskii Zrelishchnyi Plakat.* London; Harmondsworth: Penguin, 1990. Bib. pp. 205-207.

[VPO-060] Barnicoat, John. *Concise History of Posters.* World of Art Series.

538

New York: Oxford University Press; New York: Harry N. Abrams, 1972. Reprint. New York: Thames and Hudson, 1985. 288 pp. Bib. pp. 262-265. Also titled *Posters: A Concise History*.

[VPO-070] Barkhatova, E[lena] V[alentinovna]. *Russian Constructivist Posters*. Paris: Flammarion, 1992. Dist. Abbeville Press, New York. 214 pp. Bib. refs.

[VPO-080] Block, Jane, and T. Victoria Hansen. *Homage to Brussels: The Art of Belgian Posters, 1895-1915*. New Brunswick: Jane Voorhees Zimmerli Art Museum, Rutgers University, 1992. Bib. refs. pp. 117-119.

[VPO-090] Campbell, Colin. *The Beggarstaff Posters: The Work of James Pryde and William Nicholson*. London: Barie and Jenkins, 1990. Bib. refs. pp. 121-123.

[VPO-100] Cirker, Hayward, and Blanche Cirker. *Golden Age of the Poster*. New York: Dover Publications, 1971.

[VPO-110] Cole, Beverley, and Richard Durack. *Railway Posters, 1923-1947: From the Collection of the National Railway Museum, York, England*. New York: Rizzoli International Publications, 1992. Bib. refs. p. 158.

[VPO-120] Collins, Bradford Ray. "Jules Cheret and the Nineteenth-Century French Poster." Ph.D. Thesis, Yale University, 1980. Bib. pp. 220-231.

[VPO-130] Constantino, Maria. *Picasso Posters*. New York: Crescent Books, 1991. 112 pp.

[VPO-140] Copland, Brian Dalton. *A Review of Poster Research*. London: Business Publications for Institute of Practitioners in Advertising and British Poster Advertising Association, 1963. 178 pp. Bib.

[VPO-150] Corredor Matheos, Jose, and Gloria Picazo. *Miró's Posters*. Trans. *Los Carteles de Miró*. Secaucus, N.J.: Chartwell Books, 1980. Reprint. Barcelona: Edicionees Poligrafa, S.A., 1987. Bib. p. 269.

[VPO-160] Darracott, Joseph, and Belinda Loftus. *First World War Posters*. [2nd ed.] [London]: Imperial War Museum, 1981. 72 pp. Bib. pp. 11-12.

[VPO-170] ------. *Second World War Posters*. [2nd ed.] [London]: Imperial War Museum, 1981. 72 pp. Bib. p. 11.

[VPO-180] Davis, Harold. *Publishing Your Art as Cards and Posters: The Complete Guide to Creating, Designing and Marketing*. New York: Consultant Press, 1990. Bib. refs. pp. 65-73.

[VPO-190] Delhaye, Jean. *Art Deco Posters and Graphics*. New York: St. Martin's Press, 1984. 96 pp.

[VPO-200] DeLong, Lea Rosson, Michael Gontesky, and Julie D. Nelson. *New Deal Art of the Upper Midwest: An Anniversary Exhibition: Paintings, Drawings and Sculpture, Prints, Posters, Farm Security Administration Photographs, October 8--December 31, 1988*. Sioux City, Iowa: Sioux City Art Center, 1988. 40 pp. Bib. refs.

[VPO-210] DeNoon, Christopher. *Posters of the WPA*. Los Angeles: Wheatley Press, with University of Washington Press, Seattle, 1987. Bib. p. 172.

[VPO-220] Dooijes, Dick, and Pieter Brattinga. *A History of the Dutch Poster 1890-1960*. [Trans. D. A. S. Reid and Raymond Garlick]. Amsterdam: Scheltema and Holkema, 1968. 156 pp. Bibs.

[VPO-230] Edwards, Gregory J. *The Book of the International Film Poster*. Salem, N.H.: Salem House; London: Columbus, 1985. Reprint. London: Tiger, 1988. Also titled *The International Film Poster Book: The Role of the Poster in Cinema Art, Advertising and History*. N.p.: Merrimack Pub. Cir., 1985. Bib. pp. 220-221.

[VPO-240] Edwards, Gregory J., and Robin Cross. *Worst Movie Posters of all Time: A Treasury of Trash*. London: Sphere Books, 1984. 63 pp.

[VPO-250] Ehses, Hanno H. J. *Design and Rhetoric: An Analysis of Theatre Posters*. Halifax, N.S.: Nova Scotia College of Art and Design, Design Division, 1986. Bib. refs. pp. 35-36.

[VPO-260] Feinblatt, Ebria, Bruce Davis. *Toulouse-Lautrec and his Contemporaries: Posters of the Belle Epoque from the Wagner Collection*. Exhibition, Los Angeles County Museum of Art, 11 April to 16 June 1985. [Los Angeles]; New York: Los Angeles County Museum of Art with Harry N. Abrams, 1985. Bib. p. 261.

[VPO-270] Fern, Alan Maxwell. *Off the Wall: Research into the Art of the Poster*. Hanes Lecture, no. 5. Chapel Hill: Hanes Foundation, Rare Book Collection, University Library, University of North Carolina at Chapel Hill, 1985. Bib. refs. pp. 15-20.

[VPO-280] Fraser, James Howard. *The Rebel Image as a Requiem for the*

540

Soviet Empire: Posters of Perestroika and Glasnost. Tokyo: Gendaikikakushitsu Publishers, 1992. Bib. pp. 154-163. English and Japanese.

[VPO-290] Fraser, Stewart E. One Hundred Great Chinese Posters. New York: Images Graphiques, 1977.

[VPO-300] Freeman, Larry, and American Life Foundation. Victorian Posters. Watkins Glen, N.Y.: N.p., 1969. Dist. Century House. 304 pp. Bib. p. 278.

[VPO-310] Fusco, Tony. The Official Identification and Price Guide to Posters. New York: House of Collectibles, 1990. Dist. Ballantine Books. Bib. refs. pp. 545-558.

[VPO-320] Gallo, Max, and Arturo Carlo Quintavalle. The Poster in History. Trans. Alfred Mayor and Bruni Mayor. Trans. I manifesti nella storia e nel costume. Secaucus, N.J.: Wellfleet Press, 1989. Bib. p. 255.

[VPO-330] Goddu, Joseph. American Art Posters of the 1890s. Exhibition, Hirschl and Adler Galleries, 25 November 1989 to 6 January 1990. New York: Hirschl and Adler Galleries, 1989. Bib. pp. 78-79.

[VPO-340] Green, Oliver. Underground Art: London Transport Posters, 1908 to the Present. London: Studio Vista, 1990. 144 pp. Bib.

[VPO-350] Grushkin, Paul. The Art of Rock: Posters from Presley to Punk. New York: Abbeville Press, 1987. Bib. pp. 498-503.

[VPO-360] Hockney, David. Hockney Posters. New York: Harmony Books, 1987. 47 pp. London: Pavilion, 1987. 128 pp.

[VPO-370] Hofstatter, Hans H[elmut], W[ladyslawa] Jaworska, and S. Hofstatter. Art Nouveau: Prints, Illustrations and Posters. Trans. from German. Ware: Omega, 1984. Bib. pp. 287-291.

[VPO-380] Hyman, Helen S. Design to Persuade: American Literary Advertising Posters of the 1890's: A Catalogue Accompanying an Exhibition at the Yale Center for American Art and Material Culture, Yale University Art Gallery, April 8 Through May 28, 1978. [New Haven]: Yale University Art Gallery, 1978. Bib. p. 92.

[VPO-390] Johnson, J. Stewart. The Modern American Poster. [New York]: Museum of Modern Art, 1983. 178 pp.

[VPO-400] Kauffer, E[dward] McKnight, ed. The Art of the Poster, Its Origin,

Evolution and Purpose. London: C. Palmer, 1924. Bib. pp. 187-188.

[VPO-410]   King, Julia. *The Flowering of Art Nouveau Graphics.* London: Trefoil, 1990. Bib. refs. pp. 138-139.

[VPO-420]   Leijonhufvud, Goran. *Going Against the Tide: On Dissent and Big-Character Posters in China.* Scandinavian Institute of Asian Studies Monograph Series, no. 58. London: Curzon Press, 1990. 284 pp. Bib. refs. pp. 180-184.

[VPO-430] Lethbridge, Roger. *Techniques for Successful Seminars and Poster Presentations.* Melbourne: Longman Cheshire, 1991. 126 pp. Bibs.

[VPO-440]   Longhauser, Elsa Weiner. *The Basel School of Design and Its Philosophy: The Armin Hofmann Years, 1946-1986: An Exhibition of Posters, Goldie Paley Gallery, Moore College of Art, November 7--December 17, 1986, Rhode Island School of Design, Providence, Rhode Island, Virginia Commonwealth University, Richmond, Virginia.* [Philadelphia]: Goldie Paley Gallery, Moore College of Art, 1986. Bib. pp. 45-46.

[VPO-450]   Lorenz, Otto. *Art Nouveau: Posters and Illustrations.* Thornbury, England: Artline Editions, 1989. 136 pp.

[VPO-460]   Madalena, Batiste. *Movie Posters: The Paintings of Batiste Madalena: Introduction by Judith Katten; An Appreciation by Anthony Slide.* New York: Harry N. Abrams, 1985.

[VPO-470]   McClelland, Doug. *Forties Film Talk: Oral Histories of Hollywood, with 120 Lobby Posters.* Jefferson, N.C.; London: McFarland, 1992. Bib. pp. 427-432.

[VPO-480]   McClelland, G. *Rick Griffin.* Limpsfield, England: Dragon's World, 1980. 96 pp. (Painting, posters, comic strips, and Griffin's Christian perspective.)

[VPO-490]   Margolin, Victor. *The Golden Age of the American Poster: A Concise Edition of the American Poster Renaissance.* New York: Ballantine Books, 1976. 31 pp.

[VPO-500]   Margolin, Victor, Ira Brichta, and Vivian Brichta. *The Promise and the Product: 200 Years of American Advertising Posters.* New York: Macmillan Publishing Co., 1979. Bib. refs. pp. 147-148.

[VPO-510]   Max, Peter. *Poster Book.* New York: Crown Publishers, [1970].

[VPO-520]   Metzl, Ervine. *The Poster: Its History and Its Art.* [New York]:

Watson-Guptill Publications, 1963. 183 pp.

[VPO-530] Mourlot, Fernand. *Art in Posters*. Monte Carlo: A. Sauret, 1959. Reprint. *Twentieth Century Posters: Chagall, Braque, Picasso, Dufy, Matisse, Miró, Leger*. Secaucus, N.J.: Wellfleet, 1989. 247 pp.

[VPO-540] Paret, Peter, Beth Irwin Lewis, Paul Paret, and Hoover Institution on War, Revolution, and Peace. *Persuasive Images: Posters of War and Revolution from the Hoover Institution Archives*. Princeton: Princeton University Press, 1992. Bib. p. 224.

[VPO-550] Pedersen, B. Martin, ed. *Graphis Poster 92: The International Annual of Poster Art*. Zurich: Graphis Press, 1992. 259 pp. Annual.

[VPO-560] Poole, Monica. *The Wood Engravings of John Farleigh*. Henley, England: Gresham Press, 1985. 137 pp. (Posters, prints, wood-engravings, and Farleigh's religious outlook.)

[VPO-570] Rademacher, Hellmut. *Masters of German Poster Art*. Trans. *Deutsche Plakatkunst und ihre Meister*. [Leipzig]: Edition Leipzig, 1966. 139 pp.

[VPO-580] Rebello, Stephen. *Reel Art: Great Posters from the Golden Age of the Silver Screen*. New York: Artabras, 1988. Bib. refs. p. 328.

[VPO-590] Rennert, Jack, and Alain Weill. *Alphonse Mucha: The Complete Posters and Panels*. Uppsala, Sweden: Hjert and Hjert, 1984. 405 pp. Bib. pp. 29-30. English, French, and German.

[VPO-600] Rudolph, G. A. *War Posters from 1914 Through 1918 in the Archives of the University of Nebraska--Lincoln*. Lincoln: University at Lincoln, 1990. 147 pp. Bib. refs. pp. v-vii.

[VPO-610] Schardt, Hermann. *Paris 1900: The Art of the Poster*. Trans. *Paris: Franzosische Plakatkunst*. New York: Portland House, 1987. 190 pp.

[VPO-620] Sloan, John. *Prints: A Catalogue Raisonne of the Etchings, Lithographs, and Posters*. Ed. Peter T. Morse. [New Haven]: Yale University Press, 1969. Bib. pp. 393-394.

[VPO-630] Sorlier, Charles. *Chagall's Posters: A Catalogue Raisonne*. New York: Crown Publishers, 1975. 142 pp.

[VPO-640] Springer, Annemarie. "Woman in French fin-de-siecle Posters." Ph.D. Thesis, Indiana University, 1971. 447 pp.

[VPO-650] Stacey, R[obert] H. *The Canadian Poster Book: 100 Years of the Poster in Canada.* Toronto; New York: Methuen, 1979. Bib. pp. 81-84.

[VPO-660] Stach, Babett, and Helmut Morsbach. *German Film Posters, 1895-1945.* Film-Television-Sound Archive Series, vol. 3. Munich; New York: K. G. Saur, 1992. 152 pp.

[VPO-670] Sumner, Peter. *Australian Theatrical Posters, 1825-1914.* Exhibition, Josef Lebovic Gallery, 18 June to 9 July 1988. Paddington, Sydney, Australia: Josef Lebovic Gallery, 1988. 64 pp.

[VPO-680] *Symbol Patterns: Ideas for Banners, Posters, Bulletin Boards.* Philadelphia: Augsburg/Fortress Press, 1981. 40 pp.

[VPO-690] Toulouse-Lautrec, Henri de. *The Posters of Toulouse-Lautrec.* Monte-Carlo: Andre Sauret, 1966. Reprint. London: Studio Editions, 1990. Bib. p. 93.

[VPO-700] Wagner, Kurt, and Lisa Pemstein. *The Posters of Paris, 1880-1900: The Terry and Louis Silver Collection.* Exhibition, Hickory Museum of Art, Hickory, North Carolina, 7 October to 30 December 1990. Boston: Silver Collection, 1990. Bib. refs. p. 129.

[VPO-710] Warren, Jon R. *Warren's Movie Poster Price Guide: The Most Comprehensive Index and Price Guide Ever Published Covering the Years 1900-1992.* 1993 ed. Chattanooga, Tenn.: American Collectors Exchange, 1992. 466 pp.

[VPO-720] Weill, Alain. *Hundred Years of the Posters of the Folies Bergere and Music Halls of Paris.* London: Hart-Davis MacGibbon, 1977. 112 pp. Bib. p. 5.

[VPO-730] ------. *The Poster: A Worldwide History and Survey.* Trans. *L'affiche dans le monde.* London: Sotheby's; Boston: G. K. Hall, 1985. Bib. pp. 400-405.

[VPO-740] White, Stephen. *The Bolshevik Poster.* New Haven: Yale University Press, 1988. Bib. refs. pp. 144-148.

[VPO-750] Wray, Vicki. *The Poster Catalogue.* Ed. Nancy McGraw. New York: Bruce McGraw Graphics, Inc., 1985. 447 pp.

[VPO-760] Wrede, Stuart. *The Modern Poster.* Exhibition, Museum of Modern Art, New York, 6 June to 6 September 1988. New York: Museum of Modern Art, 1988. Dist. New York Graphic Society Books, Boston. Bib. pp. 255-260.

544

KEY WORKS ON SCULPTURE

Of all the sections in Chapters 12 and 13 on the visual arts, sculpture has been the most difficult to represent well. In its broadest sense, sculpture refers to three dimensional art in clay, metal, stone, wood, or virtually any medium lending itself to shaping, including balloons (covered in Chapter 5 as part of clowning), ice, snow, paper, and plastic. Furthermore, the term "sculpture" is applied to projects of greatly differing sizes. On the one hand, sculpture includes projects as large as André Le Nôtre's Gardens of Versailles, or Gutzon Borglum's monumental work on Mt. Rushmore, or Cristo's twenty-five mile long conceptualist project *Running Fence*; on the other hand, sculpture includes the delicate ivory carvings from China or the miniature figurines created in most cultures around the world. With the advent of modern interpretations of art, one could concievably include in the category of sculpture virtually any three dimensional objects, including silhouetted figures cut from sheet metal, or arrangements of painted pipes, like those found in the Laumeier International Sculpture Park in St. Louis, Missouri.

As one can anticipate, the number of books covering all these sundry forms of sculpture is far too large to represent fully in the following bibliography. Although some works listed below date back to the 1880s, most are drawn from the past two decades, and then not exhaustively. The bibliographies listed below offer a wide variety of options for conducting research on sculpture in the following categories: African [VSC-070], [VSC-110], American [VSC-020], [VSC-040], [VSC-090]; architectural terra cotta [VSC-150]; ceramic and sculpture [VSC-160]; church portals [VSC-170]; English [VSC-050]; European [VSC-010], [VSC-090]; French [VSC-120]; general [VSC-080]; Greek [VSC-100]; Irish [VSC-130]; Italian [VSC-060], [VSC-180]; sculpture gardens [VSC-140]. Also note Michael S. Edge's *Directory of Art Bronze Foundries*[VSC-030], which will be of interest to the practicing sculptor and to the researcher trying to trace the work of specific artists, or study the techniques used to produce their work. For additional lists of resources for studying sculpture, see the bi-monthly journal *Sculpture* [VSC-1460], the first three sections of Chapter 12, and the bibliographies of key works listed below.

As an introduction to the study of sculpture, one will do well to consult any of several general texts, including John Edwin Canaday's *What is Art? An Introduction to Painting, Sculpture and Architecture* [VSC-450], Ronald L. Coleman's *Sculpture: A Basic Handbook for Students* [VSC-480], Rudolf Distelberger's recent general volume, *Sculpture and Decorative Arts: Medieval, Renaissance, and Other Periods* [VSC-530], James J. Kelly's *The Sculptural Idea* [VSC-930], Judith Klausner's *Enjoying the Arts: Sculpture* [VSC-950], Judith Peck's *Sculpture: A Fifteen-Week Multimedia Program* [VSC-1260], Herbert Read's fine Bollingen Series lecture, *Art of Sculpture* [VSC-1360], and William Tucker's *The Language of Sculpture* [VSC-1580]. Furthermore, for those interested in the techniques of sculpting, several texts will prove helpful, including John W. Mills's *The Encyclopedia of Sculpture Techniques* [VSC-1160], David Orchard's *The Techniques of Wood Sculpture* [VSC-1230], Auguste Rodin's older but intriguing general text, *Art* [VSC-1400], Wilbert Verhelst's *Sculpture: Tools, Materials, and Techniques* [VSC-1590], and Arthur Williams' substantial recent study, *Sculpture: Technique, Form, Content* [VSC-1660].

Most of the works listed below fit into national or regional categories, as follows: Africa [VSC-860], [VSC-940], [VSC-1190], [VSC-1300], [VSC-1450], [VSC-1600]; America [VSC-270], [VSC-500], [VSC-640], [VSC-690], [VSC-720], [VSC-920], [VSC-1040], [VSC-1050], [VSC-1120], [VSC-1220], [VSC-1340], [VSC-1410]; Australia [VSC-1540]; Bosnia and Herzegovina [VSC-880]; Brazil [VSC-830]; China [VSC-260], [VSC-590], [VSC-1320], [VSC-1500]; Cyprus [VSC-300], [VSC-910]; Denmark [VSC-1150]; Egypt [VSC-1420], [VSC-1650]; Europe [VSC-550], [VSC-670], [VSC-1130], [VSC-1200], [VSC-1630], [VSC-1640], [VSC-1720]; France [VSC-230], [VSC-240], [VSC-310], [VSC-340], [VSC-370], [VSC-620], [VSC-680], [VSC-770], [VSC-840], [VSC-1030]; Germany [VSC-1310]; Great Britain [VSC-510], [VSC-810], [VSC-900], [VSC-1350], [VSC-1680]; Greece [VSC-220], [VSC-350], [VSC-420], [VSC-600], [VSC-660], [VSC-1110], [VSC-1280], [VSC-1370], [VSC-1530], [VSC-1690]; India [VSC-320], [VSC-380], [VSC-490], [VSC-570], [VSC-580], [VSC-700], [VSC-1170]; Italy [VSC-390], [VSC-430], [VSC-470], [VSC-520], [VSC-540], [VSC-1060], [VSC-1070], [VSC-1210], [VSC-1290]; Japan [VSC-970], [VSC-1240], [VSC-1390]; Mayan Empire [VSC-1140];

Nepal [VSC-280]; Parthia [VSC-870]; Roman Empire [VSC-650], [VSC-820], [VSC-960]; Spain [VSC-1270]; western [VSC-440].

Numerous artists have distinguished themselves by their sculpture, such as Michelangelo, whose work is treated above as a subsection on painters. The following artists are listed to offer a glimpse of some noteworthy names for research in sculpture: Eric Gill [VSC-1700]; Alfred David Lenz [VSC-1020]; Henri Matisse [VSC-740]; Joan Miró [VSC-1520]; Henry Moore [VSC-1180], [VSC-1550]; Pablo Picasso [VSC-1570]; Frederic Remington [VSC-800]; Auguste Rodin [VSC-990], [VSC-1560]; George Segal [VSC-850]. For a more complete list of artists and their works, see Ann Sutherland Harris's *Entering the Mainstream: Women Sculptors of the Twentieth Century* [VSC-790], and Julia Ann Clark Shedd's work of 1881, *Famous Sculptors and Sculpture* [VSC-1490]. For additional studies of famous sculptors, see the bibliographies at the beginning of this section on sculpture, and consult bibliographies given in general works on the visual arts presented in Chapter 12.

Sculpture is often classified according to the era it represents. While the books already mentioned cover these eras to varying degrees, the following works specialize in period studies and their respective styles: Classical [VSC-200], [VSC-350]; Gothic [VSC-230], [VSC-340], [VSC-710], [VSC-1670]; Hellenistic [VSC-1510]; Medieval [VSC-1430]; Modern [VSC-750], [VSC-760], [VSC-1010], [VSC-1080]; Nineteenth Century [VSC-890], [VSC-1350]; Renaissance [VSC-360], [VSC-1210], [VSC-1330], [VSC-1630]; Romanesque [VSC-240], [VSC-840], [VSC-900], [VSC-1710]; Twentieth Century [VSC-250], [VSC-400], [VSC-1100], [VSC-1380], [VSC-1470]. Sculpture can also be divided into media, which the following works treat in particular: bronze [VSC-610]; paper [VSC-210]; plaster [VSC-1100]; silver [VSC-780]; stone [VSC-1250]; wood [VSC-460], [VSC-730], [VSC-1090], [VSC-1230].

One of the most interesting categories for students of religion and the arts is a small selection of books treating religious subjects in sculpture. While many of the books on Medieval and Renaissance sculpture also treat these themes, the following works specialize in these religious subjects: Adam and Eve in sculpture [VSC-1680], Bible in sculpture [VSC-1610], early Christian sculpture [VSC-410], ecclesiastical sculpture [VSC-330], Jewish history in sculpture [VSC-1620], misericords (carved choir loft seats) [VSC-980], religion and sculpture [VSC-830] and [VSC-1480], tombs [VSC-1250], women of the Bible in sculpture [VSC-1440]. For those seeking a promising area of research in Christianity and the arts, sculpture offers a particularly fruitful opportunity. Computer searches for books published since 1960 on Christianity and sculpture reveal that little has been published on this subject. Some art critics--such as Jane Dillenberger in *Secular Art with Sacred Themes* [VAR-350], and in various essays and papers presented during the past few decades, and Doug Adams in *Transcendence with the Human Body in Art: George Segal, Stephen De Staebler, Jasper Johns, and Christo* [VSC-190]--have begun the process of interpreting modern and contemporary sculpture from a Christian perspective. Much work remains to be done in this area. One will find considerable information about non-Christian religions in studies of classical mythology and sculpture [VSC-200], and in the general categories of Chinese, Indian, and African sculpture, which have been discussed above and are listed below. For additional works including discussions of sculpture and religion, see works listed in the section on visual arts and religion in Chapter 12.

Special Bibliographies

[VSC-010] Brenner, Mildred, and Betty Feldman. *European and American Sculpture: The Nineteenth Century, 1770-1870: Bibliography.* [New York]: [New York University Fine Arts], 1940. 27 pp.

[VSC-020] Demeter, Mary, Helen Horvath, James Slayman, and Helen Horvath. *Selected Bibliography of Writings on American and British Architecture, American Sculpture, and the Minor Arts During the Victorian Period.* [Urbana, Ill.]: N.p., 1956. 74 pp.

[VSC-030] Edge, Michael S. *Directory of Art Bronze Foundries.* Springfield, Oreg.: Artesia Press, 1990. 132 pp.

[VSC-040] Ekdahl, Janis. *American Sculpture: A Guide to Information Sources.* Art and Architecture Information Guide Series, vol. 5. Detroit: Gale Research, 1977. 260 pp.

[VSC-050] Farrar, Charles Samuel. *Art Topics in the History of Sculpture, Painting and Architecture, with Specific References to Most of the English Standard Works of Art.* 4th ed., rev. and en-

548

larged. Chicago: C. S. Farrar and Co., 1986. 206 pp.

[VSC-060] Glass, Dorothy F. *Italian Romanesque Sculpture: An Annotated Bibliography*. A Reference Publication in Art History. Boston: G. K. Hall, 1983. xxvi, 302 pp.

[VSC-070] Green, Esther. *African Tribal Sculpture: A Bibliography Based Principally on Works Available in South African Libraries*. Cape Town: University of Cape Town, School of Librarianship, 1967. 64 pp.

[VSC-080] Hobbs, Thomas C. *Sculpture and Sculptors: A Bibliography*. [Eunice]: LeDoux Library, Louisiana State University at Eunice, 1974. 11 pp.

[VSC-090] Johnson, Ivan, and Elizabeth Poucher. *European and American Sculpture: The Twentieth Century, 1870-1940: Bibliography*. [New York]: [New York University Fine Arts], 1940. 41 pp.

[VSC-100] Lehmann, Karl. *Excavation Sites [Bibliography]*. New York: New York University, Institute of Fine Arts, n.d. Bound with: 1: *Aegean Art [With Bibliography]*; 2: *Ancient Athens and Archaic Greek Art [Bibliography]*; 3: *Great Masters of Greek Sculpture*; and 4: *Classical Greek Sculpture*.

[VSC-110] Louw, Helene A. *South African Sculpture, 1910-1959: A Bibliography*. Cape Town: University of Cape Town, School of Librarianship, 1959. 37 pp.

[VSC-120] Lyman, Thomas W., and Daniel Smartt. *French Romanesque Sculpture: An Annotated Bibliography*. Boston: G. K. Hall, 1987. 450 pp.

[VSC-130] Sexton, Eric Hyde Lord. *A Descriptive and Bibliographical List of Irish Figure Sculptures of the Early Christian Period, with a Critical Assessment of Their Significance*. Portland, Maine: The Southworth-Anthoensen Press, 1946. xxvii, 300 pp.

[VSC-140] Teague, Edward H. *Sculpture Gardens: A Bibliography of Periodical Literature*. Monticello, Ill.: Vance Bibliographies, 1985. 4 pp.

[VSC-150] Tindall, Susan M. *American Architectural Terra Cotta: A Bibliography*. Monticello, Ill.: Vance Bibliographies, 1981. 48 pp.

[VSC-160] Triance, Ann. *A Ceramic and Sculpture Bibliography*. [Adelaide]: Croydon Park College of Technical and Further Education, North Adelaide School of Art, 1985. 95 pp.

[VSC-170] Vance, Mary A. *Church Portals: A Bibliography*. Monticello, Ill.:

Vance Bibliographies, 1985. 7 pp.

[VSC-180] Wilk, Sarah Blake. *Fifteenth-Century Central Italian Sculpture: An Annotated Bibliography.* A Reference Publication in Art History. Boston: G. K. Hall, 1986. xxvi, 401 pp.

Key Works

[VSC-190] Adams, Doug. *Transcendence with the Human Body in Art: George Segal, Stephen De Staebler, Jasper Johns, and Christo.* New York: Crossroad, 1991. Bib. refs. pp. 149-159.

[VSC-200] Agard, Walter Raymond. *Classical Myths in Sculpture.* [Madison]: University of Wisconsin Press, [1951]. Bib. pp. 177-183.

[VSC-210] Ansill, Jay. *Practical and Decorative Origami.* N.p.: Cassell, 1992. 96 pp.

[VSC-220] Archaeological Institute of America, Princeton Society. *Athens Comes of Age: From Solon to Salamis: Papers of a Symposium Sponsored by the Archaeological Institute of America, Princeton Society and the Department of Art and Archaeology, Princeton University.* Princeton: Archaeological Institute of America, 1978. 108 pp. Bib. refs.

[VSC-230] Armi, C. Edson. *The "Headmaster" of Chartres and the Origins of "Gothic" Sculpture.* University Park, Pa.: Pennsylvania State University Press, 1993. Bib. refs.

[VSC-240] ------. *Masons and Sculptors in Romanesque Burgundy: The New Aesthetic of Cluny III.* 2 vols. University Park, Pa.: Pennsylvania State University Press, 1984. 384 pp. Bib. Vol. 1, pp. 191-199.

[VSC-250] Armstrong, Richard, Richard Marshall, John G. Hanhardt, and Robert Pincus-Witten. *The New Sculpture 1965-1975: Between Geometry and Gesture.* Exhibition, Whitney Museum of American Art, New York, 20 February to 3 June 1990, and Museum of Contemporary Art at the Temporary Contemporary, Los Angeles, 17 February to 7 July 1991. New York: Whitney Museum of American Art, 1990. Bib. refs. pp. 346-351.

[VSC-260] Asselberghs, Roger. *Chinese Ceramics and Oriental Works of Art Selected from a European Collection.* Louvain-la-Neuve, Belgium: Editions Duculot, 1992. Unpaged. Preface in French. Also titled *Passion for Asia.*

550

[VSC-270]   Ballatore, Sandy. *Singular Visions: Contemporary Sculpture in New Mexico: [Exhibition] April 27 to September 29, 1991.* Santa Fe: Museum of Fine Arts, Museum of New Mexico, 1991. 53 pp. Bib. refs. p. 26.

[VSC-280]   Bangdel, Lain Singh. *Stolen Images of Nepal.* Kathmandu, Nepal: Royal Nepal Academy, 1989. Bib. refs. pp. 324-328.

[VSC-290]   Bartman, Elizabeth. *Ancient Sculptural Copies in Miniature.* Leiden; New York: E. J. Brill, 1992. Bib. refs. pp. 198-203.

[VSC-300]   Begg, Patrick. *Late Cypriote Terracotta Figurines: A Study in Context.* Studies in Mediterranean Archaeology and Literature, Pocket-Book, no. 101. Jonsered: P. Astrom, 1991. 108 pp. Bib. refs. pp. 55-59.

[VSC-310]   Beretz, Elaine Marie. "Fortune Denied: The Theology Against Chance at Saint-Étienne, Beavais." Ph.D. Thesis, Yale University, 1989. Bib. refs. pp. 307-343.

[VSC-320]   Bhaskara Reddy, G[untaka] V[ijaya]. *Erotic Sculptures of Ancient India: A Critical Study from the Earliest Times to 1200 A.D..* New Delhi: Inter-India Publications, 1991. Bib. refs. pp. 110-125.

[VSC-330]   Bingham, William Philip Strong. *Ecclesiastical Sculpture: A Lecture on the Connexion Between Sculpture and Christianity, Delivered in the New Hall, Chippenham, at the Third Annual Meeting of the Wiltshire Archaeological and Natural History Society, On Wednesday, September 12, 1855.* London: Joseph Masters, 1855. 36 pp. Bib. refs.

[VSC-340]   Blum, Pamela Z. *Early Gothic Saint-Denis: Restorations and Survivals.* Berkeley: University of California Press, 1992. Bib. refs. pp. 179-182.

[VSC-350]   Boardman, John. *Greek Sculpture: The Classical Period: A Handbook.* New York: Thames and Hudson, 1985. Reprint, with corrections. 1991. Bib. pp. 242-247.

[VSC-360]   Bober, Phyllis Pray, Ruth Rubinstein, and Susan Woodford. *Renaissance Artists and Antique Sculpture: A Handbook of Sources.* London: H. Miller; New York: Oxford University Press, 1987. Reprint. 1991. Bib. pp. 481-506.

[VSC-370]   Boisselier, Jean. *La statuaire du Champa: recherches sur les cultes et l'iconographie.* École française d'Extreme-Orient, Publications, v. 54. Paris: École française d'Extreme-Orient, 1963. 468 pp. French.

[VSC-380] Boner, Alice. *Principles of Composition in Hindu Sculpture: Cave Temple Period.* N.p.: Kegan Paul, 1991. 290 pp.

[VSC-390] Bossaglia, R., et al. *1200 Years of Italian Sculpture.* New York: Harry N. Abrams, 1973. Bib. pp. 441-450.

[VSC-400] Brades, Susan Ferleger, and Christine Taylor. *Gravity and Grace: The Changing Condition of Sculpture 1965-1975.* Exhibition, Hayward Gallery, London, 21 January to 14 March 1993. London: South Bank Centre, 1993. 132 pp. Bib. refs.

[VSC-410] Brinkerhoff, Dericksen M. *A Collection of Sculpture in Classical and Early Christian Antioch.* College Art Association Monograph Series, vol. 22. 1970. Reprint. University Park, Pa.: Pennsylvania State University Press, 1985. 144 pp.

[VSC-420] Buitron-Oliver, Diana, and Nicholas Gage. *The Greek Miracle: Classical Sculpture from the Dawn of Democracy: The Fifth Century B.C.* Washington, D.C.: National Gallery of Art, 1992. 164 pp. Bib. refs.

[VSC-430] Bule, Steven, Alan Phipps Darr, and Fiorella Superbi Gioffredi, eds. *Verrocchio and Late Quattrocento Italian Sculpture.* Firenze: Le Letters, 1992. 527 pp. Bib. refs.

[VSC-440] Butler, Ruth. *Western Sculpture: Definitions of Man.* New York: Harper and Row, 1979.

[VSC-450] Canaday, John [Edwin]. *What is Art? An Introduction to Painting, Sculpture and Architecture.* New York: Alfred A. Knopf, 1980.

[VSC-460] Cartmell, Ronald. *Wood Sculpture.* London: Allman, 1970. Bib.

[VSC-470] Cellini, Benvenuto. *The Treatises of Benvenuto Cellini on Goldsmithing and Sculpture.* Trans. C. R. Ashbee. 1888. Reprint. New York: Dover Publications, [1967]. 164 pp.

[VSC-480] Coleman, Ronald L. *Sculpture: A Basic Handbook for Students.* 2nd ed. Dubuque, Iowa: W. C. Brown Co., 1980. 336 pp. Bib.

[VSC-490] Collins, Charles Dillard. *The Iconography and Ritual of Siva at Elephanta.* Sri Barib Das Oriental Series, no. 119. Delhi: Sri Satguru, 1991. Bib. pp. 217-236.

[VSC-500] Conrads, Margaret C. *American Paintings and Sculpture at the Sterling and Francine Clark Art Institute.* New York: Hudson Hills Press, 1990. Dist. Rizzoli International Publications 219 pp. Bib. refs.

552

[VSC-510] Darke, Jo. *The Monument Guide to England and Wales: A National Portrait in Bronze and Stone*. London: Macdonald Illustrated, 1991. 256 pp.

[VSC-520] Desloge, Nora W., and Laura Lewis Meyer. *Italian Paintings and Sculpture*. Saint Louis Art Museum Bulletin, 1988 Winter. St. Louis, Mo.: Saint Louis Art Museum, 1988.

[VSC-530] Distelberger, Rudolf. *Sculpture and Decorative Arts: Medieval, Renaissance, and Other Periods*. Washington, D.C.: National Gallery of Art; [New York]: Cambridge University Press, 1992. Bib. refs.

[VSC-540] Draper, James David. *Bertoldo di Giovanni, Sculptor of the Medici Household: Critical Reappraisal and Catalogue Raisonne*. [Columbia, Mo.]: University of Missouri Press, 1992. 376 pp.

[VSC-550] Duby, Georges, Xavier Barral i Altet, and Sophie Guillot de Suduiraut. *Sculpture: The Great Art of the Middle Ages from the Fifth to the Fifteenth Century*. Trans. Michael Hero. New York: Skira/Rizzoli, 1990. 318 pp.

[VSC-560] Duncan, J. P., and K. K. Law. *Computer-Aided Sculpture*. N.p.: Cambridge University Press, 1989.

[VSC-570] Dutta, Monoranjan. *Sculpture of Assam*. Delhi: Agam Kala Prakashan, 1990. 173 pp. Bib. refs. pp. 142-145.

[VSC-580] Dwivedi, Shiva Kant. *Temple Sculptures of India: With Special Reference to the Sculptures of the Bhumija Temples of Malwa*. Delhi: Agam Kala Prakashan, 1991. Bib. refs. pp. 191-202.

[VSC-590] *Eskenazi: Ancient Chinese Sculpture from the Alsdorf Collection and Others: 12 June--6 July 1990, Foxglove House, London*. [London: Eskenazi London], 1990. Bib. pp. 72-74.

[VSC-600] Fleischer, Robert. *Artemis von Ephesos und verwandte Kultstatuen aus Anatolien und Surien*. Études préliminaires aux religions orientales dans l'Empire roman, t. 35. Leiden: Brill, 1973. German.

[VSC-610] Forrest, Michael. *Art Bronzes*. West Chester, Penn.: Schiffer Pub., 1988. Bib. pp. 487-488.

[VSC-620] Forsyth, William H. *The Pieta in France: A Regional Study of Fifteenth- and Sixteenth-Century Sculpture*. New York: Metropolitan Museum of Art, 1993. Bib. refs.

[VSC-630] Franc, Helen Margaret. *An Invitation to See: 150 Works from the*

Museum of Modern Art. [Rev. ed.] New York: Museum of Modern Art, 1992. Bib. refs. pp. 181-184.

[VSC-640] Freedman, Paula B., Robin Jaffee Frank, and Marianne Bernstein. *A Checklist of American Sculpture at Yale University.* New Haven: Yale University Art Gallery, 1992.

[VSC-650] Fullerton, Mark D. *The Archaistic Style in Roman Statuary.* Mnemosyne, Bibliotheca Classica Batava, Supplementum, 110 0169-8958. Leiden; New York: E. J. Brill, 1990. Bib. refs. pp. 207-210.

[VSC-660] Gardner, Ernest Arthur. *Six Greek Sculptors.* 1910. Reprint. Freeport, N.Y.: Books for Libraries Press, 1967. Bib. pp. 253-254.

[VSC-670] Gardner, Julian. *The Tomb and the Tiara: Curial Tomb Sculpture in Rome and Avignon in the Later Middle Ages.* Clarendon Studies in the History of Art. Oxford: Clarendon Press, 1991. xxiv, 183 pp. .

[VSC-680] Gazzola, Piero. *San Zeno [Maggiore], Bible des pauvres.* 2nd ed. [Lausanne]: Mermod, 1957. 136 pp. French.

[VSC-690] Gerdts, Abigail Booth. *An American Collection: Paintings and Sculpture from the National Academy of Design.* Exhibition, Cheekwood Fine Arts Center, Nashville, Tennessee, 7 October to 7 January 1990. New York: National Academy of Design, 1989. 208 pp. Bib. refs.

[VSC-700] Gichner, Lawrence Ernest. *Erotic Aspects of Hindu Sculpture.* Washington, D.C.: N.p., 1949. 56 pp.

[VSC-710] Gillerman, Dorothy, ed. *Gothic Sculpture in American Collections: The New England Museums.* Vol. 1. Hamden, Conn.: Garland Publishing, n.d. 434 pp. Also titled *Gothic Sculpture in America: Vol. 1: The New England Museums.* Publications of the International Center of Medieval Art, no. 2. New York: Garland Publishing, 1989. Bib. pp. 391-399.

[VSC-720] Greenberg, Jan, and Sandra [Jane Fairfax] Jordan. *The Sculptor's Eye: Looking at Contemporary American Art.* New York: Delacorte Press, 1993. Bib. refs.

[VSC-730] Gross, Chaim. *The Technique of Wood Sculpture.* New York: Arco Publishing, 1976.

[VSC-740] Guse, Ernst-Gerhard. *Henri Matisse: Drawings and Sculpture.* Munich: Prestel-Verlag; New York: Neues Publishing, 1991. Bib. refs. pp. 221-222.

554

[VSC-750] Hamilton, George Heard. *Painting and Sculpture in Europe 1880-1940.* New York: Penguin Books, 1981. Bib. pp. 550-581.

[VSC-760] Hammacher, Abraham Marie. *Modern Sculpture: Tradition and Innovation.* New York: Harry N. Abrams, 1988. Bib. pp. 437-440. Enlarged ed. of *The Evolution of Modern Sculpture,* 1969.

[VSC-770] Hargrove, June Ellen. *The Statues of Paris: An Open Air Pantheon: The History of Statues of Great Men.* Antwerp: Mercatorfonds, 1989. Bib. refs. p. 377.

[VSC-780] Harmsen, William, and Dorothy Harmsen. *Sculpture in Silver: Art of the Future.* Rev. ed. Denver: Harmsen Publishing Co., 1992. Bib. refs. p. 109.

[VSC-790] Harris, Ann Sutherland. *Entering the Mainstream: Women Sculptors of the Twentieth Century.* [North Vancouver, British Columbia]: Gallerie Publications, 1991. Unpaged. Bib. refs.

[VSC-800] Hassrick, Peter H. *Frederic Remington: Paintings, Drawings, and Sculpture in the Amon Carter Museum and the Sid W. Richardson Foundation Collections.* New York: Harry N. Abrams, 1973. Reprint. Avenel, N.J.: Wing Books, 1993. Bib. refs.

[VSC-810] Hawkes, Alexandra Jane. "The Non-Crucifixion Iconography of the Pre-Viking Sculpture in the North of England: Carvings at Hovingham, Masham, Rothbury, Sandbach and Wirksworth." 2 vols. Ph.D. Thesis, University of Newcastle upon Tyne, 1989.

[VSC-820] Henig, Martin, ed. *Architecture and Architectural Sculpture in the Roman Empire.* Monograph/Oxford University Committee for Archaeology, no. 29. Oxford: Oxford University Committee for Archaeology, 1990. Dist. Oxbow Books. Bib. refs. pp. 161-162.

[VSC-830] Herstal, Stanislaw. *Imagens religiosas do Brasil.* Sao Paulo: N.p., 1956. 97 pp. and 304 pp. of illus. Italian.

[VSC-840] Horste, Kathryn. *Cloister Design and Monastic Reform in Toulouse: Romanesque Sculpture of La Dauraude.* Clarendon Studies in the History of Art Series. Oxford: Clarendon; Oxford University Press, 1992. 416 pp. Bib. pp. 247-252.

[VSC-850] Hunter, Sam. *George Segal.* New York: Rizzoli International Publications, 1989. 128 pp. Bib. p. 23.

[VSC-860]   *Important African and Modern Masterworks: [Exhibition] 24 October--4 December 1992.* New York: Kent Gallery, 1992. 75 pp. Bib. refs.

[VSC-870]   Ingholt, Harald. *Parthian Sculptures from Hatra: Orient and Hellas in Art and Religion.* New Haven: Connecticut Academy of Arts and Sciences, 1954. 55 pp.

[VSC-880]   Jandric, Ljubo, ed. *The Treasures of the Franciscan Monasteries of Bosnia and Herzegovina: Paintings and Sculpture, Metalwork, Textiles, Archive Material, Books, Stone Monuments.* Exhibition, Collegium Artisticum, Sarajevo, 14 March to 2 April 1988, Sarajevo Winter Festival, 1988. Serajevo: Institute for the Protection of Cultural, Historical and Natural Heritage of Bosnia and Herzegovina, 1988. 171 pp.

[VSC-890]   Janson, H[orst] W[oldemar]. *Nineteenth Century Sculpture.* San Bernadino, Calif.: Group Three Publishing, 1990.

[VSC-900]   Kahn, Deborah. *Canterbury Cathedral and its Romanesque Sculpture.* London: Harvey Millér, 1991. 232 pp. Bib.

[VSC-910]   Karageorghis, Vassos. *The Coroplastic Art of Ancient Cyprus.* 2 vols. Nicosia: A. G. Leventis Foundation, 1991.

[VSC-920]   Kasson, Joy S. *Marble Queens and Captives: Women in Nineteenth-Century American Sculpture.* New Haven: Yale University Press, 1990. 293 pp. Bib. refs.

[VSC-930]   Kelly, James J. *The Sculptural Idea.* 3rd ed. Minneapolis: Burgess Publishing Co., 1981. Bib. pp. 211-215.

[VSC-940]   Kerchache, Jacques, Jean Louis Paudrat, and Lucien Stephan. *Art of Africa.* New York: Harry N. Abrams, 1993. 619 pp. Bib. refs.

[VSC-950]   Klausner, Judith. *Enjoying the Arts: Sculpture.* Ed. Ruth C. Rosen. New York: Richard Rosen Press, 1981. 140 pp.

[VSC-960]   Kleiner, Diana E. E. *Roman Sculpture.* New Haven: Yale University Press, 1992. Bib. p. 464.

[VSC-970]   Koplos, Janet. *Contemporary Japanese Sculpture.* Abbeville Modern Art Movements. New York: Abbeville Press, 1991. 175 pp. Bib. refs.

[VSC-980]   Kraus, Dorothy, and Henry Kraus. *The Hidden World of the Misericords.* [New York]: George Braziller, 1975. 192 pp.

[VSC-990]   Laurent, Monique. *Rodin.* Trans. from French. London: Barrie

556

and Jenkins, 1990. Bib. p. 160.

[VSC-1000] Lawrence, Sidney, and George Foy. *Music in Stone: Great Sculpture Gardens of the World*. Ed. P. Tompkins. New York: Scala Books, 1984. 204 pp.

[VSC-1010] Legg, Alicia, and Mary Beth Smalley. *Painting and Sculpture in the Museum of Modern Art, with Selected Works on Paper: Catalog of the Collection to January 1988*. New York: Museum of Modern Art, 1988. Bib. pp. 130-133.

[VSC-1020] [Lenz, Hugh F.] *The Alfred David Lenz System of Lost Wax Casting*. New York: National Sculpture Society, 1933. 37 pp.

[VSC-1030] Levey, Michael. *Painting and Sculpture in France 1700-1789*. New Haven; London: Yale University Press, 1993. Bib. refs. pp. 307-310.

[VSC-1040] Lowe Art Museum. *Before Discovery: Artistic Development in the Americas Before the Arrival of Columbus*. Coral Gables, Fla.: University of Miami, 1990. Bib. refs. pp. 154-155.

[VSC-1050] McCue, George, David Finn, and Amy Binder. *Sculpture City, St. Louis: Public Sculpture in the "Gateway to the West"*. New York: Hudson Hills Press with Laumeier International Sculpture Park, St. Louis, 1988. Dist. Rizzoli International Publications Bib. p. 183.

[VSC-1060] McHam, Sarah Blake. *The Chapel of St. Anthony at the Santo and the Development of Venetian Renaissance Sculpture*. Cambridge, [England]; New York: Cambridge University Press, 1993. Bib. refs.

[VSC-1070] Magni, Mariaclotilde. *Architettura religiosa e scultura romanica nella Valle d'Aosta*. Aosta: Musumeci, 1974. Italian.

[VSC-1080] Marlborough Gallery. *Modern Sculpture*. Exhibition, Marlborough Gallery, 20 September to 28 November 1992. New York: Marlborough Gallery, 1992. 79 pp. Bib. refs.

[VSC-1090] Maskell, Alfred. *Wood Sculpture*. The Connoisseur's Library. New York: G. P. Putnam's Sons, 1911. xxxii, 425 pp. Bib.

[VSC-1100] Matilsky, Barbara C. *The Expressionist Surface: Contemporary Art in Plaster*. Exhibition, Queens Museum, New York, 9 June to 26 August 1990. New York: Queens Museum, 1990. Bib. p. 48.

[VSC-1110] Mattusch, Carol C. *Greek Bronze Statuary: From the Beginnings Through the Fifth Century B.C.* Ithaca: Cornell University

Press, 1988. 246 pp. Bib. refs.

[VSC-1120] Menconi, Susan E. *Primary Models: American Plasters, 1880-1945.* Exhibition, Hirschl and Adler Galleries, 3 March to 14 April 1990. New York: Hirschl and Adler Galleries, 1990. 67 pp. Bib. refs.

[VSC-1130] Middeldorf, Ulrich. *Sculptures from the Samuel H. Kress Collection: European Schools 14th to 19th Century.* Montclair, N.J.: Abner Schram, Ltd., 1976.

[VSC-1140] Miller, Arthur G. *Maya Rulers of Time: A Study of Architectural Sculpture at Tikal, Guatemala.* Philadelphia: University Museum, 1986. Bib. refs. pp. 95-96.

[VSC-1150] Mills, James A. *Medieval Danish Wooden Sculpture: Roods.* 2 vols. Glen Head, N.Y.: Aggersborg Press, 1991.

[VSC-1160] Mills, John W. *The Encyclopedia of Sculpture Techniques.* New York: Watson-Guptill Publications, 1989. Bib. refs. p. 239.

[VSC-1170] Misra, Ratanalala. *The Mortuary Monuments in Ancient and Medieval India.* Delhi: B. R. Publishing Corporation, 1991. Bib. refs. pp. 133-141.

[VSC-1180] Moore, Henry. *Henry Moore: Sculpture and Drawings.* 3rd ed. London: Lund, Humphries and Co., Ltd., A. Zwemmer, 1949. xliv, 292 pp. Bib. p. xxxiii-xxxviii.

[VSC-1190] Museum of Modern Art [New York]. *African Negro Art.* New York: Museum of Modern Art, 1935. 58 pp. Bib. pp. 25-29.

[VSC-1200] Newton, Eric. *European Painting and Sculpture.* 4th ed. Baltimore: Penguin, 1962. 266 pp.

[VSC-1210] Olson, Roberta J. M. *Italian Renaissance Sculpture.* London: Thames and Hudson, 1992. Bib. pp. 213-214.

[VSC-1220] Opitz, Glenn B., ed. *Dictionary of American Sculptors: 18th Century to the Present.* Poughkeepsie, N.Y.: Apollo Book, 1984. 680 pp.

[VSC-1230] Orchard, David. *The Techniques of Wood Sculpture.* Cincinnati: North Light Books, 1985. 144 pp.

[VSC-1240] Paine, Robert Treat, and Alexander Coburn Soper. *The Art and Architecture of Japan.* 3rd ed. Pelican History of Art. New Haven: Yale University Press, 1981. 521 pp. Bib. refs. pp. 455-489.

558

[VSC-1250] Panofsky, Erwin. *Tomb Sculpture: Four Lectures on its Changing Aspects from Ancient Egypt to Bernini.* New York: Harry N. Abrams, 1992. Bib. refs. pp. 301-310.

[VSC-1260] Peck, Judith. *Sculpture: A Fifteen-Week Multimedia Program.* Old Tappan, N.J.: Prentice-Hall Press, 1986. 144 pp.

[VSC-1270] Permanyer, L., and Melba Levick. *Barcelona: Open-Air Sculpture Gallery.* Trans. *Barcelona: Un Museo de Esculturas al Aire libre.* New York: Rizzoli International Publications, 1992. 299 pp.

[VSC-1280] Petrakos, Valiseios. *National Museum: Sculpture, Bronzes, Vases.* Trans. *Ethniko Mouseio.* Athens: Clio Editions, 1981.

[VSC-1290] Poeschke, Joachim. *Donatello and His World: Italian Renaissance Sculpture.* [New York]: Harry N. Abrams, 1993. Bib. refs.

[VSC-1300] Ponter, Anthony, Laura Ponter, and Robert Holmes. *Spirits in Stone: The New Face of African Art.* Sebastopol, Calif.: Ukama Press, 1992. 202 pp. Bib. refs. (Zimbabwe Shona sculpture.)

[VSC-1310] Powe, Norma Faye. "Sculpture of the Cathedral Cloister, Elne." 3 vols. Ph.D. Thesis, University of Minnesota, 1989. Bib. pp. 212-235.

[VSC-1320] Priest, Alan. *Chinese Sculpture in the Metropolitan Museum of Art.* New York: [Metropolitan Museum of Art], 1944. 81 pp., 132 plates. Bib. pp. 69-75.

[VSC-1330] Radcliffe, Anthony. *Renaissance and Later Sculpture: Thyssen-Bornemisza Collection.* [London]: Philip Wilson, 1992. 434 pp.

[VSC-1340] Rawls, Walton H. *A Century of American Sculpture: Treasures from Brookgreen Gardens.* 2nd ed. New York: Abbeville Press, 1988. Bib. p. 126.

[VSC-1350] Read, Benedict, Joanna Barnes, and John Christian. *Pre-Raphaelite Sculpture: Nature and Imagination in British Sculpture, 1848-1914.* Exhibition, Matthiesen Gallery, London, 31 October to 12 December 1991; Birmingham City Museum and Art Galery, 15 January to 15 March 1992. London: Henry Moore Foundation with Lund Humphries, 1991. Bib. refs. pp. 168-172.

[VSC-1360] Read, Herbert. *Art of Sculpture.* 2nd ed. Bollingen Series, vol.

35. Princeton: Princeton University Press, 1961.

[VSC-1370] Riis, P[oul] J[orgen], Mette Moltesen, and Pia Guldager. *Catalogue of Ancient Sculptures: Vol. 1: Aegean, Cypriote, and Graeco-Phoenician.* Copenhagen: Department, Nationalmuseet (Denmark), Antiksamlingen, 1989. Bib. pp. 110-113.

[VSC-1380] Ritchie, Andrew Carnduff. *Sculpture of the Twentieth Century.* New York: Museum of Modern Art, [1952]. Bib. pp. 233-237.

[VSC-1390] Roberts, Laurance P. *A Dictionary of Japanese Artists: Painting, Sculpture, Ceramics, Prints, Lacquer.* Tokyo; New York: Weatherhill, 1990. 299 pp. Bib. refs. pp. 223-232.

[VSC-1400] Rodin, Auguste. *Art.* Trans. Romilly Fedden. New York: Dodd, Mead, 1928. 259 pp.

[VSC-1410] Rubinstein, Charlotte Streifer. *.American Women Sculptors: A History of Women Working in Three Dimensions.* Boston: G. K. Hall, 1990. 638 pp. Bib. refs. pp. 575-603.

[VSC-1420] Russman, Edna R., and David Finn. *Egyptian Sculpture: Cairo and Luxor.* London: British Museum Publications, 1990. Bib. pp. 222-226.

[VSC-1430] St. Clair, Archer, and Elizabeth Parker McLachlan. *The Carver's Art: Medieval Sculpture in Ivory, Bone, and Horn: September 10--November 21, 1989, the Jane Voorhees Zimmerli Art Museum, Rutgers, the State University of New Jersey.* New Brunswick: Jane Voorhees Zimmerli Art Museum, Rutgers University, 1989. Bib. refs. pp. 123-132.

[VSC-1440] Sandys, Edwina, and James P. Morton. *Women of the Bible: Sculpture.* N.p.: Everson Museum, 1986. 24 pp.

[VSC-1450] Schadler, Karl-Ferdinand, and Jo-Anne Birnie Danzker. *Gods Spirits Ancestors: African Sculpture from Private German Collections.* Exhibition, Villa Stuck München, 28 October 1992 to 10 January 1993. Munich: Panterra, 1992. Bib. refs. pp. 240-247.

[VSC-1460] *Sculpture.* Washington, D.C.: International Sculpture Center, 1981-. Bi-monthly. Formerly *International Sculpture.*

[VSC-1470] Senie, Harriet. *Contemporary Public Sculpture: Tradition, Transformation, and Controversy.* New York: Oxford University Press, 1992. Bib. pp. 235-265.

560

[VSC-1480] Seta, Alessandro della. *Religion and Art: A Study in the Evolution of Sculpture, Painting and Architecture.* New York: Charles Scribner's Sons, 1914. 415 pp.

[VSC-1490] Shedd, Julia Ann Clark. *Famous Sculptors and Sculpture.* Boston: J. R. Osgood, 1881. 319 pp.

[VSC-1500] Sickman, Laurence, and Alexander Coburn Soper. *The Art and Architecture of China.* Pelican History of Art. Harmondsworth, Middlesex, England: Penguin Books Ltd., 1956. Reprint. 1991. 527 pp. Bib. pp. 493-499.

[VSC-1510] Smith, R. R. R. *Hellenistic Sculpture: A Handbook.* World of Art. New York: Thames and Hudson, 1991. Bib. refs. pp. 277-282.

[VSC-1520] South Bank Centre. *Joan Miró: Sculpture.* Exhibition, Southampton City Art Gallery, Ikon Gallery, Birmingham and Aberdeen Art Gallery. London: South Bank Centre, 1989. Bib. p. 59.

[VSC-1530] Sparkes, Brian A. *Greek Art.* Greece and Rome. New Surveys in the Classics, no. 22 0017-3835. Oxford; New York: Oxford University Press for Classical Association, 1991. 77 pp.

[VSC-1540] Sturgeon, Graeme. *Contemporary Australian Sculpture.* Roseville, NSW, Australia: Craftsman House, 1991. xxiii, 127 pp. Bib. refs. pp. 113-116.

[VSC-1550] Sylvester, David. *Henry Moore: Complete Sculpture.* 5th ed. London: Lund Humphries, 1988. Bib. refs. vol. 1, pp. xli-xliii.

[VSC-1560] Taillandier, Yvon. *Rodin.* New York: Crown Publishers, 1988. Bib. pp. 93-96.

[VSC-1570] Tate Gallery. *Late Picasso: Paintings, Sculpture, Drawings, Prints, 1953-1972.* Exhibition, Musée National d'art Moderne, Paris, 17 February to 16 May 1988; the Tate Gallery, London, 23 June to 18 September, 1988. London: Tate Gallery, 1988. Bib. pp. 303-305.

[VSC-1580] Tucker, William. *The Language of Sculpture.* New York: Thames and Hudson, 1985.

[VSC-1590] Verhelst, Wilbert. *Sculpture: Tools, Materials, and Techniques.* Englewood Cliffs, N.J.: Prentice-Hall Press, [1973]. Bib. pp. 261-263.

[VSC-1600] Vogel, Susan Mullin, and Mario Carrieri. *African Aesthetics: The Carlo Monzino Collection.* Exhibition, 7 May to 7 September 1986. New York: Center for African Art, 1986. Bib.

[VSC-1610] Wartenbergh, Henk. *Ik zie, ik zie . . . De bijbel langs Amsterdams straten.* Amsterdam: Buijten and Schipperheijn, 1972. 237 pp. Dutch. (The Bible in pictures and sculpture of Amsterdam.)

[VSC-1620] Weber, Robert, and Fred Bertram. *An Epic in Sculpture: The Medallic History of the Jewish People.* N.p.: Judaic Heritage, 1974. 180 pp. Bib. refs. in footnotes.

[VSC-1630] Weinberger, Martin. *Renaissance Art of Northern Europe, Gothic and Renaissance Sculpture in Northern Europe, and Northern High Renaissance and Baroque Sculpture.* New York: University, 1935. Bib.

[VSC-1640] *Western European Sculpture from Soviet Museums, 15th and 16th Centuries.* Trans. *Zapadnoevropeiskaia Skulptura XV-XVI Vekov v Sovetskikh Muzeiakh.* Leningrad: Aurora Art Publishers, 1988. 261 pp. Bibs.

[VSC-1650] Wilkinson, Richard H. *Reading Egyptian Art: A Hieroglyphic Guide to Ancient Egyptian Painting and Sculpture.* London: Thames and Hudson, 1992. Bib. pp. 220-222.

[VSC-1660] Williams, Arthur. *Sculpture: Technique, Form, Content.* Worcester, Mass.: Davis Publications, 1989. Bib. refs. pp. 353-355.

[VSC-1670] Williamson, Paul, and Peta Evelyn. *Northern Gothic Sculpture 1200-1450.* Catalog of holdings. London: Victoria and Albert Museum, 1988. Bib. pp. 201-209.

[VSC-1680] Wizowaty, Judith Vaughan. "The Iconography of Adam and Eve on Sculptured Stones in Anglo-Saxon England." Ph.D. Thesis, University of Texas at Austin, 1989. Bib. refs. pp. 501-565.

[VSC-1690] Woodford, Susan. *An Introduction to Greek Art.* Ithaca: Cornell University Press, 1986. Bib. p. 181.

[VSC-1700] Yorke, M. *Eric Gill: Man of Flesh and Spirit.* London: Constable, 1981. 304 pp. Bib.

[VSC-1710] Young, Brian. *The Villein's Bible: Stories in Romanesque Carving.* London: Barrie and Jenkins, 1990. Bib. refs. p. 149.

[VSC-1720] Ziegler, Joanna E. *Sculpture of Compassion: The Pieta and the*

Beguines in the Southern Low Countries, c. 1300--c. 1600. Brussels, [Belgium]: [Dist. Brepols Publishers], 1992. 412 pp. Bib. refs.

CHAPTER 14

WIT AND HUMOR

BIBLIOGRAPHIES ON WIT AND HUMOR

Wit and humor have traditionally been treated as integral parts of drama, literature, music, and other art forms, and have only occasionally been examined as subjects in their own right. When studied as discrete elements in literature or oral tradition, wit and humor quickly become complex and difficult to classify. For example, wit is usually considered more intellectual while humor is considered more light hearted in its treatment of human foibles and incongruities. Yet even these basic distinctions are difficult to maintain. Wit and humor also overlap with satire. Satire, whose literal meaning is "a dish filled with mixed fruits," can be Juvenalian (caustic, biting, and angry) or Horatian (gentle, urbane, and smiling). Furthermore, satire can be expressed through the methods of irony, burlesque, parody, sarcasm, invective, or innuendo, each method embodying varying degrees of wit and humor. Furthermore, comedy is also associated with wit and humor and similarly involves a complex array of forms ranging from comedy of manners to black comedy. To make matters more difficult to assess, wit and humor are culture specific and vary radically from country to country, and even from community to community. What one person considers witty or humorous, may not seem amusing at all to another person. For these reasons, the study of wit and humor must be conducted carefully to make a meaningful contribution to research in the arts.

While numerous books containing cartoons, humorous stories, and jokes are available, few treat humor as a subject worthy of systematic research and scholarly analysis. The few works which could be obtained for this section are the product of numerous searches, especially for works with bibliographies. The following list of bibliographies includes a variety of texts ranging from strict bibliographies of research in humor to catalogs of collections. The most analytically oriented of the bibliographies listed below are James E. Evans' *Comedy: An Annotated Bibliography of Theory and Criticism* [BWH-060], Jeffrey H. Goldstein's *Humour, Laughter and Comedy: A Bibliography of Empirical and Non-Empirical Analyses in the English Language* [BWH-080], Paul E. McGhee's and Jeffrey H. Goldstein's *Handbook of Humor Research* [BWH-130], and Don Lee Fred Nilsen's *Humor Scholarship: A Research Bibliography* [BWH-160], all of which are reasonably current.

Many of the bibliographies given below treat American humor, including the following: [BWH-020], [BWH-030], [BWH-090], [BWH-100], [BWH-120], [BWH-140], [BWH-150], [BWH-180]. The catalogs and indexes of collections of wit and humor include works on the following topics: the Schmulowitz Collection [BWH-010], recordings of comedy [BWH-040], musical comedy [BWH-050], humorous books for children [BWH-070], comic-strip characters [BWH-110], and the Theodore H. Koundakjian Collection [BWH-120]. Note especially the work of Don Lee Fred Nilsen [BWH-150 to BWH-160] for his skillful treatment of language, as illustrated well by his earlier work on clichés. For additional bibliographies, see those given in the key works listed below.

[BWH-010] *Catalog of the Schmulowitz Collection of Wit and Humor: Supplement One*. San Francisco: San Francisco Public Library, 1977. 132 pp.

[BWH-020] Corrin, Brownlee Sands, and Arthur Power Dudden. "An Annotated Audio-Videography of Socio-Political Wit, Humor, and Satire." *American Humor: An Interdisciplinary Newsletter*, vol. 2, no. 2 (1975): 3-60.

565

[BWH-030] Davis, C. E., and M. B. Hudson. "Humor of the Old Southwest: A Checklist of Criticism." *Mississippi Quarterly* 27 (Spring 1974): 179-199.

[BWH-040] Debenham, Warren. *Laughter on Record: A Comedy Discography.* Metuchen, N.J.: Scarecrow Press, 1988. 387 pp.

[BWH-050] Drone, Jeanette M. *Index to Opera, Operetta and Musical Comedy Synopses in Collections and Periodicals.* Metuchen, N.J.: Scarecrow Press, 1978. 177 pp.

[BWH-060] Evans, James E. *Comedy: An Annotated Bibliography of Theory and Criticism.* Metuchen, N.J.: Scarecrow Press, 1987. 419 pp.

[BWH-070] Fakih, Kimberly Olson. *The Literature of Delight: A Critical Guide to Humorous Books for Children.* New Providence, N.J.: R. R. Bowker, 1993.

[BWH-080] Goldstein, J[effrey] H., et al. *Humour, Laughter and Comedy: A Bibliography of Empirical and Non-Empirical Analyses in the English Language.* Oxford: Pergamon Press, 1977. Bib. pp. 464-504.

[BWH-090] Griffith, Nancy Snell. *Humor of the Old Southwest: An Annotated Bibliography of Primary and Secondary Sources.* Bibliographies and Indexes in American Literature, 0742-6860, no. 10. New York: Greenwood Press, 1989. 220 pp.

[BWH-100] Inge, M. Thomas. *"One Priceless Universal Trait": American Humor, A Bibliographic Guide.* Ashland, Va.: Randolph-Macon College, 1987. 42 pp.

[BWH-110] Kinnard, Roy. *The Comics Come Alive: A Guide to Comic-Strip Characters in Live-Action Productions.* Metuchen, N.J.: Scarecrow Press, 1991. 255 pp.

[BWH-120] Koundakjian, Theodore H. *A Revised Check List of the Theodore H. Koundakjian Collection of Native American Humor of the Nineteenth Century.* Berkeley, Calif.: N.p., 1973. 142 pp. (20 copies)

[BWH-130] McGhee, Paul E., and Jeffrey H. Goldstein, eds. *Handbook of Humor Research.* 2 vols. New York: Springer-Verlag, 1983. Bibs.

[BWH-140] Mott, Howard S. *Three Hundred Years of American Humor [1637-1936].* New York: H. S. Mott, Jr., 1937. 32 pp.

[BWH-150] Nilsen, Don Lee Fred. *Humor in American Literature: A Select-

566

ed *Annotated Bibliography.* Garland Reference Library of the Humanities, no. 1049. New York: Garland Reference, 1992. 580 pp.

[BWH-160] ------. *Humor Scholarship: A Research Bibliography.* Bibliographies and Indexes in Popular Culture, no. 1. Westport, Conn.: Greenwood Press, 1993.

[BWH-170] Salway, Lance. *Humorous Books for Children.* 2nd ed. Stroud, England: Thimble Press, 1980. 46 pp.

[BWH-180] Sloane, David E. E., ed. *American Humor Magazines and Comic Periodicals.* Historical Guides to the World's Periodicals and Newspapers, 0742-5538. New York: Greenwood Press, 1987. xxxv, 648 pp. Bib. pp. 593-595.

KEYWORKS ON WIT AND HUMOR

Research on humor has increased greatly during the past decade. One of the most interesting aspects of this research has been the application of the social scientific methods to studies of humor. Some of the most recent and intriguing of these social scientific studies are Madahev L. Apte's *Humor and Laughter: An Anthropological Approach* [WHU-020], Jean-Louis Barsoux's *Funny Business: Humour, Management and Business Culture* [WHU-060], Norman Cousins' *Anatomy of an Illness as Perceived by the Patient: Reflections on Healing and Regeneration* [WHU-240], R. Johnson's "Jokes, Theories, Anthropology" [WHU-480], and Michael Joseph Mulkay's *On Humour: Its Nature and Its Place in Modern Society* [WHU-640]. Other important studies exploring the theoretical and philosophical aspects of humor include the following items: [WHU-100], [WHU-160], [WHU-170], [WHU-270], [WHU-310], [WHU-330], [WHU-350], [WHU-530], [WHU-590], [WHU-620], [WHU-630], [WHU-650], [WHU-670], [WHU-680], [WHU-760], [WHU-810]. One of the best journals for research in humor is one edited by Victor Raskin, *Humor: International Journal of Humor Research* [WHU-470]. The oldest surviving periodical including humor is the London based weekly, *Punch* [WHU-740], whose issues since 1841 provide a useful resource for analyzing the changes in humor during the past century and a half.

567

Much of the study of wit and humor can be classified according to nationalities. For assistance in analyzing national styles, see Avner Ziv's recent work, *National Styles of Humor* [WHU-910]. The following studies fit into the categories of these national styles: American [WHU-080], [WHU-090], [WHU-150], [WHU-200], [WHU-360], [WHU-400], [WHU-440], [WHU-780], [WHU-820], [WHU-860], [WHU-880]; Arab [WHU-500]; Australian [WHU-770]; Canadian [WHU-410], [WHU-870]; Chinese [WHU-460]; English [WHU-520], [WHU-610], [WHU-720], [WHU-830]; Japanese [WHU-110]; Korean [WHU-180]; Oriental [WHU-120]; Russian [WHU-210]; Scottish [WHU-600]; Soviet [WHU-510]; Tamil [WHU-280]; Vietnamese [WHU-850]. Although the individuals represented in this section offer only a small sampling of humorists and wits even during the twentieth century, the following works will suggest the kinds of studies which have been done on or by humorists, and those which still need to be written: Jilly Cooper [WHU-230], Luigi Pirandello [WHU-700], Marcel Proust [WHU-800], and Sydney Smith [WHU-690]. For additional works on individual humorists, see the full-length bibliographies listed above, and the reference sections of the key works listed below.

Several of the works listed below are also designed to cover specific eras, including the following: eighteenth century [WHU-040], [WHU-140], [WHU-220]; Renaissance [WHU-050], [WHU-130]; seventeenth century [WHU-030], [WHU-390]; twentieth century [WHU-560]. Still more works are devoted to a wide variety of topics related to humor and wit, as follows: art [WHU-380], [WHU-790]; black humor [WHU-260]; cartoons [WHU-340], [WHU-430], [WHU-890]; children [WHU-580], [WHU-900]; graveyards [WHU-070]; hypocrisy [WHU-660]; law [WHU-420]; literature [WHU-370], [WHU-540], [WHU-750], [WHU-840]; medicine [WHU-190]; music [WHU-250], [WHU-550]; parody [WHU-560], [WHU-570]; politics [WHU-320], [WHU-490], [WHU-730]. Two additional general works which cover a wide variety of topics are Joey Adams' *Encyclopedia of Humor* [WHU-010], and Evan Esar's *20,000 Quips and Quotes* [WHU-290]. Aside from exploring the bibliographies of works in this section for clues about valuable books treating wit and humor, also consider works listed in earlier chapters treating cinema, dance and mime and clowning, drama and rhetoric, electronic communications, and literature.

[WHU-010] Adams, Joey. *Encyclopedia of Humor*. New York: Bonanza, 1968.

[WHU-020] Apte, Madahev L. *Humor and Laughter: An Anthropological Approach*. Ithaca: Cornell University Press, 1985. Bib. pp. 275-308.

[WHU-030] Ashton, John. *Humour, Wit, and Satire of the Seventeenth Century*. London: Chatto and Windus, 1883. Reprint. New York: Dover Publications; Detroit: Singing Tree Press, 1968. Bib. pp. 437-448.

[WHU-040] Auty, Susan G. *Comic Spirit of Eighteenth Century Novels*. Port Washington, N.Y.: Kennikat Press Corporation, 1975. Bib. pp. 190-195.

[WHU-050] Barolsky, Paul. *Infinite Jest: Wit and Humor in Italian Renaissance Art*. Columbia: University of Missouri Press, 1978. Bib. pp. 217-222.

[WHU-060] Barsoux, Jean-Louis. *Funny Business: Humour, Management and Business Culture*. London; New York: Cassell, 1993. 200 pp. Bib. refs.

[WHU-070] Beable, William Henry. *Epitaphs: Graveyard Humour and Eulogy*. 1925. Reprint. Detroit: Singing Tree Press, 1971. 246 pp.

[WHU-080] Blair, Walter. *Native American Humor (1800-1900)*. New York: American Book Co., 1931. 573 pp. Bib. pp. 163-196.

[WHU-090] ------. *Native American Humor*. San Francisco: Chandler Publishing Co., 1960. 565 pp. Bib.

[WHU-100] Blistein, Elmer M. *Comedy in Action*. Durham, N.C.: Duke University Press, 1964. Bib. pp. 131-139.

[WHU-110] Blyth, Reginald Horace. *Japanese Humour*. Tourist Library, vol. 24. Tokyo: Japan Travel Bureau, [1957]. 184 pp.

[WHU-120] ------. *Oriental Humour*. [Tokyo]: Hokuseido Press, [1959]. Bib. pp. 567-573.

[WHU-130] Bowen, Barbara C. *One Hundred Renaissance Jokes: A Critical Anthology*. Birmingham, Ala.: Summa Publications, 1988. 128 pp.

569

[WHU-140] Browning, J. D., ed. *Satire in the 18th Century.* New York: Garland Publishing, 1983. 231 pp. Bib. refs.

[WHU-150] Cerf, Bennett. *An Encyclopedia of American Humor.* New York: Random House, 1954.

[WHU-160] Chapman, Anthony J., and Hugh C. Foot, eds. *Humour and Laughter: Theory, Research, and Applications.* London; New York: Wiley, 1976. 348 pp. Bibs.

[WHU-170] ------, eds. *It's a Funny Thing, Humour.* Illus. Roy R. Behrens. International Conference on Humour and Laughter, 1976, Cardiff, Wales. Oxford; New York: Pergamon Press, 1977. Bib. pp. 469-507.

[WHU-180] Chun, Shin-Yong, ed. *Humour in Korean Literature.* Rev. Korean Culture Series, vol. 1. Seoul, Korea: International Cultural Foundation, 1977. 298 pp.

[WHU-190] Cocker, John. *Stitches: Side-Splitting Humour from the Doctor's Office, Hospital and Operating Room.* Don Mills, Ontario: Stoddart, 1993.

[WHU-200] Cohen, Hennig, and William B. Dillingham, eds. *Humor of the Old Southwest.* 2nd ed. Athens, Ga.: University of Georgia Press, 1975. Bib. pp. 413-427.

[WHU-210] Coleman, Arthur Prudden. *Humor in the Russian Comedy from Catherine to Gogol.* New York: Columbia University Press, 1925. Bib. pp. 93-94.

[WHU-220] Cooper, Anthony Ashley, Earl of Shaftesbury. *Sensus Communis: An Essay on the Freedom of Wit and Humour.* 1709. Reprint. New York: Garland Publishing, 1971. 120 pp.

[WHU-230] Cooper, Jilly. *Angels Rush in: The Best of Her Satire and Humour.* London: Methuen, 1990. 370 pp.

[WHU-240] Cousins, Norman. *Anatomy of an Illness as Perceived by the Patient: Reflections on Healing and Regeneration.* New York: Bantam Books, 1981.

[WHU-250] Crowest, Frederick James. *Musicians' Wit, Humour, and Anecdote.* Illus. J. P. Donne. 1902. Reprint. Ann Arbor: Gryphon Books, 1971. 423 pp.

[WHU-260] Davis, Douglas M. *The World of Black Humor: An Introductory Anthology of Selections and Criticism.* New York: E. P. Dutton and Co., [1967]. 350 pp.

570

[WHU-270]   Durant, John R., and Jonathan Miller. *Laughing Matters: A Serious Look at Humour.* New York: Halsted Press, 1988. 134 pp. Essex, England: Longman Scientific and Technical; New York: Wiley, 1988. 136 pp.

[WHU-280]   Eichinger Ferro-Luzzi, Gabriella. *The Taste of Laughter: Aspects of Tamil Humour.* Wiesbaden: O. Harrasowitz, 1992. Bib. refs. pp. 201-211.

[WHU-290]   Esar, Evan. *20,000 Quips and Quotes.* Garden City, N.Y.: Doubleday, 1968.

[WHU-300]   Feaver, William. *Masters of Caricature: From Hogarth and Gillray to Scarfe and Levine.* New York: Alfred A. Knopf, 1981. Bib. p. 233.

[WHU-310]   Feinberg, Leonard. *The Secret of Humor.* Amsterdam: Rodopi, 1978. 205 pp. Bib. refs.

[WHU-320]   Fitzgerald, Richard. *Art and Politics: Cartoonists of the Masses and Liberator.* Westport, Conn.: Greenwood Press, 1973. Bib. pp. 235-241.

[WHU-330]   Fleet, F. R. *A Theory of Wit and Humour.* 1890. Reprint. Port Washington, N.Y.: Kennikat Press, [1970]. 278 pp.

[WHU-340]   Friedwald, Will, and Jerry Beck. *The Warner Bros. Cartoons.* Metuchen, N.J.: Scarecrow Press, 1981. 287 pp.

[WHU-350]   Fry, William F. *Sweet Madness: A Study of Humor.* Palo Alto, Calif.: Pacific Books, [1963]. Bib. pp. 173-178.

[WHU-360]   Gale, Steven H. *Encyclopedia of American Humorists.* Garland Reference Library of the Humanities, vol. 633. New York: Garland Publishing, 1988.

[WHU-370]   Galligan, Edward L. *The Comic Vision in Literature.* Athens: University of Georgia Press, 1984. Bib. pp. 195-196.

[WHU-380]   Getlein, Frank, and Dorothy Getlein. *The Bite of the Print: Satire and Irony in Woodcuts, Engravings, Etchings, Lithographs and Serigraphs.* New York: C. N. Potter, [1963]. Bib. pp. 269-272. (See [VLI-300])

[WHU-390]   Gilman, Ernest B. *The Curious Perspective: Literary and Pictorial Wit in the Seventeenth Century.* New York: Yale University Press, 1978. 267 pp. Bib. refs.

[WHU-400]   Glanz, Rudolf. *The Jew in Early American Wit and Graphic Humor.* New York: KTAV Publishing House, 1973.

269 pp.

[WHU-410] Gould, Allan, ed. *The Great Big Book of Canadian Humour*. Toronto: Macmillan Canada, 1992. 283 pp.

[WHU-420] Harvey, Cameron. *Legal Wit and Whimsy: An Anthology of Legal Humour*. Toronto: Carswell, 1988. 156 pp. Bib. refs.

[WHU-430] Hewison, William. *The Cartoon Connection: The Art of Pictorial Humour*. London: Elm Tree Books, 1977. 144 pp.

[WHU-440] Holliday, Carl. *The Wit and Humor of Colonial Days (1607-1800)*. Philadelphia: J. B. Lippincott Co., 1912. Bib. pp. 309-315.

[WHU-450] Horn, Maurice, and Richard E. Marschall, eds. *The World Encyclopedia of Cartoons*. 2 vols. Detroit: Gale Research with Chelsea House Pub., New York, 1980. Bib. Vol. 2, pp. 623-627.

[WHU-460] Hua, Junwu. *Satire and Humour from a Chinese Cartoonist's Brush: Selected Cartoons of Hua Junwu, 1983-1989*. Trans. Gladys Yang. Bilingual Ed. Beijing: China Today Press, 1991. 276 pp.

[WHU-470] *Humor: International Journal of Humor Research*. Tempe, Ariz.: International Society for Humor Studies, English Department, Arizona State University, 1988-. Quarterly.

[WHU-480] Johnson, R. "Jokes, Theories, Anthropology." *Semiotica* 22, no. 3/4 (1978): 331-334.

[WHU-490] Kallen, Horace M. *Liberty, Laughter, and Tears: Reflections on the Relations of Comedy and Tragedy to Human Freedom*. DeKalb, Ill.: Northern Illinois University Press, 1968.

[WHU-500] Kishtainy, Khalid. *Arab Political Humour*. London; New York: Quartet Books, 1985. Bib. pp. 201-203.

[WHU-510] Kolasky, John, comp. *Look Comrade--The People are Laughing: Underground Wit, Satire and Humour from Behind the Iron Curtain*. Toronto: P. Martin Association, 1972. 135 pp.

[WHU-520] L'Estrange, Alfred Guy Kingan. *History of English Humour, With an Introduction upon Ancient Humour*. 2 vols. Essays in Literature and Criticism, no. 46. 1878. Reprint. New York: Burt Franklin, [1970].

[WHU-530] Levin, Harry, ed. *Veins of Humor*. Cambridge, Mass.: Harvard University Press, 1972. 284 pp. Bib. refs.

[WHU-540]   Lewis, Paul. *Comic Effects: Interdisciplinary Approaches to Humor in Literature*. Albany, N.Y.: State University of New York Press, 1989. 179 pp. Bib. refs.

[WHU-550]   Loesser, Arthur, comp. *Humor in American Song*. 1942. Reprint. Detroit: Gale Research, 1974. 315 pp.

[WHU-560]   Lowrey, Burling, ed. *Twentieth Century Parody*. New York: Harcourt Brace, 1960.

[WHU-570]   Macdonald, Dwight. *Parodies: An Anthology from Chaucer to Beerbohm*. New York: Random House, 1960.

[WHU-580]   McGhee, Paul E., and Anthony J. Chapman. *Children's Humour*. Illus. Patty Inkley. Chichester; New York: J. Wiley, 1980. Bib. pp. 307-317.

[WHU-590]   MacHovec, Frank J. *Humor: Theory, History, Applications*. Springfield, Ill.: Charles C. Thomas Pub., 1988. Bib. pp. 197-200.

[WHU-600]   Mackay, Charles. *A Dictionary of Lowland Scotch: With an Introductory Chapter on the Poetry, Humour, and Literary History of the Scottish Language*. London: Whittaker, 1888. Detroit: Gale Research, 1968. xxxii, 398 pp.

[WHU-610]   McKnight, George Harley, ed. *Middle English Humorous Tales in Verse*. New York: AMS Press, 1972. lxxv, 156 pp. Bib. pp. 81-91.

[WHU-620]   Mendel, Werner M. *Celebration of Laughter*. N.p.: Mara Books, 1970. Bib.

[WHU-630]   Mikes, George. *Laughing Matter: Towards a Personal Philosophy of Wit and Humor*. New York: Library Press, 1970. 133 pp. Bib. refs. Also titled *Humour in Memoriam*, London, 1968.

[WHU-640]   Mulkay, M[ichael] J[oseph]. *On Humour: Its Nature and Its Place in Modern Society*. Cambridge: Polity Press; Oxford; New York: Basil Blackwell Publishing, 1988. Bib. refs. pp. 224-229.

[WHU-650]   Nash, Walter. *The Language of Humour*. English Language Series, vol. 16. London; New York: Longman, 1985. Bib. pp. 173-176.

[WHU-660]   Oliver, Edward James. *Hypocrisy and Humor*. New York: Sheed and Ward, [1960]. Bib. pp. 166-167.

[WHU-670]   O'Neill, Patrick. *The Comedy of Entropy: Humour, Narrative,*

Reading. Toronto: University of Toronto Press, 1990. 325 pp. Bib. refs.

[WHU-680] Palmer, Jerry. *Taking Humour Seriously*. London; New York: Routledge, 1993. Bib. refs.

[WHU-690] Pearson, Hesketh. *The Smith of Smiths: Being the Life, Wit and Humour of Sydney Smith*. New York; London: Harper and Brothers, 1934. Bib. refs. pp. 327-329.

[WHU-700] Pirandello, Luigi. *On Humor*. Trans. Antonio Illiano and Daniel P. Testa. Chapel Hill: University of North Carolina Press, [1974]. 150 pp. Bib. refs.

[WHU-710] Powell, Chris, and George E. C. Paton, eds. *Humour in Society: Resistance and Control*. New York: St. Martin's Press, 1988. xxii, 279 pp. Bibs.

[WHU-720] Priestley, J[ohn] B[oynton]. *English Humour*. London; New York: Longmans, Green and Co., 1929. 180 pp. New York: Stein and Day, [1976]. 208 pp.

[WHU-730] Press, Charles. *The Political Cartoon*. Rutherford, [N.J.]: Fairleigh Dickinson University Press, 1978. Bib. pp. 379-389.

[WHU-740] *Punch*. London: Punch Publications, 1841-. Weekly.

[WHU-750] Raabe, Tom. *Biblioholism: The Literary Addiction*. Golden, Colo: Fulcrum Pub., 1991. Bib. refs. p. 175-179.

[WHU-760] Schaeffer, Neil. *The Art of Laughter*. New York: Columbia University Press, 1981. 166 pp. Bib. refs.

[WHU-770] Sharkey, Michael, ed. *Illustrated Treasury of Australian Humour*. Melbourne; New York: Oxford University Press Australia, 1988. Bib. refs. pp. 283-310.

[WHU-780] Sharma, R. K. *Contemporary Black Humour in American Novels, from Nathanael West to Thomas Berger*. Delhi: Ajanta Publications, 1988. Bib. pp. 175-195.

[WHU-790] Shikes, Ralph E., and Steven Heller. *Art of Satire: Painters as Caricaturists and Cartoonists from Delacroix to Picasso*. New York: Horizon Press, 1984. Bib. pp. 119-123.

[WHU-800] Slater, Maya. *Humour in the Works of Marcel Proust*. Oxford Modern Languages and Literature Monographs. Oxford; New York: Oxford University Press, 1979. Bib. pp. 205-212.

574

[WHU-810] Storey, Mark. *Poetry and Humour from Cowper to Clough*. Totowa, N.J.: Rowman and Littlefield, 1979. 192 pp. Bib. refs.

[WHU-820] *Studies in American Humor*. San Marcos, Tex.: Humor Publications, Inc., Department of English, Southwest Texas State University, 1974-. Quarterly. Incorporating *American Humor*.

[WHU-830] Thackeray, William Makepeace. *The English Humourists; Charity and Humour; The Four Georges*. Everyman's Library, no. 610. London: J. M. Dent, 1968. 423 pp. Bib. p. xix.

[WHU-840] *Thalia: Studies in Literary Humor*. Ottawa, Ontario, Canada: Thalia, Department of English, University of Ottawa, 1978-. Semi-annual.

[WHU-850] *Vietnamese Folk Tales: Satire and Humour*. 4th ed. Hanoi: Foreign Languages Publishing House, 1990. 88 pp.

[WHU-860] Trachtenberg, Stanley, ed. *American Humorists, 1800-1950*. 2 pts. Dictionary of Literary Biography, vol. 11. Detroit: Gale Research, 1982.

[WHU-870] Walker, Alan, ed. *The Treasury of Great Canadian Humour*. Toronto; New York: McGraw-Hill Ryerson, 1974. 413 pp.

[WHU-880] Weiss, Harry B[ischoff]. *A Brief History of American Jest Books*. New York: The New York Public Library, 1943. Bib. p. 19.

[WHU-890] White, David Manning, and Robert H. Abel, eds. *The Funnies: An American Idiom*. New York: Free Press of Glencoe, 1963. Bib. pp. 293-304.

[WHU-900] Wolfenstein, Martha. *Children's Humor: A Psychological Analysis*. Glencoe, Ill.: Free Press, [1954]. 224 pp.

[WHU-910] Ziv, Avner, ed. *National Styles of Humor*. Westport, Conn.: Greenwood Press, 1988. 243 pp. Bib. pp. 215-219.

KEY WORKS ON WIT AND HUMOR AND RELIGION

Finding literature which treats wit and humor from a religious perspective, especially a Christian one, is not easy, particularly if one is looking for works with bibliographies. The list given below is the product of numerous searches in sundry libraries and several computer search programs. The brevity of this list suggests that the study of wit and humor is a particularly promising subject for those seeking new areas of research in Christianity and the arts.

The works listed below range from collections of jokes to detailed studies of humor and the Bible. For collections of humor with a religious emphasis, see the following books: [WHR-020], [WHR-040], [WHR-050], [WHR-070], [WHR-120], [WHR-150], [WHR-160], [WHR-200], [WHR-220], [WHR-340], [WHR-420], [WHR-430]. For studies of humor and religion, see Tal D. Bonham's *Humor: God's Gift* [WHR-060], Leslie B. Flynn's *Serve Him with Mirth: The Place of Humor in the Christian Life* [WHR-130], Marilyn Meberg's *Choosing the Amusing: What Difference Does it Make?* [WHR-250], Colin Morris' *The Hammer of the Lord* [WHR-260], Thomas James Mullen's *Laughing Out Loud and Other Religious Experiences* [WHR-270], Ward Patterson's "Holy Humor: The Religious Rhetoric of Grady Nutt" [WHR-280], John Bill Ratliff's *Humor as a Religious Experience* [WHR-300], and Nelvin Vos's *For God's Sake Laugh!* [WHR-410]. For studies which explore the comic view of life in a more eclectic context, see M. Conrad Hyers' *The Comic Vision: Comic Heroism in a Tragic World* [WHR-180], and his *The Laughing Buddha: Zen and the Comic Spirit* [WHR-190]. Also see several additional studies which explore popular expressions of religious humor, including [WHR-230], [WHR-240], [WHR-350], [WHR-360], and [WHR-370].

Some of the most intriguing studies of religious humor are those treating preaching. The best recent books on this topic are Doug Adams' *Humor in the American Pulpit: From George White Through Henry Ward Beecher* [WHR-010], James R. Barnette's "Humor in Preaching: The Contributions of Psychological and Sociological Research" [WHR-030], John W. Drakeford's *Humor in Preaching* [WHR-110], John Gatta's *Gracious Laughter: The Meditative Wit of Edward Taylor* [WHR-140], and Ruth Reitz's "Notes Toward Understanding the Use of Humor to Communicate Christian Messages" [WHR-310]. Several of the studies given below treat wit and humor from a theological perspective, including Peter Bouteneff's recent thesis, "The History, Hagiography and Humor of the Fools for Christ" [WHR-080], Henri Cormier's substantial analysis, *The Humor of Jesus* [WHR-090], Bob W. Parrott's philosophical treatment of humor, *God's Sense of Humor--Where?--*

576

When?--How? [WHR-290], Cal Samra's closely related works on Christ's use of humor and joy in healing, [WHR-320] and [WHR-330], and Elton Trueblood's older but noteworthy exploratory study, *The Humor of Christ* [WHR-400]. For studies which examine the role of humor in the Bible, see Jakob Jonsson's recent and substantial work, *Humor and Irony in the New Testament, Illuminated by Parallels in Talmud and Midrash* [WHR-210], and, for a perspective from the late nineteenth century, Marion Daniel Shutter's *Wit and Humor of the Bible* [WHR-380]. In a lighter vein, also consider Robert L. Short's *The Gospel According to Peanuts* [WHR-360] and *The Parables of Peanuts* [WHR-370]. For a practical study of the relationship between biblical humor and daily life, read Charles R. Swindoll's *Laugh Again* [WHR-390]. While the number of books given here is small, this list will at least alert readers to some of the prominent writers on this topic whose articles may be found in various journals and denominational publications.

[WHR-010]   Adams, Doug. *Humor in the American Pulpit: From George White Through Henry Ward Beecher.* 4th ed. Austin, Tex.: Sharing Co., 1986. Bib. pp. 226-239.

[WHR-020]   Autry, Ronald. *Heaven Inc.* Oxford, Miss.: Yoknapatawpha Press, 1990. 121 pp.

[WHR-030]   Barnette, James R. "Humor in Preaching: The Contributions of Psychological and Sociological Research." Ph.D. Thesis, Southern Baptist Theological Seminary, 1992. Bib. refs. pp. 265-288.

[WHR-040]   Bentall, Shirley. *Amusings: For Christians with a Sense of Humor.* Toronto: Canadian Baptist, 1980. 111 pp. Bib. refs.

[WHR-050]   Bonham, Tal D. *Another Treasury of Clean Jokes.* Nashville: Broadman Press, 1983. 160 pp.

[WHR-060]   ------. *Humor: God's Gift.* Nashville: Broadman Press, 1988. Bib. pp. 299-316.

[WHR-070]   ------. *The Treasury of Clean Jokes.* Nashville: Broadman Press, 1981. 160 pp.

[WHR-080]   Bouteneff, Peter. "The History, Hagiography and Humor of the Fools for Christ." M.Div. Thesis, St. Vladimir's Orthodox

Theological Seminary, 1990. Bib. pp. 72-73.

[WHR-090] Cormier, Henri. *The Humor of Jesus.* Trans. *L'humour de Jésus.* New York: Alba House, 1977. 154 pp. Bib. refs.

[WHR-100] Demoray, Donald E. *Laughter, Joy, and Healing.* Grand Rapids: Baker Book House, 1986.

[WHR-110] Drakeford, John W. *Humor in Preaching.* Grand Rapids, Mich.: Ministry Resources Library, 1986. Bib. pp. 107-110.

[WHR-120] Fisher, Ben C. *Mountain Preacher Stories: Laughter Among the Trumpets.* Boone, N.C.: Appalachian Consortium Press, 1990. 75 pp.

[WHR-130] Flynn, Leslie B. *Serve Him with Mirth: The Place of Humor in the Christian Life.* Grand Rapids: Zondervan, 1960. 191 pp. Bib. refs.

[WHR-140] Gatta, John. *Gracious Laughter: The Meditative Wit of Edward Taylor.* Columbia: University of Missouri Press, 1989. Bib. pp. 212-223.

[WHR-150] Hart, Johnny. *Back to B.C.* London: Coronet Books, 1977.

[WHR-160] Holloway, Gary. *Saints, Demons, and Asses: Southern Preacher Anecdotes.* Bloomington, Ind.: Indiana University Press, 1989. Bib. pp. 117-120.

[WHR-170] Hyers, M. Conrad. *And God Created Laughter: The Bible as Divine Comedy.* Atlanta: John Knox Press, 1987. Bib. pp. 122-124.

[WHR-180] ------. *The Comic Vision: Comic Heroism in a Tragic World.* Wakefield, N.H.: Longwood Academic, 1991. Bib. refs. Rev. ed. of *The Comic Vision and the Christian Faith: A Celebration of Life and Laughter.* New York: Pilgrim Press, 1982. Bib. p. 192.

[WHR-190] ------. *The Laughing Buddha: Zen and the Comic Spirit.* Wolfeboro, N.H.: Longwood Academic, 1989. 195 pp. Rev. ed. of *Zen and the Comic Spirit,* 1974.

[WHR-200] Jones, Loyal. *The Preacher Joke Book.* Little Rock: August House, 1989. 109 pp.

[WHR-210] Jonsson, Jakob. *Humor and Irony in the New Testament, Illuminated by Parallels in Talmud and Midrash.* Reykjavik: Bokautgafa Menningarsjols, 1965. Reprint. Leiden: E. J. Brill, 1985. 299 pp. Bib. pp. 276-284.

578

[WHR-220] Mantz, Douglas. *Let There be Laughter: The Best of Humour, Anecdotes, Cartoons by, for and About Canadian Baptists.* Burlington, Ontario: Welch Pub., 1989. 81 pp.

[WHR-230] Marsh, Spencer. *Edith the Good.* San Francisco: Harper and Row, 1977.

[WHR-240] ------. *God, Man, and Archie Bunker.* New York: Harper and Row, 1975.

[WHR-250] Meberg, Marilyn. *Choosing the Amusing: What Difference Does it Make?* Portland, Oreg.: Multnomah Press, 1986. 132 pp. Bib. refs.

[WHR-260] Morris, Colin. *The Hammer of the Lord.* New York: Abingdon Press, 1973.

[WHR-270] Mullen, Thomas James. *Laughing Out Loud and Other Religious Experiences.* Waco, Tex.: Word Books, 1983. 133 pp. Bib. refs.

[WHR-280] Patterson, Ward. "Holy Humor: The Religious Rhetoric of Grady Nutt." Ph.D. Thesis, Indiana University, 1983. Bib. pp. 470-485.

[WHR-290] Parrott, Bob W. *God's Sense of Humor--Where?--When?--How?* New York: Philosophical Library, 1984. 205 pp.

[WHR-300] Ratliff, John Bill. *Humor as a Religious Experience.* Louisville: Southern Baptist Theological Seminary, [1971]. Bib. pp. 205-225.

[WHR-310] Reitz, Ruth. "Notes Toward Understanding the Use of Humor to Communicate Christian Messages." M.A. Thesis, Regent University, 1991. Bib. pp. 93-103.

[WHR-320] Samra, Cal. *Jesus Put on a Happy Face: The Healing Power of Joy and Humor.* Kalamazoo, Mich.: Rosejoy Publications, 1985. Bib. pp. 194-198.

[WHR-330] ------. *The Joyful Christ: The Healing Power of Humor.* San Francisco: Harper and Row, 1986. Bib. pp. 207-210.

[WHR-340] Samra, Cal, and Rose Samra. *Holy Hilarity: Playshop Guidebook of the Fellowship of Merry Christians.* Portage, Mich.: Merry Christians, 1992. 81 pp.

[WHR-350] Schulz, Charles M. *I Take my Religion Seriously.* Anderson, Ind.: Warner Press, 1989. 132 pp.

[WHR-360] Short, Robert L. *The Gospel According to Peanuts*. Richmond: John Knox, 1964.

[WHR-370] ------. *The Parables of Peanuts*. Greenwich: Fawcett Publications, 1968.

[WHR-380] Shutter, Marion D[aniel]. *Wit and Humor of the Bible*. Boston: Arena, 1892. 219 pp.

[WHR-390] Swindoll, Charles R. *Laugh Again*. Dallas: Word Publishing, 1991. Bib. refs. in notes, pp. 245-250.

[WHR-400] Trueblood, Elton. *The Humor of Christ*. New York: Harper and Row, 1964.

[WHR-410] Vos, Nelvin. *For God's Sake Laugh!* Richmond: John Knox Press, 1967. Bib. pp. 73-75.

[WHR-420] Willimon, William H. *And the Laugh Shall be First: A Treasury of Religious Humor*. Nashville: Abingdon Press, 1986. 156 pp.

[WHR-430] ------. *William H. Willimon's Last Laugh*. Nashville: Abingdon Press, 1991. 156 pp.

INDEX OF AUTHORS

628

INDEX OF TITLES

650

662

672

684

694

696

698

702

704

712

718

720

728

738

754

764

STUDIES IN ART AND RELIGIOUS INTERPRETATION